Pontiac Phoenix & Oldsmobile Omega Automotive Repair Manual

by Rik Paul
and John H Haynes
Member of the Guild of Motoring Writers

Models covered:
Pontiac Phoenix, LJ and SJ models and Oldsmobile Omega,
Brougham and SX models with 2.5 liter (151 cu in) L4
and 2.8 liter (173 cu in) V6 engines
1980 thru 1984

ISBN 1 85010 146 9

Haynes Publishing Group
Sparkford Nr Yeovil
Somerset BA22 7JJ England

Haynes Publications, Inc
861 Lawrence Drive
Newbury Park
California 91320 USA

Acknowledgements

Thanks are due to the Pontiac and Oldsmobile divisions of the General Motors Corporation for their assistance with technical information and supply of certain illustrations.

The Champion Spark Plug Company supplied the illustrations showing the various spark plug conditions. The bodywork repair photographs used in the manual were provided by Holt Lloyd Limited who supply 'Turtle Wax', 'Dupli-Color Holts', and other Holts range products.

About this manual

Its aim

The aim of this manual is to help you get the best value from your car. It can do so in several ways. It can help you decide what work must be done (even should you choose to get it done by a garage), provide information on routine maintenance and servicing, and give a logical course of action and diagnosis when random faults occur. However, it is hoped that you will use the Manual by tackling the work yourself. On simpler jobs it may be quicker than booking the car into a garage, and going there twice, to leave and collect it. Perhaps most important, a lot of money can be saved by avoiding the costs the garage must charge to cover its labor and overheads.

The manual has drawings and descriptions to show the function of the various components so that their layout can be understood. Then the tasks are described and photographed in a step-by-step sequence so that even a novice can do the work.

Its arrangement

The manual is divided into thirteen Chapters, each covering a logical sub-division of the vehicle. The Chapters are each divided into Sections, numbered with single figures, e.g. 5; and the Section into photographs (or sub-sections), with decimal numbers following on from the Section they are in, e.g. 5.1, 5.2, 5.3 etc.

It is freely illustrated, especially in those parts where there is a detailed sequence of operations to be carried out. There are two forms of illustration: figures and photographs. The figures are numbered in sequence with decimal numbers, according to their position in the Chapter: e.g. Fig. 6.4 is the 4th drawing/illustration in Chapter 6. Photographs are numbered (either individually or in related groups) the same as the Section or sub-section of the text where the operation they show is described.

There is an alphabetical index at the back of the manual as well as a contents list at the front.

References to the left or right of the vehicle are in the sense of a person in a seat facing forward.

While every care has been taken to ensure that the information in this manual is correct, no liability can be accepted by the authors or publishers for loss, damage or injury caused by any errors in, or omissions from, the information given.

Introduction to the Pontiac Phoenix and Oldsmobile Omega

Although the original Phoenix was introduced into the Pontiac line-up in 1977 and the original Omega was introduced into the Oldsmobile line-up in 1973, both of the models covered in this manual are actually totally re-engineered cars, bearing little resemblance to the early models.

These redesigned Phoenix and Omega cars were introduced in 1979, for the 1980 model year as part of the ambitious X-Body program, and represents the most revolutionary new design in the modern history of General Motors.

The company's traditional front-engine/rear-wheel drive design was replaced with a front-wheel drive design that used a transverse-mounted engine and transaxle combination. This arrangement placed all of the major mechanical components in the engine compartment, leaving the rest of the vehicle open for passenger and storage space. This allows the car to be lighter and smaller in its external dimensions, while still maintaining spacious internal dimensions.

In the process of building this totally new American car, GM utilized features found on some of the more popular foreign models, such as MacPherson Strut independent front suspension, rack and pinion steering and a trailing arm.

Two engines are available with both the Phoenix and Omega; a 2.5 liter four-cylinder (L4) and a 2.8 liter six-cylinder (V6). The L4 is a re-engineered version of the Pontiac Iron Duke engine, that has been adapted to transverse mounting for the X-bodies. The V6 is a totally new engine that utilizes a 60° cylinder angle design instead of the previously used 90° angle design. This change was needed in order to fit the V6 sideways into the engine compartment.

Each engine is available with either a 4-speed manual transaxle with a self-adjusting clutch or a Turbo Hydramatic 125 automatic transaxle.

Further information on the various systems and components of both cars, as well as complete specifications, can be found in the appropriate individual chapters.

Contents

Oldsmobile Omega Brougham four-door sedan

Pontiac Phoenix four-door hatchback

Vehicle identification numbers

Modifications are a continuing and unpublicized process in vehicle manufacture. Since spare parts manuals and lists are compiled on a numerical basis, the individual vehicle numbers are essential to identify correctly the component required.

Vehicle identification Number (VIN): This very important identification number is located on a plate attached to the left top of the dashboard and can be easily seen while looking through the windshield from the outside of the car. The VIN also appears on the Vehicle Certificate of Title and Registration. It gives such valuable information as where and when the vehicle was manufactured, the model year of manufacture and the body style (Fig. 0.1).

Body identification plate: This metal plate is located on the top right side of the radiator support behind the right headlight. Like the VIN it contains valuable information about the manufacture of the car, as well as information about the way in which the vehicle is equipped.

This plate is especially useful for matching the color and type of paint for repair work.

Engine identification numbers (L4 engine): The engine VIN number for the L4 engine can be found on a pad at the right front of the cylinder block, below the cylinder head. The engine unit and code number label is located on the timing cover, and the engine code stamping is found on a pad at the left front of the cylinder block below the cylinder head. Refer to Fig. 0.2.

Engine identification numbers (V6 engine): The V6 engine's VIN location is on a pad on the front of the cylinder block below the right cylinder head. The engine unit and code label is located on the front and rear of the left rocker cover. Refer to Fig. 0.2.

Manual transaxle number: The identification number for the manual 4S transaxle is located on a pad on the forward side of the transaxle case, next to the middle mounting bolt. Refer to Fig. 0.3.

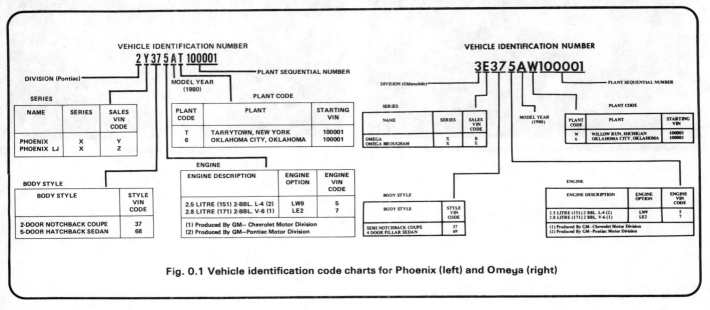

Fig. 0.1 Vehicle identification code charts for Phoenix (left) and Omega (right)

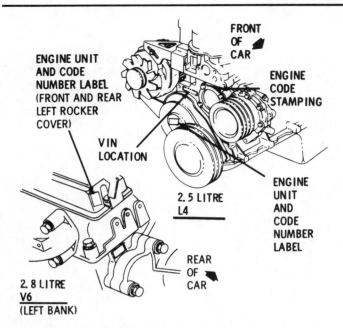

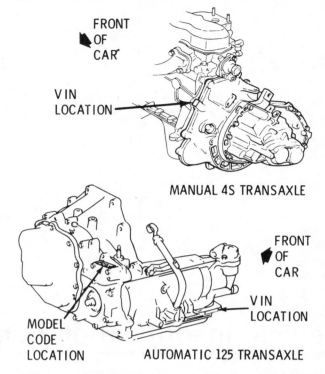

Fig. 0.2 Engine VIN (Vehicle Identification Number) locations

Fig. 0.3 Transaxle VIN (Vehicle Identification Number) locations

Automatic transaxle number: The identification number for the automatic 125 transaxle is located on the oil pan flange pad, to the right side of the oil dipstick at the rear of the transaxle. Refer to Fig. 0.3 The model tag is found next to the manual shift shaft, and may be partially obstructed by the shift cable (photo).

Starter number: Stamped on the outer case toward the rear.

Generator number: Located on top of the drive end frame.

Battery number: Located on the top left of the battery, on the cell cover.

Tune-up decal: Located on the left front shock tower inside the engine compartment (photo).

The automatic transaxle model tag is located next to the manual shift shaft

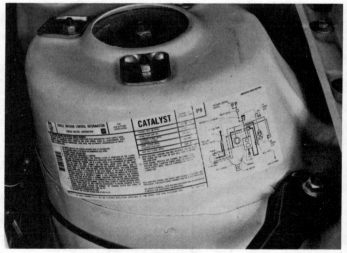

Tune-up decal location

Buying parts

Once you've found all the identification numbers, record them for reference when buying parts. Since the manufacturers change specifications, parts and vendors (who subcontract various components on the vehicle), providing the I.D. numbers is about the only way to be reasonably sure that you are buying parts for your particular vehicle. Still, that isn't absolute.

Whenever possible, take the worn part down to the parts house or dealer so that direct comparison with the new or rebuilt unit can be made. Along the trail from manufacturer to parts shelf there are a dozen places that the part can end up with the wrong number or be listed incorrectly.

The two places to purchase new parts for your vehicle, the parts house and the dealer, differ in the type of parts that they carry. While the dealer can obtain virtually every part for your vehicle, the parts house is usually limited to normal high-wear items such as: shocks, tune-up parts, various engine gaskets, V-belts, water pumps, clutches, brake parts, etc. Rarely will a parts house that specializes in foreign or domestic parts have body or interior parts, large suspension components, engine blocks, transmission gears or cases. It's always best to call the parts house and ask first, because many times you'll end up going to the vehicle dealer.

Used parts can be obtained for roughly half the price of new parts, but you don't always know what you're getting. Once again, take your worn part to the wrecking yard for direct comparisons.

Whether new, used or rebuilt, the best course is to buy from someone who specializes in your vehicle.

Basic maintenance techniques

There are a number of techniques involved in maintenance and repair that will be referred to throughout the manual. Use of these techniques will help the home mechanic be more efficient, better organized and able to perform the tasks properly. This will help ensure that the repair job is thorough and complete.

Fastening systems

Fasteners, basically, are any nut, bolt, pin or clamp that is used to hold one or more parts together. There are a few things to keep in mind when dealing with fasteners. Almost all fasteners use a locking device of some type; either a lock washer, locknut or key, or are secured with thread cement. All threaded fasteners should be clean and have good threads, not bent, and not rounded off on the shoulders where the wrench fits. Replace all damaged nuts and bolts.

Rusted nuts and bolts should be treated with a specific rust-penetrating fluid. Some mechanics use turpentine in a spout-type oil can, and it works quite well. After applying the rust penetrant, let it "work" on the threads for a few minutes, or longer, before attempting to loosen the bolt or nut. Badly rusted bolts may have to be chiseled off or removed with a special nut-breaker available at tool stores.

Flat washers and lock washers, when removed in an assembly, should always be replaced if damaged. Always use a flat washer between a lock washer and any soft metal surface, such as aluminium or thin sheet metal. Special locknuts can only be used once or at most a few times before they lose their locking ability. Replace as necessary.

If a bolt or stud breaks off in an assembly, it can be drilled and pulled out with a special tool called an E-Z Out. Most machine shops can perform this task. They can also repair holes that are stripped out and have to be rethreaded.

Torqueing sequence and procedures

When all threaded fasteners are tightened down, they are tightened to a specific torque value. Over-tightening the fastener can weaken it and cause it to break, while under-tightening can cause it to come loose. Each bolt, depending on the type of material that it's made of and the diameter of the threaded shaft, has a specific torque value. The size and strength of a bolt is determined by the job it must do. Small bolts hold down small jobs, and larger ones take care of the heavy duty, high-strength requirements determined by the manufacturer. The torque values given will never be higher than the maximum strength of the bolt. Throughout the manual references will be made to torque values and those specific to the operations covered will be listed at the beginning of each chapter. For those nuts and bolts not listed specifically, refer to the general torque values chart (Fig. .05).

Bolts and nuts used in a pattern on an assembly (i.e., head bolts, oil pan bolts, differential cover bolts, etc.) must be loosened and torqued in a sequence to avoid warping the assembly. Initially the bolts should go on finger-tight only. Then they should be tightened gradually: at first one turn each and diagonally tightening one opposite the first one, then back to the one next to the first one, then opposite that one, until the assembly is criss-crossed one complete time. The second time, each bolt should be torqued only $\frac{1}{2}$ turn, and again sequentially. The third and subsequent times should be $\frac{1}{4}$ turn each until the bolt is torqued to the proper specifications. The reverse sequence is followed to loosen the bolts.

Disassembly sequence

Tearing an assembly down should be done with care and purpose to help ensure that the assembly goes back together with all the right parts in the right places with nothing left over. Always keep track of the sequence in which parts are removed. Make note of special bevels or markings on parts that can be reinstalled more than one way, such as a grooved thrust washer on a shaft. It's a good idea to lay the assembly out on clean shop towels in the order of, or in reference to, its disassembly.

When removing fasteners from an assembly, keep track of which ones went on which location. Sometimes threading a bolt back in a part, or a nut and washers back on a stud can help keep track of the location of these fasteners. If these nuts and bolts cannot be returned to their respective locations, then they should be kept in a compartmentalized box or series of small boxes. A cupcake or muffin tin is ideal for this purpose, since each cavity can hold the bolts and nuts from a particular area; ie., pan bolts, valve cover bolts, engine mount bolts, etc. This plan is especially helpful when working on assemblies with very small parts, such as the carburetor, alternator or generator, valve train, and for screws and finish washers in the dash and interior, among others. The cupcake cavities can be marked with paint, nail polish or tape as to their function.

Whenever wiring looms, harnesses or wiring groups are separated, it's a good idea to identify them with masking take and a marker as to location point or mate. They can be numbered or designated alphabetically.

Gasket sealing surfaces

Throughout the vehicle, gaskets are used to seal the mating surface between two parts, and keep lubricants, fluids, coolant, vacuum or pressure contained in the assembly.

Many times these gaskets are installed with the use of a liquid or paste-type gasket sealing compound. Age, heat and pressure can sometimes cause the two parts to stick together so tightly that they are very difficult to separate. Many times the assembly can be loosened by striking it with a rubber or plastic mallet around the sealing edges. A regular hammer can be used if a block of soft wood is placed between the hammer and the part. Do not hammer against any cast parts, or any parts that can be easily damaged with a hammer blow. With any stubborn part, always recheck to see that every fastener has been removed.

Avoid using a screwdriver or bar to pry apart an assembly, because this can easily mar the gasket sealing surface of the parts, which must remain smooth. If prying becomes necessary, use a broom handle, but keep in mind that extra clean-up is necessary if the wood splinters.

After the parts are separated, the old gasket must be carefully scraped off and the gasket surfaces cleaned. Stubborn gasket material can be soaked with rust penetrant or treated with a special chemical to soften it so that it can be easily scraped off. A scraper can be fashioned from a piece of copper tubing by flattening and sharpening one end. Copper is chosen because it is usually softer than the surfaces to be scraped, thereby reducing the chances of gouging the part. Some gaskets can be removed with a wire brush, but regardless of the method, the surfaces should be clean and smooth. If for some reason the gasket surface is gouged, then a gasket sealer thick enough to fill scratches will have to be used. For most applications, a non-drying, or semi-drying gasket compound should be used as indicated in the manual.

Hose removal tips

Removal of any hoses follows the same rules as for gaskets. Avoid scratching or gouging the surface that the hose mates against or the connection may leak. Because of various chemical reactions the rubber in hoses can literally bond itself to the metal spigot it fits over. To remove a hose, loosen the hose clamp that secures it to the spigot. Then, with a pair of slip-joint (water-pump) pliers, grab the hose at the clamp and rotate it around the spigot. Work it back and forth until the hose is free. Silicone or other lubricant safe for rubber can then be applied at the joint and the hose will slip off. Use the same lubricant to install hoses as well. Apply it to the mouth of the hose and the spigot to which it will be attached. If a hose clamp is broken or appears to be weak, replace it with a new one. Badly deteriorated hoses should be replaced. Check for cracks, splits, tears and leaks.

Tools and working facilities

Introduction

A selection of good tools is a basic requirement for anyone who plans to maintain and repair his vehicle. For the owner who has few tools, if any, the initial investment might seem expensive, but when compared to the spiraling costs of routine maintenance and repair, it is a wise investment.

To help the owner decide which tools are needed to perform the tasks detailed in this manual, we offer three lists of tools: *Maintenance and minor repair, Repair and Overhaul,* and *Special.* The newcomer to practical mechanics should start off with the Maintenance and Minor Repair tool set for the simplest jobs around the vehicle. Then, as his confidence and experience grow, he can tackle more difficult tasks, buying extra tools as they are needed. Eventually he will build the basic kit into the Repair and Overhaul tool set over a period of time. The experienced do-it-yourselfer will have a tool kit complete enough for most repair and overhaul procedures and will add tools from the Special category when he feels the expense is justified by the frequency of use.

It is obviously not possible to cover the subject of tools fully here. For those who wish to learn more about tools and their use there is a book entitled How to Choose and Use Car Tools available from the publishers of this Manual.

Maintenance and minor repair tool kit

The tools in this list should be considered as a minimum requirement if one expects to perform routine maintenance, servicing and minor repair. We recommend the purchase of combination wrenches (box at one end, open at the other); while more expensive than just the open-ended ones, they do offer the advantages of both types of wrenches.

> *Combination wrenches 6, 7, 8, 9, 10, 11, 12, 13, 14, 17 and 19 mm*
> *Adjustable wrench — 9 inch*
> *Engine oil pan/transmission/rear axle drain plug key (where applicable)*
> *Spark plug wrench (with rubber insert)*
> *Spark plug gap adjustment tool*
> *Set of feeler gauges*
> *Break adjuster wrench (where applicable)*
> *Brake bleed nipple wrench*
> *Screwdriver — 4-in long x $\frac{1}{4}$-in dia. (flat blade)*
> *Screwdriver — 4-in long x $\frac{1}{4}$-in dia. (Phillips)*
> *Combination pliers — 6-inch*

> *Hacksaw, junior*
> *Tire pump*
> *Tire pressure gauge*
> *Grease gun (where applicable)*
> *Oil can*
> *Fine emery cloth (1 sheet)*
> *Wire brush (small)*
> *Funnel (medium size)*
> *Safety goggles*
> *Axle or jack stands*

Note: *If basic tune-ups are going to be a large part of the normal maintenance it would be imperative to invest in a good stroboscopic timing light and a combination tach/dwell meter. Although they are listed in the special tools, they are invaluable in properly tuning late-model vehicles*

Repair and overhaul tool kit

These tools are virtually essential for anyone who plans to perform major repairs and are additional to those given in the basic list. Included is a comprehensive set of sockets. Although these are expensive they will be found invaluable because they are so versatile, especially if various extensions and drives are included.

We recommend the $\frac{1}{2}$ in square-drive type over the $\frac{3}{8}$ in drive. Although the larger drive is more bulky and expensive, it has the capability of accepting a very wide range of large sockets. Ideally, the mechanic would have a $\frac{3}{8}$ in drive set for 6 to 14 mm sockets and a $\frac{1}{2}$ in drive set from 15 on up.

> *Sockets to cover a range from 6 to 24 mm*
> *Reversible ratchet drive (for use with sockets)*
> *Extension piece, 10-inch (for use with sockets)*
> *Universal joint (for use with sockets)*
> *Torque wrenches (for use with sockets)*
> *Self-grip wrench — 8-inch*
> *Ballpeen hammer*
> *Soft-faced hammer, plastic or rubber*
> *Screwdriver — 6-in long x $\frac{5}{16}$-in dia. (flat blade)*
> *Screwdriver — 2-in long x $\frac{5}{16}$-in square (flat blade)*
> *Screwdriver — 1$\frac{1}{2}$-in long x $\frac{1}{4}$ dia. (Phillips)*
> *Screwdriver 3-in long x $\frac{1}{8}$ in dia. (electricians)*
> *Pliers — electricians side cutters*
> *Pliers — needle-nosed*

Pliers – circlip (internal and external)
Cold chisel – ½ inch
Scriber (this can be made by grinding the end of a broken hacksaw blade
Scraper (this can be made by flattening and sharpening one end of a piece of copper tubing
Centerpunch
Pin punch
Hacksaw
Valve grinding tool
Steel rule/straightedge
Allen keys
Selection of files
Wire brush (large)
Jack stands (second set)
Jack (strong scissor or hydraulic type)

Special tools

The tools in this list are those which are not used regularly, are expensive to buy, or which need to be used in accordance with their manufacturers' instructions. Unless these tools are used frequently, it is not economical to purchase many of them. A consideration would be to split the cost and use between a friend or friends (i.e., members of a car club) to help defray the expense. In addition, most of these tools can be borrowed from a tool rental shop or a garage.

This list contains only those tools and instruments freely available to the public, and not those special tools produced by the vehicle manufacturer specifically for its dealer network. Occasionally, references to these manufacturer's special tools are found in the text of this manual. Generally, an alternative method of doing the job without the special tool is offered. However, sometimes there is no alternative to their use. Where this is the case and the tool cannot be purchased or borrowed, then the work should be turned over to the dealer, repair garage or automotive machine shop.

Valve spring compressor (photo)
Piston ring compressor (photo)
Balljoint separator
Universal hub/bearing puller (photo)
Impact screwdriver
Micrometer and/or vernier gauge (photos)
Carburetor flow balancing device (where applicable)
Dial gauge (photo)
Stroboscopic timing light
Dwell angle meter/tachometer
Universal electrical multi-meter
Cylinder compression gauge
Lifting tackle
Floor jack

Light with extension lead
Vacuum tester (photo)
Brake shoe spring tool (photo)

Special engine overhaul tools:
Piston ring expander (photo)
Hydraulic lifter retractor (photo)
Piston ring groove cleaner (photo)
Cylinder hone (photo)
Cylinder ridge reamer (photo)
Cylinder bore taper gauge (photo)

Buying tools

For the home mechanic who is just starting to get involved in the repair of his vehicle, but has few tools, there are a couple of ways to go on tool buying. If tune-up and maintenance is the extent of the work planned, then the purchase of individual tools is satisfactory. If, on the other hand, repair and overhaul work is planned, then the best course is to purchase a modest tool set from one of the large department stores. Usually, they can be had at a substantial savings over the individual tool price, and normally include a metal tool box. As the mechanic tackles larger jobs, purchase add-on sets (i.e., ¼-in and ⅜-in drive socket sets, box end wrench sets, chisel and punch sets, etc.) and a larger tool chest can be purchased to expand the tool selection. Also the cost of the tools will be spread over a longer time period, as opposed to buying a very large tool set at one time.

Specific tool shops will many times be the only sources of some of the special tools that are needed. They usually have good selections, especially of the larger tools, wrenches and sockets.

Regardless of where tools are bought, avoid cheap ones especially screwdrivers and sockets, because they usually won't last very long due to poor quality. Replacement expense of cheap tools will eventually outweigh the cost of quality tools.

Care and maintenance of tools

Having purchased a tool set, it is necessary to keep the tools in a clean and usable condition. Always wipe off any dirt, grease and metal filings off the tools before putting them away. Never leave them lying around in the work area. Always check closely under the hood for tools used so that they don't get lost during a test drive.

Some tools can be hung from a rack in the garage or workshop wall, while others should be kept in a toolbox or tray. Any measuring instruments, gauges, meters etc., must be carefully stored where they cannot be damaged by impact or weather.

Take a little care when tools are used, and they will last a lot longer. Tools, even with the best of care, will wear out if they are used frequently. When a screwdriver top is damaged or a socket gets cracked or rounds out, then replace it. Not only is it safer, but it will make each job a simple, enjoyable task.

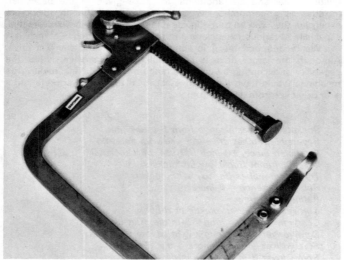

Valve spring compressor

Piston ring compressor

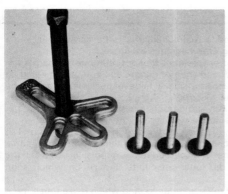

Universal hub puller

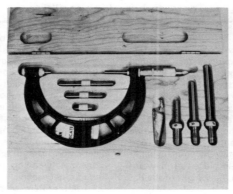

Micrometer set

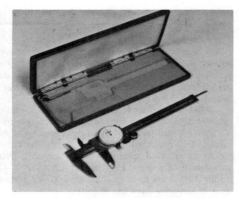

Vernier caliper

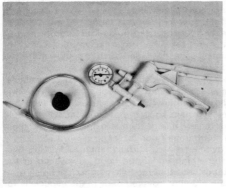

Vacuum tester

Brake shoe spring tool

Dial gauge set

Hydraulic lifter retractor

Piston ring groove cleaner

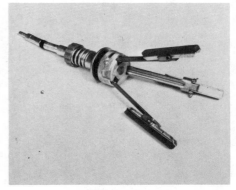

Cylinder hone

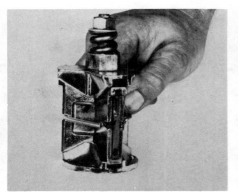

Cylinder ridge reamer

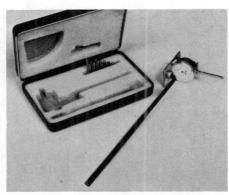

Cylinder bore taper gauge set

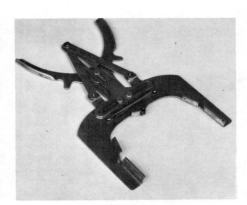

Piston ring expander

Tool Safety

Along with replacement of damaged or worn tools, other safety rules must be followed. Always wear eye protection (safety goggles) when working over a running engine, while under the car or when prying, striking, sawing or working with power tools. Safety goggles are available from an outlet that sells tools.

Always maintain a clean work area. Clean up spills of antifreeze, oil, hydraulic fluids, water, etc., immediately to avoid an accident.

Always use jack stands under the vehicle when the body must be raised. Don't trust this function to the jack itself, concrete or wood blocks or other dubious forms of support. (Note: On some asphalt surfaces it is a good idea to put 12 X 12 X $\frac{1}{2}$-in pieces of plywood under the stands to keep them from sinking from the weight of the car as it is lowered onto the stands).

Whenever removing or installing major components (i.e., engine, transmission, axle, etc), always have a helper on hand to avoid becoming pinned if the large assembly should fall or shift.

When using wrenches, combination or ratchet, always try to pull the wrench toward you. If the situation calls for pushing the wrench away to either tighten or loosen a nut or bolt, always push with an open hand to avoid scraped knuckles if the wrench should break loose. Whenever possible, use a long extension on a ratchet to get clear of things that can scratch hands. Always use the right tool for the job. Obviously, don't use a screwdriver as a chisel, or a ratchet handle as a hammer.

Gasoline or other flammable solvents should never be used to clean parts. If there is, however, no alternative available, and gasoline has to be used, keep the cleaning confined to a well-ventilated shop or garage, that does not have a gas heater or other appliance with an open flame. For these reasons, it's best to clean parts outside.

By obeying these few safety rules, repair and maintenance of a vehicle can be a safe, fun operation, that is quite rewarding.

Working facilities

Not to be overlooked when discussing tools is the workshop. If anything more than routine maintenance is to be carried out, some form of suitable working area becomes essential.

It is understood and appreciated that many home mechanics are without the use of good workshop or garage and end up removing an engine or doing major repair outside. Whenever possible, complete the overhaul under the cover of a roof.

If possible, overhauling and repair should be done on a clean, flat workbench or table of suitable working height.

Any workbench needs a vise, and one with a jaw opening of 4 in (100 mm) is suitable for most jobs. As mentioned previously, some clean, dry storage space is also required for tools, as well as the lubricants, cleaning fluids, touch-up paints and so on which soon become necessary.

Another item which may be required, and which has a much more general use, is an electric drill with a chuck capacity of $\frac{3}{8}$ in (19.5 mm). Together with a good selection of twist drill bits, the drill is essential for installing many aftermarket accessories, such as luggage racks, mirrors etc. Sometimes, waste oil and fluids drained from the engine or transmission during normal maintenance or repairs can become a problem with their disposal. To avoid pouring oil on the ground or in the sewage system, simply pour the used fluids into large bottles or jugs, seal them with caps and take them to a reclamation center or service station for disposal. Plastic jugs (such as old antifreeze containers) are ideal.

Always keep a supply of old newspapers and clean rags available. Old towels and other rags are excellent for mopping up spills. Many home mechanics use rolls of paper towels for most work because they don't have to be cleaned. To help keep the area under your vehicle from becoming stained or messy, a large carboard box can be cut open and flattened to protect the garage floor.

Whenever working over a painted surface, such as leaning over the fenders to service something under the hood, always cover the fender with an old blanket or bedspread to help protect the finish from tools and chemicals. There are vinyl covered pads made especially for this which are available in automotive parts stores and are recommended.

Jacking and towing

The jack supplied with the car should be used only for changing a wheel due to a roadside flat or for raising the car enough to allow jack stands to be placed under the car to support its weight. Under no circumstances should repair work be done under the car while it is supported by this jack, nor should the engine be started or run while this jack is being used.

All Phoenix and Omega cars come equipped with a ratchet-type bumper jack designed to lift one corner of the car by engaging in one end of either the front or rear bumper.

The car should be on level ground with the transaxle in 'Park' (automatic) or 'Reverse' (manual). The parking brake should be firmly set. Blocking the front and rear of the wheel on the same side as the one being lifted will further prevent the car from rolling.

With the jack column securely seated in the base and the lever in the 'Up' position, insert the jack hook into the bumper. The jack base must sit flat, with the column angled slightly away from the vehicle.

Operate the jack with a slow, smooth motion, and be attentive to any shifting in the weight of the car. The flexible body panels may deform during jacking, but will return to their original shape.

Raise the vehicle just enough so either the wheel and tire to be changed just clears the ground, or so jack stands can be placed into position, under the car. If jack stands are being used put the jack lever into the 'down' position and lower it until the weight of the car is off the jack.

The proper procedure for removing and installing a wheel and tire is described in Chapter 11, Section 2.

To remove the jack stands, the jack must be used once more to lift the vehicle enough so the stands can be removed from under the car. Then the car can be lowered to the ground and the jack removed.

Towing

The vehicle can be towed on all four wheels providing that speeds do not exceed 35 mph and the distance is not over 50 miles. Towing equipment specifically designed for this purpose should be used and should be attached to the main structural members of the car and not the bumper or brackets.

Safety is a major consideration when towing, and all applicable state and local laws should be obeyed. A safety chain system must be used for all towing.

While towing, the parking brake should be fully released and the transmission should be in 'Neutral'. The steering must be unlocked (ignition switch in the 'Off' position). Remember that power steering and power brakes will not work with the engine off.

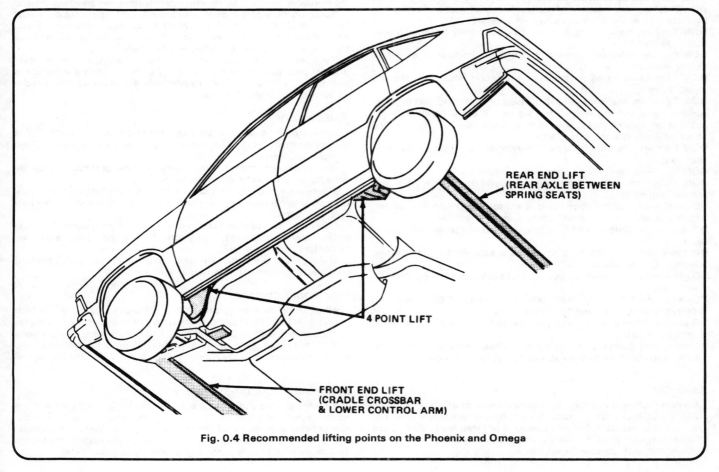

Fig. 0.4 Recommended lifting points on the Phoenix and Omega

Safety first!

Regardless of how enthusiastic you may be about getting on with the job at hand, take the time to ensure that your safety is not jeopardized. A moment's lack of attention can result in an accident, as can failure to observe certain simple safety precautions. The possibility of an accident will always exist, and the following points should not be considered a comprehensive list of all dangers. Rather, they are intended to make you aware of the risks and to encourage a safety conscious approach to all work you carry out on your vehicle.

Essential DOs and DON'Ts

DON'T rely on a jack when working under the vehicle. Always use approved jackstands to support the weight of the vehicle and place them under the recommended lift or support points.

DON'T attempt to loosen extremely tight fasteners (i.e. wheel lug nuts) while the vehicle is on a jack — it may fall.

DON'T start the engine without first making sure that the transmission is in Neutral (or Park where applicable) and the parking brake is set.

DON'T remove the radiator cap from a hot cooling system — let it cool or cover it with a cloth and release the pressure gradually.

DON'T attempt to drain the engine oil until you are sure it has cooled to the point that it will not burn you.

DON'T touch any part of the engine or exhaust system until it has cooled sufficiently to avoid burns.

DON'T siphon toxic liquids such as gasoline, antifreeze and brake fluid by mouth, or allow them to remain on your skin.

DON'T inhale brake lining dust — it is potentially hazardous (see *Asbestos* below)

DON'T allow spilled oil or grease to remain on the floor — wipe it up before someone slips on it.

DON'T use loose fitting wrenches or other tools which may slip and cause injury.

DON'T push on wrenches when loosening or tightening nuts or bolts. Always try to pull the wrench toward you. If the situation calls for pushing the wrench away, push with an open hand to avoid scraped knuckles if the wrench should slip.

DON'T attempt to lift a heavy component alone — get someone to help you.

DON'T rush or take unsafe shortcuts to finish a job.

DON'T allow children or animals in or around the vehicle while you are working on it.

DO wear eye protection when using power tools such as a drill, sander, bench grinder, etc. and when working under a vehicle.

DO keep loose clothing and long hair well out of the way of moving parts.

DO make sure that any hoist used has a safe working load rating adequate for the job.

DO get someone to check on you periodically when working alone on a vehicle.

DO carry out work in a logical sequence and make sure that everything is correctly assembled and tightened.

DO keep chemicals and fluids tightly capped and out of the reach of children and pets.

DO remember that your vehicle's safety affects that of yourself and others. If in doubt on any point, get professional advice.

Asbestos

Certain friction, insulating, sealing, and other products — such as brake linings, brake bands, clutch linings, torque converters, gaskets, etc. — contain asbestos. *Extreme care must be taken to avoid inhalation of dust from such products since it is hazardous to health.* If in doubt, assume that they *do* contain asbestos.

Fire

Remember at all times that gasoline is highly flammable. Never smoke or have any kind of open flame around when working on a vehicle. But the risk does not end there. A spark caused by an electrical short circuit, by two metal surfaces contacting each other, or even by static electricity built up in your body under certain conditions, can ignite gasoline vapors, which in a confined space are highly explosive. Do not, under any circumstances, use gasoline for cleaning parts. Use an approved safety solvent.

Always disconnect the battery ground (−) cable *at the battery* before working on any part of the fuel system or electrical system. Never risk spilling fuel on a hot engine or exhaust component.

It is strongly recommended that a fire extinguisher suitable for use on fuel and electrical fires be kept handy in the garage or workshop at all times. Never try to extinguish a fuel or electrical fire with water.

Fumes

Certain fumes are highly toxic and can quickly cause unconsciousness and even death if inhaled to any extent. Gasoline vapor falls into this category, as do the vapors from some cleaning solvents. Any draining or pouring of such volatile fluids should be done in a well ventilated area.

When using cleaning fluids and solvents, read the instructions on the container carefully. Never use materials from unmarked containers.

Never run the engine in an enclosed space, such as a garage. Exhaust fumes contain carbon monoxide, which is extremely poisonous. If you need to run the engine, always do so in the open air, or at least have the rear of the vehicle outside the work area.

If you are fortunate enough to have the use of an inspection pit, never drain or pour gasoline and never run the engine while the vehicle is over the pit. The fumes, being heavier than air, will concentrate in the pit with possibly lethal results.

The battery

Never create a spark or allow a bare light bulb near the battery. The battery normally gives off a certain amount of hydrogen gas, which is highly explosive.

Always disconnect the battery ground (−) cable *at the battery* before working on the fuel or electrical systems.

If possible, loosen the filler caps or cover when charging the battery from an external source. Do not charge at an excessive rate or the battery may burst.

Take care when adding water and when carrying a battery. The electrolyte, even when diluted, is very corrosive and should not be allowed to contact clothing or skin.

Always wear eye protection when cleaning the battery to prevent the caustic deposits from entering your eyes.

Household current

When using an electric power tool, inspection light, etc., which operates on household current, always make sure that the tool is correctly connected to its plug and that, where necessary, it is properly grounded. Do not use such items in damp conditions and, again, do not create a spark or apply excessive heat in the vicinity of fuel or fuel vapor.

Secondary ignition system voltage

A severe electric shock can result from touching certain parts of the ignition system (such as the spark plug wires) when the engine is running or being cranked, particularly if components are damp or the insulation is defective. In the case of an electronic ignition system, the secondary system voltage is much higher and could prove fatal.

Troubleshooting

Contents

Introduction

This section provides an easy-reference guide to the more common faults which may occur during the operation of your car. These faults and their probable causes are grouped under their respective systems, e.g. 'Engine', 'Cooling system', etc., and refer to the Chapter and/or Section which seals with the problem.

Remember that successful fault diagnosis is not a mysterious 'black art' practiced only by professional mechanics, it's simply the result of a bit of knowledge combined with an intelligent, systematic approach to the problem. Always work by a process of elimination, starting with the simplest solution and working through to the most complex — and never overlook the obvious. Even the most thorough and organized motorists have been known to forget to fill the gas tank or have the car lights on overnight, so don't assume that you are above such oversights.

Finally, always get clear in your own mind why a fault has occurred and take steps to ensure that it doesn't happen again. If the electrical system fails owing to a poor connection, check all other connections in the system to make sure that they don't fail as well; if a particular fuse continues to blow, find out why — don't just go on replacing fuses. Remember, failure of a small component can often be indicative of potential failure or incorrect functioning of a more important component or system.

Engine

1   Engine will not rotate when attempting to start

1   Battery terminal connections loose or corroded. Check the cable terminals at the battery; tighten or clean corrosion as necessary.
2   Battery discharged or faulty. If the cable connections are clean and tight on the battery posts, turn the key to the 'On' position and switch on the headlights and/or windshield wipers. If these fail to function, the battery is discharged.
3   Automatic transmission not fully engaged in Park or manual transmission clutch not fully depressed.
4   Broken, loose or disconnected wiring in the starting circuit. Inspect all wiring and connectors at the battery, starter solenoid (at lower left front of engine) and ignition switch (on steering column).
5   Starter motor pinion jammed on flywheel ring gear. If manual transmission, place gearshift in gear and rock the car to manually turn the engine. Remove starter (Chapter 5) and inspect pinion and flywheel (Chapter 2) at earliest convenience.
6   Starter solenoid faulty (Chapter 5).
7   Starter motor faulty (Chapter 5).
8   Ignition switch faulty (Chapter 10).

2   Engine rotates but will not start

1   Fuel tank empty.
2   Battery discharged (engine rotates slowly). Check the operation of electrical components as described in previous Section (Chapter 11).
3   Battery terminal connections loose or corroded. See previous Section.
4   Carburetor flooded and/or fuel level in carburetor incorrect. This will usually be accompanied by a strong fuel odor from under the hood. Wait a few minutes, depress the accelerator pedal all the way to the floor and attempt to start the engine.
5   Choke control inoperative (Chapter 1).
6   Fuel not reaching carburetor. With ignition switch in 'Off' position, open hood, remove the top plate of air cleaner assembly and observe the top of the carburetor (manually move choke plate back if necessary). Have an assistant depress accelerator pedal fully and check that fuel spurts into carburetor. If not, check fuel filter, fuel lines and fuel pump (Chapter 1 and 4).
7   Excessive moisture on, or damage to, ignition components (Chapter 1 and 5).
8   Worn, faulty or incorrectly adjusted spark plugs (Chapter 1).
9   Broken, loose or disconnected wiring in the starting circuit (see previous Section).
10   Distributor loose, thus changing ignition timing. Turn the distributor body as necessary to start the engine, then set ignition timing as soon as possible (Chapter 1 and 5).
11   Broken, loose or disconnected wires at the ignition coil, or faulty coil (Chapter 5).

3   Starter motor operates without rotating engine

1   Starter pinion sticking. Remove the starter (Chapter 5) and inspect.
2   Starter pinion or engine flywheel teeth worn or broken. Remove the inspection cover on the left side of the engine and inspect.

4   Engine hard to start when cold

1   Battery discharged or low. Check as described in Section 1.
2   Choke control inoperative or out of adjustment (Chapter 1).
3   Carburetor flooded (see Section 2).
4   Fuel supply not reaching the carburetor (see Section 2).
5   Carburetor worn and in need of overhauling (Chapter 4).

5   Engine hard to start when hot

1   Choke sticking in the closed position (Chapter 1).

2   Carburetor flooded (see Section 2).
3   Air filter in need of replacement (Chapter 1).
4   Fuel not reaching the carburetor (see Section 2).
5   Thermac air cleaner faulty (Chapter 1 and 6).
6   EFE (heat riser) sticking in the closed position (Chapter 1).

6   Starter motor noisy or excessively rough in engagement

1   Pinion or flywheel gear teeth worn or broken. Remove the inspection cover on the left side of the engine and inspect.
2   Starter motor retaining bolts loose or missing.

7   Engine starts but stops immediately

1   Loose or faulty electrical connections at distributor, coil or generator.
2   Insufficient fuel reaching the carburetor. Disconnect the fuel line at the carburetor and remove the filter (Chapter 1). Place a container under the disconnected fuel line. Disconnect wiring connector marked "BAT" from distributor cap. This will prevent the engine from starting. Have an assistant crank the engine several revolutions by turning the ignition key. Observe the flow of fuel from the line. If little or none at all, check for blockage in the lines and/or replace the fuel pump (Chapter 4).
3   Vacuum leak at the gasket surfaces of the intake manifold and/or carburetor. Check that all mounting bolts (nuts) are tightened to specifications and all vacuum hoses connected to the carburetor and manifold are positioned properly and are in good condition.

8   Engine 'lopes' while idling or idles erratically

1   Vacuum leakage. Check mounting bolts (nuts) at the carburetor and intake manifold for tightness. Check that all vacuum hoses are connected and are in good condition. Use a doctor's stethoscope or a length of fuel line hose held against your ear to listen for vacuum leaks while the engine is running. A hissing sound will be heard. A soapy water solution will also detect leaks. Check the carburetor and intake manifold gasket surfaces.
2   Leaking EGR valve or plugged PCV valve (see Chapter 6).
3   Air cleaner clogged and in need of replacement (Chapter 1).
4   Fuel pump not delivering sufficient fuel to the carburetor (see Section 7).
5   Carburetor out of adjustment (Chapter 4).
6   Leaking head gasket. If this is suspected, you are best to take the car to a repair shop or GM dealer where this can be pressure checked without the need to remove the heads.
7   Timing chain or gears worn and in need of replacement (Chapter 2).
8   Camshaft lobes worn, necessitating the removal of the camshaft for inspection (Chapter 2).

9   Engine misses at idle speed

1   Spark plugs faulty or not gapped properly (Chapter 1).
2   Faulty spark plug wires (Chapter 1).
3   Excessive moisture and/or damage on distributor components (Chapter 1).
4   Carburetor choke not operating properly (Chapter 4).
5   Sticking or faulty emissions systems (see Troubleshooting in Chapter 6).
6   Clogging fuel filter and/or foreign matter in fuel. Remove the fuel filter (Chapter 1 and 4) and inspect.
7   Vacuum leaks at carburetor, intake manifold or at hose connections. Check as described in Section 8.
8   Incorrect idle speed (Chapter 1) or idle mixture (Chapter 4).
9   Incorrect ignition timing (Chapter 1).
10   Uneven or low cylinder compression. Remove plugs and use compression tester as per manufacturer's instructions.

10   Engine misses throughout driving speed range

1   Carburetor fuel filter clogged and/or impurities in the fuel system

(Chapter 1). Also check fuel output at the carburetor (see Section 7).
2 Faulty or incorrectly gapped spark plugs (Chapter 1).
3 Incorrectly set ignition timing (Chapter 1).
4 Cracked distributor cap, disconnected distributor wires, or damage to the distributor components (Chapter 1).
5 Leaking spark plug wires (Chapter 1).
6 Emissions system components faulty (see Troubleshooting section, Chapter 6).
7 Low or uneven cylinder compression pressures. Remove spark plugs and test compression with gauge.
8 Weak or faulty ignition coil (Chapter 5).
9 Weak or faulty HEI ignition system (Chapter 5).
10 Vacuum leaks at carburetor, intake manifold or vacuum hoses (see Section 8).

11 Engine stalls

1 Carburetor idle speed incorrectly set (Chapter 1).
2 Carburetor fuel filter clogged and/or water and impurities in the fuel system (Chapter 1).
3 Choke improperly adjusted or sticking (Chapter 1).
4 Distributor components damp, or damage to distributor cap, rotor, etc. (Chapter 1).
5 Emissions system components faulty (Troubleshooting section, Chapter 6).
6 Faulty or incorrectly gapped spark plugs. (Chapter 1). Also check spark plug wires (Chapter 1).
7 Vacuum leak at the carburetor, intake manifold or vacuum hoses. Check as described in Section 8.
8 Valve lash incorrectly set (Chapter 2).

12 Engine lacks power

1 Incorrect ignition timing (Chapter 1).
2 Excessive play in distributor shaft. At the same time check for faulty distributor cap, wires, etc. (Chapter 1).
3 Faulty or incorrectly gapped spark plugs (Chapter 1).
4 Carburetor not adjusted properly or excessively worn (Chapter 4).
5 Weak coil or condensor (Chapter 5).
6 Faulty HEI system coil (Chapter 5).
7 Brakes binding (Chapters 1 and 9).
8 Automatic transmission fluid level incorrect, causing slippage (Chapter 1).
9 Manual transmission clutch slipping (Chapter 8).
10 Fuel filter clogged and/or impurities in the fuel system (Chapter 1 and 4).
11 Emissions control systems not functioning properly (see Troubleshooting, Chapter 6).
12 Use of sub-standard fuel. Fill tank with proper octane fuel.
13 Low or uneven cylinder compression pressures. Test with compression tester, which will also detect leaking valves and/or blown head gasket.

13 Engine backfires

1 Emissions systems not functioning properly (see Troubleshooting, Chapter 6).
2 Ignition timing incorrect (Section 1).
3 Carburetor in need of adjustment or worn excessively (Chapter 1 and 4).
4 Vacuum leak at carburetor, intake manifold or vacuum hoses. Check as described in Section 8.
5 Valve lash incorrectly set, and/or valves sticking (Chapter 2).

14 Pinging or knocking engine sounds on hard acceleration or uphill

1 Incorrect grade of fuel. Fill tank with fuel of the proper octane rating.
2 Ignition timing incorrect (Chapter 1).
3 Carburetor in need of adjustment (Chapter 1 and 4).

4 Improper spark plugs. Check plug type with that specified on tune-up decal located inside engine compartment. Also check plugs and wires for damage (Chapter 1).
5 Worn or damaged distributor components (Chapter 1).
6 Faulty emissions systems (see Troubleshooting, Chapter 6).
7 Vacuum leaks. (Check as described in Section 8).

15 Engine "diesels" (continues to run) after switching off

1 Idle speed too fast (Chapter 1).
2 Electrical solenoid at side of carburetor not functioning properly (Chapter 4).
3 Ignition timing incorrectly adjusted (Chapter 1).
4 Thermac air cleaner valve not operating properly (see Troubleshooting, Chapter 6).
5 Excessive engine operating temperatures. Probable causes of this are: malfunctioning thermostat, clogged radiator, faulty water pump (Chapter 3).

Engine — electrical

16 Battery will not hold a charge

1 Generator drive belt defective or not adjusted properly (Chapter 1).
2 Battery terminals loose or corroded (Chapter 1).
3 Generator not charging properly (Chapter 5).
4 Loose, broken or faulty wiring in the charging circuit (Chapter 5).
5 Short in vehicle circuitry causing a continual drain on battery.
6 Battery defective internally.

17 Ignition light fails to go out

1 Fault in generator or charging circuit (Chapter 5).
2 Generator drive belt defective or not properly adjusted (Chapter 1).

18 Ignition light fails to come on when key is turned

1 Ignition light bulb faulty (Chapter 10).
2 Generator faulty (Chapter 5).
3 Fault in the printed circuit, dash wiring or bulb holder (Chapter 10).

Engine fuel system

19 Excessive fuel consumption

1 Dirty or choked air filter element (Chapter 1).
2 Incorrectly set ignition timing (Chapter 1).
3 Choke sticking or improperly adjusted (Chapter 1).
4 Carburetor idle speed and/or mixture not adjusted properly (Chapters 1 and 4).
5 Carburetor internal parts excessively worn or damaged (Chapter 4).
6 Low tire pressure or incorrect tire size (Chapter 1).

20 Fuel leakage and/or fuel odor

1 Leak in a fuel feed or vent line (Chapter 4).
2 Tank overfilled. Fill only to automatic shut-off.
3 EEC emissions system filter in need of replacement (Chapter 6).
4 Vapor leaks from EEC system lines (Chapter 6).
5 Carburetor internal parts excessively worn or out of adjustment (Chapter 4).

Engine cooling system

21 Overheating

1 Insufficient coolant in system (Chapter 1).

2   Fan belt defective or not adjusted properly (Chapter 1).
3   Radiator core blocked or radiator grille dirty and restricted (Chapter 3).
4   Thermostat faulty (Chapter 3).
5   Fan not functioning properly. (Chapter 3).
6   Radiator cap not maintaining proper pressure. Have cap pressure tested by gas station or repair shop.
7   Ignition timing incorrect (Chapter 1).

22 Overcooling

1   Thermostat faulty (Chapter 3).
2   Inaccurate temperature gauge (Chapter 10).

23 External water leakage

1   Deteriorated or damaged hoses. Loose clamps at hose connections (Chapter 1).
2   Water pump seals defective. If this is the case, water will drip from the 'weep' hole in the water pump body (Chapter 3).
3   Leakage from radiator core or header tank. This will require the radiator to be professionally repaired (see Chapter 3 for removal procedures).
4   Engine drain plugs or water jacket freeze plugs leaking (see Chapters 1 and 2).

24 Internal water leakage

Note: *Internal coolant leaks can usually be detected by examining the oil. Check the dipstick and inside of valve cover for water deposits and an oil consistency like that of a milkshake.*
1   Faulty cylinder head gasket. Have the system pressure-tested professionally or remove the cylinder heads (Chapter 2) and inspect.
2   Cracked cylinder bore or cylinder head. Dismantle engine and inspect (Chapter 2).

25 Water loss

1   Overfilling system (Chapter 1).
2   Coolant boiling away due to overheating (see causes in Section 15).
3   Internal or external leakage (see Sections 22 and 23).
4   Faulty radiator cap. Have the cap pressure-tested.

26 Poor coolant circulation

1   Inoperative water pump. A quick test is to pinch the top radiator hose closed with your hand while the engine is idling, then let loose. You should feel a surge of water if the pump is working properly (Chapter 3).
2   Restriction in cooling system. Drain, flush and refill the system (Chapter 1). If it appears necessary, remove the radiator (Chapter 3) and have it reverse-flushed or professionally cleaned.
3   Loose water pump drive belt (Chapter 3).
4   Thermostat sticking (Chapter 3).

Clutch

27 Fails to release (pedal pressed to the floor – shift lever does not move freely in and out of reverse

1   Improper linkage adjustment (Chapter 8).
2   Fork shaft improperly installed (Chapter 8)
3   Clutch disc warped, bent or excessively damaged (Chapter 8).

28 Clutch slips (engine speed increases with no increase in road speed)

1   Linkage in need of adjustment (Chapter 8).

2   Clutch disc oil-soaked or facing worn. Remove disc (Chapter 8) and inspect.
3   Clutch disc not seated in. It may take 30 or 40 normal starts for a new disc to seat.

29 Grabbing (chattering) on take-up

1   Oil on clutch disc facings. Remove disc (Chapter 8) and inspect. Correct any leakage source.
2   Worn or loose engine or transmission mounts. These units may move slightly when clutch is released. Inspect mounts and bolts.
3   Worn splines on clutch gear. Remove clutch components (Chapter 8) and inspect.
4   Warped pressure plate or flywheel. Remove clutch components and inspect.

30 Squeal or rumble with clutch fully engaged (pedal released)

1   Improper adjustment; no lash (Chapter 8).
2   Release bearing binding on transmission bearing retainer. Remove clutch components (Chapter 8) and check bearing. Remove any burrs or nicks, clean and relubricate before reinstallation.
3   Weak linkage return spring. Replace the spring.

31 Squeal or rumble with clutch fully disengaged (pedal depressed)

1   Worn, faulty or broken release bearing (Chapter 8).
2   Worn or broken pressure plate springs (or diaphragm fingers) (Chapter 8).

32 Clutch pedal stays on floor when disengaged

1   Bind in linkage or release bearing. Inspect linkage or remove clutch components as necessary.
2   Linkage springs being over-extended. Adjust linkage for proper lash. Make sure proper pedal stop (bumper) is installed.

Manual transaxle

Note: *All service information on the manual transaxle is contained within Chapter 7.*

33 Noisy in Neutral with engine running

1   Input shaft bearing worn.
2   Damaged main drive gear bearing.

34 Noisy in all gears

1   Either of the above causes, and/or:
2   Insufficient lubricant.
3   Worn or damaged output gear bearings or shaft.

35 Noisy in one particular gear

1   Worn, damaged or chipped gear teeth for that particular gear.
2   Worn or damaged synchronizer for that particular gear.

36 Slips out of high gear

1   Transaxle loose on clutch housing.
2   Stiff shift lever seal.
3   Shift linkage binding.
4   Broken or loose input gear bearing retainer.
5   Dirt between clutch lever and engine housing
6   Worn or improperly adjusted linkage.

37 Difficulty in engaging gears

1   Clutch not releasing fully.
2   Loose, damaged or maladjusted shift linkage. Make a thorough inspection, replacing parts as necessary.

38 Fluid leakage

1   Excessive amount of lubricant in transaxle (see Chapter 1 for correct checking procedures. Drain lubricant as required).
2   Loose or improperly sealed clutch cover.
3   Drive axle shaft seals in need of replacement.
4   Loose or broken input gear bearing retainer O-ring.

Automatic transaxle

Note: *Due to the complexity of the automatic transaxle, it is difficult for the home mechanic to properly diagnose and service this component. For problems other than the following, the vehicle should be taken to a reputable mechanic.*

39 Fluid leakage

1   Automatic transaxle fluid is a deep red color, and fluid leaks should not be confused with engine oil which can easily be blown by air flow to the transaxle.
2   To pinpoint a leak, first remove all built-up dirt and grime from around the transaxle. Degreasing agents and/or steam cleaning will achieve this. With the underside clean, drive the car at low speeds so the air flow will not blow the leak far from its source. Raise the car and determine where the leak is coming from. Common areas of leakage are:
    a) Fluid pan: tighten mounting bolts and/or replace pan gasket as necessary (see Chapter 1).
    b) Drive axle shaft seals. Replace seals as necessary (Chapter 7).
    c) Filler pipe: replace the rubber oil seal where pipe enters transaxle case.
    d) Transaxle oil lines: tighten connectors where lines enter transaxle case and/or replace lines.
    e) Vent pipe: transaxle over-filled and/or water in fluid (see checking procedures, Chapter 1).

40 General shift mechanism problems

1   Section 9 in Chapter 7 seals with checking and adjusting the shift linkage on the automatic transaxle. Common problems which may be attributed to maladjusted linkage are:
    a) Engine starting in gears other than Park or Neutral.
    b) Indicator on quadrant pointing to a gear other than the one actually being used.
    c) Vehicle will not hold firm when in Park position.

41 Transaxle will not downshift with accelerator pedal pressed to the floor

1   Section 10 in Chapter 7 deals with adjusting the downshift cable or downshift switch to enable the transaxle to downshift properly.

42 Engine will start in gears other than Park or Neutral

1   Neutral start switch not working or clutch pedal self-adjusting mechanism not functioning properly (see Chapter 8).

43 Transaxle slips, shifts rough, is noisy or has no drive in forward or reverse gears

1   There are many probable causes for the above problems, but the

home mechanic should concern himself only with one possibility; fluid level.
2   Before taking the vehicle to a specialist, check the level of the fluid and condition of the fluid as described in Chapter 1. Correct fluid level as necessary or change the fluid and filter if needed. If problem persists, have a professional diagnose the probable cause.

Drive axles

44 Clicking noise in turns

1   Worn or damaged outboard joint. Check for cut or damaged seals. Repair as necessary (Chapter 8).

45 Knock or clunk when accelerating from a coast

1   Worn or damaged inboard joint. Check for cut or damaged seals. Repair as necessary (Chapter 8).

46 Shudder or vibration during acceleration

1   Excessive joint angle. Have checked and correct as necessary (Chapter 8).
2   Worn or damaged inboard or outboard joints. Repair or replace as necessary (Chapter 8).
3   Sticking inboard joint assembly. Correct or replace as necessary (Chapter 8).

Brakes
Note: *Before assuming a brake problem exists, check that the tires are in good condition and are inflated properly (see Chapter 1): the front end alignment is correct (see Chapter 11): and that the vehicle is not loaded with weight in an unequal manner.*

47 Vehicle pulls to one side under braking

1   Defective, damaged or oil-contaminated disc pad on one side. Inspect as described in Chapter 1. Refer to Chapter 9 if replacement is required.
2   Excessive wear of brake pad material or disc on one side. Inspect and correct as necessary.
3   Loose or disconnected front suspension components. Inspect and tighten all bolts to specifications (Chapter 1).
4   Defective caliper assembly. Remove caliper and inspect for stuck piston or damage (Chapter 9).

48 Noise (high-pitched squeak without brake applied)

1   Front brake pads worn out. This noise comes from the wear sensor rubbing against the disc. Replace pads with new ones immediately (Chapter 9).

49 Excessive brake pedal travel

1   Partial brake system failure. Inspect entire system (Chapter 1) and correct as required.
2   Insufficient fluid in master cylinder. Check (Chapter 1) and add fluid and bleed system if necessary (Chapter 9).
3   Rear brakes not adjusting properly. Make a series of starts and stops while the vehicle is in Reverse. If this does not correct the situation remove drums and inspect self-adjusters (Chapter 1).

50 Brake pedal appears spongy when depressed

1   Air in hydraulic lines. Bleed the brake system (Chapter 9).
2   Faulty flexible hoses. Inspect all system hoses and lines. Replace parts as necessary.

3   Master cylinder mountings insecure. Inspect master cylinder bolts (nuts) and torque tighten to specifications.
4   Master cylinder faulty (Chapter 9).

51 Excessive effort required to stop vehicle

1   Power brake booster not operating properly (Chapter 9).
2   Excessively worn linings or pads. Inspect and replace if necessary (Chapter 1).
3   One or more caliper pistons (front wheels) or wheel cylinders (rear wheels) seized or sticking. Inspect and rebuild as required (Chapter 9).
4   Brake linings or pads contaminated with oil or grease. Inspect and replace as required (Chapter 1).
5   New pads or linings fitted and not yet "bedded in". It will take a while for the new material to seat against the drum (or rotor).

52 Pedal travels to floor with little resistance

1   Little or no fluid in the master cylinder reservoir caused by: leaking wheel cylinder(s); leaking caliper piston(s); loose, damaged or disconnected brake lines. Inspect entire system and correct as necessary.

53 Brake pedal pulsates during brake application

1   Wheel bearings not adjusted properly or in need of replacement (Chapter 1).
2   Caliper not sliding properly due to improper installation or obstructions. Remove and inspect (Chapter 9).
3   Rotor not within specifications. Remove the rotor (Chapter 9) and check for excessive lateral run-out and parellelism. Have the rotor professionally machined or replace it with a new one.
4   Out-of-round rear brake drums. Remove the drums (Chapter 9) and have them professionally machined, or replace them.

Suspension and steering

54 Car pulls to one side

1   Tire pressures uneven (Chapter 1).
2   Defective tire (Chapter 1).
3   Excessive wear in suspension or steering components (Chapter 1).
4   Front end in need of alignment. (Chapter 11).
5   Front brakes dragging. Inspect braking system as described in Chapter 1.

55   Shimmy, shake or vibration

1   Tire or wheel out of balance or out of round. Have professionally balanced.
2   Loose or worn wheel bearings (Chapter 1). Replace as necessary (Chapter 11)
3   Shock absorbers and/or suspension components worn or damaged (Chapter 11).

56 Excessive pitching and/or rolling around corners or during braking

1   Defective shock absorbers. Replace as a set (Chapter 11).
2   Broken or weak coil springs and/or suspension components. Inspect as described in Chapter 11.

57 Excessively stiff steering

1   Lack of lubricant in power steering fluid reservoir (Chapter 1).
2   Incorrect tire pressures (Chapter 1).
3   Lack of lubrication at ball joints (Chapter 1).

4   Front end out of alignment.
5   Rack and pinions out of adjustment or lacking lubrication.
6   See also Section 63 'Lack of power assistance'.

58 Excessive play in steering

1   Loose wheel bearings (Chapter 1).
2   Excessive wear in suspension or steering components (Chapter 1).
3   Rack and pinion out of adjustment (Chapter 11).

59 Lack of power assistance

1   Steering pump drive belt faulty or not adjusted properly (Chapter 1).
2   Fluid level low (Chapter 1).
3   Hoses or pipes restricting the flow. Inspect and replace parts as necessary.
4   Air in power steering system. Bleed system (Chapter 11).

60 Excessive tire wear (not specific to one area)

1   Incorrect tire pressures (Chapter 1).
2   Tires out of balance. Have professionally balanced.
3   Wheels damaged. Inspect and replace as necessary.
4   Suspension or steering components excessively worn (Chapter 1).

61 Excessive tire wear on outside edge

1   Inflation pressures not correct (Chapter 1).
2   Excessive speed on turns.
3   Front-end alignment incorrect (excessive toe-in). Have professionally aligned (Chapter 11).
4   Suspension arm bent or twisted.

62 Excessive tire wear on inside edge

1   Inflation pressures incorrect (Chapter 1).
2   Front-end alignment incorrect (toe-out). Have professionally aligned (Chapter 11).
3   Loose or damaged steering components (Chapter 1).

63 Tire tread worn in one place

1   Tires out of balance. Balance tires professionally.
2   Damaged or buckled wheel. Inspect and replace if necessary.
3   Defective tire.

64 General vibration at highway speeds

1   Out-of-balance front wheels or tires. Have them professionally balanced.
2   Front or rear wheel bearings. Check (Chapter 1) and replace as necessary (Chapter 11).
3   Defective tire or wheel. Have them checked and replaced if necessary.

65 Noise – whether coasting or in drive

1   Road noise. No corrective procedures available.
2   Tire noise. Inspect tires and tire pressures (Chapter 1).
3   Front wheel bearings loose, worn or damaged. Check (Chapter 1) and replace if necessary (Chapter 11).
4   Lack of lubrication in the balljoints or tie rod ends (Chapter 1).
5   Damaged shock absorbers or mountings. (Chapter 1).
6   Loose wheel nuts. Check and tighten as necessary (Chapter 11).

Chemicals and lubricants

A wide variety of automotive chemicals and lubricants are available for use in maintaining and repairing a vehicle. They cover a number of areas from cleaning solvents and degreasers to lubricants and protectants for rubber, plastic and vinyl.

Note: *The use of any chemical or lubricant should be in accordance with the manufacturer's instructions on each label. Always read first for the proper application of these chemicals and lubricants.*

Points and plug cleaner is a solvent used to clean oily film and dust from points, oil deposits from spark plugs and grime from electrical connections. It is oil free and leaves no residue. It can also be used to spray through carburetor jets and other orifices to dislodge gum.

Carburetor cleaner is similar to points and plug cleaner but it usually has a stronger solvent and may leave a slightly oil residue. It is not recommended for cleaning electrical connections.

Brake cleaner is much like points and plug spray in that it leaves no residue. It is used for cleaning grease or brake fluid off brake parts where clean surfaces are absolutely necessary.

Silicone lubricant is used to protect rubber parts such as hoses, weatherstripping and grommets and is used as a light lubricant for hinges etc.

White grease is a light lubricant used on cable ends, controls and other areas where lubrication is needed, but the parts are not subjected to high temperatures or extreme friction.

Bearing grease is a heavy, high-temperature lubricant used in all bearings where there is high friction, heavy loads or high temperatures, such as wheel bearings, universal joints, water pump bearings, etc.

Gear oil (sometimes called gear grease) is a heavy oil used in the differential, standard transmission, and steering gear box, or other areas where high-friction, high-temperature lubrication is needed. It is viscosity weight rated at between 80 and 120.

Motor oil, of course, is the lubricant specially formulated for use in the engine. They normally contain a wide range of additives to prevent corrosion, reduce foaming and reduce wear, among other things. Oil comes in various weights (viscosity ratings) of anywhere from 5 to 80 weight. The weight of the oil recommended depends on the seasonal temperature and the demands on the engine. Light oil is used in very cold climates and very light-duty engines, whereas heavy oil is used in hot climates and under heavy-duty running conditions. Multiple-viscosity oils are formulated to have advantages of both light and heavy oils. When the engine and temperature are cold, the oil is thin, but as the engine heat goes up the oil becomes thicker to help combat heat. Multiple-viscosity oils have a multitude of a ratings from 5W-20 to 20W-50.

Gas additives perform several functions depending on the type of additive. They contain certain solvents that can help remove gum that builds up on carburetor and intake parts, and they can dissolve the lacquer that bonds carbon deposits together on the inside surfaces of the combustion chamber. They may also contain upper cylinder lubrication for valves and rings.

Oil additives range from viscosity index improvers (thickeners) to slick chemical treatments that reduce friction. Viscosity improvers make the motor oil thicker to withstand higher temperatures and reduce oil consumption in older engines.

Undercoating is a petroleum-based, tar-like substance that is used to protect metal surfaces on the underside of a vehicle from rain, snow and road salts. It also acts as a sound deadening agent by insulating the bottom of the vehicle.

Weatherstrip cement is used to adhere rubber weatherstripping around doors, windows, the trunk lid and other places where sealing weather out is important.

Waxes and polishes, of course, are used to help protect the painted and shiny metal surfaces from weather elements. There are certain waxes that are developed for particular types of paint. Some car polishes utilize a chemical or abrasive cleaner to help take off the top layer of oxidized (dull) paint on older cars. In recent years many other non-wax polishes have been introduced, and they contain a wide variety of chemicals, including polymers, co-polymers and silicones among others.

Degreasers are heavy-duty solvents that are used to dissolve grease that accumulates on various parts. They can be sprayed or brushed on and are either removed with water or solvent depending on the type.

Solvents are used alone or in combination with degreasers to clean parts and assemblies during repair and overhaul. A proper solvent for use in a garage by the home mechanic is one that is non-flammable and does not produce irritating fumes. Stoddard solvent is the most common type used in automotive work.

Gasket sealing compounds help seal joints where gaskets are used or this can be used on metal-to-metal joints. There are some that withstand extreme heat, others that are impervious to fuels, some that can seal large cavities, and types that either dry hard or stay pliable. Usually, gasket compounds can be applied with a brush, squeezed from a tube or sprayed on.

Thread cement is a locking compound that helps keep threaded fasteners from loosening from vibration. They are usualy either a liquid or a paste, and varieties are available for light-duty and heavy-duty applications.

Moisture dispersants are usually sprays that can be used to dry out electrical components such as the distributor, fuse block and wiring connections. Some moisture dispersants can also be used as treatment for rubber and as a lubrication for hinges, cables, etc.

Chapter 1 Tune-up and routine maintenance

Refer to Chapter 13 for specifications and information related to 1981 through 1984 models

Contents

Specifications

Note: *Additional specifications and torque settings can be found in each individual Chapter.*

Quick reference capacities

	U.S.	Liters	Imperial
Crankcase, with filter (L4 engine)	3 qt	2.8	$2\frac{1}{2}$ qt
Crankcase, with filter (V6 engine)	4 qt	3.8	$3\frac{1}{4}$ qt
Fuel tank	14 gal	53	$11\frac{3}{4}$ gal
Transaxle (Automatic)	5 qt	4.6	$4\frac{1}{4}$ qt
Transaxle (Manual)	3 pt	1.5	$2\frac{1}{2}$ pt
Cooling system (L4 engine) without A/C	$9\frac{1}{2}$ qt	9.0	8 qt
Cooling system (L4 engine) with A/C	$9\frac{3}{4}$ qt	9.3	8 qt
Cooling system (V6 engine) without A/C	$11\frac{1}{2}$ qt	10.8	$9\frac{1}{4}$ qt
Cooling system (V6 engine) with A/C	$11\frac{3}{4}$ qt	11.2	$9\frac{3}{4}$ qt

Recommended fluids and lubricants

Engine*

-30° F to 20°F	SAE 5W – 20
	SAE 5W – 30
	SAE 10W
0°F to 60°F	SAE 5W – 30
	SAE 10W – 30
	SAE 10W – 40
20°F to 100°F	SAE 20W
	SAE 10W – 30
	SAE 10W – 40
	SAE 20W – 40
	SAE 20W – 50

*All engine lubricants should be labeled SE.

Manual and automatic transaxles	Dextron-II automatic transmission fluid
Automatic transaxle shift linkage	Engine oil
Manual transaxle shift linkage	
Column shift	Chassis grease
Floor shift	Engine oil
Clutch linkage	
Pivot points	Engine oil
Pushrod to clutch fork joint	Chassis grease
Power steering pump and system	GM power steering fluid or equivalent
Brake system and master cylinder	Delco Supreme II fluid or DOT-3 fluids
Engine coolant	Mixture of good quality ethylene glycol based antifreeze and water, in at least a 50/50 ratio but not to exceed 70/30 ratio of antifreeze to water
Windshield washer solvent	GM Optikleen washer solvent ot equivalent
Parking brake cables	Chassis grease
Chassis lubrication	Chassis grease
Manual steering gear	GM Lubricant No. 1052182 or equivalent
Hood and door hinges	Engine oil
Hood latch assembly	
Pivots and spring anchor	Engine oil
Release pawl	Chassis grease
Key lock cylinders	WD-40 spray lubricant or equivalent

Filters

Engine oil filter (L4 engine)	AC Type PF40
Engine oil filter (V6 engine)	AC Type PF51
Air filter (L4 engine)	AC Type A734C
Air filter (V6 engine)	AC Type A735C
Fuel filter (L4 engine)	AC Type GF470
Fuel filter (V6 engine)	AC Type GF471
ECS filter (L4 and V6 engines)	GM 7026014

General data

PCV valve (L4)	AC Type CV795C
PCV valve (V6)	AC Type CV789C
Thermostat	195°F (91°C)
Radiator pressure cap	15 psi
Idle speed adjustments	Refer to Tune-up decal in engine compartment or Tune-up and emissions data
Spark plug gap (L4 engine)	.060 in
Spark plug gap (V6 engine)	.045 in
Ignition timing	Refer to Tune-up decal in engine compartment or Tune-up and emissions data

Torque specifications

	ft-lb	m-kg
Oil pan drain plug	20	2.7
Spark plugs	15	2.0
Carburetor mounting nuts	12	1.6
Fuel inlet nut	18	2.5
Manual transaxle fill plug	18	2.5
Automatic transaxle pan bolts	12	1.6
Brake caliper mounting bolts	28	3.8
Wheel lug nuts	103	14.2

Tune-up and emissions data

Engine & Code	Ignition timing BTDC degrees	Spark plug type gap	Solenoid screw rpm	Carburetor screw rpm base (B) curb (C)	Fast idle rpm	Carburetor identification choke spec.	Emission control devices	EGR valve model	Back pressure transducer	Distributor Dist. model	Distributor vacuum model	Vacuum advance Crankshaft degrees start @ in.hg	full @ in.hg	max. advance	Mechanical advance crankshaft
2.5 Liter 2-BBL, L-4, Manual Trans. Low Alt., VIN Code 5, Engine code(s) – WA, WB	10° 1000N	R43 TSX .060	1300N 1000N	1000N(C) 500N(B)	2400N 2600N 2400N 2600N	17059617(1) 17059621(1) 17059615(2) 17059619(2) NA	TAC,OC,BP-EGR,PAIR,EEC PCV,Decel. valve,DS-TVS DS-VRV,DS-VDV,EGR-TVS	17057238	Integral	1110783	1973703	4"	10.5"	19°-20° @ 10.5" hg.	0°-3° @ 1400 rpm 4°-9° @ 1700 rpm 19°-23° @ 4000 rpm
2.5 Liter 2-BBL, L-4, Auto. Trans. Low Alt., VIN Code 7, Engine code(s) – XA, XB	10° 650D	R43 TSX .060	900D 650D	650D(C) 500D(B)	2600N 2600N	17059616(1) 17059620(1) 17059614(2) NA	TAC,OC,BP-EGR,PAIR,EEC PCV,Decel. valve,DS-TVS DS-VRV,DS-VDV,EGR-TVS	17057220	Integral	1110782	1973675	3.5"	8"	16.5°-21° @ 8" hg.	0°-4° @ 1050 rpm 2.5°-9° @ 1300 rpm 19°-23° @ 4000 rpm
2.5 Liter 2-BBL, L-4, Manual Trans. Calif., VIN Code 5, Engine code(s) – A3, AU	10° 1000N	R43 TSX .060	1200N 1000N	1000N(C) 500N(B)	2200N 2200N	17059717(1) NA 17059715(2) NA	TAC,ORC,C-4 EGR,EEC PCV,Decel. valve,DS-TVS DS-VDV,EGR-TVS	17058400	NA	1110787	1973787	3.5"	9"	20° @ 9" hg.	0° @ 1050 rpm 7° @ 1700 rpm 21° @ 4000 rpm
2.5 Liter 2-BBL, L-4, Calif., VIN Code 5, Engine code(s) – Z9, Z4, Z6	10° 650D	R43 TSX .060	900D 650D	650D(C) 500D(B)	2600N 2600N	17059716(1) NA 17059714(2) NA	TAC,ORC,C-4 EGR,EEC PCV,Decel. valve,DS-TVS DS-VDV,EGR-TVS	17058357	NA	1110786	1973701	3.5"	9"	21° @ 9" hg.	0°-3° @ 1050 rpm 2.5°-7° @ 1300 rpm 19°-23° @ 4000 rpm
2.8 Liter 2-BBL, V-6, Manual Trans. Low Alt., VIN code 7, Engine code(s) – CNF, CNH	2° 750N	R44 TS	1200N 1200N	750N(B) 750N(B)	1900N 1900N	17059653(1) NA 17059651(2) NA	TAC,OC,EGR,PAIR,EFE EEC,PCV,Decel. valve, SVB-TVS,DS/CAN,PURGE-TVS	17058349	NA	1103362	1973644	3.5"	8.5"	8.5°-11.5° @ 20" hg.	0°-4.5° @ 1100 rpm 16.5°-21° @ 2500 rpm 24°-28° @ 4800 rpm
2.8 Liter 2-BBL, V-6, Auto. Trans. Low Alt., VIN code 7, Engine code(s) – CNJ, CNK, DCZ, DDB	6° 700P	R44 TS	850D NA	700D(C) 700D(C)	2000P 2000P	17059652(1) NA 17059650(2) NA	TAC,OC,EGR,PAIR,EFE EEC,PCV,Decel. valve, SVB-TVS,DS/CAN,PURGE-TVS EGR-TVS,EFE-TVS,EFE-CV	17058348	NA	1103361	1973626	3.5"	9"	8.5°-11.5° @ 20" hg.	0°-4.5° @ 1100 rpm 11.5°-16° @ 2200 rpm 20°-24° @ 4800 rpm
2.8 Liter 2-BBL, V-6, Manual Trans. Calif., VIN code 7, Engine code(s) – CNL, CNM	6° 750N	R44 TS .045	NA NA	750N(B) 750N(B)	2000N 2000N	17059763(1) NA 17059763(2) NA	TAC,ORC,C-4 PAIR,EFE BP-EGR,EEC,PCV,PAIR-SOL, Decel. valve,SVB-TVS EGR/CAN,PURGE-TVS,EFE-TVS EFE-CV,DS-TVS,DS-VDV	17061106	Integral	1103362	1973626	3.5"	8.5"	8.5°-11.5° @ 20" hg.	0°-4.5° @ 1100 rpm 16.5°-21° @ 2500 rpm 24°-28° @ 4800 rpm
2.8 Liter 2-BBL, V-6, Auto. Trans. Calif., VIN code 7, Engine code(s) – CNR, CNS	10° 700P	R44 TS .045	800D NA	700D(C) 700D(C)	2000P 2000P	17059762(1) NA 17059760(2) NA	TAC,ORC,C-4 PAIR,EFE BP-EGR,EEC,PCV,PAIR-SOL, Decel. valve,SVB-TVS EGR/CAN,PURGE-TVS,EFE-TVS EFE-CV,DS-TVS,DS-VDV	17061105 17061106	Integral	1103361	1973626	3.5"	9"	8.5°-11.5° @ 20" hg.	0°-4.5° @ 1100 rpm 11.5°-16° @ 2200 rpm 20°-24° @ 4800 rpm

AIR = Air injection reaction
AIR-DV = Air-diverter valve
C-4 = Computer controlled catalytic converter system
CTS = Coolant temperature sensor
CP-TVS = Canister purge-thermal vacuum switch
DS-TVS = Distributor spark-thermal vacuum switch
DS-\ DV = Distributor spark-vacuum delay valve
DS-VMW = Distributor spark-vacuum modulator valve
ECM = Electronic control module (C-4 system)
EECS = Evaporative emission control system
EFE = Early fuel evaporation
EFE-CV = Early fuel evaporation-check valve
EFE-EGR-TVS = Early fuel evaporation-exhaust gas recirculation-thermal vacuum switch
EGR-TVS = Exhaust gas recirculation-thermal vacuum switch
EGR-TVV = Exhaust gas recirculation-thermal vacuum valve
(B) = Base idle
(C) = Curb idle

OC = Oxidizing catalyst
ORC = Oxidation reduction catalyst
OS = Oxygen sensor
PAIR = Pulse air injection reactor
PCV = Positive crankcase ventilation
PVB-TVS = Primary vacuum break-thermal vacuum switch
SVB-TVS = Secondary vacuum break-thermal vacuum switch
THERMAC = Thermostatic air cleaner
TAC-TCV = Thermostatic air cleaner-thermal check valve
VCS = Vacuum control switch
VCV = Vacuum check valve
VMV = Vacuum modulator valve
VRV = Vacuum regulator valve
(1) = With air conditioning
(2) = Without air conditioning
NA = Not applicable
N = Neutral-manual trans.
P = Park-auto. trans.

1 Introduction

1 This Chapter was designed to help the home mechanic maintain his (or her) car for peak performance, economy, safety and longevity.
2 On the following pages you will find a maintenance schedule along with Sections which deal specifically with each item on the schedule. Included are visual checks, adjustments and item replacements. Location of the various components mentioned can be aided by referring to the engine compartment figures included.
3 Servicing you car using the time/mileage maintenance schedule and the sequenced Sections will give you a planned progam of maintenance. Keep in mind that it is a full plan, and maintaining only a few items at the specified intervals will not give you the same results.
4 You will find as you service your car that many of the procedures can, and should, be grouped together due to the nature of the job at hand. Examples of this are as follow:
5 *If the car is fully raised* for a chassis lubrication, for example, this is the ideal time for the following checks: manual transaxle fluid, exhaust system, suspension, steering and the fuel system.
6 *If the tires and wheels are removed*, as during a routine tire rotation, go ahead and check the brakes and wheel bearings at the same time.
7 *If you must borrow or rent a torque wrench*, you will do best to service the spark plugs and check the carburetor mounting torque both in the same day to save time and money.
8 The first step of this or any maintenance plan is to prepare yourself before the actual work begins. Read through the appropriate Sections for all work that is to be performed before you begin. Gather together all necessary parts and tools. If it appears you could have a problem during a particular job, don't hesitate to ask advice from your local parts man or dealer service department.

2 Routine maintenance intervals

Every 250 miles or weekly – whichever comes first

Check the engine oil level (Section 3)
Check the engine coolant level (Section 3)
Check the windshield washer fluid level (Section 3)
Check the tires and tire pressures (Section 4)
Check the automatic transaxle fluid level (Section 3)
Check the power steering fluid level, if so equipped (Section 3)

Every 3750 miles or 6 months – whichever comes first

Change engine oil and filter (Section 6)
Lubricate the chassis components (Section 32)
Inspect and service the cooling system (Section 22)
Inspect the exhaust system (Section 35)
Inspect the suspension and steering components (Section 34)
Check the drivebelts (Section 12)
Check the fuel system components (Section 23)
Check all fluid levels (Section 3)
Replace the PCV valve (Section 28)
Replace the air filter (Section 9)
Replace the PCV filter (Section 9)

Every 7500 miles or 12 months – whichever comes first

Check the Thermo Controlled Air Cleaner (Section 27)
Check the carburetor choke (Section 15)
Check the EFE system (Section 24)
Check the engine idle speed adjustments (Section 11)
Check the carburetor mounting torque (Section 18)
Check the vacuum advance system (Section 31)
Rotate the tires (Section 5)
Replace the fuel filter (Section 13)
Inspect the disc brakes (Section 19)
Check the EGR valve (Section 25)

Every 15 000 miles or 12 months – whichever comes first

Replace the spark plugs (Section 7)
Check the parking brake (Section 21)
Inspect the drum brakes (Section 19)
Check the throttle linkage (Section 16)
Check the spark plug wires (Section 18)
Check the wheel bearings (Section 20)
Change the automatic transaxle fluid and filter if car is driven under abnormal conditions (Section 36)

Every 30 000 miles or 24 months – whichever comes first

Check the drive axle and output shaft seals (Section 33)
Check the balljoints (Section 33)
Check the idle speed solenoid (Section 17)
Check the engine timing (Section 10)
Check the distributor (Section 14)
Check the EEC system and replace the EEC filter (Section 26)
Service the catalytic converter (Section 29)
Change the oxygen sensor (if so equipped) (Section 30)
Change the automatic transaxle fluid and filter (Section 36)

3 Fluid levels check

1 There are a number of components on a vehicle which rely on the use of fluids to perform their job. Through the normal operation of the car, these fluids are used up and must be replenished before damage occurs. See the Recommended Lubricants Section for the specific fluid to be used when adding is required. When checking fluid levels, it is important that the car is on a level surface.

Engine oil

2 The engine oil level is checked with a dipstick which is located at the side of the engine block. This dipstick travels through a tube and into the oil pan at the bottom of the engine.
3 The oil level should be checked preferably before the car has been driven, or about 15 minutes after the engine has been shut off. If the oil is checked immediately after driving the car, some of the oil will remain in the upper engine components, thus giving an inaccurate reading on the dipstick.
4 Pull the dipstick from its tube and wipe all the oil from the end with a clean rag. Insert the clean dipstick all the way back into the oil pan and pull it out again. Observe the oil at the end of the dipstick. At its highest point, the level should be between the 'Add' and 'Full' marks.
5 It takes approximately 1 quart of oil to raise the level from the 'Add' mark to the 'Full' mark on the dipstick. Do not allow the level to drop below the 'Add' mark, as this may cause engine damage due to oil starvation. On the other hand, do not overfill the engine by adding oil above the 'Full' mark, as this may result in oil-fouled spark plugs, oil leaks or oil seal failures.
6 Oil is added to the engine after removing a twist-off cap located on the rocker arm cover. An oil can spout or funnel will reduce spills as the oil is poured in (photo).
7 Checking the oil level can also be a step toward preventative maintenance. If you find the oil level dropping abnormally, this is an indication of oil leakage or internal engine wear which should be corrected. If there are water droplets in the oil, or it is milky-looking, this also indicates component failure, and the engine should be checked immediately. The condition of the oil can also be checked along with the level. With the dipstick removed from the engine, take your thumb and index finger and wipe the oil up the dipstick, looking for small dirt particles or engine filings which will cling to the dipstick. This is an indication that the oil should be drained and fresh oil added (Section 6).

Engine coolant

8 Most vehicles are equipped with a pressurized coolant recovery system which makes coolant level checks very easy. A clear or white coolant reservoir is attached to the inner fender panel and is connected by a hose to the radiator cap. As the engine heats up during operation,

coolant is forced from the radiator, through the connecting tube and into the reservoir. As the engine cools, this coolant is automatically drawn back into the radiator to keep the level correct.

9   The coolant level should be checked when the engine is cold. Merely observe the level of fluid in the reservoir, which should be at or near the 'Full cold' mark on the side of the reservoir. If the system is completely cooled, also check the level in the radiator by removing the cap. Some systems also have a 'Full hot' mark to check the level when the engine is hot.

10   Under no circumstances should the radiator cap be removed while the system is hot, as escaping steam could cause serious injury. Wait until the engine has completely cooled, then wrap a thick cloth around the cap and turn it to its first stop. If any steam escapes from the cap, allow the engine to cool further. Then remove the cap and check the level in the radiator. It should be 2 – 3 inches below the bottom of the filler neck.

11   If only a small amount of coolant is required to bring the system up to the proper level, regular water can be used. However, to maintain the proper antifreeze/water mixture in the system, both should be mixed together to replenish a low level. High-quality antifreeze offering protection to -20° should be mixed with water in the proportion specified on the container. Do not allow antifreeze to come in contact with your skin or painted surfaces of the car. Flush contacted areas immediately with plenty of water.

12   Coolant should be added to the reservoir after removing the cap at the top of the reservoir.

13   As the coolant level is checked, observe the condition of the coolant. It should be relatively clear. If the fluid is brown or a rust color, this is an indication that the system should be drained, flushed and refilled.

14   If the cooling system requires repeated additions to keep the proper level, have the pressure radiator cap checked for proper sealing ability. Also check for leaks in the system (cracked hoses, loose hose connections, leaking gaskets, etc.).

Windshield washer

15   The fluid for the windshield washer system is located in a plastic reservoir behind the left shock well. The level inside the reservoir

Fig. 1.1 Overall view of the L4 engine compartment (typical)

1 Right front shock well	7 Windshield wiper motor assembly	13 Tune-up decal	21 Exhaust manifold
2 Generator	8 A/C accumulator	14 Thermostat housing	22 Front engine strut
3 Heater/A/C blower assembly	9 Power brake vacuum booster filter	15 Coolant temperature sensor	23 Rocker arm cover
4 A/C vacuum tank	10 Brake master cylinder	16 Engine lifting bracket	24 Radiator filler cap
5 Carburetor	11 Windshield washer tank	17 Engine oil dipstick	25 A/C compressor
6 Air filter element and housing	12 Left front shock well	18 Spark plug wires	26 PCV valve
		19 Hood latch assembly	27 Engine oil filler cap
		20 Thermac motor assembly	28 Fender brace

should be maintained at the 'Full' mark (photo).

16 General Motors 'Optikleen' washer solvent or its equivalent should be added through the plastic cap whenever replenishing is required. Do not use plain water alone in this system, especially in cold climates where the water could freeze.

Battery

17 X-Body cars are equipped with 'Freedom, or maintenance-free batteries. These require no maintenance, as the battery case is sealed and has no removal caps for adding water.

18 If a maintenance-type battery is installed, the caps on the top of the battery should be removed periodically to check for a low water level. This check will be more critical during the warm summer months. Remove each of the caps and add distilled water to bring the level of each cell to the split ring in the filler opening.

19 Note: There are certain precautions to be taken when working on or near the battery: a) Never expose a battery to open flame or sparks which could ignite the hydrogen gas given off by the battery. b) Wear protective clothing and eye protection to reduce the possibility of the

corrosive sulfuric acid solution inside the battery harming you (if the fluid is splashed or spilled, flush the contacted area immediately with plenty of water). c) Remove all metal jewelery which could contact the positive terminal and another grounded metal source, thus causing a short circuit. d) Always keep batteries and battery acid out of the reach of children.

20 At the same time the battery water level is checked, the overall condition of the battery and its related components should be inspected. If corrosion is found on the cable ends or battery terminals, remove the cables and clean away all corrosion using a baking soda/water solution or a wire brush cleaning tool designed for this purpose. See Chapter 5 for complete battery care and servicing.

Brake master cylinder

21 The brake master cylinder is located on the left side of the engine compartment firewall and has a cap which must be removed to check the fluid level.

22 Before removing the cap, use a rag to clean all dirt, grease, etc., from around the cap area. If any foreign matter enters the master

Fig. 1.2 Overall view of the V6 engine compartment (typical)

1 Right front shock well	7 Power brake vacuum booster	13 Front PULSAIR valve	19 Engine oil filler cap
2 Heater/A/C blower assembly	filter	assembly	20 Front engine strut
3 A/C vacuum tank	8 Brake master cylinder	14 Spark plug wires	21 Intake manifold
4 Rear PULSAIR valve	9 Windshield washer tank	15 Radiator support	22 A/C compressor
assembly	10 Left front shock well	16 Hood latch assembly	23 Fender brace
5 A/C accumulator	11 Air cleaner duct	17 PCV valve	24 EGR valve
6 Windshield wiper motor	12 Distributor	18 Carburetor	
assembly			

3.6 Oil filler cap location on the L4 engine

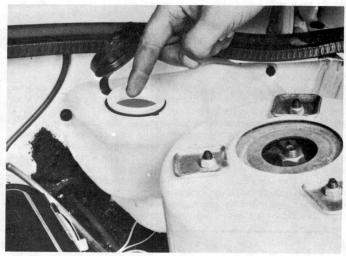

3.15 Windshield washer fluid tank

3.25 Adding brake fluid to the brake master cylinder

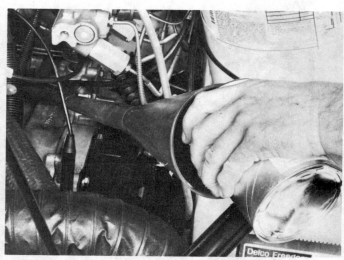

3.38 Using a funnel to add fluid to the automatic transaxle

cylinder with the cap removed, blockage in the brake system lines can occur. Also make sure all painted surfaces around the master cylinder are covered, as brake fluid will ruin paintwork.
23 Release the clip(s) securing the cap to the top of the master cylinder.
24 Carefully lift the cap off the cylinder and observe the fluid level. It should be approximately ¼-inch below the top edge of each reservoir.
25 If additional fluid is necessary to bring the level up to the proper height, carefully pour the specified brake fluid into the master cylinder (photo). Be careful not to spill the fluid on painted surfaces. Be sure the specified fluid is used, as mixing different types of brake fluid can cause damage to the system. See Recommended Lubricants in the front of this Chapter or your owner's manual.
26 At this time the fluid and master cylinder can be inspected for contamination. Normally, the braking system will not need periodic draining and refilling, but if rust deposits, dirt particles or water droplets are seen in the fluid, the system should be dismantled, drained and refilled with fresh fluid.
27 Reinstall the master cylinder cap. Make sure the lid is properly seated to prevent fluid leakage and/or system pressure loss.
28 The brake fluid in the master cylinder will drop slightly as the brake shoes or pads at each wheel wear down during normal operation. If the master cylinder requires repeated replenishing to keep it at the proper level, this is an indication of leakage in the brake system which should be corrected immediately. Check all brake lines and their

connections, along with the wheel cylinders and booster (see Chapter 9 for more information).
29 If upon checking the master cylinder fluid level you discover that one or both reservoirs is empty or nearly empty, the braking system should be bled (Chapter 9). When the fluid level gets low, air can enter the system and should be removed by bleeding the brakes.

Manual transaxle
30 Manual transaxles do not have a dipstick. The fluid level is checked by removing a plug in the left side of the transaxle case (Fig. 1.4). Locate this plug and use a rag to clean the plug and the area around it.
31 With the vehicle components cold, remove the plug. If fluid immediately starts leaking out, thread the plug back into the transaxle because the fluid level is all right. If there is no fluid leakage, completely remove the plug and place your little finger inside the hole. The fluid level should be just at the bottom of the plug hole.
32 If the transaxle needs more fluid, use a syringe to squeeze the appropriate lubricant into the plug hole to bring the fluid up to the proper level.
33 Thread the plug back into the transaxle and tighten it securely. Drive the car and check for leaks around the plug.

Automatic transaxle
34 Due to the shape of the filler tube, fluid level readings may be

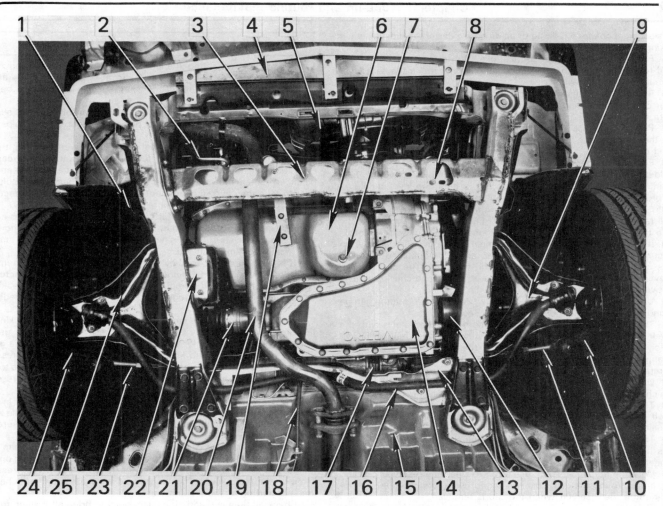

Fig. 1.3 Typical view of the underside of the engine compartment

1	Fender splash shield	8	Front transaxle mount	14	Transaxle	20	Front exhaust pipe
2	Power steering pump	9	Left lower control arm	15	Floor pan	21	Right drive axle
3	Cradle	10	Left steering knuckle	16	Stabilizer bar	22	Engine mount
4	Front bumper skirt	11	Left tie rod	17	Rack and pinion assembly	23	Right tie rod
5	Fan and fan shroud	12	Left drive axle	18	Parking brake cable	24	Right steering knuckle
6	Engine drain pan	13	Rear transaxle mount	19	Damper (L4)	25	Right lower control arm
7	Engine oil drain plug						

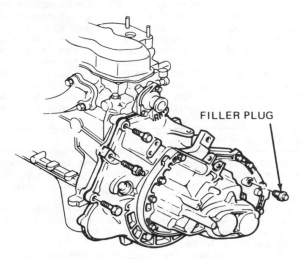

Fig. 1.4 Manual transaxle filler plug location (Sec 3)

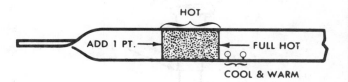

Fig. 1.5 Automatic transaxle dipstick (Sec 3)

misleading. Look for a full ring of oil on both sides of the dipstick when taking a reading.

35　Park the car on a level surface, place the selector lever in 'Park' and leave the engine running at an idle. Do not move the shift lever through all of the gears.

36　Remove the transaxle dipstick (located on the left side, near the rear of the engine) and wipe all the fluid from the end of the dipstick with a clean rag.

37　Push the dipstick back into the transaxle until the cap seats firmly on the dipstick tube. Now remove the dipstick again and observe the fluid on the end.

38　Feel the temperature of the fluid on the dipstick. If the fluid feels cold or warm the level should be between the dimples above the 'Full' mark. See Fig. 1.5. If the fluid is too hot to hold, the level should be at or in the hatched area near the 'Full' mark. If the fluid is below the 'Add' mark, add sufficient fluid to bring the level up. One pint of fluid will raise the level from 'Add' to 'Full'. Fluid should be added directly into the dipstick guide tube, using a funnel to prevent spills (photo).

39　It is important that the transaxle must not be overfilled. Under no circumstances should the fluid level be above its specified mark, as this could cause internal damage to the transaxle. The best way to prevent overfilling is to add fluid a little at a time and check the level between additions.

40　Use only transaxle fluid specified by GM. This information can be found in the Recommended Lubricants Section.

41　The condition of the fluid should also be checked along with the level. If the fluid at the end of the dipstick is a dark reddish-brown color, or if the fluid has a 'burnt' smell, the transaxle fluid should be changed with fresh. If you are in doubt about the condition of the fluid, purchase some new fluid and compare the two for color and smell.

42　Unlike manual steering, the power steering system relies on fluid which may, over a period of time, require replenishing.

43　The reservoir for the power steering pump is inside the pump itself, and the combination cap/dipstick is located on top of the pump housing.

44　The power steering fluid level should be checked only after the car has been driven, with the fluid at operating temperature. The front wheels should be pointed straight ahead.

45　With the engine shut off, use a rag to clean the reservoir cap and the areas around the cap. This will help prevent foreign material from falling into the reservoir when the cap is removed.

46　Twist off the reservoir cap, which has a built-in dipstick attached to it. Pull off the cap and clean off the fluid at the bottom of the dipstick with a clean rag. Now reinstall the dipstick/cap assembly to get a fluid level reading. Remove the dipstick/cap and observe the fluid level. When the fluid is hot, it should be between the 'Hot' and 'Cold' marks on the dipstick (Fig. 1.6).

47　If additional fluid is required, pour the specified lubricant directly into the reservoir, using a funnel to prevent spills.

48　If the reservoir requires frequent fluid additions, all power steering hoses, hose connections, the power steering pump and the rack and pinion assembly should be carefully checked for leaks.

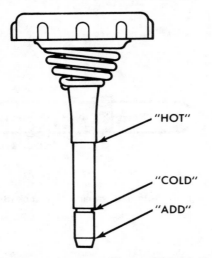

Fig. 1.6 Power steering pump filler cap/dipstick (Sec 3)

4　Tire and tire pressure checks

1　Periodically inspecting the tires can not only prevent you from being stranded with a flat tire, but can also give you clues as to possible problems with the steering and suspension systems before major damage occurs.

2　Proper tire inflation add miles to the lifespan of the tires, allows the car to achieve maximum miles-per-gallon figures, and helps the overall riding comfort of the car.

3　When inspecting the tire, first check the wear on the tread. Irregularities in the tread pattern (cupping, flat spots, more wear on one side than the other) are indications of front end alignment and/or balance problems. If any of these conditions are found you would do best to take the car to a competent repair shop which can correct the problem. See Chapter 11 for more information.

4　Also check the tread area for cuts or punctures. Many times a nail or tack will imbed itself into the tire tread and yet the tire will hold its air pressure for a short time. In most cases, a repair shop or gas station can repair the punctured tire.

5　It is also important to check the sidewalls of the tire, both inside and outside. Check for the rubber being deteriorated, cut or punctured. Also inspect the inboard side of the tire for signs of brake fluid leakage, which indicates that a thorough brake inspection is needed immediately (Section 19).

6　Incorrect tire pressure cannot be determined merely by looking at the tire. This is especially true for radial tires. A tire pressure gauge must be used. If you do not already have a reliable gauge, it is a good idea to purchase one and keep it in the glove box. Built-in pressure gauges at gas stations are often unreliable. If you are in doubt as to the accuracy of your gauge, many repair shops have 'master' pressure gauges which you can use for comparison purposes.

7　Always check tire inflation when the tires are cold. Cold, in this case, means that the car has not been driven more than one mile after sitting for three hoours or more. It is normal for the pressure to increase 4 to 8 pounds or more then the tires are hot.

8　Unscrew the valve cap protruding from the wheel or hubcap and firmly press the gauge onto the valve stem. Observe the reading on the gauge and check this figure against the recommended tire pressure listed on the tire placard. This tire placard is usually found attached to the rear portion of the driver's door.

9　Check all tires and add air as necessary to bring all tires up to the recommended pressure levels. Do not forget the spare tire. Be sure to reinstall the valve caps, which will keep dirt and moisture out of the valve stem mechanism.

5　Tire rotation

1　Radial tires, as used on the X-Body cars, tend to wear faster in the shoulder area than other tire designs. This is especially so for the front tires. Therefore, in order to obtain the maximum life from the tires, they should be rotated at 7500 miles, and then again at every 15 000-mile intervals, as shown in the Routine Maintenance schedule.

2　Rotating the tires simply means that the rear tires are removed from the rear axle and remounted on the front axle. At the same time, the front tires are likewise transferred to the rear axle.

3　It is important with radial tires that the tires be kept on the same side of the car during rotation. For example, the right rear tire should be remounted in the right front position, while the right front tire is remounted in the right rear position. The same goes for the left side.

6　Oil and filter change

1　Frequent oil changes may be the best form, of preventative maintenance available for the home mechanic. When engine oil get old, it gets diluted and contaminated, which ultimately leads to premature parts wear.

2　Although some sources recommend oil filter changes every other oil change, we feel that the minimal cost of an oil filter and the relative ease with which it is installed dictate that a new filter be used whenever the oil is changed.

3　The tools necessary for a normal oil and filter change are: a wrench to fit the drain plug at the bottom of the oil pan; and oil filter wrench to remove the old filter; a container with at least a 6 quart capacity to drain the old oil into; and a funnel or oil can spout to help pour fresh oil into the engine.

4   In addition, you should have plenty of clean rags and newspapers handy to mop up any spills. Access to the underside of the car is greatly improved if the car can be lifted on a hoist, driven onto ramps or supported by jack stands. Do not work under a car which is supported only by a bumper, hydraulic or scissors-type jack.

5   If this is your first change on the car, it is a good idea to crawl underneath and familiarize yourself with the locations of the oil drain plug and the oil filter. Since the engine and exhaust components will be warm during the actual work, it is best to figure out any potential problems before the car and its accessories are hot.

6   Allow the car to warm up to normal operating temperature. If the new oil or any tools are needed, use this warm-up time to gather everything necessary for the job. The correct type of oil to buy for your application can be found in Recommended Lubricants in the front of this Chapter.

7   With the engine oil warm (warm engine oil will drain better and more built-up sludge will be removed with the oil), raise the vehicle for access beneath. Make sure the car is firmly supported.

8   Move all necessary tools, rags and newspapers under the car. Position the drain pan under the drain plug. Keep in mind that the oil will initially flow from the pan with some force, so place the pan accordingly.

9   Being careful not to touch any of the hot exhaust pipe components, use the wrench to remove the drain plug near the bottom of the oil pan (photo). Depending on how hot the oil has become, you may want to wear gloves while unscrewing the plug the final few turns.

10 Allow the old oil to drain into the pan. It may be necessary to remove the pan farther under the engine as the oil flow reduces to a trickle.

11 After all the oil has drained, clean the drain plug thoroughly with a clean rag. Small metal filings may cling to this plug which could immediately contaminate your new oil.

12 Clean the area around the drain plug opening and reinstall the drain plug. Tighten the plug securely with your wrench. If a torque wrench is available, the torque setting is 20 ft-lb.

13 Move the drain pan into position under the oil filter (photo).

14 Now use the filter wrench to loosen the oil filter. Chain or metal band-type filter wrenches may distort the filter canister, but don't worry too much about this as the filter will be discarded anyway.

15 If the filter is on so tight it cannot be loosened, or is inaccessible with a filter wrench, as a last resort you can punch a metal bar or long screwdriver directly through the bottom of the canister and use this as a T-bar to turn the filter. If this must be done, be prepared for oil to spurt out of the canister as it is punctured.

16 Completely unscrew the old filter. Be careful, it is full of oil. Empty the old oil inside the filter into the drain pan.

17 Compare the old filter with the new one to make sure they are of the same type.

18 Use a clean rag to remove all oil, dirt and sludge from the area where the oil filter mounts to the engine. Check the old filter to make sure the rubber gasket is not stuck to the engine mounting surface. If this gasket is stuck to the engine (use a flashlight if necessary), remove it.

19 Open one of the cans of new oil and fill the new filter with fresh oil. Also smear a light coat of this fresh oil onto the rubber gasket of the new filter.

20 Screw the new filter to the engine following the tightening directions printed on the filter canister or packing box. Most filter manufacturers recommend against using a filter wrench due to possible overtightening or damage to the canister.

21 Remove all tools, rags, etc., from under the car, being careful not to spill the oil in the drain pan. Lower the car off its support devices.

22 Move to the engine compartment and locate the oil filler cap on the rocker arm cover.

23 If an oil can spout is used, push the spout into the top of the oil can and pour the fresh oil through the filler opening. A funnel placed into the opening may also be used.

24 Pour about 3 quarts of fresh oil into the engine. Wait a few minutes to allow the oil to drain to the pan, then check the level on the oil dipstick (see Section 2 if necessary). If the oil level is at or near the lower 'Add' mark, start the engine and allow the new oil to circulate.

25 Run the engine for only about a minute and then shut it off. Immediately look under the car and check for leaks at the oil pan drain plug and around the oil filter. If either is leaking, tighten with a bit more force.

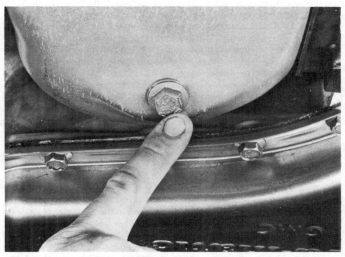

6.9 Crankcase oil drain plug location

6.13 The V6 oil filter is located between the starter and the fuel pump

26 With the new oil circulated and the filter now completely full, recheck the level on the dipstick and add enough oil to bring the level to the 'Full' mark on the dipstick.

27 During the first few trips after an oil change, make a point to check for leaks, and also check the oil level.

28 The old oil drained from the engine cannot be reused in its present state and should be disposed of. Oil reclamation centers, auto repair shops and gas stations will normally accept the oil which can be refined and used again. After the oil has cooled, it can be drained into a suitable container (capped plastic jugs, topped bottles, milk cartons, etc.) for transport to one of these disposal sites.

7   Spark plug – replacement

1   The spark plugs are located on the front side of an L4 engine and on the front and rear sides of a V6. If the car is equipped with air-conditioning or power steering, some of the plugs may be tricky to service, in which case special extension or swivel tools will be necessary. Make a survey under the hood to ascertain if special tools will be needed.

2   If most cases the tools necessary for a spark plug replacement job are: a plug wrench or spark plug socket which fits onto a ratchet wrench (this special socket will be insulated inside to protect the porcelain insulator) and a feeler gauge to check and adjust the spark

plug gap. A special spark plug wire removal tool is available for separating the wire boot from the spark plug (photo).

3   The best policy to follow when replacing the spark plugs is to purchase the new spark plugs beforehand, adjust them to the proper gap and then replace each plug one at a time. When buying the new spark plugs it is important that the correct plug is purchased for your specific engine. This information can be found in the Specifications Section of this Chapter, but should be checked against the information found on the Tune-up decal located under the hood of your car or in the factory owner's manual. If differences exist between these sources, purchase the spark plug type specified on the Tune-up decal, as this information was printed for your specific engine.

4   With the new spark plugs at hand, allow the engine to thoroughly cool before attempting the removal. During this cooling time, each of the new spark plugs can be inspected for defects and the gap can be checked.

5   The gap is checked by inserting the proper thickness gauge between the electrodes at the tip of the plug. The gap between these electrodes should be the same as that given in the Specifications or on the Tune-up decal. The wire should just touch each of the electrodes. If the gap is incorrect, use the notched adjuster on the feeler gauge body to bend the curved side electrode slightly until the proper gap is achieved. Also at this time check for cracks in the spark plug body, indicating the spark plug should be replaced with a new one. If the side electrode is not exactly over the center one, use the notched adjuster to align the two.

6   Cover the fenders of the car to prevent damage to exterior paint.

7   With the engine cool, remove the spark plug wire from one spark plug. Do this by grabbing the boot at the end of the wire, not the wire itself. Sometimes it is necessary to use a twisting motion while the boot and plug wire is pulled free. Using a plug wire removal tool is the easiest and safest method.

8   If compressed air is available, use this to blow any dirt or foreign material away from the spark plug area. A common bicycle pump will also work. The idea here is to eliminate the possibility of foreign material falling into the engine cylinder as the spark plug is replaced.

9   Now place the spark plug wrench or socket over the plug and remove it from the engine by turning in a counterclockwise motion.

10 Compare the spark plug with those shown on page 129 to get an indication of the overall running condition of the engine.

11 Insert one of the new plugs into the engine, tightening it as much as possible by hand. The spark plug should screw easily into the engine. If it doesn't, change the angle of the spark plug slightly, as chances are the threads are not matched (cross-threaded).

12 Firmly tighten the spark plug with the wrench or socket. It is best to use a torque wrench for this to assure that the plug is seated correctly. The correct torque figure is shown in the Specifications.

13 Before pushing the spark plug wire onto the end of the plug, inspect it following the procedures outlined in Section 18.

14 Install the plug wire to the new spark plug, again using a twisting motion on the boot until it is firmly seated on the spark plug. Make sure the wire is routed away from the hot exhaust manifold.

15 Follow the above procedures for the remaining spark plugs, replacing each one at a time to prevent mixing up the spark plug wires.

8   Spark plug wires check

1   The spark plug wires should be checked at the recommended intervals or whenever new spark plugs are installed.

2   The wires should be inspected one at a time to prevent mixing up the order which is essential for proper engine operation.

3   Disconnect the plug wire from the spark plug. A removal tool can be used for this, or you can grab the rubber boot, twist slightly and then pull the wire free. Do not pull on the wire itself, only on the rubber boot.

4   Inspect inside the boot for corrosion, which will look like a white, crusty powder. Some models use a conductive white grease which should not be mistaken for corrosion.

5   Now push the wire and boot back onto the end of the spark plug. It should be a tight fit on the plug end. If not, remove the wire and use a pair of pliers to carefully crimp the metal connector inside the wire boot until the fit is secure.

6   Now, using a clean rag, clean the entire length of the wire. Remove all built-up dirt and grease. As this is done, inspect for burns, cracks, or any other form of damage. Bend the wires in several places to ensure that the conductive inside wire has not hardened.

7   Next the wires should be checked at the distributor in the same manner as the spark plugs. On the V6 engine the distributor boots are connected to a circular retaining ring. Release the locking tabs, turn the ring upside-down and check all wire boots at the same time.

8   After checking each wire, one at a time, reinstall them (or the retaining ring), making sure they are securely fastened at the distributor and spark plug.

9   A visual check of the spark plug wires can also be made. In a darkened garage (make sure there is ventilation) start the engine and observe each plug wire. Be carefull not to come into contact with any moving engine parts. If there is a break or fault in the wire, you will be able to see arcing or a small spark at the damaged area.

10 If it is decided that the spark plug wires are in need of replacement, purchase a new set for your specific engine model. Wire sets can be purchased which are pre-cut to the proper size and with the rubber boots already installed. Remove and replace each wire individually to prevent mix-ups in the firing sequence.

9   Air filter and PCV filter replacement

1   At the specified intervals, the air filter and PCV filter should be replaced with new ones. A thorough program of preventative mainten-

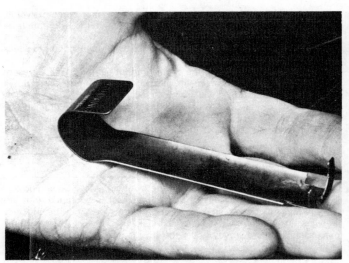

7.2 A spark plug wire removing tool prevents damaging the wire when removing it from the plug

9.2 The L4 air filter and housing

ance would call for the two filters to be inspected periodically between changes.

2 The air filter is located inside the air cleaner housing on the top of the engine. To reach the filter, first remove the top plate (photo).

3 While the top plate is off, be careful not to drop anything down into the carburetor.

4 Lift the air filter out of the housing.

5 To check the filter, hold it up to strong sunlight, or place a flashlight or droplight on the inside of the ring-shaped filter. If you can see light coming through the paper element, the filter is all right. Check all the way around the filter.

6 Wipe the inside of the air cleaner clean with a rag.

7 Place the old filter (if in good condition) or the new filter (if specified interval has elapsed) back into the air cleaner housing. Make sure it seats properly in the bottom of the housing.

8 Reinstall the top plate.

9 The PCV filter is also located inside the air cleaner housing. Remove the top plate as described previously and locate the filter on the side of the housing.

10 Loosen the hose clamp, if equipped, at the end of the PCV hose leading to the filter. Disconnect the hose from the filter.

11 Remove the metal locking clip which secures the filter holder to the air cleaner housing. Pliers can be used for this.

12 Remove the filter and plastic holder from the inside of the air cleaner.

13 Compare the new filter with the old one to make sure they are the same.

14 Place the new filter assembly into position and install the metal locking clip on the outside of the air cleaner.

15 Connect the PCV hose and tighten the clamp around the end of the hose.

16 Reinstall the air cleaner top plate.

17 For more information on these filters and the systems they are a part of, see Chapter 6.

10 Ignition timing

1 The proper ignition timing setting for your car is printed on the Tune-Up decal located on the left shock well inside the engine compartment. It can also be found in Specifications. If there are any discrepancies between these specs, the Tune-Up decal should be given preference.

2 Locate the timing mark pointer plate located alongside the crankshaft pulley (Fig. 1.7). The 'O' mark is Top Dead Center. To locate which mark the notch in the pulley must line up with to achieve correct timing, count back from the 'O' mark the number of degrees BTDC as noted in your specifications. Each mark on the timing plate equals one degree. Now locate the notch in the pulley and mark it with a dab of paint or chalk so it will be visible under the strobe light.

3 Follow all of the preliminary instructions printed on your Tune-Up decal.

4 Disconnect the vacuum advance line from the vacuum advance mechanism.

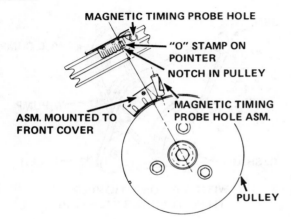

MAGNETIC TIMING PROBE HOLE

"O" STAMP ON POINTER

NOTCH IN PULLEY

ASM. MOUNTED TO FRONT COVER

MAGNETIC TIMING PROBE HOLE ASM.

PULLEY

Fig. 1.7 Location of the ignition timing marks plate mounted by the crank pulley (Sec 10)

5 Connect a tachometer according to the manufacturer's instructions and set the idle speed to the setting noted on the Tune-Up decal. Refer to Section 11 for setting the idle speed.

6 With the ignition off, connect the pick-up lead of the timing light to the number one spark plug. Use either a jumper lead between the wire and plug or an inductive-type pick-up. Do not pierce the wire or attempt to insert a wire between the boot and the wire. Connect the timing light power leads according to the manufacturer's instructions.

7 Start the engine and aim the timing light at the timing mark by the crankshaft pulley, and note which timing mark the notch on the pulley is lining up with.

8 If the notch is not lining up with the correct mark, loosen the distributor hold-down clamp bolt at the base of the distributor, and rotate the distributor until the notch is lining up with the correct timing mark.

9 Retighten the hold-down bolt and recheck the timing.

10 Turn off the engine and remove the timing light. Reconnect the number one spark plug wire, if removed.

11 Reconnect the vacuum line to the vacuum advance mechanism.

11 Idle speed adjustments

1 Engine idle speed is the speed at which the engine operates when no accelerator pedal pressure is applied. This speed is critical to the performance of the engine itself, as well as many engine sub-systems.

2 A hand-held tachometer must be used when adjusting idle speed to get an accurate reading. The exact hook-up for these meters varies with the manufacturer, so follow the particular directions included.

3 Set the parking brake and block the front wheels. If the car has an automatic transaxle, place it in 'Drive', and have an assistant keep the brake pedal depressed. If it has a manual transaxle, place it in 'Neutral'. This will energize the idle speed solenoid.

4 Disconnect the air conditioning compressor clutch lead, if so equipped.

5 Start the engine and allow it to run until it reaches normal operating temperature and the choke is fully opened. The A/C switch should be off.

6 Disconnect and plug the distributor vacuum advance hose.

7 Check the distributor timing and adjust if necessary as described in Section 10.

8 Reconnect the vacuum advance hose.

9 Disconnect the purge hose from the EEC canister.

10 Connect a tachometer to the engine according to the manufacturer's instructions. In the following steps, consult the Vehicle Emission Control Information label on the left front shock well for your car's proper idle speed settings. For location of the various carburetor idle adjustment screws, consult the component layout photos in Chapter 4.

11 *Cars equipped with air conditioning:* Turn the idle speed screw until the inactive solenoid idle speed is obtained. Then turn on the A/C switch. Open the throttle slightly to allow the idle speed solenoid's plunger to fully extend. Now turn the solenoid screw to set the active solenoid idle speed. Turn the A/C switch off.

12 *Cars not equipped with air conditioning:* Open the throttle slightly to allow the idle speed solenoid's plunger to fully extend. Then turn the solenoid screw to adjust the idle speed to the active solenoid specification. Disconnect the solenoid's electrical lead and turn the idle speed screw to adjust for the inactive solenoid specification.

13 Switch the automatic transaxle from 'Drive' to 'Park'. Leave the manual transaxle in 'Neutral'.

14 Disconnect and plug the EGR valve vacuum hose.

15 Place the fast idle screw on the highest step of the fast idle cam. Then turn the fast idle screw in or out to obtain the correct fast idle setting.

16 Turn off the engine.

17 Disconnect the tachometer.

18 Reconnect the EGR vacuum hose.

19 Reconnect the purge hose to the EEC canister.

20 Reconnect the A/C compressor clutch lead.

12 Engine drive belt check and adjustment

1 The drivebelts, or V-belts as they are sometimes called, at the front of the engine play an important role in the overall operation of the car and its components. Due to their function and material make-up,

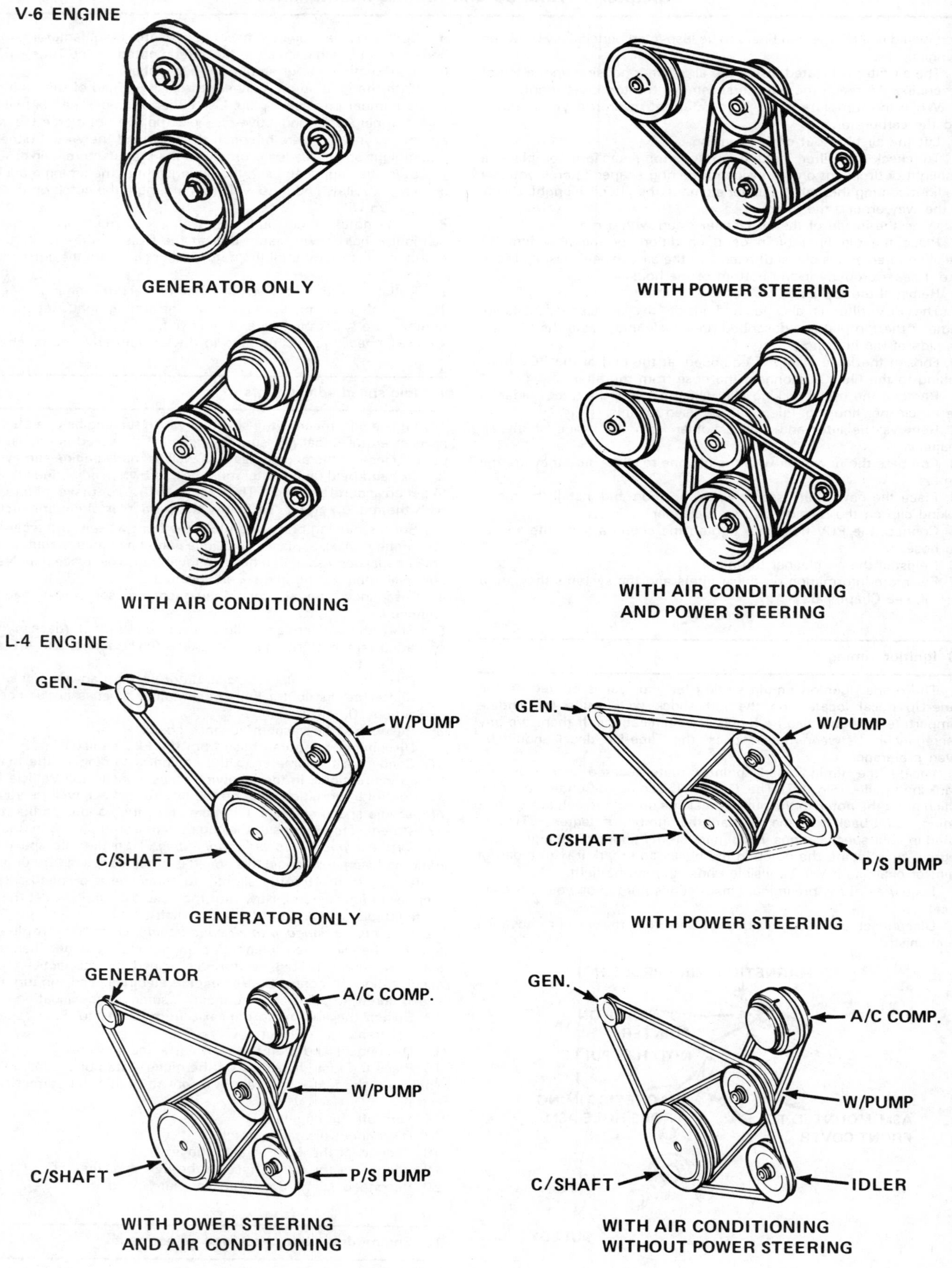

V-6 ENGINE

GENERATOR ONLY

WITH POWER STEERING

WITH AIR CONDITIONING

**WITH AIR CONDITIONING
AND POWER STEERING**

L-4 ENGINE

GEN.

W/PUMP

C/SHAFT

GENERATOR ONLY

GEN.

W/PUMP

C/SHAFT

P/S PUMP

WITH POWER STEERING

GENERATOR

A/C COMP.

W/PUMP

C/SHAFT

P/S PUMP

**WITH POWER STEERING
AND AIR CONDITIONING**

GEN.

A/C COMP.

W/PUMP

C/SHAFT

IDLER

**WITH AIR CONDITIONING
WITHOUT POWER STEERING**

Fig. 1.8 Drivebelt and pulley arrangements used on the L4 and V6 engines (Sec 12)

the belts are prone to failure after a period of time and should be inspected and adjusted periodically to prevent major engine damage.
2   The number of belts used on a particular car depends on the accessories installed. Drive belts are used to turn the generator, power steering pump, water pump and air conditioning compressor. The various belt arrangements found on X-Bodies are shown in Fig. 1.8.
3   With the engine off, open the hood and locate the various belts on the right side of the engine compartment. Using your fingers (and a flashlight if necessary) move along the belts checking for cracks or separation. Also check for fraying and glazing, which gives the belt a shiny appearance. Both sides of the belts should be inspected, which means you will have to twist the belt to check the underside.
4   The tension of each belt is checked by pushing on the belt at a distance halfway between the pulleys. Push firmly with your thumb and see how much the belt moves downward (deflects). A rule of thumb, so to speak, is that if the distance (pulley center to pulley center) is between 7 inches and 11 inches, the belt should deflect $\frac{1}{4}$ inch. If the belt is longer and travels between pulleys spaced 12 inches to 16 inches apart, the belt should deflect $\frac{1}{2}$-inch.
5   If it is found necessary to adjust the belt tension, either to make the belt tighter or looser, this is done by moving the belt-driven accessory on its bracket. For more detailed information, refer to the appropriate Chapter for each belt-driven component.
6   It will often be necessary to use some sort of pry bar to move the accessory while the belt is adjusted. If this must be done to gain the proper leverage, be very careful not to damage the component being moved, or the part being pried against.

13 Fuel filter replacement

1   Disconnect the fuel line connection at the fuel inlet nut on the carburetor (photo).
2   Remove the fuel inlet nut from the carb (photo).
3   Remove the filter and spring.
4   When reinstalling the spring and filter, the end of the filter with the hole should face toward the inlet nut (photo).

5   Place a new gasket on the fuel inlet nut necessary and install the nut into the carb.
6   Install the fuel line and tighten the connector to its proper torque while holding the fuel inlet fitting with a wrench.

14 Distributor check

1   Although the breakerless distributor used on the X-Body cars requires much less maintenance than conventional distributors, periodic inspections should be performed at the intervals specified in the routine maintenance schedule and whenever any work is performed on the distributor.
2   Remove the distributor cap by placing a screwdriver on the slotted head of each latch. Press down on the latch and turn it $\frac{1}{4}$ turn to release the hooked end at the bottom of the latch. Due to the inaccessible location of the L4 distributor, a stubby screwdriver will be easier to work with.
3   With all latches disengaged from the distributor body, place the cap (with the spark plug wire still attached) out of the way (photo). Use a length of wire or tape if necessary.
4   Remove the rotor, which is now visible at the top of the distributor shaft. The rotor is held in place with two screws. Place the rotor in a safe place where it cannot be damaged.
5   Visually inspect the various distributor components for any obvious signs of wear or damage. If dirt or oil has built up in the distributor, remove it by using a contact cleaner or other electrical parts solvent.
6   Before installing the rotor, inspect it for cracks or damage. Carefully check the condition of the metal contact at the top of the rotor for excessive burning or pitting. If in doubt as to its quality, replace it with a new one.
7   The rotor has raised pegs on the bottom. When installing it, make sure it is firmly seated.
8   Before installing the distributor cap, inspect it for cracks or damage. Closely examine the contacts on the inside of the cap for excessive corrosion or damage (photo). Slight scoring is normal. Again,

13.1 Removing the fuel inlet nut from the carburetor (V6)

13.2 The fuel filter fits inside the fuel inlet nut (L4)

13.4 When installing the fuel filter the end with the hole and rubber gasket should face the inlet nut

14.3 Removing the distributor cap (V6)

14.8 The distributor cap should be replaced when the terminals become corroded

if in doubt as to the quality of the cap, replace it with a new one as described in Chapter 5.
9   Install the distributor cap, locking the latches under the distributor body.

15 Carburetor choke inspection

1   The choke only operates when the engine is cold, and thus this check can only be performed before the car has been started for the day.
2   Open the hood and remove the top plate of the air cleaner assembly.
3   Look at the top of the carburetor at the center of the air cleaner housing. You will notice a flat plate at the carburetor opening.
4   Have an assistant press the accelerator pedal to the floor. The plate should close fully. Start the engine while you observe the plate at the carburetor. Do not position your face directly over the carburetor, as the engine could backfire, causing serious burns. When the engine starts, the choke plate should open slighty.
5   Allow the engine to continue running at an idle speed. As the engine warms up to operating temperature, the plate should slowly open, allowing more cold air to enter through the top of the carburetor.
6   After a few minutes, the choke plate should be fully open to the vertical position.
7   You will notice that the engine speed corresponds with the plate opening. With the plate fully closed, the engine should run at a fast idle speed. As the plate opens, the engine speed will decrease.
8   With the engine off and the throttle held half open, open and close the choke several times. Check the linkage to see that all the connections are secure and that there is no damage or binding.
9   If the choke or linkage is binding, sticking or working sluggishly, clean with a choke cleaner. If the condition continues after cleaning, replace the troublesome parts.
10   Visually inspect all vacuum hoses to be sure that they are securely connected and that there is no cracking or other signs of deterioration. Replace as necessary.
11   Check to see that the vacuum break diaphragm shafts are fully extended when the engine is off. If the shafts are not fully extended, replace the vacuum break assembly.
12   Start the engine and check that the primary vacuum break diaphragm shaft fully retracts. If it does not fully retract, replace the vacuum break assembly.
13   If an electric choke fails to open with the engine running, check the voltage at the choke heater connection. If the voltage is between 12 and 15 volts, replace the electrical choke unit. If the voltage is much lower than 12 volts, check all wires and connections to be sure that they are tight, clean and in good condition. Repair as necessary. Note: If the oil pressure switch connection is faulty, the temperature pressure warning light will be off with the key 'on' and the engine not running.

16 Throttle linkage check

1   The throttle linkage is a cable-type system, in which there are no linkage adjustments to be made.
2   While an assistant operates the accelerator pedal, check that the linkage is operating smoothly and opening completely. If any binding is noted, check the routing of the throttle cable and correct as necessary. Figures 1.9 and 1.10 show the routing of the throttle cables on the L4 and V6 engines.

17 Idle speed solenoid checking

1   The idle speed solenoid is mounted next to the carburetor and is used to maintain the proper idle speed under various conditions. The carburetor photos showing component layout in Chapter 4 can be used to identify the solenoid.
2   An improperly functioning idle speed solenoid can cause stalling or rough idling. If the car is exhibiting these problems, check that the idle speed solenoid plunger is extended when the solenoid is energized by performing the following test.
3   Turn on the ignition, but do not start the engine. If so equipped, the air conditioner switch must be on.

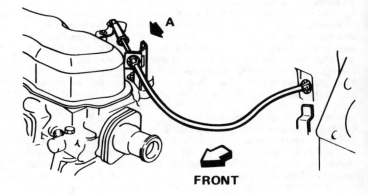

Fig. 1.9 Routing of the accelerator cable (L4) (Sec 16)

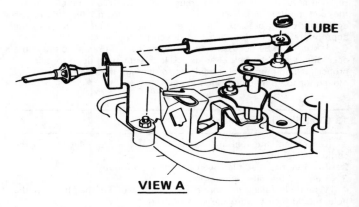

CAUTION: FLEXIBLE COMPONENTS (HOSES, WIRES, CONDUITS, ETC.) MUST NOT BE ROUTED WITHIN 50.0 mm (2 IN.) OF MOVING PARTS OF ACCELERATOR LINKAGE FORWARD OF SUPPORT, UNLESS ROUTING IS POSITIVELY CONTROLLED.
CAUTION: CABLE IS NOT TO BE KINKED OR DAMAGED IN ANY WAY DURING ASSEMBLY OPERATION.

Fig. 1.10 Routing of the accelerator cable (V6) (Sec 16)

4   Open the throttle to allow the solenoid plunger to extend, then close the throttle again.

5   When the wire at the solenoid is disconnected the plunger should drop away from the throttle lever. When the wire is connected the plunger should move out and contact the throttle lever.

6   If the solenoid plunger does not move in or out as described in then preceding paragraph, check the voltage in the solenoid feed wire. If the voltage is between 12 and 15 volts, replace the solenoid. If it is much lower than 12 volts, check the solenoid feed wire and connections to be sure they are tight, clean, and in good condition.

18 Carburetor mounting torque

1   The carburetor is attached to the top of the intake manifold by four nuts. These fasteners can sometimes work loose through normal engine operation and cause a vacuum leak.

2   To properly tighten the carburetor mounting nuts, a torque wrench is necessary. If you do not own one, they can usually be rented on a daily basis.

3   Remove the air cleaner assembly, labeling each hose to be disconnected to make reassembly easier.

4   Locate the mounting nuts at the base of the carburetor. Decide what special tools or adapters, if any, will be necessary to tighten the nuts with a properly sized socket and the torque wrench.

5   Tighten the nuts to a torque of about 12 ft-lb. Do not overtighten the nuts, as this may cause the threads to strip.

6   If you suspect a vacuum leak exists at the bottom of the carburetor, get a length of spare hose about the diameter of fuel hose. Start the engine and place one end of the hose next to your ear as you probe around the base of the carburetor with the other end. You will be able to hear a hissing sound if a leak exists. A soapy water solution brushed around the suspect area can also be used to pinpoint pressure leaks.

7   If, after the nuts are properly tightened, a vacuum leak still exists, the carburetor must be removed and a new gasket used. See Chapter 4 for more information.

8   After tightening nuts, reinstall the air cleaner, connecting all hoses to their original positions.

19 Brakes check

1   The brakes should be inspected every time the wheels are removed or whenever a fault is suspected, Indication of a potential braking system fault are: the car pulls to one side when brake pedal is depressed; noises coming from the brakes when they are applied; excessive brake pedal travel; pulsating pedal; and leakage of fluid, usually seen on the inside of the tire or wheel.

Rear brakes inspection

2   Loosen the lug nuts on the rear wheels, but do not remove them.

3   Raise the rear end of the car and support it with jackstands. Be sure the parking brake is released.

4   Remove the rear wheels.

5   Mark the position of the drum on the axle and remove the drum. If the drum does not pull off its studs easily apply penetrating oil around the lug and hub holes and tap lightly with a rubber mallet (photo). In some cases the brake shoes may have to be adjusted inward as described in Chapter 9, Section 11.

6   Clean the dirt and dust from the inside of the drum by wiping with a damp cloth. If the dust is blown out with compressed air be careful not to breath it, as the brake dust contains asbestos and can be hazardous to your health.

7   Inspect the inside surface of the brake drum. If any scoring, deep scratching or heat damage is evident, or if new brake shoes are being installed, have the drums resurfaced at an automotive machine shop. If the drum is cracked it must be replaced. A drum should also be measured to check that it is not out-of-round or tapered, both of which can diminish braking performance and accelerate tire wear. These measurements can be taken with an inside micrometer at the open and closed edges of the drum's machined surface and at right angles to each other as shown in Figure 1.11. See the specifications in Chapter 9 for the allowable tolerances and have the drums turned if the measurements exceed them. NOTE: If the drum is grooved but the brake linings are only sightly worn, the drum should not be resurfaced

19.5 Removing the brake drum

Fig. 1.11 Measuring the inside diameter of the rear brake drum for ovaling or warping (Sec 19)

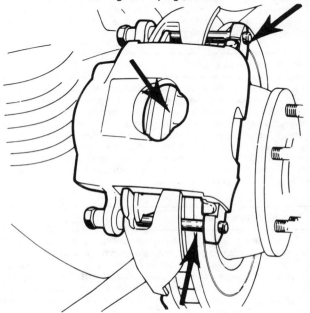
Fig. 1.12 Location of the disc brake inspection hole (Sec 18)

but only polished with fine emery cloth. Turning the drum and smoothing the lining surface would necessitate the removal of too much metal and lining, while if left as is, the grooves and ridges match, giving satisfactory braking performance.

8   Observe the thickness of the lining material on both the front and rear brake shoes. If the material has worn away to within $\frac{1}{32}$ in of the recessed rivets or metal backing, the shoes should be replaced. If the linings look worn, but you are unable to determine their exact thickness, compare them with a new set at the auto parts store. The shoes should also be replaced if they are cracked, glazed (shiny surface) or they are wet with brake fluid. Refer to Chapter 9, Section 9.

9   Inspect the wheel cylinder for signs of leakage and if any is evident overhaul the cylinder as described in Chapter 9, Section 10.

10 Inspect all brake lines for leakage, cracking or other damage and be sure all brake lines, hoses and connectors are tight.

11 Install the brake drum to its original position using the marks made on removal as a reference.

12 Install the rear wheels and wheel lug nuts.

13 Lower the car to the ground and tighten the lug nuts fully.

Disc brake inspection

14 The thickness of the lining on the front disc pads should be checked on a regular basis as damage can occur if the linings become excessively worn. All four pads (two on each front wheel) should be replaced at the same time. Also, do not mix different types of replacement pads. All should be manufactured from the same material to give uniform performance.

15 To perform a visual inspection of the disc pad linings, first remove the wheel in the same way described under rear brake inspection. Now visible is the disc brake caliper which contains the pads. There is an outer pad and an inner pad. Both should be inspected. Check both ends of the outer pad by looking in at each end of the caliper. This is where the highest rate of wear occurs. Also check the thickness of the inner pad lining by looking down through the inspection hole in the top of the caliper.

16 If there is doubt whether to replace the pads or not, a more accurate check can be made by removing the pads as described in Chapter 9, Section 5 and measuring how close the surface of the lining has worn to the rivets in the shoe. Whenever the thickness of any lining is worn to within 0.76 mm (0.030 in) of a rivet at either end of the shoe, it should be replaced.

17 While checking the pad linings, also inspect the rotor surface for scoring or 'hot spots' indicated by small discolored blemishes. Light scoring is acceptable but if the damage is excessive the rotor should be resurfaced or replaced.

18 Before installing the wheels, check for any leakage around the brake hose connections leading to the caliper or damage (cracking, splitting, etc) to the brake hose. Replace the hose or fittings as necessary, referring to Chapter 9.

20 Wheel bearings check

1   In most cases, the front wheel bearings will not need servicing until the brake pads are changed. However, these bearings should be checked whenever the front wheels are raised for any reason.

2   With the vehicle securely supported on jack stands, spin the wheel and check for noise, rolling resistance or free play. Now grab the top of the tire with one hand and the bottom of the tire with the other. Move the tire in and out on the spindle. If it moves more than 0.005 in, the bearings should be checked, and replaced if necessary. Refer to Chapter 11 for the proper procedure.

21 Parking brake adjustment

1   The parking brake does not need routine maintenance but the cable may stretch over a period of time necessitating adjustment. Also, the parking brake should be checked for proper adjustment whenever the rear brake cables have been disconnected. If the parking brake pedal travel is less than nine ratchet clicks or more than sixteen ratchet clicks under heavy foot pressure, the parking brake needs adjustment.

2   Depress the parking brake pedal exactly two ratchet clicks.

3   Raise the rear of the car and support it with jackstands.

4   Turn the adjusting nut (photo) until the left rear wheel can just be turned rearward using two hands but is locked when you attempt to turn it forward. The adjusting nut is located in the equalizer set-up that connects the front parking brake cable to the rear cables.

5   Release the parking brake and check that both rear wheels turn freely and that there is no brake drag in either direction.

6   Lower the car to the ground.

22 Cooling system check and servicing

1   Many major engine failures can be attributed to a faulty cooling system. If equipped with an automatic transaxle, the cooling system also plays an integral role in transaxle longevity.

2   The cooling system should be checked with the engine cold. Do this before the car is driven for the day or after it has been shut off for one or two hours.

3   Remove the radiator cap and thoroughly clean the cap (inside and out) with clean water. Also clean the filler neck on the radiator. All traces of corrosion should be removed.

4   Carefully check the upper and lower radiator hoses along with the smaller diameter heater hoses. Inspect their entire length, replacing any hose which is cracked, swollen or shows signs of deterioration. Cracks may become more apparent if the hose is squeezed.

5   Also check that all hose connections are tight. A leak in the cooling system will usually show up as white or rust-colored deposits on the areas adjoining the leak.

6   Use compressed air or a soft brush to remove bugs, leaves, etc., from the front of the radiator or air-conditioning condensor. Be careful not to damage or cut yourself on the sharp cooling fins.

7   Finally, have the cap and system tested for proper pressure. If you do not have a pressure tester, most gas stations and repair shops will do this for a minimal charge.

8   At the same time the cooling system is checked, as per the maintenance schedule, it should also be drained, flushed and refilled. This is to replenish the antifreeze mixture and prevent rust and corrosion which can impair the performance of the cooling system and ultimately cause engine damage.

9   As antifreeze is a poisonous solution, take care not to spill any of the cooling mixture on the vehicle's paint or your own skin. If this happens, rinse immediately with plenty of clear water. Also, it is advisable to consult your local authorities about the dumping of antifreeze before draining the cooling system. In many areas reclamation centers have been set up to collect automobile oil and drained antifreeze/water mixtures rather than allowing these liquids to be added to the sewage and water facilities.

10 With the engine cold, remove the radiator pressure fill cap.

11 Move a large container under the radiator to catch the water/antifreeze mixture as it is drained.

12 Drain the radiator by opening the radiator drain valve, located on the right side of the radiator. If this drain has excessive corrosion and

21.4 Loosening the parking brake adjusting nut

cannot be turned easily, disconnect the lower radiator hose to allow the coolant to drain. Be careful that none of the solution is splashed on your skin or in your eyes.

13 If accessible, remove the two engine drain plugs located in the engine block. These will allow the coolant to drain from the engine itself.

14 Disconnect the radiator overflow pipe and remove the reservoir. Flush it out with clean water.

15 Place a cold water hose (a common garden hose is fine) in the radiator filler neck at the top of the radiator and flush the system until the water runs clean at all drain points.

16 In severe cases of contamination or clogging of the radiator, remove it (see Chapter 3) and reverse-flush it. This involves simply inserting the cold pressure hose in the bottom radiator outlet to allow the clear water to run against the normal flow, draining through the top. A radiator repair shop should be consulted if further cleaning or repair is necessary.

17 Where the coolant is regularly drained and the system refilled with the correct antifreeze/inhibitor mixture there should be no need to employ chemical cleaners or descalers.

18 To refill the system, reconnect the radiator hoses and install the drain plugs securely in the engine. Special thread sealing tape (available at auto parts stores) should be used on the drain plugs going into the engine block. Install the expansion reservoir and the overflow hose.

19 Fill the radiator to the base of the filler neck and then add more coolant to the expansion reservoir so that it reaches the 'FULL COLD' mark.

20 Run the engine until normal operating temperature is reached, and with the engine idling, add coolant up to the correct level (see Section 3), then fit the radiator cap so that the arrows are in alignment with the overflow pipe. Install the reservoir cap.

21 Always refill the system with a mixture of high-quality antifreeze and water in at least a 50/50 proportion. The antifreeze should not exceed a 70/30 ratio with the water, however.

22 Keep a close watch on the coolant level and the various cooling hoses during the first few miles of driving. Tighten the hose clamps and/or add more coolant mixture as necessary.

23 Fuel system check

1 There are certain precautions to take when inspecting or servicing the fuel system components. Work in a well-ventilated area and do not allow open flames (cigarettes, appliance pilot lights, etc.) to get near the work area. Mop up spills immediately and do not store fuel-soaked rags where they could ignite.

2 The fuel system is under some amount of pressure, so if any fuel lines are disconnected for servicing, be prepared to catch the fuel as it spurts out. Plug all disconnected fuel lines immediately after disconnection to prevent the tank from emptying itself.

3 The fuel system is most easily checked with the car raised on a hoist where the components under the car are readily visible and accessible.

4 If the smell of gasoline is noticed while driving, or after the car has sat in the sun, the system should be thoroughly inspected immediately.

5 Remove the gas filler cap and check for damage, corrosion, and a proper sealing imprint on the gasket. Replace the cap with a new one if necessary.

6 With the car raised, inspect the gas tank and filler neck for punctures, cracks or any damage. The connection between the filler neck and the tank is especially critical. Sometimes a rubber filler neck will leak due to loose clamps or deteriorated rubber – problems a home mechanic can usually rectify.

7 Carefully check all rubber hoses and metal lines leading away from the fuel tank. Check for loose connections, deteriorated hose, crimped lines or damage of any kind. Follow these lines up to the front of the car, carefully inspecting them all the way. For fuel system repairs refer to Chapter 4.

8 If a fuel odor is still evident after the inspection, refer to Section 26 on the evaporative emissions system and Chapter 4 for carburetor adjustments.

24 EFE (Early Fuel Evaporation) system check

1 The EFE system uses a valve located in between the exhaust

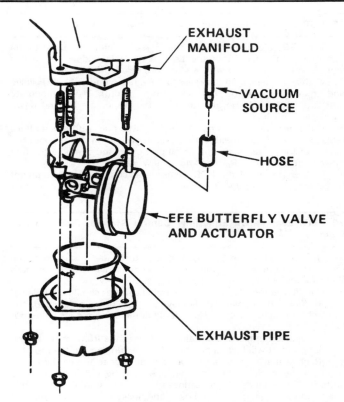

Fig. 1.13 Location of the EFE valve between the exhaust manifold and the front exhaust pipe (Sec 24)

manifold and the exhaust pipe (Fig. 1.13) to recirculate exhaust gases to help pre-heat the carburetor and choke. This valve is vacuum-operated and controlled by a thermal vacuum switch (TVS) which senses coolant temperature.

2 When the engine is cold the TVS will apply a vacuum signal to the valve, causing it to close. When the engine coolant reaches the TVS's calibration point, the switch will shut off the vacuum signal, thus allowing the EFE valve to open once more allowing the exhaust gases to exit through the exhaust pipe.

3 If the EFE valve should stick in the open position, the engine will run poorly and waste gas until it has warmed up on its own. If the valve sticks in the closed position, the engine will run as if it is out of tune due to the constant flow of hot air to the carburetor.

4 Because of the high exhaust temperatures and the EFE valve's location which leaves it open to the elements, corrosion can set in, impairing the valve's operation.

5 To check the system, locate the actuator and rod assembly, which is on a bracket between the exhaust manifold and the exhaust pipe. With the engine cold, have an assistant start the engine. Observe the movement of the actuator rod which leads to the heat valve inside the exhaust pipe. It should immediately be drawn into the diaphragm, moving the valves to the closed position. If this is the case, the system is operating correctly.

6 If the actuator rod did not move, disconnect the vacuum hose at the actuator and place your thumb over the open end. With the engine cold and at idle, you should feel a suction indicating proper vacuum. If there is vacuum at this point, replace the actuator with a new one.

7 If there is no vacuum in the line, this is an indication that either the hose is crimped or plugged, or the thermal vacuum switch threaded into the water outlet is not functioning properly. Replace the hose or switch as necessary.

8 To make sure the EFE system is disengaging once the engine has warmed, continue to observe the actuating rod as the engine reaches normal operating temperature. The rod should again move, indicating the valve is in the open position.

9 If after the engine has warmed, the valve does not open, pull the vacuum hose at the actuator and check for vacuum with your thumb. If there is no vacuum, replace the actuator. If there is vacuum, replace the TVS switch.

Labels on figure: EXHAUST MANIFOLD, VACUUM SOURCE, HOSE, EFE BUTTERFLY VALVE AND ACTUATOR, EXHAUST PIPE

25 EGR (Exhaust Gas Recirculation) valve check

1   The EGR valve is located on the intake manifold, adjacent to the carburetor. The majority of the time, when a fault develops in this emissions system it is due to a stuck or corroded EGR valve.

2   With the engine cold to prevent burns, reach under the EGR valve and manually push on the diaphragm (photo). Using moderate pressure, you should be able to press the diaphragm up and down within the housing.

3   If the diaphragm does not move or moves only with much effort, replace the EGR valve with a new one. If you are in doubt about the quality of the valve, go to your local part store and compare the free movement of your EGR valve with a new valve.

4   Further testing of the EGR system and component replacement procedures can be found in Chapter 6.

26 EEC (Evaporative Emissions Control System) filter replacement

1   The function of the EEC system is to draw fuel vapors from the tank and carburetor, store them in a charcoal canister, and then burn these fumes during normal engine operation.

2   The filter at the bottom of the charcoal canister should be replaced at the specified intervals. If, however, a fuel odor is detected, the canister, filter and system hoses should immediately be inspected for fault.

3   To replace the filter, locate the canister at the front of the engine compartment. It will have a number of hoses running out the top of it.

4   Remove the bolts which secure the canister to the car body.

5   Turn the canister upside-down and pull the old filter from the bottom of the canister. If you cannot turn the canister enough for this due to the short length of the hoses, the hoses must be duly marked with pieces of tape and then disconnected from the top.

6   Push the new filter into the bottom of the canister, making sure it is seated all the way around.

7   Place the canister back into position and tighten the mounting bolts. Connect the various hoses if disconnected.

8   The EEC system is explained in more detail in Chapter 6.

27 Thermac (Thermo Controlled Air Cleaner) check

1   All models are equipped with a thermostatically controlled air cleaner which draws air to the carburetor from different locations depending upon engine temperature.

2   This is a simple visual check, however, if access is tight, a small mirror may have to be used.

3   Open the hood and find the vacuum flapper door on the air cleaner assembly. It will be located inside the long 'snorkel' of the metal air cleaner (photo). Check that the flexible air hose(s) are securely attached and are not damaged.

4   If there is a flexible air duct attached to the end of the snorkel, leading to an area behind the grille, disconnect it at the snorkel. This will enable you to look through the end of the snorkel and see the flapper door inside (photo).

5   The testing should preferably be done when the engine and outside air are cold. Start the engine and look through the snorkel at the flapper door, which should move to a closed position. With the door closed, air cannot enter through the end of the snorkel, but rather air enters the air cleaner through the flexible duct attached to the exhaust manifold.

6   As the engine warms up to operating temperature, the door should open to allow air through the snorkel end. Depending on ambient temperature, this may take 10 to 15 minutes. To speed up this check, you can reconnect the snorkel air duct, drive the car and then check that the door is fully open.

7   If the Thermo Controlled Air Cleaner is not operating properly, see Chapter 6 for more information.

28 PCV (Positive Crankcase Ventilation) valve replacement

1   The PCV valve is located on a rocker arm cover. There is a hose connected to the valve which runs to the carburetor (photos).

2   When purchasing a replacement PCV valve, make sure it is for your particular vehicle, model year and engine size.

3   Pull the valve (with the hose attached) from its rubber grommet in the rocker arm cover, and remove the PCV valve from the hose, noting its installed position and direction.

4   Compare the old valve with the new one to make sure they are the same.

5   Push the new valve into the end of the hose until it is fully seated.

6   Inspect the rubber grommet in the cover for damage and replace it with a new one if faulty.

7   Push the PCV valve and hose securely into the rocker arm cover.

8   More information on the PCV system can be found in Chapter 6.

29 Catalytic converter servicing

1   The catalytic converter is a muffler-like unit located underneath the vehicle and is incorporated in the exhaust system. The converter is designed to reduce the amount of hydrocarbon (HC) and carbon monoxide (CO) pollutants released into the atmosphere.

2   49 States and High Altitude model X-Bodies use a bead-type converter. This type contains small beads placed in layers called a bed. These beads are coated with platinum and palladium which cause chemical reactions to occur that convert CO to CO_2 (carbon dioxide) and HC to CO_2 and H_2O (water). The volume of the bed provides over 100 square yards of surface area exposure to the exhaust gases which pass through it.

3   All California version X-Bodies use the Phase II Monolith converter which utilizes a honeycomb-type internal design which is coated with platinum and rhodium. This type of catalyst helps reduce oxides of nitrogen in addition to HC and CO.

4   Since lead and phosphorus additives in gasoline can poison the beads' catalytic elements, thus rendering the converter ineffective in altering the gases' toxic elements, only unleaded fuel should be used in the vehicle.

5   Periodic maintenance of the converter is not required, but it has a limited working life after which it must be renewed. This is usually at intervals of around 30 000 miles (48 000 km). At the approximate end of these intervals a 'catalyst' reminder light will appear on the speedometer, indicating that the useful life of the catalyst has been depleted.

6   If, through physical damage, the use of leaded fuels or because its active elements have been depleted, a bead-type converter is rendered ineffective, the unit can be replaced with a new one or the beads drained and replaced. Replacing the catalyst can be done either on or off of the car. The off-car servicing procedure is detailed in Chapter 4, Section 23. The on-car servicing procedure, however, should be done by a qualified mechanic with the proper equipment. The catalyst in the Monolith converter cannot be replaced separately from the rest of the unit.

7   If the bottom of a bead-type converter is damaged, it can be replaced without replacing the entire converter. Again, the operation should be performed by a qualified mechanic with the proper equipment.

8   It should be noted that since the internal chemical conversions occur between 600° and 1200° F, the converter operates at a very high temperature. Before performing any work on or near the converter, be sure it has cooled sufficiently to avoid serious burns.

30 Oxygen sensor replacement

1   The oxygen sensor is a screw-in type sensor located in the exhaust manifold on L4 engines and in the exhaust pipe in V6 engines (photo). The sensor may be difficult to remove when the engine is cold, so the operation is best done with the engine at operating temperature.

2   On V6 models, raise the front of the car and support it on jack stands for working clearance.

3   On L4 models, remove the air cleaner.

4   Remove the electrical connector from the oxygen sensor.

5   Apply a penetrating oil to the threads of the oxygen sensor and allow it to soak in for about 5 minutes.

6   Carefully unscrew the sensor and remove it. Be careful that you do not damage the threads in the exhaust manifold/pipe while removing the sensor.

7   Coat the threads on the new sensor completely with an anti-seize compound and install it.

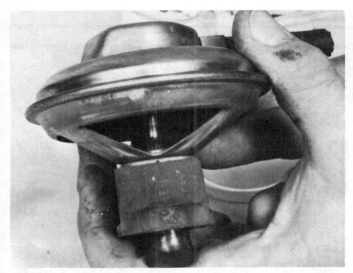

25.2 Check the EGR valve by pressing on the diaphragm from underneath

27.3 The Thermac motor assembly is located in the snorkel of the air cleaner

27.4 Removing the flexible air duct prior to checking the Thermac vacuum valve

28.1a Removing the L4 PCV valve from the rocker arm cover

28.1b Removing the V6 PCV valve from the rocker arm cover

30.1 The V6 oxygen sensor is located in the front exhaust pipe

8   Carefully torque the sensor to 30 ft-lb (4.1 m-kg).
9   Reconnect the electrical connector to the sensor.
10   On L4 models reinstall the air cleaner, and on V6 models lower the
car to the ground.
11   Whenever the oxygen sensor is replaced the 'sensor' flag in the
instrument panel must be reset as described in Chapter 10.
12   More information on the oxygen sensor can be found in Chapter 6.

31 Vacuum advance system check

1   If the vacuum advance system malfunctions you may notice a
decrease in gas mileage as well as a drop in power, though neither
effect will be dramatic. Because of this, it is important that the vacuum
advance system be checked at its proper interval in the routine
maintenance schedule.
2   Unfortunately, the vacuum advance system on X-Body cars is
fairly complex and is tied into various emissions control systems as
well as the C-4 computer control system, making it impractical for the
home mechanic to perform a complete inspection of the system. The
two simple checks described below, however, are often enough to find
a problem.
3   Begin by visually inspecting all vacuum lines used in the system to
be sure they are not cracked, hardened or otherwise damaged and
they are securely attached to their connections. The proper vacuum
lines used in your particular system can be identified by referring to the
vacuum line schematics in Chapter 6.
4   A check that the vacuum advance diaphragm attached to the
distributor is in good condition can be performed with a hand vacuum
pump. Disconnect the vacuum line from the diaphragm canister and
attach the vacuum pump to the canister fitting. Remove the distributor
cap and rotor. Then apply vacuum to the diaphragm canister and check
that the linkage arm inside the distributor is drawn into the canister
and that the distributor's magnetic pickup rotates with it. Keep the
vacuum applied for several seconds to make sure the diaphragm does
not retract to its original position prematurely. If the diaphragm does
not respond to the vacuum as described or if it returns to its original
position before the vacuum signal is released, it is defective and must
be replaced. This procedure, as well as further information on the
vacuum advance system can be found in Chapter 5.
5   More complete testing of the vacuum advance system should be
performed by a GM dealer or other qualified mechanic with the proper
testing equipment.

32 Chassis lubrication

1   A grease gun and a cartridge filled with the proper grease (see
Recommended Lubricants) are the only equipment necessary to
lubricate the balljoints and tie rods.
2   The balljoint grease fitting is located on the underside of each
balljoint (photo), while the tie rod fitting is located on top of the tie rod
(photo).
3   For easier access under the car, raise the vehicle with a jack and
place jack stands under the frame. Make sure the car is firmly
supported by the stands.
4   Before you do any greasing, force a little of the grease out of the
nozzle to remove any dirt from the end of the gun. Wipe the nozzle
clean with a rag.
5   Wipe the grease fitting nipple clean and push the nozzle firmly
over the fitting nipple. Squeeze the trigger on the grease gun to force
grease into the component. Both the balljoints and tie rods should be
lubricated until the rubber reservoir is firm to the touch. Do not pump
too much grease into these fittings as this could rupture the reservoir.
If the grease seeps out around the grease gun nozzle, the nipple is
clogged or the nozzle is not fully seated around the fitting nipple.
Resecure the gun nozzle to the fitting and try again. If necessary,
replace the fitting.
6   Wipe any excess grease from the components and the grease
fitting.
7   While you are under the car, clean and lubricate the brake cable
along with its cable guides and levers. This can be done by smearing
some of the chassis grease onto the cable and its related parts with
your fingers.
8   Lower the car to the ground for the remaining body lubrication
process.

32.2a Balljoint grease fitting location

32.2b The tie rod grease fitting is located on top of the outer tie rod

9   Open the hood and smear a little chassis grease on the hood latch
mechanism. Have an assistant pull the release knob from inside the car
as you lubricate the cable at the latch.
10   Lubricate all the hinges (door, hood, trunk) with a few drops of
light engine oil to keep them in proper working order.
11   Finally, the key lock cylinders can be lubricated with spray-on
graphite, which is available at auto parts stores.

33 Drive axles, output shafts and balljoint seals check

1   At the recommended intervals the seals on the driveshafts,
transaxle output shafts and balljoints should be inspected for wear,
cracking or other damage.
2   The drive axle boot seals are very important in that they prevent
dirt, water and other foreign matter from getting into and damaging the
the ball bearing joints. To check these, raise the car for clearance and
support it on jack stands. Slide under the car and inspect the condition
of all four boot seals (two on each shaft) You will probably have to
clean the boots prior to inspection. A mirror may be necessary in order
to inspect the tops of the boots. If there are any tears or cracking in the
boots or if there is any evidence of leaking grease they must be
replaced as described in Chapter 8. Check also the tightness of the
boot clamps and tighten if necessary.

3   Also at this time check the transaxle output shaft seals located at the point where the drive axles exit from the transaxle. Again, this area will probably have to be cleaned before inspection. If there is any oil leaking from either drive axle/transaxle junction, the output shaft seals must be replaced. Refer to Chapter 7.

4   The balljoint seals should, likewise, be checked at this time. After cleaning around the balljoints, inspect the seals for wear, cracking or damage, and replace if necessary as described in Chapter 11.

34 Suspension and steering check

1   Whenever the front of the car is raised for service it is a good idea to visually check the suspension and steering components for wear.

2   Indication of a fault in these systems are: excessive play in the steering wheel before the front wheels react; excessive sway around corners or body movement over rough roads, and binding at some point as the steering wheel is turned.

3   Before the car is raised for inspection, test the shock absorbers by pushing downwards to rock the car at each corner. If you push the car down and it does not come back to a level position within one or two bounces, the shocks are worn and need to be replaced. As this is done, check for squeaks and strange noises from the suspension components. Information on shock absorber and suspension components can be found in Chapter 11.

4   Now raise the front end of the car and support it firmly with jack stands. Because of the work to be done, make sure the car cannot fall from the stands.

5   Grab the top and bottom of the front tire with your hands and rock the tire/wheel on its spindle. If there is movement of more than 0.005 in, the wheel bearings should be replaced (see Chapter 11).

6   Crawl under the car and check for loose bolts, broken or disconnected parts and deteriorated rubber bushings on all suspension and steering components. Look for grease or fluid leaking from around the rack and pinion assembly. Check the power steering hoses and their connections for leaks.

7   Have an assistant turn the steering wheel from side to side and check the steering components for free movement, chafing or binding. If the steering does not react with the movement of the steering wheel, try to determine where the slack is located.

35 Exhaust system check

1   With the exhaust system cold (at least 3 hours after being driven), check the complete exhaust system from its starting point at the engine to the end of the tailpipe. This is best done on a hoist where full access is available.

2   Check the pipes and their connections for signs of leakage and/or corrosion indicating a potential failure. Check that all brackets and

35.2 The exhaust system hangers and brackets should be strong and tight

hangers are in good condition and are tight (photo).

3   At the same time, inspect the underside of the body for holes, corrosion, open seams, etc., which may allow exhaust gases to enter the trunk or passenger compartment. Seal all body openings with silicone or body putty.

4   Rattles and other driving noises can often be traced to the exhaust system, especially the mounts and hangers. Try to move the pipes, muffler and catalytic converter. If the components can come into contact with the body or driveline parts, secure the exhaust system with new mountings.

5   This is also an ideal time to check the running condition of the engine by inspecting the very end of the tailpipe. The exhaust deposits here are an indication of engine tune. If the pipe is black and sooty, or bright white deposits are found here, the engine is in need of a tune-up including a thorough carburetor inspection and adjustment.

36 Automatic transaxle fluid change

1   At the specified time intervals, the transaxle fluid should be changed and the filter replaced with a new one. The routine maintenance chart calls for an automatic transaxle fluid change only once every 30 000 miles. This interval should be shortened to every 15 000 miles if the car is normally driven under one or more of the following conditions: heavy city traffic; where the outside temperature normally reaches 90°F or higher; in very hilly or mountain areas; or if a trailer is frequently pulled.

2   Since there is no drain plug, the transaxle oil pan must be removed from the bottom of the transaxle to drain the fluid. Before doing any draining, purchase the specified transmission fluid (see Recommended Lubricants in the front of this Chapter) and a new filter. The necessary gaskets should be included with the filter; if not, purchase an oil pan gasket and a filter O-ring seal.

3   Other tools necessary for this job include: jack stands to support the vehicle in a raised position; wrench to remove the oil pan bolts; a standard screwdriver; a drain pan capable of holding at least 8 pints; newspaper and clean rags.

4   The fluid should be drained immediately after the car has been driven. This will remove any built-up sediment better than if the fluid were cold. Because of this, it may be wiser to wear protective gloves (fluid temperature can exceed 350° in a hot transaxle).

5   After the car has been driven to warm up the fluid, raise the vehicle and place it on jack stands for access underneath.

6   Move the necessary equipment under the car, being careful not to touch any of the hot exhaust components.

7   Place the drain pan under the transaxle oil pan and loosen, but do not remove, the bolts at one end of the pan (photo).

8   Moving around the pan, loosen all the bolts a little at a time. Be sure the drain pan is in position, as fluid will begin dripping out (photo). Continue in this fashion until all of the bolts are removed, except for one at each of the corners.

9   While supporting the pan, remove the remaining bolts and lower the pan (photo). If necessary, use a screwdriver to break the gasket seal, but be careful not to damage the pan or transaxle. Drain the remaining fluid into the drain receptacle. As this is done, check the fluid for metal filings which may be an indication of internal failure.

10 Now visible on the bottom of the transaxle is the filter/strainer.

11 Remove the filter and its O-ring seal (photo).

12 Thoroughly clean the transaxle oil pan with solvent. Inspect for metal filings or foreign matter. Dry with compressed air if available. It is important that all remaining gasket material be removed from the oil pan mounting flange. Use a gasket scraper or putty knife for this.

13 Clean the filter mounting surface on the valve body. Again, this surface should be smooth and free of any leftover gasket material.

14 Install the new filter into position, complete with a new O-ring seal.

15 Apply a bead of gasket sealant around the oil pan mounting surface, with the sealant to the inside of the bolt holes. Press the new gasket into place on the pan, making sure all bolt holes line up.

16 Lift the pan up to the bottom of the transaxle and install the mounting bolts. Tighten the bolts in a diagonal fashion, working around the pan. Using a torque wrench, tighten the bolts to about 12 ft-lb.

17 Lower the car off its jack stands.

18 Open the hood and remove the transaxle fluid dipstick from its guide tube.

36.7 Begin the automatic transaxle drain pan removal by loosening the bolts at one end

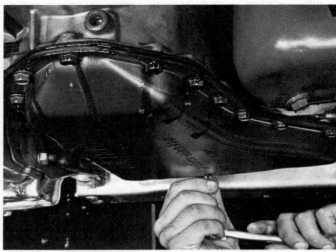

36.8 Move around the pan loosening all of the bolts a little at a time

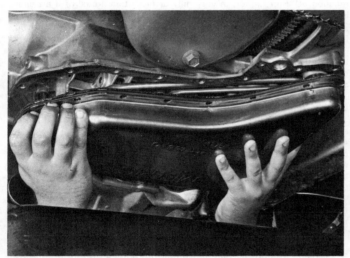

36.9 Lowering the drain pan from the automatic transaxle

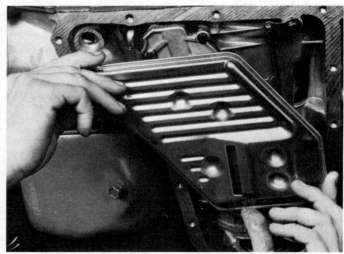

36.11 Removing the automatic transaxle filter

19 It is best to add a little fluid at a time, continually checking the level with the dipstick. Allow the fluid time to drain into the pan. Add fluid until the level just registers on the end of the dipstick. A good starting point will be 4 to 5 pints added to the transaxle through the filler tube (use a funnel to prevent spills).

20 With the selector lever in 'Park', apply the parking brake and start the engine without depressing the accelerator pedal (if possible). Do not race the engine at a high speed; run at slow idle only.

21 Check the level on the dipstick (with the engine still idling). Look under the car for leaks around the transaxle oil pan mating surface.

22 Add more fluid through the dipstick tube until the level on the dipstick is $\frac{1}{4}$-inch below the 'Add' mark on the dipstick. Do not allow the fluid level to go above this point, as the transaxle would then be overfilled, necessitating the removal of the pan to drain the excess fluid.

23 Push the dipstick firmly back into its tube and drive the car to reach normal operating temperature (15 miles of highway driving or its equivalent in the city). Park the car on a level surface and check the fluid level on the dipstick with the engine idling and the transaxle in 'Park'. The level should now be at the 'Full Hot' mark on the dipstick. If not, add more fluid as necessary to bring the level up to this point. Again, do not overfill.

Chapter 2 Engine

Refer to Chapter 13 for specifications and information related to 1981 through 1984 models

Contents

Specifications – L4 engines

Engine – general (L4)

Type	In-line 4 cylinder, vertical
Displacement	2.5 liter (151 cu in)
Sales code	LX8
Bore	101.6 mm (4.0 in)
Stroke	76.2 mm (3.0 in)
Compression ratio	8.3 : 1
Compression pressure (wide open throttle with all spark plugs removed)	140 psi at 160 rpm
Firing order	1, 3, 4, 2
Number one cylinder	Front cylinder

Cylinder block (L4)

Bore diameter	101.6 mm (4.0 in)
Bore out-of-round	0.0127 mm (0.005 in) maximum
Bore taper	0.0127 mm (0.005 in) maximum

Pistons and rings (L4)

Piston clearance in bore
    Top .... 0.0635 to 0.0838 mm (0.0025 to 0.0033 in)
    Bottom .... 0.043 to 0.104 mm (0.0017 to 0.0041 in)
Piston diameter (measured 90° from piston pin center line) .... 101.526 to 101.536 mm (3.9971 to 3.9975 in)
Compression ring side clearance
    Top .... 0.062 mm (0.0030 in)
    Bottom .... 0.0762 mm (0.0030 in)
Compression ring width
    Top .... 1.968 to 1.981 mm (0.0775 to 0.0780 in)
    Bottom .... 1.968 yo 1.981 mm (0.0775 to 0.0780 in)
Upper compression ring gap .... 0.381 to 0.635 mm (0.015 to 0.025 in)
Lower compression ring gap .... 0.2286 to 0.4826 mm (0.009 to 0.019 in)
Oil ring width .... 4.8006 mm (0.189 in)
Oil ring gap .... 0.381 to 1.397 mm (0.015 to 0.055 in)
Piston pin diameter .... 23.8252 to 23.9268 mm (0.938 to 0.942 in)
Piston pin length .... 76.2 mm (3.0 in)
Pin-to-piston
    Clearance .... 0.00508 to 0.01016 mm (0.0002 to 0.0004 in loose)
    Fit in rod .... Press

Crankshaft and connecting rods (L4)

Main bearing journal
    Diameter .... 59.182 mm (2.30 in)
    Out-of-round .... 0.0127 mm (0.0005 in) maximum
    Taper .... 0.0127 mm (0.005 in) maximum
    Clearance limit (new) .... 0.0127 to 0.05588 mm (0.0005 to 0.0022 in)
    Crankshaft end play (new) .... 0.0889 to 0.2159 mm (0.0035 to 0.0085 in)
Rod bearing journal
    Diameter .... 50.8 mm (2.000 in)
    Out-of-round .... 0.0127 mm (0.0005 in) maximum
    Taper .... 0.0127 mm (0.0005 in) maximum
    Clearance limit (new) .... 0.0127 to 0.0660 mm (0.0005 to 0.0026 in)
    Rod side clearance .... 0.1524 to 0.5588 mm (0.006 to 0.022 in)

Camshaft (L4)

Lobe lift
    Intake .... 10.3124 mm (0.406 in)
    Exhaust .... 10.3124 mm (0.406 in)
Journal diameter .... 47.4726 mm (1.869 in)
Journal clearance .... 0.01778 to 0.0685 mm (0.0007 to 0.0027 in)
End play clearance .... 0.0381 to 0.127 mm (0.0015 to 0.0050 in)

Valve train (L4)

Lash (intake and exhaust) 0
Rocker arm ratio .... 1.75 : 1
Pushrod length .... 242.316 mm (9.754 in)
Valve lifter
    Leak-down rate .... 12 to 90 seconds with 50-lb load
    Lifter body diameter .... 21.3868 to 21.4046 mm (0.8420 to 0.8427 in)
    Plunger travel .... 3.175 mm (0.125 in)
    Clearnace in boss .... 0.635 mm (0.0025 in)
    Lifter bore diameter .... 21.425 to 21.450 mm (0.8435 to 0.8445 in)

Valves and valve springs (L4)

Intake
    Face angle .... 45°
    Seat angle .... 46°
    Head diameter .... 43.688 mm (1.72 in)
    Stem diameter .... 8.6995 to 8.6817 mm (0.3425 to 0.3418 in)
    Overall length .... 125.0696 mm (4.924 in)
    Stem to guide clearance .... 0.0254 to 0.0686 mm (0.0010 to 0.0027 in)
    Valve seat width .... 0.897 to 1.897 mm (0.353 to 0.747 in)
    Valve installed height .... 42.926 mm (1.69 in)
Exhaust
    Face angle .... 45°
    Seat angle .... 46°
    Head diameter .... 38.1 mm (1.50 in)
    Stem diameter .... 8.6817 to 8.9665 mm (0.3418 to 0.3425 in)
    Overall length .... 124.968 mm (4.92 in)
    Stem to guide clearance; top .... 0.0254 to 0.0686 mm (0.0010 to 0.0027 in)
    Stem to guide clearance; bottom .... 0.0508 to 0.0939 mm (0.0020 to 0.0037 in)
Valve seat width .... 1.468 to 2.468 mm (0.058 to 0.971 in)
Valve installed height .... 42.926 mm (1.69 in)

Valve spring pressure and length, intake and exhaust
    Valve closed .... 78 to 86 lb at 1.66 in
    Valve open .... 122 to 180 lb at 1.254 in

Lubrication (L4)

Oil capacity, with filter .... 2.838 liters (3 qt)
Filter type .... PF 40 or equivalent
Oil pressure .... 36 to 41 lb at 2000 rpm

Torque specifications

L4 engines

	ft-lb	m-kg
Main bearing to block bolts	70	9.6
Connecting rod nuts	32	4.4
Oil pan bolts	6	0.8
Oil pan drain plug	25	3.4
Oil screen support nut	37	5.1
Oil pump to block bolts	22	3.0
Oil pump cover bolts	10	1.4
Pushrod cover to block bolts	7	1.0
Crank pulley hub bolt	200	27.6
Flywheel to crankshaft bolts	44	6.0
Carburetor to manifold nuts	15	2.0
Intake manifold to cylinder head bolts	29	4.0
Carb spacer to intake manifold bolts	15	2.0
Exhaust manifold to cylinder head bolts	44	6.0
Fuel pump to block bolts	18	2.5
Distributor retaining clamp bolt	22	3.0
EGR valve to manifold bolts	10	1.4
Water outlet housing bolts	20	2.7
Thermostat housing bolts	20	2.7
Water pump bracket to block bolts	25	3.4
Timing cover to block bolts	7	1.0
Rocker arm studs	75	10.3
Cylinder head to block bolts	85	11.7
Rocker arm to stud nuts	20	2.7
Rocker arm cover bolts	6	0.8
Camshaft thrust plate to block bolts	7	1.0
Oil pump drive shaft retainer plate bolts	10	1.4
Engine mount to cradle nuts	41	5.6

Specifications – V6 engines

Engine – general (V6)

Type .... 60° V6, six-cylinder
Displacement .... 2.8 liters (173 cu in)
Sales code LE2
Bore .... 89 mm (3.50 in)
Stroke .... 76 mm (2.99 in)
Compression ratio .... 8.6 : 1
Firing order 1, 2, 3, 4, 5, 6

Cylinder block (V6)

Bore diameter .... 88.992 to 89.070 mm (3.504 to 3.507 in)
Out-of-round .... 0.02 mm (0.0008 in) maximum
Taper – thrust side .... 0.02 mm (0.0008 in) maximum
Piston clearance in bore .... 0.043 to 0.069 mm (0.0017 to 0.0027 in)

Piston rings (V6)

Top compression ring groove clearance .... 0.030 to 0.070 mm (0.0019 to 0.0028 in)
2nd compression ring groove clearance .... 0.040 to 0.095 mm (0.0016 to 0.0037 in)
Oil ring groove clearance .... 0.199 mm (0.0078 in) maximum
Top compression ring gap .... 0.25 to 0.50 mm (0.0098 to 0.0196 in)
2nd compression ring gap .... 0.25 to 0.50 mm (0.0098 to 0.0196 in)
Oil ring gap .... 0.51 to 0.40 mm (0.0201 to 0.0157 in)

Piston pin (V6)

Diameter .... 22.9937 to 23.0015 mm (0.90526 to 0.90557 in)
Clearance .... 0.0065 to 0.0091 mm (0.00026 to 0.00036 in)
Fit in rod (pressed) .... 0.0187 to 0.0515 mm (0.00074 to 0.00203 in)

Camshaft (V6)

Intake lift .... 5.87 mm (0.231 in)
Exhaust lift .... 6.67 mm (0.262 in)

Journal diameter .... 47.44 to 47.49 mm (1.868 to 1.870 in)
Journal clearance .... 0.026 to 0.101 mm (0.0010 to 0.0040 in)

Crankshaft (V6)

Main journal diameter .... 63.340 to 63.364 mm (2.4937 to 2.4946 in)
Main journal taper .... 0.005 mm (0.0002 in) maximum
Main journal out-of-round .... 0.005 mm (0.0002 in) maximum
Main bearing clearance (all) .... 0.044 to 0.076 mm (0.0017 to 0.0030 in)
Crankshaft end play .... 0.05 to 0.20 mm (0.002 to 0,008 in)
Crankpin diameter .... 50.758 to 50.784 mm (1.9983 to 1.9994 in)
Crankpin taper .... 0.005 mm (0.0002 in) maximum
Crankpin out of round .... 0.005 mm (0.0002 in) maximum
Rod bearing clearance .... 0.036 to 0.091 mm (0.0014 to 0.0036 in)
Rod side clearance .... 0.16 to 0.44 mm (0.006 to 0.017 in)

Valve system (V6)

Lifter type .... Hydraulic
Rocker arm ratio .... 1.5 : 1
Valve lash adjustment .... $1\frac{1}{2}$ turns from zero lash
Face angle (all) .... 45°
Seat angle (all) .... 46°
Seat runout .... 0.05 mm (0.002 in)
Seat width (intake) .... 1.25 to 1.50 mm (0.049 to 0.059 in)
Seat width (exhaust) .... 1.60 to 1.90 mm (0.063 to 0.075 in)
Stem clearance (all) .... 0.026 to 0.068 mm (0.0010 to 0.0028 in)
Valve spring free length .... 48.5 mm (1.91 in)
Valve spring installed height .... 40.0 mm (1.57 in)
Valve spring pressure (closed) .... 391 N at 40 mm (87.9lb at 1.57 in)
Valve spring pressure (open) .... 867 N at 30 mm (194.9lb at 1.18 in)
Damper free length .... 47.2 mm (1.86 in)
Damper — number of coils (approx) 4

Torque specifications
V6 engines

	ft-lb	m-kg
A/C compressor bracket to head bolts	35	4.8
A/C compressor mounting bolts	25	3.4
Camshaft sprocket bolts	18	2.5
Clutch cover to flywheel bolts	15	2.0
Rear camshaft cover bolts	7	1.0
Cylinder head bolts	68	9.4
Connecting rod cap nuts	37	5.1
Crankshaft pulley bolts	25	3.4
Crankshaft pulley hub bolt	75	10.3
Distributor hold-down clamp bolt	25	3.4
EGR valve mounting bolts	15	2.0
Engine mounting bracket bolts	80	11.0
Engine strut bracket	35	4.8
Exhaust manifold mounting bolts	25	3.4
Flex plate to torque converter bolts	27	3.7
Flywheel mounting bolts	50	7.0
Front cover mounting bolts (small)	15	2.0
Front cover mounting bolts (large)	25	3.4
Fuel pump mounting bolts	15	2.0
Generator bracket to head bolts	35	4.8
Generator brace to cover bolts	25	3.4
Generator adjusting bolt	23	3.8
Generator pivot bolt	25	3.4
Intake manifold mounting bolts	23	3.8
Main bearing cap bolts	70	9.6
Oil dipstick tube mounting bolts	25	3.4
Oil pan mounting bolts (small)	7	1.0
Oil pan mounting bolts (large)	18	2.5
Oil pump mounting bolt	30	4.1
Oil pump cover bolts	8	1.1
Oil pressure switch	5	0.7
Oil drain plug	18	2.5
Power steering pump adjusting bolts and nut	28	3.9
Power steering pump bracket to head bolts	25	3.4
Power steering pump brace to block bolts	25	3.4
Power steering pump attaching bolts and nuts	25	3.4
Rear lifting bracket bolt	25	3.4
Rocker arm cover bolts	8	1.1
Rocker arm studs	45	6.2
Spark plugs	12	1.6
Starter motor mounting bolts	32	4.4
Starter motor brace to case bolts	15	2.0

	ft-lb	m-kg
Strut bracket assembly nut and bolt	35	4.8
Timing chain tensioner bolts	15	2.0
Transaxle to engine block bolts	55	7.6
Water outlet housing bolts	25	3.4
Water pump mounting bolts (small)	7	1.0
Water pump mounting bolts (medium)	15	2.0
Water pump mounting bolts (large	25	3.4
Water pump pulley bolt	15	2.0

1 Engines – general information

1   Two different engines are available with the X-Body cars: a 2.5-liter four-cylinder (L4) and a 2.8-liter six-cylinder (V6). The L4 engine is standard equipment, with the V6 engine being offered as an option.
2   The L4 engine is basically a modified Pontiac "Iron Duke" engine, adapted to fit sideways in the engine compartment, due to the X-Bodys' transverse-mounted engine design. The V6 engine is a completely new GM engine design, specifically built for the X-Body cars.
3   The L4 cylinder block is made of cast iron and has 4 in-line cylinders numbered sequentially from front to rear. These cylinders are completely encircled by coolant jackets. The crankshaft is retained by 5 main bearings.
4   The cylinder block of the V6 engine is made of cast alloy iron and has 6 cylinders arranged in a 60° "V" design with 3 cylinders on each side. The right (rear) bank of cylinders is numbered front to rear 1, 3 and 5. The left (front) bank is numbered 2, 4 and 6. The crankshaft is supported by 4 main bearings.
5   The cylinder heads of both engines are also cast iron and incorporate individual intake and exhaust ports for each cylinder. Valve guides are cast integrally in the heads.
6   The valve train is of the simple ball pivot type. Camshaft motion is transmitted through the hydraulic lifters and pushrods to the rocker arms, which, by pivoting on their balls, transmit the motion to the valves. The hydraulic lifters keep all parts of the valve train in constant contact. Each lifter acts as an automatic adjuster maintaining zero lash at all times. Manual readjustment is not necessary after the original adjustment has been set.
7   The camshaft in the L4 engine is supported by 3 bearings and is gear-driven off of the crankshaft.
8   The V6 camshaft is supported by 4 journals and incorporates a drive gear for the distributor and oil pump and a fuel pump eccentric. The camshaft is driven off of the crankshaft by a $\frac{3}{8}$ in pitch timing chain.
9   The pistons used in both engines are cast aluminium and utilize 2 compression rings and 1 oil control ring on each piston.
10   The L4 engine is lubricated by a system which uses an oil sump pump to pick up oil from the oil pan and route it through the full flow oil filter and into an oil passage which runs along the right side of the block. Oil is then pumped to the camshaft and crankshaft bearings through small passages. Lubrication is supplied to the rocker arms through holes in the hydraulic lifters and pushrods. The timing gears are lubricated by way of a passage from the front of the camshaft to a calibrated nozzle above the crankshaft gear.
11   The V6 lubrication system is similar to that of the L4 engine. From the oil filter, oil in the V6 is routed to the main oil gallery located in the left cylinder bank, above and to the left of the camshaft. Oil from this gallery supplies the left bank hydraulic lifters, which, in turn, lubricate the left cylinder head valve mechanisms through the lifters and pushrods as in the L4. From this gallery oil is also directed, by means of intersecting passages, to the camshaft bearings, crankshaft main bearings, connecting rods, and the right cylinder bank oil gallery. Oil draining back from the rocker arms is directed by way of dams in the crankcase casting to the camshaft lobes.
12   Procedures in this chapter that are specific to only one of the engines are noted as such. Procedures which do not have this notation are intended for both engines.
13   Whenever engine work is required, there are some basic steps which the home mechanic should perform before any work is begun. These preliminary steps will help prevent delays during the operation. They are as follows:

(a)   Read through the appropriate sections in this manual to get an understanding of the processes involved, tools necessary and replacement parts which will be needed

(b)   Contact your local GM dealer or automotive parts store to check on replacement parts availability and cost. In many cases, a decision must be made beforehand whether to simply remove the faulty component and replace it with a new or rebuilt unit or to overhaul the existing part
(c)   If the vehicle is equipped with air-conditioning, it is imperative that a qualified specialist depressurize the system if this is required to perform the necessary engine repair work. The home mechanic should never disconnect any of the air-conditioning system while it is still pressurized, as this can cause serious personal injury as well as possibly damage the air-conditioning system. Ascertain if depressurization is necessary while the vehicle is still operational

NOTE: *Although many of the procedures described in this chapter are performed with the engine in the car, some of the accompanying photos show the engine out of the car. Because of the greater photographic clarity, these photos were taken during a complete overhaul of the engine. They are used with the in-car operations because of the important visual information they provide.*

2 Rocker arm cover (L4) – removal and installation

NOTE: *If the engine has been removed from the car, disregard the following steps which do not apply.*
1   Remove the air cleaner.
2   Remove the PCV valve and hose.
3   If equipped, remove the PULSAIR air hose from the air valve.
4   Remove the spark plug wires from the plugs and mounting clips, labeling each wire as to its proper position.
5   Remove the rocker cover bolts (photo).
6   Remove the rocker arm cover (photo). To break the gasket seal it may be necessary to tap the cover with your hand or a rubber mallet. Do not pry on the cover.
7   Prior to installation, clean all dirt, oil and old gasket material from the sealing surfaces of the cover and cylinder head with a degreaser.
8   Place a continuous $\frac{3}{16}$ in (5 mm) diameter bead of RTV or equivalent sealer around the sealing lip of the cover (photo). Be sure to apply the sealant to the inside of the mounting bolt holes (Fig. 2.3).
9   Place the rocker arm cover on the cylinder head while the sealant is still wet, and install the mounting bolts, torquing them to specs.
10   Complete the installation by reversing the sequence of the removal procedure.

3 Rocker arm covers (V6) – removal and installation

NOTE: *If the engine has been removed from the car, disregard the following steps which do not apply.*
1   Disconnect the negative battery cable.
2   Remove the air cleaner.
3   Remove the front engine strut and bracket, mounted between the radiator support and the front cylinder head.
4   Remove the PCV valve from the front cylinder head.
5   Disconnect the spark plug wires from the spark plugs, labelling each as to its proper location.
6   Remove the accelerator linkage and springs from the carburetor.
7   If equipped with an automatic transaxle, disconnect the T.V. linkage from the carburetor (photo).
8   If equipped with cruise control, remove the diaphragm actuator mounting bracket.
9   Remove the rocker arm cover mounting bolts and lift off the rocker cover (photo). To break the gasket seal, it may be necessary to tap the cover lightly with your hand or a rubber mallet. Do not pry on the cover.

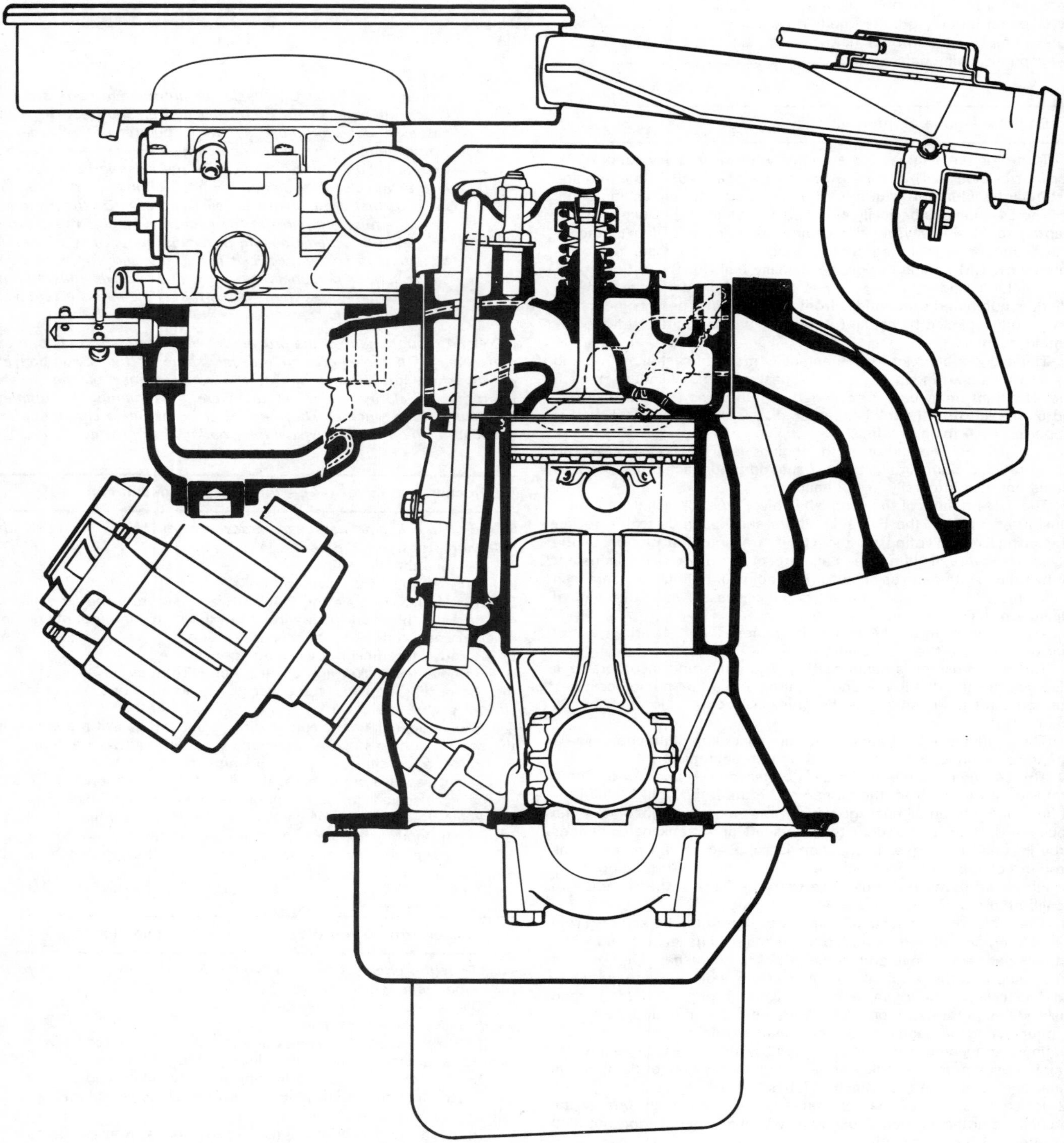

Fig. 2.1 Cross sectional view of the L4 engine

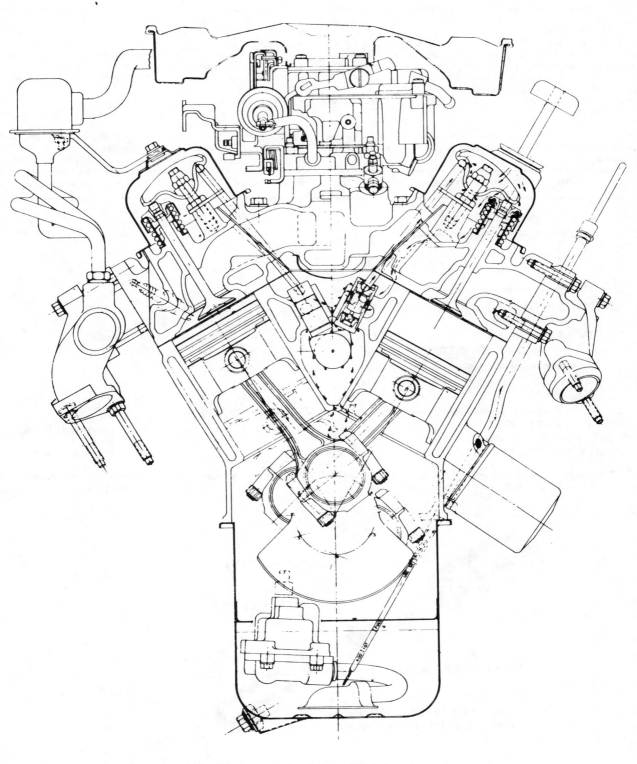

Fig. 2.2 Cross sectional view of the V6 engine

10 Prior to installation clean all dirt, oil and old gasket material from the sealing surfaces of the covers and cylinder heads. Clean the surfaces with a degreaser.

11 Place a continuous $\frac{1}{8}$ in (3 mm) diameter bead of RTV or equivalent sealant around the sealing lip of the covers. Be sure to apply the sealant to the inside of the mounting bolt holes (Fig. 2.4).

12 Install the cover while the sealant is still wet, and install the mounting bolts, torquing them to specs.

13 Complete the installation by reversing the sequence of the removal procedure.

---

4 Rocker arm, pushrod and valve spring – removal and installation (engine in car)

NOTE: *Valve mechanism components must be re-installed to their original positions. Place all removed components in a compartmented box to aid in identification.*

1 Remove the rocker arm cover as described in Section 2 (L4) or Section 3 (V6).

2 If only the pushrod is to be replaced, loosen the rocker nut enough so the rocker arm can be rotated away from the pushrod. If the rocker arm or valve spring is to be replaced, remove the rocker arm nut and ball, and lift off the rocker arm.

3 Pull the pushrod out of its hole.

4 If the valve spring is to be removed, remove the spark plug from the cylinder being serviced.

5 There are two methods of keeping the valve in place while the valve spring is removed. If you have access to compressed air, attach an air hose adapter (GM part number J-22794) or equivalent to your air hose and insert it into the spark plug hole. When air pressure is applied the valves will be held in place by the pressure.

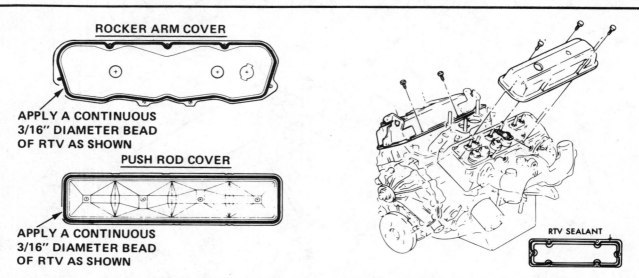

ROCKER ARM COVER

APPLY A CONTINUOUS 3/16" DIAMETER BEAD OF RTV AS SHOWN

PUSH ROD COVER

APPLY A CONTINUOUS 3/16" DIAMETER BEAD OF RTV AS SHOWN

Fig. 2.3 Recommended sealant application for installation of the L4 rocker arm cover and push rod cover (Secs 2 and 5)

RTV SEALANT

Fig. 2.4 Recommended sealant application for installation of the V6 rocker arm cover (Sec 3)

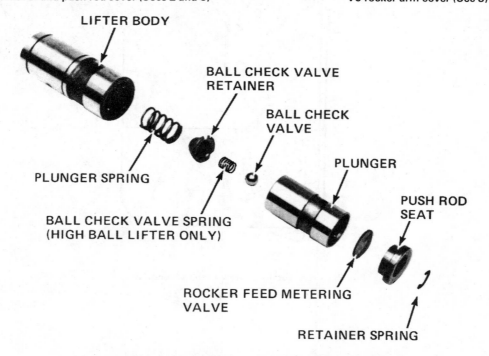

LIFTER BODY

BALL CHECK VALVE RETAINER

BALL CHECK VALVE

PLUNGER

PUSH ROD SEAT

PLUNGER SPRING

BALL CHECK VALVE SPRING (HIGH BALL LIFTER ONLY)

ROCKER FEED METERING VALVE

RETAINER SPRING

Fig. 2.5 Exploded view of a hydraulic valve lifter assembly (Sec 6)

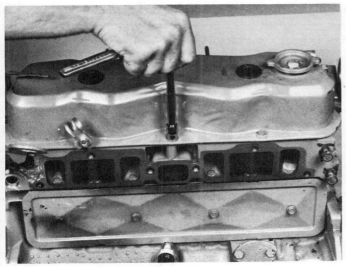

2.5 Removing the rocker arm cover bolts

2.6 Removing the rocker arm cover

2.8 Applying sealant to the rocker cover sealing lip prior to installation

3.7 Disconnecting the automatic transaxle throttle valve linkage from the carburetor

3.9 Removing the rocker arm cover.

5.2 Removing the push rod cover (L4)

6   If you do not have access to compressed air, bring the piston of that cylinder to top dead center (TDC). Feed a long piece of $\frac{1}{4}$ in nylon cord in through the spark plug hole until it fills the combustion chamber. Be sure to leave the end of the cord hanging out of the spark plug hole so it can be removed easily.

7   Thread the rocker arm nut onto the rocker arm stud. Position a valve spring compressor tool over the spring and hook it under the rocker arm nut. Using the nut to secure the tool, apply downward pressure to the valve spring. If care is taken, a screwdriver can also be used in this fashion to compress the spring. Compress the spring just enough to allow the removal of the valve spring retaining cups. Then let up on the spring.

8   Remove the valve spring retainer, cup shield, valve spring and valve stem oil seal. The valve stem oil seal must always be replaced whenever the spring locks have been disturbed.

9   Inspection procedures for the various valve components are detailed in Section 16.

10 Installation is the reverse of the removal procedure. Prior to installing the rocker arms, coat the bearing surfaces of the arms and rocker arm balls with 'Molykote' or its equivalent. The L4 engine valve mechanisms require no special lash adjustment. The rocker arm nuts simply need to be torqued to the proper specifications. On V6 engines be sure to adjust the lash as described in Section 7 once the valve mechanism is completely assembled.

5   Pushrod cover (L4) – removal and installation

1   Remove the intake manifold as described in Section 8.

2   Remove the pushrod cover bolts and lift off the cover (photo). If the gasket seal is difficult to break, tap on the cover lightly with a rubber mallet. Do not pry on the cover.

3   Using a degreaser, thoroughly clean the sealing surfaces on the cover and engine block of all oil and old gasket material.

4   Prior to installation of the cover, place a continuous $\frac{3}{16}$ in (5 mm) bead of RTV or equivalent sealant to the sealing lip of the pushrod cover (Fig. 2.6).

5   With the sealant still wet, place the cover in position on the block and install the cover bolts, torquing them to specs.

6   Install the intake manifold, and related components.

6   Hydraulic lifter – removal, inspection and installation

1   A noisy valve lifter is best traced when the engine is idling. Place a length of hose or tubing near the position of each intake and exhaust valve while listening at the other end of the tube. Another method is to remove the rocker arm cover and, with the engine idling, place a finger on each of the valve spring retainers in turn. If a valve lifter is faulty in operation, it will be evident from the shock felt from the retainer as the valve seats.

2   Provided adjustment is correct, the most likely cause of a noisy valve lifter is a piece of dirt being trapped between the plunger and lifter body.

3   Remove the L4 rocker arm cover as described in Section 2, or the V6 covers as described in Section 3.

4   Remove the L4 rocker arm cover as described in Section 2, or the V6 covers as described in Section 3.

5   Remove the intake manifold as described in Section 8 (L4) or Section 9 (V6).

6   On L4 engines remove the pushrod cover as described in Section 5.

7   Loosen the rocker arm nut and rotate the rocker arm away from the pushrod.

8   Remove the pushrod.

9   To remove the lifters, a special hydraulic lifter removal tool can be used (photo), or a sharp scribe can be positioned at the top of the lifter and used to force the lifter upward. Do not use pliers or other tools on the outside of the lifter body, as this will damage the finished surface and render the lifter useless.

10 The lifters should be kept separate for reinstallation in their original positions.

11 To dismantle a valve lifter, hold the plunger down with a pushrod and then extract the pushrod seat retainer using a small screwdriver.

12 Remove the pushrod seat and the metering valve.

13 Remove the plunger, ball check valve and the plunger spring. Remove the ball check valve and spring by prying with a small screwdriver.

14 Examine all components for wear, especially the ball for flat spots. If any faults are observed, replace the complete lifter assembly.

15 Examine each lifter for scoring, wear or erosion of the camshaft lobe mating surface. Any imperfections on the lifter body surface is cause for replacement. Wear in the lifter bore in the block is rare.

16 Reassembly should be performed in the following manner:

   (a) Place the check ball on the small hole in the bottom of the plunger.

   (b) Insert the check ball spring on the seat in the ball retainer and place the retainer over the ball so that the spring rests on the ball. Using a small screwdriver, carefully press the retainer into position in the plunger.

   (c) Place the plunger spring over the ball retainer, invert the lifter body and slide it over the spring and plunger. Make sure the oil holes in the body and plunger line up.

   (d) Fill the assembly with SAE 10 oil. Place the metering valve and pushrod seat into position, press down on the seat and install the pushrod seat retainer.

17 When installing the lifters, make sure they are in their original bores, and coat their surfaces with Molykote or its equivalent.

18 Complete the installation by reversing the steps on the removal procedure.

6.9 Removing the hydraulic lifters (L4)

7   Valve mechanism (V6) – lash adjustment

1   The valve mechanism need only be adjusted when valve components have been removed or loosened.

2   Once the valve mechanism has been completely reassembled, tighten the rocker arm nuts until all lash has been eliminated.

3   Turn the engine over until the number 1 piston is at top dead center (TDC).

4   Back off the rocker arm nut until lash is felt at the pushrod, then turn it back in just until all lash is removed. This can be determined by rotating the pushrod while tightening the nut. After the point where the lash has been removed, turn the nut in an additional $1\frac{1}{2}$ turns. This will center the lifter plunger.

5   With the number 1 piston at TDC, the 1, 2 and 3 exhaust valves and the 1, 5 and 6 intake valves can be adjusted in this way.

6   Turn the engine until the number 4 piston is at TDC and repeat the adjustment on the 4, 5 and 6 exhaust valves and the 2, 3 and 4 intake valves.

7   To be sure you do not mix up the TDC firing positions of the number 1 and 4 pistons, check the position of the rotor in the distributor to see which cylinder it is firing. Another method is to place your fingers on the number 1 rocker arms as the timing marks at the crank pulley line up. If the valves are not moving, the engine is in the number 1 firing position. If the valves move as the timing marks line up, the engine is in the number 4 firing position.

8   Intake manifold (L4) – removal and installation

1   Remove the air cleaner, being sure to label the lines and hoses as to their proper location.
2   Remove the PCV hose.
3   Disconnect the negative battery terminal.
4   Drain the cooling system as described in Chapter 1.
5   Remove the carburetor as described in Chapter 4.
6   Remove the carburetor base gasket (photo).
7   Disconnect the vacuum lines from the carburetor spacer.
8   Remove the EGR valve.
9   Remove the carburetor spacer (photo).
10 Remove the carburetor spacer gasket (photo).
11 Remove the bell crank and throttle linkage brackets and set to one side for clearance.
12 Remove the heater hose from the intake manifold (photo).
13 Remove the upper generator bracket.
14 If equipped, remove the PULSAIR air valve bracket.
15 Remove the bolts that secure the intake manifold to the cylinder head and lift off the intake manifold (photo).
16 Remove the manifold gasket.
17 If the intake manifold is to be replaced with another, transfer any remaining components still attached to the old manifold to the new one.
18 Before installing the manifold, place clean, lint-free rags in the engine cavity and scrupulously clean the engine block, cylinder heads and manifold gasket surfaces. All extra gasket material and sealing compound must be removed prior to installation. Remove all dirt and gasket remnants from the engine cavity.
19 Apply a thin bead of RTV or an equivalent sealer to the intake manifold and cylinder head mating surfaces. Be certain that the sealant will not spread into the air or water passages when the manifold is installed.
20 Place a new intake manifold gasket on the manifold, place the manifold in position against the cylinder head and install the mounting bolts fingertight.
21 Tighten the manifold mounting bolts in the sequence shown in Fig. 2.6 a little at a time until they are all torqued to specs.
22 Install the remaining components in the reverse order of removal.
23 Fill the radiator with coolant, start the engine and check for leaks. Check the carburetor idle speeds and adjust if necessary, as described in Chapter 1.

9   Intake manifold – removal and installation

NOTE: *If the engine has been removed from the car, disregard the following steps which do not apply.*
1   If the vehicle is equipped with air conditioning, carefully examine the routing of the A/C hoses and the mounting of the compressor. You may be able to remove the intake manifold without disconnecting the A/C system. If you are in doubt, take the car to a certified dealer or refrigeration specialist to have the system de-pressurized. Do not under any circumstances disconnect the A/C hoses while the system is under pressure.
2   Disconnect the negative battery cable.
3   Drain the coolant from the radiator (Chapter 1).
4   Remove the air cleaner assembly (photo).
5   Disconnect the upper radiator hose and the heater hose from the intake manifold.
6   Disconnect the accelerator linkage at the carburetor. If the cable is supported by a bracket on the manifold, this must also be removed.
7   With a container handy to catch any spillage, disconnect the fuel inlet hose at the carburetor. Plug the end of this hose to prevent dirt from entering the system and excessive fuel seepage.
8   Disconnect all other hoses connected to the carburetor. Make sure each hose is identified as to its location with strips of numbered tape. This will prevent confusion upon reassembly.
9   Remove the distributor following closely the instructions given in Chapter 5. The distributor cap with the spark plug wires attached should be taped or wired out of the way.
10 Remove both rocker arm covers as described in Section 3.
11 Disconnect the vacuum hose leading to the power brake booster (if equipped with power brakes).
12 Remove any accessory brackets attached to the intake manifold.
13 Remove the external EFE pipe from the rear of the manifold.

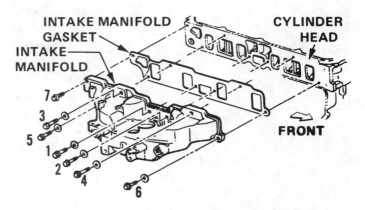

Fig. 2.6 Recommended torquing sequence for the L4 intake manifold mounting bolts (Sec 8)

8.6 Removing the carburetor base gasket

8.9 Removing the carburetor spacer

8.10 Removing the carburetor spacer gasket

8.12 Removing the heater hose from the intake manifold

8.15a Locations of the intake manifold mounting bolts

8.15b Lifting the intake manifold from the cylinder head

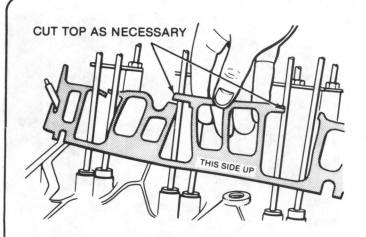

CUT TOP AS NECESSARY

THIS SIDE UP

Fig. 2.7 The V6 intake manifold gasket must be cut as shown during installation so the top can be positioned behind the pushrods (Sec 9)

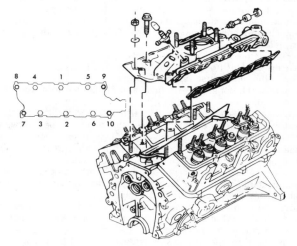

Fig. 2.8 Recommended torquing sequence for the V6 intake manifold mounting bolts (Sec 9)

9.4 Note the position of all hoses and pipes when removing the air cleaner assembly

14 Remove the intake manifold-to-cylinder head attaching bolts.

15 Lift the manifold, complete with carburetor, free from the engine. Do not pry on the mating surfaces to break the seal as this may cause damage.

16 If the intake manifold is to be replaced with another, transfer all components that have not yet been removed. These include:

(a) Carburetor and carburetor attaching bolts or studs (see Chapter 4 for procedures)
(b) Temperature and/or oil pressure sending unit
(c) Heater hose and water pump hose adapter fittings
(d) EGR valve (use new gasket, see Chapter 6)
(e) Emission system TVS switches (Chapter 6)
(f) Carburetor choke assembly

17 Before installing the manifold, place clean lint-free rags in the engine cavity and scrupulously clean the engine block, cylinder heads and manifold gasket surfaces. All extra gasket material and sealing compound must be removed prior to installation. Remove all dirt and gasket remnants from the engine cavity.

18 Clean the sealing surfaces of the cylinder case's front and rear ridges with degreaser. Then apply a $\frac{3}{16}$ in (5 mm) diameter bead of RTV or equivalent sealant on each ridge.

19 Install the new intake gaskets on the cylinder heads. Notice that the gaskets are marked "Right" and "Left". Be sure to use the correct gasket on each cylinder head.

20 Hold the gaskets in place by extending the bead of RTV up about $\frac{1}{4}$ in onto the gasket ends. The new gasket will have to be cut where indicated in Fig. 2.7 so they can be installed behind the pushrods.

21 Carefully lower the intake manifold into position, making sure you do not disturb the gaskets.

22 Install the intake manifold mounting bolts and tighten them using the sequence shown in Fig. 2.8. Tighten them a little at a time until they are all torqued to specs.

23 Install the remaining components in the reverse order of removal. Refer to Chapter 5 for the installation of the distributor.

24 Fill the radiator with coolant, start the engine and check for leaks. Adjust the ignition timing and carburetor idle speeds (Chapter 1) as necessary.

10 Exhaust manifold (L4) – removal and installation

1   If the car is equipped with air-conditioning, carefully examine the routing of the A/C hoses and the mounting of the compressor. You may be able to remove the exhaust manifold without disconnecting the A/C system. If you are in doubt, take the car to a GM dealer or other qualified automotive shop to have the system depressurized. Do not under any circumstances disconnect any A/C lines while the system is under pressure.

2   Remove the air cleaner.

3   Remove the carburetor pre-heat tube.

4   Remove the flexible engine strut mounted between the radiator support and the cylinder head (photo).

5   Remove the engine oil dipstick tube to the left of the exhaust manifold (photo).

6   Remove the exhaust sensor located on the left side of the exhaust manifold.

7   Remove the A/C compressor mounting bracket mounted to the center of the exhaust manifold.

8   Label the four spark plug wires as to their positions. Disconnect them and secure to the side for working clearance.

9   Disconnect the exhaust pipe from the exhaust manifold. The exhaust pipe can be hung from the frame using wire.

10 Remove the exhaust manifold end bolts first (photo). Then remove the center bolts and the exhaust manifold.

11 Remove the exhaust manifold gasket.

12 Before installing the exhaust manifold, clean the mating surfaces on the cylinder head and manifold. All leftover gasket material should be removed.

13 Place a new exhaust manifold gasket into position on the cylinder head. Then place the manifold into position and install the mounting bolts fingertight.

14 Tighten the manifold mounting bolts in the sequence shown in Fig. 2.9 a little at a time until all of the bolts are torqued to specs.

15 Install the remaining components in the reverse order of removal, using new gaskets wherever one has been removed.

16 Start the engine and check for exhaust leaks between the manifold and cylinder head and between the manifold and exhaust pipe.

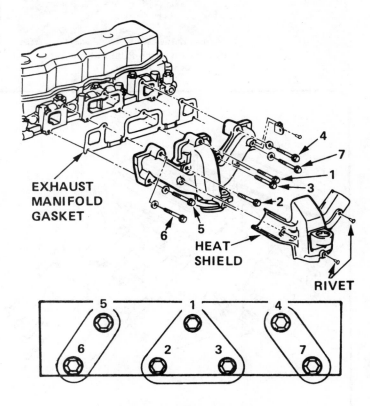

BOLT LOCATIONS

Fig. 2.9 Recommended torquing sequence for the L4 exhaust manifold (Sec 10)

11 Exhaust manifold (V6) – removal and installation

Note: *If the engine has been removed from the car, disregard the following steps which do not apply.*

10.4 Location of the front engine strut

10.5 Removing the engine oil dipstick tube

10.10 The exhaust manifold end bolts should be removed before the center bolts

11.6 Location of the PULSAIR bracket on the right rocker cover

12.5 Disconnecting a vacuum line from the cylinder head

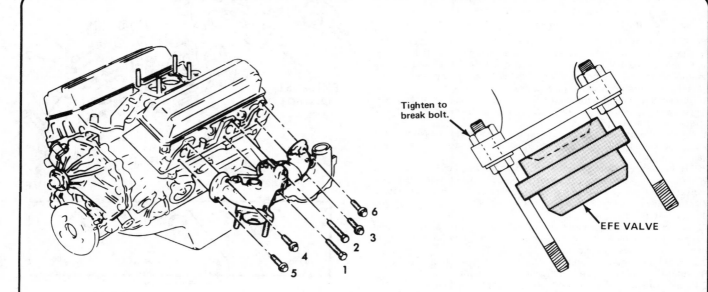

Fig. 2.10 Recommended torquing sequence for the V6 exhaust manifold (Sec 11)

Tighten to break bolt.

EFE VALVE

Fig. 2.11 When removing the exhaust pipe from the right side V6 exhaust manifold, the upper bolts must be tightened until the flange bolts break (Sec 11)

1 If the vehicle is equipped with air conditioning, carefully examine the routing of the A/C hoses and the mounting of the compressor. You may be able to remove the exhaust manifolds without disconnecting the A/C system. If you are in doubt, take the car to a certified dealer or refrigeration specialist to have the system depressurized. Do not under any circumstances disconnect the A/C hoses while the system is under pressure.
2 Disconnect the negative battery cable.
3 Disconnect the carburetor hot air pipe routed from the right exhaust manifold to the air cleaner.
4 Mark each spark plug wire with a piece of coded tape and then remove each plug wire from its spark plug. Remember to pull on the rubber boot and not the wire itself. It is important that the order of these wires should not be mixed up.
5 Remove the air cleaner.
6 Remove the PULSAIR bracket bolt from the right rocker cover (photo) and remove the system's plumbing from both exhaust manifolds.
7 Remove any remaining hoses.
8 Raise the front of the car and support it on jackstands.
9 Disconnect the left exhaust pipe from the exhaust manifold. If the bolts are tight, penetrating oil will help loosen them.
10 The EFE valve is mounted between the right exhaust manifold and exhaust pipe. To disconnect these, tighten the upper manifold flange nuts, as shown in Fig. 2.11, until the bolts break. Then remove the exhaust pipe from the manifold. The front exhaust crossover pipe can be hung from the cradle using wire.
11 If equipped with bolt locking strips, use a screwdriver to pry the metal locking strips away from the exhaust manifold bolt heads. This will enable you to put a standard wrench on the bolts.
12 Remove the exhaust manifold end bolts first, followed by the center bolts. Lift the manifold away from the engine.
13 Before installing the exhaust manifolds, clean the mating surfaces on the cylinder heads and exhaust manifolds. All leftover gasket material should be removed.
14 Place new gaskets into position on the cylinder head, using a thin film of sealer to hold them in place.
15 Install the manifold and tighten the bolts a little at a time using the sequence shown in Fig. 2.10 until they are all torqued to specs.
16 Install the remaining components in the reverse order of removal. When connecting the right exhaust manifold to the exhaust pipe, use new exhaust pipe bolts.
17 Start the engine and check for exhaust leaks where the manifold meets the cylinder head and where the manifold joins with the exhaust pipes.

12 Cylinder head (L4) – removal

Note: If the engine has been removed from the car, disregard the following steps which do not apply.
1 Remove the intake manifold as described in Section 8.
2 Remove the exhaust manifold as described in Section 10.
3 Remove the bolts that secure the generator bracket to the cylinder head.
4 Disconnect the A/C compressor and swing it out of the way for clearance. Be sure not to disconnect any of the A/C lines unless the system has been depressurized.
5 Disconnect all electrical and vacuum lines from the cylinder head (photo). Be sure to label the lines as to their location.
6 Remove the upper radiator hose.
7 Disconnect the spark plug wires and remove the spark plugs. Be sure to label the plug wires as to their correct locations.
8 Remove the rocker arm cover. To break the gasket seal it may be necessary to strike the cover with your hand or a rubber mallet. Do not pry on the sealing surfaces.
9 In disassembling the valve mechanisms it is important that all of the components be kept separate once removed, so they can be installed in their original positions. A cardboard box or rack numbered according to engine cylinders, can be used for this.
10 Remove each of the rocker arm nuts (photo).
11 Lift the rocker arms off of their studs (photo).
12 Remove the pushrods (photo).
13 Remove the thermostat housing from the cylinder head (photo).
14 Remove all vacuum valves and switches from the cylinder head (photo).

15 Remove the engine lifting "eyes" (photo).
16 Remove the A/C compressor mounting bracket.
17 Loosen each of the 10 cylinder head mounting bolts one turn at a time until they can be removed (photo). Note the length and position of each bolt to aid in reinstallation.
18 Lift the head free of the engine (photo). If the head is stuck to the engine block, do not attempt to pry it free, as this may ruin the sealing surfaces. Instead, use a hammer and a block of wood, tapping upward at each end. Place the head on a block of wood to prevent damage.
19 Remove the cylinder head gasket (photo). Refer to the following Sections for overhaul, inspection and installation procedures.

13 Cylinder heads (V6) – removal

Note: If the engine has been removed from the car, disregard the following steps which do not apply.
1 Remove the intake manifold as described in Section 9.
2 Remove the exhaust manifolds as described in Section 11.
3 Remove the upper generator bracket and stud.
4 Remove the dipstick tube bracket from the left cylinder head.
5 Loosen the rocker arm nuts enough to pivot the rocker arms away from the pushrods.
6 Remove the pushrods. It is important that all valve mechanism components that are removed from the cylinder head be kept separate so they can be reinstalled in their original positions.
7 Loosen each of the cylinder head mounting bolts a little at a time until they can be removed. Note the length of each bolt as it is removed, to aid in the installation procedure.
8 Lift the heads free of the engine. As they are heavy, you may need the help of an assistant. If the head is stuck to the engine block, do not attempt to pry it free, as this may ruin the sealing surfaces. Instead, use a hammer and a block of wood, tapping upward at each end.
9 Remove the cylinder head gaskets. Place the heads on wood blocks to prevent damage. Refer to the following Sections covering overhaul, inspection and installation procedures.

14 Cylinder head – dismantling

Note: New and rebuilt cylinder heads are commonly available for GM engines at dealerships and auto parts stores. Due to the fact that some specialized tools are necessary for the dismantling and inspection of the heads, and replacement parts may not be readily available, it may be more practical and economical for the home mechanic to purchase replacement heads and install them referring to Section 19.
1 Another alternative at this point is to take the cylinder heads complete to a competent automotive machine shop or GM dealership for the overhaul process.
2 If the complete engine is being overhauled at the same time, it may be wise to refer to Section 48 before a decision is made.
3 If it is decided to overhaul the cylinder heads, read through the following Sections first to gain an understanding of the steps involved and the tools and replacement parts necessary for the job. Proceed as follows.
4 Remove the rocker arm nuts, balls and rocker arms, if not previously removed. Using a valve spring compressor (available at GM dealers or auto parts stores), compress each of the valve springs and remove the valve locking keys. Work on one valve at a time, removing the keys, then releasing the spring and removing the spring cap, spring shield (if equipped), spring and spring dampers (photo). Place these components together on a numbered box or rack used during cylinder head removal. All valve mechanism components must be kept separate so they can be returned to their original positions (photos).
5 Remove the oil seals from the stem of each valve. New seals should be used upon reassembly
6 Remove any spring shims used at the bottom of the valve spring.
7 Remove each valve, in turn, and place in the numbered box or rack to complete the valve mechanism removal. Place the valve components in an area where they will not be able to be mixed-up.

15 Cylinder head – cleaning

1 Clean all carbon from the combustion chambers and valve ports. GM tool J 8089 is designed for this purpose; however, most auto parts

12.10 Removing the rocker arm nuts

12.11 Lifting the rocker arms from their studs

12.12 Removing the push rods

12.13 Removing the thermostat housing

12.14 Removing a vacuum switch from the cylinder head

12.15 Removing an engine lifting bracket

12.17 Loosening the cylinder head mounting bolts

12.18 Lifting the cylinder head from the engine

12.19 Removing the cylinder head gasket

14.4a Using a valve spring compressor to compress the springs

14.4b With the valve spring compressed, the valve locking keys can be removed

14.4c The valve spring components removed from the head

stores will carry this cleaning attachment which is connected to a common hand drill motor.

2   Thoroughly clean the valve guides. GM tool J-8101 is available for this, as are many similar devices found at auto parts stores.

3   Use parts cleaner to remove all sludge and dirt from the rocker arms, rocker balls, pushrods and valve springs. Work on one set of components at a time, returning each set to its numbered location on your box or rack.

4   A buffing wheel should be used to remove all carbon deposits from the valves. Do not mix up the order of the valves while cleaning them.

5   Clean all carbon deposits from the head gasket mating surface. Be careful not to scratch this sealing surface.

6   Clean the threads on all cylinder head attaching bolts thoroughly.

16 Cylinder head – inspection

1   Carefully inspect the head for cracks around the exhaust ports and combustion chambers, and for external cracks in the water chamber.

2   Check the valve stem-to-bore clearance in the following fashion. Using a micrometer, check the diameter of the valve stem in three places: top, center and bottom (photo). Exhaust valves have tapered stems and are approximately .001-in larger at the top of the stem than at the head end. Next, insert a telescope hole gauge in the valve guide bore to obtain the bore's diameter. The valve clearance can now be figured out from these measurements. If the valve stem clearance exceeds the specifications, an oversize valve must be used, and the valve guide bore must be reamed. This is a job for your dealer or machine shop. Excessive clearance will cause excessive oil consumption while insufficient clearance will result in noisy operation and may cause the valve to stick, resulting in harsh engine operation.

3   Another method of checking this clearance is as follows: one at a time, place a valve in its installed position, with the valve head slightly (about $\frac{1}{16}$-in) off its seat. Now attach a dial indicator to the head with the indicator point just touching the valve stem where it exits the cylinder head. Grab the top of the valve and move it from side to side noting the movement on the dial indicator.

4   Inspect each of the valve springs and its damper. Replace any spring which is deformed, cracked or broken.

5   Check the valve spring tension using GM tool J-8056. The springs are compressed to a specified height and then the tension required for this is measured. This is done without the dampers. If not within 10 lb of the specified load, the spring should be replaced with a new one.

6   Inspect the rocker arm studs for wear or damage. These studs can be unscrewed using a deep socket. When assembling, coat the new stud with a gasket sealant and torque-tighten.

7   Check the pushrods for warping by rolling each on a clean, flat piece of glass. Any pushrod which is not perfectly straight and free from damage should be replaced with a new one.

8   Check the cylinder head for warpage. Do this by placing a straightedge across the length of the head and measuring any gaps between the straightedge and the head surface with a feeler gauge (photo). This should be done at three points across the head gasket surface, and also in a diagonal fashion across this surface.

9   If warpage exceeds .006-in at any point when a straightedge which spans the entire head is used, the cylinder head should be resurfaced. Using a straightedge with a span of 6 inches, the warpage should not exceed .003-in. Cylinder head resurfacing is a job for a professional automotive machine shop. Also note that if a cylinder head is resurfaced, the intake manifold position will be slightly altered, requiring the manifold to be resurfaced a proportionate amount.

17 Valves and valve seats – inspection and valve grinding

1   Examine the heads of the valves for pitting and burning, especially the heads of the exhaust valves. The valves' seatings should be examined at the same time. If the pitting on valve and seat is very slight the marks can be removed by grinding the seats and valves together with coarse, and then fine, valve grinding paste.

2   Valve grinding is carried out as follows: smear a trace of coarse carborundum paste on the seat face and apply a suction grinder tool to the valve head. With a semi-rotary motion, grind the valve head to its seat, lifting the valve occasionally to redistribute the grinding paste. When a dull, matte even surface finish is produced on both the valve seat and the valve, wipe off the paste and repeat the process with fine

16.2 Using a micrometer to check the valve stem diameter

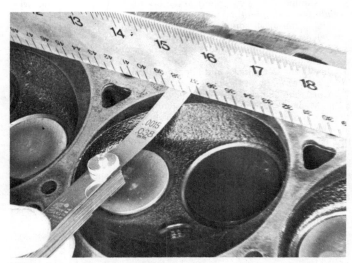
16.8 Using a straightedge and feeler gauge to check for cylinder head warpage

17.3 Using a micrometer to check the valve head diameter

carborundum paste, lifting and turning the valve to redistribute the paste as before. A light spring placed under the valve head will greatly ease this operation. When a smooth, unbroken ring of light grey matte finish is produced, on both valve and valve seat faces, the grinding operation is completed.

3   Where the valve or seat shows signs of bad pitting or burning, then the valve should be refaced by your dealer and the seat recut. If the refacing of the valve will reduce the edge of the valve head (seat width) to less than that given in the Specifications, replace the valve (photo).

4   Scrape away all carbon from the valve head and the valve stem. Carefully clean away every trace of grinding compound, taking great care to leave none in the ports or in the valve guides. Clean the valves and valve seats with a solvent-soaked rag, then with a clean rag, and finally, if an air line is available, blow the valves, valve guides and valve ports clean.

18 Cylinder head – assembly

1   Make sure all valve mechanism components are perfectly clean and free from carbon and dirt. The bare cylinder head should also be clean and free from abrasive agents which may have been used for valve grinding, reaming etc.

2   Insert a valve in the proper port.

3   Assemble the valve spring assembly for that cylinder. This will include the spring and damper, shield and cap.

4   Using the valve spring compressor, compress the assembly over the valve stem and hold in this position.

5   Install a new oil seal in the lower groove of the valve stem. Make sure it is flat and not twisted.

6   Install the valve locks and release the compressor. Make sure the lock seats properly in the upper groove of the valve stem.

7   Check the installed height of the valve springs using a narrow, thin scale. Measure from the top of the shim (if present) or the spring seat to the top of the valve spring or spring shield (if used). If necessary, $\frac{1}{16}$-in shims can be used under the valve spring to bring the unit to the proper specifications. Shims are used to correct springs which are too high, as the shims will act to compress the springs slightly. At no time should the spring be shimmed to give an installed height under the minimum specified length. If the spring is too short, it should be replaced with a new one.

8   Each valve stem oil seal should be checked with a vacuum tester as shown in the photo. A properly installed seal should not leak vacuum.

18.8 Using a vacuum tester to check the valve stem oil seal

19 Cylinder heads – installation

1   If not already done, thoroughly clean the gasket surfaces on both the cylinder heads and the engine block. Do not scratch or otherwise damage these sealing areas.

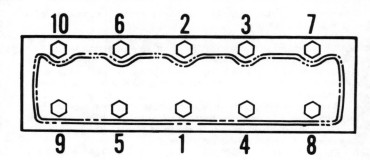

Fig. 2.12 Recommended tightening sequence of the L4 cylinder head mounting bolts (Sec 19)

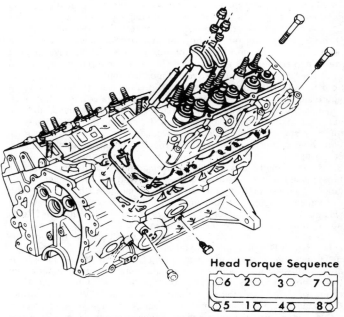

Head Torque Sequence

Fig. 2.13 Recommended tightening sequence for the V6 cylinder head mounting bolts (Sec 19)

2   To get the proper torque readings, the threads of the attaching bolts must be free of dirt. This also goes for the threaded holes in the engine block. Run a tap through these holes to ensure they are clean.

3   Place the gasket in place over the engine block dowel pins (photo).

4   Carefully lower the cylinder head onto the engine, over the dowel pins and the gaskets (photo). Be careful not to move the gasket while doing this.

5   Coat both the threads of the cylinder head attaching bolts and the point at which the head and stem meet with a sealing compound and install each finger-tight. Do not tighten any of the bolts at this time (photo).

6   Tighten each of the bolts, a little at a time, in the sequence shown in Fig. 2.12 for L4 engines or Fig. 2.13 for V6 engines. Continue tightening in this sequence until the proper torque reading is obtained. As a final check, work around the head in a logical front to rear sequence to make sure none of the bolts have been left out of the sequence.

7   Install the exhaust manifold(s) as described in Section 10 (L4) or Section 11 (V6).

8   Install each of the valve lifters (if removed) into its proper bore. Molykote or its equivalent should be used as a coating on each lifter.

9   Place a small amount of Molykote or its equivalent on each end of the pushrods and install each in its original position. Make sure the pushrods are seated properly in the lifter cavity.

10 Place each of the rocker arms and corresponding rocker balls onto its original stud. The rocker balls and valve stem end of the rocker arms should receive a small amount of Molykote or its equivalent.

11 On L4 engines, torque the rocker arm nuts to specs. On V6

engines, refer to Section 7 for the lash adjustment.

12 Install the rocker arm covers. Apply a bead of RTV sealer (or its equivalent) around the entire sealing surface of the cylinder head. This bead should be $\frac{1}{8}$ in wide. When going around bolt holes always go around the inboard side of the holes. Install the cover while the sealer is still wet and torque the bolts to specs.

13 Install the intake manifold with new gaskets as described in Section 8 (L4) or Section 9 (V6).

14 Install the remaining engine components in the reverse order of removal.

15 Fill the radiator with coolant, start the engine and check for leaks. Adjust the ignition timing as required. Be sure to recheck the coolant level once the engine has warmed up to operating temperature.

20 Crank pulley hub and front oil seal (L4) – removal and installation

NOTE: *If the engine has been removed from the car, disregard the following steps which do not apply.*

1 Remove the engine drive belts. Refer to the appropriate chapters for each accessory.

2 Remove the right front fender inner splash shield to provide working clearance.

3 With the parking brake applied and the shifter in "Park" (automatic) or in gear (manual) to prevent the engine from turning over, remove the crank pulley bolt (photo). As there is considerable torque on this bolt, a breaker bar will probably be necessary.

4 Mark the position of the pulley to the hub (photo). Remove the bolts that secure the crank pulley to the hub, and lift out the pulley (photo).

5 Using a crank hub puller, remove the hub from the crankshaft (photo).

6 Carefully pry out the oil seal from the front cover with a large screwdriver. Be sure not to distort the cover.

7 Install the new seal with the helical lip toward the rear of the engine. Drive the seal into place using a special GM front oil seal installing tool or an appropriate sized socket. If there is enough room, a flat block of wood can also be used in a similar fashion as shown.

8 Apply a light coat of oil to the inside lip of the seal.

9 Position the pulley hub on the crankshaft and, using a slight twisting motion, slide it through the seal until it bottoms against the crankshaft gear. The crank pulley hub bolt can also be used to press the hub into position (photo).

10 Install the crank pulley onto the hub, noting the alignment marks made during removal.

11 Install the crank pulley hub bolt and torque it to specs.

12 Complete the installation by reversing the removal steps, tightening the drive belts to their proper tension.

21 Timing gear cover (L4) – removal and installation

NOTE: *If the engine has been removed from the car, disregard the following steps which do not apply.*

1 Remove the crank pulley hub as described in Section 20.

2 Remove the lower generator bracket.

3 Remove the nuts that secure the front engine mount to the cradle.

4 Attach an engine hoist to the lifting 'eyes' mounted on the engine. One 'eye' is located at the right front corner of the cylinder head and the other at the left rear corner of the cylinder head. Make sure the chain is looped properly through the engine brackets and secured with strong nuts and bolts through the chain loops. The hook on the hoist should be over the center of the engine with the lengths of chain at equal distances.

5 Raise the engine just enough so you can remove the bolts that secure the engine mount bracket to the engine block and remove the support bracket and mount as an assembly.

6 Remove the bolts that secure the timing gear cover to the engine block and oil pan (photo).

7 Pull the cover forward slightly and, using a sharp knife or other suitable cutting tool, cut the front oil pan seal flush with the cylinder block at both sides of the cover.

8 Remove the timing gear cover.

9 Remove the timing gear cover gasket.

10 Using a degreaser clean all dirt and old gasket material from the sealing surfaces of the timing gear cover, engine block and oil pan.

11 Replace the front oil seal by carefully prying it out of the timing gear cover with a large screwdriver. Be sure not to distort the cover.

12 Install the new seal with the helical lip toward the inside of the cover. Drive the seal into place using a special GM front oil seal installing tool or an appropriate sized socket. A flat block of wood will also work (photo).

13 Prior to installing the cover, install a new front oil pan gasket. Cut the ends off of the gasket as shown in Fig. 2.17 and install it on the cover by pressing the rubber tips into the holes provided.

14 Apply a thin coat of gasket sealant to the timing gear cover gasket and place it in position on the cover.

15 Apply a bead of RTV to the joint between the oil pan and engine block.

16 Using the crank pulley hub as a centering tool, insert the hub in the front cover seal and place the cover in position on the block with the hub on the crankshaft.

17 Install the oil pan-to-cover bolts and partially tighten them.

18 Install the bolts that secure the cover to the block and torque all of the mounting bolts to specs (photo).

19 Remove the hub from the front cover seal.

20 Complete the installation by reversing the removal procedure.

22 Torsional damper (V6) – removal and installation

NOTE: *If the engine has been removed from the car, disregard the following steps which do not apply.*

1 Loosen the generator, power steering pump and air-conditioning compressor (as required) to relieve tension on the drive belts.

2 Remove the inner fender splash shield to provide working clearance.

3 Remove the drive belts, noting the installed positions of each.

4 Remove the accessory drive pulley from the torsional damper. Then remove the torsional damper retaining bolt at the center.

5 Install a special torsional damper (harmonic balancer) remover to the damper. Draw the damper off the crankshaft, being careful not to drop it as it breaks free. A common gear puller should not be used to draw the damper as this may separate the outer portion of the damper from the inner hub. Only a puller which bolts to the inner hub should be used.

6 Before installing the torsional damper, coat the front cover seal area (on damper) with engine oil.

7 Place the damper in position over the key on the crankshaft. Make sire the damper keyway lines up with the key.

8 Using a torsional damper installer (GM tool J-23523 or equivalent), draw the damper onto the crankshaft. This tool distributes the draw evenly around the inner hub.

9 Remove the installation tool and install the torsional damper center retaining bolt. Torque to specifications.

10 Follow the removal procedure in the reverse order for the remaining components.

11 Adjust the tension of the various drive belts by referring to the appropriate chapter for each accessory.

23 Crankcase front cover (V6) – removal and installation

NOTE: *If the engine has been removed from the engine disregard the following steps which do not apply.*

1 Remove the water pump as described in Chapter 3, Section 5.

2 If equipped with air-conditioning, remove the A/C compressor from its mounting bracket and secure it out of the way. NOTE: Under no circumstances disconnect any of the air-conditioning system hoses without first having the system depressurized by a GM dealer or other qualified automotive shop.

3 Remove the A/C compressor mounting bracket.

4 Remove the torsional damper as described in Section 22.

5 Disconnect the lower radiator hose at the front cover.

6 Remove the front cover mounting bolts and remove the cover.

7 Clean all oil, dirt and old gasket material from the sealing surfaces of the front cover and engine block. Replace the front cover oil seal as described in Section 24.

8 Prior to installation, apply a continuous $\frac{1}{8}$-in (3 mm) diameter bead of RTV or equivalent sealant to the front cover sealing surface. Apply

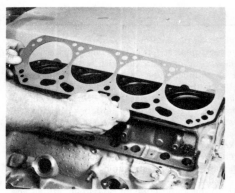

19.3 Installing a new cylinder head gasket (L4)

19.4 Installing the head onto the engine block (L4)

19.5 The cylinder head mounting bolts should be coated with sealant as described in the text prior to installation

20.3 Removing the crank pulley bolt

20.4a Marking the position of the pulley to the hub prior to pulley removal

20.4b Lifting the pulley from the hub

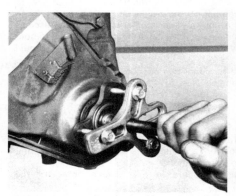

20.5 Using a crank hub puller to remove the hub from the crankshaft

20.9 Using the crank pulley hub bolt to press the hub onto the crankshaft

21.6 Removing the timing gear cover mounting bolts

21.12 Using a block of wood to install the front oil seal into the timing gear cover

21.18 Installing the timing gear cover mounting bolts

the sealant to the inboard side of the mounting bolt holes. Also completely encircle the water inlet and outlet holes with the sealant.
9   Place the front cover in position on the engine block and install the front cover mounting bolts, torquing them to specs.
10   Complete the installation by reversing the removal procedure.

24   Oil seal (front cover) (V6) – replacement

With front cover installed on engine
1   With the torsional damper removed (Section 22), pry the old seal out of the crankcase front cover with a large screwdriver. Be careful not to damage the front surface of the crankshaft.
2   Place the new seal into position with the open end of the seal (seal 'lip') toward the inside of the cover.
3   Drive the seal into the cover until it is fully seated. GM tool J-23042 or an equivalent is available for this purpose. These tools are designed to exert even pressure around the circumference of the seal as it is hammered into place. A section of large-diameter pipe or a large socket could also be used.
4   Take care not to distort the front cover.

With front cover removed from engine
5   This method is preferred, as the cover can be supported as the new seal is driven into place, preventing the possibility of cover distortion.
6   Remove the crankcase front cover as described in Section 23.
7   Pry the old seal out of its bore with a large screwdriver.
8   Support the inside of the cover, around the seal area and install the new seal in the same fashion as described above.

25   Timing chain and sprockets (V6) – removal and installation

Note: If the engine has been removed from the car, disregard the following steps which do not apply.
1   Remove the torsional damper and crankcase cover as described in Sections 22 and 23 respectively.
2   Turn the engine until the marks on the camshaft and crankshaft sprockets are in alignment. Do not attempt to remove either sprocket or the chain until this is done.
3   Remove the 3 camshaft sprocket retaining bolts and lift the camshaft sprocket and timing chain together off the front of the engine. In some cases it may be necessary to tap the sprocket with a soft-faced mallet.
4   If it is found necessary to remove the crankcase sprocket, it can be pulled from the crankshaft using a puller designed for this purpose.
5   Install the crankshaft sprocket to the crankshaft by using a bolt and washer from the puller set.

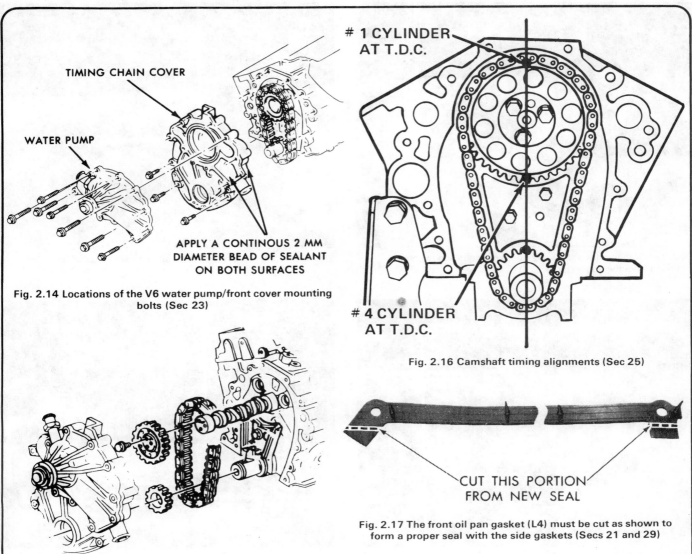

Fig. 2.14 Locations of the V6 water pump/front cover mounting bolts (Sec 23)

TIMING CHAIN COVER

WATER PUMP

APPLY A CONTINOUS 2 MM DIAMETER BEAD OF SEALANT ON BOTH SURFACES

Fig. 2.15 V6 timing chain and gears arrangement (Sec 25)

1 CYLINDER AT T.D.C.

4 CYLINDER AT T.D.C.

Fig. 2.16 Camshaft timing alignments (Sec 25)

CUT THIS PORTION FROM NEW SEAL

Fig. 2.17 The front oil pan gasket (L4) must be cut as shown to form a proper seal with the side gaskets (Secs 21 and 29)

6   Install the timing chain over the camshaft sprocket with slack in the chain hanging down over the crankshaft sprocket.

7   With the timing marks aligned, slip the chain over the crankshaft sprocket and then draw the camshaft sprocket into place with the 3 retaining bolts. Do not hammer or in any way attempt to drive the camshaft sprocket into place, as this would dislodge the welsh plug at the rear of the engine.

8   With the chain and both sprockets in place, check again that the timing marks on the two sprockets are perfectly in line with each other. If not, remove the camshaft sprocket and move until the marks align.

9   Lubricate the chain with engine oil and install the remaining components in the reverse order of removal.

26 Oil pump drive shaft (L4) – removal and installation

1   Remove the air cleaner.
2   Remove the carburetor bowl vent line at the rocker arm cover.
3   Remove the upper generator bracket.
4   Remove the generator.
5   Remove the oil pump drive shaft retainer plate bolts.
6   Remove the bushing (photo).
7   Remove the shaft and gear assembly (photo).
8   Thoroughly clean the sealing surfaces on the cylinder block and retainer plate.

9   Inspect the gear teeth to see that they are not chipped or broken. Replace if necessary.

10   Install the oil pump drive shaft into the block and turn it until it engages with the camshaft drive gear in the oil pump body.

11   Apply a $\frac{1}{16}$-in (1.5 mm) diameter bead of RTV or equivalent sealant to the retainer plate so that it completely seals around the oil pump drive shaft hole in the block (photo). Install the retainer plate mounting bolts and torque them to specs.

12   Complete the installation by reversing the removal procedure.

27 Oil pan (L4) – removal and installation

Note: *If the engine has been removed from the car, proceed to paragraph 11.*

1   Raise the front of the car and support it with jack stands.
2   Drain the oil from the crankcase as described in Chapter 1.
3   Remove the nuts that secure the front engine mount to the cradle.
4   Remove the exhaust crossover pipe.
5   Disconnect the wires from the starter.
6   Remove the flywheel housing inspection cover.
7   Remove the upper generator bracket.
8   Attach an engine hoist to the lifting 'eyes' mounted to the engine. One 'eye' is located at the right front corner of the cylinder head and the other is at the left rear corner of the cylinder head. Make sure the

26.6 The oil pump drive shaft retainer plate, bolts and bushing removed from the engine block

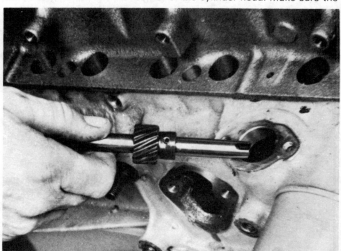

26.7 Removing the oil pump drive shaft and gear assembly

26.11 Sealant should be applied to the retainer plate prior to installation

27.11 Removing the oil pan

chain is looped properly through the engine brackets and secured with strong nuts and bolts through the chain loops. The hook on the hoist should be over the center of the engine with the lengths of chain at equal distances so the engine can be lifted straight up.

9   Remove the lower generator bracket and the engine support bracket.

10 Lift the engine just enough to provide adequate clearance to remove the oil pan.

11 Remove the oil pan retaining bolts and lift off the oil pan (photo). It may be necessary to use a rubber mallet to break the seal.

12 Prior to installing the oil pan, clean any dirt or old gasket material from the sealing surfaces of the oil pan and engine block.

13 The oil pan gasket consists of four separate gasket pieces. Each must be carefully installed in its proper place to form a good junction with the other pieces it joins with.

   (a) *Install the rear oil pan gasket in the rear main bearing cap and apply a small quantity of RTV or a similar sealant in depressions where the pan gasket engages in the block.*

   (b) *Install the front oil pan gasket on the timing gear cover, pressing the tips into the holes provided in the cover (photo).*

   (c) *Install the side gaskets on the oil pan, using grease to hold it in place.*

   (d) *Trim the ends off of the front gasket as indicated in Fig. 2.17 to form a good joint with the side gaskets.*

   (e) *Apply a bead of RTV at the split lines between the front gasket and the side gaskets. The pan can now be installed (photo).*

14 Place the oil pan into position against the block (photo) and insert the rear and side mounting bolts. Tighten these bolts snugly before installing the front bolts into the timing cover. Torque all of the bolts to specs.

15 To complete the installation, reverse the removal steps.

28 Oil pan (V6) – removal and installation

Note: *If the engine has been removed from the car, proceed to paragraph 13.*

1   Disconnect the negative battery terminal.

2   Raise the front of the car and support it on jack stands.

3   Drain the engine oil into a suitable container.

4   Remove the front exhaust crossover pipe.

5   Remove the flywheel inspection cover.

6   Remove the starter as described in Chapter 5, Section 20.

7   If equipped with a manual transaxle, remove the nuts that secure the engine mounting bracket to the engine mount.

8   If equipped with a manual transaxle, it will be necessary to raise the front of the engine about $\frac{3}{4}$-in (19 mm) in order to provide clearance for the oil pan removal.

9   Prior to lifting, a spacer can be fabricated out of a block of wood. Measure the height of the engine mount studs and choose a solid block of wood approximately $\frac{3}{4}$-in thicker than this measurement. Measure the diameter of the studs and the distance between tham and drill holes in the block so it can be slipped over the tops of the studs.

10 If an engine hoist is not available for the lifting, an alternative method can be used. Use a floor jack and a block of wood placed under the oil pan. The wood block should spread the load across the

oil pan, preventing damage or collapse of the oil pan metal. The oil pump pick-up and screen is very close to the oil pan bottom, so any collapsing of the pan may damage the pick-up or prevent the pump from drawing oil properly.

11 With either method, raise the engine slowly until the wood block spacer can be placed between the engine mount and the engine mount bracket. Check clearances all around the engine as it is raised, particularly at the front engine strut.

12 Lower the engine onto the wood block. Make sure it is firmly supported. If a hoist is being used, keep the lifting chains secured to the engine. If a jack is being used, remove it at this time.

13 Remove the oil pan bolts.

14 Remove the oil pan. It may be necessary to use a rubber mallet to break the seal.

15 Before installing the oil pan, thoroughly clean the gasket sealing surfaces on the engine block and on the oil pan with degreaser. All sealer and gasket material must be removed.

16 Before installing the oil pan, apply a $\frac{1}{8}$-in (3 mm) diameter bead of RTV or equivalent sealer around the pan's sealing flange.

17 Using a new rear oil pan seal, position the oil pan against the engine block and install the mounting bolts, torquing them to specs.

18 If the engine has been raised, lower it onto the engine mount and install the retaining nuts, torquing them to specs.

19 The remainder of the installation is the reverse of the removal procedure.

20 Fill the engine with the correct grade of oil, start the engine and check the pan for leaks.

29 Oil pump – removal and installation

1   Remove the oil pan as described in Section 27 (L4) or Section 28 (V6).

2   On L4 engines, remove the two oil pump flange mounting bolts (photo) and the nut from the main bearing cap bolt. On V6 engines, remove the bolt that secures the pump to the rear main bearing cap.

3   Lift off the oil pump and screen as an assembly (photo).

4   If the oil pump is to be overhauled, refer to Section 30.

5   To install, align the pump shaft so it mates with the oil pump drive shaft tang.

6   Place the oil pump housing flange in position and install the mounting bolt(s). No gasket is needed between the pump flange and the block.

7   On L4 engines, install the oil pump screen bracket over the main bearing cap bolt and install the nut (photo).

8   Torque the pump mounting bolt(s) and main bearing nut (L4) to specs.

9   Install the oil pan.

30 Oil pump – dismantling, examination and reassembly

1   In most cases it will be more practical and economical to replace a faulty oil pump with a new or rebuilt unit. If it is decided to overhaul the oil pump, check on internal parts availability before beginning.

2   Remove the pump cover retaining screws and the pump cover. Index mark the gear teeth to permit reassembly in the same position.

27.13a During installation the rubber tips on the front oil pan gasket should be pressed into the holes in the timing gear cover

27.13b All four sections of the oil pan gasket in position on the engine block

27.14 Be sure not to disturb the gaskets when positioning the oil pan on the block

29.2 Removing the oil pump flange mounting bolts (L4)

29.3 Removing the oil pump and screen assembly (L4)

29.7 Installing the oil pump screen bracket over the rear main bearing cap bolt (L4)

30.3 Removing the drive gear and shaft and the idler gear from the oil pump body

30.4a Removing the pressure regulator valve retaining pin

30.4b Removing the pressure regulator valve assembly

3   Remove the idler gear, drive gear and shaft from the body (photo).
4   Remove the pressure regulator valve retaining pin (photo), the regulator valve and the related parts (photo).
5   If necessary on V6 engines, the pick-up screen and pipe assembly can be extracted from the pump body. On L4 engines, the screen assembly is factory-fitted to the pump body and cannot be separated.
6   Wash all the parts in solvent and thoroughly dry them. Inspect the body for cracks, wear or other damage. Similarly inspect the gears (photo).
7   Check the drive gear shaft for looseness in the pump body, and the inside of the pump cover for wear that would permit oil leakage past the ends of the gears (photo). If either the gears or body are worn or damaged, the entire assembly must be replaced.
8   Inspect the pick-up screen and pipe assembly for damage to the screen, pipe or relief grommet. If the V6 screen assembly was removed, it must be replaced with a new one.
9   Apply a gasket sealant to the end of the pipe (pick-up screen and pipe assembly) and tap it into the pump body taking care that no damage occurs.
10 Install the pressure regulator valve and related parts.
11 Install the drive gear and shaft in the pump body, followed by the idler gear with the smooth side toward the pump cover opening. Lubricate the parts with engine oil.
12 Install the cover and torque tighten the screws.
13 Turn the driveshaft to ensure that the pump operates freely.

31 Rear main oil seal (V6) – replacement (engine in car)

1   Always service both halves of the rear main oil seal as a unit. While the replacement of this seal is much easier with the engine removed from the car, as in a total engine rebuild, the job can be done with the engine in place.
2   Remove the oil pan and oil pump as described previously in this Chapter.
3   Remove the rear main bearing cap from the engine.
4   Using a screwdriver, pry the lower half of the oil seal from the bearing cap.
5   To remove the upper half of the seal, use a small hammer and a brass pin punch to roll the seal around the crankshaft journal. Tap one end of the seal with the hammer and punch (be careful not to strike the crankshaft) until the other end of the seal protrudes enough to pull the seal out with a pair of pliers.
6   Clean all sealant and foreign material from the cylinder bearing cap and case. Do not use an abrasive cleaner for this.
7   Inspect components for nicks, scratches or burrs at all sealing surfaces.
8   Coat the seal lips of the new seal with light engine oil. Do not get oil on the seal mating ends.
9   Included in the purchase of the rear main oil seal should be a small plastic installation tool.

10 Position the narrow end of this installation tool between the crankshaft and the seal seat. The idea is to protect the new seal from being damaged by the sharp edge of the seal seat.
11 Raise the new upper half of the seal into position with the seal lips facing toward the front of the engine. Push the seal onto its seat, using the installation tool as a protector against the seal contacting the sharp edge.
12 Roll the seal around the crankshaft, all the time using the tool as a shoehorn for protection. When both ends of the seal are flush with the engine block, remove the installation tool being careful not to withdraw the seal as well.
13 Install the lower half of the oil seal to the bearing cap, again using the installation tool to protect the seal against the sharp edge. Make sure the seal is firmly seated, then withdraw the installation tool.
14 Smear a bit of sealant to the bearing cap areas immediately adjacent to the seal ends.
15 Install the bearing cap (with seal) and torque the attaching bolts to about 10 to 12 ft-lb only. Now tap the end of the crankshaft first rearward, then forward to line up the thrust surfaces. Retorque the bearing cap bolts to the proper specification and install the oil pump and oil pan.

32 Flywheel and rear main bearing seal (L4 only) – removal and installation

1   To gain access to the flywheel, either the engine or the transaxle must be removed from the car. If other engine work is needed remove the engine as described in Section 34 (L4) or Section 35 or 36 (V6). If no other work needs to be done necessitating the removal of the engine, it would be easier to remove the transaxle as described in Chapter 7.
2   If equipped with a manual transaxle, remove the clutch from the flywheel as described in Chapter 8, Section 3.
3   The flywheel can be unbolted from the rear flange of the crankshaft. To prevent the flywheel from turning, a long screwdriver or similar tool can be run through the flywheel and against the engine block (photo).
4   Once the bolts are removed, the flywheel can be lifted off (photo).
5   Remove the flywheel spacer if equipped (photo).
6   On L4 engines, if the rear main bearing seal needs to be replaced, pry it out of its bore (photo).
7   Examine the flywheel teeth for any that are broken or chipped. If this condition exists, the flywheel must be replaced with a new one.
8   On manual transaxle flywheels, inspect the clutch friction face for scoring. Light scoring may be corrected using emery cloth, but where there is deep scoring the flywheel must be replaced with a new one or clutch damage will soon occur.
9   On automatic transaxle flywheels, examine the converter securing bolt holes for elongation. This condition, too, necessitates the replacement of the flywheel.

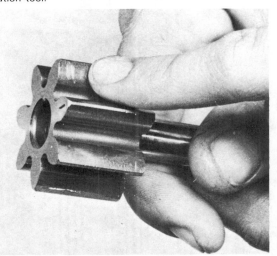

30.6 If the gears show signs of wear or damage they should be replaced

30.7 Inspect the pump cover for wear

32.3 A long screwdriver can be positioned as shown to prevent the flywheel from turning during mounting bolt removal

32.4 Lifting the flywheel from the crankshaft

32.5 Removing the flywheel spacer

32.6 Removing the rear oil seal from its bore

10 Before installing the flywheel, clean the mating surfaces of the flywheel and the crankshaft.

11 On L4 engines, if the oil seal was removed, apply a light coat of engine oil to the inside lip of the new seal and install it in its bore.

12 To install, position the flywheel in place against the crankshaft using a new spacer, if equipped, and insert the mounting bolts, securing them only fingertight. It is a good idea to use a thread sealing agent such as Locktite or an equivalent on the bolt threads.

13 Again, while preventing the flywheel from turning, tighten the bolts a little at a time until they are all torqued to specs.

14 Complete the remainder of the installation procedure by reversing the removal steps.

33 Engine mounts – general

1   Engine mounts are non-adjustable and seldom require service. Periodically, they should be inspected for hardening or cracking of the rubber, or separation of the rubber from its metal backing.

2   The various powertrain mounts for both the engine and transaxle, are illustrated in Figs. 2.18, 2.19 and 2.20. General instructions on raising the engine enough to replace the mounts are included in Sections 27 and 28.

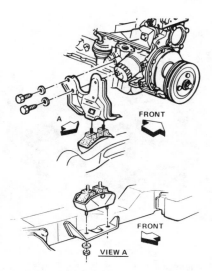

Fig. 2.18 Location of the L4 engine support bracket and engine mount (Sec 33)

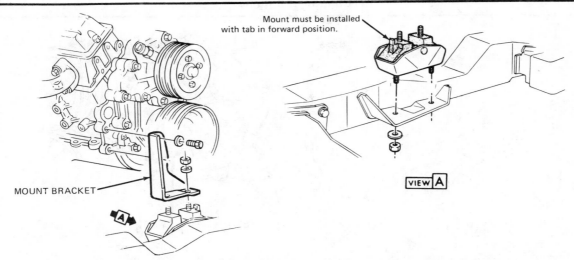

Mount must be installed with tab in forward position.

VIEW A

MOUNT BRACKET

A

Fig. 2.19 Location of the V6 engine support bracket and engine mount (Sec 33)

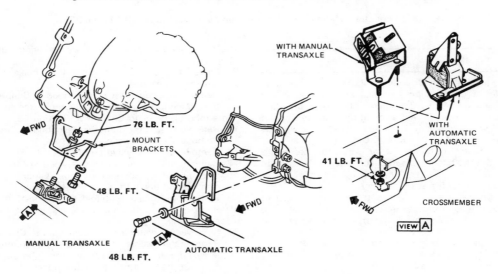

WITH MANUAL TRANSAXLE

WITH AUTOMATIC TRANSAXLE

FWD

76 LB. FT.

MOUNT BRACKETS

48 LB. FT.

41 LB. FT.

A

FWD

CROSSMEMBER

VIEW A

MANUAL TRANSAXLE

FWD

A

48 LB. FT.

AUTOMATIC TRANSAXLE

FRONT TRANSAXLE MOUNTS

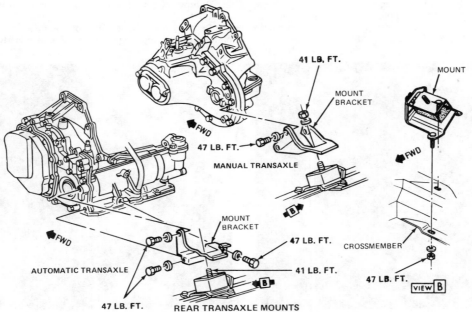

41 LB. FT.

MOUNT BRACKET

MOUNT

FWD

47 LB. FT.

MANUAL TRANSAXLE

FWD

B

FWD

MOUNT BRACKET

47 LB. FT.

CROSSMEMBER

FWD

47 LB. FT.

41 LB. FT.

47 LB. FT.

VIEW B

AUTOMATIC TRANSAXLE

B

47 LB. FT.

REAR TRANSAXLE MOUNTS

Fig. 2.20 Locations of the front and rear transaxle mounts (Sec 33)

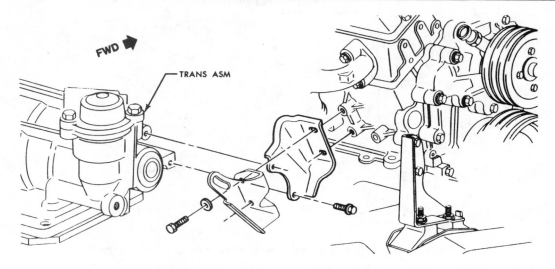

Fig. 2.21 Location of the transaxle-to-engine support bracket (V6) (Sec 33)

34 Engine (L4) – removal

1   If the vehicle is equipped with air-conditioning, the car should be driven to a GM dealer or refrigeration specialist to have the system depressurized. The air-conditioning system cannot be simply unbolted and laid aside for engine removal. Do not attempt to disconnect any of the air-conditioning system while it is under pressure as serious damage to the system, as well as to yourself, can occur.

2   Remove the hood. Refer to Chapter 12 for the correct procedure to follow for this job. Set the hood in a safe place where it will not be damaged.

3   Disconnect the battery cables at the battery.

4   Remove the air cleaner assembly and set aside. Make sure to identify all hoses with pieces of tape to make reassembly easier.

5   Drain the radiator and engine block, referring to Chapter 1, if necessary.

6   Raise the front of the car and support it on jack stands.

7   Drain the oil from the crankcase. Refer to Chapter 2.

8   Remove the flywheel access plate (photo).

9   Remove the starter as described in Chapter 5, Section 20. NOTE: Before disconnecting or removing any electrical wires, vacuum lines, hydraulic hoses or any other hoses or lines, always mark them with pieces of tape as to their installed locations. This will eliminate possible problems and confusion in the installation procedure.

10   If equipped, remove the power steering pump as described in Chapter 11, Section 31.

11   Lower the car to the ground to make work in the engine compartment easier.

12   Remove the generator as described in Chapter 5, Section 16.

13   If equipped, remove the A/C compressor and its related components (photo). Refer to Chapter 3, Section 19.

14   Remove the water pump as described in Chapter 3, Section 5.

15   Remove the EGR valve.

16   Remove the PCV valve and hose

17   Remove the carburetor as described in Chapter 4, Section 7.

18   If equipped, disconnect the fuel vapor hoses to the charcoal canister located behind the left front headlight.

19   Remove the intake manifold as described in Section 8.

20   Remove the spark plug wires, being sure to identify them with pieces of tape.

21   Remove the distributor as described in Chapter 5, Section 9.

22   Remove the flexible front engine strut, mounted between the front of the cylinder and the radiator support (photo).

23   Remove the radiator and heater hoses.

24   Remove the fan assembly and radiator as described in Chapter 3.

25   Remove the oil dipstick tube, mounted to the left of the exhaust manifold.

26   Remove the exhaust manifold as described in Section 10. Completely remove the front exhaust pipe in this step.

34.8 Removing the flywheel access plate mounting bolts

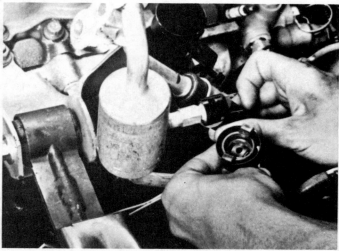

34.13 Removing the A/C compressor muffler assembly

27 Disconnect all remaining electrical and vacuum connections to the engine, carefully labeling each as to its location (photo).
28 Remove the bolts that secure the transaxle to the engine.
29 Remove the nuts that secure the transaxle to the cradle.
30 Remove the spark plugs.
31 If equipped with an automatic transaxle, remove the bolts that secure the torque converter to the flywheel. To do this, it will be necessary to turn the engine by the bolt at the center of the crankshaft pulley to bring all of the flywheel bolts into view. Mark the relative position of the flywheel to the converter with a scribe so it can be installed in the same position. Use a long screwdriver in the teeth of the flywheel to prevent movement as the bolts are loosened.
32 Remove the two rear transaxle support bracket bolts.
33 Remove the fuel supply line at the fuel pump. Have an empty can and some rags handy to catch excess fuel in the system. Immediately plug the hose to keep dirt out of the system and prevent later fuel drainage.
34 Remove the fuel pump.
35 Remove the nuts that secure the front engine mount to the cradle (photo).
36 With a block of wood placed between a jack and the bottom of the transaxle, raise the engine and transaxle just until the front mounting studs clear the cradle.
37 Attach an engine hoist to the lifting 'eyes' mounted to the engine. One 'eye' is located at the right front corner of the cylinder head and the other is at the left rear corner of the head. Make sure the chain is looped properly through the engine brackets and secured with strong nuts and bolts through the chain loops. The hook on the hoist should be over the center of the engine with the lengths of chain at equal distances, so the engine can be lifted straight up.
38 Raise the engine just until all slack is out of the chains.
39 Remove the two upper transaxle-to-engine bolts (photo).
40 Lift the engine slightly, and pull it toward the right side of the car until the flywheel clears the transaxle housing.
41 Carefully lift the engine straight up and out of the engine compartment, continually checking clearances around the engine (photo). Be particularly careful that the engine does not hit the brake master cylinder, firewall or the body nosepiece as it is rolled free of the car.
42 The transaxle should remain supported by the floor jack or wood blocks while the engine is out of place.

34.22 Removing the front engine strut

34.27 Disconnecting vacuum and electrical connections from the engine

35 Engine (V6, automatic transaxle) – removal

1   If the vehicle is equipped with air-conditioning, the car should be driven to a GM dealer or automative refrigeration specialist to have the system depressurized. Under no circumstances disconnect any part of the air-conditioning system without first having this done.
2   Remove the hood as described in Chapter 12 and set it in a safe place where it will not be damaged.
3   Disconnect the battery cables from the battery.
4   Remove the air cleaner.
5   Drain the radiator and engine block, referring to Chapter 1 if necessary.
6   Disconnect the vacuum hosing to all non-engine mounted components (photos). NOTE: Before disconnecting or removing any electrical wires, vacuum lines, hydraulic hoses, etc., always mark them with pieces of tape to identify their installed locations. This will eliminate possible problems and confusion in the installation procedure.
7   Disconnect the detent (TV) cable from the carburetor lever.
8   Disconnect the accelerator linkage.
9   Disconnect the engine wire harness connector.
10 Disconnect the ground strap at the engine forward strut.
11 Remove the radiator hoses.
12 Remove the heater hoses.
13 If equipped, remove the power steering pump and bracket as described in Chapter 11.
14 Raise the front of the car and support it on jack stands for working clearance.
15 Remove the front exhaust crossover pipe.
16 Disconnect the fuel lines where they connect with the rubber hoses at the right side of the engine.
17 Remove the nuts that secure the front engine mount to the right side of the cradle.
18 Remove the battery cables from the engine where they are connected at the starter and the transaxle housing bolt.
19 Remove the flywheel inspection cover.
20 Remove the bolts that secure the torque converter to the flywheel. To do this, it will be necessary to turn the engine by the crankshaft pulley bolt in order to bring all of the flywheel bolts into view. Mark the relative position of the flywheel to the converter with a scribe so it can be installed in the same position. Use a screwdriver in the teeth of the flywheel to prevent movement as the bolts are loosened.
21 Remove the transaxle-to-crankcase support bracket.
22 Lower the car to the ground.
23 Support the transaxle with a floor jack and a block of wood placed under the rear extension.
24 Remove the engine strut bracket mounted between the radiator support and the front (left) cylinder head (photo).
25 Remove the bolts that hold the transaxle to the engine.
26 If equipped with air-conditioning, remove the A/C compressor from its mounting bracket.
27 Attach an engine hoist to the lifting 'eyes' mounted to the engine. Make sure the chain is looped properly through the engine brackets and secured with strong nuts and bolts through the chain loops. The hook of the hoist should be over the center of the engine with the lengths of chain at equal distances, so the engine can be lifted straight up.
28 Lift the engine slightly and pull it toward the right side of the car until the flywheel clears the transaxle housing.

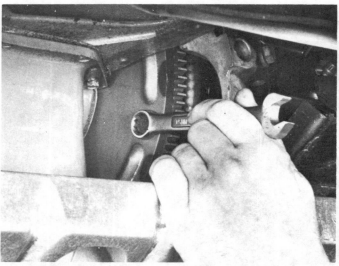
34.31 Removing the torque converter mounting bolts

34.35 Removing the front engine mount nuts

34.39 With the engine supported by a hoist, the two upper transaxle-to-engine bolts can be removed

34.41 Lifting the engine from the car

35.6 Disconnecting the vacuum hosing from all non-engine mounted connections

35.24 Removing the front engine strut

29 Carefully lift the engine straight up and out of the engine compartment, continually checking clearances around the engine. Be particularly careful that the engine does not hit the brake master cylinder, firewall or the body nosepiece as it is rolled free of the car.
30 The transaxle should remain supported by either the floor jack or wood blocks while the engine is out of place.

36 Engine (V6, manual transaxle) – removal

1 If the vehicle is equipped with air-conditioning, the car should be taken to a GM dealer or automotive refrigeration specialist to have the system depressurized. Under no circumstances disconnect any part of the air-conditioning system without first having this done.
2 Remove the hood, as described in Chapter 12, and set it in a safe place where it will not be damaged.
3 Disconnect the battery cables from the battery.
4 Remove the air cleaner.
5 Drain the radiator and engine block, referring to Chapter 1 if necessary.
6 Disconnect the vacuum hosing to all non-engine mounted components. NOTE: Before disconnecting or removing any electrical wires, vacuum lines, hydraulic hoses, etc., always mark them with pieces of tape to identify their installed locations. This will eliminate possible problems and confusion in the installation procedure.
7 Disconnect the accelerator linkage from the carburetor.
8 Disconnect the engine wiring harness connector.
9 Remove the radiator hoses.
10 Remove the heater hoses.
11 If equipped, remove the power steering pump and bracket, as described in Chapter 11.
12 Disconnect the clutch cable from the transaxle.
13 Disconnect the shift linkage from the transaxle shift levers, and remove the cables from their bosses.
14 Disconnect the speedometer cable from the transaxle.
15 Unlock the steering column and raise the front of the car. Support it on jack stands.
16 Attach an engine hoist to the lifting 'eyes' mounted to the engine, Make sure the chain is looped properly through the engine brackets and secured with strong nuts and bolts through the chain loops. The hook on the hoist should be over the center of the engine with the lengths of chain at equal distances so the engine can be lifted straight up.
17 Raise the engine just enough to relieve the weight from the engine and transaxle mount assemblies.
18 Remove all engine-to-transaxle bolts but one.
19 Remove the front exhaust crossover pipe. If the bolts are frozen penetrating oil may help to loosen them.
20 Remove the bolts that secure the rear front transaxle mount plate to the transaxle cradle mount assembly.
21 Loosen the bolts that secure the rear transaxle mount bracket to the cradle mount.
22 Remove the nuts that secure the stabilizer bar to the lower control arms.
23 Remove all the engine and transaxle mounting nuts.
24 Remove the left front wheel.
25 Remove the cradle as described in Chapter 12.
26 Remove the drive axles from the transaxle as described in Chapter 8, Section 7.
27 Place a floor jack under the transaxle and lower the engine and transaxle just until the transaxle weight is on the jacks. A second jack or block may be necessary to help support the transaxle.
28 Remove the final transaxle-to-engine bolt and separate the transaxle from the engine. Be sure the transaxle is adequately supported from underneath.
29 Lower the front of the car to the ground. Loosen the engine hoist chain as this is done, to lower the engine with the car.
30 If equipped with air-conditioning, remove the A/C compressor.
31 Remove the front engine strut mounted between the radiator support and the front (left) cylinder head.
32 Carefully lift the engine straight up and out of the engine compartment, continually checking clearances around the engine compartment. Be particularly careful that the engine does not hit the brake master cylinder, firewall or the body nosepiece as it is rolled free of the car.
33 The transaxle should remain supported by either the floor jack(s) or wood blocks while the engine is out of place

37 Engine – dismantling (general)

1 It is best to mount the engine on a dismantling stand, but if one is not available, then stand the engine on a strong bench so as to be at a comfortable working height.
2 During the dismantling process the greatest care should be taken to keep the exposed parts free from dirt. As an aid to achieving this, it is a sound practice to thoroughly clean down the outside of the engine, removing all traces of oil and dirt.
3 Use a water-soluble grease solvent. The latter compound will make the job easier, as, after the solvent has been applied and allowed to stand for a time, a vigorous jet of water will wash off the solvent and all the grease and filth. If the dirt is thick and deeply embedded, work the solvent into it with a wire brush.
4 Finally, wipe down the exterior of the engine with a rag and only then, when it is quite clean, should the dismantling process begin. As the engine is stripped, clean each part in a bath of parts cleaner.
5 Never immerse parts which have internal oilways in solvent (such as the crankshaft), but wipe them carefully with a solvent-soaked rag. Probe the oilways with a length of wire and if an air line is available, blow the oilways through to clean them.
6 Be extremely careful using combustible cleaning agents near an open flame or inside an enclosed work area. Fumes can ignite from a lighted cigarette or a hot water heater pilot light. Wipe up any fuel or cleaner spills immediately, and do not store greasy or solvent-soaked rags where they can ignite.
7 Re-use of old engine gaskets is false economy and can give rise to oil and water leaks, if nothing worse. To avoid the possibility of trouble after the engine has been reassembled, *always* use new gaskets throughout.
8 Do not throw the old gaskets away, as it sometimes happens that an immediate replacement cannot be found and the old gasket is then very useful as a template. Hang up the old gaskets as they are removed on a suitable hook or nail.
9 Wherever possible, replace nuts, bolts and washers finger-tight from wherever they were removed. This helps avoid later loss and muddle. If they cannot be replaced, then lay them out in such a fashion that it is clear from where they came.

38 Engine – major overhaul dismantling sequence

The sections in this chapter deal with removal, installation, overhaul and inspection of the various engine components. Reference should be made to appropriate chapters for removing and servicing the ancillary engine accessories. These parts include the generator, carburetor, etc.
2 If the engine is removed from the vehicle for a major overhaul, the entire engine should be stripped of its components including:
Generator (Chapter 5)
Accessory drive belts and pulleys (if not previously removed during engine removal).
Water pump and related hoses (Chapter 3).
Fuel pump and fuel pump pushrod (Chapter 4).
Distributor with cap and spark plug wires (Chapter 5).
Carburetor and fuel lines (Chapter 4)
Oil filter (Chapter 1).
Clutch pressure plate and disc (Chapter 8).
Oil dipstick and dipstick tube.
Spark plugs (Chapter 1).
3 With those components removed, the general engine sub-assemblies can be removed, serviced and installed using the following sections in this chapter.
4 If at any time during the dismantling procedure damage is found to any of the major engine components (cylinder heads, cylinder block, crankshaft, etc), consider the possibility of purchasing new or rebuilt assemblies as described in Section 48). This decision will in most cases alter your particular rebuilding sequence, as dismantling, inspection and assembly will not be required.

39 Camshaft and bearings (L4) – removal and installation

1 Remove the engine as described in Section 34 and install it on a suitable stand.

2   Remove the rocker arm cover.
3   Loosen the rocker arm nuts and pivot the rocker arms clear of the pushrods.
4   Remove the pushrods.
5   Remove the pushrod cover.
6   Remove the valve lifters as described in Section 6.
7   Remove the distributor.
8   Remove the fuel pump.
9   Remove the oil pump drive shaft and gear assembly.
10   Remove the front pulley hub as described in Section 20.
11   Remove the timing gear cover as described in Section 21.
12   Remove the two camshaft thrust plate screws by working through the holes in the camshaft gear (photo).
13   While supporting the camshaft with your fingers inserted through the fuel pump hole to prevent damaging the camshaft bearings, carefully and slowly pull the camshaft straight out from the block (photo).
14   If the gear must be removed from the camshaft, it must be pressed out. If you do not have access to a press, take it to your dealer or an automotive machine shop. The thrust plate must be positioned so that the woodruff key in the shaft does not damage it when the shaft is pressed out.
15   Examine the bearing surfaces and the surfaces of the cam lobes. The oil pan may have to be removed to thoroughly inspect the bearings. Surface scratches, if very shallow, can be removed by rubbing with a fine emery cloth or oilstone. Any deep scoring will necessitate a new camshaft.
16   Mount the camshaft on V-blocks and use a dial gauge to measure lobe lift and run-out. Reject a camshaft which does not meet the specified limits.
17   Using a micrometer, measure the journal diameter (photo). Again, reject a camshaft which does not meet the specified limits.
18   If the camshaft bearings are worn, they must be replaced by using the following procedure:
   (a)   Remove the oil pan if not already off.
   (b)   Remove the flywheel.
   (c)   Driving from the inside out, drive out the expansion plug from the rear cam bearing.
   (d)   Using a camshaft bearing remover set, available from a GM dealer or auto parts store, drive out the front bearing toward the rear.
   (e)   Drive out the rear bearing toward the front.
   (f)   Using an extension on the bearing remover, drive out the center bearing toward the rear.
   (g)   Install the new bearings by reversing the removal procedure. Be sure all of the oil holes are aligned. **Note:** *The front bearing must be driven approximately $\frac{1}{8}$-in from the front of the cylinder block in order to uncover the oil hole to the timing gear oil nozzle.*
   (h)   After installing the new bearings, install a new camshaft rear expansion plug flush with the rear surface of the block.
   (i)   Reinstall the flywheel and oil pan.
19   If the camshaft gear has been removed from the camshaft, it must be pressed on prior to installation.
   (a)   Support the camshaft in an arbor press by using press plate adaptors behind the front journal.
   (b)   Place the gear spacer ring and the thrust plate over the end of the shaft.
   (c)   Install the woodruff key in the shaft keyway.
   (d)   Install the camshaft gear and press it onto the shaft until it bottoms against the gear spacer ring.
   (e)   Use a feeler gauge to check the end clearance of the thrust plate. It should be .0015- to .0050-in. If the clearance is less than .0015-in the spacer ring should be replaced. If the clearance is more than .0050-in the thrust plate should be replaced.
20   Prior to installing the camshaft, verify that number 1 cylinder is at TDC. Coat each of the lobes and journals liberally with a lithium-based grease.
21   Slide the camshaft into the engine block, again taking extra care not to damage the bearings (photo).
22   Position the camshaft and crankshaft gears so that the valve timing marks line up (photo). With the shafts in this position, the engine is in the number 4 cylinder firing position.
23   Install the camshaft thrust plate mounting screws and torque to specs.

24   Complete the installation by reversing the removal procedure. When installing the distributor, be sure to rotate the engine 360° to the number 1 cylinder firing position (see Chapter 5).

40 Camshaft (V6) – removal and installation

1   Remove the engine from the car as described in Section 35 or Section 36.
2   Remove the rocker arm covers.
3   Remove the pushrods.
4   Remove the valve lifters as described in Section 6.
5   Remove the crankshaft front cover as described in Section 23.
6   Remove the fuel pump and fuel pump pushrod.
7   Remove the distributor as described in Chapter 5.
8   Remove the timing chain and camshaft sprocket.
9   Install 2 bolts into the camshaft bolt holes to be used as grips to pull on the camshaft.
10   Carefully draw the camshaft out of the engine block. Do this very slowly to avoid damage to the camshaft bearings as the journals pass through the bearing surfaces. Always support the camshaft with one hand near the engine block.
11   Refer to Section 41 for inspection and servicing of the camshaft and camshaft bearings.
12   Prior to installing the camshaft, coat each of the lobes and journals liberally with a lithium-based grease.
13   Slide the camshaft into the engine block, again taking extra care not to damage the bearings.
14   Install the camshaft sprocket and timing chain so that the marks on the crankshaft and camshaft sprockets line up. Be sure that the number 1 piston is at top dead center. This should be checked with a dial gauge.
15   Install the remaining components in the reverse order of removal.

41 Camshaft and bearings (V6) – inspection and servicing

1   Examine the bearing surfaces and the surface of the cam lobes. Surface scratches, if very shallow, can be removed by rubbing with a fine emery cloth or an oilstone. Any deep scoring will necessitate a new camshaft.
2   Mount the camshaft on V-blocks and use a dial gauge to measure lobe lift and run-out. Reject a camshaft which does not meet the specified limits.
3   Measure the journal diameters using a micrometer. Again, reject a camshaft which does not meet the specified limits.
4   If the camshaft bearings are worn or damaged, they must be replaced. To begin this operation, remove the crankshaft, leaving the

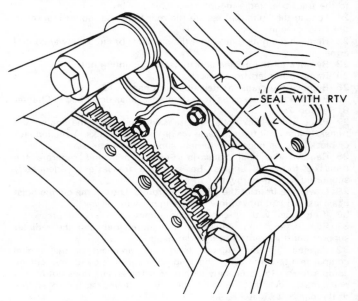

Fig. 2.22 Location of the camshaft rear cover (V6) (Sec 41)

39.12 Removing the camshaft thrust plate screws

39.13a The camshaft should be supported from inside the block during removal

39.13b Removing the camshaft from the block

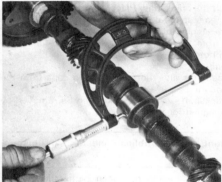

39.17 Using a micrometer to measure the journal diameter

39.21 The camshaft lobes and journals should be lubricated prior to installing the shaft into the block. Dial indicator is used here to verify that piston is at Top Dead Center

39.22 The camshaft and crankshaft gears should be positioned so their timing marks line up

42.2 Using a ridge reamer to remove the carbon deposits from the top of the cylinders

42.5 Pieces of rubber hosing should be slipped over the connecting rod studs during removal and installation

42.6 The piston and connecting rod assembly should be removed through the top of the cylinder

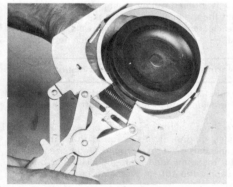

42.9 Using a piston ring expanding tool to remove the piston rings

43.9 Removing the main bearing caps

43.10 Lifting the crankshaft from the engine block

cylinder heads and pistons in place. The threads of the connecting rod bolts should be taped prior to removing the crankshaft to prevent damage to the shaft. Also tape the connecting rods to the side of the engine so they will not be in the way during removal of the bearings.
5   Remove the camshaft rear cover from the cylinder block (Fig. 2.22).
6   To extract the bearings, use GM tool J-6098 or an equivalent bearing remover/installer tool. To remove the bearings, follow the instructions that should be included with the tool set.
7   This same tool set is used to install the camshaft bearings. Install the front and rear bearings first, as these will act as guides for centering the remaining bearings. When installing the camshaft bearings, be sure that the oil holes in the bearings line up with their respective oil holes in the block.
8   Clean any dirt, oil or old gasket material from the camshaft rear cover. To install the cover, apply a $\frac{1}{8}$-in (3 mm) diameter bead of RTV or equivalent sealant around the sealing surface, and bolt the cover to the engine block.
9   Reinstall the crankshaft as described in Section 51.

42 Pistons, connecting rods and bearings – removal

1   Remove the oil pan, oil pump and cylinder heads as described previously in this chapter.
2   Before the piston assemblies can be forced up through the top of the engine block, a ridge reamer should be used to remove the ridge and/or carbon deposits at the top of each cylinder (photo). Working on one cylinder at a time, turn the engine so the piston is at the bottom of its stroke. Then place a rag on top of the piston to catch the cuttings. After the ridge is removed, crank the engine until the piston is at the top of the cylinder and remove the cloth and cuttings. Failure to remove this ridge may cause damage to the piston rings, pistons or cylinder walls.
3   Inspect the connecting rods and connecting rod caps for cylinder identification. If these components are not plainly marked, identify each using a small punch to make the appropriate number of indentations to identify the cylinders they belong to.
4   Working in sequence, remove the nuts on the connecting rod stud and lift the cap (with bearing inside) off the crankshaft. Place the connecting rod cap and bearing on a clean work surface marked cylinder number 1, 2, 3, etc.
5   Push a piece of rubber or plastic tubing over the connecting rod studs to completely cover the studs. This is important as these studs could easily damage the crankshaft or cylinder wall when the piston assembly is removed (photo).
6   Push the piston/connecting rod assembly out through the top of the cylinder (photo). Place the piston with its connecting rod next to its rod cap on the sequenced work area.
7   Repeat these procedures for the remaining cylinders, turning the crankshaft as necessary to gain access to the connecting rod nuts. Reuse the rubber or plastic tubing for each assembly.
8   Remove the bearings from the connecting rods and the connecting rod caps. This is easily done with a small screwdriver. If the engine has many miles on it, it is false economy to reuse the bearings, but if they are to be reinstalled, place them in a numbered rack.
9   If a piston ring expanding tool is available, use this to remove each of the rings from the piston (photo). An alternative method is to expand the ring just enough to clear the lands of the piston body. Then place strips of tin (about $\frac{1}{4}$-in wide) under the ring at equal distances around the piston. Using a slight twisting motion, 'walk' the ring up the piston and off the top.
10   Place the rings in their 'installed' order adjacent to the piston/connecting rod on your numbered work area.
11   Separating the connecting rod from the piston requires the removal of the piston pin. This job is best left to a dealer or automotive machine shop equipped with the proper support tools and an arbor press.
12   Do not take the time to clean and inspect the piston/rod assemblies at this time, as they may have to be replaced with new units depending on the condition of the cylinder block and/or crankshaft.

43 Crankshaft – removal

1   Remove the engine from the car as described in Section 34(L4) or

Section 35 or 36(V6) amd support it on a suitable stand.
2   On L4 engines, remove the crankshaft pulley and hub assembly as described in Section 20. On V6 engines, remove the crankshaft pulley and torsional damper as described in Section 22.
3   Remove the oil pan.
4   Remove the oil pump assembly.
5   On L4 engines, remove the timing gear cover. On V6 engines, remove the water pump, cracnkcase front cover, camshaft sprocket and timing chain.
6   Remove the pistons and connecting rods from the crankshaft as described in Section 42.
7   Remove the flywheel as described in Section 32.
8   Check that each of the main bearing caps is marked in respect of its location in the engine block. If not, use a punch to make small indentions in each cap: one indentation for the first main bearing cap, two indentations for the second cap, etc. The main bearing caps must be reinstalled in their original positions.
9   Unbolt the main bearing caps (photo) and lift each cap and its corresponding bearing off the crankshaft. Place all of the main bearing caps and bearings on a work space numbered to correspond with the position of the cap in the engine block.
10   Lift the crankshaft from the engine block, being careful not to damage it in any way (photo).
11   Remove the rear main oil seal.
12   Remove the main bearings and the main bearing caps from the block, keeping them separated as to their positions.
13   If necessary, the crankshaft gear or sprocket can be removed by using a special puller designed for this purpose.

44 Piston and connecting rod assemblies – cleaning and inspection

1   In most cases where the engine has seen high mileage, the original pistons will have to be replaced with new ones. This is because the cylinders will have to be bored to a larger size to compensate for normal wear. If however the cylinder walls require only a slight finish honing, the old pistons may be reused if they are in good condition.
2   Wash the connecting rods and pistons in a cleaning solvent and dry with compressed air, if available.
3   Don't use a wire brush or any abrasive cleaning tools on any part of the piston.
4   Clean the ring grooves of the piston with a groove cleaner tool and make sure the oil ring holes and slots are clean.
5   Insect the rods for twisting, bending, nicks or cracks. If any of the above items are found, the rod must be replaced with a new one.
6   Inspect the piston for cracked ring lands, skirts or pin bosses. Check for worn or wavy ring lands, scuffed or damaged skirts and eroded areas at the top of the piston. Replace any pistons that are damaged or show signs of excessive wear.
7   Inspect the ring grooves for nicks which may cause the rings to hang up.
8   With the piston still connected to the connecting rod, swivel the rod back and forth, noting the degree of difficulty. Compare all piston/rod assemblies. If the rods seem loose on the piston pins, and move with little or no drag, the piston pins have worn and the piston pin must be replaced.
9   If the cylinder block is in need of any machine work, even finish honing, chances are that the machinist will want the pistons on hand to check piston-to-bore clearance as the cylinder walls are cut. This measurement is critical and should be left to the machine shop.

45 Crankshaft and bearings – inspection and servicing

1   Examine the crankpin and main journal surfaces for scoring, scratches or corrosion. If evident, then the crankshaft will have to be reground professionally.
2   Using a micrometer, test each journal and crankpin at several different points for ovality (photo). If this is found to be more than 0.001-inch, then the crankshaft must be reground. Undersize bearings are available to suit the recommended reground diameter, but normally your dealer will supply the correct matching bearings with the reconditioned crankshaft.
3   After a high mileage, the main bearings and the connecting rod bearings may have worn to give an excessive running clearance. The

correct running clearance for the different journals is given in the Specifications.

The clearance is best checked using a product such as 'Plastigage', having refitted the original bearings and caps and tightened the cap bolts to the torque settings specified in Specifications. *Never attempt to correct excessive running clearance by filing the caps but always fit new shell bearings, having first checked the crankshaft journals and crankpins for ovality and to establish whether their diameters are of standard or reground sizes.*

4   Checking the connecting rod bearings is carried out in a similar manner to that described for the main bearings. The correct running clearance is given in the Specifications.

5   It is good practice to check the running clearance of rod and main bearings even if new bearings are installed. The use of 'Plastigage' is described in Section 46.

6   The crankshaft endplay should be checked by forcing the crankshaft to the extreme front position, then using a feeler gauge at the front end of the rear main bearing. Refer to the Specifications for the permissible clearance. This procedure is detailed in Section 51.

7   The connecting rod side clearance should be measured with a feeler gauge between the connecting rod caps. If the side clearance is outside the specified tolerance, replace the rod assembly. This procedure is detailed in Section 53.

45.2 Using a micrometer to measure the crankshaft journals

46 Main bearings and rod bearings – checking clearance

Note: *There are three precautions to take when working with Plastigage. These are:*

(a)   *Plastigage is soluble in oil, so all oil and grease should be removed from the crankshaft and bearing surfaces while the testing is done.*

(b)   *Do not rotate the crankshaft while the Plastigage is installed in the engine, as this may cause damage to the crankshaft or engine surfaces.*

(c)   *Remove all traces of the Plastigage when testing is complete. Be very careful not to harm the crankshaft or bearing surfaces as the Plastigage is removed. Do not use sharp tools or abrasive cleaners, instead, remove the used Plastigage with your fingernail or a blunt wood stick.*

1   Whenever an engine is overhauled the bearing clearances should be checked. This should be done for reused bearings as well as for new bearings.

2   The procedure is basically the same for both the main bearings and the connecting rod bearings.

3   With the crankshaft set into the engine block, install the main bearings into the engine block and the main bearing caps.

4   Remove all oil, grime and foreign material from the crankshaft and bearing surfaces.

5   Place a piece of Plastigage (available at most auto supply shops) along the length of each main bearing journal on the crankshaft (photo).

6   Install each main bearing cap and tighten the attaching bolts to specification. The arrow on each cap should face toward the front of the engine.

7   Now remove each bearing cap and measure the width of the Plastigage strip which will have flattened out when the caps were tightened. A scale is provided on the Plastigage envelope for measuring the width of the Plastigage strip, and thus, bearing clearance (photo).

8   If the Plastigage is flattened more at the ends than in the middle, or vice versa, this is an indication of journal taper which can be checked in the Specifications Section.

9   To test for an out-of-round condition, remove all traces of the Plastigage (be careful not to damage the crankshaft or bearing surfaces) and rotate the crankshaft 90 degrees. With the crankshaft rotated to this point, use the Plastigage to check the clearances again. Compare these measurements with those taken previously to arrive at eccentricity or out of round.

10 To check connecting rod bearing clearances, install each piston/rod assembly (Section 52) and use the Plastigage as described above.

11 Connecting rod side clearance (Section 53) can also be checked at this time.

12 If the bearings have shown to be within all tolerances, they may

46.5 To measure main and rod bearing clearances place a piece of Plastigage on the journal

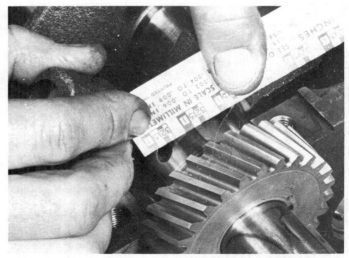

46.7 Using the provided scale to measure the Plastigage

be installed following the steps outlined in the appropriate sections.
13 If not within specifications, the bearings should be replaced with the correctly sized bearings. Upper and lower bearings should always be replaced as a unit.

47 Cylinder block – inspection

1   It is important that the cylinder block be inspected carefully and as described. The cylinder block was designed to operate with exacting tolerances, and if the engine is reassembled without first properly inspecting the block, all work and cost involved in the rebuild may be for nothing.
2   Clean the cylinder block as necessary to remove built-up sludge and grime. Clean all excess gasket material from the sealing surfaces.
3   Inspect the cylinder block for cracks in the cylinder walls, water jacket, valve lifter bores and main bearing webs. Use a flashlight where necessary. In most cases, cracks will require that a new engine block be purchased.
4   The cylinder bores must be examined for taper, ovality, scoring and scratches. These checks are important for proper operation of the pistons and piston rings.
5   Scoring and scratches can usually be seen with the naked eye and felt with the fingers. If they are deep, the engine block may have to be replaced with a new one. If the imperfections are slight, a qualified machine shop should be able to hone or bore the cylinders to a larger size.
6   There are two indications for excessive wear of the cylinders. First, if the vehicle was emitting blue smoke from the exhaust system before engine dismantling. This blue smoke is caused by oil seeping past the piston rings due to the wear of the cylinder walls. Second, the thickness of the ridge at the top of the cylinder (which may have been removed during piston removal) can give an indication about overall cylinder wear.
7   Using an internal-type dial gauge, measure each bore at three different points (photo). Take a measurement near the top of the bore and then near the bottom of the bore. Finally, measure at the center. Jot down all measurements to determine the taper of the cylinder (slightly larger at the top than the bottom or vice versa).
8   An out-of-round condition can be found in a similar fashion, except measure the cylinder first parallel with the engine centerline and then turn the micrometers until they are perpendicular with the centerline (180 degrees from first measurement).
9   Where the cylinder bores are worn beyond the permitted tolerances as shown in the Specifications Section, the block will have to be replaced with a new one, honed or bored.
10 A final check of the cylinder block would include an inspection for warpage. This is done with a straight edge and feeler gauges in the same manner as for the cylinder heads. The tolerances described in Section 16 also apply to the cylinder block. If warpage is slight, a machine shop can resurface the block.

48 Engine – rebuilding alternatives

1   At this point in the engine rebuilding process the home mechanic is faced with a number of options for completing the overhaul. The decision to replace the cylinder block, piston/rod assemblies and crankshaft depends on a number of factors with the number one consideration being the condition of the cylinder block. Other considerations are: cost, competent machine shop facilities, parts availability, time available to complete the project and experience.
2   Some of the rebuilding alternatives are as follows:

Individual parts – If the inspection procedures prove that the engine block and most engine components are in reusable condition, this may be the most economical alternative. The block, crankshaft and piston/rod assemblies should all be inspected carefully. Even if the block shows little wear, the camshaft bearing bores and cylinder bores should receive a finish hone; both jobs for a machine shop.

Master kit (crankshaft kit) – This rebuild package usually consists of a reground crankshaft and a matched set of pistons and connecting rods. The pistons will come already installed with new piston pins to the connecting rods. Piston rings and the necessary bearings may or may not be included in the kit. These kits are commonly available for

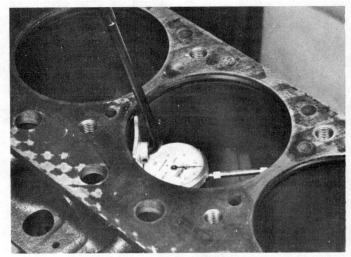
47.7 Using an internal-type dial gauge to measure the cylinder bore

49.2a Removing an old freeze plug

49.2b Using a hammer and socket to install a new freeze plug

standard cylinder bores, as well as for engine blocks which have been bored to a regular oversize.

Short block – A short block consists of a cylinder block with a crankshaft and piston/rod assemblies already installed. All new bearings are incorporated and all clearances will be within tolerances. Depending on where the short block is purchased, a guarantee may be included. The existing camshaft valve mechanism, cylinder heads and ancillary parts can be bolted to this short block with little or no machine shop work necessary for the engine overhaul.

Long block – A long block, called a 'Target or Target Master' engine by GM dealerships consists of a short block plus oil pump, oil pan, cylinder heads, valve covers, camshaft and valve mechanism, camshaft gear, timing chain and crankcase front cover. All components are installed with new bearings, seals and gaskets incorporated throughout. The installation of manifolds and ancillary parts is all that is necessary. Some form of guarantee is usually included with purchase.

3   Give careful thought to which method is best for your situation and discuss the alternatives with local machine shop owners, parts dealers or GM dealership partsmen.

49 Engine – general overhaul information

1   Before assembling any parts to the engine block, the block should have all necessary machine work completed and the engine block should be thoroughly cleaned. If machine work was performed, chances are that the block was hot-tanked afterwards to remove all traces of the machine cuttings.
2   The oil galleys and water passages of the block should also be thoroughly clean and free from dirt or machining leftovers. It's good practice to install new freeze plugs in the engine whenever it is stripped for a total overhaul. These plugs are difficult to replace once the engine has been assembled and installed. If the engine was sent out for machine work and hot-tanking, it may be best to let the machine shop remove and install new plugs. If they are to be done at home, proceed as follows:

(a)   Use a hammer and punch to press one side of the plug into the block.
(b)   Use pliers to pry the old freeze plug out of its recess (photo).
(c)   Place a suitable replacement plug into position and hammer into place until flush with the engine block. Special installation tools are available for pressing the plug into place, however a suitable sized socket will work fine (photo).

3   Clean and examine all bolts, nuts and fasteners. Replace any that are damaged.
4   Clean and cover all engine components to keep dirt and dust away from them until they can be installed.
5   Have assembly grease and an oil can filled with engine oil handy to lubricate parts as they are installed.
6   Lay out all necessary tools and a reliable torque wrench on a clean work table for easy retrieval.
7   New gaskets and seals must be used throughout. These are commonly available together in a master rebuild gasket set.
8   In almost all cases, parts to be replaced during a major overhaul include: camshaft bearings, connecting rod bearings, main bearings, piston rings, timing chain, spark plugs and oil filter. These are in addition to any parts found damaged or excessively worn during dismantling or the various inspection processes.

50 Pistons and piston rings – assembly

1   The piston should be attached to its appropriate connecting rod. As mentioned previously, this is a job for a professional equipped with the proper supports and an arbor press.
2   The new piston rings should be comparable in size to the piston being used.
3   The installation of the piston rings on the piston is critical to the overall performance of the rebuilt engine.
4   Measure the ring end gap of each ring before it is installed in the piston. This is done as follows:

(a)   Arrange the piston rings into sets for each piston. The set will contain a top ring, 2nd ring and a 3 piece oil control ring (2 rails and a spacer).

(b)   Slip a top ring into the appropriate cylinder bore. Push the ring into the cylinder bore about $\frac{1}{4}$-inch below the upper limit of ring travel (a total of about 1 inch below block deck). Push the ring down into position with the top of a piston to make sure the ring is square with the cylinder wall.
(c)   Using a feeler gauge, measure the gap between the ends of the ring (photo). If the gap is less than specified (see Specifications), remove the ring and try another top ring for fit.
(d)   Check all top rings in the same manner and if necessary use a fine file to remove a slight amount of material from the ends of the ring(s). If inadequate end gap is used, the rings will break during operation.
(e)   Measure the end gap of each 2nd ring and oil control ring as described above.

5   Check the fit of each piston ring into its groove by holding the ring next to the piston and then placing the outer surface of the ring into its respective groove. Roll the ring entirely around the piston and check for any binding. If the binding is due to a distorted ring, replace the ring with a new one. Perform this check for the top and 2nd rings of each piston.
6   Install the piston rings as follows:

(a)   Study Fig. 2.23 thoroughly to understand exactly where each ring gap should be located in relation to the piston and other rings. The location of each ring gap is important.
(b)   If a piston ring expander tool is available, use this to install the rings. If not, small lengths of tin can be used to prevent the rings from entering the wrong groove (see Section 42 on piston ring removal).
(c)   Install the bottom oil ring spacer in its groove and insert the anti-rotation tang in the oil hole. Hold the spacer ends butted and install the lower steel oil ring rail with the gap properly located. Install the upper steel oil ring rail and properly set its gap. Flex or squeeze the oil ring assembly to make sure it is free in the groove. If not, dress the groove with a file or replace the oil control ring assembly as necessary.
(d)   Install the end ring and properly locate its gap.
(e)   Install the top ring with gap properly positioned.
(f)   Repeat the above procedures for all piston assemblies.

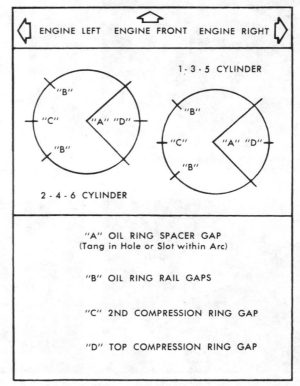

Fig. 2.23 Recommended positioning of the piston ring gaps when installed on the piston (V6) (Sec 50)

7   Proper clearance of the piston rings in their grooves is very important. Clearance between the ring and its groove is checked with a blade feeler gauge, sliding the appropriately sized feeler gauge (see Specifications) between the top of the ring and the inside of the groove (photo). Rotate the feeler blade all the way around the piston, checking for proper clearance. Replace rings or clean and dress the groove as necessary for proper clearance.

51 Crankshaft, main bearings and oil seal – installation

Note: *If a new or reground crankshaft is being installed, or if the original crankshaft has been reground, make sure the correct bearings are being used.*

1   On V6 engines, install the rear main bearing oil seal. The upper half of the seal should be positioned on its cylinder block seat and the lower half on the rear main bearing cap. Install with the lips toward the front of the engine. Where two lips are incorporated, install lip with helix toward the front of the engine. Use the protector installation tool when installing the seal halves. (See Section 31 for use of installation tool and further information).

2   On V6 engines, lubricate the seal lips with engine oil.

3   Install the main bearings in the cylinder block and main bearing caps (photo). Lubricate the bearing surfaces with engine oil or a lithium-based grease (photo).

4   Lower the crankshaft into position, being careful not to damage the bearing surfaces.

5   Apply a thin coat of brush-on sealer to the block mating surface and the corresponding surface of the bearing cap. Do not allow sealer or get on the crankshaft or seal (see Section 31).

6   Install the main bearing caps (with bearings) over the crankshaft and onto the cylinder block. The arrows should point toward the front of the engine.

7   Torque all main bearing cap attaching bolts to the proper specification, except the number 5 (L4) or number 3 (V6) main bearing cap. Torque this bearing cap bolt to about 10 to 12 ft-lb only at this time. Tap the end of the crankshaft with a lead hammer, first to the

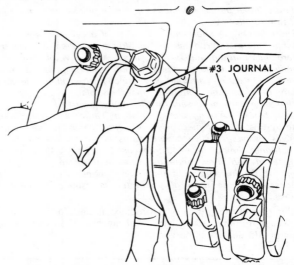

Fig. 2.24 Using a feeler gauge to measure crankshaft end play (V6) (Sec 51)

rear and then to the front to line up the rear bearing properly. Now retorque all bearing cap bolts to the proper specification.

8   To measure crankshaft end play, force the crankshaft as far forward as it will go and use a feeler gauge to measure the gap between the front of the main bearing and the crankshaft thrust surface (photo).

9   Install the rear oil seal and flywheel as described in Section 32 to ease in engine rotation during reassembly.

10   On L4 engines, install the Woodruff key into the keyway in the end of the crankshaft. Then install the crankshaft timing gear and rotate the crankshaft so the timing marks on the crankshaft and camshaft gears line up.

50.4 Using a feeler gauge to measure the piston ring end gap

50.7 Using a feeler gauge to measure piston ring groove clearance

51.3a Installing the main bearings in the cylinder block

51.3b Lubricating the main bearings prior to installation of the crankshaft

51.8 Using a feeler gauge to measure crankshaft end play

52.5 A piston ring compressor and pieces of rubber hose should be in place when installing the piston and connecting rod assembly

52 Pistons, connecting rods and bearings – installation

1   With the pistons complete with piston rings and connecting rods, they can be installed in the engine.
2   Make sure the cylinder bores are perfectly clean. Wipe the cylinder walls several times with a light engine oil and a clean, lint-free cloth.
3   Lubricate the connecting rod bearings and install them into their appropriate rod and rod cap.
4   Lightly coat the pistons, rings and cylinder walls with light engine oil.
5   Install a length of rubber or plastic tubing over the connecting rod studs on one rod assembly. This will prevent the threaded bolts from possibly damaging the cylinder wall or crankshaft journal as the piston/rod assembly is pushed into place (photo).
6   Check that all the piston ring gaps are positioned properly (see Section 50).
7   Check that the piston/rod assembly is properly positioned. Most pistons will be marked with an 'F' or a drilled-out area indicating the piston should be installed with these marks toward the front of the engine. The rod bearing tang slots should be toward the outside of the engine block once installed.
8   Place a piston ring compressor around the piston, with the base of the compressor flush with the cylinder block. Tighten the compressor until the rings are flush with the piston surface and then push the piston assembly into the bore. A wooden hammer handle can be used to tap the top of the piston slightly (photo). Hold the ring compressor solidly against the cylinder block until all rings are inside the bore. Continue pushing until the connecting rod is near its installed position.
9   Ensure that all bearing surfaces and the crankshaft journal are coated with engine oil and remove the tubing protector pieces. Install the connecting rod bearing cap (with bearing) to the connecting rod (photo).
10 Torque the nuts to specifications.
11 Repeat this procedure for all cylinders, using the rubber or plastic tubing on each assembly to prevent damage as the pistons are pushed into place. Rotate the crankshaft as necessary to make the connecting rod nuts accessible for tightening.

53 Connecting rod – checking side clearance

1   Side clearance can be checked with the piston/rod assemblies temporarily installed for bearing clearance checking.
2   With the piston/rod assemblies installed and the bearing caps tightened to specifications, use feeler gauges to check the clearance between the sides of the connecting rods and the crankshaft (photo).
3   If the clearance at this point is below the minimum tolerance, the rod may be machined for more clearance at this area.
4   If the clearance is too excessive, a new rod must be used or the crankshaft must be reground or replaced with a new one.

54 Engine – final assembling and pre-oiling after overhaul

1   After the crankshaft, piston/rod assemblies and the various associated bearings have been installed in the engine block, the remainder of the components (cylinder heads, oil pump, camshaft, etc.,) can be installed following the installation procedures located in the various Sections of this Chapter.
2   Follow the engine disassembly sequence in the reverse order of installation, using new gaskets where necessary.
3   On V6 engines, adjust the valve lash as described in Section 7.
4   After a major overhaul it is a good idea to pre-oil the V6 engine before it is installed and initially started. This will tell you if there are any faults in the oiling system at a time when corrections can be made easily and without major damage. Pre-oiling the engine will also allow the parts to be lubricated thoroughly in a normal fashion, but without heavy loads placed upon them.
5   The engine should be assembled completely with the exception of the distributor and the valve covers.
6   A modified distributor will be needed for this job. This pre-oil tool is a distributor body with the bottom gear ground off and the counterweight assembly removed from the top of the shaft.
7   Place the pre-oiler into the distributor shaft access hole at the rear of the intake manifold and make sure the bottom of the shaft mates

52.8 A wooden hammer handle can be used to tap the piston into the cylinder

52.9 Fitting the connecting rod bearing cap over the crankshaft and connecting rod studs

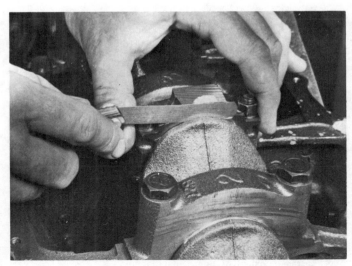

53.2 Using a feeler gauge to check connecting rod side clearance

with the oil pump. Clamp the modified distributor into place just as you would an ordinary distributor. Now attach an electric drill motor to the top of the shaft.

8   With the oil filter installed, all oil gallery ways plugged (oil pressure sending unit at rear of block) and the crankcase full of oil as shown on the dipstick, rotate the pre-oiler with the drill. Make sure the rotation is in a clockwise direction. Soon, oil should start to flow from the rocker arms, signifying that the oil pump and oiling system is functioning properly. It may take 2 to 3 minutes for the oil to flow to each rocker arm. Allow the oil to circulate throughout the engine for a few minutes.

9   Check for oil leaks at all locations and correct as necessary.

10   Remove the pre-oiler and install the normal distributor and valve covers.

55 Engine (L4) – installation

1   If the engine has been completely stripped for overhaul, the installation procedure will be made easier if the following components are installed to the engine block prior to installing the engine in the car:

    (a)   *Cylinder head, including rocker arms, nuts and pivots.*
    (b)   *Hydraulic lifters and pushrods.*
    (c)   *Exhaust manifold (photo).*
    (d)   *Oil dipstick tube.*
    (e)   *Lower rear A/C compressor mount (photo).*
    (f)   *Forward A/C compressor mount.*
    (g)   *Water pump and bracket assembly.*
    (h)   *Power steering pump bracket (photo).*
    (i)   *Water jacket access plate (photo).*
    (j)   *Intake manifold.*
    (k)   *Upper generator bracket.*
    (l)   *Lower generator bracket and motor mount (photo).*
    (m)   *Rocker arm cover.*
    (n)   *Fuel pump (photo).*
    (o)   *Oil pressure sender.*
    (p)   *Distributor (photo).*
    (q)   *Thermal vacuum switches (photo).*
    (r)   *Thermostat housing.*
    (s)   *Water temperature sensors.*
    (t)   *Flywheel.*

2   Prior to installing the engine, ensure that the transaxle is securely supported and is as parallel to the floor as possible.

3   Connect an engine hoist to the engine and lift it off of its stand. The chains should be positioned as during removal, with the engine sitting level.

4   Lower the engine into place inside the engine compartment, closely watching the clearances on all sides as it is lowered (photo).

Possible interference points are at the water pump (photo), the flywheel (photo), the generator (photo) and the hoses and wiring harnesses near the firewall. With a manual transaxle, carefully guide the engine onto the transaxle input shaft. With the two components at the same angle, the shaft should slide easily into the engine. With an automatic transaxle, the flywheel needs to be guided past the torque converter guide pin, located in the center of the torque converter (photo).

5   With the engine mated with the transaxle bellhousing, install the two upper transaxle-to-engine bolts.

6   Remove the transaxle support jack.

7   Lower the engine onto the chassis mounts.

8   Disconnect the engine hoist from the engine.

9   Install the front engine mount nuts.

10   Install the remaining components in the reverse order of removal.

11   Fill the cooling system.

12   Fill the engine with the correct grade of oil.

13   Check the transaxle fluid level, adding fluid as necessary.

14   Connect the positive battery cable, followed by the negative battery cable. If sparks or arcing occur as the negative cable is connected to the battery, check that all electrical accessories are turned off (check dome light). If arcing still occurs, check that all electrical wiring is connected properly to the engine and transaxle.

15   See Section 58 for the starting-up procedure.

56 Engine (V6, with automatic transaxle) – installation

1   Prior to installing the engine, ensure that the transaxle is securely supported and is as parallel to the floor as possible.

2   Connect an engine hoist to the engine and lift it off of its stand. The chains should be positioned as during removal, with the engine sitting level.

3   Lower the engine into place inside the engine compartment, closely watching the clearances on all sides as it is lowered. Check that the front engine mount studs are properly located in the cradle bracket. On automatic transaxles, the flywheel needs to be guided past the torque converter guide pin, located in the center of the torque converter.

4   Line the transaxle up with the cylinder case and install the attaching bolts, torquing them to specs.

5   Disconnect the engine hoist from the engine.

6   Install the forward engine strut bracket between the radiator support and the front (left) cylinder head.

7   Raise the vehicle and install the transaxle case-to-cylinder case support bracket bolts.

8   Install the engine mount nuts.

9   Install the remaining components in the reverse order of removal.

10   Fill the cooling system.

55.1a Installed position of the exhaust manifold

55.1b Installed position of the lower rear A/C compressor mount and water pump

55.1c Installed position of the power steering pump bracket

55.1d Installed position of the water jacket access plate

55.1e Installed position of the lower generator bracket and engine mount

55.1f Installed position of the fuel pump

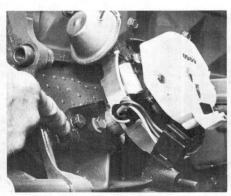

55.1g Installed position of the distributor

55.1h Sealing tape should be applied to the threads of all thermal vacuum switches prior to installation

55.4a Lowering the engine into the engine compartment

55.4b Check clearance at water pump during engine installation

55.4c Check clearance at the flywheel during engine installation

55.4d Check clearance at the generator during engine installation

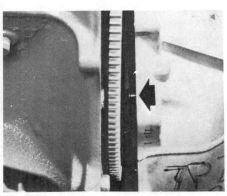

55.4e With an automatic transaxle the flywheel must be guided past the torque converter guide pin during engine installation

11 Fill the engine with the correct grade of oil.
12 Check the transaxle fluid level, adding fluid as necessary,
13 Connect the positive battery cable, followed by the negative battery cable. If sparks or arcing occur as the negative cable is connected to the battery, check that all electrical accessories are turned off (check dome light). If arcing still occurs, check that all electrical wiring is connected properly to the engine and transaxle.
14 See Section 58 for the starting-up procedure.

57 Engine (V6, with manual transaxle) – installation

1   Prior to installing the engine, ensure that the transaxle is securely supported and is as parallel to the floor as possible.
2   Connect an engine hoist to the engine and lift it off of its stand. The chains should be positioned as during removal, with the engine sitting level.
3   Lower the engine into the engine compartment, closely watching the clearances on all sides as it is lowered.
4   With the engine still supported by the hoist, install the forward engine strut bracket between the front (left) cylinder head and the radiator support.
5   Raise the transaxle so it is even and at the same angle as the engine. Start the right drive axle into the transaxle. Carefully guide the engine onto the transaxle input shaft, and insert at least one transaxle-to-engine bolt.
6   Start the left drive axle into the transaxle.
7   Install the cradle.
8   Install all the nuts that secure the transaxle and engine mounts to the cradle.
9   Install the remaining components in the reverse order of removal.
10 Fill the cooling system.
11 Fill the engine with the correct grade of oil.
12 Check the transaxle fluid level, adding fluid as necessary.
13 Connect the positive battery cable, followed by the negative battery cable. If sparks or arcing occur as the negative battery cable is connected to the battery, check that all electrical accessories are

turned off (check dome light). If arcing still occurs, check that all electrical wiring is connected properly to the engine and transaxle.
14 See Section 58 for the starting-up procedure.

58 Engine start-up after major repair or overhaul

1   With the engine in place in the vehicle and all components connected, make a final check that all pipes and wiring have been connected and that no rags or tools have been left in the engine compartment.
2   Connect the negative battery cable. If it sparks or arcs, power is being drawn from someplace and all accessories and wiring should be checked.
3   Fill the cooling system with the proper mixture and amount of coolant (Chapter 1).
4   Fill the crankcase with the correct quantity and grade of oil (Chapter 1).
5   Check the tension of all drive belts (Chapter 1).
6   Remove the 'BAT' wire connection from the HEI distributor to prevent the engine from starting. Now crank the engine over for about 15 to 30 seconds. This will allow the oil pump to distribute oil and the fuel pump to start pumping fuel to the carburetor.
7   Now connect the 'BAT' wire to the distributor cap and start the engine. Immediately check all gauges and warning lights for proper readings and check for leaks of coolant or oil.
8   If the engine does not start immediately, check to make sure fuel is reaching the carburetor. This may take a while.
9   After allowing the engine to run for a few minutes at low speed, turn it off and check the oil and coolant levels.
10 Start the engine again and check the ignition timing, emissions control settings and carburetor idle speeds (Chapter 1).
11 Run the vehicle easily during the first 500 to 1000 miles (break-in period), then check the torque settings on all major engine components, particularly the cylinder heads. Tighen any bolts which may have loosened.

Chapter 3 Cooling, heating and air conditioning systems

Refer to Chapter 13 for specifications and information related to 1981 through 1984 models

Contents

Specifications

System type	Pressurized with thermostatic control and pump/fan assistance
Radiator cap pressure setting	15 psi
Thermostat type	Wax pellet
Thermostat rating	195°F (91°C)
Water pump type	Centrifugal
Water pump bearings	Sealed ball bearings
Radiator type	Crossflow
Coolant fan	Electrically activated

Torque specifications	ft-lb	m-kg
Water outlet-to-thermostat housing bolts	6	0.8
Fan frame mounting bolts	7	1.0
Water pump mounting bolts	6	0.8
Recovery bottle mounting bolts	27 in-lb	0.3
Radiator mounting bolts	7	1.0
Engine brace-to-radiator support bolts	11	1.5
A/C muffler and hose assembly mounting bolts	24	3.3
A/C compressor mounting bolts (L4)	37	5.1
A/C compressor mounting bolts (V6)	25	3.4

1 Cooling system – general information

1   The engine cooling system is of the pressurized type with pump and fan assistance. It comprises a radiator, flow and return water hoses, water pump, thermostat and vehicle interior heater.
2   The system is pressurized by means of a spring-loaded radiator filler cap which prevents premature boiling by increasing the boiling point of the coolant. If the coolant temperature goes above this increased boiling point, the extra pressure in the system forces the radiator cap internal spring-loaded valve off its seat and exposes the overflow pipe down which displaced coolant escapes.
3   It is important to check that the radiator cap is in good condition and that the spring behind the sealing washer has not weakened or corroded. Most service stations have a machine for testing that the cap operates at the specified pressure.
4   The coolant recovery system consists of a plastic reservoir into which the overflow coolant from the radiator flows when the engine is hot. When the engine cools and the coolant contracts, coolant is drawn back into the radiator from the reservoir and thus maintains the system at full capacity.
5   The coolant level should be kept between the 'Add' and 'Full' marks on the recovery bottle. These marks are about 2 quarts apart.
6   In the L4 engine, coolant is delivered by the water pump to the water jacket chamber adjacent to the number 1 cylinder. From there it is directed through the block, around the cylinders and into the cylinder head, where it cools the valve seats. The coolant then exits at the rear of the head into the thermostat housing.
7   When the thermostat is closed, coolant is re-directed through a passage in the cylinder head and into the intake manifold, the heater core and back into the water pump. At normal temperature the thermostat is open and coolant is directed through the thermostat to the radiator.
8   The V6 engine, because of its transverse mounting, uses a parallel coolant flow system. The water pump delivers coolant to the front of the block, from where it is directed simultaneously down the block and up into the cylinder heads. It then exits through a crossover in the rear of the intake manifold.
9   The radiator is of the crossflow type. Hot engine coolant enters the radiator at the top left hand side, is cooled by the inrush of cold air through the core (this is created by the fan and ram-effect of air, resulting from forward motion of the vehicle) and returns to the engine via the outlet at the right-hand side.
10   The fan is driven by an electric motor which is attached to the radiator support. It is activated by one (two on A/C equipped cars) coolant temperature switch. **CAUTION: This fan can be activated even when the engine is off, so take great care not to reach between the fan blades when the engine is hot.**
11   **Note:** *If the radiator cap has to be removed when the engine is hot, rotate the cap slowly counter-clockwise to the detent and allow the residual pressure to escape. Do not press the cap down until any hissing has stopped and take extreme care that the hands are not scalded.*

2 Antifreeze and inhibiting solutions

1   It is recommended that the cooling system be filled with a water/ethylene glycol based antifreeze solution which will give protection down to at least − 20°F at all times. This provides protection against corrosion and increases the coolant boiling point. When handling antifreeze, take care that it is not spilled on the vehicle paintwork, since it will invariably cause damage if not removed immediately.
2   The cooling system should be drained, flushed and refilled at least every alternate Fall. The use of antifreeze solutions for periods of longer than two years is likely to cause damage and encourage the formation of rust and scale due to the corrosion inhibitors gradually losing their efficiency.
3   Before adding antifreeze to the system, check all hose connections and check the tightness of the cylinder head bolts as such solutions are searching.
4   The exact mixture of antifreeze to water which you should use depends upon the relative weather conditions. The mixture should contain at least 50 percent antifreeze, offering protection to -34°F. Under no circumstances should the mixture contain more than 70 percent antifreeze.

3 Water pump drivebelts – adjustment and replacement

1   The water pump is driven by the same belts that drive the generator and power steering pump (when equipped), and is also connected to the A/C compressor belt. See Chapter 1, for applicable illustrations. To adjust or replace any of these belts see the procedure described under the appropriate accessory.

4 Water pump – testing

1   A failure in the water pump can cause serious engine damage due to overheating. The pump will not be able to circulate cooled water through the engine.
2   There are three ways to check the operation of the water pump while it is still installed on the engine. If the pump is suspect, it should be replaced with a new or factory rebuilt unit.
3   With the engine warmed up to normal operating temperature, squeeze the upper radiator hose. If the water pump is working properly, a pressure surge should be felt as the hose is released.
4   Water pumps are equipped with weep or vent holes. If a failure occurs to the bladder of the pump, small amounts of water will leak from these weep holes. In most cases it will be necessary to use a flashlight from under the car to see evidence from this point in the pump body.
5   If the water pump shaft bearings fail there may be a squealing sound at the front of the engine while it is running. Shaft wear can be felt if the water pump pulley is forced up and down. Do not mistake drivebelt slippage, which also causes a squealing sound, for water pump failure.

5 Water pump – removal and installation

Note: *It is not economical or practical to overhaul a water pump. If failure occurs, a new or rebuilt unit should be purchased to replace the faulty water pump.*
1   Disconnect the negative battery cable.
2   Drain the radiator, referring to Chapter 1 if necessary.
3   Remove the generator drivebelt as described in Chapter 10.
4   Remove the power steering drivebelt, if equipped, as described in Chapter 11.
5   Remove the A/C compressor drivebelt, if equipped, as described in Section 17.
6   Disconnect the coolant hoses from the water pump.
7   Remove the water pump mounting bolts and lift out the pump. Note: On L4 engines equipped with air conditioning, it may be necessary to remove the A/C compressor from its mounts in order to gain enough clearance to remove the water pump. Refer to Section 19.
8   If installing a new or rebuilt pump, transfer the pulley from the old unit to the new one.
9   Be sure the sealing surfaces are clean of any foreign material. Then place a $\frac{1}{8}$ in bead of gasket sealant on the pump sealing surface. While the sealant is still wet, install the pump and torque the mounting bolts to specs.
10   The remainder of the installation is the reverse of the removal procedure.
11   Adjust all drivebelts to the proper tension (see Chapter 1).
12   Connect the negative battery cable and fill the radiator with a mixture of ethylene glycol antifreeze and water in a 50/50 mixture. Start the engine and allow to idle until the upper radiator hose gets hot. Check for leaks. With the engine hot, fill with more coolant mixture until the level is at the bottom of the filler neck. Install radiator cap and check coolant level periodically over the next few miles of driving.

6 Thermostat – removal and installation

1   The thermostat is basically a restriction valve which is actuated by a thermostatic element. It is mounted inside a housing on the engine and is designed to open and close at predetermined temperatures to allow coolant to warm up or cool the engine.
2   To remove the thermostat for replacement or testing, begin by disconnecting the negative battery cable.

3   Open the coolant drain valve on the lower right side of the radiator and drain the coolant into a suitable container.

4   If the car is equipped with cruise control, remove the vacuum modulator mounting bracket from the thermostat housing.

5   Remove the bolts that secure the water outlet to the thermostat housing (photo).

6   The thermostat will now be visible and can be removed from the engine (photo). Note how the thermostat sits in the recess, as it must be replaced in this same position.

7   Before installation, use a gasket scraper or putty knife to carefully remove all traces of the old gasket on the thermostat housing and the water outlet cover (photo). Do not allow the gasket particles to drop down into the water passage.

8   Place a $\frac{1}{8}$ in bead of RTV or equivalent sealer around the sealing surface on the thermostat housing and place the thermostat into its recess.

9   Immediately place the water outlet and a new gasket into position and torque-tighten the attaching bolts.

10   Where applicable, install the vacuum modulator bracket onto the thermostat housing.

11   Connect the negative battery cable and fill the radiator with the proper amount of antifreeze and water, as described in Chapter 1.

12   With the radiator cap removed, start the engine and run it until the upper radiator hose becomes hot. When this hose is hot, the thermostat should be in the open position. At this point, add more coolant if necessary to reach the top of the filler neck.

13   Install the radiator cap, making sure the arrows are aligned with the overflow hose.

6.5 Removing the water outlet from the thermostat housing (all)

7   Thermostat – testing

1   The only way to test the operation of the thermostat is with the unit removed from the engine. In most cases if the thermostat is suspect it is more economical to merely buy a replacement thermostat as they are not very costly.

2   To test, first remove the thermostat as described in Section 6.

3   Inspect the thermostat for excessive corrosion or damage. Replace the thermostat with a new one if either of these conditions is found.

4   Place the thermostat in hot water 25 degrees above the temperature stamped on the thermostat. The water temperature should be approximately 220. When submerged in this water (which should be agitated thoroughly), the valve should be fully open.

5   Now remove the thermostat using a piece of bent wire and place it in water which is 10 degrees below the temperature on the thermostat, or about 185 degrees. At this temperature the thermostat valve should close fully.

6   Reinstall the thermostat if it checks out OK, if not purchase a new thermostat of the same temperature rating.

6.6 Removing the thermostat from the thermostat housing

8   Recovery bottle – removal and installation

1   Remove the bottle's mounting bolts and lift the bottle free from the body.

2   Disconnect the rubber hose from the bottle. If the bottle still holds fluid, immediately plug the outlet hole with your finger so the bottle can be lifted from the engine compartment without spilling coolant on the car's exterior. Then drain the coolant from the bottle.

3   When installing, place the empty bottle into position and install the mounting bolts, torquing them to specs.

4   Attach the coolant hose to the bottle.

5   Fill the botle to the appropriate mark with coolant solution.

9   Fan – removal and installation

1   Disconnect the negative battery cable.

2   Unplug the forward wiring harness (photo) from the fan motor and remove the harness from the fan frame.

3   Remove the bolts that secure the fan frame to the radiator support and remove the fan (photo).

4   To install, place the fan in position, making sure the lower leg of the frame engages the mounting grommet in the radiator support.

5   Install the fan mounting bolts and torque to specs.

6.7 Use a scraper to clean the thermostat sealing surface of all gasket material

9.2 Disconnecting the fan wiring harness

9.3 Removing the fan from the engine compartment

10.3 Removing the front engine brace

11.1 Coolant temperature switch (L4)

6   Attach the forward lamp wiring harness to the fan frame and plug the connector into the fan.
7   Reconnect the negative battery cable.

10 Radiator – removal and installation

1   Disconnect the negative battery cable.
2   Open the drain valve on the lower right side of the radiator and drain the coolant into a suitable container.
3   Remove the pivoting engine mount brace that attaches to the radiator support (photo).
4   Remove the fan as described in Section 9.
5   Mark the position of the hood latch on the radiator support with a sharp scribe or pencil and remove the hood latch.
6   Remove the coolant recovery tank hose from the radiator neck.
7   Disconnect the upper and lower coolant hoses from the radiator.
8   Disconnect the transmission oil cooler lines from the radiator. Immediately plug the lines so fluid does not leak from them.
9   Remove the radiator mounting bolts and clamps.
10 Lift the radiator out of the engine compartment. Note: If the car is equipped with air conditioning it may be necessary to raise the left-hand side of the radiator first to clear the radiator neck from the A/C compressor. If coolant drips on any body paint, immediately wash it off with water as the anti-freeze solution can damage the finish.

11 With the radiator removed, it can be inspected for leaks or damage. If in need of repairs, have a professional radiator shop or dealer perform the work as special welding techniques are required.
12 Bugs and dirt can be cleaned from the radiator by using compressed air and a soft brush. Do not bend the cooling fins as this is done.
13 To install the radiator, place it in position so the bottom of the radiator is in the lower mounting pads and install the mounting clamp and bolts. Torque the bolts to specs.
14 The remainder of the installation procedure is the reverse of the removal procedure.
15 After installation, fill the cooling system as described in Chapter 1.
16 Start the engine and check for leaks. Allow the engine to reach normal operating temperature (upper radiator hose hot) and add coolant until the level reaches the bottom of the filler neck.

11 Coolant temperature switch – fault diagnosis and replacement

1   The coolant temperature indicator system is comprised of a lamp mounted on the instrument panel and a coolant temperature switch or sender, located at the left rear of the cylinder head on L4 engines (photo), and at the rear of the right head on V6 engines. If a temperature gauge is used on the instrument cluster, the temperature switch is replaced by a transducer.

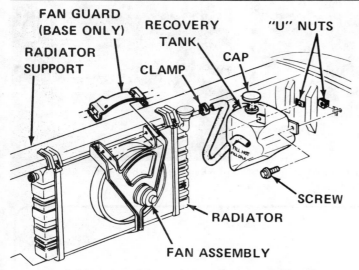

Fig. 3.1 Location of the coolant recovery bottle (Sec 8)

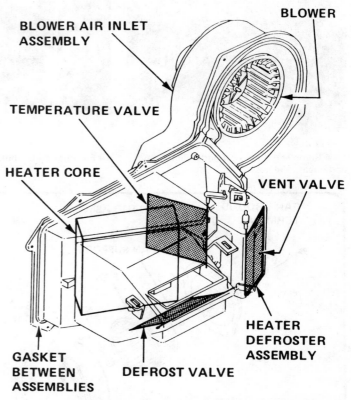

Fig. 3.2 Components of the heater/vent module (Sec 12)

2   In the event of an unusual indication or a fault developing, check the coolant level in the system and then ensure that the connecting wiring between the gauge and the sender unit is secure.
3   When the ignition switch is turned on and the starter motor is turning, the indicator lamp should be illuminated (overheated engine indication). If the lamp is not on, the bulb may be burned out, the ignition switch may be faulty or the circuit may be open.
4   As soon as the engine starts, the lamp should go out and remain so unless the engine overheats. Failure of the lamp to go out may be due to the wiring being grounded between the lamp and the sender unit, a defective temperature sender unit or a faulty ignition switch.
5   If the sender unit is to be replaced, it is simply unscrewed from the cylinder head and a replacement installed. There will be some coolant spillage, so check the level after the replacement has been installed.

12 Heating system – general information

1   The main components of the heater/vent assembly are the blower/air inlet assembly, the heat/defroster assembly (which contains the heater core), temperature valve, defroster valve/vent valve, and the air ducts which deliver the air to the various outlet locations.
2   Outside air is drawn into the system through vent openings in the shroud grill panel, located between the rear of the hood and the windshield. From there it is directed through the blower (motor/fan assembly) and into the heat/defroster assembly (Fig. 3.2). The various valves in this assembly determine how much air will be directed past the heater core, which is heated by the engine coolant, and where it will be delivered in the vehicle.
3   The temperature valve controls the temperature of the heated air and the mix of heated and ambiant air by regulating the amount of air passing through the heater core.

13 Heater core (without air-conditioning) – removal and installation

1   Open the drain valve on the lower right side of the radiator and drain the coolant into a suitable container. Disconnect the negative battery cable.
2   Remove the heater inlet and outlet hoses.
3   Remove the radio noise suppression strap from the heater core cover.
4   Remove the heater core cover mounting screws, and remove the cover from within the engine compartment.
5   Remove the heater core.
6   If the heater core is in need of repair, have a professional radiator shop or dealer perform the work.
7   Installation is the reverse of the removal procedure. Be sure to fill the radiator with coolant to the proper level and connect the battery cable.

14 Heater core (with air conditioning) – removal and installation

1   Open the drain valve on the lower right side of the radiator and drain the coolant into a suitable container. Disconnect the negative battery cable.
2   Working in the engine compartment, remove the heater inlet and outlet hoses from the heater core.
3   Remove the noise absorbing panel from under the dash, if equipped.
4   Remove the heater outlet duct (photo).
5   Remove the heater core cover (photo).
6   Remove the heater core (photo).
7   If the heater core is in need of repair, have a professional radiator shop or dealer perform the work.
8   Installation is the reverse of the removal procedure. Be sure to refill the radiator with coolant to the proper level, and connect the battery cable.

15 Blower motor – removal and installation

1   Disconnect the negative battery cable.
2   Unplug the electrical connections from the blower motor.
3   Remove the blower motor mounting screws and remove the motor from the blower case.
4   Installation is the reverse of the removal procedure.

16 Air conditioning system – general information

1   The X-Body cars use a cycling clutch orifice tube (C.C.O.T) type of refrigeration system. With this system the proper temperature is maintained by cycling the compressor on and off, and by maintaining a mix of cooled, ambient and heated air, using the same blower and outlet duct system that the heating system uses.
2   The on and off operation of the compressor is controlled by a

14.4 Removing the heater outlet duct from underneath the dash

14.5 Removing the heater core cover

14.6 Removing the heater core

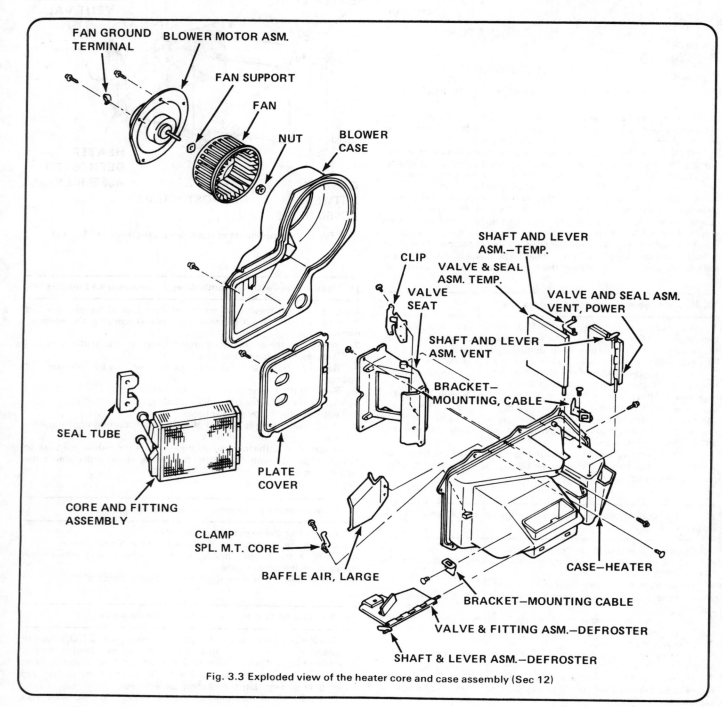

FAN GROUND TERMINAL

BLOWER MOTOR ASM.

FAN SUPPORT

FAN

NUT

BLOWER CASE

CLIP

VALVE SEAT

VALVE & SEAL ASM. TEMP.

SHAFT AND LEVER ASM.—TEMP.

VALVE AND SEAL ASM. VENT, POWER

SHAFT AND LEVER ASM. VENT

BRACKET— MOUNTING, CABLE

SEAL TUBE

CORE AND FITTING ASSEMBLY

PLATE COVER

CLAMP SPL. M.T. CORE

BAFFLE AIR, LARGE

CASE—HEATER

BRACKET—MOUNTING CABLE

VALVE & FITTING ASM.—DEFROSTER

SHAFT & LEVER ASM.—DEFROSTER

Fig. 3.3 Exploded view of the heater core and case assembly (Sec 12)

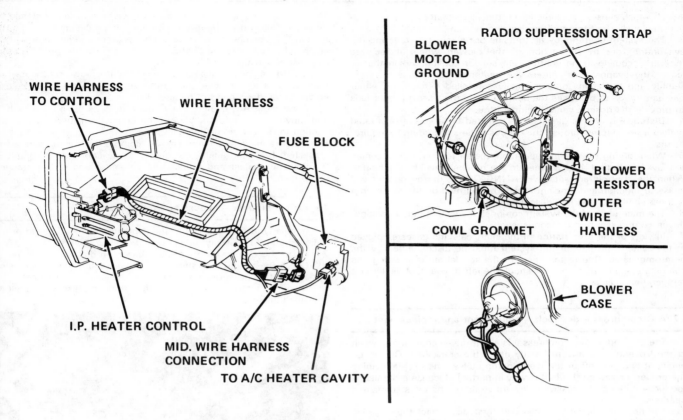

Fig. 3.4 Routing of the heater control wiring harness (Sec 12)

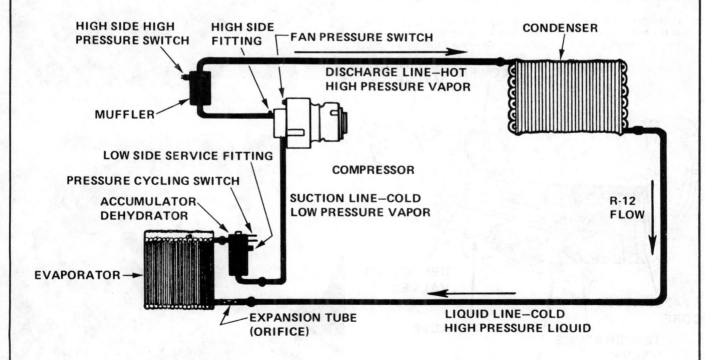

Fig. 3.5 Diagram of the major components of the air conditioning system and direction of the refrigerant flow (Sec 16)

switch which senses pressures inside the accumulator, as opposed to the previously used temperature-sensing system.

3   The system operates by air (outside or recirculated) entering the evaporator core by the action of the blower, where it receives maximum cooling if the controls are set for cooling. When the air leaves the evaporator, it enters the heater/air conditioner duct assembly and by means of a manually controlled deflector, it either passes through or bypasses the heater core in the correct proportions to provide the desired vehicle temperature.

4   Distribution of this air is then regulated by a vacuum-actuated deflector and passes through the various outlets according to requirements.

5   When during the cooling operation, the air temperature is cooled too low for comfort, it is warmed to the required level by the heater. When the controls are set to 'HEATING ONLY', the evaporator will cease to function and ambient air will be warmed by the heater in a manner similar to that just described.

6   The main units of the system comprise the evaporator, an engine-driven compressor and the condenser.

7   In view of the toxic nature of the chemicals and gases employed in the system, no part of the system must be disconnected by the home mechanic. Due to the need for the specialized evacuating and charging equipment, such work should be left to your GM dealer or a refrigeration specialist.

17 A/C compressor drivebelt – adjustment and replacement

1   The air conditioning compressor is a belt-driven component which in the V6 engine is driven directly off of the crankshaft. On the L4 engine it is driven off of the water pump pulley (photo). Maintaining the proper tension on this belt is very important, because if the belt is too loose it can put excessive sideward strain on the units shafts and bearings.

2   To check the tension of this belt, first disconnect the negative battery cable then find the longest stretch of the belt and, gripping it in the center of this stretch, move the belt back and forth to gauge its slack. The distance that the belt can be moved back-and-forth should be about $\frac{1}{2}$-in (13 mm). If the slack allows the belt to move more than this distance, the belt should be adjusted using the following procedure.

3   Loosen the compressor's adjusting bolts and mounting bolts and adjust the belt by moving the compressor away from the engine. Tighten the adjusting and mounting bolts and recheck the adjustment.

4   If the A/C compressor drivebelt is frayed or cracked it should be replaced. This is done by using the following procedure.

5   On L4 engines, first remove the power steering drivebelt, if equipped, as described in Chapter 11. Then remove the generator belt as described in Chapter 5.

6   On V6 engines, first remove the generator belt as described in Chapter 5. Then remove the power steering pump drive belt, if equipped, as described in Chapter 11.

7   Loosen the A/C compressor's adjusting bolts as in paragraph 3, and move the compressor toward the engine until the belt is loose enough to remove from the pulleys.

8   Install a new belt over the A/C compressor, water pump and crankshaft (V6), and adjust and tighten as described in paragraph 3.

9   Reinstall, adjust and tighten the generator and power steering pump belts.

18 Air conditioner – checks and maintenance

1   Regularly inspect the fins of the condenser (located ahead of the radiator) and if necessary, brush away leaves and bugs.

2   Clean the evaporator drain tubes free from dirt.

3   Check the condition of the system hoses and if there is any sign of deterioration or hardening, have them replaced by your dealer.

4   At similar intervals, check and adjust the compressor drivebelt as described in Section 17.

17.1 The L4 A/C compressor is driven off the water pump pulley

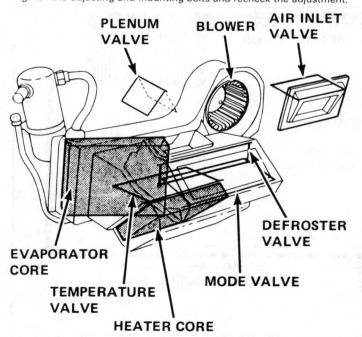

PLENUM VALVE   BLOWER   AIR INLET VALVE

DEFROSTER VALVE

EVAPORATOR CORE

MODE VALVE

TEMPERATURE VALVE

HEATER CORE

Fig. 3.6 Components of the heater/A/C module (Sec 16)

19.3a Removing the electrical connections from the A/C compressor (shown removed from its bracket for accessibility)

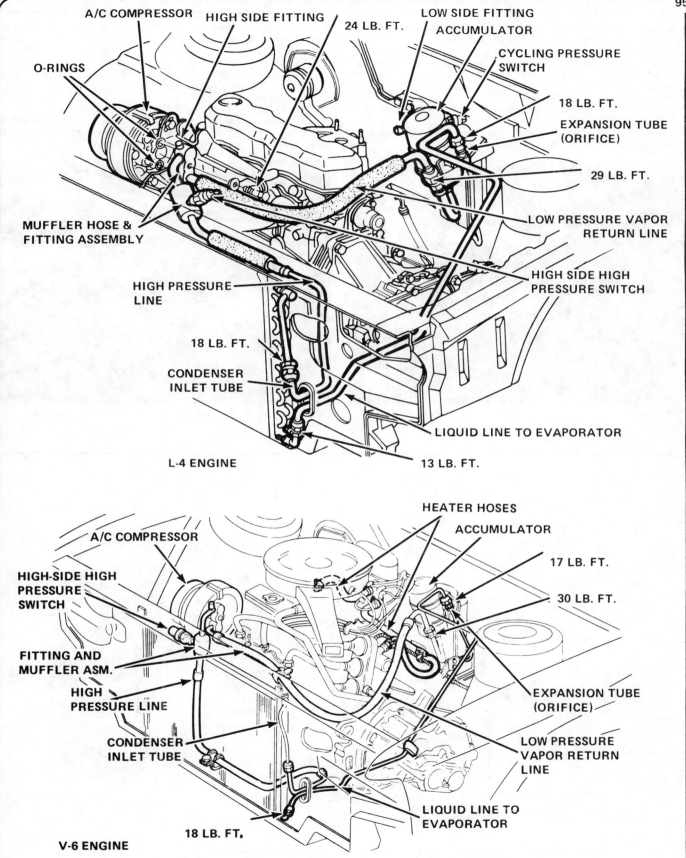

Fig. 3.7 Routing of the air conditioning system hoses and tubes (Sec 16)

19 A/C compressor – removal and installation

1   Prior to disconnecting any A/C lines anywhere in the system the car should be taken to a GM dealer or other qualified automotive air conditioning repair shop to have the system discharged.
2   Disconnect the negative battery cable.
3   Remove all electrical and vacuum connections from the A/C compressor (photos).
4   Remove the muffler fitting and hose assembly from the rear head of the compressor.

5   Loosen the compressor's adjusting bolts and nut (photo), pivot the compressor to loosen the drivebelt and remove the belt from the compressor pulley.
6   Remove the upper A/C adjustment bolt and spacer.
7   Remove the lower A/C bracket bolt and lower pivot bolt.
8   Remove the lower rear compressor adjustment nut.
9   Remove the compressor.
10   Installation is the reverse of the removal procedure.
11   Once the compressor and all A/C lines have been securely connected again, the car must once again be taken to a GM dealer or other qualified shop to have the system charged.

19.3b Disconnecting the vacuum connections from the A/C compressor

19.5 Loosening the A/C compressor mounting bolts and nut

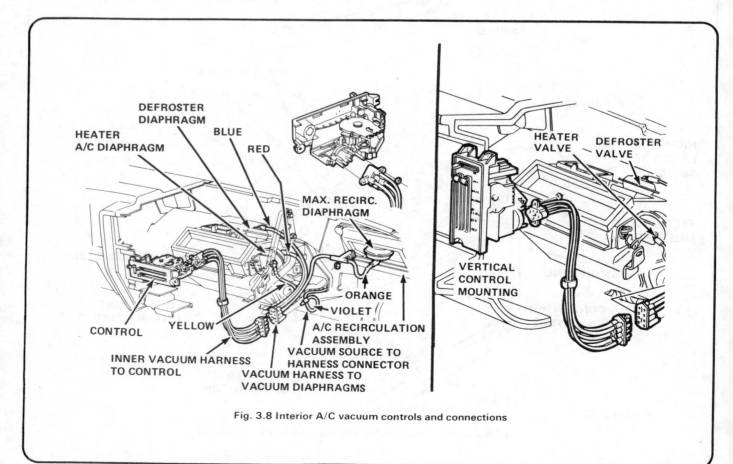

Fig. 3.8 Interior A/C vacuum controls and connections

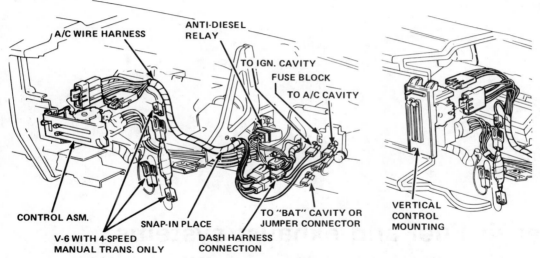

Fig. 3.9 Interior A/C electrical connections

A/C WIRE HARNESS
ANTI-DIESEL RELAY
TO IGN. CAVITY
FUSE BLOCK
TO A/C CAVITY
CONTROL ASM.
V-6 WITH 4-SPEED MANUAL TRANS. ONLY
SNAP-IN PLACE
DASH HARNESS CONNECTION
TO "BAT" CAVITY OR JUMPER CONNECTOR
VERTICAL CONTROL MOUNTING

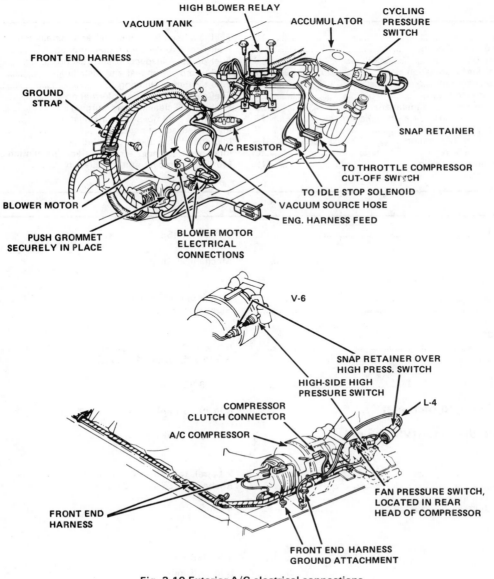

HIGH BLOWER RELAY
VACUUM TANK
ACCUMULATOR
CYCLING PRESSURE SWITCH
FRONT END HARNESS
GROUND STRAP
SNAP RETAINER
A/C RESISTOR
BLOWER MOTOR
TO THROTTLE COMPRESSOR CUT-OFF SWITCH
TO IDLE STOP SOLENOID
VACUUM SOURCE HOSE
ENG. HARNESS FEED
PUSH GROMMET SECURELY IN PLACE
BLOWER MOTOR ELECTRICAL CONNECTIONS

V-6
SNAP RETAINER OVER HIGH PRESS. SWITCH
HIGH-SIDE HIGH PRESSURE SWITCH
L-4
COMPRESSOR CLUTCH CONNECTOR
A/C COMPRESSOR
FAN PRESSURE SWITCH, LOCATED IN REAR HEAD OF COMPRESSOR
FRONT END HARNESS
FRONT END HARNESS GROUND ATTACHMENT

Fig. 3.10 Exterior A/C electrical connections

Chapter 4 Fuel and exhaust systems

Refer to Chapter 13 for specifications and information related to 1981 through 1984 models

Contents

Specifications

Fuel tank capacity .... 14 gallons (53 liters)

Fuel pump type .... Mechanical, diaphragm

Fuel pump location
  L4 engine .... Center rear of engine
  V6 engine .... Right front of engine

Fuel pump pressure
  L4 engine .... 6.5 to 8.0 psi (45 to 55 kPa)
  V6 engine .... 6.0 to 7.5 psi (41.4 to 51.7 kPa)

Fuel feed pipe diameter .... $\frac{3}{8}$ in (9.52 mm)

Fuel tank emission pipe diameter .... $\frac{5}{16}$ in (9.38 mm)

Vapor return pipe diameter (V6 engine) .... $\frac{1}{4}$ in (6.4 mm)

Carburetor
  Type .... 2-barrel, two stage down draft
  Models .... Rochester 2ES and E2ES
  Primary stage bore .... 35 mm
  Secondary stage bore .... 46 mm

Float adjustment
Carb number
17059614 .... $\frac{3}{16}$ in (5.5 mm)
17059615 .... $\frac{3}{16}$ in (5.5 mm)
17059616 .... $\frac{3}{16}$ in (5.5 mm)
17059617 .... $\frac{3}{16}$ in (5.5 mm)

17059650	$\frac{3}{16}$ in (5.5 mm)
17059651	$\frac{3}{16}$ in (5.5 mm)
17059652	$\frac{3}{16}$ in (5.5 mm)
17059653	$\frac{3}{16}$ in (5.5 mm)
17059714	$\frac{11}{16}$ in (17.8 mm)
17059715	$\frac{11}{16}$ in (17.8 mm)
17059716	$\frac{11}{16}$ in (17.8 mm)
17059717	$\frac{11}{16}$ in (17.8 mm)
17059760	$\frac{1}{8}$ in (3.4 mm)
17059762	$\frac{1}{8}$ in (3.4 mm)
17059763	$\frac{1}{8}$ in (3.4 mm)
17059618	$\frac{3}{16}$ in (5.5 mm)
17059619	$\frac{3}{16}$ in (5.5 mm)
17059620	$\frac{3}{16}$ in (5.5 mm)
17059621	$\frac{3}{16}$ in (5.5 mm)

Pump adjustment
Carb number

17059614	$\frac{1}{2}$ in (12.44 mm)
17059615	$\frac{5}{32}$ in (3.8 mm)
17059616	$\frac{1}{2}$ in (12.44 mm)
17059617	$\frac{5}{32}$ in (3.8 mm)
17059650	$\frac{3}{32}$ in (2.5 mm)
17059651	$\frac{3}{32}$ in (2.5 mm)
17059652	$\frac{3}{32}$ in (2.5 mm)
17059653	$\frac{3}{32}$ in (2.5 mm)
17059714	$\frac{5}{32}$ in (3.8 mm)
17059715	$\frac{3}{32}$ in (2.45 mm)
17059716	$\frac{5}{32}$ in (3.8 mm)
17059717	$\frac{3}{32}$ in (2.45 mm)
17059760	$\frac{5}{64}$ in (2.2 mm)
17059762	$\frac{5}{64}$ in (2.2 mm)
17059763	$\frac{5}{64}$ in (2.2 mm)
17059618	$\frac{1}{2}$ in (12.44 mm)
17059619	$\frac{5}{32}$ in (3.8 mm)
17069620	$\frac{1}{2}$ in (12.44 mm)
17059621	$\frac{5}{32}$ in (3.8 mm)

Fast idle adjustment (bench setting) .... 3 turns out after cam contact

Choke coil lever adjustment .... .085 in (2.16 mm)

Air valve rod adjustment .... .025 in (.6 mm)

Fast idle adjustment

Carb number	rpm
17059614, 618	2600
17059615	2600
17059616, 620	2000
17059617	1900
17059650	2000
17059651	1900
17059652	2600
17059653	2200
17059714	2600
17059715	2200
17059716	2000
17059717	2000
17059760	2000
17059762	2600
17059763	2600
17059619	See Vehicle Emissions Control Label
17059621	See Vehicle Emissions Control Label

Idle speed adjustment (with air conditioning)

Carb number	rpm sol	curb
17059616	650D	900D
17059617	1000N	1300N
17059716	650D	850D
17059717	1000N	1200N
17059652	700D	850D
17059653	750N	1200N
17059762	700D	800D
17059763	750N	NA
17059620	650D	900D
17059621	1000N	1300N

Idle speed adjustment (without air conditioning)

Carb number	rpm sol	curb
17059614	650D	500D
17059615	1000N	500N
17059714	650D	500D
17059715	1000N	500N
17059650	700N	NA
17059651	750N	1200N
17059760	700D	NA
17059763	750N	NA
17059618	650D	500D
17059619	1000N	500N

Unloader adjustment

Carb number	
17059614	36°
17059615	36°
17059616	36°
17059617	36°
17059650	30°
17059651	30°
17059652	30°
17059653	30°
17059714	32°
17059715	32°
17059716	32°
17059717	32°
17059760	35°
17059762	35°
17059763	35°
17059618	36°
17059619	36°
17059620	36°
17059621	36°

Primary vacuum break adjustment (L4 engine)

Carb number	
17059614	17°
17059615	19°
17059616	17°
17059617	19°
17059714	23°
17059715	25°
17059716	23°
17059717	25°
17059618	17°
17059619	19°
17059620	17°
17059621	19°

Primary vacuum break adjustment (V6 engine)

Carb number	
17059650	30°
17059651	22°
17059652	30°
17059653	22°
17059760	20°
17059762	20°
17059763	20°

Secondary vacuum break adjustment (V6 engine)
Carb number

17059650	38°
17059651	23°
17059652	38°
17059653	23°
17059760	33°
17059762	33°
17059763	33°

Choke rod adjustment (L4 engine) 18°

Choke rod adjustment (V6 engine)
Carb number

17059650	27°
17059651	27°
17059652	27°
17059653	27°
17059760	17.5°
17059762	17.5°
17059763	17.5°

Torque specifications

	ft-lb	m-kg
Carburetor mounting nuts	60 to 96 in-lb	.69 to 1.10
Fuel inlet nut	18	2.48

1 Fuel system – general information

1 The X-Bodies use a fuel system of a conventional design. Simply put, fuel is pumped from the fuel tank, through the fuel pump and fuel filter into the carburetor, where it is mixed with air for combustion. The fuel system, as well as the exhaust system, is interrelated with and works in conjunction with the emissions control systems covered in Chapter 6. Thus, some elements that relate directly to the fuel system and carburetor functions are covered in that Chapter.

2 The X-Bodies use two basic carburetor models: the Rochester 2SE and E2SE. Both are 2-barrel, 2-stage down draft designs. All models use aluminum die castings for the air horn, float bowl, throttle body and choke housing. The exceptions are models used on the L4 engine, which have a zinc die-cast choke housing to reduce heat transfer for good cold engine operation. The E2SE model carb incorporates several design features used in conjunction with the car's C-4 computer control system, described in Chapter 6. For location of the various carburetor components, refer to the L4 and V6 carburetor component location figures included in this Chapter.

3 The idle mixture needle in all carb models is recessed in the throttle body and sealed with a hardened steel plug. The idle mixture setting is pre-set at the factory and should not be altered. If mixture control adjustments are improperly set, the C-4 system will not maintain precise control of carburetor air/fuel mixtures. Proper adjustment must be done while using special emission sensing equipment, making it impractical for the home mechanic. To have the carb mixture settings checked or readjusted, take your car to a GM dealer or other qualified mechanic with the proper equipment.

4 The choke system on all L4 engine carb models uses a single vacuum break unit that is mounted on the idle speed solenoid bracket. A dual vacuum break system is used on V6 engine carb models, with the secondary vacuum break unit mounted on a bracket located on the secondary side of the carburetor. On all models, an electrically-heated thermostatic choke coil is mounted in the choke housing.

5 Alphabetical code letters are imprinted on the air horn, float bowl and throttle body to identify air and vacuum hose connections.

6 The carburetor model identification number is stamped vertically on the float bowl in a flat area adjacent to the vacuum tube, as shown in Fig. 4.7. Refer to this number when servicing the carburetor.

7 L4 engine carbs use a 1-in pleated paper fuel filter located in the float bowl behind the fuel inlet nut. V6 engine carbs use a 2-in filter. A clogged fuel filter will stop the flow of fuel and cause the engine to stop. This is usually preceded by hesitation and sluggish operation.

8 The X-Bodies use a conventional diaphragm-type, mechanical fuel pump. Pumps used on V6 engine have a metering outlet for a fuel return system. Any vapor that forms is returned to the fuel tank along with hot fuel through a separate line. This system greatly reduces the

chance of vapor lock by keeping fresh fuel constantly recirculating through the pump.

9 The fuel tank is located under the body floor pan, forward of the rear axle. The tank has an emission venting line going to the charcoal canister and a fuel feed line leading to the fuel pump. Tanks of V6 engine models also have a fuel return line from the fuel pump. A woven plastic filter is located on the lower end of the fuel pickup pipe inside the tank. This filter is self-cleaning and normally requires no maintenance, unless there is an abnormal amount of sediment and water in the tank.

10 Prior to any operation in which a fuel line will be disconnected, remove the negative terminal from the battery to eliminate the possibility of sparks occurring while open fuel is present.

2 Idle speed adjustments

1 As idle speed adjustments are an integral part of the tune-up operation, information on these procedures is described in Chapter 1, Section 11.

3 Choke – inspection and cleaning

1 As inspection of the choke is included in the car's routine maintenance schedule, this information is covered in Chapter 1, Section 15.

4 Idle speed solenoid – checking

1 As checking of the carburetor idle speed solenoid is included in the car's routine maintenance schedule, this procedure is described in Chapter 1, Section 17.

5 Idle speed solenoid – removal and installation

1 Remove the air cleaner.

2 Disconnect the idle speed solenoid's electrical connector.

3 Bend back the retaining tabs on the lock washer and remove the solenoid's retaining nut.

4 Install by reversing the removal procedure.

5 Check the idle speed adjustment and adjust if necessary as described in Chapter 1, Section 11.

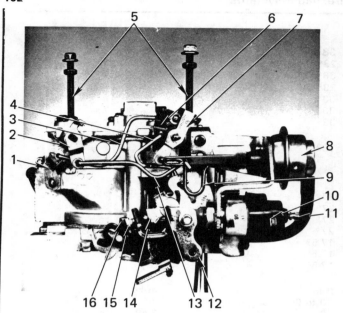

Fig. 4.1 Component locations on a typical L4 carburetor
(left side view, also see Figs. 4.2 - 4.4)

1	Intermediate choke lever	10	Idle speed solenoid
2	Air valve lever	11	Idle speed solenoid
3	Intermediate choke rod		adjustment screw
4	Fast idle cam rod	12	Primary throttle valve
5	Air cleaner bolts	13	Air valve rod
6	Choke lever	14	Fast idle cam
7	Vacuum break lever	15	Fast idle adjustment
8	Vacuum break and air		screw
	valve control diaphragm	16	Slow idle adjustment
9	Vacuum break rod		screw

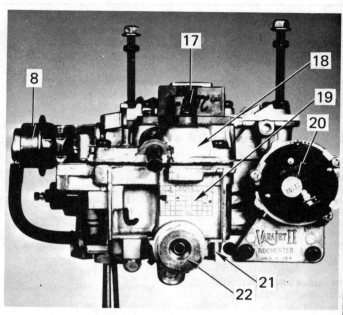

Fig. 4.2 Component locations on a typical L4 carburetor
(right side view, also see Figs. 4.1, 4.3, 4.4)

8	Vacuum break and air	19	Float bowl
	valve control diaphragm	20	Thermostatic choke
17	Mixture control		assembly
	solenoid	21	Throttle body
18	Air horn	22	Fuel inlet nut

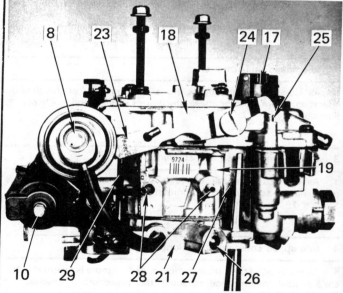

Fig. 4.3 Component locations on a typical L4 carburetor
(rear view, also see Figs. 4.1, 4.2, 4.4)

8	Vacuum break and air	24	Pump lever attaching
	valve control diaphragm		screw
10	Idle speed solenoid	25	Pump plunger stem
17	Mixture control solenoid	26	Idle mixture needle
18	Air horn		(sealed)
19	Float bowl	27	Carb identification
21	Throttle body		number
23	Pump lever	28	Vacuum line fittings
		29	Pump rod

Fig. 4.4 Component locations on a typical L4 carburetor
(top view, also see Figs. 4.1 - 4.3)

8	Vacuum break and air	30	Vent screen assembly
	valve control diaphragm	31	Choke valve
17	Mixture control	32	Secondary air valve
	solenoid	33	Vapor return tube

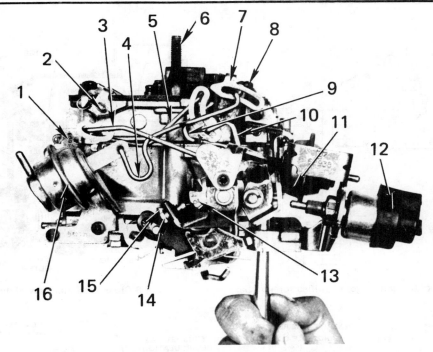

Fig. 4.5 Component locations on a typical V6 carburetor
(rear view, also see Fig. 4.6)

1 Intermediate choke lever
2 Air valve lever
3 Air valve rod
4 Secondary vacuum break rod
5 Intermediate choke rod
6 Air cleaner stud
7 Vacuum break lever
8 Choke lever
9 Fast idle cam rod
10 Primary vacuum break rod
11 Primary vacuum break unit (air valve dashpot)
12 Idle speed solenoid
13 Fast idle cam
14 Fast idle adjustment screw
15 Slow idle adjustment screw
16 Secondary vacuum break unit

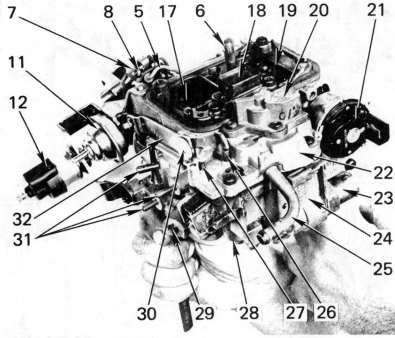

Fig. 4.6 Component locations on a typical V6 carburetor
(right side, front and top view, also see Fig. 4.5)

5 Intermediate choke rod
6 Air cleaner stud
7 Vacuum break lever
8 Choke lever
11 Primary vacuum break unit (air valve dashpot)
12 Idle speed solenoid
17 Choke lever
18 Vent screen assembly
19 Secondary air valve
20 Mixture control solenoid
21 Thermostatic choke assembly
22 Air horn
23 Fuel inlet nut
24 Float bowl
25 Vapor return tube
26 Pump plunger stem
27 Throttle position Sensor plunger stem
28 Throttle body
29 Idle mixture needle (sealed)
30 Pump lever attaching screw
31 Vacuum line fittings
32 Pump lever

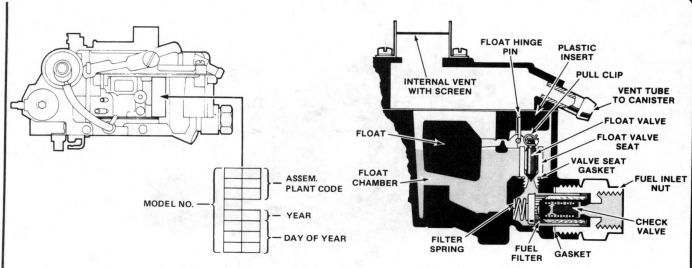

Fig. 4.7 Location of the carburetor identification number

Fig. 4.8 Cross sectional view of the float system

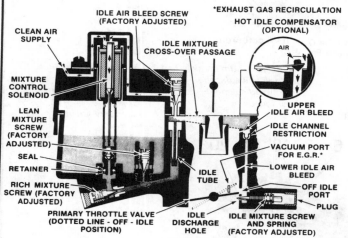

Fig. 4.9 Cross sectional view of the E2SE idle system

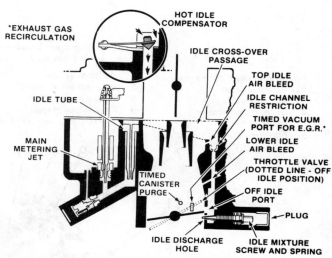

Fig. 4.10 Cross sectional view of the 2SE idle system

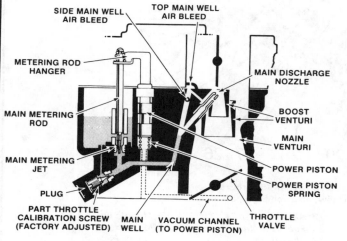

Fig. 4.11 Cross sectional view of the 2SE main metering system

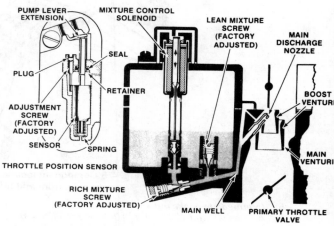

Fig. 4.12 Cross sectional view of the E2SE main metering system

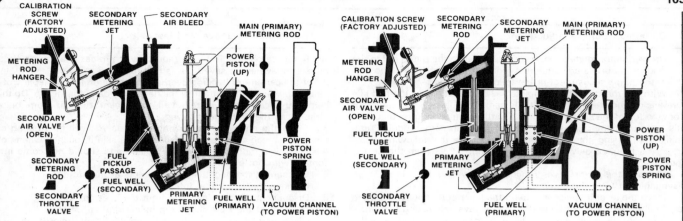

Fig. 4.13 Cross sectional view of the 2SE power system (L4)

Fig. 4.14 Cross sectional view of the 2SE power system (V6)

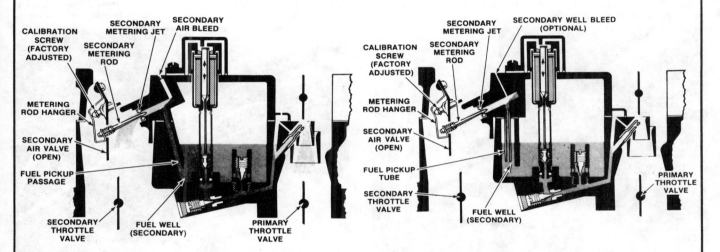

Fig. 4.15 Cross sectional view of the E2SE power system (L4)

Fig. 4.16 Cross sectional view of the E2SE power system (V6)

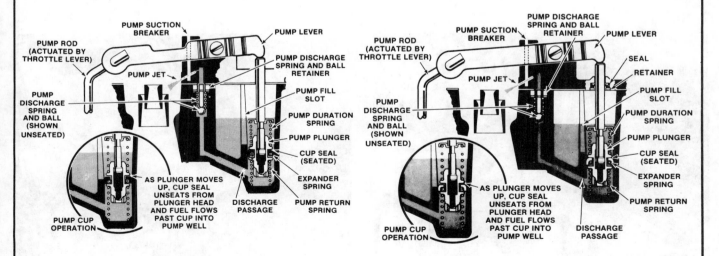

Fig. 4.17 Cross sectional view of the 2SE pump system

Fig. 4.18 Cross sectional view of the E2SE pump system

6 Carburetor pump – adjustment

1   On carburetor models that use a clip to retain the pump rod to the pump lever, no pump adjustment is required. On models with no clip, check the pump adjustment in the following manner.

2   With the throttle valve completely closed, make sure the fast idle screw is off the steps of the fast idle cam. Then, take a measurement from the top of the air horn to the top of the pump stem (photo). Check this measurement against the specs for your carb model. Pump adjustment, using the procedure described in the following paragraphs, is required only if this measurement differs from that in the specs.

3   Remove the pump lever retaining screw and the pump lever, disengaging it from the pump rod.

4   Place the lever in a vise and bend the lever at its thinest point the required amount. Do not bend it in a sideways or twisting motion.

5   Remount the pump lever on the air horn. Then open and close the throttle several times, checking the linkage for freedom of movement and checking the pump lever alignment.

6   Recheck the pump adjustment measurement as described in paragraph 1 and readjust as necessary.

7   When the proper adjustment has been obtained, engage the pump lever with the pump rod and secure it to the air horn once more with the pump lever attaching screw.

7 Carburetor – removal and installation

1   If the carburetor is to be rebuilt by a professional repair shop, much money can be saved if it is first removed at home.

2   If the carburetor is being overhauled, check on the availability of a rebuilt kit which will contain all the necessary parts for the job. Do this before the carburetor is removed to prevent the car from being disabled as the parts are received.

3   Allow the engine to completely cool, as you will be working on areas which can cause serious burns to the skin if touched when hot. Also, fuel will more than likely be spilled and should not come into contact with hot parts.

4   Disconnect the negative battery cable at the battery.

5   Remove the air cleaner (photo).

6   Disconnect the fuel inlet line from the inlet nut (photo).

7   Disconnect the PCV hose from its carb fitting (photo).

8   Disconnect all vacuum hoses from the carb (photo). As you disconnect them, label the hoses as to their position, so there will be no confusion during installation.

9   Disconnect all electrical leads and connectors (photo). Again, label them as they are removed to eliminate confusion during installation.

10 Disconnect the accelerator linkage from the carburetor. On LY models, both the accelerator cable and the automatic transaxle's T.V. cable are attached to the accelerator linkage bracket, but neither of

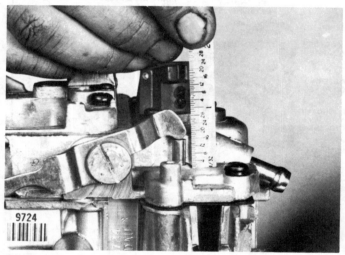

6.2 Checking pump adjustment

7.5 Note position of all hoses when removing the air cleaner

7.6 Disconnecting the fuel inlet line from the inlet nut (L4)

7.7 Disconnecting the PCV hose from its carb fitting (L4)

7.8 Disconnecting vacuum hoses from the carb

7.9 Disconnecting electrical leads from the carb

7.10 The accelerator linkage has the accelerator cable and T.V. cable attached to it, and unsnaps from the carb at the point indicated by arrow (L4)

7.11 Disconnecting vapor lines from the carb

7.13a Removing the carburetor (L4)

7.13b Removing the carburetor (V6)

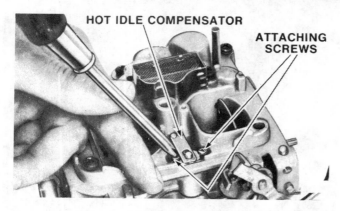

Fig. 4.19 Location of the idle compensator (Sec 8)

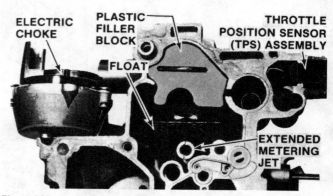

Fig. 4.20 Layout of the float bowl components. The TPS assembly is removed from the float bowl by pushing up from the bottom on the electrical connector (Sec 8)

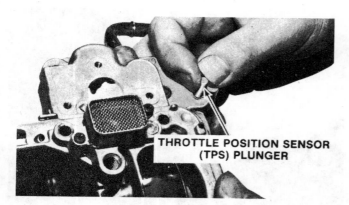

Fig. 4.21 The TPS plunger is removed from the air horn by pushing it out toward the bottom (Sec 8)

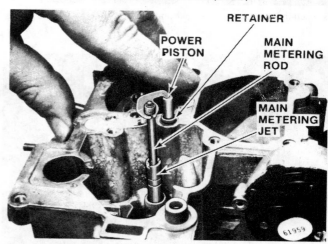

Fig. 4.22 The power piston and metering rod assembly (2SE) is removed from the float bowl by depressing the piston stem and allowing it to snap free. This may take several attempts. Do not use pliers. (Sec 8)

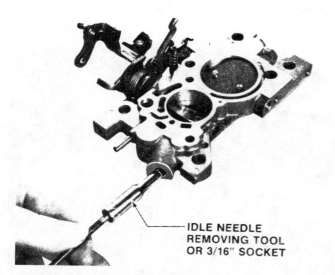

Fig. 4.23 Removing the idle mixture needle after breaking the sealing plug (Sec 8)

these have to be disconnected, as the entire linkage system unsnaps from the carburetor (photo).

11   Remove any other hoses or lines attached to the carb (photo).

12   Remove the 4 carb mounting nuts.

13   Lift off the carburetor (photos).

14   Remove the carburetor base gasket.

15   If the carburetor needs to be disassembled or overhauled, refer to Section 8.

16   Before installing the carburetor, check that the 4 mounting studs are in good shape and their threads are not damaged. Run the carb nuts over the studs to make sure they can be installed easily.

17   Installation is the reverse of the removal procedure.

8   Carburetor – disassembly

1   Prior to disassembling the carburetor, purchase a carburetor rebuild kit for your particular model. This kit will have all of the necessary replacement parts for the overhaul procedure.

2   It will be necessary to have a relatively large, clean workshop to lay out all of the parts as they are removed from the carb. Many of the parts are very small and thus can be lost if the work space is cluttered.

3   The steps involved with disassembling the carburetor are illustrated in the following step-by-step photo sequence to make the operation as easy as possible. Work slowly through the procedure and if at any point you feel the reassembly of a certain component may prove confusing, stop and make a rough sketch or apply identification marks. The time to think about reassembling the carburetor is when it is being taken apart. The carb disassembly photo sequence begins with photo 8.3/1.

8.3/1 Remove the gasket from around the top of the air horn

8.3/2 Remove the fuel inlet nut along with the fuel filter

8.3/3 Removing the pump lever attaching screw

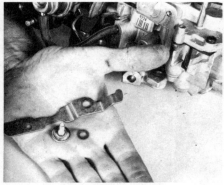
8.3/4 Disconnect the pump rod from the pump lever and remove the pump lever

8.3/5 Disconnect the vacuum break diaphragm hose from the throttle body

8.3/6 Remove the screws that secure the idle speed solenoid/vacuum break diaphragm bracket

8.3/7 Lift off the idle speed solenoid/vacuum break diaphragm assembly and disconnect the air valve rod from the outside vacuum break plunger

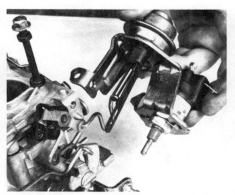
8.3/8 Disconnect the vacuum break rod from the inside vacuum break diaphragm plunger. Note: On V6 models disconnect the vacuum break and air valve rods from their respective levers. It is not necessary to disconnect these rods from the vacuum break plungers unless either the rods or vacuum break unit are being replaced

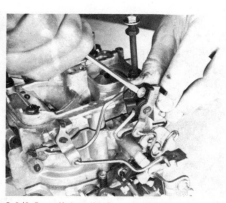
8.3/9 Pry off the clip that secures the intermediate choke rod to the choke lever and seperate the rod from the lever

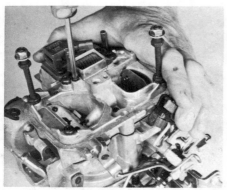

8.3/10 Remove the screws that secure the vent/screen assembly to the air horn and lift off the assembly

8.3/11 Remove the screws that secure the mixture control solenoid and, using a slight twisting motion, lift the solenoid out of the air horn

8.3/12 Remove the 6 (L4) or 7 (V6) screws and 2 air cleaner bolts (L4) that secure the air horn to the float bowl. If so equipped, the hot idle compensator must be removed to gain access to the short air horn screw (Fig. 4/19)

8.3/13 Rotate the fast idle cam upwards, lift off the air horn and disconnect the fast idle cam rod from the fast idle cam

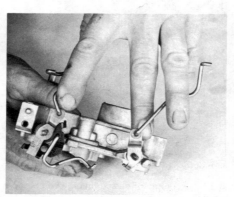

8.3/14 On L4 models, the air valve rod and the vacuum break rod are clipped to their respective levers and need not be removed unless replacement is necessary

8.3/15 Disengage the fast idle cam rod from the choke lever and save the bushing for reassembly

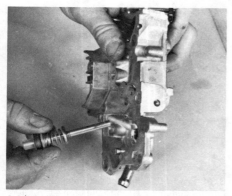

8.3/16 The pump plunger will probably come out with the air horn and must be removed. If not, remove the plunger from the pump well in the float bowl. Note: For Throttle Position Sensor-equipped carbs, see Figs. 4.20 and 4.21 for further instructions

8.3/17 Compress the pump plunger spring and remove the spring retainer clip and spring from the piston

8.3/18 Remove the air horn gasket from the float bowl

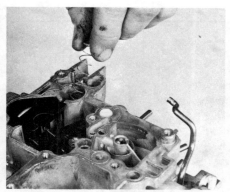

8.3/19 Remove the pump return spring from the pump well

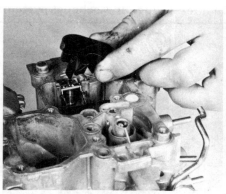

8.3/20 Remove the plastic filler block that covers the float valve

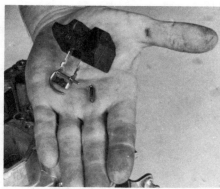

8.3/21 Remove the float assembly and float valve by pulling up on the retaining pin

8.3/22 On E2SE carbs remove the float valve seat and gasket (left) and the extended metering jet (right) from the float bowl. On 2SE carbs see Fig. 4.22 for power piston removal

8.3/23 Using needle-nosed pliers, pull out the white plastic retainer and remove the pump discharge spring and check ball. Do not pry on the retainer to remove it as this will damage the sealing surface around it

8.3/24 Remove the screws that secure the choke housing to the throttle body

8.3/25 Remove the 4 screws that attach the float bowl to the throttle body

8.3/26 Separate the float bowl from the throttle body

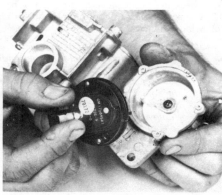

8.3/27 Carefully file off the heads of the pop-rivets that secure the choke cover to the choke housing and remove the cover. Tap out the remainder of the rivets

8.3/28 Remove the choke coil lever screw and lift out the lever

8.3/29 Remove the intermediate shaft and lever assembly by sliding it out the lever side of the float bowl

8.3/30 The plug covering the idle mixture needle should not be removed unless the needle needs replacing or normal cleaning procedures fail to clean the idle mixture passages. If removal is necessary, use a punch at the locater point as shown, and break out the throttle body casting, then drive out the plug. Finally remove the needle and spring as shown in Fig. 4.23. Further disassembly of the air horn, float bowl and throttle body is not necessary for normal cleaning purposes

9 Carburetor – cleaning and inspection

1   Clean the air horn, float bowl, throttle body and related components with clean solvent and blow them out with compressed air. A can of compressed air such as is shown in the photo can be used if an air compressor is not available. Do not use a piece of wire for cleaning the jets and passages.
2   The idle speed solenoid, mixture control solenoid, Throttle Position Sensor, electric choke, pump plunger, diaphragm, plastic filler block and other electrical, rubber and plastic parts should *not* be immersed in carburetor cleaner, as they will harden, swell or distort.
3   Make sure all fuel passages, jets and other metering parts are free of burrs and dirt.
4   Inspect the upper and lower surfaces of the air horn, float bowl and throttle body for damage. Be sure all material has been removed.
5   Inspect all lever holes and plastic bushings for excessive wear or out-of-round conditions and replace if necessary,
6   Inspect the float valve and seat for dirt, deep wear grooves and scoring and replace if necessary.
7   Inspect the float valve pull clip for proper installation and adjust if necessary.
8   Inspect the float, float arms and hinge pin for distortion or binding and correct or replace as necessary.
9   Inspect the rubber cup on the pump plunger for excessive wear or cracking.
10 Check the choke valve and linkage for excessive wear, binding or distortion and correct or replace as necessary.
11 Inspect the choke vacuum diaphragm for leaks and replace if necessary.
12 Check the choke valve for freedom of movement.
13 Check the mixture control solenoid for binding or leaking in the following manner.

   a) Connect one end of a jumper wire to either end of the solenoid connector and the other end to the positive terminal of a battery.
   b) Connect another jumper wire between the other terminal of the solenoid connector and either the negative terminal of a battery or a ground.
   c) Remove the rubber seal and retainer from the end of the solenoid stem and attach a hand vacuum pump to it (photo).
   d) With the solenoid fully energized (lean position), apply at least 25 Hg-in of vacuum and time the leak-down rate from 20 Hg-in to 15 Hg-in. The leak-down rate should not exceed 5 Hg-in in 5 seconds. If leakage exceeds that amount, replace the solenoid.
   e) To check if the solenoid is sticking in the down position, again pump about 25 Hg-in of vacuum into it, then disconnect the jumper lead to the battery and watch the pump gauge reading. It should fall to zero in less than 1 second.

10 Carburetor – assembly

1   Prior to reassembling the carburetor, compare all old and new gaskets back-to-back to be sure they match perfectly. Check especially that all the necessary holes are present and in the proper position in the new gaskets.
2   If the idle mixture needle and spring have been removed, reinstall by lightly seating the needle, then back it off 3 turns. This will provide a preliminary idle mixture adjustment. Final idle mixture adjustment must be made on the car. Refer to Section 1, paragraph 3.
3   Install a new gasket on the bottom of the float bowl (photo).
4   Mount the throttle body on the float bowl so that it is properly fitted over the locating dowels on the bowl (photo), and reinstall the 4 attaching screws, tightening them evenly and securely (photo). Be sure that the steps on the fast idle cam face toward the fast idle screw on the throttle lever when installed.
5   Inspect the linkage to make sure that the lockout tang properly engages in the slot of the secondary lockout lever and that the linkage moves freely without binding (photo).
6   Install the choke housing onto the throttle body making sure the locating lug on the rear of the housing sits in its recess in the float bowl (photos).
7   Install the intermediate choke shaft and lever assembly into the float bowl by pushing it through from the throttle lever side.
8   Position the intermediate choke lever in the 'up' position and install the thermostatic coil lever onto the end sticking into the choke housing. The coil lever is properly aligned when the coil pick-up tang is in the 12 o'clock position (photo). Install the attaching screw into the end of the intermediate shaft to secure the coil lever.
9   3 self-tapping screws supplied in the overhaul kit are used in place of the original pop-rivets to secure the choke cover and coil assembly onto the choke housing. Start the 3 screws into the housing, checking that they start easily and are properly aligned (photo), then remove them again.
10 Place the fast idle screw on the highest step of the fast idle cam, then install the choke cover onto the housing, aligning the notch in the cover with the raised casting projection on the housing cover flange (photo). When installing the cover, be sure the coil pick-up tang engages the inside choke lever. Note: On V6 models the thermostatic coil tang is formed so that it will completely encircle the coil pick-up lever. Make sure the lever is inside of this tang when installing the cover.
11 With the choke cover installed, install the 3 self-tapping screws and tighten securely.
12 Install the pump discharge check ball and spring in the passage next to the float chamber, then place a new plastic retainer in the hole

9.1 A can of compressed air such as this can be used to blow out the carb passeges

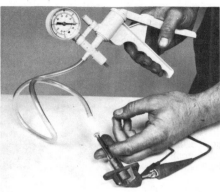

9.13 Using a vacuum pump to test the mixture control solenoid

10.3 Installing a new float bowl-to-throttle body gasket

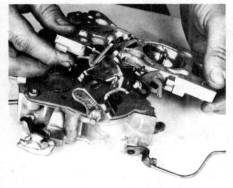

10.4a Fitting the throttle body onto the float bowl

10.4b Installing the throttle body attaching screws

10.5 Inspecting the linkage for proper engagement and free movement

10.6a Installing the choke housing onto the throttle body

10.6b The lug on the rear of the choke housing should sit in the float bowl recess

10.8 Install the thermostatic coil lever so it sits in the 12 o'clock position when the intermediate choke lever is in the up position

10.9 The choke cover is reinstalled with the self-tapping screws supplied in the overhaul kit

10.10 Be sure the notch in the choke cover is aligned with the raised casting projection on the housing cover flange

10.13 Installing the main metering jet

so that its end engages the spring and tap it lightly into place until the retainer top is flush with the bowl surface.

13 Install the main metering jet into the bottom of the float chamber (photo).

14 Install the float valve seat assembly with its gasket (photo).

15 To make float level adjustments easier, bend the float arm upward slightly at the notch shown in the photo before installing.

16 Install the float valve onto the float arm by sliding the lever under the pull clip. The correct installation of the pull clip is to hook the clip over the edge of the float on the float arm facing the float pontoon (photo). Install the float retaining pin into the float arm, then install the float assembly by aligning the valve into its seat and the float retaining pin into its locating channels in the float bowl.

17 Adjust the float level in the following manner: While holding the float retaining pin firmly in place, push down on the float arm at its outer end, against the top of the float valve, so that the top of the float is the specified distance from the float bowl surface (photo). Bend the float arm as necessary to achieve the proper measurement by pushing down on the pontoon. See the specification table for the proper float measurement for your car. Check the float level visually following adjustment.

18 On 2SE carbs, install the power piston spring into the piston bore. If the metering rod has been removed from the power piston assembly, reinstall the rod into its holder, making sure the spring is on top of the arm. Refer to Fig. 4.24. Then install the assembly into the float bowl. Use care when installing the metering rod into the main metering jet so as not to damage the metering rod tip. Press down firmly on the power piston's plastic retainer until it is firmly seated in its recess and the top is flush with the top of the bowl casting. Light tapping may be required.

19 Install the plastic filler block over the float valve so that it is flush with the float bowl surface (photo).

20 If the carb is equipped with a Throttle Position Sensor, install the TPS return spring in the bottom of its well in the float bowl. Then install the TPS and connector assembly by aligning the groove in the electrical connector with the slot in the float bowl. When properly installed, the assembly should sit below the float bowl surface.

21 Install a new air horn gasket on the float bowl (photo).

22 Install the pump return spring in the pump well (photo).

23 Reassemble the pump plunger assembly, lubricate the plunger cap with a thin coat of engine oil, and install the pump plunger into the pump well (photo).

24 If used, remove the old pump plunger seal and retainer and the old TPS plunger seal and retainer in the air horn. See Fig. 4.25. Install new seals and retainers in both locations and lightly stake both seal retainers in 3 places other than the original staking locations.

25 Install the fast idle cam rod into the lower hole of the choke lever.

26 If so equipped, apply a light coating of silicone grease or engine oil on the TPS plunger and push it through its seal in the air horn, so that about one-half of the plunger extends above the seal.

27 Prior to installing the air horn, apply a light coating of silicone grease or engine oil to the pump plunger stem to aid in slipping it through its seal in the air horn.

28 Rotate the fast idle cam to the 'up' position so it can be engaged with the lower end of the fast idle cam rod (photo) and, while holding down on the pump plunger assembly, carefully lower the air horn onto the float bowl, guiding the pump plunger stem through its seal.

29 Install the 6 (L4) or 7 (V6) air horn attaching screws and lock washers and 2 air cleaner bolts (L4) (photos), tightening them in the proper sequence as shown in Fig. 4.26.

30 If so equipped, install a new seal in the recess of the float bowl and the hot idle compensator valve.

31 Install a new rubber seal on the end of the mixture control solenoid stem until it is up against the boss on the stem (photo).

32 Using a $\frac{3}{16}$-in socket or other appropriate tool and a hammer (photo) drive the retainer over the mixture control solenoid stem just far enough to retain the rubber seal, while leaving a slight clearance between them for seal expansion.

33 Apply a light coat of engine oil on the rubber seal and, using a new gasket, install the mixture control solenoid in the air horn. Use a slight twisting motion while installing the solenoid to help the rubber seal slip into its recess.

34 Install the vent/screen assembly onto the air horn.

35 Install a plastic bushing in the hole in the choke lever, with the small end facing outward. Then with the intermediate choke lever at the 12 o'clock position, install the intermediate choke rod in the

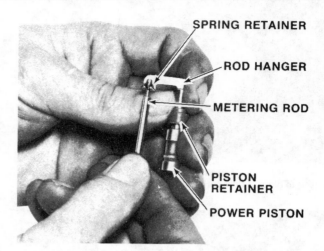

Fig. 4.24 The metering rod can be removed from the power piston assembly (2SE) by compressing the spring on top of the metering rod and aligning the rod's groove with the slot in the holder (Sec 10)

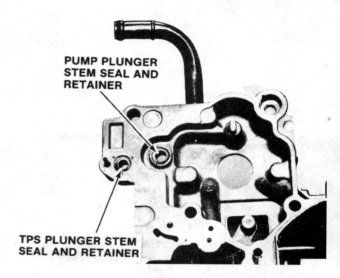

Fig. 4.25 Locations of the pump and TPS plunger seals and retainers in the air horn (Sec 10)

bushing. Install a new retaining clip on the end of the rod. An effective way of doing this is to use a broad flat-head screwdriver and a $\frac{3}{16}$-in socket as shown in the photo. Make sure the clip is not seated tightly against the bushing and that the linkage moves freely.

36 Engage the vacuum break rod with the inside vacuum break diaphragm plunger and the air valve rod with the outside plunger and mount the idle speed solenoid/vacuum break diaphragm assembly to the car (photo). Note: On V6 models, prior to mounting this assembly, connect the vacuum break rod and the air valve rod to their respective levers.

37 Engage the pump rod with the pump rod lever (photo) and mount the pump lever on the air horn with its washer in between the lever and the air horn (photo). On V6 models, install a new retaining clip on the pump rod after engaging it with the pump lever.

38 Reconnect the vacuum break diaphragm hose to its fitting on the carb body.

39 Install the fuel filter so that the hole faces toward the inlet nut.

40 Place a new gasket on the inlet nut and install, torquing it to specs. Be careful not to overtighten the nut, as this could damage the gasket, causing a fuel leak.

41 Install a new gasket on the top of the air horn (photo).

10.14 Installing the float valve seat assembly

10.15 Prior to installation bend the float arm up slightly at the point shown

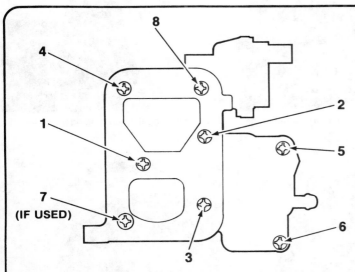

Fig. 4.26 Recommended tightening sequence for the air horn mounting screws (Sec 10)

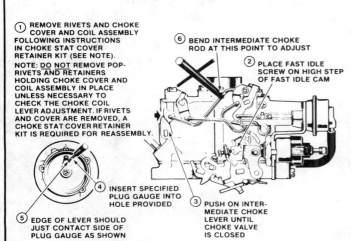

① REMOVE RIVETS AND CHOKE COVER AND COIL ASSEMBLY FOLLOWING INSTRUCTIONS IN CHOKE STAT COVER RETAINER KIT (SEE NOTE).
NOTE: DO NOT REMOVE POP-RIVETS AND RETAINERS HOLDING CHOKE COVER AND COIL ASSEMBLY IN PLACE UNLESS NECESSARY TO CHECK THE CHOKE COIL LEVER ADJUSTMENT. IF RIVETS AND COVER ARE REMOVED, A CHOKE STAT COVER RETAINER KIT IS REQUIRED FOR REASSEMBLY.

⑥ BEND INTERMEDIATE CHOKE ROD AT THIS POINT TO ADJUST

② PLACE FAST IDLE SCREW ON HIGH STEP OF FAST IDLE CAM

④ INSERT SPECIFIED PLUG GAUGE INTO HOLE PROVIDED

③ PUSH ON INTER-MEDIATE CHOKE LEVER UNTIL CHOKE VALVE IS CLOSED

⑤ EDGE OF LEVER SHOULD JUST CONTACT SIDE OF PLUG GAUGE AS SHOWN

Fig. 4.27 Choke coil lever adjustment procedure (L4 and V6)(Sec 10)
Note: A hex wrench of the specified size can be used in place of the plug gauge shown

FIGURE 1
1. CHOKE COIL LEVER ADJUSTMENT MUST BE CORRECT AND FAST IDLE ADJUSTMENT MUST BE MADE BEFORE PROCEEDING.
2. USE CHOKE VALVE MEASURING GAUGE J-26701 OR BT-7704. TOOL MAY BE USED WITH CARBURETOR ON OR OFF ENGINE. IF OFF ENGINE, PLACE CARBURETOR ON HOLDING FIXTURE SO THAT IT WILL REMAIN IN SAME POSITION WHEN GAUGE IS IN PLACE.
3. ROTATE DEGREE SCALE UNTIL ZERO (0) IS OPPOSITE POINTER.
4. WITH CHOKE VALVE COMPLETELY CLOSED, PLACE MAGNET SQUARELY ON TOP OF CHOKE VALVE.
5. ROTATE BUBBLE UNTIL IT IS CENTERED.

FIGURE 2
6. ROTATE SCALE SO THAT DEGREE SPECIFIED FOR ADJUSTMENT IS OPPOSITE POINTER.
7. PLACE FAST IDLE SCREW ON SECOND STEP OF CAM AGAINST RISE OF HIGH STEP.
8. CLOSE CHOKE BY PUSHING ON INTERMEDIATE CHOKE LEVER.
9. PUSH ON VACUUM BREAK LEVER TOWARD OPEN CHOKE UNTIL LEVER IS AGAINST REAR TANG ON CHOKE LEVER.
10. TO ADJUST, BEND FAST IDLE CAM ROD UNTIL BUBBLE IS CENTERED.
11. REMOVE GAUGE.

Fig. 4.28 Choke rod adjustment procedure (L4 and V6) (Sec 10)

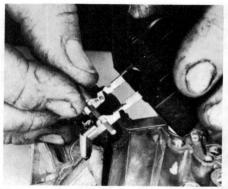
10.16 During installation the float valve should be positioned on the float arm as shown

10.17 Measuring float adjustment

10.19 Installing the plastic filler block

10.21 Installing a new air horn gasket on the float bowl

10.22 Installing the pump return spring in the pump well

10.23 Installing the pump plunger into the pump well

10.28 Engage the fast idle cam rod into the fast idle cam prior to installation of the air horn

10.29a Installing the air cleaner bolts into the L4 air horn

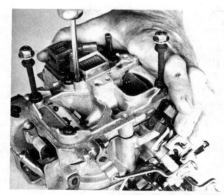
10.29b Installing the air horn mounting screws (L4)

10.31 Fitting a new rubber seal on the end of the mixture control solenoid

10.32 Using a hammer and the end of a drift to tap the seal retainer onto the mixture control solenoid stem

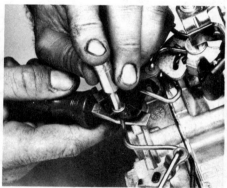
10.35 Installing a retaining clip onto the intermediate choke rod to secure it to the choke lever

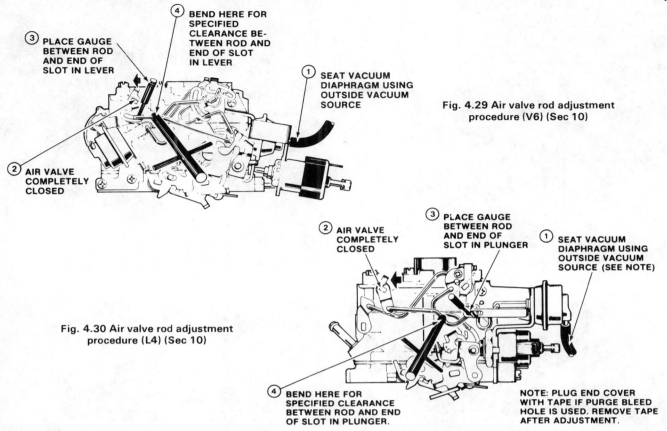

③ PLACE GAUGE BETWEEN ROD AND END OF SLOT IN LEVER

④ BEND HERE FOR SPECIFIED CLEARANCE BE-TWEEN ROD AND END OF SLOT IN LEVER

① SEAT VACUUM DIAPHRAGM USING OUTSIDE VACUUM SOURCE

② AIR VALVE COMPLETELY CLOSED

Fig. 4.29 Air valve rod adjustment procedure (V6) (Sec 10)

② AIR VALVE COMPLETELY CLOSED

③ PLACE GAUGE BETWEEN ROD AND END OF SLOT IN PLUNGER

① SEAT VACUUM DIAPHRAGM USING OUTSIDE VACUUM SOURCE (SEE NOTE)

Fig. 4.30 Air valve rod adjustment procedure (L4) (Sec 10)

④ BEND HERE FOR SPECIFIED CLEARANCE BETWEEN ROD AND END OF SLOT IN PLUNGER.

NOTE: PLUG END COVER WITH TAPE IF PURGE BLEED HOLE IS USED. REMOVE TAPE AFTER ADJUSTMENT.

FIGURE 1

1. USE CHOKE VALVE MEASURING GAUGE J-26701 OR BT-7704. TOOL MAY BE USED WITH CARBURETOR ON OR OFF ENGINE. IF OFF ENGINE, PLACE CARBURETOR ON HOLDING FIXTURE SO THAT IT WILL REMAIN IN SAME POSITION WHEN GAUGE IS IN PLACE.

2. ROTATE DEGREE SCALE UNTIL ZERO (0) IS OPPOSITE POINTER.

3. WITH CHOKE VALVE COMPLETELY CLOSED, PLACE MAGNET SQUARELY ON TOP OF CHOKE VALVE.

4. ROTATE BUBBLE UNTIL IT IS CENTERED.

FIGURE 2

5. ROTATE SCALE SO THAT DEGREE SPECIFIED FOR ADJUSTMENT IS OPPOSITE POINTER.

6. SEAT CHOKE VACUUM DIAPHRAGM USING VACUUM SOURCE.

7. HOLD CHOKE VALVE TOWARD CLOSED POSITION BY PUSHING ON INTERMEDIATE CHOKE LEVER. MAKE SURE PLUNGER BUCKING SPRING (IF USED) IS COMPRESSED AND SEATED.

8. TO ADJUST, BEND VACUUM BREAK ROD UNTIL BUBBLE IS CENTERED.

9. REMOVE GAUGE.

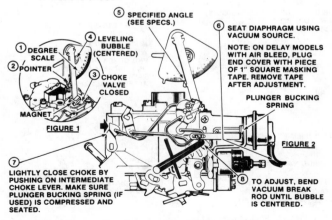

⑤ SPECIFIED ANGLE (SEE SPECS.)

⑥ SEAT DIAPHRAGM USING VACUUM SOURCE.

NOTE: ON DELAY MODELS WITH AIR BLEED, PLUG END COVER WITH PIECE OF 1" SQUARE MASKING TAPE. REMOVE TAPE AFTER ADJUSTMENT.

PLUNGER BUCKING SPRING

④ LEVELING BUBBLE (CENTERED)

① DEGREE SCALE

② POINTER

③ CHOKE VALVE CLOSED

MAGNET

FIGURE 1

FIGURE 2

⑦ LIGHTLY CLOSE CHOKE BY PUSHING ON INTERMEDIATE CHOKE LEVER. MAKE SURE PLUNGER BUCKING SPRING (IF USED) IS COMPRESSED AND SEATED.

⑧ TO ADJUST, BEND VACUUM BREAK ROD UNTIL BUBBLE IS CENTERED.

Fig. 4.31 Primary vacuum break adjustment procedure (L4 shown, V6 uses same procedure) (Sec 10)

10.36 Installing the idle speed solenoid/vacuum break diaphragm assembly

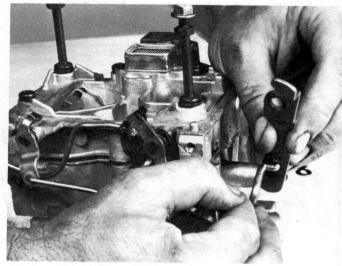

10.37a Engaging the pump rod with the pump rod lever

10.37b Inserting the pump rod mounting screw through the pump rod prior to installation

10.41 Installing a new gasket on top of the air horn

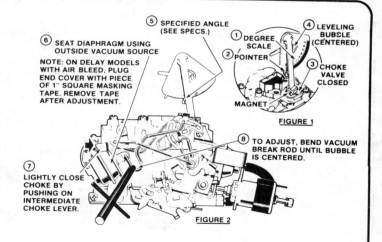

FIGURE 1

1. USE CHOKE VALVE MEASURING GAUGE J-26701 OR BT-7704. TOOL MAY BE USED WITH CARBURETOR ON OR OFF ENGINE. IF OFF ENGINE, PLACE CARBURETOR ON HOLDING FIXTURE SO THAT IT WILL REMAIN IN SAME POSITION WHEN GAUGE IS IN PLACE.

2. ROTATE DEGREE SCALE UNTIL ZERO (0) IS OPPOSITE POINTER.

3. WITH CHOKE VALVE COMPLETELY CLOSED, PLACE MAGNET SQUARELY ON TOP OF CHOKE VALVE.

4. ROTATE BUBBLE UNTIL IT IS CENTERED.

FIGURE 2

5. ROTATE SCALE SO THAT DEGREE SPECIFIED FOR ADJUSTMENT IS OPPOSITE POINTER.

6. SEAT CHOKE VACUUM DIAPHRAGM USING VACUUM SOURCE.

7. HOLD CHOKE VALVE TOWARD CLOSED POSITION BY PUSHING ON INTERMEDIATE CHOKE LEVER. MAKE SURE PLUNGER BUCKING SPRING (IF USED) IS COMPRESSED AND SEATED.

8. TO ADJUST, BEND VACUUM BREAK ROD UNTIL BUBBLE IS CENTERED.

9. REMOVE GAUGE.

⑤ SPECIFIED ANGLE (SEE SPECS.)
④ LEVELING BUBBLE (CENTERED)
① DEGREE SCALE
② POINTER
③ CHOKE VALVE CLOSED
MAGNET

⑥ SEAT DIAPHRAGM USING OUTSIDE VACUUM SOURCE
NOTE: ON DELAY MODELS WITH AIR BLEED, PLUG END COVER WITH PIECE OF 1" SQUARE MASKING TAPE. REMOVE TAPE AFTER ADJUSTMENT.

FIGURE 1

⑧ TO ADJUST, BEND VACUUM BREAK ROD UNTIL BUBBLE IS CENTERED.

⑦ LIGHTLY CLOSE CHOKE BY PUSHING ON INTERMEDIATE CHOKE LEVER.

FIGURE 2

Fig. 4.32 Secondary vacuum break adjustment procedure (V6) (Sec 10)

FIGURE 1

1. USE CHOKE VALVE MEASURING GAUGE J-26701 OR BT-7704. TOOL MAY BE USED WITH CARBURETOR ON OR OFF ENGINE. IF OFF ENGINE, PLACE CARBURETOR ON HOLDING FIXTURE SO THAT IT WILL REMAIN IN SAME POSITION WHEN GAUGE IS IN PLACE.

2. ROTATE DEGREE SCALE UNTIL ZERO (0) IS OPPOSITE POINTER.

3. WITH CHOKE VALVE COMPLETELY CLOSED, PLACE MAGNET SQUARELY ON TOP OF CHOKE VALVE.

4. ROTATE BUBBLE UNTIL IT IS CENTERED.

FIGURE 2

5. ROTATE SCALE SO THAT DEGREE SPECIFIED FOR ADJUSTMENT IS OPPOSITE POINTER.

6. INSTALL CHOKE THERMOSTATIC COVER AND COIL ASSEMBLY IN HOUSING. ALIGN INDEX MARK WITH SPECIFIED POINT ON HOUSING.

7. HOLD PRIMARY THROTTLE VALVE WIDE OPEN.

8. ON WARM ENGINE, CLOSE CHOKE VALVE BY PUSHING CLOCKWISE ON INTERMEDIATE CHOKE LEVER (HOLD IN POSITION WITH RUBBER BAND).

9. TO ADJUST, BEND TANG ON THROTTLE LEVER UNTIL BUBBLE IS CENTERED.

10. REMOVE GAUGE.

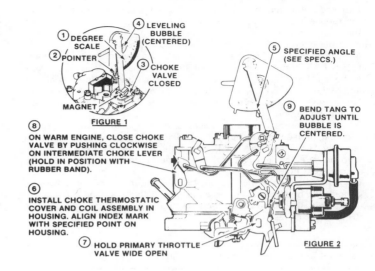

Fig. 4.33 Unloader adjustment procedure (Sec 10)

11 Fuel system – cleaning

1 With time it is likely that sediment will collect in the bottom of the fuel tank. Condensation, resulting in rust and other impurities, will usually be found in the fuel tank of any car more than 3 or 4 years old. The following procedure should be performed to eliminate foreign material or contaminated fuel from the fuel system.
2 Disconnect the negative battery cable.
3 Drain and remove the fuel tank as described in Section 16.
4 Remove the fuel inlet line and fuel filter from the carburetor. If the filter is clogged, replace it.
5 Remove the fuel level sender from the fuel tank as described in Section 17. Check condition of filter and replace if necessary.
6 Purge and clean the fuel tank as necessary using one of the methods described in Section 18.
7 Disconnect the fuel inlet line at the fuel pump and clean the line out by applying air pressure through it in the direction of the fuel flow.
8 Use low air pressure to clean the pipes on the tank unit.
9 Reinstall the fuel level sender with a new gasket as described in Section 17.
10 Reinstall the fuel tank.
11 Connect all wires and lines except the fuel pump-to-carburetor line.
12 Connect a rubber hose to the fuel pump-to-carb line at the carb end. Place the other end of the hose into a 1-gallon fuel can.
13 Disconnect the wire leading to the 'BATT' terminal of the distributor and connect the negative battery cable.
14 Put about 6 gallons of clean fuel into the fuel tank and operate the pump by turning the engine over until about two quarts of fuel has flowed through the pump. This will clean the pump out.
15 Remove the rubber hose and connect the fuel line to the carburetor.
16 Connect the ignition coil's positive lead.
17 Check all the connections to be sure they are tight.

12 Fuel line – repair and replacement

1 If a section of metal fuel line needs to be replaced only brazed seamless steel should be used, as copper or aluminum tubing does not have enough durability to withstand normal operating vibrations.
2 If only one section of a metal fuel line is damaged, it can be cut out and replaced with a piece of rubber tubing. The rubber tubing should be cut 4 inches (100 mm) longer than the section it's replacing, so there is about 2 inches of overlap between the rubber and metal tubing at either end of the section. Hose clamps should be used to

Fig. 4.34 Identification of the fuel pump lines (V6) (Sec 12)
A Vapor return line, B Fuel outlet line, C Fuel inlet line

secure both ends of the repaired section.
3 If a section of metal line longer than 6 inches is being removed, use a combination of metal tubing and rubber hose so that the hose lengths will not be longer than 10 inches.
4 Never use rubber hose within 4 inches of any part of the exhaust system.

13 Fuel filter – removal and installation

1 As replacement of the fuel filter is included in the car's routine maintenance schedule, this procedure is described in Chapter 1, Section 13.

14 Fuel pump – inspection and testing

1 Check that there is adequate fuel in the fuel tank.
2 With the engine running, examine all fuel lines between the fuel

tank and fuel pump for leaks, loose connections, kinks or flattening in the rubber hoses. Air leaks before the fuel pump can seriously affect the pump's output.
3   Check the pump diaphragm flange for leaks.
4   Disconnect the fuel line into the carb. Disconnect the wire leading to the 'BATT' terminal of the distributor, so the engine can be cranked without it firing. Place a clean container such as a coffee can at the end of the detached fuel line and crank the engine for several seconds. There should be a strong spurt of gasoline from the line on every second revolution.
5   If little or no gasoline emerges from the line during engine cranking, then either the line is clogged or the fuel pump is not working properly. Disconnect the fuel line from the pump and blow air through it to be sure the line is clear. If the line is clear, then the pump is suspect and needs to be replaced.
6   A more accurate method of testing fuel pump flow capacity is to perform the previous test using a measuring container and a watch. At engine idle, the pump should be able to pump one pint of gasoline in 30 seconds or less.

15 Fuel pump – removal and installation

1   Disconnect the negative battery cable.
2   To provide extra working room, raise the front of the car and support it on jackstands.
3   On V6 engines remove the fuel pump shield and oil filter.
4   Disconnect the fuel inlet hose from the fuel pump.
5   Disconnect the vapor return hose, if so equipped.
6   Loosen the fuel pump-to-carb line at the carb end.
7   Disconnect the fuel outlet line at the pump.
8   Remove the two hex bolts that secure the fuel pump and remove the pump. As the pump is sealed and cannot be disassembled, if defective it must be replaced as a unit.
9   Installation is the reverse of the removal procedure with the following note: If the fuel outlet pipe is difficult to fit on the fuel pump nozzle, time can be saved by disconnecting the upper end of the pipe from the carburetor. Tighten the fitting while holding the fuel pump nut with a wrench. Then reinstall and tighten the carburetor fitting.

16 Fuel tank – removal and installation

Note: *Any repairs to the fuel tank or filler neck should be carried out by a professional who has experience in this critical and potentially dangerous work.*
1   **CAUTION: While performing any work on the fuel tank, it is advisable to have a CO$_2$ fire extinguisher on hand and to wear safety glasses. All precautions should be taken to keep any kind of combustion (lighted cigarettes, etc.) or sparks away from the area of the tank and siphoned fuel.**

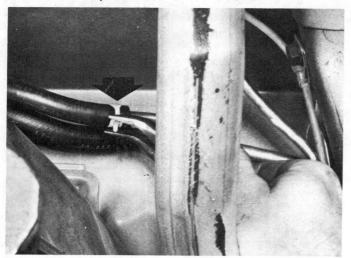

16.6 Disconnecting the fuel pressure and fuel return hoses

2   Raise the rear of the car and support it on jackstands.
3   Disconnect the negative battery terminal.
4   Disconnect the fuel feed line at the pump.
5   Siphon or pump the fuel from the tank. Since there is no drain plug in the tank and due to the restrictor in the filler neck, the fuel must be siphoned or pumped out through the fuel feed line. It's advisable when pumping, to use a hand-operated pump.
6   Disconnect the fuel pressure and fuel return hose at the point where the rubber lines connect with the rigid steel lines (photo).
7   Remove the ground wire screw (photo).
8   Disconnect the fuel fill and vapor return lines (photo).
9   Remove the heat shield located between the exhaust pipe and forward end of the fuel tank (photo).
10 While the tank is supported either by an assistant or by a jack, remove the two rear support strap bolts (photo).
11 Lower the tank slightly and disconnect the fuel level sensor wire located on top of the tank (photo).
12 Lower and remove the tank (photo).
13 CAUTION: Never perform any repair work involving heat or flame on the tank until it has been purged of gas and vapors as described in Section 18.
14 Before installing the tank, make sure that all traces of dirt and corrosion are cleaned from it. A coat of rust-preventative paint is recommended. If the tank is rusted internally, however, it should be replaced with a new one.
15 Installation is the reverse of the removal procedure.

17 Fuel level sender – removal and installation

1   Lower the fuel tank as described in Section 16.
2   Using either a special GM tool or equivalent wrench, unscrew the sender cam ring.
3   Remove the fuel gauge tank unit.
4   Install the new tank unit, being careful not to bend or damage it.
5   When reinstalling the cam lock with a new gasket it may be necessary to compress the gasket slightly by pressing down on the wrench. Once the lock is started under the retaining tangs, pressure can be released.
6   Install the fuel tank.

18 Fuel tank – cleaning and purging

1   Drain and remove the fuel tank as described in Section 16.
2   Remove the fuel level sender as described in Section 17.
3   Turn the tank over and empty out any remaining fuel.
4   If repair work needs to be done to the fuel tank that does not involve heat or flame, the tank can be satisfactorily cleaned by running hot water into it and letting it overflow out the top for at least five minutes. **This method, however, does not remove gas vapors.**
5   If repair work involving heat or flame is necessary, have it done by an experienced professional. The following, more thorough procedures should be used to remove all fuel and vapors from the tank.
6   Fill the tank completely with tap water, agitate vigorously and drain.
7   Add a gasoline emulsifying agent to the tank according to the manufacturer's instructions, refill with water, agitate for approximately 10 minutes and drain.
8   Flush to overflowing once again with water for several minutes and drain.
9   The tank is now ready for repair work.
10 Under no circumstances perform repair work involving heat or flame without first carrying out the above precautions.

19 Exhaust system – general information

1   The exhaust system consists of the muffler, catalytic converter and exhaust pipes and includes four main pieces: the front crossover pipe which attaches to the exhaust manifold, the front intermediate pipe, the catalytic converter and the rear intermediate pipe/muffler/tailpipe assembly. See Figure 4.35.
2   On V6 engine models and on L4 California models, the connection between the exhaust manifold and the front crossover pipe is of the ball type and does not need a gasket. The connection on the L4 49

16.7 Disconnecting the ground wire screw

16.8 Disconnecting the fuel fill and vapor return hoses

16.9 Removing the heat shield

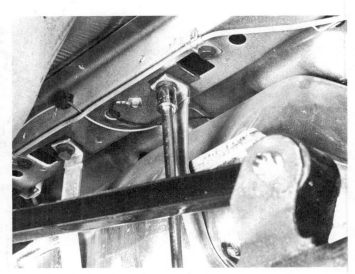
16.10 Removing the rear support strap bolts

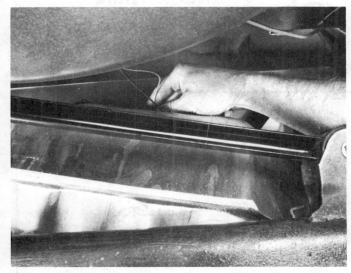
16.11 Disconnecting the fuel level sensor wire from the top of the fuel tank

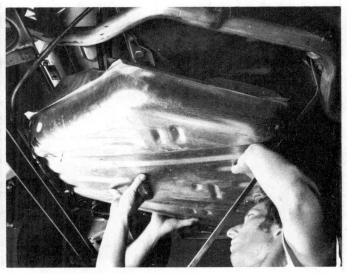
16.12 Lowering the fuel tank

States version, on the other hand, has a machined surface and requires a gasket.

3   The entire exhaust system is supported by hangers which help eliminate vibration from the system to the chassis. Two types of hangers are used: rubber straps which are designed to flex, and rubber blocks which are rigid. For maximum vibration dampening it's important to use the correct hanger in each location.

4   The catalytic converter is attached to the exhaust pipes by clamps. The muffler, on the other hand, is welded to the rear intermediate pipe and the tailpipe.

5   When replacing exhaust system parts, be sure you allow enough clearance from all points on the underbody to avoid overheating the floor pan and possibly damaging the interior carpet and insulation.

6   Regular inspection of the exhaust system should be made to keep it at maximum efficiency. Look for any damage or mispositioned parts, open seams, holes, loose connections, excessive corrosion or other defects which could allow exhaust fumes to seep into the car.

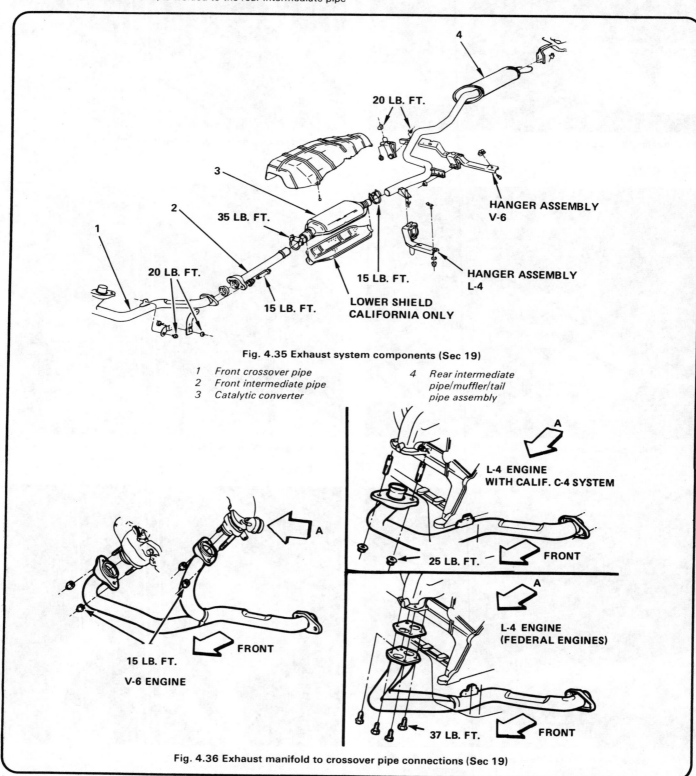

Fig. 4.35 Exhaust system components (Sec 19)

1   Front crossover pipe
2   Front intermediate pipe
3   Catalytic converter
4   Rear intermediate pipe/muffler/tail pipe assembly

Fig. 4.36 Exhaust manifold to crossover pipe connections (Sec 19)

20 Exhaust system – one-piece removal and installation

1   While the procedures on removing and installing individual parts of the exhaust system are described in following Sections, if the entire exhaust system must be removed, and if a hydraulic lift is available, most of the system can be easily removed in one piece.
2   Raise the car on a hydraulic lift.
3   Remove the spring-loaded bolts that connect the front crossover pipe to the front intermediate pipe and separate the pipes (photo).
4   Remove all nuts and bolts of the hangers that attach the exhaust pipes, converter and muffler to the chassis.
5   Slide the assembly as one piece toward the front of the car so that the muffler clears the rear axle and remove. To clear the rear axle the muffler must be turned on end to fit between the fuel tank and right rear spring (photo).
6   Installation is the reverse of the removal procedure.

20.3 Separating the front exhaust pipe from the front intermediate pipe

20.5 During removal the muffler must be turned on end to clear the rear axle, fuel tank and right rear spring

21 Catalytic converter – general

1   As catalytic converter servicing is included in the car's routine maintenance schedule, information on the system in general, as well as the servicing of it is detailed in Chapter 1, Section 29.

22 Catalytic converter – removal and installation

1   To obtain sufficient working clearance, raise the front of the car and support it on jackstands.
2   Remove the clamps at either end of the converter.
3   Remove the spring-loaded bolts that secure the front intermediate pipe to the front crossover pipe and separate the pipes.
4   The converter can now be slid off of the rear intermediate pipe, and then separated from the front intermediate pipe. Penetrating oil and slight tapping with a rubber mallet may be necessary to separate them.
5   Note: If the converter flanges are heavily corroded or have been crimped onto the intermediate pipes so that they will not separate easily, it will not be possible to remove the converter without damaging it. In such a case, the converter should only be removed if it is being replaced as a unit. If catalyst replacement is desired, it will necessitate the on-car procedure mentioned in Chapter 1, Section 29. To remove the converter under these conditions, either have it cut off and the new converter welded on at a muffler shop, or follow the following procedure outlined in paragraphs 6 through 9.
6   After the front intermediate and crossover pipes have been separated, disconnect the exhaust hangers forward of the muffler and gently lower the entire assembly out of its cradle.
7   Use a hacksaw or torch to cut the rear outlet pipe of the converter before it enters the rear intermediate pipe's flange. Remove the converter and front intermediate pipe.
8   Using an exhaust flange chisel, cut the front flange of the converter and separate it from the front intermediate pipe.
9   Before the new converter can be installed, the piece of outlet pipe still in the rear intermediate pipe flange must be removed. This can be done with pliers and a chisel by bending the pipe inward until it frees itself of the flange. Be careful not to damage the flange itself. The rear intermediate pipe can now be reattached to its hangers.
10 To install the new or serviced converter, reverse the removal procedure outlined in paragraphs 1 through 4.

23 Catalytic converter (bead type) – catalyst replacement; off-car procedure

1   Remove catalytic converter as described in Section 22. Take particular note of paragraph 5.
2   Remove the pressed fill plug on the bottom of the converter by driving a small chisel between the converter shell and the fill plug to raise the lip of the plug. Once the lip is raised, pliers can be used to twist the plug out. Note: Do not pry the fill plug loose as this will damage the sealing surface around the plug.

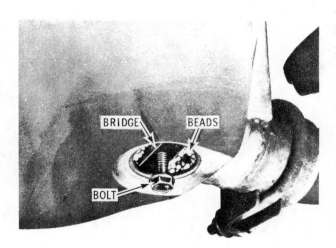

Fig. 4.37 During catalyst replacement, the bridge should be worked into the fill hole as shown prior to installing the fill plug (Sec 23)

3   Hold the converter over a suitable container and shake the beads out into it until the converter is empty.

4   Support the converter at approximately a 45° position with the front end up. Place a suitable funnel in the fill hole and put the new catalyst beads into it. Tapping lightly with a hammer on the edge of the converter belt will help settle the beads into the converter. Continue pouring until the converter is full.

5   Install the service fill plug in the fill hole in the following manner: Install the bolt into the bridge and work the bridge into the fill hole until it's positioned as shown in Fig. 4.37.

6   Remove the bolt from the bridge and put the washer and fill plug, dished side out, over the bolt.

7   Hold the fill plug and washer against the bolt head and thread the bolt about 5 turns into the bridge.

8   When the fill plug is seated in the fill hole, tighten the bolt to 28 ft-lb (3.8 m-kg).

9   Reinstall the converter.

10 Start the engine and check for leaks.

11 Reset the catalyst maintenance reminder flag in the dash instrument cluster, if so equipped, using the procedure described in Chapter 10.

24 Muffler – removal and installation

1   The muffler is welded onto both the rear intermediate pipe and the tail pipe, and the entire assembly is designed to be replaced as a unit. However, if the muffler needs replacing but the rear intermediate pipe is in good condition, a muffler shop will be able to cut off the old muffler and weld on a new one without having to replace the pipes as well. If you wish to replace the entire section as one piece, access to a hydraulic lift is needed for clearance reasons.

2   Raise the car on a hydraulic lift.

3   Remove the clamp at the junction between the rear intermediate pipe and converter and separate the two parts. If the junction is corroded, crimped, or otherwise won't separate easily, use an exhaust flange chisel to cut the rear intermediate pipe flange in order to separate the parts.

4   Disconnect the hangers that attach the rear section to the chassis.

5   Remove the rear section by sliding it toward the front of the car so that the muffler clears the rear axle and remove. In order to clear the rear axle the muffler must be turned on end to fit between the fuel tank and right rear spring.

6   Installation is the reverse of the removal procedure.

Chapter 5 Ignition and starting systems

Refer to Chapter 13 for specifications and information related to 1981 through 1984 models

Contents

Specifications

System type	12v, negative ground
Battery type	Delco 'Freedom'; sealed battery, lead acid
Distributor type	Designated High Energy Ignition (HEI) (breakerless)
Distributor direction of rotation	Clockwise
Firing order	
L4 engine	1, 3, 4, 2
V6 engine	1, 2, 3, 4, 5, 6
Coil	
Primary resistance	0.41 to 0.51 ohms
Secondary resistance	3000 to 20000 ohms
Resistor	0.43 to 0.68 ohms
Generator output current	Varies according to vehicle specifications and generator type
Starter motor	
Type	5MT
Voltage	9V

Torque specifications	ft-lb	m-kg
Battery cables	9	1.2
Battery hold-down clamp	6	0.8
Generator shaft nut	50	6.9
Generator bracket to head	35	4.8
Generator brace to cover	25	3.4
Generator pivot bolt	25	3.4
Generator adjusting bolt	22	3.0
Distributor hold-down clamp bolt	22	3.0
Starter motor mounting bolts	30	4.0
Starter motor brace to motor	27	3.7
Starter motor brace to case	15	2.0

1 Ignition system – general information

1   In order that the engine can run correctly it is necessary for an electrical spark to ignite the fuel/air mixture in the combustion chamber at exactly the right moment in relation to engine speed and load. The ignition system is based on feeding low tension (LT) voltage from the battery to the coil where it is converted to high tension (HT) voltage. The high tension voltage is powerful enough to jump the spark plug gap in the cylinders many times a second under high compression pressures, providing that the system is in good condition and that all adjustments are correct.

2   The ignition system is divided into two circuits: the low tension circuit and the high tension circuit.

3   The low tension (sometimes known as the primary) circuit consists of the battery lead to the starter motor, lead to the ignition switch, calibrated resistance wire from the ignition switch to the low tension or primary coil winding, and the lead from the low tension coil windings to the distributor.

4   The high tension circuit consists of the high tension or secondary coil windings, the heavy ignition lead from the center of the coil to the center of the distributor cap, the rotor, the spark plug leads and spark plugs.

5   The High Energy Ignition (HEI) system used on all X-Body cars is a pulse-triggered, transistor-controlled, inductive discharge system, in which a control module and magnetic pick-up replace the contact points of a conventional distributor.

6   The system functions in the following manner. Low tension voltage fed to the coil is changed into high tension voltage by the magnetic pick-up in the distributor. The magnetic pick-up contains a permanent magnet, pole-piece and pick-up coil. A timer core, rotating inside the pole piece, induces a voltage in the pick-up coil, and when the teeth on the timer and pole piece line up, a signal passes to the electronic control module to open the ignition coil primary circuit.

7   When the primary circuit current decreases, a high voltage is induced in the coil secondary winding. This is then directed to the rotor, which distributes the current to the spark plugs as in a conventional system.

8   This system features a longer spark duration and the dwell period automatically increases with engine speed. This is desirable for firing the leaner mixtures provided by the emissions control systems.

9   The ignition coil and the electronic control module are both housed in the distributor cap.

10   The distributor used on all 1980 models is equipped with both mechanical and vacuum advance mechanisms. The mechanical governor mechanism compresses two weights which move out from the distributor shaft due to centrifugal force as the engine speed increases. The weights are held in position by two light springs, and it is the tension of the springs which is largely responsible for correct spark advancement.

11   The vacuum control consists of a diaphragm, one side of which is connected via a small-bore tube to a vacuum source, and the other side to the magnetic pick-up assembly. Vacuum in the intake manifold or carburetor which varies with engine speed and throttle opening, causes the diaphragm to move, which, in turn, moves the magnetic pick-up assembly, thus advancing or retarding the spark.

12   Two types of vacuum advances are used: ported vacuum and manifold vacuum. Ported vacuum advance systems have a timed port in the carburetor throttle body above the throttle valve which provides vacuum only during open throttle operation. The manifold system uses manifold vacuum from either a manifold vacuum port on the carb or a fitting on the intake manifold. This system provides vacuum whenever the engine is running. The type of system used depends on the specifications and engine size of the car, and can be determined from the vacuum schematics in Chapter 6.

13   In addition, the vacuum advance systems also use various Thermal Vacuum Switches, Vacuum Delay Valves and Vacuum Regulator Valves which link them with various emissions control systems.

14   Due to the complexity of the systems and the special equipment needed to accurately diagnose them, suspected vacuum advance problems should be checked out by a GM dealer or other qualified mechanic. A couple of simple checks for the home mechanic are described in Chapter 1.

15   Engine oil lubricates the lower bushing of the distributor and an oil-filled reservoir provides lubrication for the upper bushing, making periodic lubrication and servicing of the distributor unnecessary.

16   CAUTION: Because of the higher voltage generated by this electronic ignition system, extreme caution should be taken whenever an operation is performed involving ignition components. This not only includes the distributor, coil, control module and ignition wires, but related items that are connected to the system as well, such as the plug connections, tachometer and any testing equipment. Consequently, before any work is performed such as replacing ignition components or even connecting testing equipment, the ignition should be turned off or the battery ground cable disconnected.

2 Ignition timing

1   As adjustment of the ignition timing is a primary part of the tune-up operation, this procedure is described in Chapter 1.

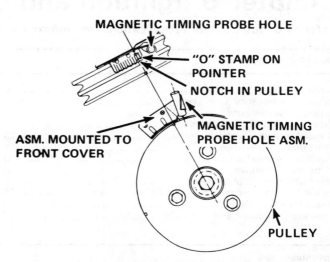

Fig. 5.1 Location of the timing marks in relation to the pulley (Sec 2)

3 Battery – maintenance

1   A sealed Delco 'Freedom' battery is used in all X-Body cars. As opposed to conventional batteries, it has no vent plugs in the top, and is completely sealed except for a small vent hole in the side. Because of its sealed design this battery never needs water added, which greatly decreases the normal maintenance of it.

2   A temperature-compensated hydrometer is built into the top of the battery which gives an indication of the electrolyte level and the battery's state of charge. A green 'dot' visible in the hydrometer's window means the battery is in a normal condition. If the hydrometer is dark with no green dot visible, the battery needs to be charged. If the hydrometer window is clear or light yellow, the battery must be replaced. CAUTION: Do not attempt to charge, test or jump the battery when the hydrometer is clear or light yellow, as the battery could explode, resulting in serious personal injury.

3   Periodically clean the top and sides of the battery, removing all dirt and moisture. This helps prevent corrosion and ensures that the battery does not become partially discharged by leakage through dampness and dirt.

4   Once every three months, remove the battery and inspect the battery securing bolts, the battery clamp plate, and battery leads for corrosion (white fluffy deposits on the metal which are brittle to touch). If any corrosion is found, clean off the deposits with an ammonia or baking soda solution. After cleaning, smear petroleum jelly on the battery terminals and lead connectors. Application of a zinc-base primer and/or underbody paint will help to prevent recurrence of corrosion on body panel metal.

5   The freezing point of electrolyte depends on its specific gravity. Since freezing can ruin a battery, it should be kept in a fully charged state to protect against freezing.

6   Some of the common causes of battery failure are:

   a) *Accessories, especially headlights, left on overnight or for several hours.*

b) Slow average driving speeds for short intervals.
c) The electrical load of the car being more than the generator output. This is especially common when several high-draw accessories are being used simultaneously, such as radios/stereos, air-conditioning, window defoggers, light systems, etc.
d) Charging system faults, such as electrical shorts, slipping generator belt, defective generator or faulty voltage regulator.
e) Battery neglect, such as loose or corroded terminals or loose battery hold-down clamp.

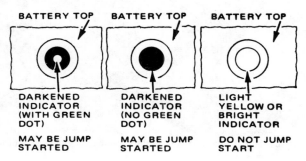

Fig. 5.2 Key to reading the built-in hydrometer in the top of the battery (Sec 3)

4 Battery charging

1 In winter time when heavy demand is placed upon the battery, such as when starting from cold, and much electrical equipment is continually in use, it's a good idea to occasionally have the battery fully charged from an external source at the rate of 3.5 to 4 amps.
2 Continue to charge the battery at this rate until the green 'dot' appears in the hydrometer window. Tipping or shaking the battery may sometimes be necessary to make the dot appear.
3 Alternatively, a trickle charger charging at the rate of 1.5 amps can be safely used overnight.
4 Special rapid 'boost' charges which are claimed to restore the power of the battery in 1 to 2 hours are most dangerous, as they can cause serious damage to the battery plates. This type of charge should only be used in a 'crisis' situation.
5 Do not charge the battery if the built-in hydrometer is a clear or light yellow color. This indicates that the battery needs replacement.

5 Battery – emergency jump starting

1 **CAUTION: Do not attempt to jump start if the hydrometer window is clear or light yellow. Replace the battery.**
2 Apply the parking brake and place the transaxle in 'Park' if automatic, or 'Neutral' if manual.
3 Remove any rings, watches, or other jewelry.
4 Do not allow any battery acid to contact eyes, skin, clothing or painted surfaces. Flush any contacted area immediately with water.
5 Hook up one end of the positive jumper cable to the positive terminal of the booster battery and the other end to the positive terminal of the discharged battery. Do not permit the vehicles to touch each other. Be sure that the positive jumper cable does not contact any metal part of either car, as this will create a short circuit.
6 Hook up one end of the negative jumper cable to the negative terminal of the booster battery and the other end to a solid engine ground at least 18 inches (450 mm) from the discharged battery. Do not connect the cable directly to the negative terminal of the dead battery. A good engine ground would be the A/C compressor or generator mounting bracket.
7 Start the engine of the car that is providing the boost and turn off all electrical accessories.
8 Start the engine of the car with the discharged battery.
9 Reverse these directions exactly when removing the jumper cables. The negative cable must be removed from the engine that was jump-started first.

6 Battery – removal and installation

1 The battery is located at the front of the engine compartment. It is held in place by a hold-down clamp near the bottom of the battery case.
2 As hydrogen gas is produced by the battery, keep open flames or lighted cigarettes away from the battery at all times.
3 Always keep the battery in the upright position. Any spilled electrolyte from the vent hole should be immediately flushed with large quantities of water. Wear eye protection when working with a battery to prevent serious eye damage from splashed fluid.
4 Always disconnect the negative (-) battery cable first, followed by the positive (+) cable.
5 After the cables are disconnected from the battery, remove the hold-down clamp.
6 Carefully lift the battery from its tray and out of the engine compartment.
7 Installation is a reversal of removal; however, make sure that the hold-down clamp is securely tightened. Do not over-tighten, however, as this may damage the battery case. The battery posts and cable ends should be cleaned prior to connection.

7 Spark plugs – general

1 Properly functioning spark plugs are a necessity if the engine is to perform properly. At the intervals specified in Routine Maintenance or your owner's manual, the spark plugs should be replaced with new ones. Removal and installation information can be found in Chapter 1.
2 It is important to replace spark plugs with new ones of the same heat range and type. A series of numbers and letters are stamped on the spark plug to help identify each variation.
3 The spark plug gap is of considerable importance, as if it is too large or too small the size of the spark and its efficiency will be seriously impaired. To set it, measure the gap with a feeler gauge, and then bend open, or close, the outer plug electrodes until the correct gap is achieved. The center electrode should never be bent as this may crack the insulation and cause plug failure, if nothing worse.
4 The condition and appearance of the spark plugs will tell much about the condition and tune of the engine. If the insulator nose of the spark plug is clean and white with no deposits, this is indicative of a weak mixture, or too hot a plug (a hot plug transfers heat away from the electrode slowly – a cold plug transfers it away quickly).
5 If the tip and insulator nose is covered with hard, black-looking deposits, then this is indicative that the mixture is too rich. Should the plug be black and oily, then it is likely that the engine is fairly worn, as well as the mixture being too rich.
6 If the insulator nose is covered with light tan to greyish brown deposits, then the mixture is correct and it is likely that the engine is in good condition.
7 If there are any traces of long, brown, tapering stains on the outside of the white portion of the plug, then the plug will have to be replaced with a new one, as this shows that there is a faulty joint between the plug body and the insulator, and compression is being allowed to leak away.
8 Always tighten a spark plug to the specified torque – no tighter.

8 Distributor cap – replacement

Note: *It is imperative that the spark plug wires be installed in the correct order on the distributor cap.*
1 If an inspection of the distributor cap terminals shows them to be burnt or crusty (photo), the cap should be replaced. Purchase a replacement distributor cap for your particular engine.
2 Disconnect the ignition switch/battery feed wire (BAT) and the tachometer lead (TACH), if equipped, from the distributor cap. Refer to Fig. 5.3.
3 Release the old cap from the distributor body by pushing downward on the slotted latches and then turning them $\frac{1}{4}$ turn (photo). Because of the distributor location, a stubby screwdriver will be needed on L4 engines.
4 On L4 engines, bring the cap into an accessible location. Place the new cap next to the old one. Use the electrical lead extension as a reference to get the new cap into the same relative position.

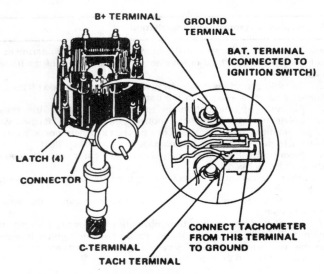

Fig. 5.3 Locations of the distributor coil connections (Sec 8)

8.1 Crusty deposits on the distributor cap terminals indicate that the cap needs replacement

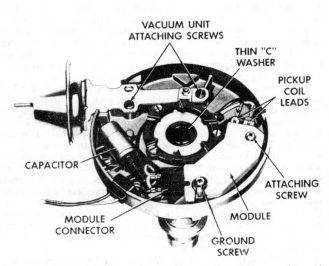

Fig. 5.4 Layout of the distributor base and components (Sec 9)

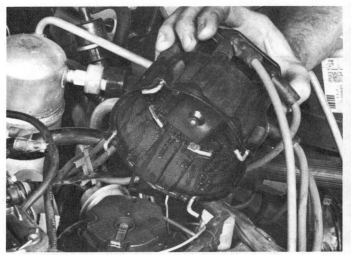

8.3 Removing the distributor cap (V6)

5   On V6 engine distributors, remove the retaining ring located on top of the cap (photo).
6   Begin transferring the spark plug wires **one at a time** from the old cap to the new one. Do not pull on the wire insulation, but rather grab the rubber boot, twist slightly and then pull the plug wire free by the boot.
7   On L4 engines, push the plug wires and boots firmly into the new distributor cap. On V6 engines, the plug wires should be fitted first into the retaining ring. Then when all wires are installed, the ring can be refitted onto the cap.
8   Place the new cap and plug wires into position over the top of the distributor and lock it into place by pushing and turning the latches. Make sure the cap is firmly seated.

9   Distributor – removal

1   Remove the distributor cap as described in Section 8. Move the cap (with the spark plug wires still attached) out of the way. Use wire or tape if necessary.
2   Remove the vacuum hose from the vacuum advance unit, and disconnect the distributor wiring harness.
3   At this point it is important to mark the position of the rotor and distributor housing for easier reassembly. At the very bottom of the

8.5 Removing the spark plug wire retaining-ring from the distributor cap on V6 engines

Measuring plug gap. A feeler gauge of the correct size (see ignition system specifications) should have a slight 'drag' when slid between the electrodes. Adjust gap if necessary

Adjusting plug gap. The plug gap is adjusted by bending the ground electrode inwards, or outwards, as necessary until the correct clearance is obtained. Note the use of the correct tool

Normal. Gray brown deposits, lightly coated core nose. Gap increasing by around 0.001 in (0.025 mm) per 1000 miles (1600 km). Plugs ideally suited to engine, and engine in good condition

Carbon fouling. Dry, black, sooty deposits. Will cause weak spark and eventually misfire. Fault: over-rich fuel mixture. Check: carburetor mixture settings, float level and jet sizes; choke operation and cleanliness of air filter. Plugs can be re-used after cleaning

Oil fouling. Wet, oily deposits. Will cause weak spark and eventually misfire. Fault: worn bores/piston rings or valve guides; sometimes occurs (temporarily) during running-in period. Plugs can be re-used after thorough cleaning

Overheating. Electrodes have glazed appearance, core nose very white – few deposits. Fault: plug overheating. Check: plug value, ignition timing, fuel octane rating (too low) and fuel mixture (too weak). Discard plugs and cure fault immediately

Electrode damage. Electrodes burned away; core nose has burned, glazed appearance. Fault: pre-ignition. Check: as for 'Overheating' but may be more severe. Discard plugs and remedy fault before piston or valve damage occurs

Split core nose (may appear initially as a crack). Damage is self-evident, but cracks will only show after cleaning. Fault: pre-ignition or wrong gap-setting technique. Check: ignition timing, cooling system, fuel octane rating (too low) and fuel mixture (too weak). Discard plugs, rectify fault immediately

distributor, scribe a mark in line with the base mark on the engine block. Also note the direction in which the rotor contact is pointed. Make a mark on the distributor housing in-line with the rotor contact strip (photo).
4   Remove the distributor clamp screw and hold-down clamp from the base of the distributor.
5   Lift the distributor straight up and out of the engine (photo). Again, note the position of the rotor. To ensure correct timing of the distributor, the rotor should be in this position prior to reinserting the distributor into the engine.
6   On L4 engines, the easiest way of removing the distributor from the engine compartment is by bringing it out to the left of the engine and under the brake master cylinder (photo).
7   Avoid rotating the engine with the distributor removed as the ignition timing will be changed.

10 Distributor – overhaul

1   Remove the distributor as previously described.
2   Remove the rotor (2 screws) (photo).
3   Remove the 2 screws retaining the module. Move the module aside and remove the connector from the 'B' and 'C' terminals
4   Remove the connections from the 'W' and 'G' terminals (photo).

5   Carefully drive out the roll pin from the drive gear (photo).
6   Remove the gear, shim and tanged washer from the distributor shaft.
7   Ensure that the shaft is not burred, then remove it from the housing (photo).
8   Remove the washer from the upper end of the distributor housing.
9   Remove 3 screws and take out the pole-piece, magnet and pick-up coil.
10 Remove the lock ring, then take out the pick-up coil retainer, shim and felt washer.
11 Remove the vacuum unit (2 screws) (photo).
12 Disconnect the capacitor lead and remove the capacitor (1 screw) (photos).
13 Disconnect the wiring harness from the distributor housing.
14 Wipe all components clean with a solvent moistened cloth and examine them for wear, distortion and other damage. Replace parts as necessary.
15 To assemble, position the vacuum unit to the housing and secure with the 2 screws.
16 Position the felt washer over the lubricant reservoir at the top of the housing, then position the shim on top of the felt washer.
17 Position the pick-up coil retainer to the housing. The vacuum advance arm goes over the actuating pin of the advance mechanism. Secure it with the lock ring.

9.3 Marking the position of the rotor on the distributor housing

9.5 Lifting the distributor from the engine (V6)

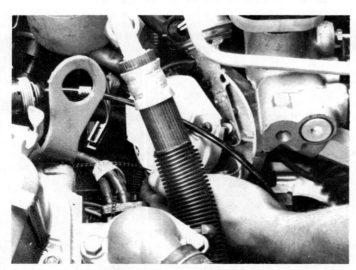
9.6 On L4 engines the distributor can be brought out to the left of the engine and under the master cylinder

10.2 Removing the rotor

10.4 Removing the module after disconnecting its leads

10.5 Driving out the roll pin from the drive gear

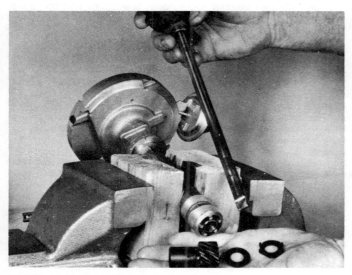
10.7 Removing the shaft from the housing

10.11 Removing the vacuum advance unit

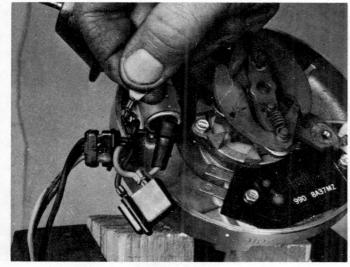
10.12a Disconnecting the capacitor leads

10.12b Removing the capacitor

18 Install the pick-up coil magnet and pole-piece. Loosely install the 3 screws to retain the pole-piece.
19 Install the washer to the top of the housing, install the distributor shaft, then rotate it and check for equal clearance all round between the shaft projections and pole-piece. Secure the pole-piece when correctly positioned.
20 Install the tanged washer, shim and drive gear. Align the gear and install a new roll pin.
21 Loosely install the capacitor with one screw.
22 Install the connector to the 'B' and 'C' terminals on the module with the tab at the top.
23 Apply silicone grease to the base of the module and secure it with 2 screws. This grease is essential to ensure good heat conduction.
24 Position the wiring harness with the grommet in the housing notch, then connect the pink wire to the capacitor stud and the black wire to the capacitor mounting screw. Tighten the screw.
25 Connect the white wire from the pick-up coil to the module 'W' terminal and the green to the 'G' terminal.
26 Install the advance weights, weight retainer (dimple downward) and springs.
27 Install the rotor and secure with the 2 screws. Ensure that the notch on the side of the rotor engages with the tab on the cam weight base.
28 Install the distributor as described in Section 11.

11 Distributor – installation

If engine was not rotated after removal
1 Position the rotor in the exact location it was in when the distributor was removed from the engine, as referred to in Section 9, paragraph 5.
2 Lower the distributor down into the engine, positioning the vacuum advance mechanism in the approximate position as removal. To mesh the gears at the bottom of the distributor it may be necessary to turn the rotor slightly.
3 With the base of the distributor all the way down against the engine block, the rotor should be pointed to the mark made on the distributor housing. If these two marks are not in alignment, repeat the previous steps.
4 Now turn the distributor housing until the scribed marks at the bottom of the distributor are in alignment.
5 Place the clamp into position and tighten the clamp bolt securely.
6 Connect the vacuum hose and wiring harness to the distributor.
7 Install the distributor cap, and connect the battery feed and tachometer wires.
8 Check the ignition timing as described in Section 2.

If engine was rotated after removal
9 Turn the crankshaft by applying a wrench to the crankshaft pulley bolt at the front of the engine until the number 1 position is at Top-Dead-Center (TDC). This can be ascertained by removing the number

1 spark plug and feeling the compression being generated. If you are careful not to scratch the cylinder, you can also use a length of stiff wire to feel the piston come to the top of the cylinder.
10 With the number 1 piston at TDC (as indicated by the timing marks on the front cover) the distributor should be firing this cylinder.
11 Position the rotor so it is pointing between the number 1 and 3 spark plug towers in the cap on L4 engines, or between the number 1 and 6 towers on V6 engines.
12 Proceed with installation as detailed in paragraphs 2 through 8. Disregard the rotor mark references in paragraph 3.

12 Ignition coil – removal and installation

1 On L4 engines, remove the distributor cap as described in Section 8.
2 On L4 engines, label the spark plug wires as to their position on the cap and remove them. On V6 engines, remove the spark plug wire retaining ring from the top of the distributor.
3 Remove the coil cover from the distributor cap (photo).
4 Note the position of each wire, duly marking them if necessary. Remove the coil ground wires then push the leads from the underside of the connectors. Remove the coil from the distributor cap (photo).
5 Installation is the reverse of the removal procedure, but ensure that the leads are connected to their original positions. Damage to the control module and ignition coil can result if the leads are connected incorrectly.

13 Charging system – general information

1 The charging system is made up of the generator, voltage regulator and the battery. These components work together to supply electrical power for the engine ignition, lights, radio, etc.
2 The generator is turned by a drivebelt on the right side of the engine. Thus, when the engine is operating, voltage is generated by the internal components of the generator to be sent to the battery for storage.
3 The generator uses a solid-state regulator that is mounted inside the generator housing. The purpose of this voltage regulator is to limit the generator voltage to a pre-set value. This prevents power surges, circuit overloads, etc., during peak voltage output. The regulator voltage setting cannot be adjusted.
4 The charging system does not ordinarily require periodic maintenance. The drivebelts, electrical wiring and connections should, however, be inspected during normal tune-ups (see Section 14).
5 All X-Body cars are equipped with either a 15-SI or 10-SI generator. The two types are similar except for the following:

- a) The 15-SI is slightly larger physically.
- b) The two types have different output ratings.
- c) They use different drive end and slip ring end bearings.
- d) The 15-SI stator uses delta windings which cannot be checked for open circuits.

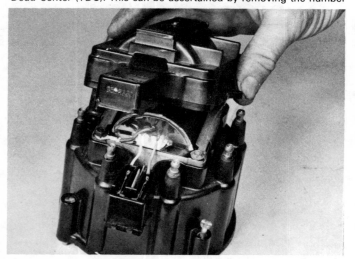

12.3 Removing the coil cover from the distributor cap

12.4 Removing the coil from the distributor cap

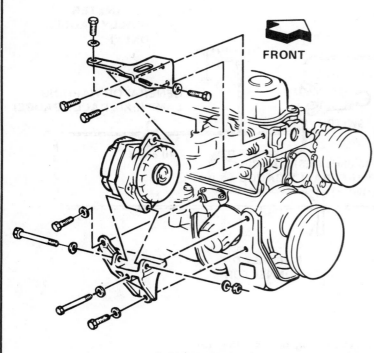

FRONT

L-4 WITHOUT A/C

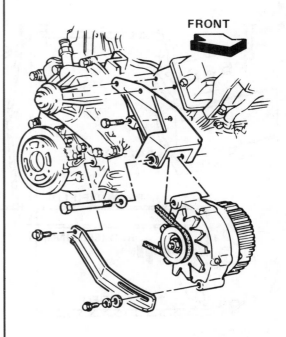

FRONT

V-6 WITHOUT A/C

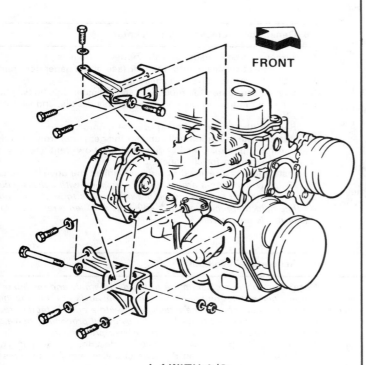

FRONT

L-4 WITH A/C

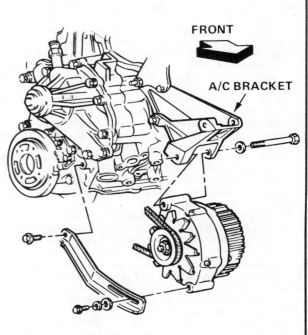

FRONT

A/C BRACKET

V-6 WITH A/C

Fig. 5.5 Generator mounting positions (Sec 13)

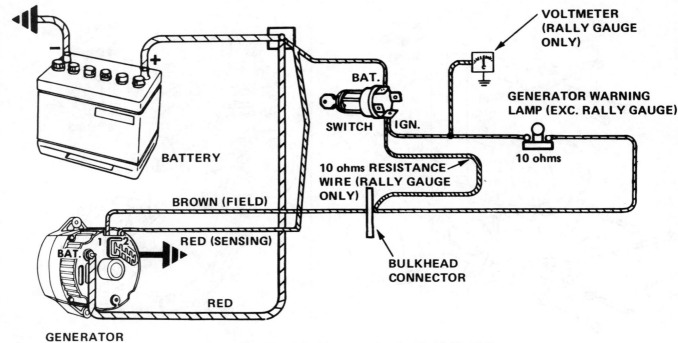

Fig. 5.6 Diagram of the SI system charging circuit (Sec 13)

14 Generator drivebelt – adjustment and replacement

1   The generator is a belt-driven component which is driven directly off of the crankshaft. See Chapter 1 for illustrations. Maintaining the proper tension on this belt is very important because if it is too loose it can put excessive strain on the belt, as well as the generator's shafts and bearings.

2   To check the tension of the belt, find the longest stretch of the belt and, gripping it in the center of this stretch, move the belt back and forth to gauge its slack. The distance that the belt can be moved back and forth should be about ½-in (13 mm). If the slack allows the belt to move more than this distance, the belt should be adjusted using the following procedure.

3   Loosen the generator's adjusting and mounting bolts and adjust the belt by moving the generator away from the engine. Tighten the adjusting and mounting bolts and recheck the adjustment.

4   If the generator drivebelt is frayed or cracked it should be replaced. This is done by using the following procedure.

5   On L4 engines, first remove the power steering pump belt, if equipped, as described in Chapter 11.

6   Loosen the generator's adjusting and mounting bolts and move the generator toward the engine until the belt is loose enough to remove from the pulley.

7   Install a new belt over the generator, crankshaft and water pump pulleys and adjust and tighten as described in paragraph 3.

8   If removed, reinstall the power steering pump belt on L4 engines.

15 Generator – maintenance and special precautions

1   Generator maintenance consists of occasionally wiping away any dirt or oil which may have collected.

2   Check the tension of the driving belt (refer to Section 14).

3   No lubrication is required as generator bearings are grease sealed for the life of the unit.

4   Take extreme care when making circuit connections to a vehicle fitted with a generator and observe the following. When making connections to the generator from a battery always match correct polarity. Before using electric-arc welding equipment to repair any part of the vehicle, disconnect the connector from the generator and disconnect the positive battery terminal. Never start the car with a battery charger connected. Always disconnect both battery leads

before using a mains charger. If boosting from another battery, always connect in parallel using heavy cable. It is not recommended that testing of a generator should be undertaken at home due to the testing equipment required and the possibility of damage occurring during test. It is best left to automotive electrical specialists.

16 Generator – removal and installation

1   Disconnect both leads from the battery terminals.

2   Disconnect the leads from the rear face of the generator, marking them first to ensure correct installation.

3   Loosen the generator mounting and adjuster link bolts (photo), push the unit in toward the engine as far as possible, and slip off the drive belts.

4   Remove the upper mounting bracket (photo).

5   Remove the mounting bolts and lift the generator from the engine compartment (photo). On L4 engines the fuel bowl vent line may have to be disconnected for clearance.

6   Installation is a reversal of removal; adjust the drive belt tension.

NOTE: *New generators are not usually supplied with pulleys. The old one should therefore be removed if a new unit is to be purchased. To do this, hold the generator shaft still with an Allen wrench while the pulley nut is unscrewed.*

17 Generator – overhaul

Note: *Due to the critical nature of the disassembly and testing of the various generator components, it may be advisable for the home mechanic to simply replace a faulty unit with a new or factory-rebuilt model. If it is decided to perform the overhaul procedure, make sure that replacement parts are available before proceeding.*

1   Remove the generator and pulley as described in Section 16.

2   Secure the generator in the jaws of a vise, applying the pressure to the mounting flange.

3   Remove the four through-bolts, and separate the slip ring end frame and stator assembly from the drive end and rotor assembly. Use a screwdriver to lever them apart and mark the relative position of the end frames to facilitate reassembly.

4   Remove the stator lead securing nuts and separate the stator from the end frame.

16.3 Loosening the generator adjusting bolts (L4)

16.4 Removing the generator upper mounting bracket (L4)

16.5 Removing the generator from the engine compartment

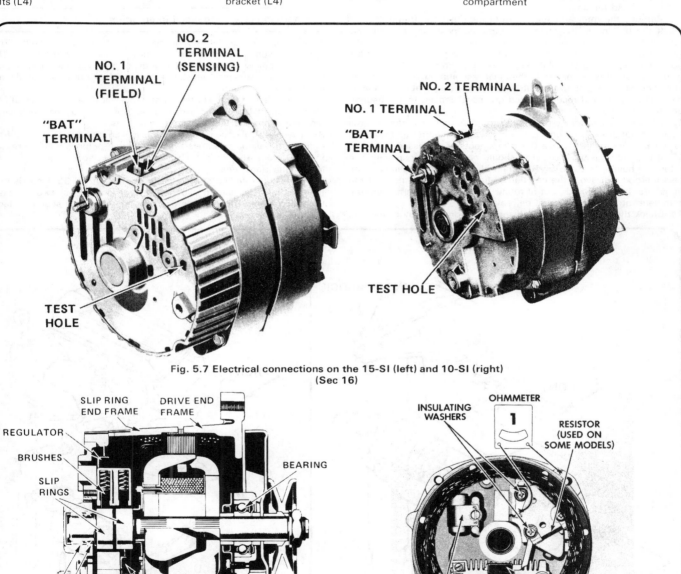

NO. 1 TERMINAL (FIELD)

NO. 2 TERMINAL (SENSING)

"BAT" TERMINAL

TEST HOLE

NO. 2 TERMINAL

NO. 1 TERMINAL

"BAT" TERMINAL

TEST HOLE

Fig. 5.7 Electrical connections on the 15-SI (left) and 10-SI (right)
(Sec 16)

SLIP RING END FRAME

DRIVE END FRAME

REGULATOR

BRUSHES

SLIP RINGS

BEARING

SEAL

BEARING

DIODE TRIO

ROTOR

RECTIFIER BRIDGE

STATOR ASSEMBLY

Fig. 5.8 Cutaway view of the 10-SI generator (15-SI is similar)
(Sec 17)

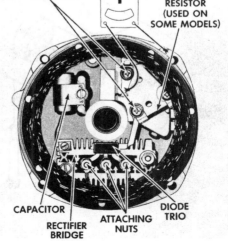

INSULATING WASHERS

OHMMETER

1

RESISTOR (USED ON SOME MODELS)

CAPACITOR

RECTIFIER BRIDGE

ATTACHING NUTS

DIODE TRIO

Fig. 5.9 Layout of the generator slip ring end frame assembly
(Sec 17)

5   Continue dismantling, by removing the rectifier bridge securing screw and the BAT terminal screw. Disconnect the capacitor lead and remove the rectifier bridge from the end-frame.

6   Unscrew the two securing screws and remove the brush holder and regulator. Carefully retain the insulating sleeves and washers.

7   Remove the capacitor (1 screw) from the end-frame.

8   If the slip ring end frame bearing is dry or noisy when rotated, it must be renewed (not greased). Greasing will not extend its service life. Press out the old bearing and discard the oil seal. Press in the new bearing, squarely, until the bearing is flush with the outside of the end frame. Install a new oil seal. During these operations, support the end frame adequately to prevent cracking or distorting the frame.

9   Now insert a $\frac{5}{16}$-in Allen wrench into the socket in the center of the shaft at the drive pulley end. Using this to prevent the shaft from rotating, unscrew the pulley retaining nut and remove the washer, pulley, fan and the spacer.

10   Remove the rotor and spacers from the drive end frame.

11   If the bearing in the drive end frame is dry or noisy it must be renewed. Do not grease it in the hope that this will extend its life. Access to the bearing is obtained after removing the retainer plate bolts and separating the plate/seal assembly. Press the bearing out using a piece of tube applied to the inner race and press the new one in by applying the . doe to the outer race. Make sure that the slinger is correctly located and recommended grease is applied to the bearing before installation.

12   With the generator completely dismantled, wipe all components clean (do not use solvent on the stator or rotor windings), and examine for wear or damage. Replace the components as necessary.

13   If the slip rings are dirty, they should be cleaned by spinning the rotor and holding a piece of 400-grain abrasive paper against them. This method will avoid the creation of flat spots on the rings. If the rings are badly scored, out-of-round or otherwise damaged, the complete rotor assembly must be replaced.

14   Check the brushes for wear. If they are worn halfway or more in length, purchase new ones. Replace the springs only if they appear weak or are distorted.

15   Reassembly is a reversal of dismantling, but observe the following points:

a)   *Tighten the pulley nut to the specified torque. Take great care to position the insulating washers and sleeves correctly on the brush clip screws.*

b)   *Clean the brush contact surfaces before installing the slip ring end frame and hold the brushes up in their holders by passing a thin rod through the opening in the clip end frame to permit the brushes to pass over the slip rings.*

c)   *Finally, make sure that the marks on the slip ring and drive end frame (which were made before dismantling) are in alignment.*

18 Starting system – general information

1   The function of the starting system is to crank the engine. This system is composed of a starting motor, solenoid and battery. The battery supplies the electrical energy to the solenoid, which then completes the circuit to the starting motor which does the actual work of cranking the engine.

2   The solenoid and starting motor are mounted together at the lower front of the engine. No periodic lubrication or maintenance is required to the starting system components.

3   The electrical circuitry of the vehicle is arranged so that the starter motor can only be operated when the clutch pedal is fully depressed (manual transaxle) or the transaxle selector lever is at 'P' or 'N' (automatic transaxle).

4   Never operate the starter motor for more than 30 seconds at a time without pausing to allow it to cool for at least two minutes. Excessive cranking can cause overheating, which can seriously damage the starter.

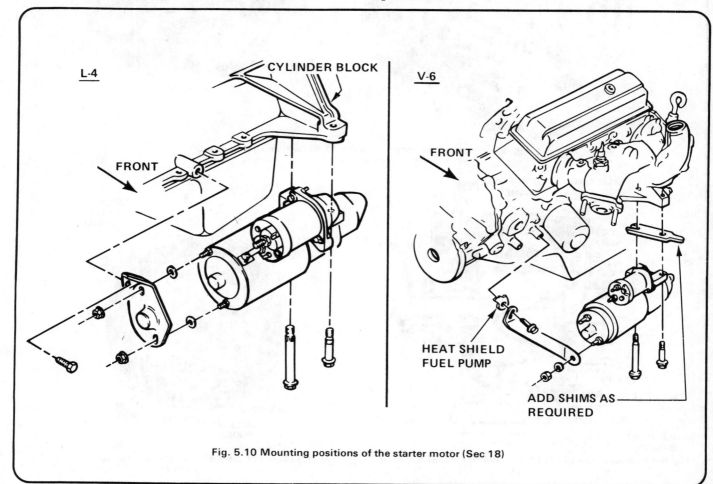

Fig. 5.10 Mounting positions of the starter motor (Sec 18)

19 Starter motor – testing in vehicle

1   If the starter motor does not rotate at all when the switch is operated, check that the speed selector lever is in 'N' or 'P' (automatic transaxle) or that the clutch pedal is depressed (manual transaxle).
2   Check that the battery is well charged and all cables, both at the battery and starter solenoid terminals, are secure.
3   If the motor can be heard spinning but the engine is not being cranked, then the overrunning clutch in the starter motor is slipping and the assembly must be removed from the engine and dismantled.
4   If, when the switch is actuated, the starter motor does not operate at all but the solenoid plunger can be heard to move with a loud 'click' then the fault lies in the main solenoid contacts or the starter motor itself.
5   If the solenoid plunger cannot be heard to move when the switch is actuated then the solenoid itself is defective or the solenoid circuit is open.
6   To check out the solenoid, connect a jumper lead between the battery (+) and the 'S' terminal on the solenoid. If the starter motor now operates, the solenoid is OK and the fault must lie in the ignition or neutral start switches or in their interconnecting wiring.
7   If the starter motor still does not operate, remove the starter/solenoid assembly for dismantling, testing and repair.
8   If the starter motor cranks the engine at an abnormally slow speed, first ensure that the battery is fully charged and all terminal connections are tight, also that the engine oil is not too thick a grade and that the resistance is not due to a mechanical fault within the power unit.
9   Run the engine until normal operating temperature is attained. Then disconnect the battery feed wire to the distributor cap so that the engine will not fire during cranking.
10 Connect a voltmeter positive lead to the starter motor terminal of the solenoid and then connect the negative lead to ground.
11 Actuate the ignition switch and take the voltmeter readings as soon as a steady figure is indicated. Do not allow the starter motor to turn for more than 30 seconds at a time. A reading of 9 volts, or more, with the starter motor turning at normal cranking speed proves it to be in good condition. If the reading is 9 volts, or more, but the cranking speed is slow, then the motor is faulty. If the reading is less than 9 volts and the cranking speed is slow, the solenoid contacts are probably at fault and should be replaced as described later in this Chapter.

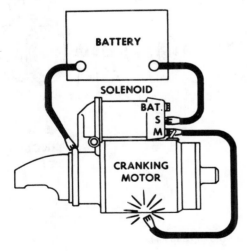

Fig. 5.11 Electrical connection set-up for checking pinion clearance of the starter motor (Sec 19)

20 Starter motor – removal and installation

1   Disconnect the ground cable from the battery.
2   Raise the vehicle to a satsifactory working height and support with jack stands.
3   Disconnect the leads at the starter solenoid, marking each with a coded piece of tape for easy identification upon reassembly. Temporarily refit each of the securing nuts to the terminals, as they have various thread types which could cause damage to the stubs if not properly reinstalled.
4   Remove the bolts that secure the plastic starter shield to the clutch bellhousing, and slide the shield back to expose the starter mounting bolts.
5   Remove the starter to engine brace.
6   Remove the 2 starter motor mounting bolts (photo).
7   Remove the starter (photo).
8   Installation is a reversal of removal, but tighten the mount bolts first to the specified torque and then tighten the front bracket bolt and nut. Be sure to replace any shims that were removed to maintain proper starter-to-flywheel alignment (photo).
9   Refit each of the wires to the solenoid terminals using your identification coding.

21 Starter motor – dismantling and component testing

Note: *Due to the critical nature of the disassembly and testing of the starter motor, it may be advisable for the home mechanic to simply purchase a new or factory-rebuilt unit. If it is decided to overhaul the starter, check on the availability of singular replacement components before proceeding.*
1   Disconnect the starter motor field coil connectors from the solenoid terminals.
2   Unscrew and remove the through bolts.
3   Remove the commutator end frame, field frame assembly and the armature from the drive housing. Remove the solenoid and shift lever assembly from the housing.
4   Slide the two-section thrust collar off the end of the armature shaft and then using a piece of suitable tube drive the stop/retainer up the armature shaft to expose the snap-ring (Fig. 5.13).
5   Extract the snap-ring from its shaft groove and then slide the stop/retainer and overrunning clutch assembly from the armature shaft.
6   Dismantle the brush components from the field frame.
7   Release the V-shaped springs from the brushholder supports.
8   Remove the brushholder support pin and then lift the complete brush assembly upwards.
9   Disconnect the leads from the brushes if they are worn down to half their original length and they are to be replaced.
10 The starter motor is now completely dismantled except for the field coils. If these are found to be defective during the tests described later in this Section removal of the pole shoe screws is best left to a service station which will have the necessary pressure driver.
11 Clean all components and replace any obviously worn components. Roller-type clutches are designed to be serviced as a complete unit and should not be disassembled.
12 *On no account attempt to undercut the insulation between the commutator segments on starter motors having the molded type commutators.* On commutators of conventional type, the insulation should be undercut (below the level of the segments) by $\frac{1}{32}$-in. Use an old hacksaw blade to do this and make sure that the undercut is the full width of the insulation and the groove is quite square at the bottom. When the undercutting is completed, brush away all dirt and dust.
13 Clean the commutator by spinning it while a piece of number '00' sandpaper is wrapped around it. On no account use any other type of abrasive material for this work.
14 If necessary, because the commutator is in such bad shape, it may be turned down in a lathe to provide a new surface. Make sure to undercut the insulation when the turning is completed.
15 *To test the armature for ground:* use a lamp-type circuit tester. Place one lead on the armature core or shaft and the other on a segment of the commutator. If the lamp lights then the armature is grounded and must be renewed.
16 *To test the field coils for open circuit:* place one test probe on the insulated brush and the other on the field connector bar. If the lamp does not light, the coils are open and must be renewed.
17 *To test the field coils for ground:* place one test probe on the connector bar and the other on the grounded bush. If the lamp lights then the field coils are grounded.
18 The overrunning clutch cannot be repaired and if faulty, it must be replaced as a complete assembly.

20.6 Removing the starter motor mounting bolts (L4)

20.7 Removing the starter (L4)

20.8 Installing shims for proper starter-to-flywheel alignment

22 Starter motor – reassembly and adjustment

1   Install the brush assembly to the field frame as follows:
2   Install the brushes to their holders.
3   Assemble the insulated and grounded brush holders together with the V-spring and then locate the unit on its support pin.
4   Push the holders and spring to the bottom of the support and then rotate the spring to engage the V in the support slot.
5   Connect the ground wire to the grounded brush and the field lead wire to the insulated brush.
6   Repeat the operations for the second set of brushes.
7   Smear silicone oil onto the drive end of the armature shaft and then slide the clutch assembly (pinion to the front) onto the shaft.
8   Slide the pinion stop/retainer onto the shaft so that its open end is facing away from the pinion.

9   Stand the armature vertically on a piece of wood and then position the snap-ring on the end of the shaft. Using a hammer and a piece of hardwood, drive the snap-ring onto the shaft.
10   Slide the snap-ring down the shaft until it drops into its groove.
11   Install the thrust collar on the shaft so that the shoulder is next to the snap-ring. Using two pairs of pliers, squeeze the thrust collar and stop/retainer together until the snap-ring fully enters the retainer (Fig. 5.14).
12   Lubricate the drive housing bush with silicone oil and after ensuring that the thrust collar is in position against the snap-ring, slide the armature and clutch assembly into the drive housing so that at the same time, the shift lever engages with the clutch.
13   Position the field frame over the armature and apply sealing compound between the frame and the solenoid case.
14   Position the field frame against the drive housing, taking care not to damage the brushes.

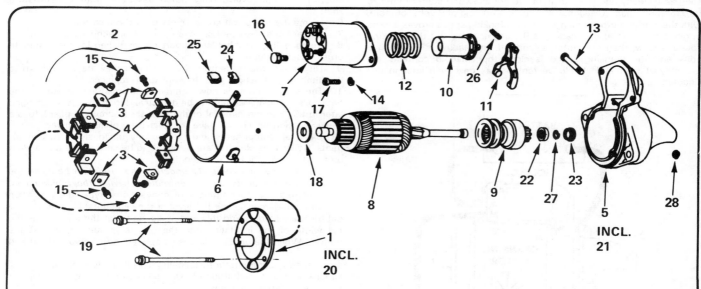

Fig. 5.12 Exploded view of the 5MT starter motor (Sec 21)

1 Frame – commutator end	10 Plunger	17 Screw – switch attaching
2 Brush and holder pkg	11 Shift lever	18 Washer – brake
3 Brush	12 Plunger return spring	19 Thru bolt
4 Brush holder	13 Shift lever shaft	20 Bushing – commutator end
5 Housing – drive end	14 Lock washer	21 Bushing – drive end
6 Frame and field asm	15 Screw – brush attaching	22 Pinion stop collar
7 Solenoid switch	16 Screw – field lead to switch	23 Thrust collar
8 Armature		24 Grommet
9 Drive asm		25 Grommet
		26 Plunger pin
		27 Pinion stop retainer ring
		28 Lever shaft retaining ring

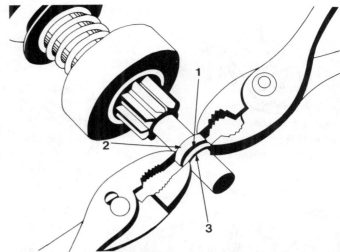

Fig. 5.14 Two pliers can be used to force the retainer over the snap ring during the installation procedure of a starter motor overhaul (Sec 21)

1	Snap ring	3	Thrust collar
2	Retainer		

Fig. 5.13 Using a hammer and $\frac{1}{2}$-in pipe coupling to remove the retainer from the snap ring during starter motor overhaul (Sec 21)

Fig. 5.15 To check the pinion clearance of the starter motor press on the clutch as shown to take up slack and measure the end clearance with a feeler gauge (Sec 22)

PRESS ON CLUTCH AS SHOWN
TO TAKE UP MOVEMENT

PINION

RETAINER

.010" TO .140"
PINION CLEARANCE

FEELER
GAUGE

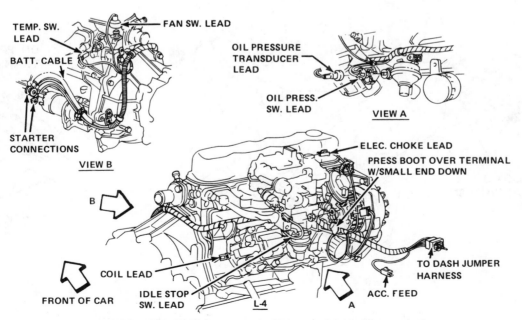

TEMP. SW. LEAD — FAN SW. LEAD

BATT. CABLE

STARTER
CONNECTIONS

VIEW B

OIL PRESSURE
TRANSDUCER
LEAD

OIL PRESS.
SW. LEAD

VIEW A

ELEC. CHOKE LEAD
PRESS BOOT OVER TERMINAL
W/SMALL END DOWN

B

COIL LEAD

IDLE STOP
SW. LEAD

FRONT OF CAR

L-4

A

ACC. FEED

TO DASH JUMPER
HARNESS

Fig. 5.16 Routing and connections of the engine wire harness (L4)

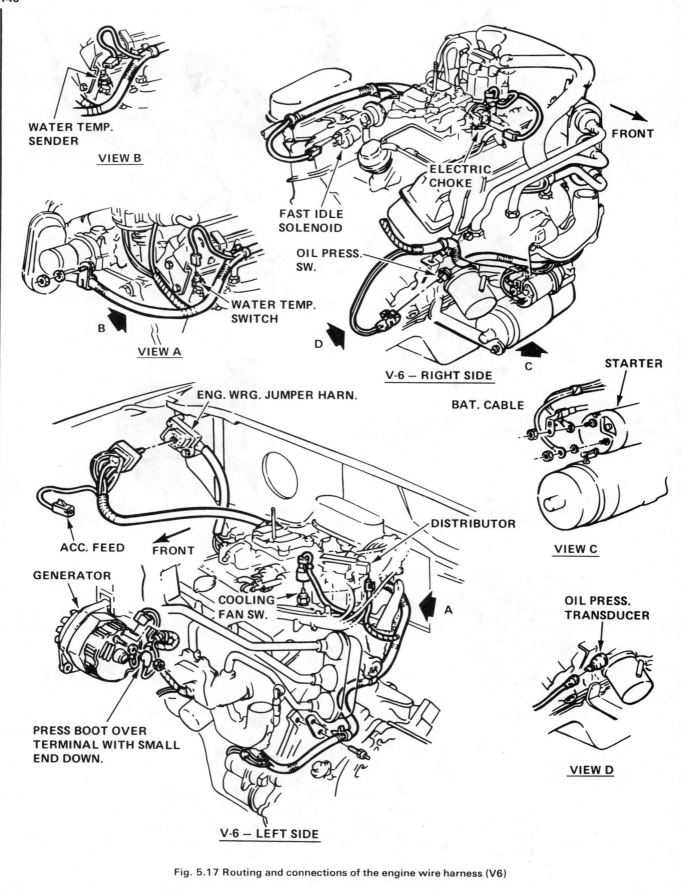

WATER TEMP.
SENDER

VIEW B

WATER TEMP.
SWITCH

B

VIEW A

ELECTRIC
CHOKE

FRONT

FAST IDLE
SOLENOID

OIL PRESS.
SW.

D

V-6 — RIGHT SIDE

C

STARTER

BAT. CABLE

VIEW C

ENG. WRG. JUMPER HARN.

DISTRIBUTOR

ACC. FEED

FRONT

GENERATOR

COOLING
FAN SW.

A

OIL PRESS.
TRANSDUCER

PRESS BOOT OVER
TERMINAL WITH SMALL
END DOWN.

VIEW D

V-6 — LEFT SIDE

Fig. 5.17 Routing and connections of the engine wire harness (V6)

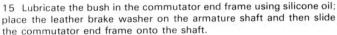

23.1 Disconnecting the connector strap between the solenoid and the starter motor

23.3 Removing the solenoid from the starter motor

15 Lubricate the bush in the commutator end frame using silicone oil; place the leather brake washer on the armature shaft and then slide the commutator end frame onto the shaft.

16 Reconnect the field coil connectors to the MOTOR terminal of the solenoid.

17 Now check the pinion clearance. To do this, connect a battery between the solenoid S terminal and ground and at the same time fix a heavy connecting cable between the MOTOR terminal and ground (to prevent any possibility of the starter motor rotating). As the solenoid is energized it will push the pinion forward into its normal cranking position and retain it there. With the fingers, push the pinion away from the stop/retainer in order to eliminate any slack and then check the clearance between the face of the pinion and the face of stop/retainer using a feeler gauge. The clearance should be between 0.010 and 0.140-in to ensure correct engagement of the pinion with the flywheel (or driveplate – automatic transaxle) ring-gear. If the clearance is incorrect, the starter will have to be dismantled again and any worn or distorted components renewed, no adjustment being provided for. Refer to Fig. 5.15.

23 Starter motor solenoid – removal, repair and installation

1 After removing the starter/solenoid unit as described in Section 20

disconnect the connector strap from the solenoid MOTOR terminal (photo).

2 Remove the two screws which secure the solenoid housing to the end-frame assembly.

3 Twist the solenoid in a clockwise direction to disengage the flange key and then withdraw the solenoid (photo).

4 Remove the nuts and washers from the solenoid terminals and then unscrew the two solenoid end-cover retaining screws and washers and pull off the end-cover.

5 Unscrew the nut washer from the battery terminal on the end-cover and remove the terminals.

6 Remove the resistor bypass terminal and contactor.

7 Remove the motor connector strap terminal and solder a new terminal in position.

8 Use a new battery terminal and install it to the end-cover. Install the bypass terminal and contactor.

9 Install the end-cover and the remaining terminal nuts.

10 Install the solenoid to the starter motor by first checking that the return spring is in position on the plunger and then insert the solenoid body into the drive housing and turn the body counter-clockwise to engage the flange key.

11 Install the two solenoid securing screws and connect the MOTOR connector strap.

Chapter 6 Emissions control systems

Refer to Chapter 13 for specifications and information related to 1981 through 1984 models

Contents

Torque specifications

	ft-lb	m-kg
EGR thermal vacuum switch	15	2.0
PULSAIR air line nuts	12	1.5
C-4 engine temperature switch	10	1.4
Oxygen sensor	30	4.1

General information

1   Despite the general bad feelings toward emissions controls, they play a necessary and integral role in the overall operation of the internal combustion engine. Your car is designed to operate with its pollution control systems, and disconnecting them or failing to properly maintain the components is illegal, not to mention being potentially harmful to the engine.

2   Through the years, as smog standards have become more stringent, emissions control systems have had to become more diverse and complex to keep the pace. Where once the anti-pollution devices incorporated were installed as peripheral components to the main engine, later-model engines work closely with, and in some cases are even controlled by, the emissions control systems. Nearly every system in the make-up of a modern-day automobile is affected in some fashion by the emissions systems.

3   This is not to say that the emissions systems are particularly difficult for the home mechanic to maintain and service. You can perform general operational checks, and do most (if not all) of the regular maintenance easily and quickly at home with common tune-up and hand tools.

4   While the end result from the various emissions systems is to reduce the output of pollutants into the air (namely hydrocarbons [HC], carbon monoxide [CO], and oxides of nitrogen [NOX]), the various systems function independently toward this goal. This is the way in which this Chapter is divided. NOTE: Information on the catalytic converter system can be found in Chapter 4.

5   If the vacuum hose schematic for your particular model, as shown in Figs. 6.13 through 6.18, does not exactly match the schematic shown on your Tune-up decal, the information on your decal should take presidence over these Figures.

2   Positive crankcase ventilation (PCV) system

General description

1   The positive crankcase ventilation, or PCV as it is more commonly called, reduces hydrocarbon emissions by circulating fresh air through the crankcase to pick up blow-by gases which are then re-routed through the carburetor to be returned by the engine.

2   The main components of this simple system are vacuum hoses and a PCV valve which regulates the flow of gases according to engine speed and manifold vacuum.

Positive crankcase ventilation system – checking

3   The PCV system can be checked for proper operation quickly and easily. This system should be checked regularly as carbon and gunk deposited by the blow-by gases will eventually clog the PCV valve and/or system hoses. When the flow of the PCV system is reduced or stopped, common symptoms are rough idling or a reduced engine speed at idle.

4   To check for proper vacuum in the system, remove the top plate of the air cleaner and locate the small PCV filter on the inside of the air cleaner housing.

5   Disconnect the hose leading to this filter. Be careful not to break the molded fitting on the filter.

6   With the engine idling, place your thumb lightly over the end of the hose. You should feel a slight pull or vacuum. The suction may be heard as your thumb is released. This will indicate that air is being drawn all the way through the system. If a vacuum is felt, the system is functioning properly. Check that the filter inside the air cleaner housing is not clogged or dirty. If in doubt, replace the filter with a new one, which is an inexpensive safeguard.

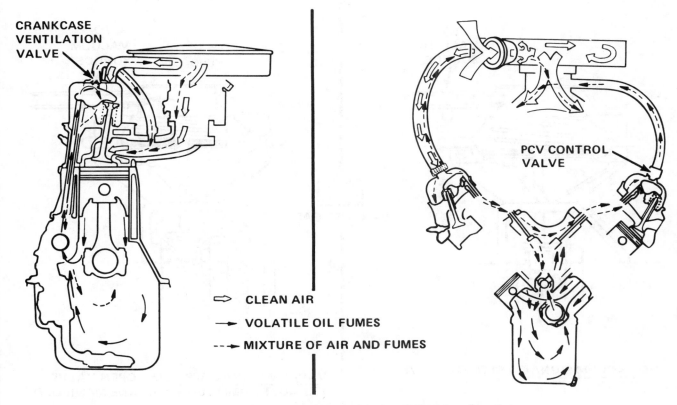

CRANKCASE VENTILATION VALVE

PCV CONTROL VALVE

⇨ CLEAN AIR

→ VOLATILE OIL FUMES

--→ MIXTURE OF AIR AND FUMES

Fig. 6.1 PCV system gas flow in the L4 and V6 engines (Sec 2)

7   If there is very little vacuum, or none at all, at the end of the hose, the system is clogged and must be inspected further.

8   Shut off the engine and locate the PCV valve. Carefully pull it from its rubber grommet. Shake it and listen for a clicking sound. That is the rattle of the valve's check needle. If the valve does not click freely, replace the valve with a new one.

9   Now start the engine and run it at idle speed with the PCV valve removed. Place your thumb over the end of the valve and feel for a suction. This should be a relatively strong vacuum which will be felt immediately.

10 If little or no vacuum is felt at the PCV valve, turn off the engine and disconnect the vacuum hose from the other end of the valve. Run the engine at idle speed and check for vacuum at the end of the hose just disconnected. No vacuum at this point indicates that the vacuum hose or inlet fitting at the engine is plugged. If it is the hose which is blocked, replace it with a new one or remove it from the engine and blow it out sufficiently with compressed air. A clogged passage at the carburetor or manifold requires that the component be removed and thoroughly cleaned of carbon build-up. A strong vacuum felt going into the PCV valve, but little or no vacuum coming out of the valve, indicates a failure of the PCV valve requiring replacement with a new one.

11 When purchasing a new PCV valve, make sure it is the proper one. See the specifications in Chapter 1. An incorrect PCV valve may pull too much or too little vacuum, possibly causing damage to the engine.

12 Information on removing and installing the PCV valve can be found in Chapter 1.

3   Exhaust gas recirculation (EGR) system

General description

1   This system is used to reduce oxides of nitrogen (NOX) emitted from the exhaust. Formation of these pollutants takes place at very high temperatures; consequently, it occurs during the peak temperature period of the combustion process. To reduce peak temperatures, and thus the formation of NOX, a small amount of exhaust gas is taken from the exhaust system and recirculated in the combustion cycle.

2   To tap this exhaust supply without an extensive array of pipes and connections in the exhaust system, additional exhaust passages are cast into the intricate runner system of the intake manifold. Because of this arrangement, most of the EGR routing components are hidden from view under the manifold.

3   Very little maintenance other than occasionally inspecting the vacuum hoses and the EGR valve is required. Beside the heart of the system – the EGR valve – the only moving part which can wear out is a Thermal Vacuum Switch (TVS) which controls the vacuum signal to the EGR valve at varying engine temperatures.

4   Two types of EGR valves are used on X-Body cars: a vacuum modulated unit and an exhaust back-pressure modulated unit. The major difference between the two valve types is the method used to control how far each valve opens.

5   In the vacuum modulated valve, the opening of the valve is controlled solely (once the TVS has opened) by a ported vacuum signal, sensitive to throttle position, which overcomes the valve's normal spring pressure (Fig. 6.2).

6   In the exhaust back-pressure type of EGR valve, a ported vacuum signal is also applied to the valve, but an air bleed prevents the valve from opening until the exhaust gas back-pressure is great enough. At this point the exhaust gases expand the valve's diaphragm and block the air bleed, allowing the vacuum signal to open the valve in the same manner as the vacuum modulated valve (Fig. 6.3).

7   Since the EGR system is determined by throttle position, it does not recirculate gases when the engine is at idle or during deceleration. In addition, the thermal vacuum switch does not allow the system to operate at all until the engine has reached normal operating temperature. This is so the EGR system won't lean out the rich gas/air mixture needed during cold engine operation.

8   Common engine problems associated with the EGR system are: rough idling or stalling when at idle, rough engine performance upon light throttle application and stalling on deceleration.

Exhaust gas recirculation system – checking

Note: *Also see Section 9 if equipped with C-4 system.*

9   Locate the EGR valve mounted on the right side of the intake manifold, adjacent to the carburetor.

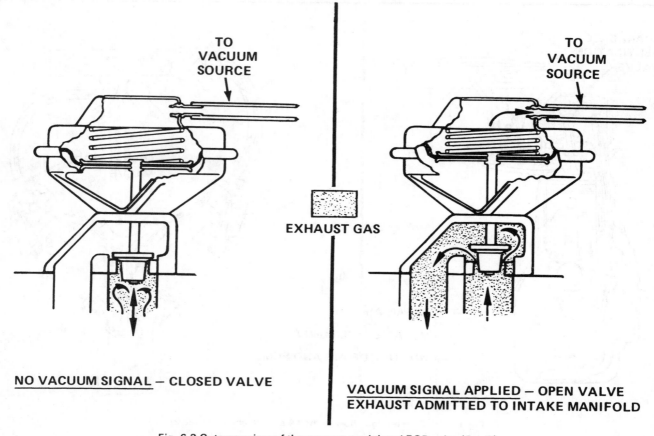

TO VACUUM SOURCE

EXHAUST GAS

TO VACUUM SOURCE

<u>NO VACUUM SIGNAL — CLOSED VALVE</u>

<u>VACUUM SIGNAL APPLIED — OPEN VALVE</u>
<u>EXHAUST ADMITTED TO INTAKE MANIFOLD</u>

Fig. 6.2 Cutaway view of the vacuum modulated EGR valve (Sec 3)

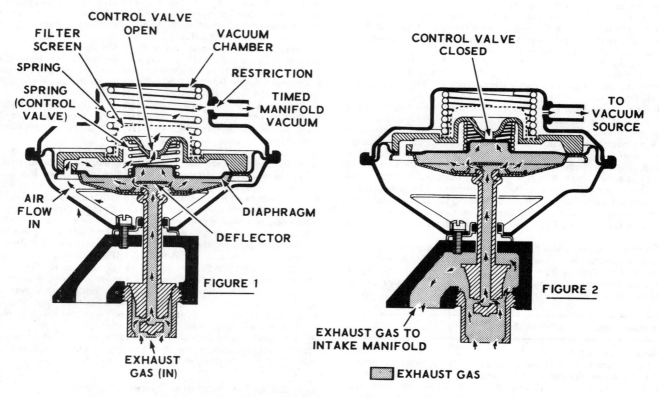

CONTROL VALVE OPEN

FILTER SCREEN

VACUUM CHAMBER

RESTRICTION

SPRING

TIMED MANIFOLD VACUUM

SPRING (CONTROL VALVE)

AIR FLOW IN

DIAPHRAGM

DEFLECTOR

FIGURE 1

EXHAUST GAS (IN)

CONTROL VALVE CLOSED

TO VACUUM SOURCE

FIGURE 2

EXHAUST GAS TO INTAKE MANIFOLD

EXHAUST GAS

Fig. 6.3 Cutaway view of the exhaust gas modulated EGR valve (Sec 3)

10 Place your finger under the EGR valve and push upward on the diaphragm plate. The diaphragm should move freely from the open to the closed position. If it doesn't, replace the EGR valve.

11 Now start the engine and run at idle speed. With your finger, manually depress the EGR diaphragm. If the valve or adjacent accessories are hot, wear gloves to prevent burning your fingers. When the diaphragm is pressed (valve closed to recirculate exhaust), the engine should lose speed, stumble or even stall. If the engine did not change speed, the EGR passages should be checked for blockage. This will require that the intake manifold be removed (See Chapter 2 for engine strip-down).

12 Now allow the engine to reach normal operating temperature. Have an assistant depress the accelerator slightly and hold the engine speed constant above idle.

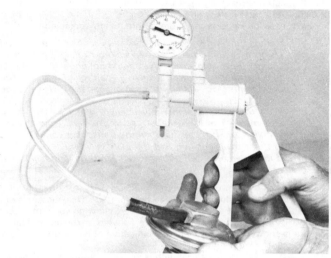

3.17 Testing the EGR valve with a vacuum tester

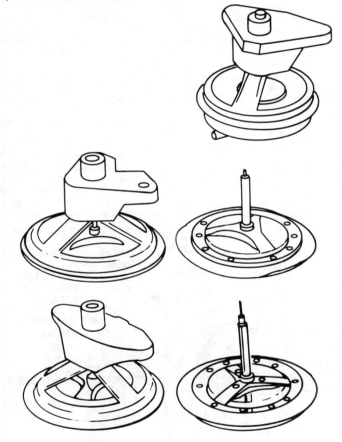

3.24 Removing the EGR valve attaching nuts

Fig. 6.4 The various EGR valves are identified by the design of the diaphragm plate. Shown are the vacuum modulated valve (top), negative pressure exhaust gas modulated valve (center) and positive pressure exhaust gas modulated valves (the latter two show the diaphragm plate isolated from the valve for greater clarity) (Sec 3)

13 Pull off the vacuum signal line at the EGR valve and check for the diaphragm plate to move downward, accompanied by an increase in engine speed.

14 Reinstall the vacuum line to the valve and the diaphragm plate should move upward with a decrease in engine speed.

15 If the diaphragm did not move, make sure the engine was at operating temperature. Repeat the test if in doubt.

16 If the diaphragm still does not move, your next check would be that vacuum is reaching the EGR valve. Pull off the vacuum hose at the valve, and with the engine running and accelerator slightly pressed, check for vacuum at the end of the hose with your thumb. If there is vacuum, replace the EGR valve with a new one. If there is no vacuum signal, follow the vacuum hose to its source, inspecting for disconnects, cracks, breaks or blockage in the lines.

3.25 Lifting the EGR valve from the intake manifold

17 If vacuum is reaching the EGR valve but the diaphragm is still not moving, one further test should be conducted if the valve is of the exhaust back-pressure type before automatically replacing it.

  a) *Remove the valve from the car, as described in this section.*
  b) *Using a vacuum tester, apply vacuum to the EGR's vacuum signal tube (photo). The valve should not open. If it does, then the transducer control, which is controlled by the back-pressure, is stuck in the 'Up' position, and the EGR valve must be replaced.*
  c) *With the vacuum signal still applied, direct a low-pressure stream of air in the exhaust gas intake hole. Now the valve should open. If it doesn't, then the transducer control is stuck in the 'Down' position and the EGR valve must be replaced.*
  d) *If the valve operated properly in these tests, reinstall it in the engine.*

18 The EGR system uses a thermal vacuum switch to regulate EGR valve operation in relation to engine temperature. This vacuum switch opens as the coolant temperature increases, allowing vacuum to reach the EGR valve. The exact temperature for your particular model and engine is shown in Fig 6.12., and is indicative of the normal operating temperature of your engine.
19 The best way to test the switch is with a vacuum gauge, checking the vacuum signal with the engine hot.
20 Disconnect the vacuum hose at the EGR valve, connect the vacuum gauge to the disconnected end of the hose and start the engine. Note the reading on the vacuum gauge with the engine at an idle and then have an assistant depress the accelerator slightly and note this reading. As the accelerator is depressed, the vacuum reading should increase.
21 If the gauge does not respond to the throttle opening, disconnect the hose which leads from the carburetor to the thermal vacuum switch. Repeat the test with the vacuum gauge installed in the vacuum hose end at the switch. If the vacuum gauge responds to accelerator opening, the thermal vacuum switch is defective and should be replaced with a new one.
22 If the gauge still does not respond to an increase in throttle opening, check for a plugged hose or defective carburetor.

EGR valve – replacement
23 Disconnect the vacuum hose at the EGR valve.
24 Remove the nuts or bolts which secure the valve to the intake manifold (photo).
25 Lift the EGR valve from the engine (photo).
26 Clean the mounting surfaces of the EGR valve. Remove all traces of gasket material (photo).
27 Place the new EGR valve, with a new gasket, on the intake manifold and tighten the attaching bolts or nuts.
28 Connect the vacuum signal hose.

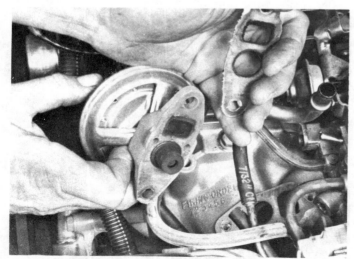

3.26 Replacing the EGR valve gasket

Thermal vacuum switch – replacement
29 Drain the engine coolant until the coolant level is beneath the switch.
30 Disconnect the vacuum hoses from the switch, noting their positions for reassembly.
31 Using a suitable wrench, remove the switch.
32 When installing the switch, apply thread sealer to the threads, being careful not to allow the sealant to touch the bottom sensor.
33 Install the switch and tighten it to specifications.

4   Evaporative emissions control system

General description
1 Although the evaporative emissions control (EEC) system is one of the most complex-looking, it is actually one of the most basic and trouble-free portions of the emissions network. Its function is to reduce hydrocarbon emissions. Basically, this is a closed fuel system which re-routes wasted fuel back to the gas tank and stores fuel vapors instead of venting them to the atmosphere.
2 Due to its very nature of having few moving parts, the EEC system requires no periodic maintenance except for replacement of the oiled fiberglass filter in the bottom of the charcoal canister at the recommended intervals.
3 A tip-off that this system is not operating properly is the strong smell of fuel vapors.
4 A pressure vacuum gasoline filler cap is used to vent the fuel tank as a standard cap would render the system ineffective and could possibly collapse the fuel tank due to pressure build-up. Other components which make up this system include: a special gas tank with fill limiters and vent connections, a charcoal canister with integral purge valve and filter which stores vapors from the fuel tank, a carburetor bowl vent valve, and various hoses linking the main components.

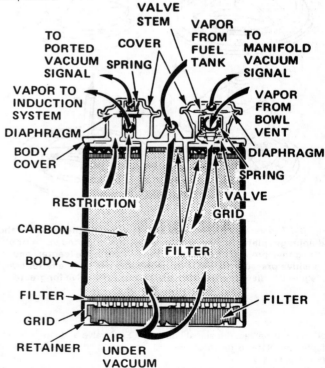

Fig. 6.5 Cutaway view of the EEC system vapor storage canister (Sec 4)

EEC system – checking
Note: *Also see Section 9 if equipped with C-4 system.*

5 As mentioned earlier, this system requires little maintenance; however, if a problem is suspected, the system should be inspected.
6 With the engine cold and at room temperature, disconnect the fuel tank line at the charcoal canister. On all models the canister is located

inside the engine compartment behind the right headlight. Each of the hose connections are duly labeled.

7   As this hose is disconnected, check for the presence of liquid fuel in the line. Fuel in this vapor hose is an indication that the vent controls or pressure-vacuum relief valve in the gas cap are not functioning properly.

8   Hook up a pressure suction device on the end of the fuel vapor line. Apply 15 psi of pressure to the line and observe for excessive loss of pressure.

9   Check for a fuel vapor smell in the engine compartment and around the gas tank.

10   Remove the fuel filler cap and check for pressure in the gas tank.

11   If there is a large loss of pressure or a fuel odor, inspect all lines for leaks or deterioration.

12   With the fuel filler cap removed, apply pressure again and check for obstructions in the vent line.

13   To check the purge valve built into the canister, start the engine and disconnect the vacuum signal line running from the engine to the canister. With your thumb over the end of the hose, raise the engine speed to about 1500 rpm and check for vacuum. If there is no vacuum signal, check the EGR operation as described in this chapter. The vacuum signal for the canister and the EGR valve originate from the same source.

14   On the V6 engine the purge line to the charcoal canister functions with the PCV vacuum when this hose is disconnected from the canister, check the PCV valve vacuum.

15   The routing of the various vacuum lines of the EEC system are shown in Figs. 6.13 through 6.18.

Charcoal canister and filter

16   See Chapter 1 for information on the servicing of the canister and filter.

5   Thermostatic air cleaner (Thermac)

General description

1   The thermostatic air cleaner (Thermac) system is provided to improve engine efficiency and reduce hydrocarbon emissions during the initial warm-up period of the car by maintaining a controlled air temperature into the carburetor. This temperature control of the incoming air allows leaner carb and choke calibrations.

2   The system uses a damper assembly located in the snorkel of the air cleaner housing to control the ratio of cold and warm air into the carburetor. This damper is controlled by a vacuum motor which is, in turn, modulated by a temperature sensor in the air cleaner. On some engines a check valve is used in the sensor, which delays the opening of the damper flap when the engine is cold and the vacuum signal is low.

3   It is during the first few miles of driving (depending on outside temperature) when this system has its greatest effect on engine performance and emissions output. When the engine is cold, the damper flap blocks off the air cleaner inlet snorkel, allowing only warm air from the exhaust manifold to enter the carb. Gradually, as the engine warms up, the flap opens the snorkel passage, increasing the amount of cold air allowed in. Once the engine reaches normal operating temperature, the flap completely opens, allowing only cold, fresh air to enter.

4   Because of this cold-engine-only function, it is important to periodically check this system to prevent poor engine performance when cold, or overheating of the fuel mixture once the engine has reached operating temperatures. If the air cleaner valve sticks in the 'no heat' position, the engine will run poorly, stall and waste gas until it has warmed up on its own. A valve sticking in the 'heat' position causes the engine to run as if it is out of tune due to the constant flow of hot air to the carburetor.

Thermac assembly – checking

5   The thermostatic air cleaner components can be quickly and easily checked for proper operation.

6   With the engine off, observe the damper door inside the air cleaner snorkel. If the car is equipped with an air duct off the end of the snorkel, this will have to be removed prior to checking (photo). If visual access to the damper door is difficult because of positioning, use a mirror. The valve should be open, meaning that in this position all air

5.6 The flexible air duct must be removed from the air cleaner snorkel prior to checking the Thermac damper door operation.

would flow through the snorkel and none through the exhaust manifold hot-air duct at the underside of the air cleaner housing.

7   Now have an assistant start the engine and continue to observe the flapper door inside the snorkel. With the engine cold and at idle the damper door should close off all air from the snorkel, allowing heated air from the exhaust manifold to enter the air cleaner as intake. As the engine warms to operating temperature the damper door should move, allowing outside air through the snorkel to be included in the mixture. Eventually, the door should recede to the point where most of the incoming air is through the snorkel and not the exhaust manifold passage.

8   If the damper door did not close off snorkel air when the cold engine was first started, disconnect the vacuum hose at the snorkel vacuum motor and place your thumb over the hose end, checking for vacuum. If there is vacuum going to the motor, check that the damper door and link are not frozen or binding within the air cleaner snorkel. Replace the vacuum motor if the hose routing is correct and the damper door moves freely.

9   If there was no vacuum going to the motor in the above test, check the hoses for cracks, crimps or disconnects. If the hoses are clear and in good condition, replace the temperature sensor inside the air cleaner housing.

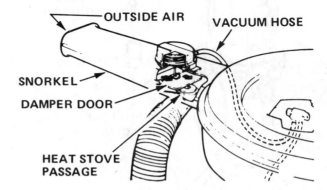

Fig. 6.6 Cutaway view of the Thermac damper door assembly (Sec 5)

Air cleaner vacuum motor – replacement

10   Remove the air cleaner assembly from the engine and disconnect the vacuum hose from the motor.

11   Drill out the two spot welds which secure the vacuum motor retaining strap to the snorkel tube.

12   Remove the motor attaching strap.

13   Lift up the motor, cocking it to one side to unhook the motor linkage at the control damper assembly.

14 To install, drill a $\frac{7}{64}$ in hole in the snorkel tube at the center of the reaining strap.

15 Insert the vacuum motor linkage into the control damper assembly.

16 Using the sheetmetal screw supplied with the motor service kit, attach the motor and retaining strap to the snorkel. Make sure the sheetmetal screw does not interfere with the operation of the damper door.

17 Connect the vacuum hose to the motor and install the air cleaner assembly.

Air cleaner temperature sensor – replacement

18 Remove the air cleaner from the engine and disconnect the vacuum hoses at the sensor.

19 Carefully note the position of the sensor. The new sensor must be installed in exactly the same position.

20 Pry up the tabs on the sensor retaining clip and remove the sensor and clip from the air cleaner.

21 Install the new sensor with a new gasket in the same position as the old one.

22 Press the retaining clip on the sensor. Do not damage the control mechanism in the center of the sensor.

23 Connect the vacuum hoses and install the air cleaner to the engine.

6   Early fuel evaporation (EFE) system

General description

1 The early fuel evaporation system is used only on V6 engines, and, like the Thermac system, is designed to increase efficiency and lower hydrocarbon emissions levels during cold engine operation by providing a rapid source of heat to the air induction system.

2 The EFE system uses a valve located in between the exhaust manifold and the exhaust pipe (Fig. 6.7) to recirculate exhaust gases to help pre-heat the carburetor and choke. This valve is vacuum-operated and controlled by a thermal vacuum switch (TVS) which senses coolant temperature. If equipped with the C-4 system (Section 9), this could also alter the function of the EFE system.

3 For information on the operation of the valve, the effects of a

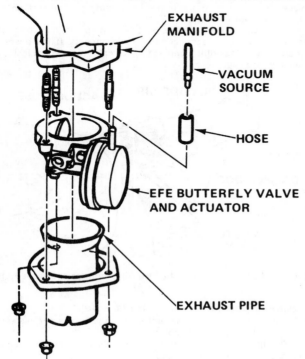

EXHAUST MANIFOLD

VACUUM SOURCE

HOSE

EFE BUTTERFLY VALVE AND ACTUATOR

EXHAUST PIPE

Fig. 6.7 The EFE valve is located between the exhaust manifold and exhaust pipe (Sec 6)

malfunctioning valve and how to check the system, refer to Chapter 1.

EFE valve – replacement

4 Disconnect the vacuum hose from the actuator fitting.

5 Remove the exhaust crossover pipe.

6 Remove the nuts that secure the valve assembly to the exhaust manifold.

7 Remove the valve assembly.

8 Installation is the reverse of the removal procedure.

Thermal vacuum switch (TVS) – replacement

9 Drain the engine coolant until the fluid level is below the level of the switch.

10 Disconnect the hoses from the TVS switch, making note of their positions for reassembly.

11 Using a suitable wrench, remove the TVS switch.

12 Apply a soft-setting sealant uniformly to the threads of the new TVS switch. Be careful that none of the sealant gets on the sensor end of the switch.

13 Install the switch and tighten to specifications.

14 Connect the vacuum hoses to the switch in their original positions and add coolant as necessary.

7   Pulse air injection reaction (PULSAIR) system

General description

1 The purpose of the PULSAIR system is to reduce hydrocarbons in the exhaust by injecting fresh air directly into the exhaust manifold ports of each engine cylinder. The fresh, oxygen-rich air helps combust the unburned hydrocarbons before they are expelled as exhaust. Not all engines are equipped with this system.

2 The PULSAIR system is extremely simple, both mechanically and functionally. The vacuum pulses created in the exhaust ports simply draw the fresh air in through the air valve and lines. One way check valves are used between each of the lines and the air valve to prevent exhaust back-pressure from forcing the gases back out through the air valve.

PULSAIR system – checking

Note: *Also see Section 9 if equipped with C-4 system.*

3 The simplicity of the system makes it very reliable one which seldom causes problems. Periodic checks should be made, however, of the condition of the components to be sure there are no leaks or cracks in the system.

4 A simple functional test of the system can be performed with the engine running. Disconnect the rubber hose from the air valve and hold your hand over the valve's inlet hole. With the engine idling, there should be a steady stream of air being sucked into it. Have an assistant apply throttle, and as the engine gains speed the suction should increase. If this does not occur, either there are leaks or blockage in the lines or the check valves are sticking. Also check that air is not being blown out of the air valve, as this is an indication also that the check valves are sticking open. Sevice or replace the components as necessary. NOTE: If your car is equipped with a C-4 system (described in this Chapter), have a dealer or other qualified mechanic diagnose PULSAIR problems as they might relate to the C-4 computor, before replacing PULSAIR components.

PULSAIR valve assembly – replacement

5 Remove the air cleaner and disconnect the negative battery cable.

6 Disconnect the rubber hose from the pulse air valve.

7 If equipped, disconnect the support bracket.

8 If equipped on V6 engines, remove the PULSAIR solenoid and bracket from the PULSAIR unit.

9 Loosen the nuts that secure the air tubes to the cylinder head and remove the assembly. Due to the high temperature at this area, these connections may be difficult to loosen. Penetrating oil applied to the threads of these nuts may help.

10 Before installing, apply a light coat of oil to the ends of the air tubes, and an anti-seize compound to the threads of the attaching nuts.

11 Installation is the reverse of the removal procedure.

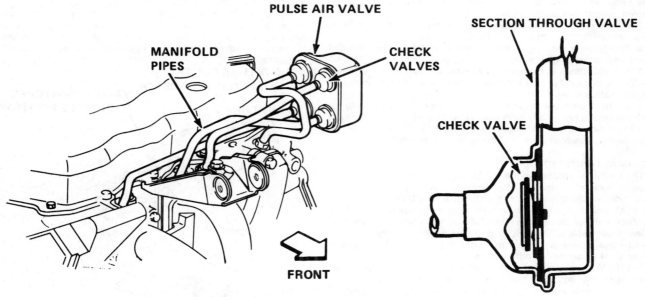

Fig. 6.8 PULSAIR system (Sec 7)

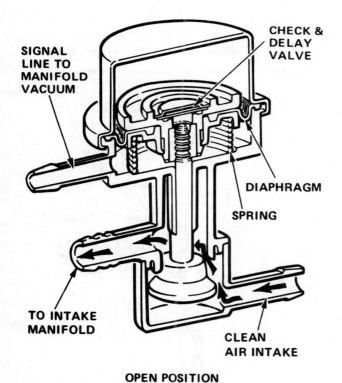

Fig. 6.9 Cutaway view of the deceleration valve (Sec 8)

8   Deceleration valve

General description

1   The deceleration valve is provided on all engines to prevent backfiring in the exhaust system during deceleration.
2   The valve is controlled by a vacuum line connected to the intake manifold. Under normal engine operation the valve remains closed.

When deceleration causes a sudden vacuum increase in the intake manifold, the vacuum signal to the valve overcomes the spring tension that holds the valve closed. This opens the valve and allows fresh air to bleed into the intake manifold, thus leaning out the air/fuel mixture and eliminating backfiring.
3   Air trapped in the chamber above the vacuum diaphragm bleeds through a check and delay valve at a calibrated rate, slowly lessening the vacuum signal within the deceleration valve, eventually allowing the spring to once more close the valve to incoming air.
4   The check valve also provides quick balancing of the chamber pressure when a sudden decrease in vacuum is caused by acceleration instead of deceleration.

Deceleration valve – checking

5   If you begin to experience backfiring while decelerating or if the engine exhibits lean mixture tendencies such as rough idling, stumbling upon acceleration or stalling, a check of the deceleration valve should be made.
6   Begin any inspection by checking the air lines and vacuum line for leaking or blockage.
7   With the engine idling, disconnect the inlet air line at the deceleration valve.
8   Place your finger over the inlet fitting. There should be no air being drawn into the valve at this time. If there is, then the valve is stuck open and should be replaced.
9   Have an assistant race the engine for a couple of moments, and then quickly let off the throttle. You should feel air being drawn in through the valve's inlet fitting immediately following the let-up on the throttle.
10   If no air was drawn in during the moments of deceleration, disconnect the vacuum line at the deceleration valve and repeat the same test. Take note that some amount of vacuum is always present in this line, but the vacuum should increase during periods of deceleration. If this is not the case, then the vacuum line is either leaking or clogged and should be cleaned or replaced as necessary.
11   If an increase in vacuum is noticeable in the vacuum line during deceleration, then the valve is stuck closed and should be replaced.

9   Computor command control (C-4) system

General description

1   The computor command control system, also known as the C-4 system, is used on various engines and controls exhaust emissions

while retaining driveability by maintaining a continuous interaction between various emission systems.

2   The main components in the system are an exhaust gas oxygen sensor, an electronic control module and a controlled air/fuel ratio carburetor. Several minor components are also used to link the C-4 system with other engine systems.

3   Any malfunctions in the computor command system are signaled by a 'Check Engine' light on the dash which goes on and remains lit until the malfunction is corrected.

4   Since the computor command system requires special tools for maintenance and repair, any work on it should be left to your dealer or a qualified technician. Although complicated, the system can be understood by examining each component and its function.

Electronic control module (ECM)

5   The electronic control module (ECM) is essentially a small onboard computer located under the dash which monitors up to 15 engine/vehicle functions and controls as many as 9 different operations. The ECM contains a programmable read only memory (PROM) calibration unit which tailors each ECM's performance to conform to the individual vehicle. The PROM is programmed with the vehicle's particular design, weight, final drive ratio, etc., and can't be used in another ECM or car which differs in any way.

6   The ECM receives continuous information from the computer command system and processes it in accordance with PROM instructions. It then sends out electronic signals to the system components, modifying their performance.

Oxygen sensor (OS)

7   The oxygen sensor (OS) is mounted in the exhaust pipe, upstream of the catalytic converter. It monitors the exhaust stream and sends information to the ECM on how much oxygen is present. The oxygen level is determined by how rich or lean the fuel mixture in the carburetor is.

8   This sensor should be replaced at specified intervals as part of the regular routine maintenance schedule. Refer to Chapter 1.

Mixture control solenoid

9   This controls the fuel flow through the carburetor idle main metering circuits. The solenoid cycles 10 times per second, constantly adjusting the fuel/air mixture. The ECM energizes the solenoid on information it receives from the oxygen sensor so as to keep emissions within limits.

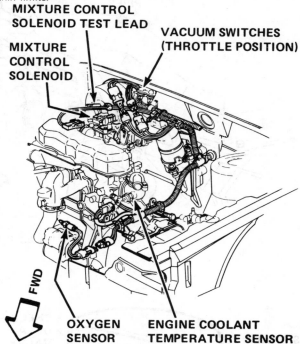

Fig. 6.10 C-4 system wiring harness (L4 engine) (Sec 9)

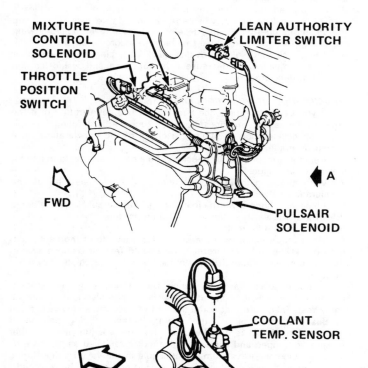

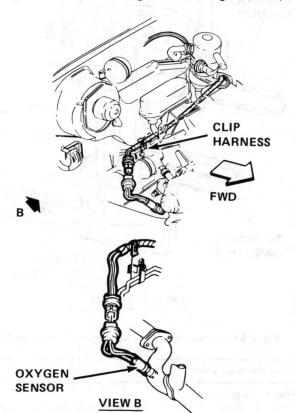

Fig. 6.11 C-4 system wiring harness (V6 engine) (Sec 9)

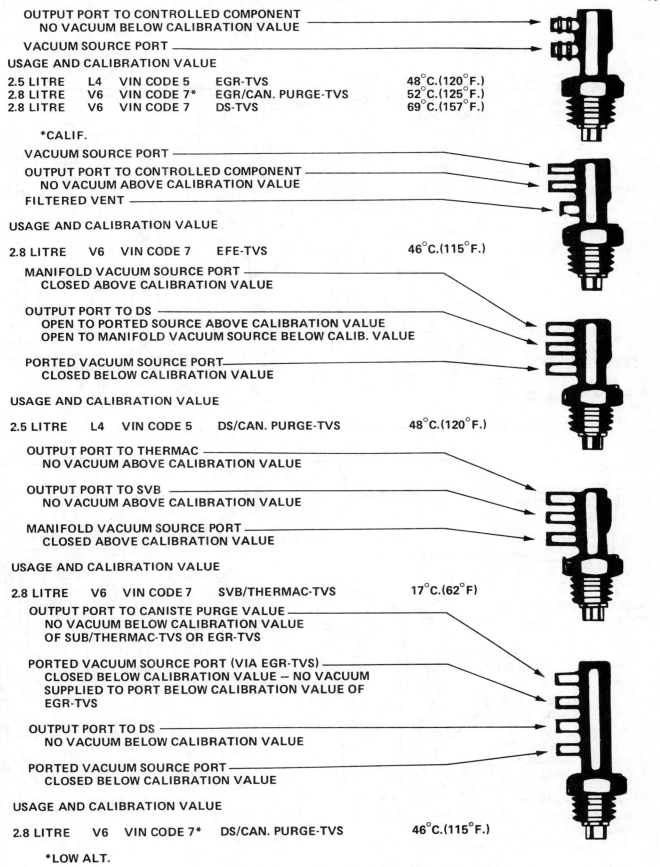

OUTPUT PORT TO CONTROLLED COMPONENT
NO VACUUM BELOW CALIBRATION VALUE

VACUUM SOURCE PORT

USAGE AND CALIBRATION VALUE

2.5 LITRE	L4	VIN CODE 5	EGR-TVS	48°C.(120°F.)
2.8 LITRE	V6	VIN CODE 7*	EGR/CAN. PURGE-TVS	52°C.(125°F.)
2.8 LITRE	V6	VIN CODE 7	DS-TVS	69°C.(157°F.)

*CALIF.

VACUUM SOURCE PORT

OUTPUT PORT TO CONTROLLED COMPONENT
NO VACUUM ABOVE CALIBRATION VALUE

FILTERED VENT

USAGE AND CALIBRATION VALUE

2.8 LITRE   V6   VIN CODE 7   EFE-TVS   46°C.(115°F.)

MANIFOLD VACUUM SOURCE PORT
CLOSED ABOVE CALIBRATION VALUE

OUTPUT PORT TO DS
OPEN TO PORTED SOURCE ABOVE CALIBRATION VALUE
OPEN TO MANIFOLD VACUUM SOURCE BELOW CALIB. VALUE

PORTED VACUUM SOURCE PORT
CLOSED BELOW CALIBRATION VALUE

USAGE AND CALIBRATION VALUE

2.5 LITRE   L4   VIN CODE 5   DS/CAN. PURGE-TVS   48°C.(120°F.)

OUTPUT PORT TO THERMAC
NO VACUUM ABOVE CALIBRATION VALUE

OUTPUT PORT TO SVB
NO VACUUM ABOVE CALIBRATION VALUE

MANIFOLD VACUUM SOURCE PORT
CLOSED ABOVE CALIBRATION VALUE

USAGE AND CALIBRATION VALUE

2.8 LITRE   V6   VIN CODE 7   SVB/THERMAC-TVS   17°C.(62°F)

OUTPUT PORT TO CANISTE PURGE VALUE
NO VACUUM BELOW CALIBRATION VALUE
OF SUB/THERMAC-TVS OR EGR-TVS

PORTED VACUUM SOURCE PORT (VIA EGR-TVS)
CLOSED BELOW CALIBRATION VALUE — NO VACUUM
SUPPLIED TO PORT BELOW CALIBRATION VALUE OF
EGR-TVS

OUTPUT PORT TO DS
NO VACUUM BELOW CALIBRATION VALUE

PORTED VACUUM SOURCE PORT
CLOSED BELOW CALIBRATION VALUE

USAGE AND CALIBRATION VALUE

2.8 LITRE   V6   VIN CODE 7*   DS/CAN. PURGE-TVS   46°C.(115°F.)

*LOW ALT.

Fig. 6.12 Thermal vacuum valves and switches used on the X-body cars

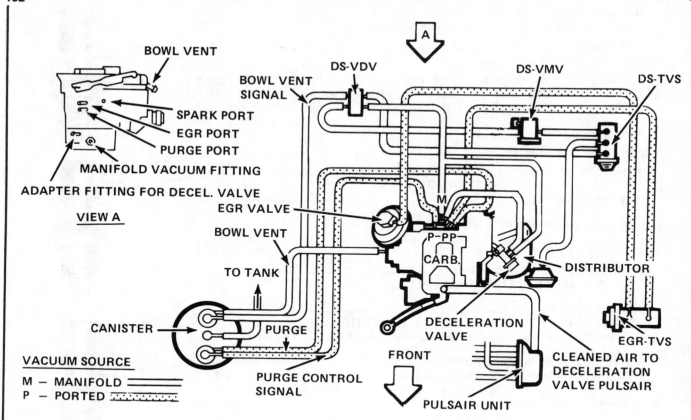

Fig. 6.13 Vacuum hose routing for L4 engine, low altitude model manual transaxle

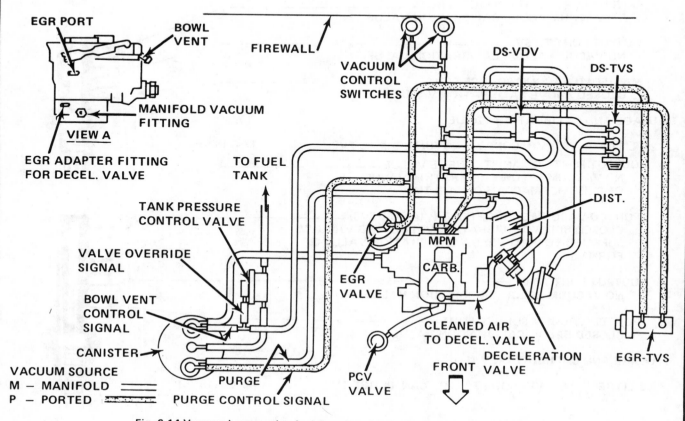

Fig. 6.14 Vacuum hose routing for L4 engine, California model, manual transaxle

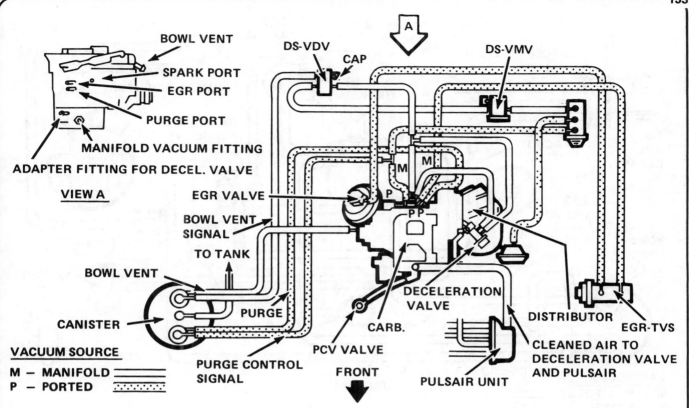

Fig. 6.15 Vacuum hose routing for L4 engine, low altitude model, automatic transaxle

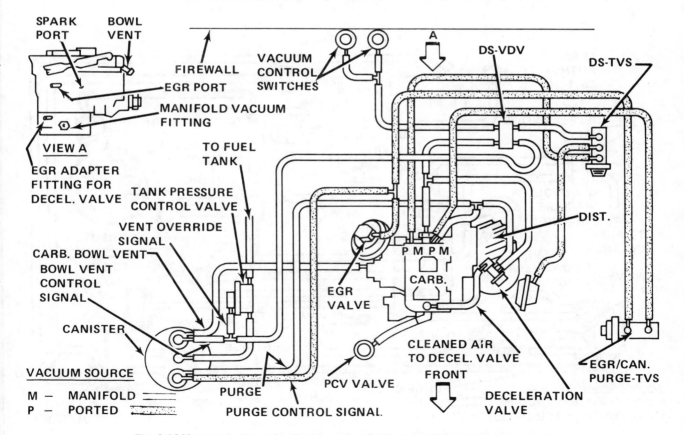

Fig. 6.16 Vacuum hose routing for L4 engine, California model, automatic transaxle

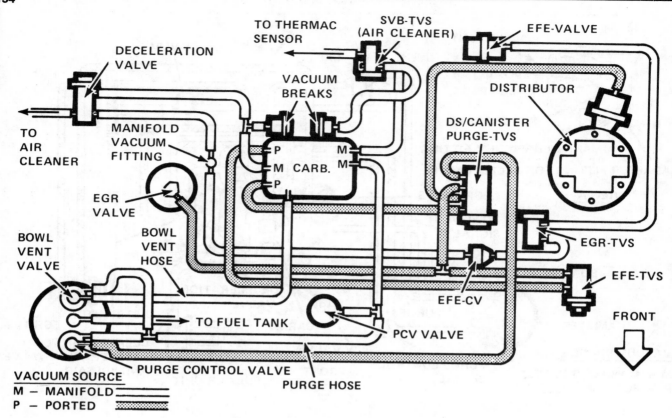

Fig. 6.17 Vacuum hose routing for V6 engine, low altitude model

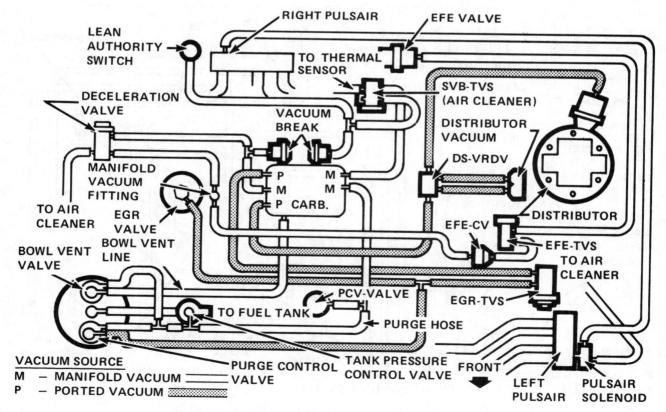

Fig. 6.18 Vacuum hose routing for V6 engine, California model

Coolant sensor

10 This sensor in the coolant stream sends information to the ECM on engine temperature. The ECM can then vary the fuel/air ratio to compensate for conditions, such as during cold engine operation. The ECM can also perform various switching functions on the EGR, EFE and PULSAIR systems according to engine temperature. This feedback from the coolant sensor to the ECM also is used to vary spark advance and activate the hot temperature light.

Pressure sensors

11 The ECM uses information from various pressure sensors to adjust engine performance. The sensors are: barometric pressure sensor (BARO), manifold absolute pressure (MAP) sensor and the throttle position sensor (TPS) as well as the above-mentioned coolant sensor.

a) Barometric pressure sensor (BARO)
12 Located in the engine compartment, the barometric pressure sensor provides a voltage to the ECM indicating ambient air pressure which varies with altitude. Not all vehicles are equipped with this sensor.

b) Manifold absolute pressure (MAPS)
13 Also located in the engine compartment, the MAPS senses engine vacuum (manifold) pressure. The ECM uses this information to adjust fuel/air mixture and spark timing in accordance with driving conditions.

c) Throttle position sensor (TPS)
14 Mounted in the carburetor body, the TPS is moved by the acclerator pump and sends a low-voltage signal to the ECM when the throttle is closed, and a higher voltage when it is opened. The ECM uses this voltage feed to recognise throttle position.

Idle speed control (ISC)

15 The idle speed control maintains low idle without stalling under changing load conditions. The ECM controls the idle speed control solenoid on the carburetor to adjust the idle.

PULSAIR system/C-4

16 When the engine is cold, the ECM energises the air valve which allows air to flow to the exhaust ports to lower carbon monoxide (CO) and hydrocarbon (HC) levels in the exhaust.

Exhaust gas recirculation (EGR)/C-4

17 The ECM controls the ported vacuum to the EGR with a solenoid valve. When the engine is cold the solenoid is energized to block vacuum to the EGR valve until the engine is warm.

Evaporative emissions system/C-4

18 When the engine is cold or idling, the ECM solenoid blocks vacuum to the valve at the top of the charcoal canister. When the engine is warm and at a specified RPM the ECM de-energizes the valve, releasing the collected vapors into the intake manifold.

Early fuel evaporation/C-4

19 The ECM controls a valve which shuts off the system until the engine is warm.

Computor command control system diagnostic circuit check

20 Using the proper equipment, the computer command control system can be used to diagnose malfunctions within itself. The 'Check Engine' light can flash trouble codes stored in the ECM 'Trouble Code Memory'. As stated before, this diagnosis should be left to your dealer or a qualified technician because of the tools required and the fact that ECM programming varies from one model vehicle to another.

10 Troubleshooting – emission systems

Note: *The following assumes the C-4 system is functioning properly. A fault in the C-4 system is indicated by a flashing 'Trouble Code' on the dashboard.*

Condition	Possible cause
Engine idles abnormally rough and/or stalls	EGR valve vacuum hoses misrouted
	Leaking EGR valve
	EFE valve malfunctioning PCV system clogged or hoses misrouted
Engine runs rough on light throttle acceleration	Malfunctioning EGR valve
	EFE valve malfunctioning
Engine stalls and/or backfires during deceleration	Restriction in EGR vacuum hoses
	Sticking EGR valve
	Malfunctioning deceleration valve
Engine detonation	EGR control valve blocked or air flow restricted
	Binding EFE valve
	Malfunctioning or restricted operation of Thermac air cleaner
	Clogged PCV valve and/or hoses
Engine dieseling on shut-off	Thermac valve sticking

Excessive engine oil consumption

Fuel odor

Clogged PCV valve and/or hoses

EEC system hoses clogged;
hoses disconnected or cracked;
charcoal canister filter in
need of replacement

Chapter 7 Transaxle

Refer to Chapter 13 for specifications and information related to 1981 through 1984 models

Contents

Specifications

Manual transaxle

Type	Synchromesh; 4 forward and reverse, with differential
Gear ratios	
1st	3.53
2nd	1.95
3rd	1.24
4th	.81 (overdrive)
Reverse	3.42
Final drive ratio	3.32
Fluid capacity	3 quarts (2.8 liters)
Recommended fluid	DEXTRON II Type B automatic transmission fluid

Automatic transaxle

Type	125, 3-speed fully atuomatic
Fluid capacity	6 quarts (3.8 liters)
Fluid refill after pan removal	4 quarts (3.8 liters)
Fluid type	DEXTRON II automatic transmission fluid

Torque specifications

	ft-lb	m-kg
Manual transaxle		
Input shaft right-hand bearing retainer	7	1.0
Reverse idler shaft lock bolt	16	2.2
Reverse inhibitor fiting	26	3.6
Transaxle case-to-clutch cover bolts	16	2.2
Ring gear bolts	54	7.5
Pinion shaft lock bolt	7	1.0
Automatic transaxle		
T.V. cable to case bolt	75 (in-lb)	0.9
Speedometer driven gear retaining bolt	75 (in-lb)	0.9
Governor cover to case bolts	8	1.1
Oil cooler connector	23	3.1
Oil pan cover bolts	12	1.6
Flywheel-to-torque converter bolts	27	3.7
Transaxle-to-engine bolts	55	7.6
Transaxle mounting bracket bolts	48	6.6
Transaxle mounting bracket-to-mount nuts	41	5.6
Transaxle mount-to-cradle nuts	41	5.6

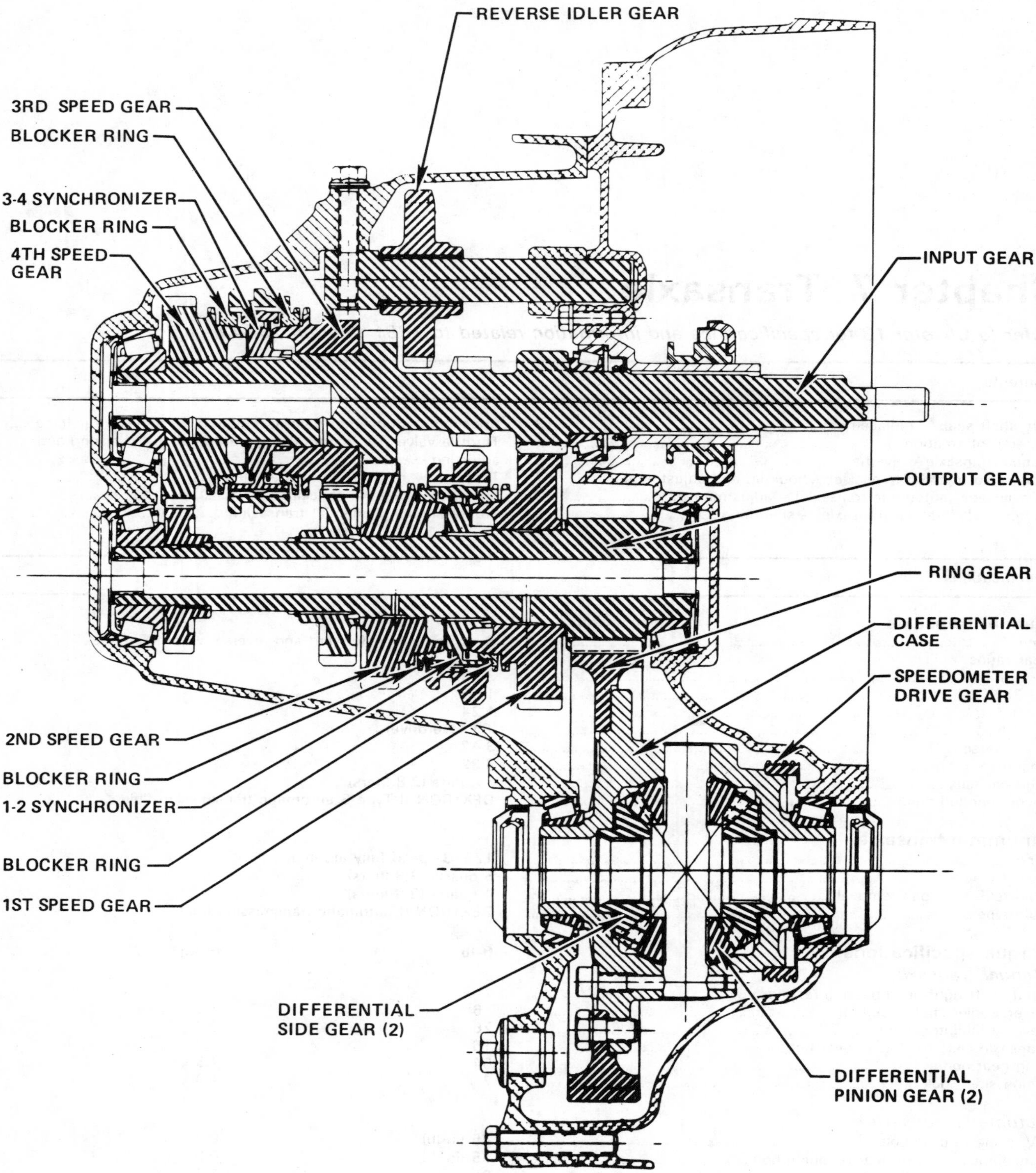

REVERSE IDLER GEAR

3RD SPEED GEAR
BLOCKER RING

3-4 SYNCHRONIZER
BLOCKER RING
4TH SPEED GEAR

INPUT GEAR

OUTPUT GEAR

RING GEAR

DIFFERENTIAL CASE

SPEEDOMETER DRIVE GEAR

2ND SPEED GEAR

BLOCKER RING

1-2 SYNCHRONIZER

BLOCKER RING

1ST SPEED GEAR

DIFFERENTIAL SIDE GEAR (2)

DIFFERENTIAL PINION GEAR (2)

Fig. 7.1 Cross sectional view of the manual transaxle

1 General information

1   All X-Body models come equipped with either a 125 3-speed, fully automatic transaxle or a 4-speed, overdrive manual transaxle. Both incorporate a differential and final drive gear set in addition to the conventional transmission components.

2   The routine maintenance chart in Chapter 1 calls for an automatic transaxle fluid change once every 30 000 miles. This interval should be shortened to every 15 000 miles if the car is normally driven under one or more of the following conditions: heavy city traffic; where the outside temperature normally reaches 90°F or higher; in very hilly or mountainous areas; or if a trailer is frequently pulled. Refer to Chapter 1 for the proper procedures for checking and changing the automatic transaxle fluid and filter.

3   The automatic transaxle uses an oil cooler, located in the side tank of the radiator, to prevent excessive temperatures from developing inside the transaxle. Should the oil cooler need flushing or other servicing, take it to a GM dealer or other radiator specialist.

4   If rough shifting or other malfunctions occur in the automatic transaxle, check the following items first before assuming the fault lies within the transaxle itself: the fluid level, the T.V. cable adjustment, manual shift linkage adjustment and engine tune. All of these elements can adversely affect the performance of the transaxle.

5   The main components of the manual transaxle are the aluminum transaxle case, aluminum clutch cover, the input gear and shaft assembly, the output gear and shaft assembly and the differential assembly. The input and output gear assemblies and the differential assembly are supported by tapered roller bearings and use shims beneath the right-hand bearing cups to set the proper preload.

6   The forward gears of the manual transaxle are of the synchromesh, or constant mesh design. The synchronizers used on the forward gears are blocker rings controlled by shift forks, while reverse uses a sliding roller gear arrangement.

2 Transaxle mounts – checking

1   Raise the car for access beneath and support it with jack stands. Make sure the vehicle is secure, as you must jostle the car somewhat to check the mounts.

2   Push upward and pull downward on the transaxle case and observe the mounts.

3   If the case can be pushed upward but cannot be pulled down, this is an indication that the rubber is worn and the mount is bottomed out.

4   If the rubber portion of the mount separates from the metal plate, this also means that the mount should be replaced.

5   Replace any mount in which the rubber exhibits hardening or cracking.

6   Check that all of the attaching nuts or bolts are tight.

7   For the transaxle mount replacement procedure, refer to Chapter 2, Section 33.

3 Axle shaft seals – replacement

1   If an oil leak develops at the point where a drive axle enters the transaxle, the seal can be replaced using the following procedure.

2   Remove the drive axle from the transaxle as described in Chapter 8, Section 7.

3   Pry the old seal out with a thin, flat-head screwdriver. Be careful that you do not damage the seal mating surface.

4   Using an appropriate sized seal installing tool or socket, install the new seal into its bore.

5   Apply a light coat of ATF to the inside lip of the seal and install the drive axle.

4 Speedometer/governor gear assembly (automatic) – servicing

1   An oil leak or other servicing needed in the area of the speedometer driven gear or governor cover can be done with the transaxle in the car.

2   Disconnect the speedometer cable from the speedometer driven gear and sleeve assembly located where the right drive axle enters the transaxle (Fig. 7.2).

3   Remove the governor cover and O-ring. Discard the O-ring.

4   If there is a problem with the speedometer/governor drive gear assembly, once the governor cover has been removed the drive gear thrust washer and drive gear assembly can be lifted out.

5   Wash the assembly in cleaning solvent and blow out the oil passage.

6   Inspect the governor driven gear for nicks and damage.

7   Inspect the governor shaft seal ring for cuts, damage and for a free fit in its groove. If the seal is damaged, cut it off the governor shaft. Lubricate a new seal with ATF and install it on the shaft.

8   Check that the governor spring is not damaged.

9   Inspect the shaft for scoring or other damage. Replace as necessary.

10   Check that there are two check balls in the assembly.

11   Install the speedometer drive gear and thrust washer onto the governor assembly.

12   Install the governor assembly into the transaxle.

13   Install a new O-ring into the governor cover and install the cover onto the transaxle, torquing the bolts to specs.

14   Install the speedometer driven gear and retainer.

15   Reconnect the speedometer cable.

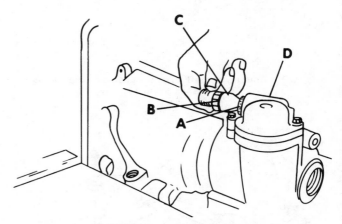

Fig. 7.2 Speedometer driven gear assembly (Sec 4)

A	Speedometer driven gear	C	Speedometer sleeve
B	O-ring seal	D	Governor cover

5 Transaxle – removal and installation

Note: *Due to the complexity of the automatic transaxle and the special equipment needed to service it, an automatic transaxle overhaul is not practical for the home mechanic to perform. Considerable money can be saved however, by removing and installing the transaxle yourself. Read through this Section to become familiar with the procedure and the tools needed for the job. The car must be raised high enough so the transaxle can be lowered from the car and slid out from underneath.*

1   Prior to removal of the transaxle, have the car test driven and diagnosed by a qualified transmission specialist, so that he may determine the nature and cause of the problem.

2   Disconnect the negative battery cable from the battery.

3   Disconnect the battery ground cable from the transaxle mounting bolt (photo). Secure the cable to the upper radiator hose with wire to keep it out of the way.

4   On automatic transaxles, remove the detent (T.V.) cable from the carburetor by sliding it in the opposite direction of the cable (Figs. 7.3 and 7.4).

5   On automatic transaxles, remove the screw that secures the detent cable to the transaxle (photo).

6   On automatic transaxles, pull up on the detent valve cable cover and disconnect the cable from the rod (photo).

7   If equipped, remove the transaxle strut.

8   Remove all of the engine-to-transaxle bolts except the one by the starter.

9   Break loose the engine-to-transaxle bolt near the starter, but do not remove it yet.

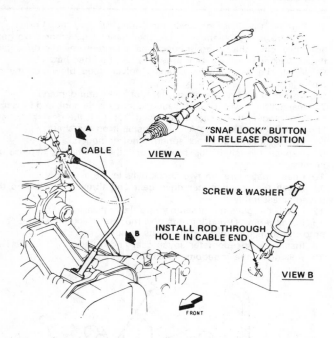

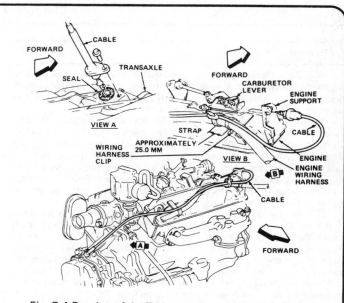

Fig. 7.3 Routing of the T.V. control cable on the L4 engine (Secs 5 and 10)

Fig. 7.4 Routing of the T.V. control cable on the V6 engine (Secs 5 and 10)

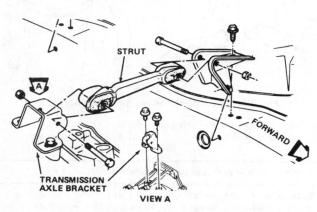

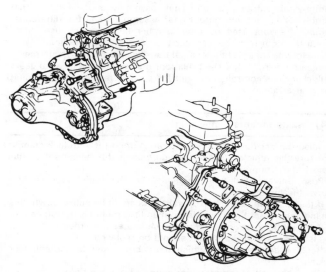

Fig. 7.5 Location of the rear transaxle strut (if equipped) (Sec 5)

Fig. 7.6 Locations of the transaxle mounting bolts (Sec 5)

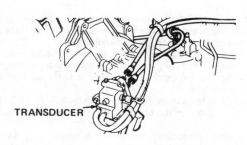

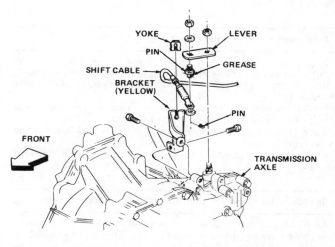

Fig. 7.7 Cruise control transducer (Sec 5)

Fig. 7.8 Exploded view of the automatic transaxle shift cable assembly (Sec 5)

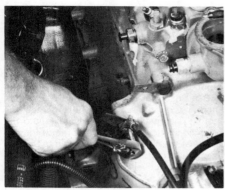

5.3 Disconnecting the battery ground cable at engine

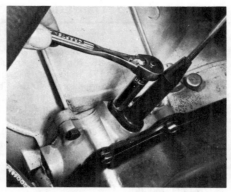

5.5 Removing the detent cable attaching screw

5.6 Disconnecting the detent cable from the actuating rod

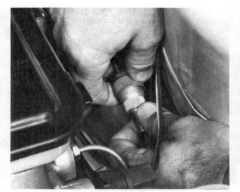

5.10 Disconnecting the speedometer cable

5.12 Removing the nut that retains the shift cable lever to the transaxle shaft

5.13 Locations of the shift linkage bracket bolts

5.14 The cooler lines should be disconnected at the transaxle

5.20a Removing the front transaxle mount nuts

5.20b Removing the rear transaxle mount nuts

5.27 Removing the flywheel shield

5.29 Removing the engine-to-transaxle bracket

5.30 The transaxle should be supported with a jack and a block of wood to distribute the weight

10 Disconnect the speedometer cable (photo).

11 If equipped with cruise control, remove the speedometer cable from the cruise transducer.

12 Remove the nut that retains the shift cable lever to the transaxle shaft (photo) and lift the lever off the shaft.

13 On automatic transaxles, remove the shift linkage bracket bolts (photo). On manual transaxles, remove the clips that secure the shift cables to the transaxle case mounting bosses.

14 On automatic transaxles, disconnect the transaxle cooler lines at the transaxle (photo). Immediately plug the lines to prevent spillage of fluid or contamination.

15 There are two principal ways of supporting the weight of the engine during the removal of the cradle and transaxle. A special support fixture can be obtained which rests on the cowl and radiator support (Chapter 12, Fig. 12.22), or an engine hoist can be used. If the engine support fixture is being used, install it at this time. Be sure its rear support is positioned in the center of the cowl. CAUTION: This fixture is not intended to support the entire weight of the engine and transaxle. If the engine hoist is being used to support the engine, the hood must be removed to gain sufficient access. Refer to Chapter 12, Section 33.

16 Unlock the steering column and raise the car.

17 On manual transaxles, remove the drain plug and drain the fluid from the transaxle.

18 Remove the stabilizer bar as described in Chapter 11.

19 If an engine hoist is being used to support the engine, now is the time to hook it to the engine. Refer to Chapter 2, Section 34, for the proper method of attaching the hoist.

20 Remove the nuts that secure the front and rear transaxle mounts to the cradle (photos).

21 If equipped, remove the top bolt from the lower transaxle damper on V6 engines (Fig. 7.10).

22 Remove the left front wheel.

23 Disconnect the left balljoint from the steering knuckle as described in Chapter 9.

24 Remove the bolts that secure the two sections of the cradle to each other. Refer to Chapter 12, if necessary.

25 Remove the left section of the cradle from the body.

26 Remove the drive axles from the transaxle as described in Chapter 8.

27 Remove the flywheel and starter shields (photo).

28 Remove the starter.

29 Remove the engine-to-transaxle bracket (photo).

30 Support the transaxle with a floor jack and a block of wood from underneath (photo).

31 On automatic transaxles, remove the bolts that secure the flywheel to the torque converter (photo). The engine will have to be turned over by hand in order to gain access to all of the bolts. This can be done by turning the crankshaft by the crank pulley nut at the front of the engine.

32 Remove the remaining transaxle bolt, located near the starter.

33 With an assistant to help you balance the transaxle on the jack, slide the transaxle away from the engine and then lower the transaxle out of the car (photo).

34 For details on repairing or overhauling a manual transaxle, refer to Section 6. If an automatic transaxle is in need of minor repair, take it to a GM dealer or other qualified transmission specialist. If an automatic transaxle is in need of a complete overhaul, it may be more economical to replace the old transaxle with a rebuilt one.

35 The engine should remain supported while the transaxle is out. The transaxle is installed by reversing the sequence of the removal procedure. NOTE: The right drive axle must be inserted into the transaxle after the transaxle has been raised into the engine compartment, but before it is mated with the engine (photo). Once the transaxle is fastened to the engine, install the left drive axle into the transaxle, then install the cradle section that has been removed.

36 On manual transaxles, adjust the shift cable by referring to Section 7. On automatic transaxles, adjust the shift linkage and TV cable by referring to Sections 9 and 10 respectively.

6   Manual transaxle – overhaul

1 Although it is feasible for the home mechanic to overhaul the manual transaxle, the operation requires some special tools. Read through this Section to become familiar with the procedure and tools needed for the job.

2 Support the transaxle on a suitable work stand and clean the outside of the transaxle thoroughly.

3 Remove the 15 bolts that secure the clutch cover to the transaxle case. The clutch cover will probably have to be tapped with a plastic hammer to break the seal between it and the case.

4 Remove the ring gear/differential assembly (Fig. 7.17).

Internal parts removal

5 Position the shifter shaft in the 'Neutral' position so that the shifter moves freely and is not engaged in any drive gear.

6 Bend back the locking tab and remove the bolt from the shifter shaft. Lift out the shifter shaft and the shift fork shaft from the synchronizer forks (Fig. 7.18).

7 Disengage the 'Reverse' shift fork from the guide pin and interlock bracket and remove it from the housing (Fig. 7.19).

8 Remove the lock bolt that secures the 'Reverse' idler gear shaft and remove the assembly (Fig. 7.20).

9 Remove the detent shift lever and interlock assembly.

10 Lift the input shaft, output shaft and shift forks out of the housing as one assembly. Note the position of the shift forks to the shafts (Fig. 7.21).

11 Remove the shift forks from the shaft assembly and separate the input and output shafts from each other (Fig. 7.22).

Input shaft disassembly

12 A press is needed to remove the gears from both the input and output shafts. Using an appropriate support plate, as shown in Fig. 7.23 (GM tool J-22912-01), press the 4th gear and the left-hand bearing from the input shaft. The terms 'left-hand' and 'right-hand' refer to the installed positions on the car, with the right-hand side being the side closest to the clutch and the left-hand side farthest from the clutch.

13 Remove the brass blocker ring.

14 Remove the snap-ring from the 3-4 synchronizer.

15 Again using support plates as shown in Fig. 7.24, press the 3rd gear and the 3-4 synchronizer from the input shaft.

5.31 Removing the 3 torque converter mounting bolts

5.33 The automatic transaxle lowered from the car

5.35 Positioning the right drive axle in the transaxle bore

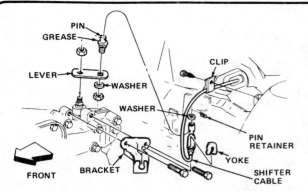

Fig. 7.9 Exploded view of the automatic transaxle column shift cable assembly (Sec 5)

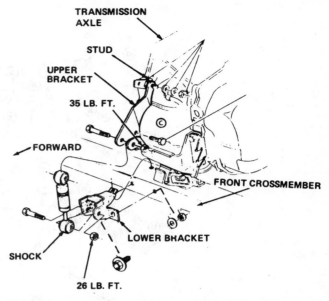

Fig. 7.10 Location of the transaxle damper (if equipped) (Sec 5)

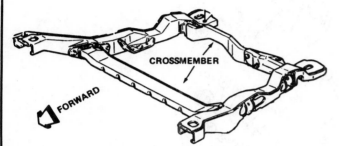

Fig. 7.11 Cradle (Sec 5)

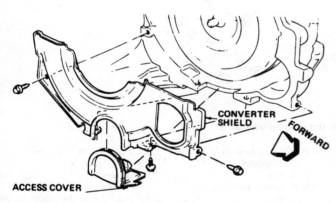

Fig. 7.13 Torque converter shield on the automatic transaxle (V6) (Sec 5)

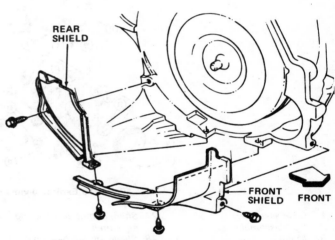

Fig. 7.12 Torque converter shield on the automatic transaxle (L4) (Sec 5)

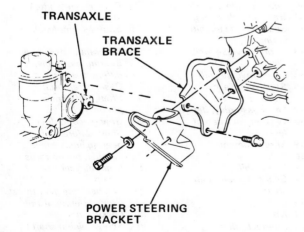

Fig. 7.15 Location of the transaxle to engine bracket (V6) (Sec 5)

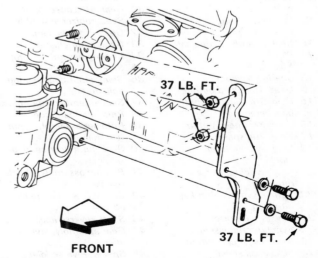

Fig. 7.14 Location of the transaxle to engine bracket (L4) (Sec 5)

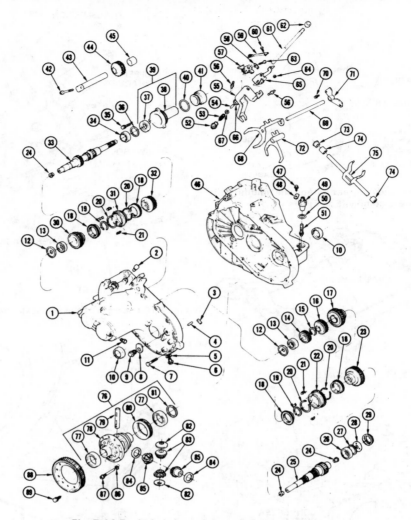

Fig. 7.16 Exploded view of the manual transaxle

1 Case assembly
2 Vent assembly
3 Magnet
4 Pin
5 Washer, drain screw
6 Screw, drain
7 Bolt
8 Washer, fill plug
9 Plug, fill
10 Seal assembly, axle shaft
11 Plug
12 Shield, oil
13 Bearing assembly
14 Gear, 4th speed output
15 Ring, 3rd speed output gear retaining
16 Gear, 3rd speed output
17 Gear, 2nd speed output
18 Ring, synchronizer blocking
19 Ring, synchronizer retaining
20 Spring, synchronizer key retaining
21 Key, synchronizer
22 Synchronizer assembly
23 Gear, 1st speed output
24 Sleeve, oil shield
25 Gear, output
26 Bearing assembly, output

27 Shim, output gear bearing adjustment
28 Shield, output bearing oil
29 Retainer, output gear bearing oil shield
30 Gear, 4th speed input
31 Synchronizer assembly
32 Gear, 3rd speed input
33 Gear, input cluster
34 Bearing assembly, input
35 Screw
36 Shim, input gear bearing adjustment
37 Seal assembly, input gear
38 Retainer, input gear
39 Retainer assembly, input gear bearing
40 Seal, input gear bearing retainer
41 Bearing assembly, clutch release
42 Screw & washer, reverse idler
43 Shaft, reverse idler
44 Gear assembly, reverse idler
45 Spacer, reverse idler shaft

46 Housing assembly, clutch & differential
47 Screw
48 Retainer, speedo gear fitting
49 Sleeve, speedo driven gear
50 Seal, speedo gear sleeve
51 Gear, speedo driven
52 Seat, reverse inhibitor spring
53 Spring, reverse inhibitor
54 Pin
55 Lever, reverse shift
56 Stud, reverse lever locating
57 Lever assembly, detent
58 Washer, lock detent lever
59 Spring, detent
60 Bolt
61 Shaft, shift
62 Seal assembly, shift shaft
63 Bolt
64 Nut
65 Interlock, shift
66 Shim, shift shaft
67 Washer, reverse inhibitor spring

68 Fork, 3rd & 4th shift
69 Shaft, shift fork
70 Screw
71 Guide, oil
72 Fork, 1st & 2nd shift
73 Seal assembly, clutch fork shaft
74 Bearing, clutch fork shaft
75 Shaft assembly, clutch fork
76 Differential assembly
77 Bearing assembly, differential
78 Case, differential
79 Shaft, differential pinion
80 Gear, speedo drive
81 Shim, differential bearing adjustment
82 Washer, pinion thrust
83 Gear, differential pinion
84 Washer, side gear thrust
85 Gear, differential side
86 Lockwasher
87 Screw, pinion shaft
88 Gear, differential ring
89 Bolt

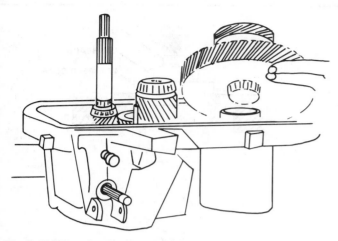

Fig. 7.17 Removing the ring gear/differential from the transaxle case (Sec 6)

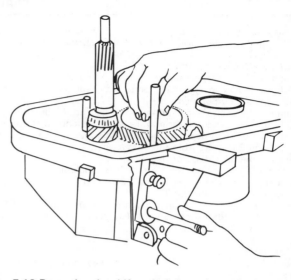

Fig. 7.18 Removing the shifter shaft from the manual transaxle case (Sec 6)

Fig. 7.19 Removing the reverse shift fork (Sec 6)

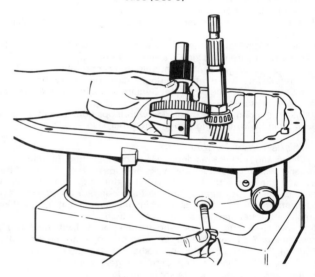

Fig. 7.20 Removing the reverse idler gear from the manual transaxle case (Sec 6)

Fig. 7.21 Input and output shaft and shift forks assembly (Sec 6)

Fig. 7.22 Input and output shaft assemblies (Sec 6)

16 Press the right-hand bearing from the shaft by using the appropriate support plate (GM Tool J26946) as shown in Fig. 7.25.

Output shaft disassembly
17 Using support plates and a bearing removal pilot (GM tool J26943) as shown in Fig. 7.26, press 4th gear and the left-hand bearing from the output shaft.
18 Remove the snap-ring that retains 3rd gear to the shaft.
19 Slide the 1-2 synchronizer into 1st gear position so the support plates can be used to support 2nd gear as shown in Fig. 7.27, and press 2nd and 3rd gears from the output shaft.
20 Remove the brass blocker ring.
21 Remove the snap-ring retaining the 1-2 synchronizer.
22 Support 1st gear as shown in Fig. 7.28 and press 1st gear and the 1-2 synchronizer from the shaft.
23 Using the appropriate support plate and bearing pilot (GM Tools J-22227-A and J-26943) as shown in Fig. 7.29, press the right-hand bearing from the output shaft.

Synchronizer overhaul
24 Carefully pry out both synchronizer key springs from each synchronizer.
25 Using a scribe, mark the relative position of the hub to the sleeve. Separate the hub, sleeve and keys.
26 Clean the parts thoroughly in solvent.
27 Inspect the parts for damage or excessive wear, and replace as necessary
28 Assemble the hub to the sleeve so that the extruded lip on the hub is directed away from the sleeve's shift fork groove. Refer to Fig. 7.30. Make sure the scribed marks made upon disassembly are lined up.
29 Carefully install one retaining ring. Then carefully pry the ring back and insert the keys, one at a time. Be sure to position the keys so that the ring is captured by them.
30 Install the ring on the other side with it positioned so that the gap is out of line with the ring gap on the other side.

Input shaft reassembly
31 Clean and inspect all input shaft components for damage or excessive wear. If there are any nicks or chips on the gear teeth, both they and the gears they mate with on the output shaft must be replaced. Check the bearing surfaces for scoring, or any roughness or noise from the rollers. If the car has high mileage on it, it is a good idea to replace the bearings as a matter of course.
32 Using an appropriate bearing installer (GM Tool J-28406) as shown in Fig. 7.31, install the right-hand bearing onto the input shaft.
33 Place 3rd gear onto the input shaft in its proper position, and install the brass blocker ring onto the gear cone. Press the 3-4 synchronizer onto the shaft as shown in Fig. 7.32.
34 Install the 3-4 synchronizer snap ring, with the beveled edges of the ring away from the synchronizer.
35 Install the brass blocker ring.
36 Place 4th gear onto the shaft in its proper position and press the left-hand bearing onto the shaft using an inner race installing tool (GM Tool J26942) as shown in Fig. 7.33.

Output shaft reassembly
37 Clean and inspect the output shaft components in the same manner as the input shaft components.
38 Using the appropriate bearing installing tool (GM Tool J-6133A) as shown in Fig. 7.34, press the right-hand bearing onto the output shaft.
39 Place the 1st gear onto the shaft in its proper position, and place the brass blocker ring onto the gear cone. Then press the 1-2 synchronizer onto the output shaft as shown in Fig. 7.35.
40 Install the 1-2 synchronizer snap-ring.
41 Place the brass blocker ring into position.
42 Place 2nd gear onto the shaft in its proper position. Using Fig. 7.36 as a guide, press 3rd gear onto the shaft with its hub toward 4th gear.
43 Install the 3rd gear snap-ring.
44 Using support plates and the inner race installer (GM Tool J-26942) as shown in Fig. 7.37, press 4th gear and the left-hand bearing onto the shaft. Be sure the 4th gear hub is toward 3rd gear.

Transaxle case overhaul
45 Remove the reverse inhibitor fitting from the case's exterior. Then

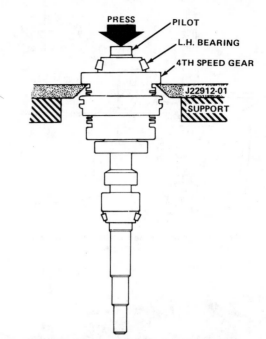

Fig. 7.23 Removing the left-hand bearing and 4th gear (input shaft) (Sec 6)

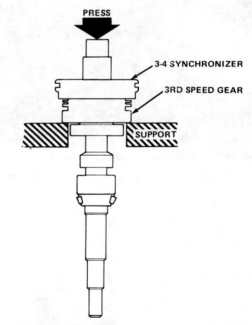

Fig. 7.24 Removing the 3-4 synchronizer and 3rd gear (input shaft) (Sec 6)

remove the spring and pilot/spacer from inside the case (Fig. 7.38).
46 Using a bearing cup removing tool (GM Tool J-26941), remove the input and output shaft left-hand bearing cups.
47 Remove the oil slingers.
48 Remove the differential side bearing cup.
49 Check the interlock bracket and 'Reverse' shift fork guide pins. Thoroughly clean all parts and inspect them for damage or wear. Replace as necessary. Clean any oil, dirt or old gasket material from the case's sealing surface.
50 Using the appropriate bearing cup installing tool (GM Tool J-23423A) or socket, reinstall the bearing cups removed in paragraphs 46 and 48.

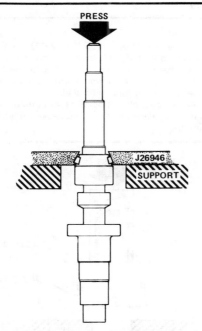

Fig. 7.25 Removing the right-hand bearing (input shaft) (Sec 6)

Fig. 7.26 Removing the left-hand bearing and 4th gear (output shaft) (Sec 6)

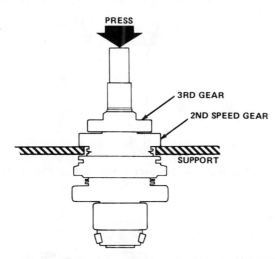

Fig. 7.27 Removing 3rd gear and 2nd gear (output shaft) (Sec 6)

Fig. 7.28 Removing the 1-2 synchronizer and 1st gear (output shaft) (Sec 6)

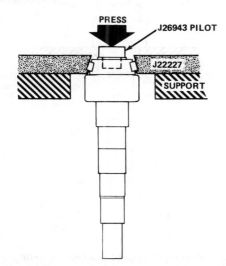

Fig. 7.29 Removing the right-hand bearing (output shaft) (Sec 6)

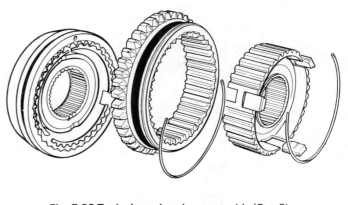

Fig. 7.30 Typical synchronizer assembly (Sec 6)

Clutch cover overhaul

51 Remove the differential bearing cup and shim.

52 Remove the input and output shaft right-hand bearing cups. Then remove the shim from the back of the input bearing cup and remove the oil shield, shim and retainer from the back of the output shaft bearing cup.

53 Remove the three bolts securing the release bearing sleeve and remove the sleeve, tapping carefully on it as needed (Fig. 7.39).

54 Remove the external oil ring and the internal oil seal from the sleeve (Fig. 7.40).

55 Remove the plastic oil scoop (Fig. 7.41).

56 The clutch fork shaft and bushings do not need to be removed unless replacement is needed. A clutch shaft bushing tool (GM Tool J-28412) can be used for removal and installation (Fig. 7.42).

57 Replace the clutch fork shaft seal.

58 Clean and inspect all components for damage or wear and replace as necessary. Clean any oil, dirt or old gasket material from the cover's sealing surface.

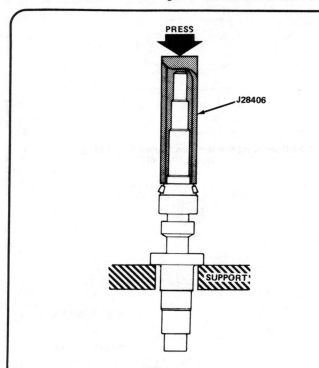

Fig. 7.31 Installing the right-hand bearing (input shaft) (Sec 6)

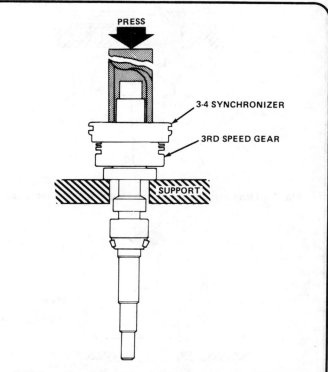

Fig. 7.32 Installing 3rd gear and the 3-4 synchronizer (input shaft) (Sec 6)

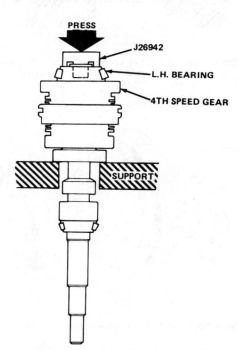

Fig. 7.33 Installing 4th gear and left-hand bearing (input shaft) (Sec 6)

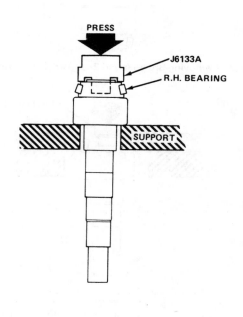

Fig. 7.34 Installing the right-hand bearing (output shaft) (Sec 6)

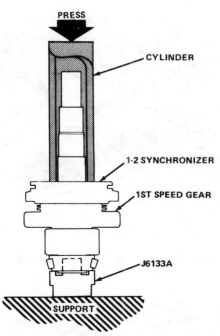

Fig. 7.35 Installing 1st gear and the 1-2 synchronizer (output shaft) (Sec 6)

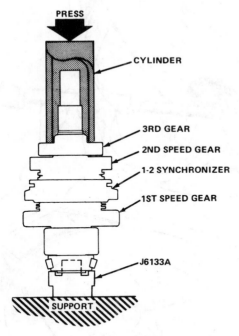

Fig. 7.36 Installing 2nd and 3rd gears (output shaft) (Sec 6)

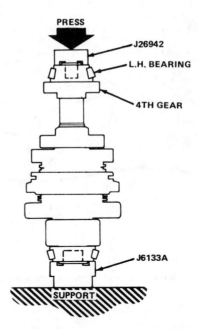

Fig. 7.37 Installing 4th gear and the left-hand bearing (output shaft) (Sec 6)

65 Inspect the differential side bearings. If there is any roughness or noise when the bearing is spun, it should be replaced. If the car has high mileage, the bearings should be replaced as a matter of course. Use GM differential side bearing puller tool set (GM Tool J-22888) or equivalent to remove the old bearings, and GM differential inner bearing installer or equivalent for installation.
66 Clean and inspect all parts for damage or wear and replace as necessary.
67 Install the gears and thrust washers into the case. Then install the pinion shaft and lock bolt. Tighten the bolts to specs.
68 Attach the ring gear to the differential housing.

Shim selection
69 Securely support the transaxle case so that the sealing surface is horizontal.
70 With the 3 left-hand bearing races installed in the case, place the input and output shaft assemblies and the differential assembly into their installed positions in the case.
71 Place the right-hand bearing races onto their respective bearings.
72 Place the appropriate shim selection gauge (from GM Tool set J-26935) onto each of the three assemblies as shown in Fig. 7.43. Be sure the bearing races fit smoothly into the bores of the gauges.
73 Install the oil shield retainer into the bore of the output shaft gauge.
74 Carefully assemble the clutch cover over the 3 gauges and onto the case, using 7 spacers provided with the shim selector set placed evenly around the perimeter, as shown in Fig. 7.44. Retain the spacers with the bolts supplied in the set. Draw the cover to the case by tightening them gradually and in a cross-pattern, torquing the bolts to 10 ft-lb (1.4 m-kg). This will compress all 3 gauge sleeves.
75 Rotate each gauge to seat the bearings, and rotate the differential case 3 revolutions in each direction.
76 Measure the gap between the outer sleeve and the base pad. This is the correct thickness for the preload shim at each location. Compare your available shims with each gap. The largest shim that can be placed into the gap and drawn through without binding is the correct shim for that location (Fig. 7.45).
77 Remove the clutch cover, spacers and gauges.
78 Place the selected shims into their appropriate bores in the clutch cover. Install the metal shield and the bearing cups, using an appropriate sized installing tool or socket for each cup.

Case reassembly
79 Place the input and output shafts together, and install the shift forks onto the assembly as shown in Fig. 7.21.

Clutch cover reassembly
59 Install the plastic oil scoop.
60 Replace the square-cut external oil ring on the release bearing sleeve.
61 Install the release bearing sleeve into the cover.
62 Use the appropriate sized installing tool (GM Tool J-26936) or socket to install the internal oil seal into the release bearing sleeve.

Differential case/ring gear overhaul
63 Separate the ring gear from the differential case.
64 Remove the pinion shaft lock bolt and the pinion shaft. Then roll the gears and the thrust washers out through the opening in the case.

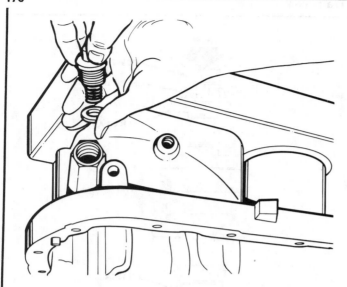

Fig. 7.38 Removing the reverse inhibitor fitting from the manual transaxle case (Sec 6)

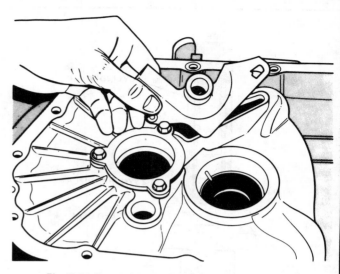

Fig. 7.41 Removing the plastic oil scoop (Sec 6)

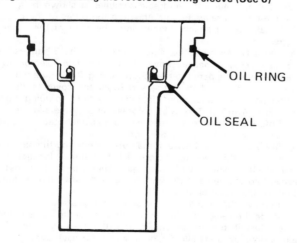

Fig. 7.39 Removing the reverse bearing sleeve (Sec 6)

OIL RING

OIL SEAL

Fig. 7.40 Locations of the oil ring and seal in the reverse bearing sleeve (Sec 6)

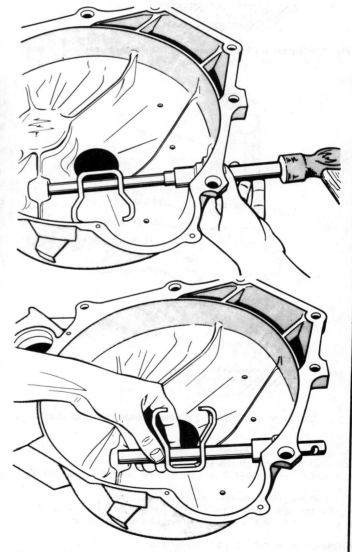

Fig. 7.42 Replacing the clutch fork shaft and bushings (Sec 6)

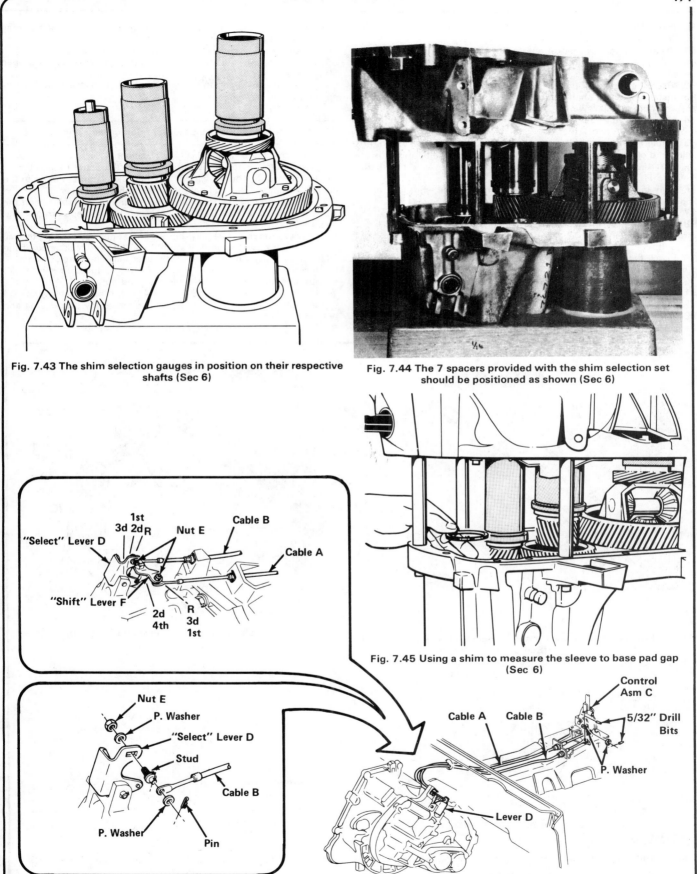

Fig. 7.43 The shim selection gauges in position on their respective shafts (Sec 6)

Fig. 7.44 The 7 spacers provided with the shim selection set should be positioned as shown (Sec 6)

1st
3d 2d R
"Select" Lever D   Nut E   Cable B
                                    Cable A
"Shift" Lever F
        2d   R
        4th   3d
              1st

Fig. 7.45 Using a shim to measure the sleeve to base pad gap (Sec 6)

Nut E
    P. Washer
        "Select" Lever D
            Stud
                Cable B
P. Washer
        Pin

Control Asm C
Cable A   Cable B   5/32" Drill Bits
                    P. Washer
                Lever D

Fig. 7.46 Manual transaxle shift cable arrangement (Sec 7)

80 Install the input and output shaft assemblies and shift forks together into the transaxle case.

81 Place the interlock bracket onto a GM shifter shaft alignment pin or equivalent. Be sure the bracket engages the fingers on the shift forks.

82 Place the detent shift lever into the bracket.

83 Install the shifter shaft just until it is through the interlock bracket and the detent shift lever.

84 Install the 'Reverse' shift fork onto the alignment pin making sure it engages the interlock bracket.

85 Install the 'Reverse' idler gear and shaft into position. Be sure the lining end of the shaft points upward, and the large chamfered ends of the gear teeth are facing up. Then install the spacer onto the shaft. Refer to Fig. 7.20.

86 Fully install the shifter shaft through the 'Reverse' shift fork, until it pilots into the inhibitor spring spacer.

87 Remove the alignment pin.

88 With the shaft in the 'Neutral' position, install the bolt and lock through the detent shift lever. Bend the locking tab over the head of the bolt.

89 Install the fork shaft through the synchronizer forks and into the bore in the case.

90 Carefully install the ring gear/differential assembly.

91 Install the magnet.

92 Apply a thin bead of sealant to the clutch cover sealing surface.

93 With the sealant still wet, carefully install the cover onto the transaxle case, using the dowel pins to guide the cover into position.

With the cover in position, tap the cover lightly with a plastic hammer to ensure that it is properly seated.

94 Install the 15 attaching bolts and torque them to specs.

95 Tighten the idler shaft retaining bolt in the case to its proper torque specification.

96 Shift through all of the gears to check that there is smooth operation with no binding.

7   Shift cable (manual transaxle) – hook-up and adjustment

1   Place the shifter in the 1st gear position.

2   Remove the shifter boot and retainer at the control assembly.

3   Install two $\frac{5}{32}$-in or No. 22 drill bits into the alignment holes in the control assembly. This will hold the assembly in 1st gear.

4   Attach both of the shift cables to the control assembly, using the studs and pin retainers. Be sure the cables are routed correctly and operate smoothly.

5   Move to the transaxle and shift it into 1st gear by pushing the rail selector shaft down (inward) just until you feel the resistance of the inhibitor spring. Then rotate the shift lever fully counterclockwise.

6   Insert the stud on cable 'A' (Fig. 7.46) into the shift lever's ('F') slotted hole. Install and tighten the retaining nut.

7   Insert the stud on cable 'B' (Fig. 7.46) into the select lever's ('D') slotted hole. Pull lightly on the lever to remove any lash. Install and tighten the retaining nut.

8   Remove the two drill bits at the control assembly.

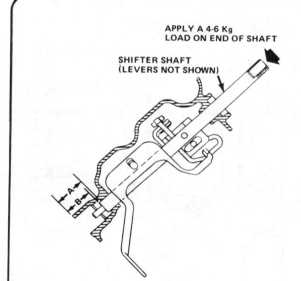

Fig. 7.47 Cross sectional view of the manual transaxle shifter shaft (Sec 8)

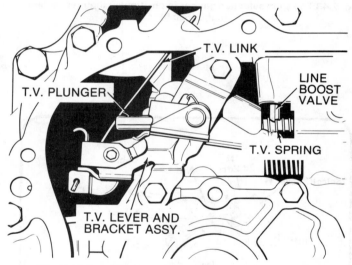

Fig. 7.48 T.V. cable mechanism (automatic) (Sec 10)

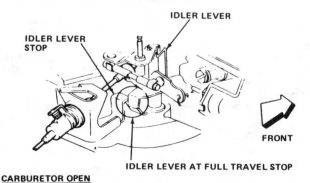

Fig. 7.49 T.V. control cable carburetor connection (automatic) (Sec 10)

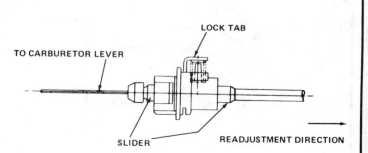

Fig. 7.50 Adjustment of the T.V. control cable (automatic) (Sec 10)

9   Road test the car, checking that the transaxle shifts smoothly, without binding, and that it engages and disengages each gear without problems. It may be necessary to fine-tune the adjustment after road testing.

8   Shifter shaft (manual transaxle) – shimming

1   When there is difficulty in shifting from 1st to 2nd, and the shift cables are properly adjusted, it may be necessary to check the shifter shaft washer (Fig. 7.47). This washer helps position the shaft so it provides proper shifting.
2   Remove the 'Reverse' inhibitor fitting spring and washer from the end of the housing.
3   Position the shifter shaft in 2nd gear.
4   Measure the distance from the end of the housing to the shoulder just behind the end of the shaft (Dimension A in Fig. 7.47).
5   Press on the end of the shaft where indicated with about 10 pounds of pressure and measure the distance from the end of the housing to the end of the shifter shaft step (Dimension B in Fig. 7.47).
6   Find the difference between these two measurements (Dimension C) on the chart below to determine which shim should be used upon reinstallation.

When Dimension C (measured in mm) is:	Use Shim
1.9 – 2.2	14008235
2.2 – 2.5	476709
2.5 – 2.8	476710
2.8 – 3.1	476711
3.1 – 3.4	476712
3.4 – 3.7	476713
3.7 – 4.0	476714
4.0 – 4.3	476715
4.3 – 4.6	476716

9   Shift linkage (automatic transaxle) – adjustment

1   The manual shift linkage on the automatic transaxles must be adjusted so that the indicator quadrant on the steering column and the shift stops correspond with the transaxle detents. If this linkage is not adjusted correctly, an internal oil leak could occur which could result in clutch or band slippage.
2   Place the shifter in the 'Neutral' position.
3   Move to the transaxle. Disconnect the shift cable from the transaxle shift lever, if not already done. Position the transaxle shift lever in the 'Neutral' position. This is done by moving the lever clockwise to the detent, then moving it counterclockwise through four detent positions ('L', 'S', 'D' and 'N') to the 'Neutral' position.
4   Reconnect the shift cable to the transaxle shift lever.

10   Throttle valve (T.V.) control cable – checking and adjustment

1   To check the T.V. cable for freeness, pull out on the upper end of the cable a short distance. A light spring resistance should be felt. This is due to the small return spring on the T.V. lever and bracket (Fig. 7.48). Pulling the cable out farther causes the lever to contact the T.V. plunger and plunger spring, and a greater resistance should be felt. Release the cable and it should return to the zero T.V. position.
2   Whenever the T.V. cable has been disconnected from the carburetor, it must be adjusted upon installation.

   a)   After the cable has been connected to the transaxle, install the cable fitting into the engine bracket and install the cable terminal to the throttle idler lever (Fig. 7.49).
   b)   Rotate the throttle idler lever to its 'full travel stop' position. This will set the automatic choke adjuster to the correct setting.
   c)   Release the throttle idler lever.

3   If, for whatever reason, once the T.V. cable is installed it should require readjustment, use the following procedure.

   a)   Depress and hold the metal lock tab (Fig. 7.50).
   b)   Move the slider back through the fitting away from the throttle idler lever until the slider stops against the fitting.
   c)   Release the metal lock tab. This disengages the automatic adjuster.
   d)   Repeat steps b and c in paragraph 2.

11   Troubleshooting (manual transaxle)

Condition	Probable cause
Noise is the same in 'Drive' or coast	Road noise. Tire noise. Front wheel bearing noise. Incorrect drive axle angle (Standing Height).
Noise changes on a different type of road	Road noise. Tire noise.
Noise tone lowers as car speed is lowered	Tire noise.
Noise is produced with engine running vehicle stopped and/or driving	Engine noise. Transaxle noise. Exhaust noise.
A knock at low speeds	Worn drive axle joints. Worn side gear hub counterbore.
Noise is most pronounced on turns	Differential gear noise
Clunk on acceleration or deceleration	Loose engine mounts. Worn differential pinion shaft in case or side gear hub counterbore in case worn oversize. Worn or damaged drive axle inboard joints.
Clicking noise in turns	Worn or damaged output joint.

Vibration	Rough wheel bearing.
	Damaged drive axle shaft.
	Out-of-round tires.
	Tire imbalance.
	Worn joint in drive axle shaft.
	Incorrect drive axle angle.
Noisy in 'Neutral' with engine running	Damaged input gear bearings.
Noisy in 'First' only	Damaged or worn first-speed constant mesh gears.
	Damaged or worn 1-2 synchronizer.
Noisy in 'Second' only	Damaged or worn second-speed constant mesh gears.
	Damaged or worn 1-2 synchronizer.
Noisy in 'Third' only	Damaged or worn third-speed constant mesh gears.
	Damaged or worn 3-4 synchronizer.
Noisy in 'High' gear	Damaged 3-4 synchronizer.
	Damaged 4th speed gear or output gear.
Noisy in 'Reverse' only	Worn or damaged 'Reverse' idler gear or idler bushing.
	Worn or damaged 1-2 synchronizer sleeve.
Noise in all gears	Insufficient lubricant.
	Damaged or worn bearings.
	Worn or damaged input gear (shaft) and/or output gear (shaft).
Slips out of gear	Worn or improperly adjusted linkage.
	Transmission loose on engine housing.
	Shift linkage does not work freely; binds.
	Bent or damaged cables.
	Input gear bearing retainer broken or loose.
	Dirt between clutch cover and engine housing.
	Stiff shift lever seal.
Leaks lubricant	Axle shaft seals.
	Excessive amount of lubricant in transmission.
	Loose or broken input gear (shaft) bearing retainer.
	Input gear bearing retainer 'O' ring and/or lip seal damaged.
	Lack of sealant between case and clutch cover or loose clutch cover.
	Shift lever seal leaks.

Chapter 8 Clutch and drive axles

Refer to Chapter 13 for specifications and information related to 1981 through 1984 models

Contents

Specifications

Clutch type .... Dry plate, diaphragm spring

Clutch operation .... Mechanical, cable linkage

Torque specifications

	ft-lb	m-kg
Clutch pedal-to-mounting bracket bolt	30	4.0
Clutch pedal mounting bracket bolts	28	3.8
Pressure plate-to-flywheel bolts	17	2.3
Hub nut	225	31

1 Clutch – general information

1   The clutch is located between the engine and the transaxle and its main components are the flywheel, clutch disc, the pressure plate assembly and the release bearing. Other components which make up the clutch system are the clutch pedal, self-adjusting mechanism, clutch cable, clutch release lever and the clutch shaft-and-fork assembly.

2   The clutch disc, pressure plate assembly and release bearing are mounted on the transaxle's input shaft. The clutch disc is sandwiched between the flywheel and the pressure plate and has a splined hub which engages and turns the input shaft. When engaged, the pressure plate is held against the clutch disc by the spring pressure of its metal fingers, and the clutch disc, in turn, is held against the engine's flywheel. The spinning of the engine is thus transmitted from the flywheel to the clutch disc and into the input shaft.

3   When the clutch pedal is depressed it pulls on the clutch cable which, in turn, pulls on the release lever at the transaxle. The other end of the release lever, located inside the clutch housing is fork-shaped. This fork engages the clutch release bearing and forces the bearing aginst the pressure plate assembly's release fingers. When the fingers receive pressure from the release bearing they withdraw the mating surface of the pressure plate from the clutch disc which disengages the clutch assembly from the engine's flywheel.

4   The self-adjusting mechanism is mounted to the clutch pedal assembly, as shown in Fig. 8.4. This mechanism controls the tension on the clutch cable, pulling it the proper amount when the clutch pedal is depressed and maintaining a constant light pressure on the cable when the pedal is released. This mechanism also automatically adjusts for any stretching the clutch cable may do over a period of time.

5   Because access to the clutch components is difficult, any time either the engine or the transaxle is removed the clutch disc, pressure plate assembly and release bearing should be carefully inspected and, if necessary, replaced. Since the clutch disc is the highest wear item, it should be replaced as a matter of course if there is any question as to its quality.

2 Clutch – inspection

1   The following check can be made to see if the clutch is releasing fully when the clutch pedal is applied. With the engine running and the brake held on, hold the clutch pedal approximately $\frac{1}{2}$ inch from the floor mat. Now shift between first and reverse gears several times. If the shift is smooth, without any noticeable vehicle movement either forward or backward, the clutch is releasing fully, If the shift is not smooth, then the clutch linkage should be inspected and corrected.

2   Another check is the travel of the release lever. With an assistant in the driver's seat, fully apply and release the clutch pedal several times, noting the length of the release lever's stroke at the transaxle. The end of the lever should have a total travel of approximately 1.6 to 1.8 inches.

3   To check if the self-adjusting mechanism is working properly, depress the clutch pedal and make sure the pawl is firmly engaging the teeth in the quadrant. Next, release the lever and check that the pawl is lifted off of the quadrant teeth by the stop on the bracket.

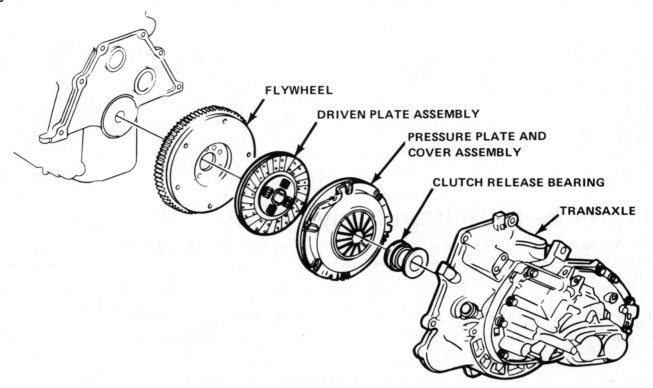

FLYWHEEL

DRIVEN PLATE ASSEMBLY

PRESSURE PLATE AND COVER ASSEMBLY

CLUTCH RELEASE BEARING

TRANSAXLE

Fig. 8.1 An exploded view of the clutch assembly (Sec 1)

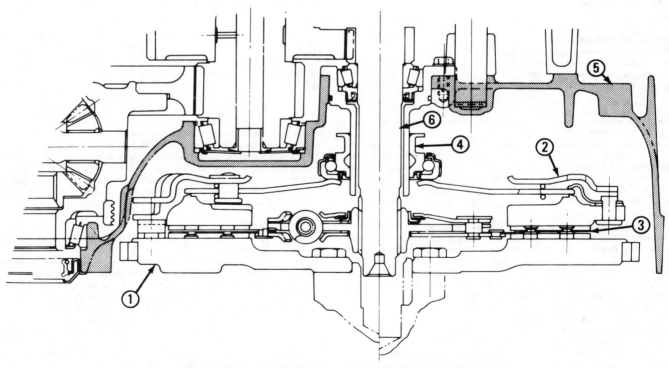

Fig. 8.2 A cross-sectional view of the clutch assembly (Sec 1)

1 Flywheel	3 Driven disc	5 Clutch housing (part of transaxle)
2 Cover and pressure plate assembly	4 Release bearing	6 Input shaft

3.8a Inspect the pressure plate surface for scoring, gouging or warping

3.8b Check that the pressure plate fingers are not bent or distorted

3.9 Inspect the clutch disc for lining wear, as well as broken rivets or springs

3   Clutch disc, pressure plate and release bearing – removal, inspection and installation

1   Because of the clutch's location between the engine and transaxle the clutch cannot be worked on without removing either the engine or transaxle. If repairs which would require removal of the engine are not needed, the quickest way to gain access to the clutch is by removing the transaxle, as described in Chapter 7.

2   With the transaxle removed mark the relationship of the pressure plate assembly to the flywheel for installation purposes.

3   Before removing the pressure plate assembly from the flywheel, check that none of the metal fingers on the pressure plate are distorted or bent. If any damage is evident the pressure plate will need to be replaced.

4   In a diagonal pattern to keep from distorting the pressure plate, loosen the attaching bolts a little at a time until the spring pressure is relieved.

5   While supporting the pressure plate assembly, remove the bolts. Then remove the pressure plate and clutch disc.

6   From the inside of the transaxle, remove the clutch release bearing and release fork.

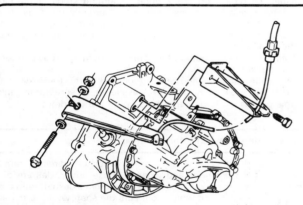

Fig. 8.3 The clutch cable linkage to the transaxle (Secs 1 and 5)

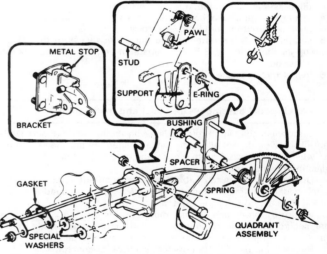

Fig. 8.4 The clutch pedal assembly, including the self-adjusting mechanism (Secs 1 and 4)

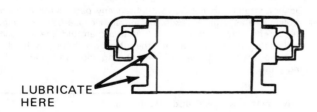

LUBRICATE HERE

Fig. 8.5 The clutch release bearing must be lubricated prior to installation on the input shaft (Sec 3)

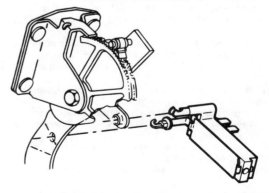

Fig. 8.6 The neutral start switch is mounted to the clutch pedal assembly (Sec 4)

7   Clean the pressure plate, flywheel mating surfaces and the bearing retainer outer surfaces of any oil and grease.

8   Examine the pressure plate surface where it contacts the clutch disc. This surface should be smooth, with no scoring, gouging or warping. Check the pressure plate cover and fingers for damage. If any fault is found with the pressure plate assembly it must be replaced as an entire unit (photo).

9   Inspect the clutch disc for lining wear. Check for loose or broken rivets or springs. (See Section 1, paragraph 5).

10 Inspect the surface of the flywheel for rivet grooves, burnt areas or scoring. If the damage is slight, the flywheel can be removed and reconditioned using a lathe. If the damage is deep, the flywheel should be replaced. Check that the ring gear teeth are not broken, cracked or seriously burned. Refer to Chapter 2 for the flywheel removal process.

11 Check that the release fork has not been cracked or bent. Slowly turn the front face of the release bearing, making sure it turns freely and without any noise. The release bearing is pre-lubricated and should not be washed in gasoline or any other solvent. Whenever a new clutch is installed a new release bearing should automatically be used.

12 If any traces of oil are detected on the clutch components the source should be found and eliminated. If oil is coming from the center of the flywheel, this indicates a failure of the rear oil seal (Chapter 2). Oil at the rear of the clutch assembly may indicate the need to replace the transaxle input shaft seal (Chapter 7).

13 To install, noting the alignment marks made during the removal procedure, hold the clutch disc and pressure plate together against the flywheel and insert a centering tool through the center of them. Since the transaxle input shaft must pass through the center of these components, they must be properly aligned to ease the installation of the transaxle. The clutch disc must be installed with the damper springs offset toward the transaxle. The flywheel side should be identified as such by stamped letters in the disc.

14 Install the mounting bolts and tighten them in steps and in a diagonal cross-pattern until they are torqued to specs.

15 Lubricate both the outer groove and inner recess of the release bearing as shown in Fig. 8.5, and reinstall it and the release fork into the transaxle.

16 Install the transaxle.

4   Clutch pedal assembly – removal and installation

1   Disconnect the clutch release lever on the transaxle (Fig. 8.3). Be careful that you do not allow the cable to snap toward the rear of the car when disconnected as this can damage the quadrant in the self-adjusting mechanism.

2   Disconnect the clutch cable from the quadrant attached to the clutch pedal by lifting the locking pawl away from the quadrant, then sliding the cable out on the right side.

3   Return to the engine compartment and remove the 2 upper nuts that secure the cable retainer to the upper mounting studs of the clutch cable bracket at the firewall, and remove the gasket.

4   Remove the neutral start switch electrical connector.

5   Remove the clutch pedal and bracket assembly from the car.

6   Remove the neutral start switch from the pedal assembly.

7   Remove the bolt securing the pedal and self-adjusting mechanism to the brackets noting the positions of the various pieces for installation.

8   Clean and inspect the various parts and replace as required.

9   To install the self-adjusting mechanism, position the quadrant spring as shown in Fig. 8.4, with a tang end inserted in the hole in the clutch pedal.

10 Carefully rotate the quadrant against the pedal, with the quadrant stop up against the back of the pedal.

11 Install the locking pawl and spring onto the stud at the top of the pedal as shown in Fig. 8.4. Be sure that the spring forces the pawl toward the quadrant.

12 Install the support to the clutch pedal and attach the E-ring to the stud at the top of the pedal.

13 Lubricate the bushings and install them and the spacer onto the pedal assembly.

14 Mount the pedal onto the bracket with the bolt and nut, making sure the bushing flanges contact the bracket on each side.

15 Check the operation of the pawl and quadrant, making sure the panel disengages from the quadrant in the released position and that the quadrant rotates fully from stop to stop.

16 Install the neutral start switch onto the pedal assembly.

17 Mount the pedal and bracket assembly to the firewall.

18 Move to the engine compartment and install the gasket onto the upper studs of the bracket.

19 Using round-edge washers on the lower studs, loosely install the nuts onto the lower studs.

20 Attach the clutch cable to the quadrant, being sure to route it underneath the pawl.

21 Position the cable retainer against the mounting bracket gasket and install the upper nuts then torque all 4 mounting nuts to specs.

22 Attach the cable to the clutch release lever. Be careful not to yank on the cable as this could damage the stop on the quadrant.

23 Connect the neutral start switch electrical connector to the switch.

5   Clutch cable – removal and installation

1   Disengage the clutch cable from the clutch release lever at the transaxle. Be careful that you do not allow the cable to snap toward the rear of the car when disconnected, as this can damage the quadrant in the self-adjusting mechanism.

2   Disengage the clutch cable from the quadrant attached to the clutch pedal by lifting the locking pawl away from the quadrant, then sliding the cable out on the right side.

3   Return to the engine compartment and remove the two upper nuts that secure the cable retainer to the upper mounting studs of the clutch cable bracket, located on the firewall.

4   Disconnect the cable from the bracket mounted on the transaxle and remove the cable.

5   Install the gasket on the 2 upper mounting studs of the clutch cable bracket and insert the new cable through the firewall and bracket, until the cable retaining flange is against the gasket.

6   Attach the cable to the quadrant, being sure to route the cable underneath the pawl.

7   Mount the 2 upper nuts to the retainer mounting studs and torque them to specs.

8   Attach the cable to the bracket mounted to the transaxle.

9   Attach the cable to the clutch release lever. Be sure not to yank on the cable as this could damage the step on the quadrant.

6   Drive axle – general information

1   The X-Body cars use 2 drive axles which run directly from the transaxle to the front hubs and wheels. These drive axles are of the double offset design in which each consists of an axleshaft with a ball-bearing joint on each end which connects the shaft with the transaxle and front hubs.

2   All of the drive axles used on the X-Bodies except for the left-hand inner joint of the automatic transaxle, incorporate a male spline which interlocks with the transaxle by the use of barrel-type snap rings. The left-hand inner joint shaft on the automatic transaxle model uses a female spline which fits over a shaft in the transaxle.

3   Each drive axle uses a helical spline end to connect with the steering knuckle and hub assembly in a tight, press fit. This design eliminates any end play between the drive axle and the hub assembly, which increases durability and reduces noise.

4   Do not attempt to heat or straighten any part of the drive axle assemblies as this could weaken the metal or cause other damage.

5   Be careful any time you work with or around the driveshaft assemblies that you do not damage the rubber seal boots on the shafts as these prevent dirt and water from entering and damaging the ball-bearing joints.

7   Drive axle – removal and installation

1   Remove the hub nut.

2   Raise the front of the car and support it with jackstands.

3   Remove the wheel.

4   Disconnect the brake line clip from the strut (photo).

5   Remove the disc brake caliper as described in Chapter 9, Section 6. Do not disconnect the brake inlet line from the caliper.

6   Make a mark on the cam bolt to ensure the same camber adjustment upon installation (photo).

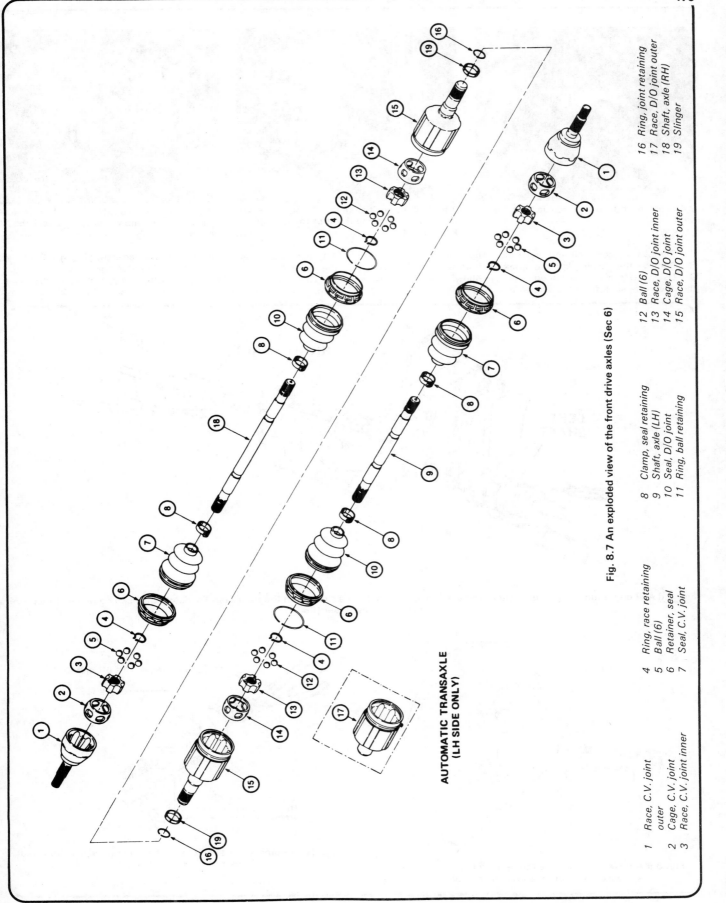

Fig. 8.7 An exploded view of the front drive axles (Sec 6)

AUTOMATIC TRANSAXLE
(LH SIDE ONLY)

1 Race, C.V. joint outer
2 Cage, C.V. joint
3 Race, C.V. joint inner

4 Ring, race retaining
5 Ball (6)
6 Retainer, seal
7 Seal, C.V. joint

8 Clamp, seal retaining
9 Shaft, axle (LH)
10 Seal, D/O joint
11 Ring, ball retaining

12 Ball (6)
13 Race, D/O joint inner
14 Cage, D/O joint
15 Race, D/O joint outer

16 Ring, joint retaining
17 Race, D/O joint outer
18 Shaft, axle (RH)
19 Slinger

7.4 Disconnect the brake line clip from the strut

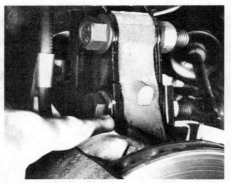

7.6 Mark the position of the camber adjusting cam before removing the strut-to-steering knuckle bolts

7.15 The hub nut is used to press the drive axle into the hub assembly. The punch keeps the rotor from turning

7   Remove the cam bolt and upper attaching bolt.
8   Remove the steering knuckle assembly from the strut bracket.
9   Using a GM special tool or equivalent as shown in Fig. 8.8 remove the drive axle shaft from the transaxle.

10 Using a GM special tool or equivalent as shown in Fig. 8.9 remove the axle shaft from the hub and bearing assembly.
11 Drive axles use seal retainers which must be installed with a press. If the drive axle needs an overhaul and you do not have direct access

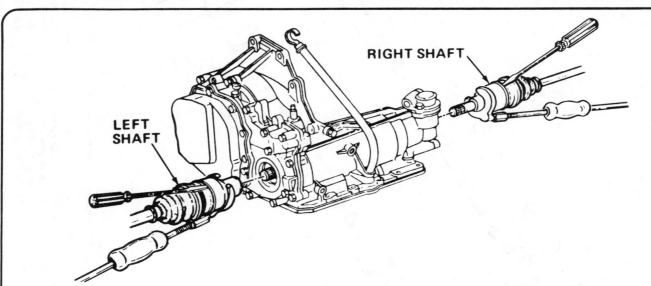

Fig. 8.8 A slide-hammer-type puller should be used to remove the drive axles from the transaxle. To install, they can be tapped into place using a screwdriver (Sec 7)

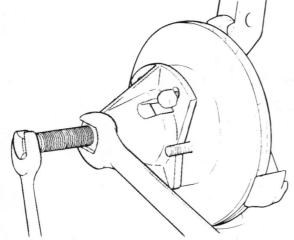

Fig. 8.9 A puller must be used to remove the hub and bearing assembly from the drive axle (Sec 7)

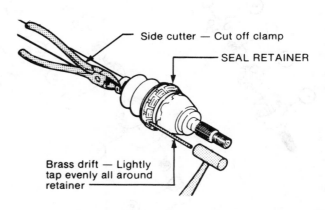

Side cutter — Cut off clamp

SEAL RETAINER

Brass drift — Lightly tap evenly all around retainer

Fig. 8.10 To remove the seal retainer from the drive axle boot seal, tap it off as shown (Sec 8)

to a press, an automotive machine shop can press the retainers for you when that step comes. See Section 8 for disassembly and reassembly of the drive axle.

12 If the drive axle is being replaced, the steering knuckle seal must also be replaced, as described in Chapter 11.

13 Loosely install the drive axle to the steering knuckle and transaxle and loosely attach the steering knuckle to the strut bracket.

14 Install the brake caliper.

15 Install the drive axle to the steering knuckle. Since the drive axle uses an interference fit, securing it to the steering knuckle is best done by installing the hub nut onto the axleshaft and tightening it. When the shaft begins to turn, insert a punch, drift or similar tool between the halves of the rotor so that it locks against the brake caliper (photo). It takes approximately 70 ft-lb (9.6 m-kg) of torque to seat the axleshaft.

16 With a jackstand or similar support under the hub assembly, lower the car just enough to align the cam bolt with the alignment marks. Torque both the cam bolt and upper nut to specs.

17 Install the axleshaft into the transaxle by placing a screwdriver in the inner retainer groove as shown in Fig. 8.8, and tapping it until the shaft is seated.

18 Connect the brake line clip to the strut bracket.

19 Mount the wheel and lower the car to the ground.

20 Torque the hub nut to specs.

8 Drive axle – disassembly and reassembly

1 Remove the drive axle from the car as described in Section 7.

2 Cut off the seal retaining clamp from the outer joint seal.

3 Remove the seal retainer from the outer joint assembly by lightly tapping it with a drift evenly all around the retainer, as shown in Fig. 8.10.

4 Using snap ring pliers, spread the retaining ring and remove the joint assembly from the axleshaft.

5 Remove the outer joint seal and seal retainer from the axleshaft.

6 Again using a drift gently tap on the bearing cage to rotate it in the outer race enough to remove the ball bearings. See Fig. 8.11.

7 When the balls are removed, pivot the cage and inner race so the cage windows align with the outer race lands, as per Fig. 8.12, and lift out the cage and inner race.

8 Rotate the inner race within the cage as shown in Fig. 8.13 and withdraw the inner race.

9 Remove the inner joint assembly, seal retainer, inner joint seal and seal retaining clamp from the axleshaft using the same procedure described in paragraphs 2 through 5.

10 Remove the separate cage, inner race and ball bearings from the inner joint assembly using the same procedure described in paragraphs 6 through 8.

11 Clean all parts in solvent. Be sure to keep the parts from the inner and outer joint assemblies separate.

12 Inspect the surfaces of the inner and outer races, the cages and the ball bearings for roughness, scoring, heat discoloration or excessive wear and replace if necessary.

13 Inspect the condition of the rubber seal boots for holes or cracking and replace if necessary.

14 Put a light coat of lithium-based grease on the ball grooves on the inner and outer races.

15 Working with the inner joint assembly components, install the inner race into the cage. Be sure the retaining ring side of the inner race faces the small end of the cage.

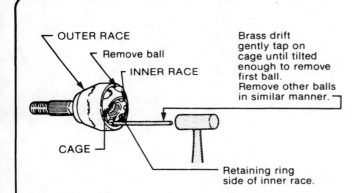

Fig. 8.11 In disassembling the joint assembly, use a drift to rotate the cage and inner race so that the balls can be removed one at a time (Sec 8)

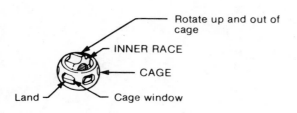

Fig. 8.13 Pivot the inner race to remove it from the cage (Sec 8)

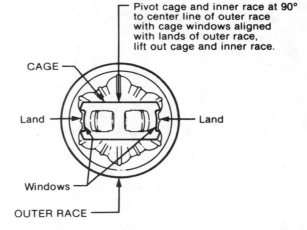

Fig. 8.12 The cage and inner race must be positioned as shown to be removed from the outer race (Sec 8)

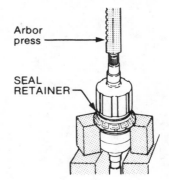

Fig. 8.14 The seal retainer must be supported in a press to be installed on the boot seal (Sec 8)

16 Install the cage and inner race into the inner joint assembly's outer race.

17 Install the balls in the same manner as they were removed.

18 Pack the joint with grease.

19 Install a new seal retaining clamp or hose clamp onto the axle shaft.

20 Install the seal retainer over the inner joint seal and install them onto the axleshaft.

21 Place the small end of the seal in its groove in the axleshaft, slip the seal retaining clamp over it and tighten the clamp.

22 Place the race retaining ring onto the axleshaft just in front of its groove. Then press the inner joint assembly onto the axleshaft until the retaining ring is seated in its groove.

23 Support the axleshaft in a suitable press with supports under the seal retainer as shown in Fig. 8.14, and press the seal retainer onto the inner joint assembly.

24 Repeat the same assembly procedure on the outer joint assembly and seal.

25 Install the drive axle into the car.

Chapter 9 Braking system

Refer to Chapter 13 for specifications and information related to 1981 through 1984 models

Contents

Specifications

Master cylinder
Piston diameter step bore ....   0.874 in (22.2 mm)

Front disc brake
Diameter ....   11.0 in (279.4 mm
Thickness:
    Maximum ....   1.040 in (26.42 mm)
    Minimum ....   0.965 in (24.47 mm)
End play (maximum) ....   0.005 in (0.127 mm)
Surface finish ....   30 to 80 micro-inch
Parallelism (thickness variation) ....   0.0005 in (0.0127 mm)
Caliper bore diameter ....   2.24 in (57.0 mm)

Rear drum brake
Maximum allowable out of round ....   (0.005 in) 0.127 mm
Drum (diameter x depth) ....   7.874 in x 1.575 in (200.0 x 40.0 mm)
Drum, maximum rebore diameter ....   7.894 in (200.64 mm)
Wheel cylinder bore diameter ....   0.689 in (17.5 mm)
Power head ....   7.874 in (200.0 mm) tandem

Pedal travel
Manual disc ....   3.5 in (89.0 mm)
Power disc ....   2.75 in (70.0 mm)

Torque specifications

	ft-lb	m-kg
Brake hose to caliper screw	22.0	45
Brake line to rear wheel cylinder	150 (in-lb)	1.7
Brake line to master cylinder nuts	150 (in-lb)	1.7
Caliper bleed screw	110 (in-lb)	1.2
Wheel cylinder bleeder screw	50 (in-lb)	0.6
Caliper mounting bolt	28	3.8
Failure warning switch	30 (in-lb)	0.3
Switch piston plug	65 (in-lb)	0.7
Proportioner valves	25	3.4
Master cylinder attaching nuts	25	3.4
Booster attaching nuts	25	3.4
Wheel lug nuts	102	14.0
Brake pedal swing bolt nut	49	6.7
Brake pedal to dash	18	2.5
Parking brake assembly attaching bolts	7	1.0

1 General information

1   The braking system on GM's X-Body cars is a diagonal split system design. It incorporates two separate circuits, each of which utilize one front and one rear brake. With this system if one circuit fails, the other circuit will still function.

2   The master cylinder is designed for the diagonal split system and incorporates a primary piston for one circuit and a secondary piston for the other.

3   This master cylinder also utilizes a quick take-up feature which provides a large volume of fluid to the brake system upon initial brake application, thus giving more immediate braking response.

4   The two front wheels use disc brakes. These consist of a flat, disc-like rotor which is attached to the front axleshaft and wheel. Around one section of the rotor is mounted a stationary caliper assembly which houses two hydraulically-operated disc brake pads. The inboard pad is mounted on a piston, while the outboard pad is mounted to the caliper housing. When the brake pedal is applied, brake fluid pressure forces the piston and inboard pad against the inside of the rotor. At the same time the caliper housing moves inward, forcing the outboard pad against the outside of the rotor. The pressure and resultant friction on the rotor is what slows the wheel.

5   The rear wheels use the conventional drum brakes. With these, fluid pressure from the master cylinder forces the rear wheel cylinder pistons outward, which in turn forces the brake shoes against the spinning brake drum attached to the rear wheel. The force of the brake shoes against the drum is what slows the wheel.

6   Both the front disc and the rear drum brakes adjust automatically to lining wear.

7   After completing any operation involving the dismantling of any part of the brake system, always test drive the car to check for proper braking performance before resuming normal driving. When testing the brakes, perform the tests on a clean, dry, flat surface. Conditions other than these can lead to inaccurate test results. Test the brakes at various speeds with both light and heavy pedal pressure. The car should brake evenly without pulling to one side or the other. Avoid locking the brakes, as this slides the tires and diminishes braking efficiency and control.

8   Tires, car load and front end alignment are factors which also affect braking performance.

9   Torque values given in the Specifications Section are for dry, unlubricated fasteners.

2 Brake lines – general inspection and replacement

1   About every six months the flexible hoses which connect the steel brake line with the rear brakes and front calipers should be inspected for cracks, chafing of the outer cover, leaks, blisters, and other damage. These are important and vulnerable parts of the brake system and inspection should be complete. A light and mirror will prove helpful for a thorough check. If a hose exhibits any of the above conditions, replace it with a new one.

2   When it becomes necessary to replace steel line, use only double-walled steel tubing. Never substitute copper tubing, as copper is subject to fatigue cracking and corrosion. The outside diameter of the tubing is used for sizing.

3   Some auto parts stores or brake supply houses carry various lengths of pre-fabricated brake line. Depending on the type of tubing used, these sections can either be bent by hand into the desired shape or must be bent in a tubing bender.

4   If pre-fabricated lengths are not available, obtain the recommended steel tubing and steel fitting nuts to match the line to be replaced. Determine the correct length by measuring the old brake line section and cut the new tubing to fit, leaving about $\frac{1}{2}$-inch extra for flaring the ends.

5   Install the fittings onto the cut tubing and flare the ends using an ISO flaring tool.

6   Using a tubing bender, bend the tubing to match the shape of the old brake line.

7   Tube flaring and bending can usually be done by a local auto parts store if the proper equipment mentioned in paragraphs 5 and 6 is not available.

8   When installing the brake line, leave at least 19 mm (0.75 in) clearance between the line and any moving or vibrating parts.

3 Bleeding the brake system

1   Anytime any part of the brake system is disassembled or develops a leak, or when the fluid in the master cylinder reservoir runs low, air will enter the system and cause a decrease in braking performance. To eliminate this air the brakes must be bled using the procedure described in this Section.

2   If air has entered the system because the master cylinder has been disconnected, or the master cylinder reservoir has been low or empty of fluid, or if a complete flushing of the system is needed, all four brakes should be bled. If a brake line serving only one brake is disconnected then only that brake need be bled. Likewise, if any line is disconnected anywhere in the system, the brakes served by that line must be bled.

3   Before beginning, have an assistant on hand, as well as a good supply of new brake fluid, an empty clear container such as a glass jar, a length of $\frac{3}{16}$-inch plastic, rubber or vinyl tubing to fit over the bleeder valve and a wrench to open and close the bleeder valve. The car may have to be raised and placed on jackstands for clearance.

4   If the car is equipped with power brakes, remove the vacuum reserve in the system by applying the brakes several times.

5   Check that the master cylinder reservoir is full of fluid and be sure to keep it at least half full during the entire operation. If, at any point, the reservoir runs low of fluid the entire bleeding procedure must be repeated.

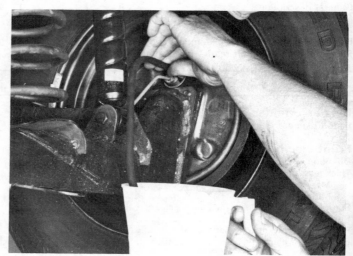

3.7 Bleeding the rear brakes

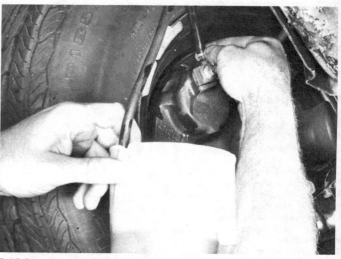

3.10 Bleeding the front brakes

6   Beginning at the right rear wheel, loosen the bleeder valve slightly to break it loose then tighten it to a point where it is snug but can still be loosened quickly and easily.
7   Place one end of the tubing over the bleeder valve and submerge the other end in brake fluid in the container (photo).
8   With your assistant sitting in the driver's seat, have him pump the brakes a few times to get pressure in the system. On the last pump have him hold the pedal firmly depressed.
9   While the pedal is held depressed, open the bleeder valve just enough to allow a flow of fluid to leave the valve. Watch for air bubbles to exit the submerged end of the tube. When the fluid flow slows after a couple of seconds, close the valve again and have your assistant release the pedal. If he releases the pedal before the valve is closed again air can be drawn back into the system.
10   Repeat paragraphs 8 and 9 until no more air is seen in the fluid leaving the tube. Then fully tighten the bleeder valve and proceed to the left front brake, left rear brake and right front brake, in that order, and perform the same operation. Be sure to check the fluid in the master cylinder reservoir frequently (photo).
11   Do not reuse any old brake fluid as it attracts moisture which will deteriorate the brake system components.
12   Refill the master cylinder with fluid at the end of the operation.

4   Front disc brakes – inspection

1   As inspection of the brakes is included in the car's routine maintenance schedule, this procedure is described in Chapter 1, Section 19.

5   Front disc brake pads – removal and installation

1   Before beginning the disc pad removal procedure, remove 2/3 of the brake fluid from the master cylinder reservoir. The easiest way of doing this is to insert a piece of hose into the reservoir, submerging it as much as possible in the fluid. Once submerged, place your thumb tightly over the end in your hand and withdraw the hose, emptying the trapped fluid into a suitable container. Repeat as necessary.
2   Raise the front of the car and support it on jackstands.
3   Remove the front wheels. If you are unfamiliar with this type of brake work, disassemble only one side at a time using the assembled side for reference.
4   Place a C-clamp on the brake, as shown in photo 5.4 and tighten it until the piston bottoms in the bore. Remove the C-clamp.
5   Disconnect the brake hose from where it is secured to the suspension bracket (photo).
6   Remove the Allen head mounting bolts (photos) and check them for galling or corrosion. Replace if necessary.
7   Remove the caliper. If only the brake pads are being replaced, the caliper can be suspended from the front suspension spring by a wire hook made from a clothing hanger. This eliminates the necessity of having to disconnect the brake line and subsequent bleeding. Never suspend the caliper only by the brake line as this could damage the line.
8   Remove the inboard pad by withdrawing the retention lug from the inner piston bore (Fig. 9.1).

5.4 Using a C-clamp to bottom the piston in the caliper bore

5.5 Disconnecting the brake hose from the strut bracket

5.6a Removing the brake caliper mounting bolts

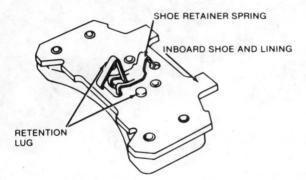

SHOE RETAINER SPRING

INBOARD SHOE AND LINING

RETENTION LUG

Fig. 9.1 Location of retainer spring and retention lugs on the front inboard brake pads (Sec 5)

5.6b Check the brake caliper mounting bolts for galling or corrosion

5.9 When removing the outer pad, the retaining tabs must be bent straight out

5.11 Removing the retaining spring from the inboard pad

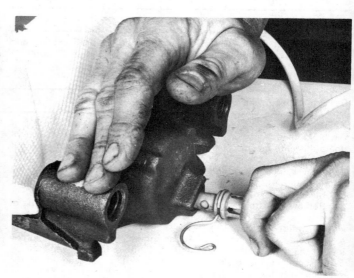

6.3 Using compressed air to force the piston from its bore

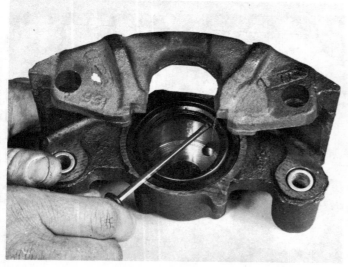

6.5a Removing the dust boot from the caliper bore

6.5b The brake caliper dust boot

9 Use channel lock pliers to bend the outer pad's retaining tabs straight out, so the pad can be removed from the caliper (photo).
10 Place the new outer pad in the caliper assembly and crimp the retaining tabs to secure it in place.
11 Remove the retainer spring from the old inboard pad (photo) and install it on the replacement pad. Ensure that it's locked firmly in place and install the inboard pad in the caliper.
12 Install new bushings in the mounting bolt holes. See Figure 9.2.
13 Place the caliper assembly in position on the caliper bracket.
14 Install the mounting bolts and torque them to the proper specifications.
15 Connect the brake line to the suspension bracket.
16 Install the wheel.
17 Repeat the procedure on the opposite brake.
18 Fill the master cylinder with brake fluid.
19 Bleed the brake system as described in Section 3.
20 Lower the car to the ground.

***

6 Front disc brake caliper – removal, overhaul and installation

1 Purchase a caliper overhaul kit which contains all of the necessary replacement parts.
2 Remove the caliper from the caliper bracket and remove the pads from the caliper as described in Section 5. In this operation, the inlet brake line should be removed from the caliper. To minimize brake fluid leakage, it can be plugged by fitting a short piece of rubber hose, the same diameter as the connection, over the line, inserting a suitable bolt in the free end and clamping it. A similar arrangement is shown in photo 10.8.
3 Use clean rags to pad the inside of the caliper. If you have access to compressed air, place an air nozzle into the caliper inlet hole and slowly apply air until the piston is forced out of its bore (photo). CAUTION: Do not use your fingers to try and catch the piston as serious injury could result. If you do not have access to compressed air, hold the caliper with the inlet hole up and carefully bang the caliper down on a block of wood to force the piston out. As a last resort, temporarily re-install the brakeline to the caliper and have an assistant depress the brake pedal. The fluid pressure will force the piston out.
4 Inspect the piston for scoring, nicks, corrosion and worn or damaged chrome plating, and replace it if necessary.
5 Remove the dust boot by prying with a screwdriver. Be careful not to scratch the housing bore (photo).
6 Remove the piston seal from its groove with a wood or plastic dowel. Do not use a metal tool here, as it could damage the bore (photo).
7 Inspect the caliper bore for scoring, nicks, corrosion or wear. Light corrosion can be removed with crocus cloth. If crocus cloth will not clean up the bore, the caliper housing must be replaced.
8 Remove the bleeder screw (photo).
9 Clean the piston and housing bore and bleeder screw with denatured alcohol. Do not use gasoline or mineral-based solvents.
10 Lubricate the bore and the new piston seal with clean brake fluid and install the seal in its groove. Be sure the seal is not twisted.
11 Install the new dust boot onto the groove of the piston as shown in Figure 9.3.
12 Insert the piston in its bore and press it down, working it through its seal until it bottoms.
13 Seat the new dust boot in the caliper bore (photo).
14 Install the bleeder screw.
15 Apply multi-purpose lithium grease at all surfaces where the caliper assembly meets the caliper bracket.
16 Complete the operation by following the procedure described in Section 5, paragraphs 10 through 20.

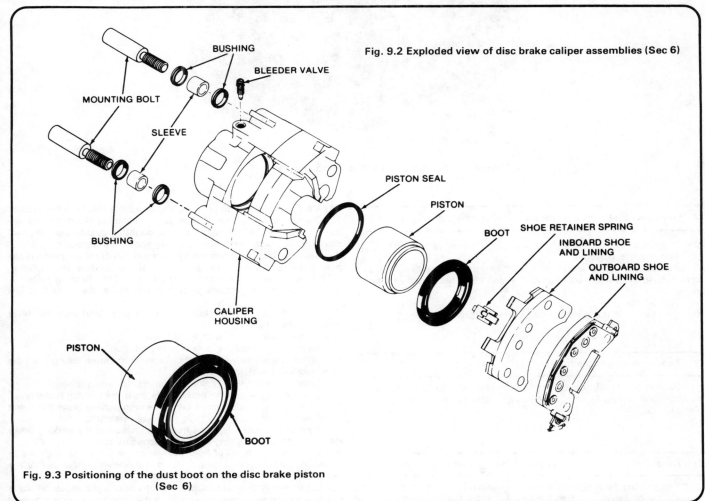

Fig. 9.2 Exploded view of disc brake caliper assemblies (Sec 6)

Fig. 9.3 Positioning of the dust boot on the disc brake piston (Sec 6)

6.6 The piston seal, removed from the caliper bore

6.8 Removing the bleeder screw from the caliper housing

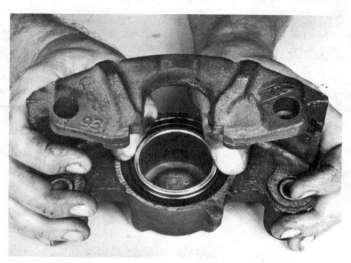

6.13 Seating the new dust boot in the caliper bore

7　Front disc brake rotor — removal and installation

1　Raise the front of the vehicle and support it on jackstands.
2　Remove the wheel(s).
3　Remove the caliper assembly from the mount as described in Section 5. Suspend it with a piece of wire — don't let it hang by the rubber hose.
4　Pull off the rotor.
5　Installation is the reverse of the removal procedure.

8　Rear brakes – inspection

1　As inspection of the brakes is included in the car's routine maintenance schedule, this procedure is described in Chapter 1, Section 19.

9　Rear brake shoes – removal and installation

1　Support the rear of the car on jackstands and remove the rear wheels and brake drums. Refer to Chapter 1, Section 19 if necessary.

Work on one side at a time, using the assembled brake for reference.
2　Disassemble the rear brakes as described in the following sequence. If any of the parts are of doubtful quality due to heat discoloration, wear, or overstress, they should be replaced.
3　Remove the hold-down spring from the primary shoe. Remove the hold-down spring and lever pivot from the secondary shoe (photo). Withdraw the hold-down pins from the rear of the backing plate.
4　Lift up on the actuating lever and remove the actuating link (photo).
5　Remove the actuator lever, actuator pivot and actuator lever return spring (photo).
6　Remove the adjusting screw (photo).
7　Remove the adjusting screw spring (photo).
8　Lift off the primary shoe and disconnect its return spring from the shoe retainer (photo).
9　Remove the parking brake strut and strut spring (photo).
10　Disconnect the parking brake cable from the parking brake lever.
11　Lift off the secondary shoe, complete with parking brake lever, and disconnect its return spring from the shoe retainer (photo).
12　Remove the return springs from the shoes and the parking brake lever and its retaining ring from the secondary shoe.
Note: *If there are signs of fluid leakage or the wheel cylinders are to be overhauled for any reason, perform this operation now, before the new linings are installed. Refer to Section 10.*
13　Before beginning the installation of the new brake shoes, lubricate the brake shoe contact surfaces with a thin coating of brake lubricant

9.3 Removing the hold-down spring and lever pivot from the secondary shoe

9.4 Removing the actuating link

9.5 Removing the actuator lever, pivot and return spring

9.6 Removing the adjusting screw

9.7 Removing the adjusting screw spring

9.8 Lifting off the primary shoe

9.9 Removing the parking brake strut and spring

9.11 Removing the secondary shoe, with parking brake lever attached

9.13 Lubricating the brake shoe contact surfaces

9.17 The assembled shoes must be spread apart to clear the axle flange when installing

9.19 Installing the actuating link

9.20 A screwdriver is helpful when installing the actuator pivot return spring

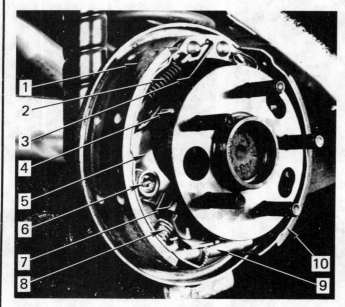

Fig. 9.4 Assembled rear brake assembly (secondary shoe side)
(Sec 9)

1	Secondary brake shoe	6	Hold-down spring and pin
2	Secondary shoe return spring	7	Actuator pivot
3	Actuating link	8	Actuator pivot return spring
4	Parking brake strut	9	Adjusting screw
5	Actuator lever	10	Primary brake shoe

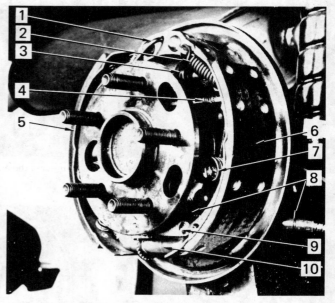

Fig. 9.5 Assembled rear brake assembly (primary shoe side)
(Sec 9)

1	Actuating link	6	Primary brake shoe
2	Primary shoe return spring	7	Hold-down spring and pin
3	Wheel cylinder assembly	8	Parking brake cable
4	Parking brake strut and spring	9	Adjusting screw spring
5	Secondary brake shoe	10	Adjusting screw

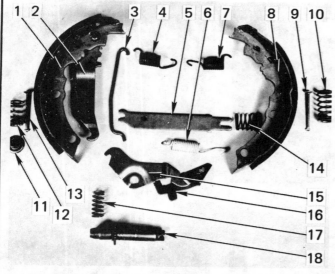

Fig. 9.6 Rear brake components (disassembled) (Sec 9)

1	Secondary brake shoe	10	Hold-down spring
2	Parking brake lever	11	Lever pivot
3	Actuating link	12	Hold-down spring
4	Secondary shoe return spring	13	Hold-down pin
5	Parking brake strut	14	Parking brake strut spring
6	Adjusting screw spring	15	Actuator lever
7	Primary shoe return spring	16	Actuator pivot
8	Primary brake shoe	17	Actuator pivot return spring
9	Hold-down pin	18	Adjusting screw

Fig. 9.7 Components of the wheel cylinder (disassembled)
(Sec 10)

1	Wheel cylinder housing	4	Pistons
2	Bleeder screw	5	Seal cups
3	Dust boots	6	Spring assembly

9.21a Installing the lever pivot onto the secondary shoe

9.21b Installing the secondary shoe hold-down spring and pin

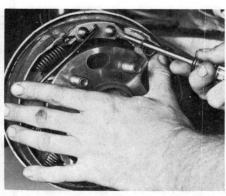
9.24 Installing the brake shoe return springs

10.4a Compressing the spring tabs on the parking brake cable

10.4b Withdrawing the parking brake cable from the backing plate

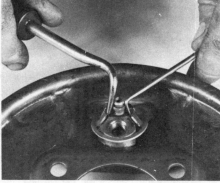
10.6 Removing the wheel cylinder retainer ring

10.7 Loosening the hub assembly mounting bolts

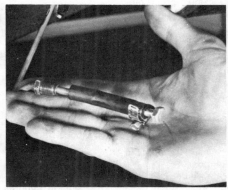
10.8 A piece of rubber tubing, a small hose clamp and a screw can be used to plug the brake fluid inlet line

10.9 Lifting off the backing plate with wheel cylinder

10.24 Installing the wheel cylinder retaining ring

12.3 Disconnecting the brake failure warning switch lead

12.4 Disconnecting the brake line connections from the master cylinder

such as white lithium grease (photo).

14 Install the parking brake lever with retaining ring on the new secondary shoe.

15 Install the adjusting screw spring onto both shoes with the long end toward the secondary shoe.

16 Insert the adjusting screw into position between the shoes with the star wheel toward the secondary shoe. Note that the coils of the adjusting screw spring must not be over the adjusting screw star wheel.

17 Spread the shoes apart to clear the axle flange (photo), connect the parking brake cable to the parking brake lever and hold the shoe assembly in place.

18 Install the parking brake strut and spring with the spring against the primary shoe and the other end on the parking brake lever.

19 Engage the actuating link into its hole in the shoe retainer (photo).

20 Install the actuator lever, pivot and spring onto the secondary shoe (photo).

21 Install the secondary shoe hold-down pin and spring, complete with lever pivot (photo).

22 Install the primary shoe hold-down pin and spring.

23 Lift on the top of the actuator lever and engage the hook of the actuating link into its hole.

24 Install the brake shoe return springs. Be sure that the short end of each spring is engaged in the outer hole of its respective shoe (photo).

25 Install the brake drums and wheels and lower the car to the ground.

10 Rear wheel cylinder – removal, overhaul and installation

1   Purchase a wheel cylinder rebuild kit which will contain all the parts needed in the overhaul procedure.

2   Support the rear of the car on jackstands and remove the rear wheels and brake drums.

3   Remove the brake shoes and related components as described in Section 9.

4   Using needle-nosed pliers compress the locking spring tabs securing the parking brake cable to the backing plate (photos) and withdraw the cable.

5   Clean any dirt from around the wheel cylinder inlet and loosen slightly, but do not remove, the brake inlet nut.

6   Using two awls or pins approximately $\frac{1}{8}$-inch in diameter or less, insert them into the access slots between the wheel cylinder pilot and the wheel cylinder retainer lock tabs on the rear of the backing plate (photo). Bending both tabs away simultaneously, remove the wheel cylinder retainer ring.

7   Loosen the four bolts that secure the hub assembly to the axle (photo).

8   Moving the rear wheel hub assembly away from the backing plate slightly, remove the inlet line nut and cover over or insert a stopper in the inlet line to stop the leakage of brake fluid (photo).

9   Lift off the backing plate complete with wheel cylinder (photo).

10 Remove the wheel cylinder from the backing plate.

11 Press on the wheel cylinder pistons to force out any remaining fluid.

12 Remove the bleeder screw.

13 Remove the dust boots at either end of the cylinder by prying them off with your fingers.

14 Remove the pistons, seal cups and spring assembly.

15 Wash all parts in clean denatured alcohol or brake fluid. Never use gasoline or other mineral-based solvents.

16 Examine the cylinder bore and pistons for wear, pitting, corrosion, roughness or scoring and replace if necessary. If damage to the cylinder bore is slight it can be honed smooth using a honing tool available at most auto supply stores.

17 Prior to reassembling the wheel cylinder components, lubricate the cylinder bore, pistons and new seal cups with brake fluid.

18 Insert the spring assembly into the bore.

19 Place the seal cups over the ends of the pistons and insert the pistons into the bore.

20 Install new dust boots over both ends of the cylinder.

21 Install the bleeder screw.

22 Insert the wheel cylinder assembly into its boss on the backing plate.

23 Place the backing plate into its position on the axle and re-install

the hub and bearing assembly onto the axle, tightening the four bolts in a cross-pattern. Torque the bolts to 74 ft-lbs (10.2 m-kg).

24 Place a block of wood between the hub and wheel cylinder (photo).

25 Place the cylinder retaining ring into its position on the wheel cylinder and seat it by using a $1\frac{1}{8}$-inch 12-point socket and plastic mallet. Be sure that the lock tabs are seated into their recesses on the wheel cylinder.

26 Re-install the brake inlet line to the wheel cylinder.

27 Insert the parking brake cable through its hole in the backing plate until it locks in place.

28 Re-install the brake shoes and related components as described in Section 9.

29 Install the brake drums and wheels.

30 Bleed the brake system as described in Section 3.

31 Lower the car to the ground and test drive, checking for proper brake operation and for leaks in the system.

11 Rear brakes – manual adjustment

1   Although the rear drum brakes are normally self-adjusting, there are times when they may have to be manually adjusted. This can be necessary when some difficulty is experienced in removing the brake drums, in which case the shoes may need to be backed off, or when the self-adjusting mechanism is not catching because the shoes are not extended far enough, usually following an overhaul.

2   For manual adjustment a hole must be made in the brake backing plate in order to get to the starred adjusting screw. Some cars have a lanced area in the backing plate which simply must be punched out. If this is done with the drum installed on the car, before driving the drum must be removed and all metal cleaned out.

3   On cars with no lanced area in the brake backing plate, a hole must be drilled. All backing plates have two round, flat areas in the lower half of the plate, through one of which the parking brake cable is routed. Drill a 13 mm ($\frac{1}{2}$-inch) hole through the round, flat area opposite the parking brake cable.

4   After a hole has been made, insert a screwdriver through the hole and, using leverage against the backing plate, turn the starred brake adjusting screw.

5   Adjust the screw so that the wheel and tire can just be turned by hand. The drag should be the same at both rear wheels. Then back off the screw 30 notches at both wheels. If the shoes still drag lightly on the drum back off the adjusting screw one or two additional notches. If there is still heavy drag at this point the parking brake may need adjusting.

6   After adjustment is complete, obtain a suitable hole cover and install it in the backing plate hole to prevent dirt and water from getting into the brakes.

7   Check the parking brake adjustment and adjust if necessary as described in Section 15.

12 Master cylinder – removal, overhaul and installation

1   A master cylinder overhaul kit should be purchased before dismantling. This kit will include all the replacement parts necessary for the overhaul procedure. The rubber replacement parts, particularly the seals, are the key to fluid control within the master cylinder. As such, it's very important that they be installed securely and facing in the proper direction. To eliminate any confusion, a step-by-step photo sequence is provided with the text. Be careful during the rebuild procedure that no grease or mineral-based solvents come in contact with the rubber parts.

2   Completely cover the front fender and cowling area of the car, as brake fluid can ruin painted surfaces if it should be spilled.

3   Disconnect the electrical lead from the brake failure warning switch (photo).

4   Disconnect the brake line connections (photo). Rags or newspapers should be placed under the master cylinder to soak up the fluid that will drain out.

5   On a manual brake set-up the master cylinder pushrod must be disconnected from the brake pedal inside the car.

6   Remove the two master cylinder mounting nuts (photo).

7   Remove the master cylinder from the car and drain any remaining fluid from it.

12.6 Removing the master cylinder mounting nuts

12.8 Removing the brake failure warning switch

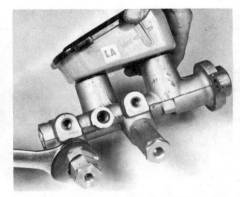
12.9 Removing the proportioner valves

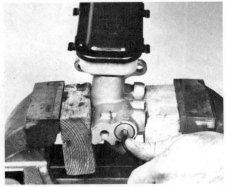
12.11 Removing the switch piston plug

12.12 Removing the switch piston assembly

12.13 Removing the primary piston circlip

12.14 Removing the primary piston assembly

12.15 Removing the secondary piston assembly

12.16 Prying the plastic reservoir from the cylinder body

12.17 Removing the quick-take-up valve retaining ring

12.18 The quick take-up valve and retaining ring

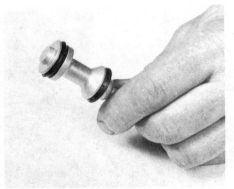
12.21 The secondary piston seals must be installed with the lips facing outwards as shown

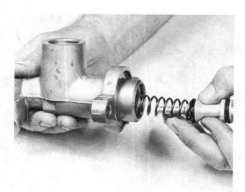

12.22 Installing the secondary piston assembly

12.23 The primary piston seal must be installed with the lip facing away from the piston

12.24a Install the seal guard over the seal

12.24b Place the primary piston spring into position

12.24c Insert the spring retainer into the spring

12.24d Insert the spring retaining bolt through the retainer and spring and thread it into the piston

12.24e Install the O-ring onto the piston

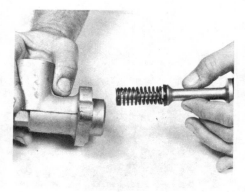

12.25 Installing the primary piston assembly into the body

12.26a Installing the small O-ring onto the switch position

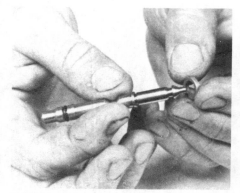

12.26b Installing the metal retainer onto the switch piston

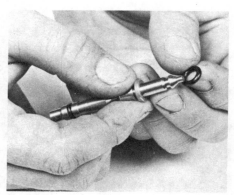

12.26c Installing the large O-ring onto the switch piston

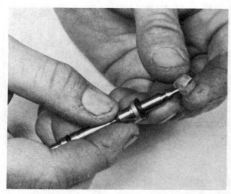

12.26d Installing the plastic retainer onto the switch piston

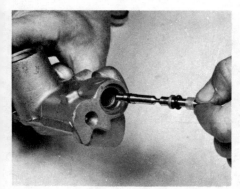

12.27 Installing the switch piston assembly into the cylinder body

12.28 Installing a new O-ring onto the switch piston plug

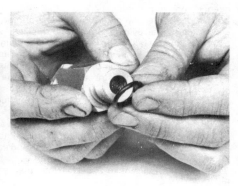

12.29 Installing new O-rings onto the proportioner valves

12.30 Installing the failure warning switch

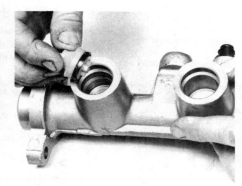

12.31 Installing the quick take-up valve

12.32 Installing the quick take-up valve retaining ring

12.33 Installing new reservoir grommets into the body

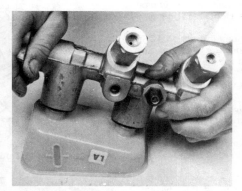

12.34 Pressing the cylinder body onto the reservoir

12.40 Installing the reservoir diaphragm into the cover

8   Remove the brake failure warning switch (photo).
9   Remove the two proportioner valves (photo). Make a note of their respective positions in the master cylinder body as the two valves are different.
10   At this point it would be advantageous for further disassembly to place the master cylinder in a vice. Two blocks of wood, one on either side of the cylinder as shown in photo 12.11 should be used to hold the cylinder. Remember that the body is made of aluminum and should not be overstressed.
11   With an Allen wrench remove the switch piston plug (photo).
12   Remove the switch piston assembly (photo). Slight tapping of the cylinder on a block of wood may be necessary to dislodge the switch piston assembly from its bore.
13   Remove the primary piston retaining ring by depressing the piston and prying out the retaining ring (photo).
14   Remove the primary piston assembly (photo).
15   Remove the secondary piston assembly (photo).
16   Remove the plastic reservoir by prying it out of the cylinder body (photo).

17   Remove the quick take-up valve retaining ring (photo).
18   Remove the quick take-up valve (photo).
19   Clean all parts in denatured alcohol. Do not use gasoline or other mineral-based solvents as these contain contaminents which soften and ruin the rubber seals (photo).
20   Inspect the cylinder bore for scoring, excessive roughness, nicks or corrosion. Slight corrosion or scratches can be taken out with crocus cloth, but always rinse the bore with clean brake fluid before attempting this. Never use crocus cloth on a dry bore. If the imperfections cannot be eliminated with crocus cloth, the cylinder should be replaced.
21   Remove the old seals from the secondary piston assembly and install the new seals so the cups face in the directions shown.
22   Lubricate the bore with clean brake fluid and insert the spring, the spring retainer and the secondary piston assembly into the cylinder bore (photo).
23   Disassemble the primary piston assembly and install the new seal so the cup faces in the direction shown (photo).
24   Reassemble the primary piston assembly by following the se-

quence shown in photos 12.24a to 12.24e.
25 Lubricate the seal and O-ring of the primary piston assembly and insert it into the cylinder bore (photo). Depress the primary piston assembly and install the primary piston retaining ring.
26 Disassemble the switch piston assembly and install new O-rings and retainers as shown in photos 12.26a through 12.26d.
27 Install the switch piston assembly into the cylinder as shown in photo 12.27.
28 Install a new O-ring on the switch piston plug and install it into the cylinder and torque to specs (photo).
29 Install new O-rings on the proportioner valves and install them into the cylinder, torquing them to specs (photo).
30 Install a new O-ring on the failure warning switch and install it into the cylinder, torquing it to specs (photo).
31 Insert the quick take-up valve into the cylinder body as shown (photo).
32 Install the quick take-up valve retaining ring into its groove in the cylinder body (photo).
33 Press new reservoir grommets into the cylinder body as shown. Be sure they are seated properly (photo).
34 Place the reservoir top down on a flat, hard surface as shown and press the cylinder body onto it, using a rocking motion (photo).
35 Place the cylinder on its mounting studs and install the mounting stud nuts. Torque them to specs.
36 On a manual brake set-up reconnect the master cylinder pushrod to the brake pedal.
37 Connect the four brake line connections to the master cylinder, torquing the tube nuts to specs.
38 Connect the electrical lead to the failure warning switch.
39 Fill the master cylinder reservoir with brake fluid and bleed the entire brake system as described in Section 3.
40 Install the reservoir diaphragm into the reservoir cover (photo) and install the cover onto the reservoir.
41 Test drive the car and check for proper braking performance and leaks.

13 Power brake booster assembly – removal and installation

1 The power brake booster assembly is located in the engine compartment on the driver's side firewall. The brake master cylinder is attached to the front of it.
2 Remove the brake master cylinder as described in Section 12.
3 Disconnect the vacuum hose from the booster assembly by loosening the clamp and removing the hose from the metal nipple (see Figure 9.9).
4 Move to the inside of the car and disconnect the pushrod from the top of the brake pedal.
5 Still inside the car, remove the four nuts which secure the booster assembly to the firewall. These attaching nuts are in a square pattern around the pushrod previously disconnected.
6 Move back to the engine compartment and pull the booster assembly away from the firewall until the studs clear. Remove the assembly from the engine compartment (photo).
7 Becuase overhauling the booster assembly is a somewhat difficult job requiring special tools to be fabricated or purchased, it's advisable to merely purchase a rebuilt assembly as a replacement unit.
8 Apply a little silicone sealer to the firewall where the booster assembly fits against it. This will provide an air-tight seal.
9 Place the booster assembly in position and push the studs through the firewall. Move to the inside of the car and secure it with the four nuts and washers.
10 Attach the pushrod to the brake pedal.
11 Connect the vacuum hose to the nipple on the shell of the assembly and tighten the clamp.
12 Install the brake master cylinder as described in Section 12.
13 Bleed the brake system as described in Section 3.
14 Check for proper operation of the power brakes with the engine running.

14 Power brake vacuum hose filter – removal and installation

1 With a pair of pliers move the clamps on either end of the filter about two inches away from the filter (see Figure 9.9).
2 Twist the filter in the hose to break the seal and remove the filter.
3 Installation is the reverse of the removal procedure.

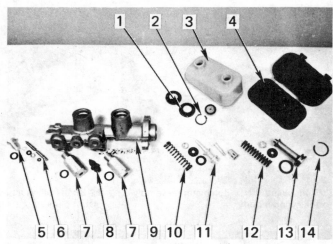

Fig. 9.8 Components of the brake master cylinder (Sec 12)

1	Reservoir grommets	7	Proportioner valves and
2	Quick take-up valve and		O-rings
	retaining ring	8	Failure warning switch
3	Reservoir	9	Master cylinder body
4	Reservoir cover and	10	Secondary piston spring
	diaphragm	11	Secondary piston assembly
5	Switch piston plug and	12	Primary piston spring
	O-ring	13	Primary piston assembly
6	Switch piston assembly	14	Primary piston retaining
			ring

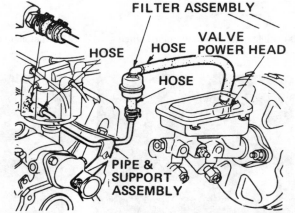

Fig. 9.9 Vacuum booster hoses, pipe and filter on the V6 engine (Sec 13)

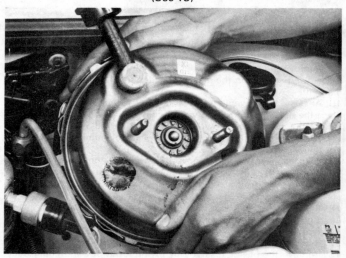

13.6 Removing the power brake booster assembly from the car

15 Parking brake – adjustment

1 The parkng brake does not need routine maintenance but the cable may stretch over a period of time necessitating adjustment. Also, the parking brake should be checked for proper adjustment whenever the rear brake cables have been disconnected. If the parking brake pedal travel is less than nine ratchet clicks or more than 16 ratchet clicks under heavy foot pressure, the parking brake need adjustment.
2 As checking of the parking brake is included in the car's routine maintenance schedule, the adjustment procedure for the parking brake is covered in Chapter 1, Section 21.

16 Parking brake release handle – removal and installation

1 Using a screwdriver, release the cable from the left side of the control assembly under the dash and slide the cable casing away from the assembly.

2 Compress the locking spring tabs behind the instrument panel and, grasping the release handle pull the cable and casing through the dash. The handle cannot be separated from the cable and is replaced as one part.
3 Installation is the reverse of the removal procedure.

17 Front parking brake cable – removal and installation

1 Depress the parking brake pedal.
2 Clamp locking pliers on the cable where it enters its casing.
3 Pull the brake release and remove the cable from the control assembly.
4 Release the locking tabs on the casing and remove the casing from the control assembly.
5 Push the grommet and cable through the cowl and into the engine compartment.
6 Remove the cable from its guide bracket attached to the engine cowl.

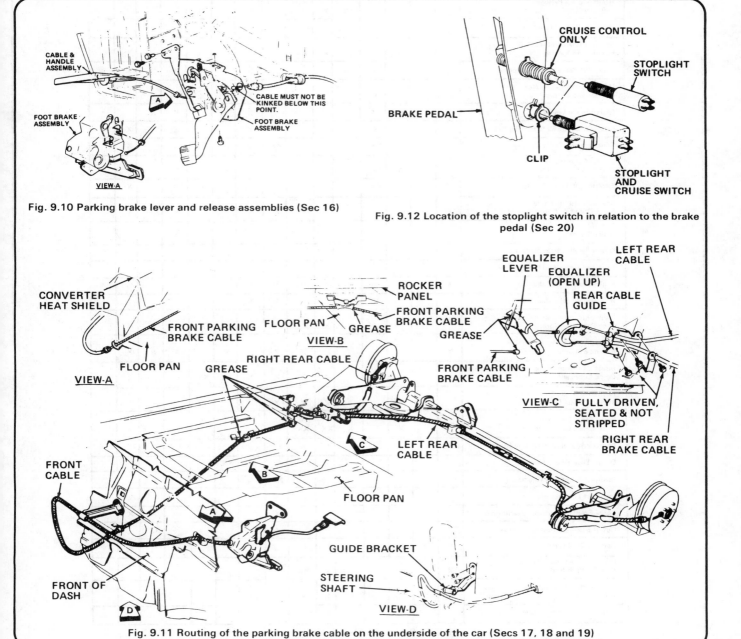

Fig. 9.10 Parking brake lever and release assemblies (Sec 16)

Fig. 9.12 Location of the stoplight switch in relation to the brake pedal (Sec 20)

Fig. 9.11 Routing of the parking brake cable on the underside of the car (Secs 17, 18 and 19)

CAUSE \ SYMPTOM	Excessive Brake Pedal Travel	Brake Pedal Travel Gradually Increases	Excessive Brake Pedal Effort	Excessive Braking Action	Brakes Slow to Respond	Brakes Slow to Release	Brakes Drag	Uneven Brake Action (Side to Side)	Uneven Brake Action (Front to Rear)	Scraping Noise from Brakes	Brake Squeak During Application	Brakes Squeak During Stop	Brakes Chatter (Roughness)	Brakes Groan at End of Stop	Brake Tell-Tale Glows During Stop
Leaking Brake Line or Connection	X	XX									X				XX
Leaking Wheel Cylinder or Piston Seal	X	XX			X					X					X
Leaking Master Cylinder	X	XX													X
Air in Brake System	XX										X				XX
Contaminated or Improper Brake Fluid								X	X	X					X
Leaking Vacuum System			XX					X							
Restricted Air Passage in Power Head					X			XX	X						
Damaged Power Head					X	X		X	X	X					
Improperly Assembled Power Head Valving					X	X		X	X	XX					
Worn Out Brake Lining - Replace					X	X				X	X	X	X	X	
Uneven Brake Lining Wear - Replace and Correct	X					X				X	X	X	XX	X	X
Glazed Brake Lining					XX			X			X	X		X	
Incorrect Lining Material - Replace					X	X					X	X		X	
Contaminated Brake Lining - Replace						XX					XX	XX	X	X	
Linings Damaged by Abusive Use - Replace					X	XX					X	X	X	X	
Excessive Brake Lining Dust					X	XX					XX	XX		X	
Heat Spotted or Scored Brake Drums or Rotors						X					X	X	XX	X	
Out-of-Round or Vibrating Brake Drums												X	XX		
Out-of-Parallel Brake Rotors													XX		
Excessive Rotor End Play													X		
Faulty Automatic Adjusters	X								X	X	X				X
Incorrect Wheel Cylinder Sizes					X	X					X	X			
Weak or Incorrect Brake Shoe Retention Springs						X		X	XX	X	X	XX	X	XX	
Brake Assembly Attachments - Missing or Loose	X									X	X	X	X	X	
Insufficient Brake Shoe Guide Lubricant									X	X	X	X	XX	XX	
Restricted Brake Fluid Passage or Sticking Wheel Cylinder Piston		X	X					X	X	X	X	X			
Brake Pedal Linkage Interference or Binding						X		X	XX	XX					
Improperly Adjusted Parking Brake										X					
Drums Tapered or Threaded													XX		
Incorrect Front End Alignment								XX							
Incorrect Tire Pressure								X	X						
Loose Front Suspension Attachments								X			XX		X	X	
Out-of-Balance Wheel Assemblies													XX		
Operator Riding Brake Pedal	X	X	X					X			X			X	
Improperly Adjusted Master Cylinder Push Rod	X							X	XX						X
Sticking Wheel Cylinder or Caliper Pistons						X		X	X	X	X				
Faulty Proportioning Valve						X			X	X	X				

Fig. 9.13 Brake troubleshooting chart

7   Remove the cable from its guide attached to the underside of the rocker panel (Figure 9.11, view B).
8   Remove the cable from the equalizer lever (Figure 9.11, View C).
9   Installation is the reverse of the removal procedure.

18 Right rear parking brake cable – removal and installation

1   Support the rear of the car on jackstands and remove the wheel and brake drum.
2   With a screwdriver inserted between the brakeshoe and the top part of the brake adjuster bracket, push the bracket to the front and release the top adjuster bracket rod.
3   Remove the rear hold-down spring and remove the actuator lever and lever return spring.
4   Remove the adjuster screw spring.
5   Remove the top rear brake shoe return spring.
6   Unhook the parking brake cable from the parking brake lever.
7   Compress the locking spring tabs securing the parking brake cable to the backing plate and withdraw the cable.
8   Mark the location of the adjusting nut so the parking brake adjustment will not be lost, then remove the adjusting nut that secures the equalizer to its retaining bolt and remove the bolt.
9   Compress the locking spring tabs of the cable casing and remove the cable from the guide bracket.
10   Unhook the cable from the connector on the rear axle, that connects it to the left rear cable.

11   Remove the cable casing from the rear axle.
12   Installation is the reverse of the removal procedure.
13   When the operation is complete check that the parking brake adjustment is correct, and adjust if necessary as described in Section 15.

19 Left rear parking brake cable – removal and installation

1   Remove the parking brake cable from the brake by following the procedure described in paragraphs 1 through 7 of Section 18.
2   Remove the cable casing from the rear axle.
3   Unhook the cable from the connector on the rear axle that connects it to the right rear cable.
4   Installation is the reverse of the removal procedure.

20 Stop light switch – removal and installation

1   Disconnect the electrical lead from the stop light switch.
2   Unscrew the switch from its mount.
3   To install, insert the switch into its mount from the rear until the switch body is up against the mounting clip.
4   Pull the brake pedal rearward until it stops. This will press the switch rearward in its clip and provide proper adjustment.
5   Reconnect the electrical lead.

Chapter 10 Electrical system

Refer to Chapter 13 for wiring diagrams related to 1981 through 1984 models

Contents

Specifications

Bulbs

	Number
Air conditioning control	194
Ash tray	1445
Back-up light	1156
Brake warning light	194
Check engine indicator (C-4 system)	194
Clock	194
Courtesy	906
Dome lamp	561
Dome reading lamp	212
Engine temperature telltale	194
Generator telltale	194
Headlamps	6052
Headlamp high beam indicator	161
Heater control panel	194
Instrument cluster illumination	194/161
License plate	194
Luggage compartment	1003
Marker lights − front and rear	194
Oil pressure indicator	194
Parking lights	1157NA
Radio illumination	1893
Seat belt warning	194
Stop light	1157
Tail light	1157
Turn signal − front	1157NA
Turn signal − rear	1156
Turn signal indicator	194

Fuses

	Amperes
Radio	10
Wiper	25
Stop, rear and front, hazard lamps, I.P. indicators	20
Dir. sig. B.U. lamps	20
Heater A/C	25
Inst. lamps, radio dial lamp, heater dial lamp, W/S wiper lamp, cigarette lighter and ash tray lamp	5
Gages warning lamps, cruise control, brake alarm, oil, rear defogger, fuel gage, headlight buzzer, seat belt warning buzzer, temp., gen., idle stop	20
Glove box lamp, dome lamp, luggage lamp, clock, hood, cigarette lighter, courtesy lamps, key warning	20
Tail, parking and side marker lamps, license lamp	20
Choke heater	20

Torque specifications

	in-lb	m-kg
Turn signal switch attaching screws	35	0.4
Ignition switch attaching screws	35	0.4
Support to lock plate screws (tilt column)	50	0.6

1 General information

1   This Chapter covers the repair and service procedures for the various lighting and electrical components not associated with the engine, as well as general information on troubleshooting the car's various electrical circuits. Information on the battery, generator, distributor and starter motor can be found in Chapter 5. Additional procedures involving body lighting can be found in Chapter 12.

2   The electrical system is of the 12 volt, negative ground type with power supplied by a lead/acid-type battery which is charged by the generator.

3   Electrical components located in the dashboard do not use ground wires or straps, but rather use grounding provisions which are integrated in the printed circuit mounted behind the instrument cluster.

4   It should be noted that whenever portions of the electrical system are worked on, the negative battery cable should be disconnected to prevent electrical shorts and/or fires.

2 Electrical troubleshooting – general

1   The wiring diagrams included in this Chapter have been designed to simplify the troubleshooting of electrical components and their circuits. Each diagram shows only the circuits which apply to the component or components specified.

2   A typical diagram starts at the top of the page with the fuse and proceeds through all of the wires, switches, connectors, splices and motors relevant to that circuit, before it ends at the ground at the bottom of the page.

3   The charging system/power distribution diagram includes all of the connections from the battery and generator to each fuse and fusible link. This diagram, combined with any one of the others, will give a complete picture of how that circuit gets its voltage and how it works.

4   To make the translation of these diagrams into practical applications easier, each diagram is accompanied by a list of the components and wires shown and their location on the car. Also, a separate Figure is included which lists the simplified electrical symbols used in these diagrams and what they mean.

5   The basic tools needed for electrical troubleshooting include a circuit tester or voltmeter (a 12 volt bulb with a set of test leads can also be used), a continuity tester (which includes a bulb, battery and set of test leads) and a jumper wire, preferably with a circuit breaker incorporated, which can be used to bypass electrical components.

6   Voltage checks should be performed if a circuit is not functioning properly. Connect one end lead of a circuit tester to either the negative battery terminal or a known good ground. Connect the other lead to a connector in the circuit being tested, preferably nearest to the battery or fuse. If the bulb of the tester goes on voltage is reaching that point, which means the part of the circuit between that connector and the battery is problem-free. Continue checking along the circuit in the same fashion. When you reach a point where no voltage is present, the problem lies between there and the last good test point. Most of the

time the problem is due to a loose connection. **NOTE:** *Keep in mind that some circuits only receive voltage when the ignition key is in the 'Accessory' or 'Run' position.*

7   A method of finding shorts in a circuit is to remove the fuse and connect a test light or voltmeter in its place to the fuse terminals. There should be no load in the circuit. Move the wiring harness from side to side while watching the test light. If the bulb goes on, there is a short to ground somewhere in that area, probably where insulation has rubbed off of a wire. The same test can be performed on other components of the circuit, including the switch.

8   A ground check should be done to see if a component is grounded properly. Disconnect the battery and connect one lead of a self-powered test light such as a continuity tester to a known good ground. Connect the other lead to the wire or ground connection being tested. If the bulb goes on, the ground is good. If the bulb does not go on, the ground is not good.

9   A continuity check is performed to see if a circuit, section of circuit or individual component is passing electricity through it properly. Disconnect the battery, and connect one lead of a self-powered test light such as a continuity tester to one end of the circuit being tested and the other lead to the other end of the circuit. If the bulb goes on, there is continuity, which means the circuit is passing electricity through it properly. Switches can be checked in the same way.

10 If several components or circuits fail at one time, chances are the fault lies in the fuse or ground connection, as several circuits often are routed through the same fuse and ground connections. This can be confirmed by referring to the fuse box and ground distribution diagrams in this Chapter.

11 Prior to any electrical troubleshooting, always visually check the condition of the wires and connections of the problem circuit. Often a connection is loose or corroded, and this simple check is all that's needed to pinpoint the problem.

3 Fuses – general

1   The electrical circuits of the car are protected by a combination of fuses, circuit breakers and fusible links.

2   The fuse box is located underneath the dash on the right side of the car. Access to the fuses is achieved by simply removing the cover of the box.

3   Each of the fuses is designed to protect a specific circuit, as is identified both on the fuse box and in Fig. 10.16.

4   If an electrical component has failed, your first check should be the fuse. A fuse which has 'blown' can be readily identified by inspecting the element inside the glass tube. If this metal element is broken the fuse is inoperable and should be replaced with a new one.

5   When removing and installing fuses, it is important that metal objects are not used to pry the fuse in or out of the holder. Plastic fuse pullers are available for this purpose.

6   It is also important that the correct fuse be installed. The different electrical circuits need varying amounts of protection, indicated by the amperage rating on the fuse. A fuse with too low a rating will blow

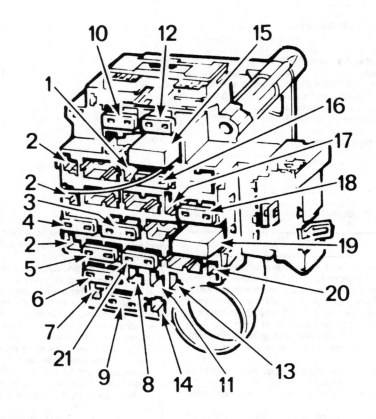

Fig. 10.1 Layout of the fuse block

Circuit	Fuse block label	Color	Amps	Type	Fuse location	Power feed location
Air conditioner blower and compressor heater; idle stop solenoid; trunk release	A/C heater	white	25	fuse	16	17
Choke heater; cooling fan	C/H	yellow	20	fuse	12	7
Air conditioner anti-dieseling relay (L4); cigar lighter; clock; computer controlled catalytic converter system; courtesy lights; ignition key warning; light-on reminder; lights: trunk/vanity mirror; lights; turn; power antenna; power door locks; radio capacitor	CTSY/CLK	yellow	20	fuse	21	11, 13 & 14
Air conditioner anti-dieseling relay (L4); brake warning indicator; choke heater; computer controlled catalytic converter system; defogger; fuel gage; gages; idle stop solenoid; ignition; light-on reminder; map light; seatbelt warning; warning indicators	GAGES	yellow	20	fuse	4	2
Lights: instrument panel; light-on reminder	INST LPS	tan	5	fuse	10	1
Defogger; power door locks; power seat	PWR ACCY	–	30	circuit breaker	19	20
Cruise control; radio	RADIO	red	10	fuse	9	8
Idle stop solenoid (V6); lights; hazard/stop/front park/front marker	STOP HAZ	yellow	20	fuse	18	–
Lights: license/rear park/rear marker	TAIL	yellow	20	fuse	3	–
Backup lights; lights: turn/hazard/front park/front marker	TURN B/U	yellow	20	fuse	5	–
Power windows	WDO	–	30	circuit breaker	15	–
Wiper/washer; wiper/washer (delay)	WIPER	white	25	fuse	6	–

prematurely, while a fuse with too high a rating may not blow soon enough to avoid serious damage.

7 At no time should the fuse be bypassed by using metal or foil. Serious damage to the electrical system could result.

8 If the replacement fuse immediately fails, do not replace it with another until the cause of the problem is isolated and corrected. In most cases this will be a short circuit in the wiring system caused by a broken or deteriorated wire.

4 Fusible links – general

1 In addition to fuses, the wiring system incorporates fusible links for overload protection. These links are used in circuits which are not ordinarily fused, such as the ignition circuit.

2 Although the fusible links appear to be of a heavier gauge than the wire they are protecting, this appearance is due to the heavy insulation. All fusible links are 4 wire gauges smaller than the wire they are incorporated into. Locations of fusible links are shown in the various wiring diagrams included in this Chapter.

3 Fusible links cannot be repaired, but rather a new link of the same wire size and Hypalon insulation can be spliced into its place. This procedure is as follows:

    a) Disconnect the negative battery cable.
    b) Disconnect the fusible link from the starter solenoid.
    c) Cut the damaged fusible link out of the wiring system. Do this just behind the connector.
    d) Strip the insulation from the circuit wiring approximately ½-inch.
    e) Position the connector on the new fusible link and crimp it into place in the wiring circuit.
    f) Use resin core solder at each end of the new link to obtain a good solder joint.
    g) Wrap the soldered joints with electrical tape. No exposed wiring should show.
    h) Connect the fusible link at the starter solenoid, and reconnect the negative battery cable. Test the circuit for proper operation.

5 Circuit breakers – general

1 A circuit breaker is used to protect the headlight wiring and is located in the light switch. An electrical overload in the system will cause the lights to go on and off, or in some cases to remain off. If this happens, check the entire headlight wiring system immediately. Once the overload condition is corrected the circuit breaker will function normally.

2 Circuit breakers are also used in the circuit of accessories such as power windows, power door locks and rear defogger.

6 Turn signals and hazard flashers – general

1 Small canister-shaped flasher units are incorporated into the electrical circuits for the directional signals and hazard warning lights.

2 When the units are functioning properly an audible check can be heard with the circuit in operation. If the turn signals fail on one side only and the flasher unit cannot be heard, a faulty bulb is indicated. If the flasher unit can be heard, a short in the wiring is indicated.

3 If the turn signal fails on both sides, the fault may be due to a blown fuse, faulty flasher unit or switch, or a broken or loose connection. If the fuse has blown, check the wiring for a short before installing a new fuse.

4 The hazard warning lamps are checked in the same manner as paragraph 3 above.

5 The hazard warning flasher unit is located in the fuse box found under the dash on the right side. The turn signal flasher is mounted on the base of the steering column support.

6 When replacing either of these flasher units it is important to buy a replacement of the same capacity. Check the new flasher against the old one to be assured of the proper replacement.

7 Horn and relay – fault testing and adjustment

1 All X-Bodies are equipped with either one or two horns, depending upon model and options, which are activiated by a horn relay located at the fuse block. The horn switch is located on the steering wheel in the form of an actuator bar. On the underside of the actuator bar is a contact plate which is 'hot' at all times. When the actuator bar is depressed, this contact touches the steel hub of the steering wheel, which provides a ground for the system, completing the circuit and activating the horn.

2 If the horn proves inoperable, your first check should be the fuse. A blown fuse can be readily identified at the fuse box under the lower right side of the dashboard.

3 If the fuse is in good condition, disconnect the electrical lead at the horn. Run a jumper wire from a 12-volt source (positive battery terminal) to the wiring terminal on the horn. If the horn does not blow, the fault lies in the grounding of the horn or the horn itself.

4 If current is not reaching the horn, indicated by the horn sounding from the above test, there is a failure in the circuit before the horn.

5 In most cases a failure of the horn relay is indicated if the circuit before the horn is at fault. Other checks would include bent metal contacts on the horn actuator or loose or broken wires in the system.

6 When checking or replacing the horn relay be aware that the

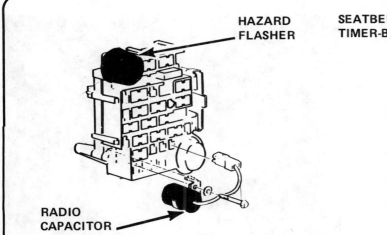

Fig. 10.2 Locations of the hazard flasher and the radio capacitor (Sec 6)

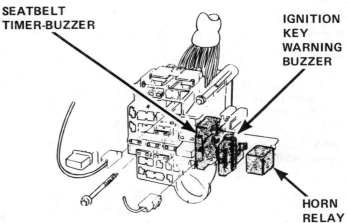

Fig. 10.3 Locations of the seatbelt timer-buzzer, ignition key warning buzzer and horn relay (Sec 7)

threaded stud is always 'hot' and shorting of this stud to a ground could destroy a fusible link, disabling the vehicle until the link is replaced.

7   On some models, the horn(s) is adjustable. If the horn emits a sputtering sound or if it sticks, particularly in cold weather, there may be too much current draw to the horn, necessitating adjustment.

8   The horn is adjusted using the following procedure:

a)   *Remove the horn from the car.*

b)   *Connect an ammeter in series with the horn and a fully-charged 12-volt battery and note the reading while the horn is blowing. It should be between 4.5 and 5.5 amperes at 12 volts.*

c)   *If the reading is higher or lower than this, turn the adjusting screw $\frac{1}{4}$ turn at a time until the current draw is within this margin. Turning the screw clockwise decreases the current draw while turning it counterlockwise increases the draw.*

d)   *On models equipped with dual horns, following adjustment sound the horns together to check for proper blending of tones. If the tone is not satisfactory the horn contacts are pitted, necessitating horn replacement.*

e)   *After reinstalling the horn(s) in the car, connect a voltmeter between the horn terminal and a ground and check the voltage reading while sounding the horn. The reading should be between 9 and 11 volts.*

8.2 Removing the speedometer cluster trim cover

8   Speedometer cluster (Phoenix) – removal and installation

1   Disconnect the negative battery cable.
2   Remove the speedometer cluster trim plate (photo).
3   Remove the steering column trim plate (photo).
4   Remove the 4 screws that retain the speedometer cluster to the instrument panel.
5   Mark the position of the shift indicator cable on the steering column shift bowl, then disconnect the cable from the bowl.
6   Disconnect the speedometer cable from the rear of the speedometer cluster and remove the cluster. The speedometer cable is disconnected by depressing the retaining spring, as shown in Fig. 10.4.
7   Disconnect the wiring harness from the cluster and remove the cluster.
8   Installation is the reverse of the removal procedure. Note: When reinstalling the shift indicator cable on the shift bowl, be sure the indicator needle is in the same position it was during removal.

8.3 Removing the steering column trim cover

9   Center instrument panel trim cover (Omega) – removal and installation

1   Remove the steering wheel trim cover.
2   Mark the position of the shift indicator on the steering column shift bowl, then disconnect the cable from the bowl.
3   Remove the 3 bolts and 1 nut that secure the steering column to the dash and carefully lower the column (photo).
4   Remove the 4 screws that retain the center trim cover to the instrument panel.
5   Pull the trim cover out from the instrument panel until you can

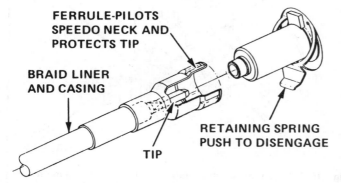

**FERRULE-PILOTS
SPEEDO NECK AND
PROTECTS TIP**

**BRAID LINER
AND CASING**

**RETAINING SPRING
PUSH TO DISENGAGE**

TIP

Fig. 10.4 Attachment method of the speedometer cable to the speedometer (Sec 8)

9.3 Locations of the steering column mounting bolts and nut

disconnect any accessory switch wiring and the remote control mirror cable, if equipped. The remote control mirror cable is removed by loosening the set screw and pulling the cable away from its bracket.
6   Remove the trim cover.
7   Installation is the reverse of the removal procedure. **Note**: *When installing the shift indicator cable on the shift bowl, be sure the indicator needle is in the same position it was during removal.*

10 Instrument cluster (Omega) – removal and installation

1   Remove the center instrument trim cover as described in Section 9.

2   Remove the 4 screws that retain the cluster to the instrument panel.
3   Pull the cluster out from the dash until you can disconnect any electrical connectors and the speedometer cable from the rear of the cluster.
4   Remove the cluster from the dash.
5   Installation is the reverse of the removal procedure.

11 Speedometer – removal and installation

Phoenix
1   Remove the speedometer cluster from the instrument panel as

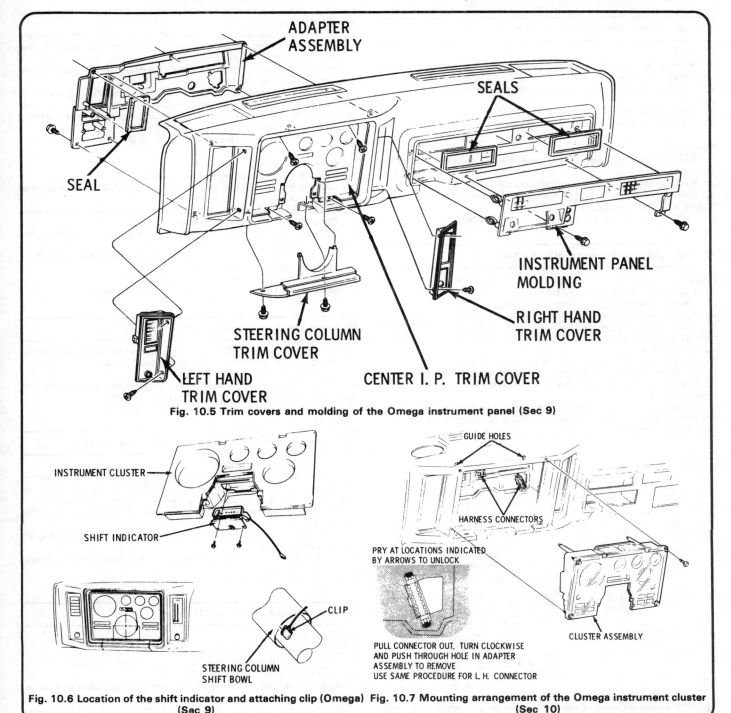

ADAPTER ASSEMBLY

SEALS

SEAL

INSTRUMENT PANEL MOLDING

RIGHT HAND TRIM COVER

STEERING COLUMN TRIM COVER

LEFT HAND TRIM COVER

CENTER I. P. TRIM COVER

Fig. 10.5 Trim covers and molding of the Omega instrument panel (Sec 9)

INSTRUMENT CLUSTER

SHIFT INDICATOR

CLIP

STEERING COLUMN SHIFT BOWL

GUIDE HOLES

HARNESS CONNECTORS

PRY AT LOCATIONS INDICATED BY ARROWS TO UNLOCK

CLUSTER ASSEMBLY

PULL CONNECTOR OUT, TURN CLOCKWISE AND PUSH THROUGH HOLE IN ADAPTER ASSEMBLY TO REMOVE
USE SAME PROCEDURE FOR L. H. CONNECTOR

Fig. 10.6 Location of the shift indicator and attaching clip (Omega) (Sec 9)

Fig. 10.7 Mounting arrangement of the Omega instrument cluster (Sec 10)

described in Section 8.
2   Remove the cluster lens, face plate and light tunnel from the cluster.
3   Remove the speedometer from the cluster.
4   Installation is the reverse of the removal procedure.

Omega
1   Remove the instrument cluster assembly as described in Section 10.
2   Remove the cluster lens from the cluster assembly.
3   Remove the 2 mounting screws from the back side of the cluster assembly and lift the speedometer out.
4   Installation is the reverse of the removal procedure.

12 Fuel gauge – removal and installation

Phoenix
1   Remove the speedometer cluster from the instrument panel as described in Section 8.
2   Remove the cluster lens, faceplate and light tunnel from the cluster.
3   Remove the fuel gauge from the cluster.
4   Installation is the reverse of the removal procedure.

Omega
1   Remove the instrument cluster assembly, as described in Section 10.
2   Remove the cluster lens from the cluster.
3   Remove the 3 fuel gauge mounting nuts from the back of the cluster and lift the gauge out.
4   Installation is the reverse of the removal procedure.

13 Headlight switch – removal and installation

Phoenix
1   Disconnect the negative battery cable.
2   Remove the steering column trim cover.
3   Pull the headlight switch shaft all of the way out (photo).
4   Reach under the dash so you can reach the headlight switch and depress the shaft release button on the switch (photo). Pull the shaft out of the switch.
5   Remove the left trim plate from the dash (photo).
6   Remove the switch from the instrument panel.
7   Disconnect the wiring harness from the switch and remove the switch (photo).
8   Installation is the reverse of the removal procedure. **Note:** *The headlight switch shaft is reinstalled simply by inserting it into the switch and pushing it in until it clicks into place.*

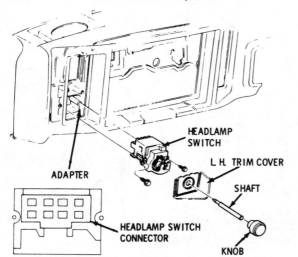

Fig. 10.8 Exploded view of the Omega headlight switch assembly (Sec 13)

Omega
1   Remove the headlight switch knob.
2   Remove the left hand trim cover from the instrument panel.
3   Remove the 2 screws that retain the headlight switch to the adapter assembly, and remove the switch.
4   Installation is the reverse of the removal procedure. **Note:** *The headlight switch shaft is reinstalled by simply inserting it into the switch and pushing it in until it clicks into place.*

14 Heater/A/C control – removal and installation

Phoenix
1   Disconnect the negative battery cable.
2   Remove the 8 screws that retain the center trim plate to the dash and lift off the panel (photo).
3   Open the glove box and reach behind the dash until you can disconnect the temperature control cable from the rear of the heater/A/C control (photo).
4   Remove the screws that retain the heater/A/C control panel to the dash instrument panel (photo).
5   Pull the control assembly out of the instrument panel and disconnect the vacuum connections (photo), electrical connections (photo) and bulb socket with bulb (photo), and remove the control from the instrument panel.
6   Installation is the reverse of the removal procedure.

Omega
1   Remove the cigar lighter unit from its outlet.
2   Remove the screws that retain the right hand trim cover from the instrument panel.
3   Disconnect the cigar lighter wiring and remove the case assembly.
4   Remove the right hand trim cover.
5   Remove the 3 screws that retain the heater/A/C control to the instrument panel.
6   Pull the control out until you can disconnect the control cable and electrical and vacuum connections.
7   Remove the control from the instrument panel.
8   Installation is the reverse of the removal procedure.

15 Glove box door – removal and installation

1   If equipped, remove the screws that retain the right hand hush panel to the dash and remove the hush panel (photo).
2   Open the glove box door.
3   Remove the screws that retain the glove box door and hinge to the instrument panel, and lift the assembly out (photo).
4   Installation is the reverse of the removal procedure.

16 Instrument panel molding – removal and installation

1   Remove the radio knobs.
2   With a small screwdriver, carefully pry the glove box light switch and the trunk release switch, if equipped out from the instrument panel molding, and disconnect the wiring connectors from the switches.
3   Remove the 2 screws that attach the glove box stop arm to the glove box door.
4   Remove the 2 screws that retain the instrument panel molding to the instrument panel.
5   To remove the molding, carefully pry it out from the instrument panel. It is retained by 5 clips.
6   Installation is the reverse of the removal procedure.

17 Radio – removal and installation

Phoenix
1   Disconnect the negative battery cable.
2   Remove the 8 screws that retain the center trim plate to the instrument panel and lift off the plate.
3   Remove the screws that retain the radio to the instrument panel (photo).
4   Pull the radio out of the dash until you can disconnect the wiring connectors (photo).

13.3 Removing the headlight switch shaft

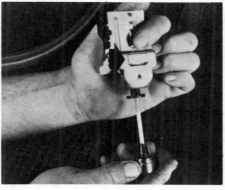
13.4 Location of the release button, used to remove the shaft from the headlight switch

13.5 The left trim plate is held on by 4 screws

13.7 Removing the wiring connector from the headlight switch

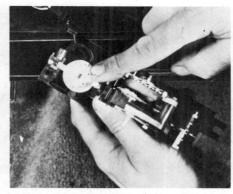
14.2 The center trim plate is held on by 8 screws

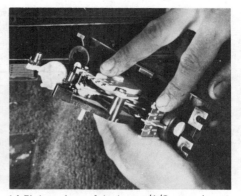
14.3 Location of the temperature control cable connection on the heater/A/C control

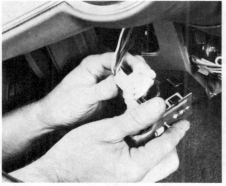
14.4 The heater/A/C control is held in by 4 screws

14.5a Location of the heater/A/C control vacuum connector

14.5b Locations of the heater/A/C control electrical connectors

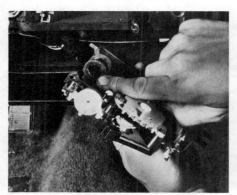
14.5c Location of the heater/A/C control bulb and socket

15.1 Removing the right hush panel

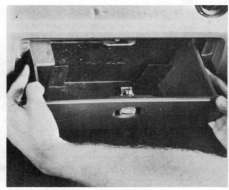
15.3 Removing the glove box

5   The radio face plates can be removed from the radio after removal of the radio knobs.
6   Installation is the reverse of the removal procedure.

Omega
1   Remove the instrument panel molding as described in Section 16.
2   Remove the ash tray drawer.
3   Remove the 4 screws that retain the ash tray bracket to the dash.
4   Remove the ash tray bulb and socket from the lamp housing.
5   Pull the radio and ash tray bracket out from the dash until you can disconnect the wiring connectors at the rear of the radio.
6   Remove the radio.
7   Installation is the reverse of the removal procedure.

18 Telltale cluster (Phoenix) – removal and installation

1   Disconnect the negative battery cable.
2   Remove the 8 screws that retain the center trim plate to the dash and lift off the plate (photos).
3   Remove the 4 screws that retain the telltale cluster to the instrument panel (photo).
4   Pull the cluster out of the dash until you can disconnect the wiring connectors from the rear of the cluster (photo).
5   Installation is the reverse of the removal procedure.

19 Ash tray assembly and map compartment – removal and installation

1   Remove the 8 screws that retain the center trim plate to the instrument panel and lift off the plate.
2   If equipped, remove the 2 screws that retain the map compartment to the instrument panel and lift it off (photo).
3   Remove the screws that retain the ash tray assembly to the instrument panel.
4   Disconnect the wire and bulb from the ash tray assembly and remove the assembly (photo).
5   Installation is the reverse of the removal procedure.

20 Clock – removal and installation

Phoenix
1   Disconnect the negative battery cable.
2   Remove the 8 screws that retain the center trim plate to the instrument panel and lift off the plate.
3   Remove the clock knob.
4   Remove the 2 screws that retain the clock to the cluster and remove the clock.
5   Installation is the reverse of the removal procedure.

Omega
1   Remove the instrument panel molding as described in Section 16.
2   Remove the screws that retain the clock to the instrument panel and lift out the clock. Refer to Fig. 10.10 to disconnect the wiring connector from the rear of the clock.
3   Installation is the reverse of the removal procedure.

21 Speakers – removal and installation

1   Remove the speaker grille by using a putty knife or similar flat instrument.
2   Remove the 4 speaker mounting screws and remove the speaker.
3   Pull the speaker outward until you can disconnect the speaker wire. Then remove the speaker.
4   Installation is the reverse of the removal procedure.

22 C-4 electronic control module – removal and installation

1   Disconnect the negative battery cable.
2   Remove the right hush panel, if equipped.
3   Remove the glove box door as described in Section 15.

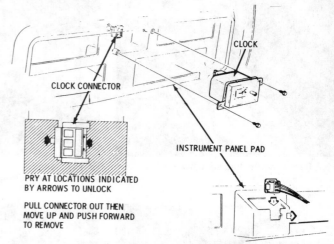

Fig. 10.9 Mounting arrangement and electrical connections of the radio (Omega) (Sec 17)

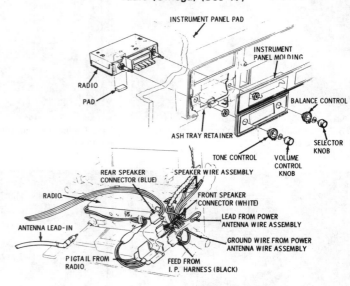

Fig. 10.10 Mounting arrangement of the clock (Omega) (Sec 20)

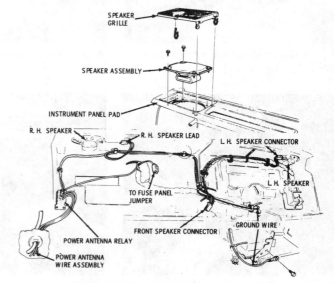

Fig. 10.11 Mounting arrangement of the front radio speaker (Omega) (Sec 21)

17.3 The radio trim plate is held to the dash by 2 screws

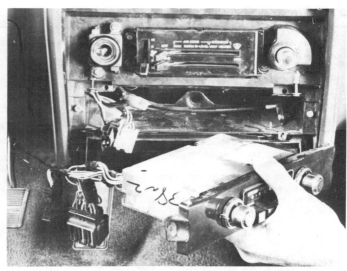

17.4 Removing the radio with trim plate from the dash

18.3 The telltale cluster is secured to the dash with 4 screws

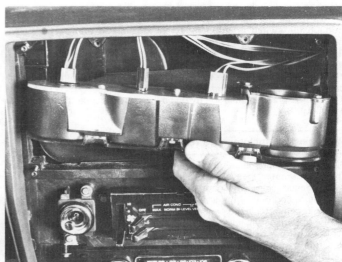

18.4 Locations of the electrical connectors on the rear of the telltale cluster

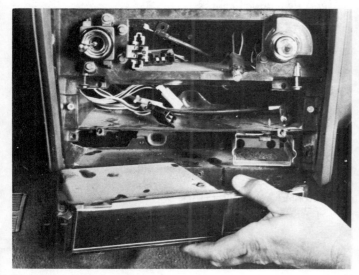

19.2 Removing the map compartment

19.4 Removing the ash tray housing

4   Remove the screws that secure the control module to the support
brackets.
5   Disconnect the electrical connectors from the control module and
remove the module from the dash.
6   Installation is the reverse of the removal procedure.

23 Pulse wiper control switch – removal and installation

1   Disconnect the negative battery cable.
2   Remove the pulse wiper control switch knob and the headlight
switch knob.
3   Remove the 4 screws that retain the left trim plate to the
instrument panel.
4   Pull the trim plate outward, rotating it if necessary to gain access
to the pulse wiper control switch.
5   Remove the pulse wiper switch lens and remove the switch
retaining screws.
6   Remove the steering column trim cover.
7   The wiring harness leading from the pulse wiper switch joins into
two other connectors located at the steering column (Fig. 10.13). In
order to remove the switch out the front of the instrument panel, the
5 wires in this harness must be cut. As the wires from the new switch
will have to be spliced into the harness, choose a convenient point
between the switch and the connectors to cut the harness.
8   To install the new switch feed the wires extending from its rear
through the switch's instrument panel location so that they hang in
back of the instrument panel.
9   Using crimp connectors, splice the wires from the new switch into
the old harness, being sure you match the color coded wires properly.
The wiring diagram for the wiper/washer (delay) circuit in this Chapter
can be used as a reference.
10 Complete the installation by reversing the sequence of paragraphs
1 through 6.

24 Emissions maintenance reminder flag – resetting

1   The emissions system maintenance reminder flag will appear in
the speedometer area at the regular intervals shown in the routine
maintenance chart in Chapter 1. On non-California cars with V6
engines, a flag with the word Catalyst will appear, indicating that the
catalytic converter needs servicing. On all California cars a flag with
the word Sensor will appear indicating that the oxygen sensor must be
replaced with a new one.
2   Prior to resetting the reminder flag, the required servicing must be
performed. For catalytic converter servicing, refer to Chapter 4. For
replacement of the oxygen sensor refer to Chapter 1.
3   Remove the speedometer cluster trim cover (Phoenix) or center
instrument panel trim cover (Omega) as described in Sections 8 and 9.
4   Remove the cluster lens from the cluster.
5   Using an awl or other pointed tool, engage it in the detents located
in the flag wheel's outer rim (Fig. 10.14) and rotate the wheel
downward until it engages in the reset position.
6   With the flag properly reset, the alignment mark shown in Fig.
10.14 should be centered in the space next to the odometer.
7   Re-install the cluster lens and trim cover.

25 Speedometer cable – inspection and replacement

1   If the speedometer is noisy during operation or if the indicator
needle wavers, the speedometer should be inspected for damage and
alignment.
2   Visually inspect the length of the speedometer cable checking that
there are no kinks, sharp bends or other damage to the outer casing.
Also, remove the speedometer cluster (Phoenix) or instrument cluster
(Omega) as described in Section 8 or 10 and check that the cable is
properly installed in the speedometer.
3   If the initial inspection reveals no damage, disconnect the cable
from the speedometer by sliding the retaining clip toward the cluster
while simultaneously pulling the cable away from the cluster. Then pull
the inner cable from the casing.
4   Inspect the cable for worn spots, breaks or kinks. Any of these
conditions necessitates replacement of the cable.
5   Prior to installing a inner cable, lubricate it with a suitable
speedometer cable lubricant, to prevent rusting.

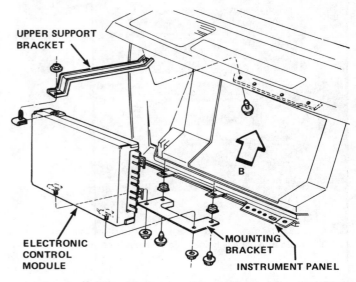

Fig. 10.12 Mounting arrangement of the C-4 electronic control
module (Sec 22)

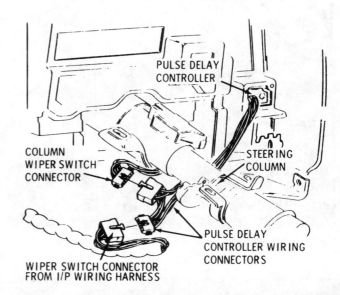

Fig. 10.13 Routing of the pulse wiper control wiring harness
(Sec 23)

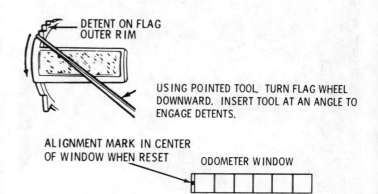

Fig. 10.14 Resetting the emissions maintenance reminder flag
(Sec 24)

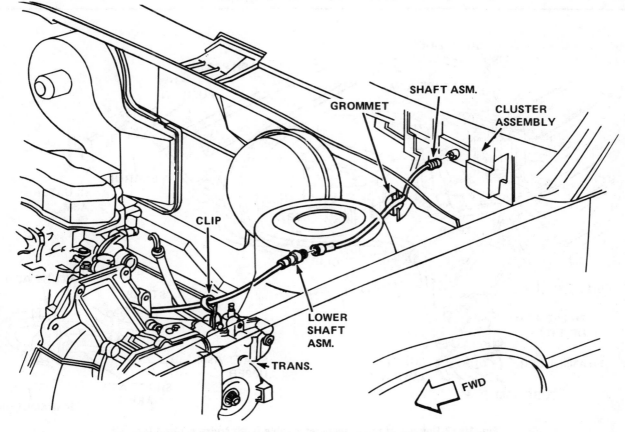

Fig. 10.15 Routing of the speedometer cable (automatic transaxle) (Sec 25)

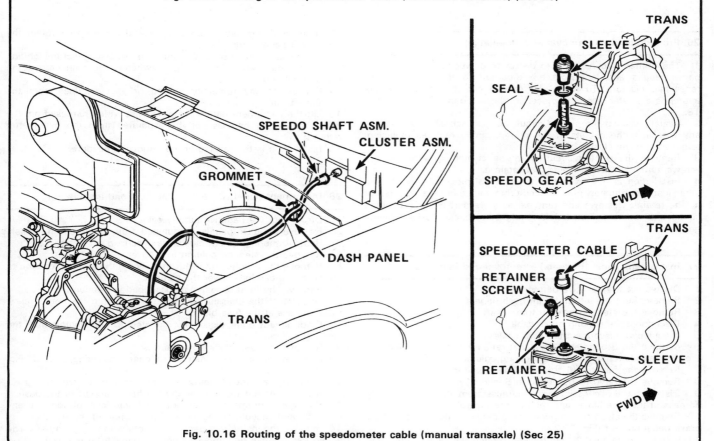

Fig. 10.16 Routing of the speedometer cable (manual transaxle) (Sec 25)

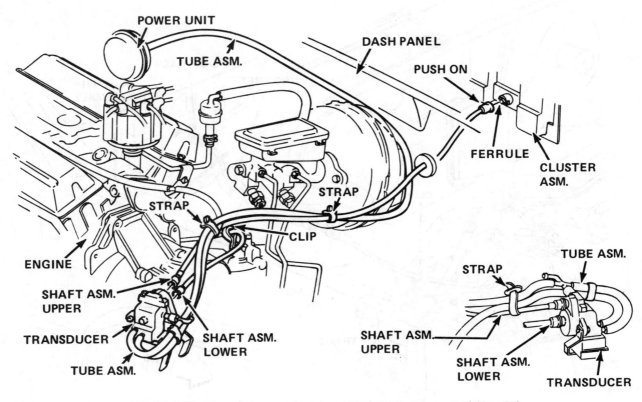

Fig. 10.17 Routing of the speedometer cable (with cruise control) (Sec 25)

26 Printed circuits – removal and installation

1   The printed circuits used to distribute power to the instrument panel gauges and indicators are mounted to the back of their respective clusters. To reach the printed circuit first remove the appropriate cluster using the procedure described in Section 8, 10 or 18.

2   Visually inspect the printed circuit on the back of the cluster for any breaks in the circuits. If the printed circuit requires replacing, remove all of the cluster bulbs.

3   Remove the printed circuit from the cluster by removing the screws, terminal nuts and clips that retain it.

4   Installation is the reverse of the removal procedure. Be careful when installing the new printed circuit that you do not tear any part of it. The retaining screws and terminal nuts are part of the grounding circuit and must be installed for the printed circuit to be properly grounded.

27 Instrument panel (Phoenix) – removal and installation

1   Disconnect the negative battery cable.
2   Remove both the left and right hush panels.
3   Remove the steering column trim cover.
4   Disconnect the parking brake cable.
5   If equipped, disconnect the vent cables.
6   Remove the 3 bolts and 1 nut that retain the steering column to the dash and carefully lower the steering column.
7   Remove the heater/A/C control as described in Section 14.
8   Remove the radio as described in Section 17.
9   Disconnect the chassis wiring harness from the engine wiring harness at the fuse block, and remove the fuse block.
10 Remove the electrical connector from the brake light switch at the brake pedal bracket (Fig. 10.23).
11 If equipped, remove the neutral start switch electrical connector at the clutch.

12 Remove the mounting bolts, nuts and screws that retain the instrument panel to the dash.
13 Pull the instrument panel out until you can disconnect the ignition switch, dimmer switch and turn signal switch wiring connectors at the steering column.
14 Disconnect any remaining wiring or vacuum lines from the instrument panel.
15 Lift the instrument panel, complete with wiring harness from the dash. The wiring harness can be separated from the panel after removal.
16 Installation is the reverse of the removal procedure.

28 Instrument panel (Omega) – removal and installation

1   Disconnect the negative battery cable.
2   Remove the hush panels, if equipped, from underneath the dash.
3   Remove the instrument cluster as described in Section 10.
4   Remove the steering column trim cover.
5   Remove the 3 bolts and 1 nut that secure the steering column to the dash and carefully lower the column.
6   Remove the front speakers as described in Section 21.
7   Disconnect the chassis electrical harness from the engine electrical harness at the fuse block.
8   If not already done, disconnect the electrical connectors from the steering column.
9   Remove the fuse block from the dash.
10 Remove the 4 upper instrument panel mounting screws (Fig. 10.24).
11 Remove the 3 lower instrument panel mounting screws.
12 Remove the nut that retains the left hand support to the dash.
13 Pull the instrument panel out until you can disconnect any electrical and vacuum connections from the rear of the panel.
14 Remove the instrument panel, complete with wiring harness. The wiring harness can be removed from the panel after removal.
15 Installation is the reverse of the removal procedure.

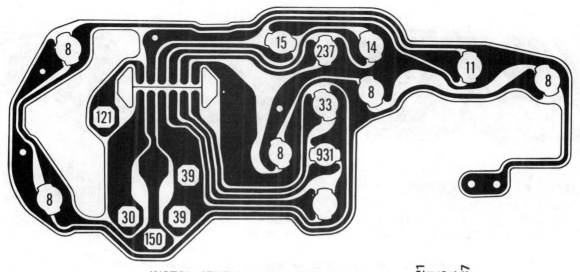

INSTRUMENT CLUSTER WITH TACH.

LEGEND OF CONNECTOR PADS

8   — ILLUMINATION
11   — HIGH BEAM INDICATOR
14   — LEFT TURN SIGNAL INDICATOR
15   — RIGHT TURN SIGNAL INDICATOR
30   — FUEL GAUGE OR TELLTALE
33   — BRAKE WARNING INDICATOR
39   — IGNITION
121 — TACHOMETER
150 — GROUND
237 — IGNITION FOR SEAT BELT WARNING TELLTALE
931 — CHOKE HEATER TELLTALE

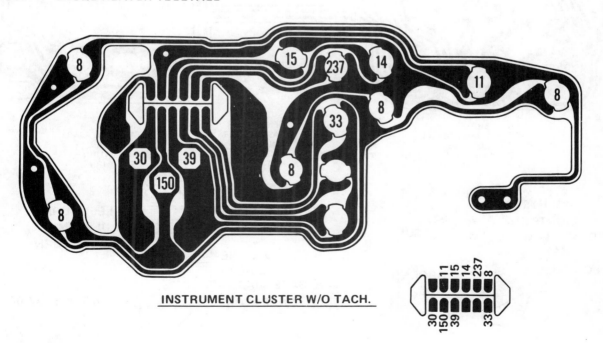

INSTRUMENT CLUSTER W/O TACH.

Fig. 10.18 Printed circuits of the speedometer cluster (Phoenix) (Sec 26)

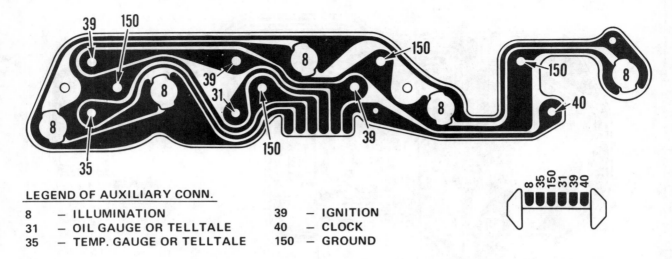

LEGEND OF AUXILIARY CONN.

8	– ILLUMINATION	39	– IGNITION
31	– OIL GAUGE OR TELLTALE	40	– CLOCK
35	– TEMP. GAUGE OR TELLTALE	150	– GROUND

Fig. 10.19 Printed circuit of the telltale cluster (Phoenix) (Sec 26)

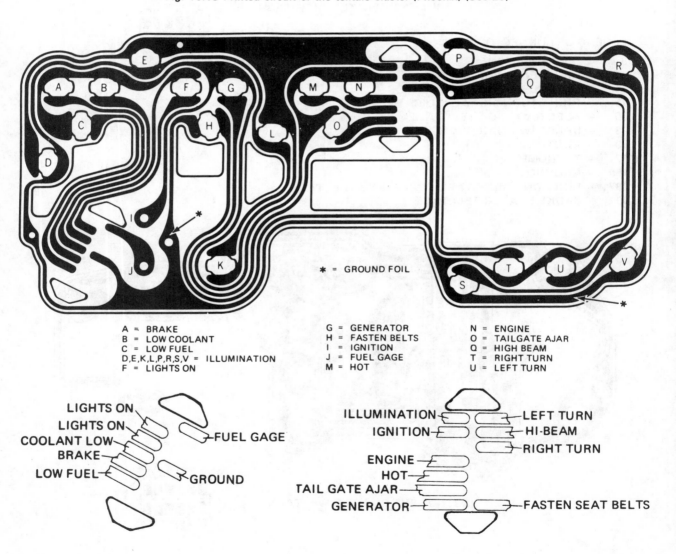

* = GROUND FOIL

A = BRAKE	G = GENERATOR	N = ENGINE
B = LOW COOLANT	H = FASTEN BELTS	O = TAILGATE AJAR
C = LOW FUEL	I = IGNITION	Q = HIGH BEAM
D,E,K,L,P,R,S,V = ILLUMINATION	J = FUEL GAGE	T = RIGHT TURN
F = LIGHTS ON	M = HOT	U = LEFT TURN

LIGHTS ON
LIGHTS ON
COOLANT LOW
BRAKE
LOW FUEL
FUEL GAGE
GROUND

ILLUMINATION
IGNITION
ENGINE
HOT
TAIL GATE AJAR
GENERATOR
LEFT TURN
HI-BEAM
RIGHT TURN
FASTEN SEAT BELTS

Fig. 10.20 Printed circuit of the standard instrument cluster (Omega) (Sec 26)

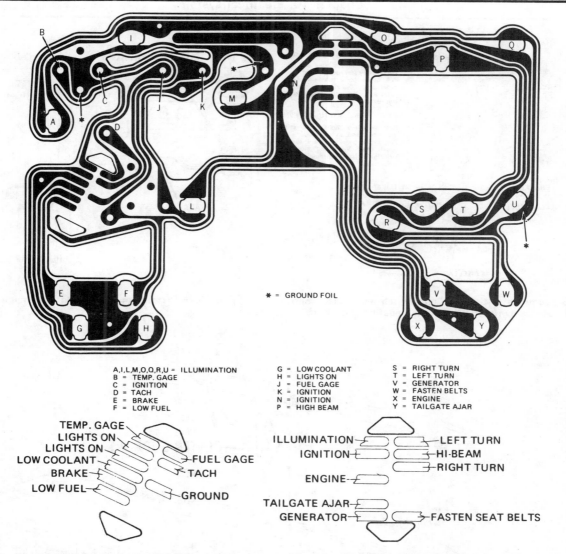

A,I,L,M,O,Q,R,U = ILLUMINATION
B = TEMP. GAGE
C = IGNITION
D = TACH
E = BRAKE
F = LOW FUEL

G = LOW COOLANT
H = LIGHTS ON
J = FUEL GAGE
K = IGNITION
N = IGNITION
P = HIGH BEAM

S = RIGHT TURN
T = LEFT TURN
V = GENERATOR
W = FASTEN BELTS
X = ENGINE
Y = TAILGATE AJAR

∗ = GROUND FOIL

TEMP. GAGE
LIGHTS ON
LIGHTS ON
LOW COOLANT
BRAKE
LOW FUEL
FUEL GAGE
TACH
GROUND

ILLUMINATION
IGNITION
ENGINE
LEFT TURN
HI-BEAM
RIGHT TURN

TAILGATE AJAR
GENERATOR
FASTEN SEAT BELTS

Fig. 10.21 Printed circuit of the instrument cluster with optional gauge package (Omega) (Sec 26)

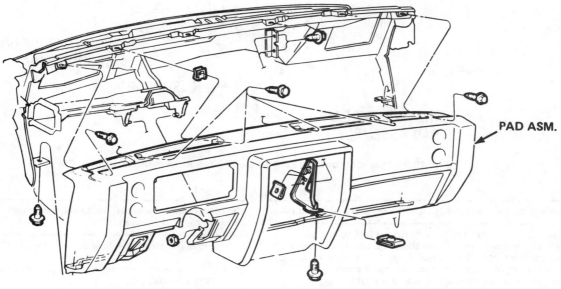

PAD ASM.

Fig. 10.22 Mounting arrangement of the Phoenix instrument panel (Sec 27)

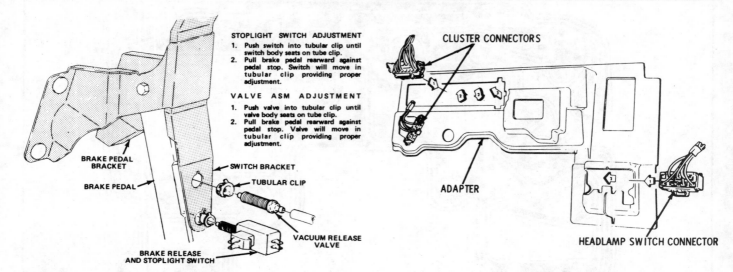

STOPLIGHT SWITCH ADJUSTMENT
1. Push switch into tubular clip until switch body seats on tube clip.
2. Pull brake pedal rearward against pedal stop. Switch will move in tubular clip providing proper adjustment.

VALVE ASM ADJUSTMENT
1. Push valve into tubular clip until valve body seats on tube clip.
2. Pull brake pedal rearward against pedal stop. Valve will move in tubular clip providing proper adjustment.

BRAKE PEDAL BRACKET
BRAKE PEDAL
SWITCH BRACKET
TUBULAR CLIP
VACUUM RELEASE VALVE
BRAKE RELEASE AND STOPLIGHT SWITCH

CLUSTER CONNECTORS
ADAPTER
HEADLAMP SWITCH CONNECTOR

Fig. 10.23 Locations of the stoplight switch and cruise control vacuum release switch on the brake pedal bracket (Sec 7)

Fig. 10.25 Instrument panel adapter (Omega) (Sec 29)

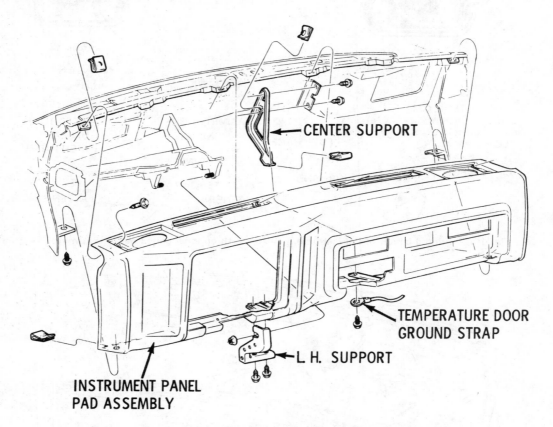

CENTER SUPPORT
TEMPERATURE DOOR GROUND STRAP
L. H. SUPPORT
INSTRUMENT PANEL PAD ASSEMBLY

Fig. 10.24 Mounting arrangement of the Omega instrument panel (Sec 28)

29 Instrument panel adapter (Omega) – removal and installation

1   Remove the instrument panel as described in Section 28.
2   Remove the headlight switch and the pulse wiper control switch, if equipped, from the instrument panel. Refer to Sections 13 and 23.
3   Remove the left air duct from the instrument panel.
4   Remove all electrical connectors from the adapter.
5   Remove the screws that retain the adapter to the instrument panel and lift off the adapter.
6   Installation is the reverse of the removal procedure.

30 Tilt steering column (including all related components) – disassembly and reassembly

1   Remove the steering wheel as described in Chapter 11, Section 22.
2   Pry the cover off by inserting a screwdriver or similar tool into the cover slots (photos).
3   The lock plate is heavily spring loaded and must be compressed to remove the retaining ring from the shaft. To compress the lock plate either use the GM lock plate compressor or fabricate one to the

dimensions shown in photo A. This tool is used with the steering wheel nut and a socket as shown in photo B. The lock plate need only be depressed slightly to remove the ring.

4   With the lock plate compressed, remove the retaining ring (photo).

5   Remove the lock plate compressing tool and lift off the lock plate (photo).

6   Lift off the canceling cam assembly (photo).

7   Lift off the upper bearing spring (photo).

8   Remove the turn signal actuator arm screw and lift off the actuator arm (photo).

9   Remove the hazard signal knob screw on the outside of the column housing (photo), and lift off the hazard knob assembly, which consists of a button, spring and the knob.

10 There are 3 screws that hold the turn signal switch assembly to the column. Remove the screws at the 6 and 9 o'clock positions first (photo). Then turn the switch to the right and remove the final screw at the 1 o'clock position.

11 Remove the screws that hold the steering column trim cover to

the dash, disconnect the vent hose if so equipped, and remove the trim cover.

12 Remove the 2 bolts on the left-hand side of the steering column colllar that secure the wiring harness (photo).

13 If only the turn signal switch is being replaced, disconnect and remove the wiring connector and extract the switch and wires from the column. The turn signal switch must be replaced as a unit complete with wiring harness. It's also recommended that you record the sequence of the wiring code to avoid confusion when connecting to the new set of wires.

14 If the turn signal switch is not being replaced, disconnect the electrical connector but leave it attached to the switch wires. Then push the wires through the column so the turn signal can hang from the column (photo).

15 Turn the ignition switch to the 'Ignition' position and pull out the key warning switch (photo). Note the position of the clip on the plastic switch for reassembly.

16 Remove the ignition lock retaining screw (photo).

30.2a A small screwdriver can be used to pry off the steering column cover

30.2b Be careful you do not deform the cover when removing it from the steering column

30.3a A lock plate compressor can be fabricated from 3 in channel iron to the dimensions shown; A(3 in), B(1 ⅜ in), C(1⅛ in), D(¾ in)

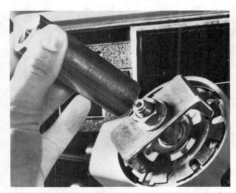
30.3b The lock spring compressor is used with the steering wheel nut and a deep socket

30.4 Removing the lock plate retaining ring

30.5 Removing the lock plate

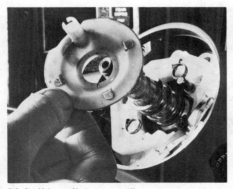
30.6 Lifting off the cancelling cam assembly

30.7 Lifting off the upper bearing spring

30.8 Removing the turn signal actuator arm

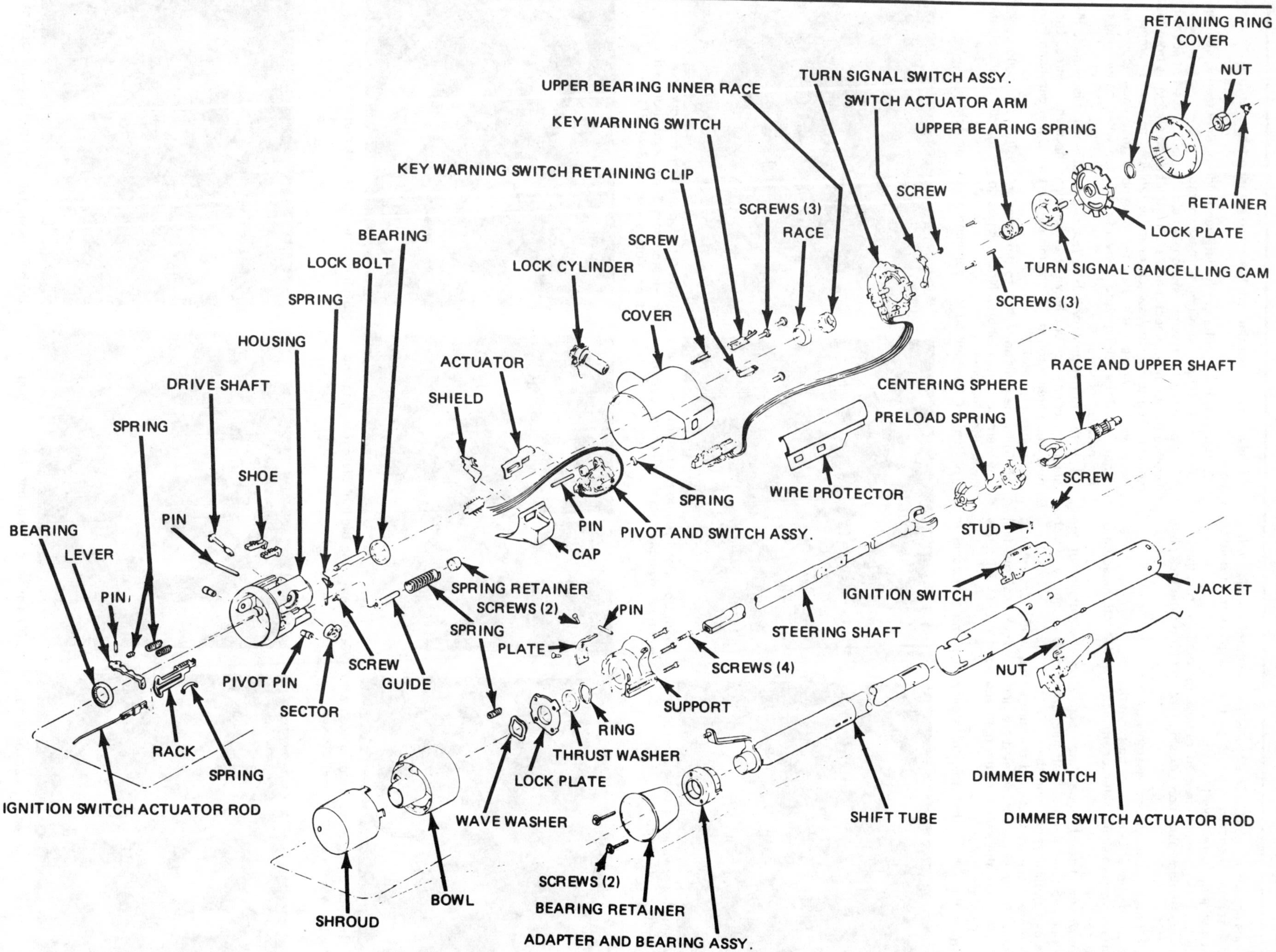

Fig. 10.26 Exploded view of the tilt steering column (Sec 30)

30.9 Removing the hazard signal knob screw

30.10 Removing the turn signal switch assembly attaching screws

30.12 Removing the bolts that secure the wiring harness

30.14 If not being replaced the turn signal switch can be left hanging from the column

30.15 Note the position of the clip on the key warning switch when removed

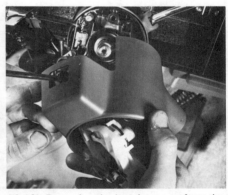
30.16 Removing the ignition lock retaining screw

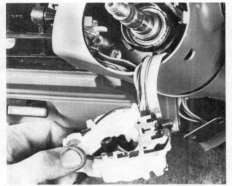
30.17 Removing the ignition lock cylinder

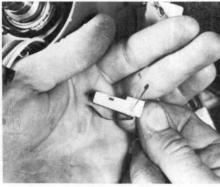
30.18a Removing the housing cover retaining screws

30.18b Removing the housing cover from the column

30.19 Location of the wiper switch pivot pin

30.22 Installed position of the dimmer actuator in the column cover

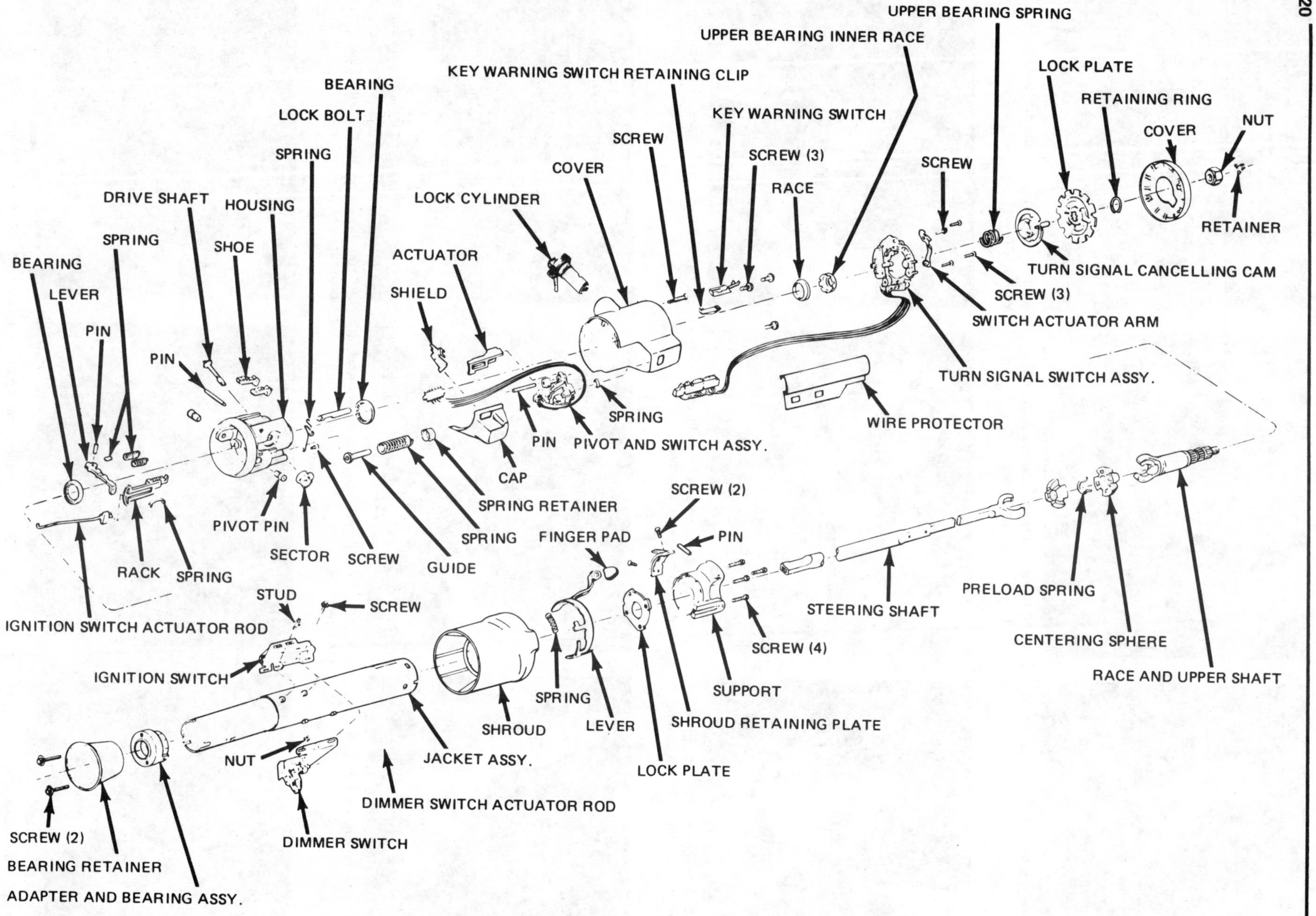

NUT

RETAINER

RETAINING RING

COVER

LOCK PLATE

TURN SIGNAL CANCELLING CAM

UPPER BEARING SPRING

SCREW (3)

SWITCH ACTUATOR ARM

SCREW

TURN SIGNAL SWITCH ASSY.

WIRE PROTECTOR

RACE AND UPPER SHAFT

CENTERING SPHERE

PRELOAD SPRING

STEERING SHAFT

UPPER BEARING INNER RACE

KEY WARNING SWITCH RETAINING CLIP

KEY WARNING SWITCH

SCREW (3)

RACE

SCREW

COVER

SCREW (4)

SUPPORT

SCREW (2)

PIN

SHROUD RETAINING PLATE

LOCK PLATE

LOCK CYLINDER

ACTUATOR

SHIELD

SPRING

PIN PIVOT AND SWITCH ASSY.

SPRING RETAINER

FINGER PAD

CAP

SPRING

LEVER

SPRING

BEARING

LOCK BOLT

SPRING

HOUSING

SHOE

GUIDE

SHROUD

JACKET ASSY.

DRIVE SHAFT

PIN

PIVOT PIN

SECTOR SCREW

STUD

SCREW

DIMMER SWITCH ACTUATOR ROD

DIMMER SWITCH

SPRING

RACK SPRING

IGNITION SWITCH ACTUATOR ROD

IGNITION SWITCH

NUT

BEARING

LEVER

PIN

BEARING RETAINER

SCREW (2)

ADAPTER AND BEARING ASSY.

Fig. 10.27 Exploded view of the key release tilt steering column (Sec 30)

17 With the ignition switch still in the 'Ignition' position, pull out the lock cylinder (photo).

18 Remove the 3 screws that hold the steering column housing cover to the column and pull off the cover (photos). When the cover is removed, the dimmer actuator may drop out. If only the wiper switch is to be replaced, the cover can be left hanging with the turn signal switch.

19 To remove the wiper switch from the housing cover punch out the pivot pin (photo). Disconnect the switch's wires at the electrical connector mounted on the column and pull the switch out. The wiper switch must be replaced as a unit.

20 If problems lie in the tilt assembly or in the column beyond this point, necessitating further disassembly of the steering column, we recommended that you let a qualified mechanic with the necessary tools correct the problem. Refer to Chapter 11 for the removal and installation procedures.

21 To install the wiper switch, reverse the removal procedure described in paragraph 19.

22 When installing the steering column cover, hold the dimmer actuator in its installed position (photos) as you slide the cover on, guiding it with a screwdriver.

23 Install the ignition switch lock cylinder by reversing the installation procedure described in steps 15 through 17.

24 To install the turn signal switch, reverse the removal procedure as described in paragraphs 8 through 14. When installing the turn signal switch actuator arm, slide it into its slot until you feel spring tension against it. Then install the actuator arm screw.

25 The remainder of the steering column is assembled by reversing the disassembly procedure described in paragraph 1 through 7. The lock plate compressor will again be needed in order to install the lock plate retaining ring.

31 Standard steering column (including all related components) – disassembly and reassembly

1 Remove the steering wheel as described in Chapter 11, Section 22.

2 Follow the tilt steering column disassembly procedure described in paragraphs 2 through 17 of Section 22.

3 Remove the dimmer switch as described in Section 24.

4 Remove the ignition switch as described in Section 25.

5 Remove the 4 screws that hold the steering column housing to the column.

6 Remove the thrust washer from the shaft and pull off the housing.

7 Remove the 3 screws that secure the shift lever gate, housing cover and upper bearing retainer to the housing and remove these pieces. See Fig. 10.28.

8 Remove the wiper switch pivot pin.

9 Remove the wiper switch.

10 Reassembly is the reverse of the disassembly procedure.

32 Dimmer switch – removal and installation

1 Disconnect the negative battery terminal.

2 Remove the steering column trim cover from the underside of the dash.

3 Disconnect the turn signal switch lead and windshield wiper switch lead extending from the steering column from the wiring harness (photo).

4 Disconnect the back-up light switch lead from its switch.

5 Disconnect the shift indicator cable by prying the clip from the shift bowl.

6 Remove the 3 bolts and 1 nut that secure the steering column to its support and lower the column. Be careful not to damage the shift cable or remaining electrical harnesses.

7 Disconnect the wiring lead from the dimmer switch (photo).

8 To remove the dimmer switch, remove the nut from the forward end of the dimmer switch bracket and the screw from the rear end that secures the switch to the column.

9 Place the new dimmer switch in position, taking care to line it up with the actuator rod.

10 Pull the turn signal/dimmer lever forward and push the dimmer switch toward the steering wheel until it clicks. Then back it off about $\frac{3}{16}$-in (5 mm) to allow for play and tighten it down.

11 Connect the wiring lead to the dimmer switch.

12 Complete the installation by reversing the removal procedure described in paragraphs 1 through 6. NOTE: When reattaching the shift indicator cable clip to the shift bowl, place the shift lever in the 'Neutral' position, then position the clip on the edge of the bowl so that the shift indicator pointer is pointing to the 'N', Push the clip onto the bowl to secure it.

33 Ignition switch – removal and installation

1 Proceed with paragraphs 1 through 6 of Section 24.

2 Disconnect the two wiring leads from the ignition switch, removing the one farthest from the steering wheel first.

3 Remove the stud and screw that secure the ignition switch to the column (photo) and lift off the switch. NOTE: Since the ignition actuator rod protrudes into the switch, the switch must be pulled up from the column to remove.

4 Before installing the new switch, use a flat-head screwdriver to move the slider inside the switch to the 'Accessory' position on the extreme right. Then slide it two detents to the left to the 'Off/unlock' position (photo). The slider must be in this position for installation.

5 Place the switch in position on the column and guide the actuator rod into the slider recess.

32.3 Location of the dimmer switch (left) and the turn signal switch and wiper switch connectors (right) on the underside of the steering column

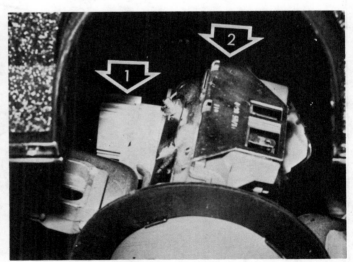

32.7 Location of the dimmer switch (1) and the ignition switch (2) as seen with the column lowered

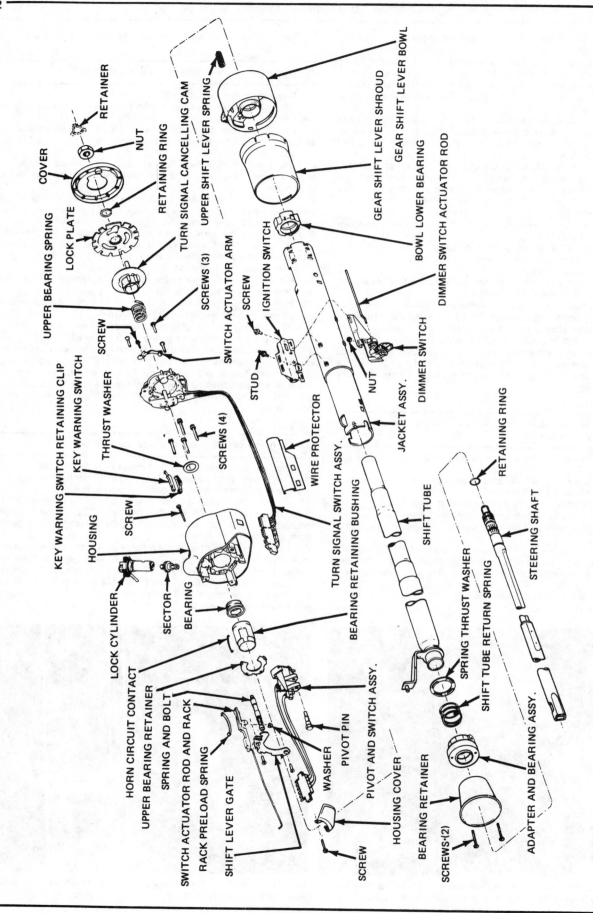

RETAINER

NUT

COVER

RETAINING RING

TURN SIGNAL CANCELLING CAM

UPPER SHIFT LEVER SPRING

LOCK PLATE

UPPER BEARING SPRING

GEAR SHIFT LEVER SHROUD

GEAR SHIFT LEVER BOWL

BOWL LOWER BEARING

DIMMER SWITCH ACTUATOR ROD

SCREWS (3)

SWITCH ACTUATOR ARM

SCREW

IGNITION SWITCH

KEY WARNING SWITCH RETAINING CLIP

KEY WARNING SWITCH

SCREW

THRUST WASHER

STUD

DIMMER SWITCH

NUT

JACKET ASSY.

SCREWS (4)

HOUSING

SCREW

WIRE PROTECTOR

TURN SIGNAL SWITCH ASSY.

BEARING RETAINING BUSHING

SHIFT TUBE

RETAINING RING

STEERING SHAFT

LOCK CYLINDER

SECTOR

BEARING

SPRING THRUST WASHER

SHIFT TUBE RETURN SPRING

HORN CIRCUIT CONTACT

UPPER BEARING RETAINER

SPRING AND BOLT

SWITCH ACTUATOR ROD AND RACK

RACK PRELOAD SPRING

SHIFT LEVER GATE

WASHER

PIVOT PIN

PIVOT AND SWITCH ASSY.

HOUSING COVER

BEARING RETAINER

SCREW

SCREWS (2)

ADAPTER AND BEARING ASSY.

Fig. 10.28 Exploded view of the standard steering column (Sec 31)

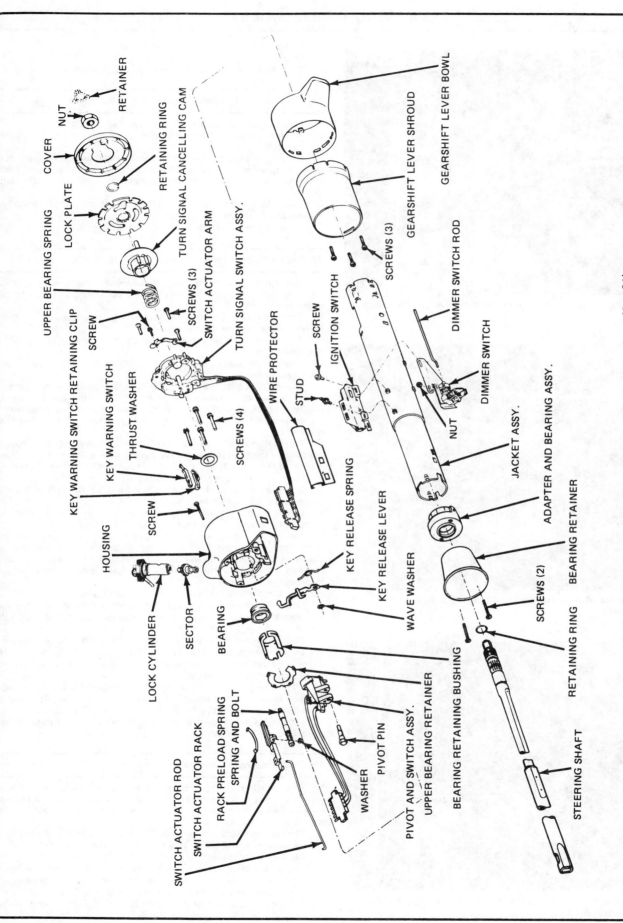

RETAINER

NUT

RETAINING RING

TURN SIGNAL CANCELLING CAM

COVER

LOCK PLATE

UPPER BEARING SPRING

SWITCH ACTUATOR ARM

TURN SIGNAL SWITCH ASSY.

SCREWS (3)

SCREW

KEY WARNING SWITCH RETAINING CLIP

KEY WARNING SWITCH

THRUST WASHER

SCREWS (4)

WIRE PROTECTOR

STUD

SCREW

IGNITION SWITCH

GEARSHIFT LEVER SHROUD

GEARSHIFT LEVER BOWL

SCREWS (3)

DIMMER SWITCH ROD

DIMMER SWITCH

NUT

JACKET ASSY.

ADAPTER AND BEARING ASSY.

BEARING RETAINER

SCREWS (2)

RETAINING RING

STEERING SHAFT

BEARING RETAINING BUSHING

UPPER BEARING RETAINER

PIVOT AND SWITCH ASSY.

PIVOT PIN

WASHER

WAVE WASHER

KEY RELEASE LEVER

KEY RELEASE SPRING

SPRING AND BOLT

RACK PRELOAD SPRING

SWITCH ACTUATOR RACK

SWITCH ACTUATOR ROD

LOCK CYLINDER

SECTOR

BEARING

SCREW

HOUSING

Fig. 10.29 Exploded view of the key release standard steering column (Sec 31)

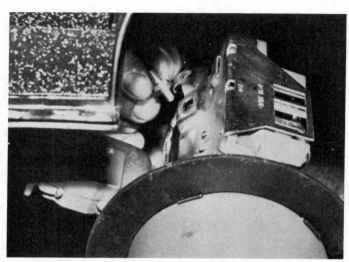

33.3 Removing the stud and screw that secures the ignition switch to the column

33.4 Use a screwdriver to move the ignition switch slider to the off/unlock position

34.3 Using an allen wrench to check that the back-up light switch is in the neutral position

6   Install the stud and screw and tighten to specs.
7   Connect the 2 wiring leads to the switch.
8   Reverse the procedure referred to in paragraph 1.

34 Back-up light switch – removal and installation

1   Proceed with paragraphs 1 through 4 of Section 24.
2   Place the shifter in the 'Neutral' position and remove the back-up light switch.
3   Before installing the switch, move the slider until it's aligned in the 'Neutral' position. This should be checked by inserting a small Allen wrench or similar tool into the 'N' hole on the back of the switch (photo).
4   Place the switch in position on the steering column and install and tighten the 2 screws that secure it.
5   Reverse the procedure referred to in paragraph 1.

35 Rear defogger (electric grid-type) – testing and repair

1   This option consists of a rear window with a number of horizontal elements that are baked into the glass surface during the glass forming operation.
2   Small breaks in the element system can be successfully repaired without removing the rear window.
3   To test the grids for proper operation, start the engine and turn on the system.
4   Ground one lead of a test lamp and lightly touch the other prod to each grid line.
5   The brilliance of the test lamp should increase as the probe is moved across the element from right to left. If the test lamp glows brightly at both ends of the grid lines, check for a loose ground wire for the system. All of the grid lines should be checked in at least two places.
6   To repair a break in a grid line it is recommended that a repair kit specifically for this purpose be purchased from a GM dealer. Included in the repair kit will be a decal, a container of silver plastic and hardener, a mixing stick and instructions.
7   To repair a break, first turn off the system and allow it to de-energize for a few minutes.
8   Lightly buff the grid line area with fine steel wool and then thoroughly clean the area with alcohol.
9   Use a decal supplied in the repair kit, or use electrician's tape above and below the area to be repaired. The space between the pieces of tape should be the same as existing grid lines. This can be checked from outside the car. Press the tape tightly against the glass to prevent seepage.
10 Mix the hardener and silver plastic thoroughly.
11 Using the wood spatula, apply the silver plastic mixture between the pieces of tape, overlapping the damaged area slightly on either end.
12 Carefully remove the decal or tape and apply a constant stream of hot air directly to the repaired area. A heat gun set at 500 to 700 degrees Fahrenheit is recommended. Hold the gun about 1 inch from the glass for 1 to 2 minutes.
13 If the new grid line appears off color, tincture of iodine can be used to clean the repair and bring it back to the proper color. This mixture should not remain on the repair for more than 30 seconds.
14 Although the defogger is now fully operational, the repaired area should not be disturbed for at least 24 hours.

36 Cruise control – general

1   This cruising speed control system is optionally available on certain models and allows the driver to maintain a constant highway speed without the necessity of continual adjustment of foot pressure on the accelerator pedal.
2   The system employs a servo unit connected to the intake manifold, a speedometer cable-driven regulator and various switches.
3   An override capability is built in.
4   Any malfunction in the performance of the system should first be checked out by inspecting the fuse, the security of the leads and terminals, and the vacuum pipes and connections.
5   The following adjustments should then be checked and if necessary altered to conform to those specified.

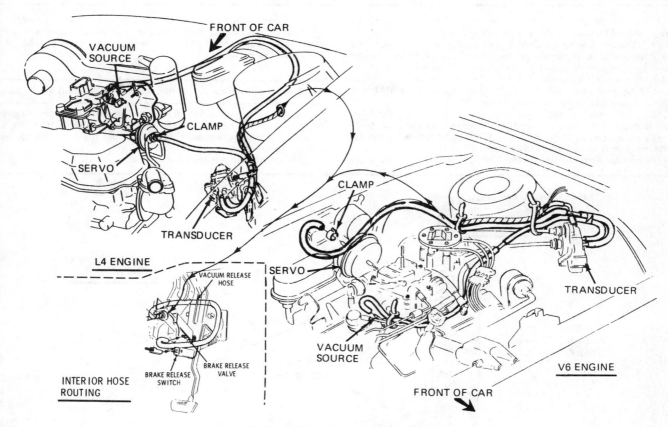

Fig. 10.30 Cruise control system (Sec 36)

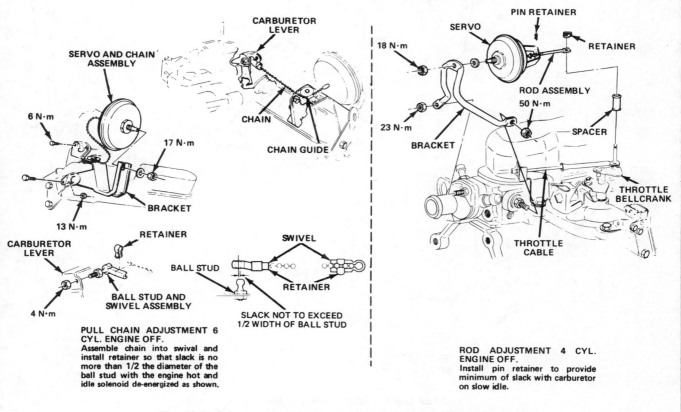

PULL CHAIN ADJUSTMENT 6
CYL. ENGINE OFF.
Assemble chain into swivel and
install retainer so that slack is no
more than 1/2 the diameter of the
ball stud with the engine hot and
idle solenoid de-energized as shown.

ROD ADJUSTMENT 4 CYL.
ENGINE OFF.
Install pin retainer to provide
minimum of slack with carburetor
on slow idle.

Fig. 10.31 Adjustment of the cruise control servo mechanism (Sec 36)

6   The servo operating rod which connects to the carburetor throttle linkage should be adjusted as shown in Fig. 10.31.

7   *The regulator* can be adjusted by turning the orifice tube in or out *(never remove it as it cannot be re-installed).* If the vehicle cruises below the engagement speed, screw the orifice tube out. If the vehicle cruises above the engagement speed, screw the orifice tube in. Each $\frac{1}{4}$ turn of the orifice tube will change the cruise speed by about 1 mph. Tighten the locknut after each adjustment.

8   *The brake release switch* contacts must open when the brake pedal is depressed between $\frac{1}{4}$ and $\frac{1}{2}$-in measured at the pedal pad.

9   The vacuum valve plunger must clear the pedal arm when the arm is moved $\frac{5}{16}$ inch measured at the switch.

10   *The column mounted engagement switch* is non-adjustable, and is serviced only as part of the complete turn signal lever assembly.

11   Faulty components should be replaced as complete assemblies after disconnecting electrical leads, vacuum hoses and control cables from them as necessary.

37 Power radio antenna – removal and installation

1   Lower the antenna mast fully by turning off the radio or ignition key switch. If the unit has failed with the antenna mast in the 'Up' position, it may be advisable to cut off the mast portion to make replacement easier.

2   Disconnect the negative battery cable.

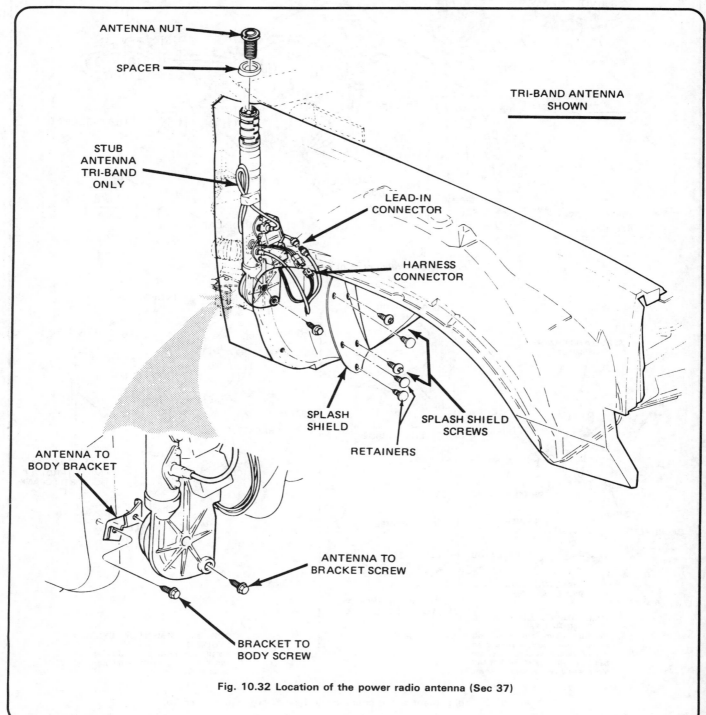

Fig. 10.32 Location of the power radio antenna (Sec 37)

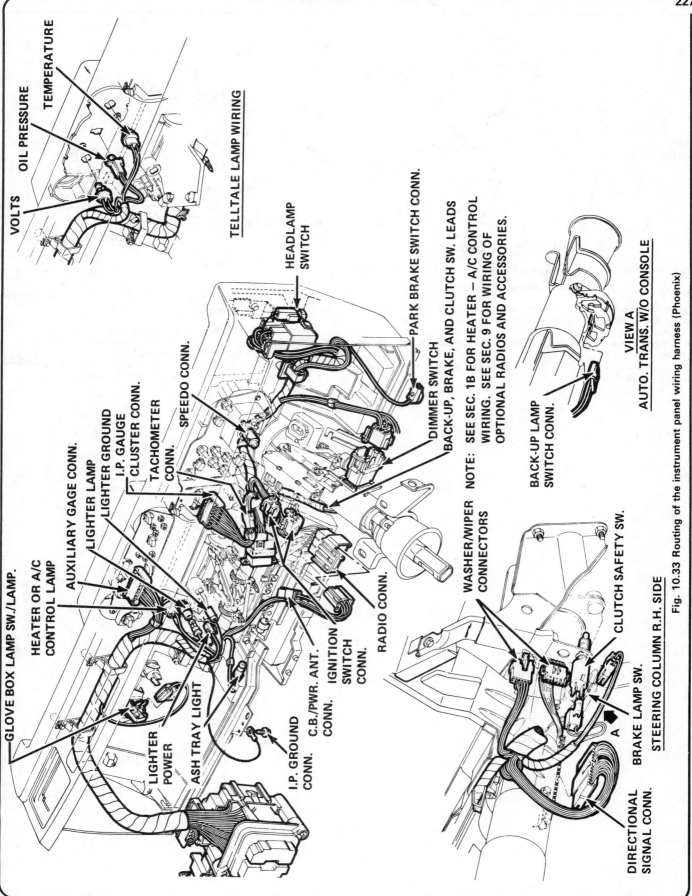

TELLTALE LAMP WIRING

TEMPERATURE
OIL PRESSURE
VOLTS

HEADLAMP SWITCH

PARK BRAKE SWITCH CONN.

DIMMER SWITCH

BACK-UP, BRAKE, AND CLUTCH SW. LEADS

SPEEDO CONN.

TACHOMETER CONN.

I.P. GAUGE CLUSTER CONN.

LIGHTER GROUND

LIGHTER LAMP

AUXILIARY GAGE CONN.

HEATER OR A/C CONTROL LAMP

GLOVE BOX LAMP SW./LAMP.

LIGHTER POWER

ASH TRAY LIGHT

I.P. GROUND CONN.

C.B./PWR. ANT. CONN.

IGNITION SWITCH CONN.

RADIO CONN.

NOTE: SEE SEC. 1B FOR HEATER – A/C CONTROL WIRING. SEE SEC. 9 FOR WIRING OF OPTIONAL RADIOS AND ACCESSORIES.

BACK-UP LAMP SWITCH CONN.

VIEW A
AUTO. TRANS. W/O CONSOLE

WASHER/WIPER CONNECTORS

CLUTCH SAFETY SW.

A

BRAKE LAMP SW.

STEERING COLUMN R.H. SIDE

DIRECTIONAL SIGNAL CONN.

Fig. 10.33 Routing of the instrument panel wiring harness (Phoenix)

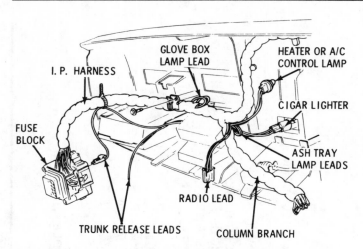

Fig. 10.34 Routing of the wiring harness on the right side of the instrument panel (Omega)

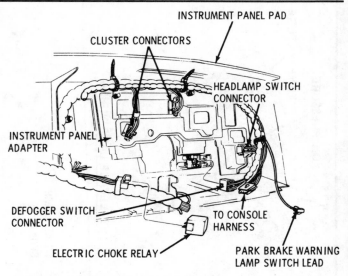

Fig. 10.35 Routing of the wiring harness on the left side of the instrument panel (Omega)

3   Access to the power antenna motor is through the inner fender panel. Raise the vehicle and remove the front tire for better access if necessary.

4   Remove the fender skirt attaching screws and pull the splash shield forward to gain access to the antenna connections. A piece of 2 x 4 lumber can be used as a spacer to keep the shield pulled away as work is performed.

5   Remove the escutcheon nut and spacer at the fender.

6   Disconnect the electrical leads and remove the antenna and motor assembly through the fender skirt opening.

7   When installing a new unit, be sure that the mast is fully retracted and the lower bracket is securely attached to the body.

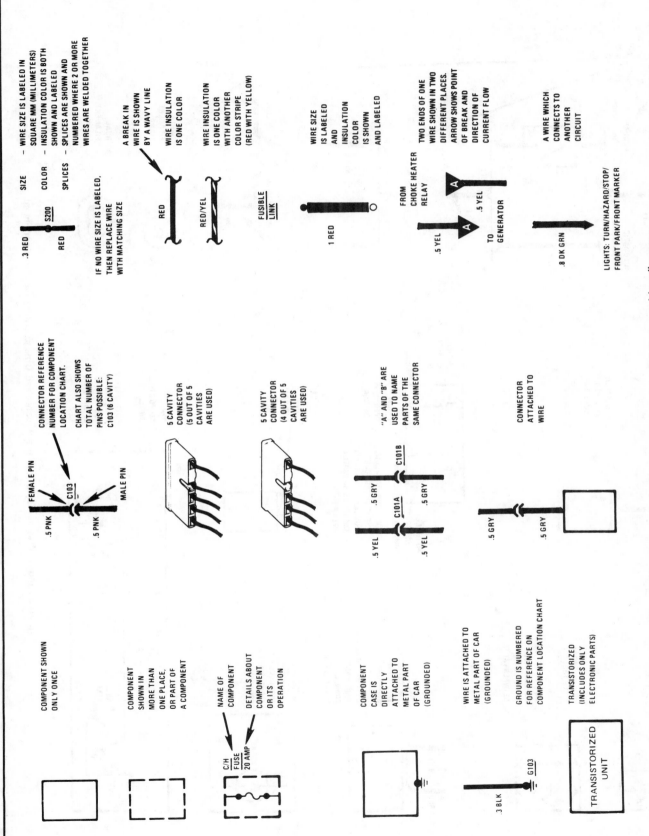

SIZE — WIRE SIZE IS LABELED IN SQUARE MM (MILLIMETERS)

COLOR — INSULATION COLOR IS BOTH SHOWN AND LABELED

SPLICES — SPLICES ARE SHOWN AND NUMBERED WHERE 2 OR MORE WIRES ARE WELDED TOGETHER

.3 RED
S200
RED

IF NO WIRE SIZE IS LABELED, THEN REPLACE WIRE WITH MATCHING SIZE

A BREAK IN WIRE IS SHOWN BY A WAVY LINE

RED — WIRE INSULATION IS ONE COLOR

RED/YEL — WIRE INSULATION IS ONE COLOR WITH ANOTHER COLOR STRIPE (RED WITH YELLOW)

FUSIBLE LINK

1 RED — WIRE SIZE IS LABELED AND INSULATION COLOR IS SHOWN AND LABELED

FROM CHOKE HEATER RELAY
.5 YEL
TO GENERATOR
A — TWO ENDS OF ONE WIRE SHOWN IN TWO DIFFERENT PLACES. ARROW SHOWS POINT OF BREAK AND DIRECTION OF CURRENT FLOW

.8 DK GRN — A WIRE WHICH CONNECTS TO ANOTHER CIRCUIT

LIGHTS: TURN/HAZARD/STOP/ FRONT PARK/FRONT MARKER

CONNECTOR REFERENCE NUMBER FOR COMPONENT LOCATION CHART.
CHART ALSO SHOWS TOTAL NUMBER OF PINS POSSIBLE: C103 (6 CAVITY)

FEMALE PIN
C103
MALE PIN
.5 PNK
.5 PNK

5 CAVITY CONNECTOR (5 OUT OF 5 CAVITIES ARE USED)

5 CAVITY CONNECTOR (4 OUT OF 5 CAVITIES ARE USED)

"A" AND "B" ARE USED TO NAME PARTS OF THE SAME CONNECTOR

C101B
.5 GRY
.5 GRY
C101A
.5 YEL
.5 YEL

CONNECTOR ATTACHED TO WIRE
.5 GRY
.5 GRY

COMPONENT SHOWN ONLY ONCE

COMPONENT SHOWN IN MORE THAN ONE PLACE, OR PART OF A COMPONENT

C/H FUSE 20 AMP
NAME OF COMPONENT
DETAILS ABOUT COMPONENT OR ITS OPERATION

COMPONENT CASE IS DIRECTLY ATTACHED TO METAL PART OF CAR (GROUNDED)

.3 BLK
G103
WIRE IS ATTACHED TO METAL PART OF CAR (GROUNDED)

GROUND IS NUMBERED FOR REFERENCE ON COMPONENT LOCATION CHART

TRANSISTORIZED UNIT
TRANSISTORIZED (INCLUDES ONLY ELECTRONIC PARTS)

Fig. 10.36 Index of symbols used in the Phoenix and Omega wiring diagrams

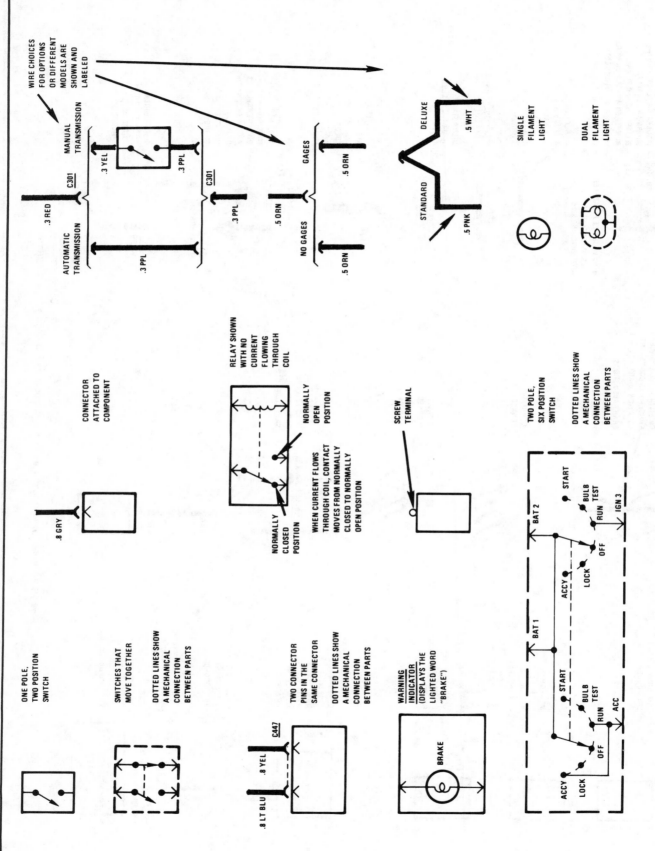

Fig. 10.36 Index of symbols used in the Phoenix and Omega wiring diagrams continued

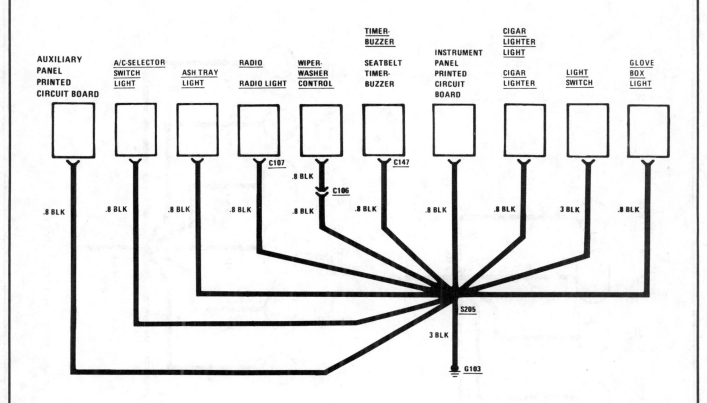

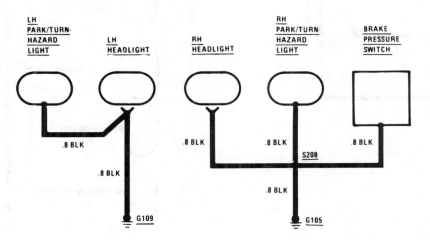

Fig. 10.37 Diagram of the instrument ground wires (top) and front light ground wires (bottom)

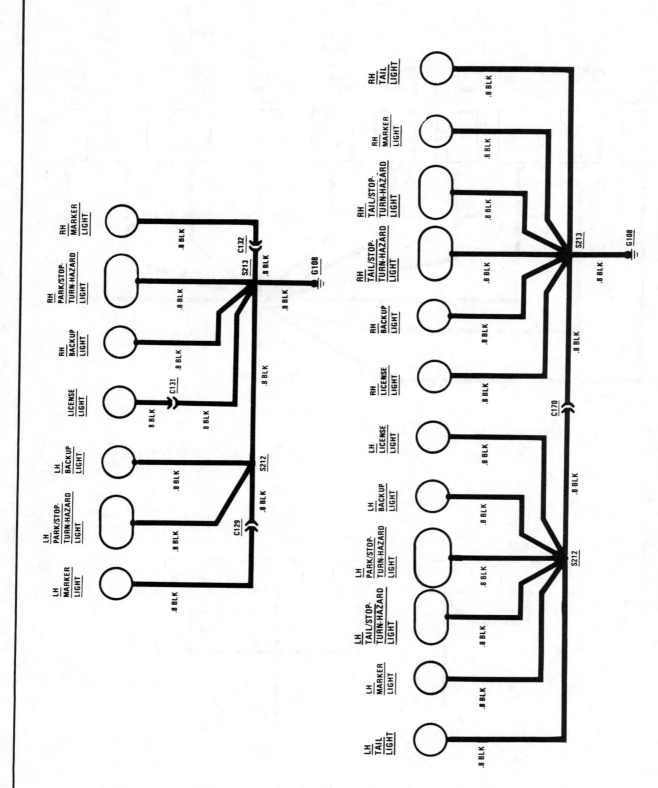

Fig. 10.38 Diagram of the Omega (top) and Phoenix (bottom) rear light ground wires

Key to wiring diagram of the charging system and general electrical power distribution

Component	Location
Fuses	Under right side of instrument panel
Fusible link A	Front center of engine, at starter solenoid
Fusible link B	Front center of engine, at starter solenoid
Fusible link C	At C101A on right cowl
Generator warning indicator	Printed circuit board
Ignition switch	Base of steering column
Starter solenoid	Front center of engine
Underhood light	Rear center of hood
Underhood light fuse	RH cowl at blower motor
C101A (20 cavities)	In engine compartment, behind fuse block
C101B (20 cavities)	In engine compartment, behind fuse block
G101	Left front of engine
G102	Left front fender

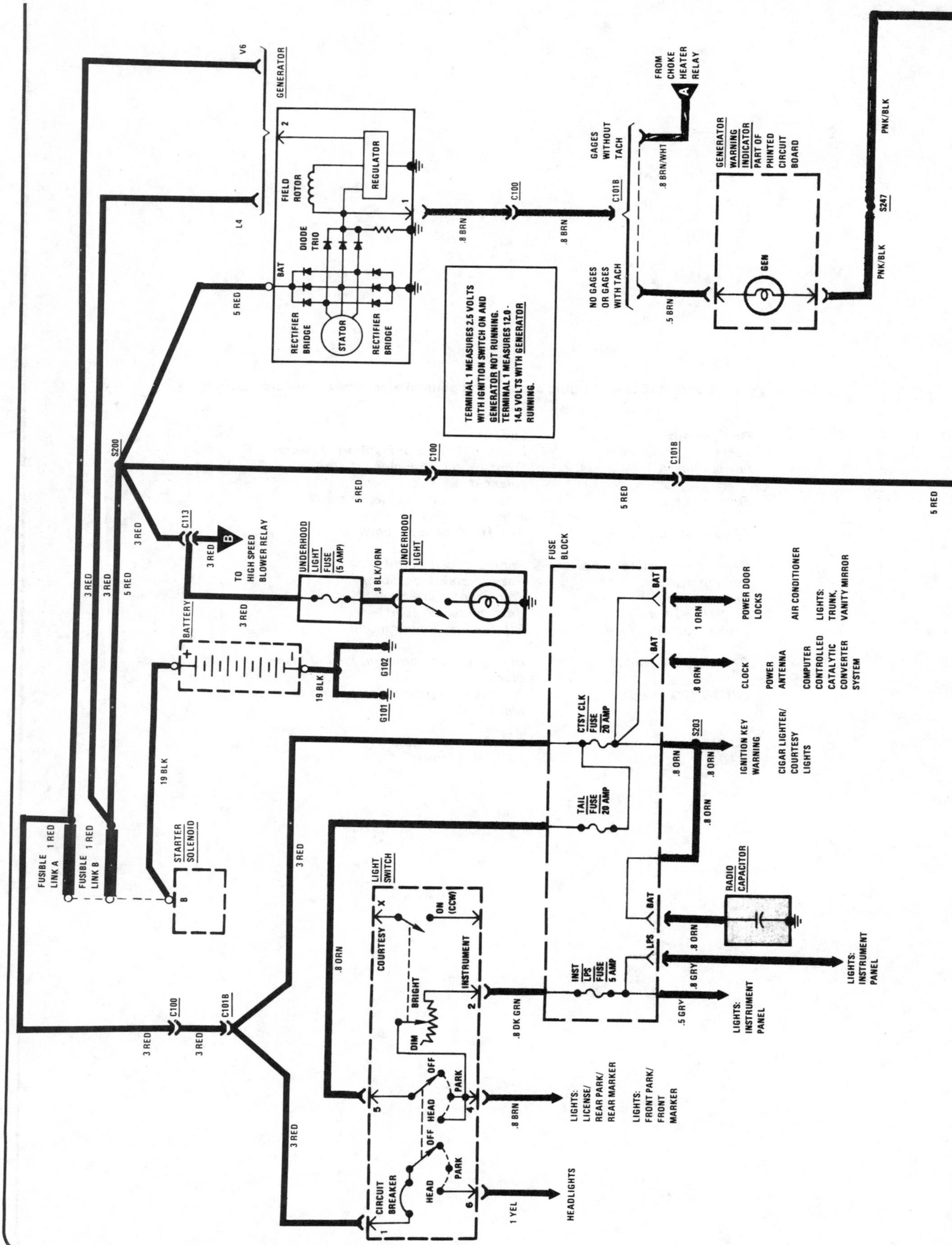

234

Fig. 10.39 Wiring diagrams of the charging system and general electrical power distribution (Omega)

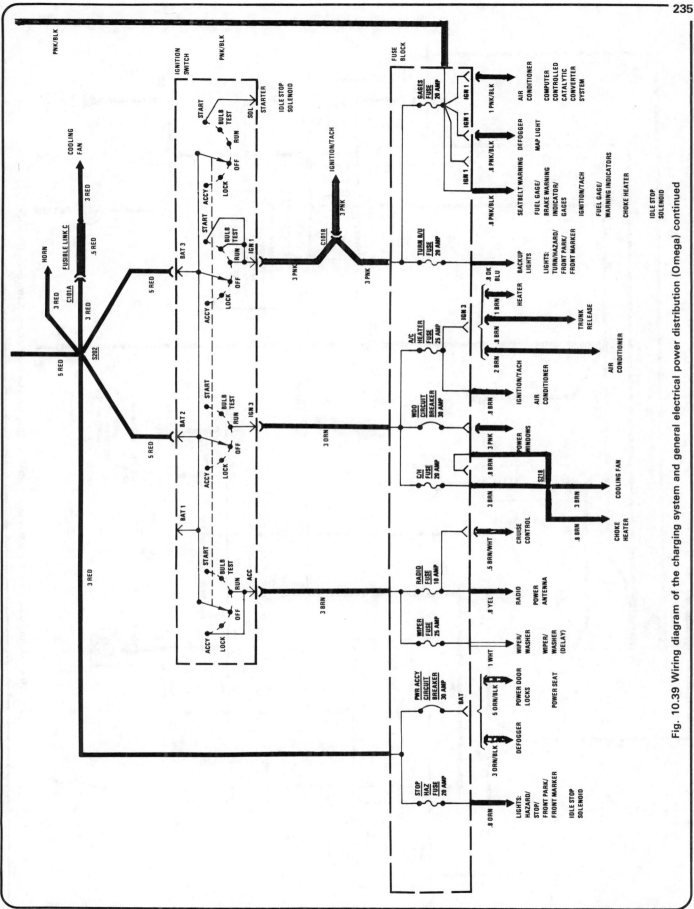

Fig. 10.39 Wiring diagram of the charging system and general electrical power distribution (Omega) continued

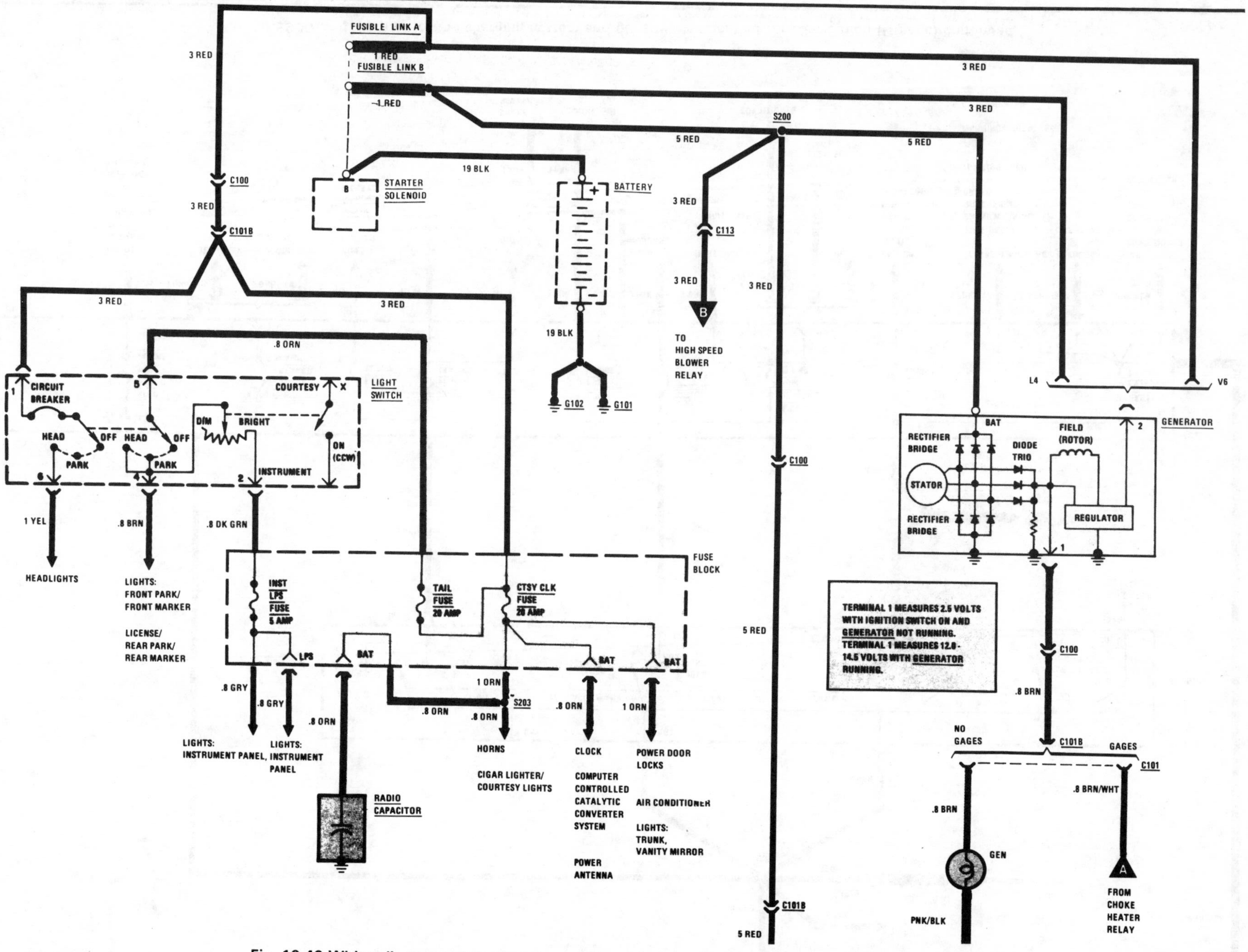

Fig. 10.40 Wiring diagrams of the charging system and general electrical power distribution (Phoenix).

237

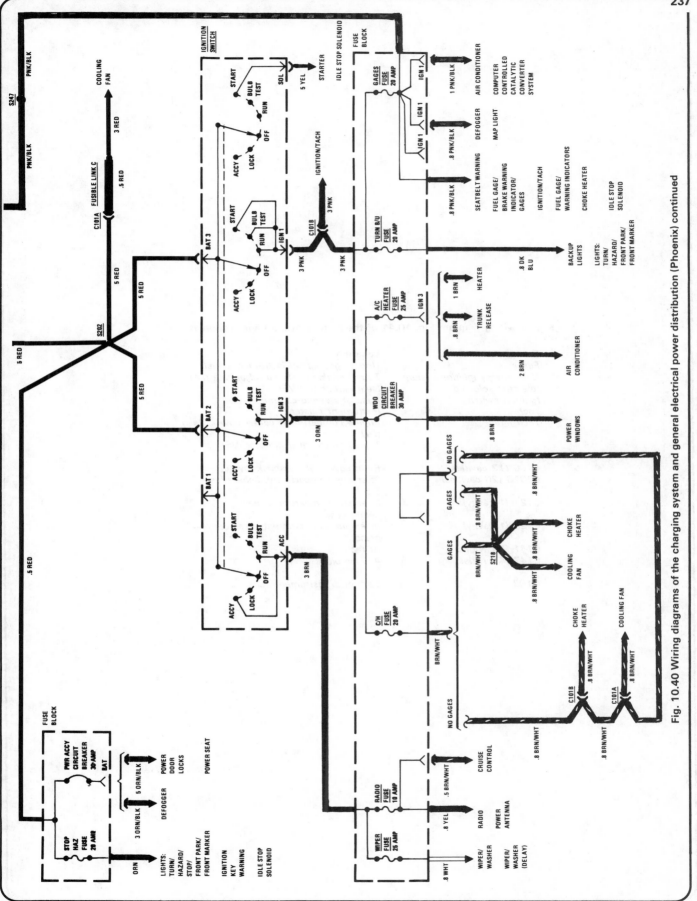

Fig. 10.40 Wiring diagrams of the charging system and general electrical power distribution (Phoenix) continued

Key to wiring diagram Fig. 10.41 of the ignition system and tachometer

Component	Location
Fuses	Under right side of instrument panel
High energy ignition system	Top of engine (V6); rear of engine (L4)
Idle stop solenoid	Near carburetor (V6)
Ignition switch	Base of steering column
Tach.	Instrument cluster
Tach filter	Engine compartment center cowl (L4)
	Top of engine at distributor (V6)
C100 (12 cavities)	Right cowl, behind shock tower
C101B (20 cavities)	In engine compartment, behind fuse block
C121 (1 cavity)	In engine compartment, near heater case
C123 (1 cavity)	In engine compartment, near compressor
C141 (3 cavities)	At tach
C147 (4 cavities)	At fuse block
G103	Bottom of instrument panel support

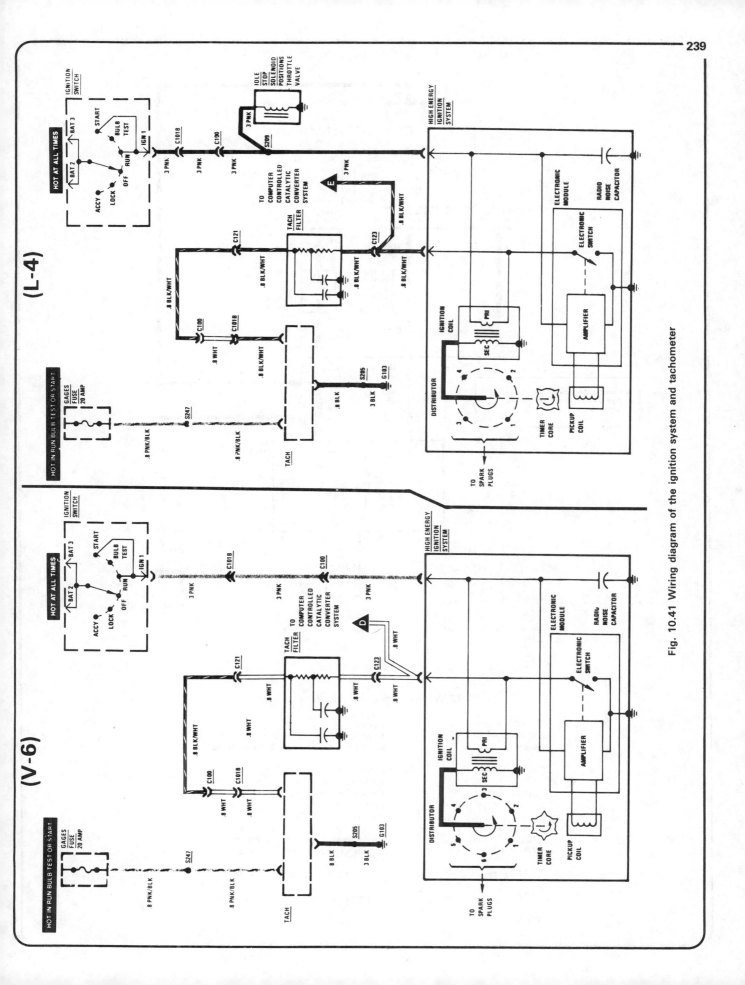

Fig. 10.41 Wiring diagram of the ignition system and tachometer

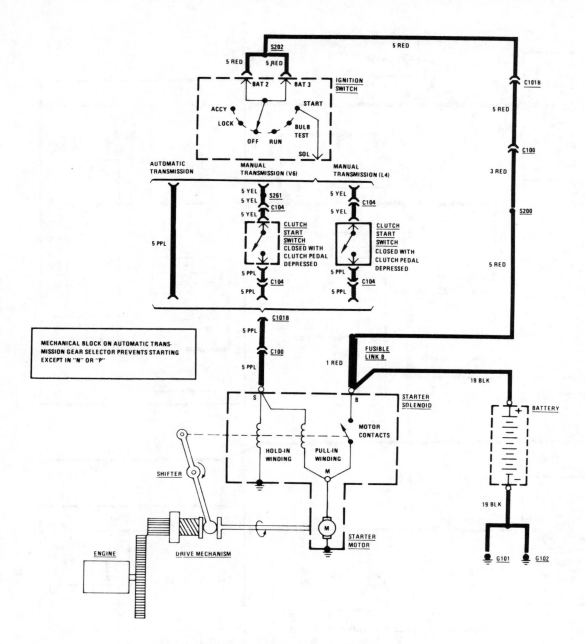

Fig. 10.42 Wiring diagram of the starter system

Component	Location
Clutch start switch	Clutch pedal lever support
Fuses	Under right side of instrument panel
Fusible link A	Front center of engine, at starter solenoid
Ignition switch	Base of steering column
Starter motor solenoid	Center front of engine
C100 (12 cavities)	Right cowl behind shock tower
C101B (20 cavities)	Engine compartment, behind fuse block
C104 (4 cavities)	Left instrument panel
G101	Transmission case, left front of engine
G102	Left front fender

Key to wiring diagram Fig. 10.43 for the turn signal, hazard, stop, front park and front marker light systems

Component	Location
Brake switch	Brake support to right of steering column
Fuses	Under right side of instrument panel
Hazard flasher	Fuse block, right instrument panel
LH turn indicator	Printed circuit board
RH turn indicator	Printed circuit board
Turn flasher	Lower steering column
Turn hazard switch assembly	Steering column
C101A (20 cavities)	In engine compartment, behind fuse block
C102A (7 cavities)	Under instrument panel, near fuse block
C103 (6 cavities)	Right rear quarter extension wall
C127 (11 cavities)	At base of steering column
C170 (1 cavity)	Inside rear light harness
G103	Bottom of left instrument panel support
G105	Above right headlight
G108	RH tail panel under light
G109	Above left headlight

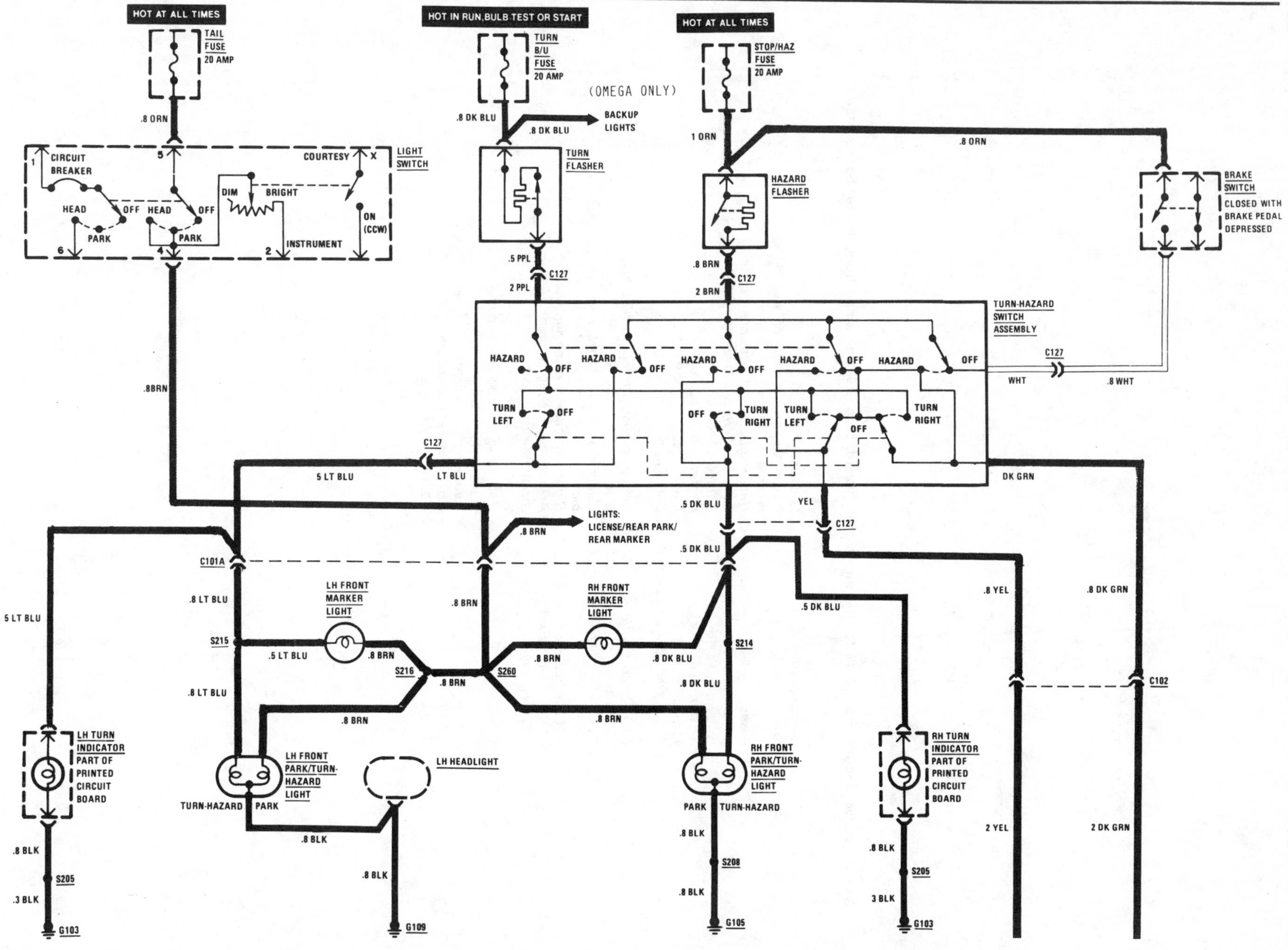

Fig. 10.43 Wiring diagram for the turn signal, hazard, stop, front park and front marker light systems

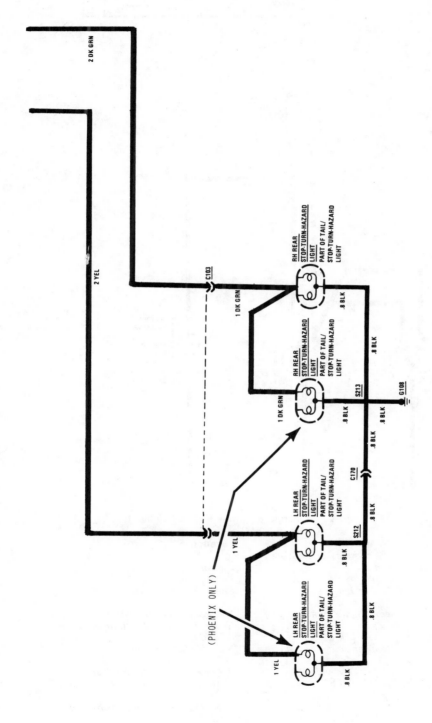

Fig. 10.43 Wiring diagram for the turn signal, hazard, stop, front park and front marker light systems continued

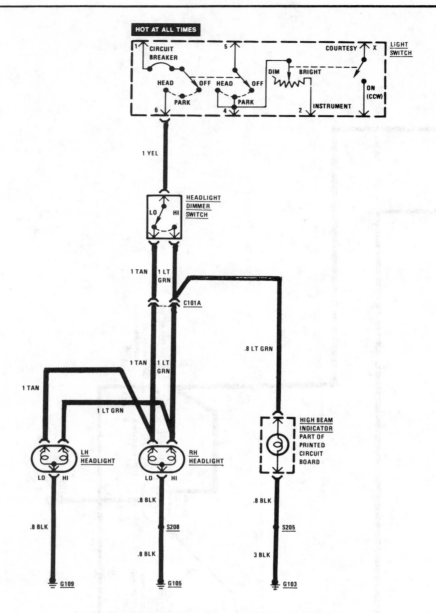

Fig. 10.44 Wiring diagrams for the headlights

Component	Location
A/C compressor pressure switch	On compressor
Cooling fan	Behind radiator
Cooling fan relay	Corner of front fender
Engine coolant temperature switch	Top front of engine (L4/V6)
Fuses	Under right side of instrument panel
Fusible link C	At C101A
Headlight dimmer switch	Base of steering column
C100 (12 cavities)	RH cowl behind shock tower
C101A (20 cavities)	In engine compartment, behind fuse block
C101B (20 cavities)	In engine compartment, behind fuse block
C145 (1 cavity)	RH front radiator support
G103	Bottom of left instrument panel support
G105	Above right headlight
G109	Above left headlight

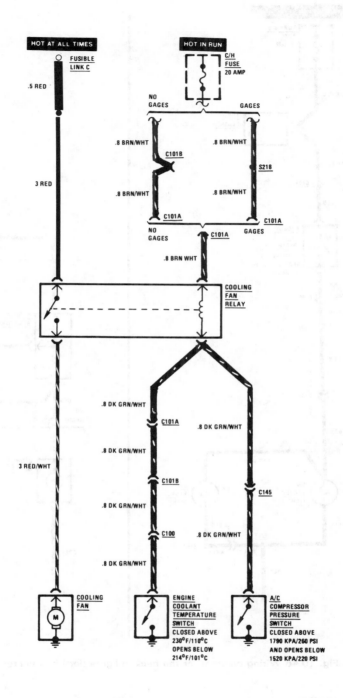

HOT AT ALL TIMES

FUSIBLE
LINK C

.5 RED

3 RED

HOT IN RUN

C/H
FUSE
20 AMP

NO
GAGES

GAGES

.8 BRN/WHT

.8 BRN/WHT

C101B

S218

.8 BRN/WHT

.8 BRN/WHT

C101A

C101A

NO
GAGES

GAGES

C101A

.8 BRN WHT

COOLING
FAN
RELAY

.8 DK GRN/WHT

C101A

.8 DK GRN/WHT

.8 DK GRN/WHT

C101B

3 RED/WHT

.8 DK GRN/WHT

C100

C145

.8 DK GRN/WHT

.8 DK GRN/WHT

COOLING
FAN

M

ENGINE
COOLANT
TEMPERATURE
SWITCH
CLOSED ABOVE
230°F/110°C
OPENS BELOW
214°F/101°C

A/C
COMPRESSOR
PRESSURE
SWITCH
CLOSED ABOVE
1790 KPA/260 PSI
AND OPENS BELOW
1520 KPA/220 PSI

Fig. 10.45 Wiring diagram for the cooling fan. For location of components, see the caption for Fig. 10.44

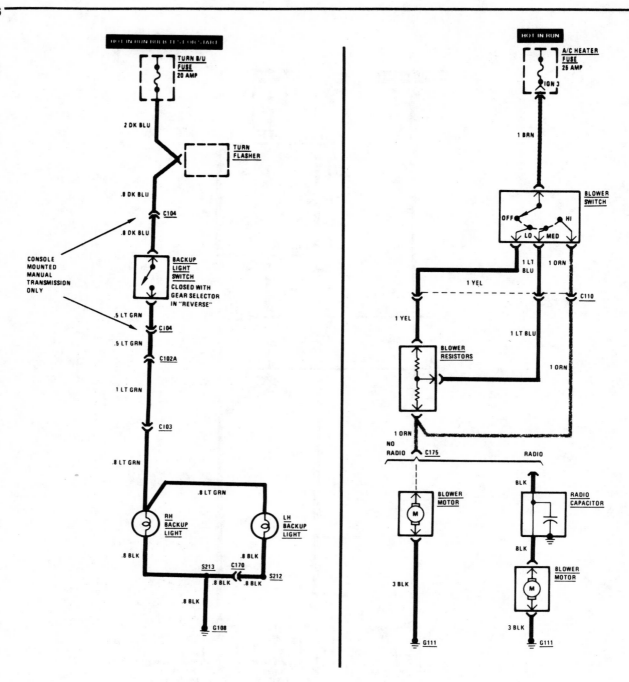

Fig. 10.46 Wiring diagram for the backup lights (left) and heater (right)

Component	Location	Component	Location
Backup light switch	Base of steering column (automatic transmission	C102A (7 cavities)	Under instrument panel, near fuse block
Backup light switch	Center console (manual transmission)	C103 (6 cavities)	Right rear quarter extension wall
		C104 (4 cavities)	Center console
Blower motor	Front of heater case	C110 (3 cavities)	Behind instrument panel at support brace
Blower resistors	Front of heater case		
Blower switch	Instrument panel to right of steering column	C170 (1 cavity)	Inside rear light harness
		C175 (3 cavities)	At heater blower case
Fuses	Under right side of instrument panel		
Radio capacitor	Attached to blower motor	G108	Right panel under light
Turn flasher	At base of steering column	G111	Right front cowl near heater blower

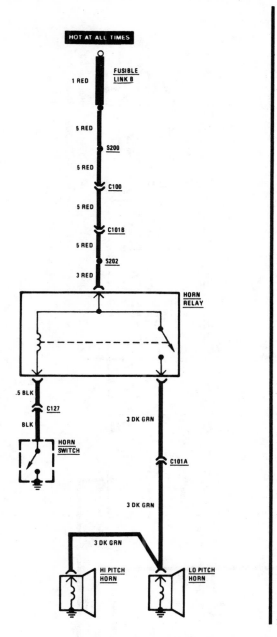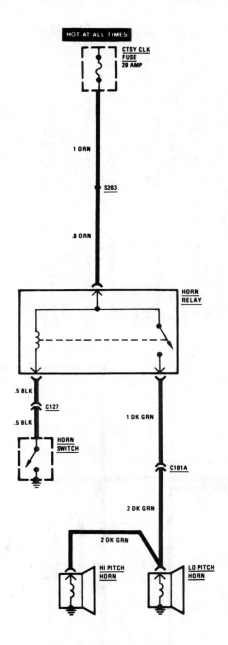

Fig. 10.47 Wiring diagrams for the horn systems of the Omega (left) and Phoenix (right)

Component	Location
Fuses	Under RH side of instrument panel at fuse block
Horn relay	On fuse block
C101A (20 cavities)	In engine compartment, behind fuse block
C107 (4 cavities)	Behind instrument panel, near radio
C108 (4 cavities)	Behind instrument panel, near radio
C109 (4 cavities)	Behind instrument panel, near radio
C127 (11 cavities)	Base of steering column
C156 (7 cavities)	Behind instrument panel, near radio
C157 (4 cavities)	Behind instrument panel, near radio
G103	Bottom of instrument panel support

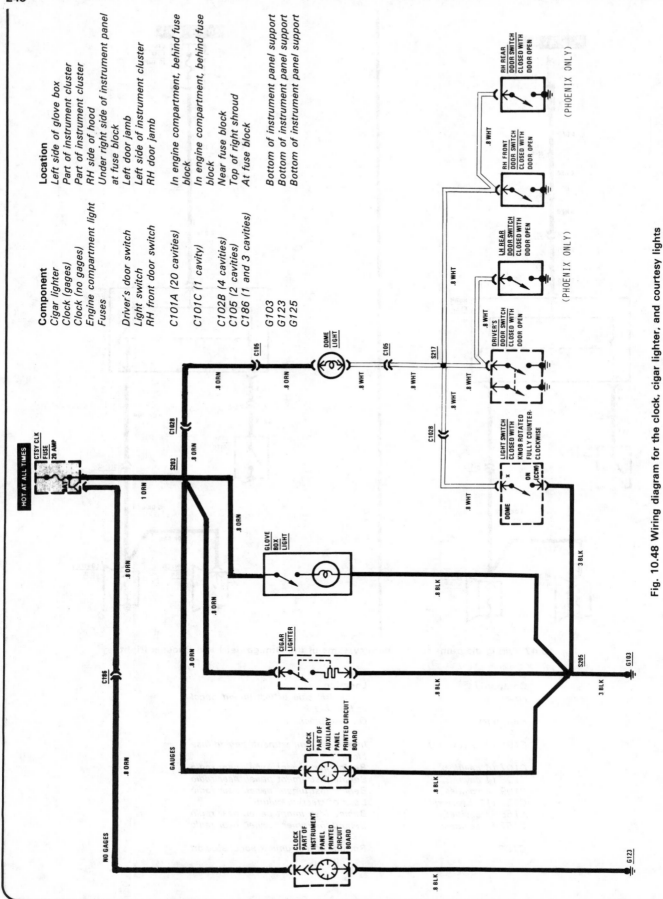

Fig. 10.48 Wiring diagram for the clock, cigar lighter, and courtesy lights

249

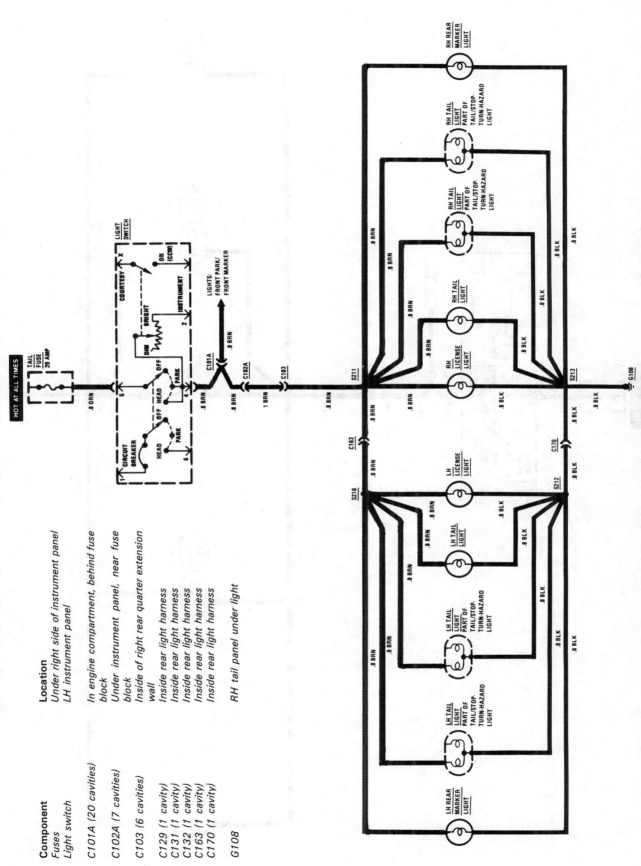

Fig. 10.49 Wiring diagram for the license, tail and rear marker light systems (Phoenix)

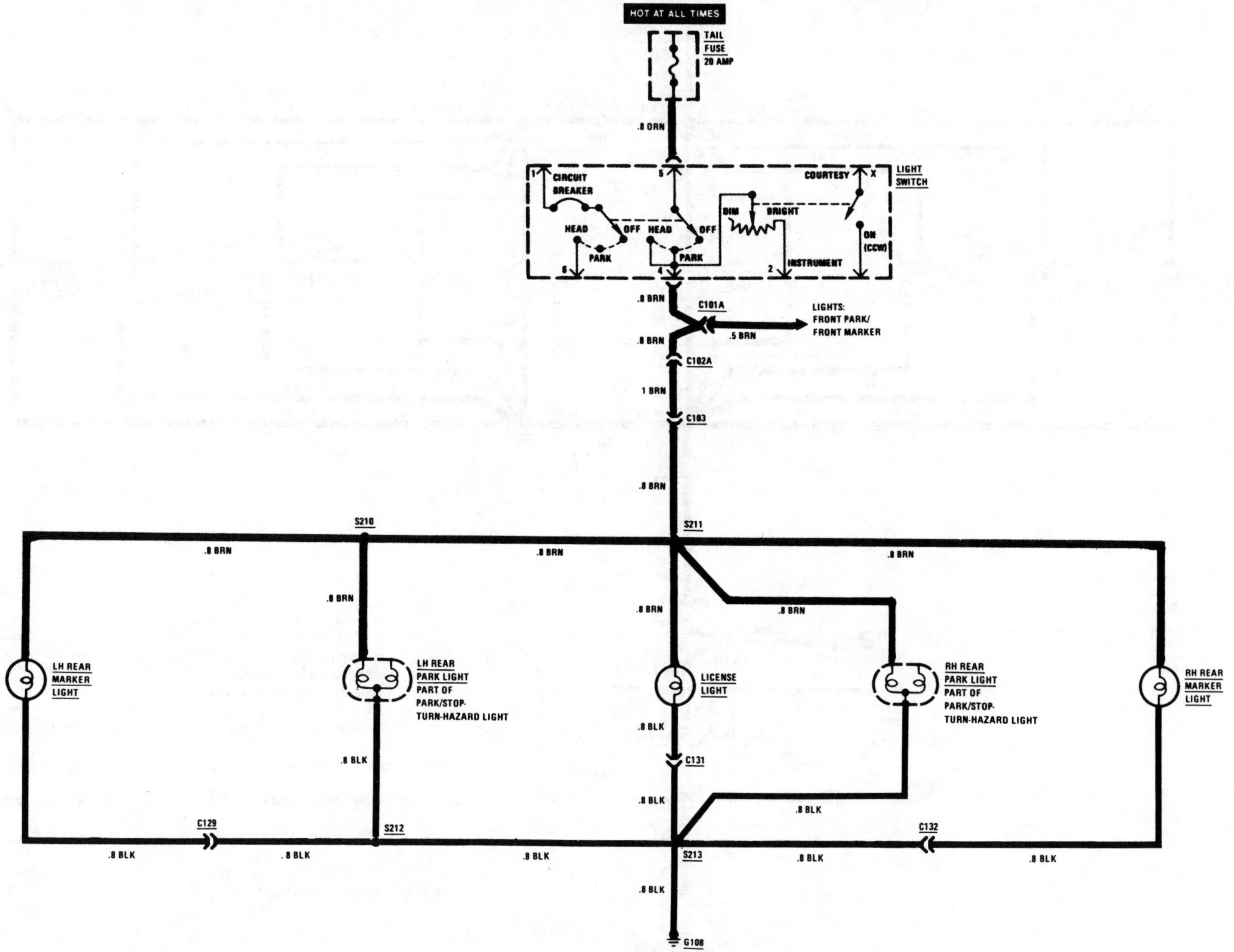

Fig. 10.50 Wiring diagram for the license, tail and rear marker light systems (Omega). For location of components see the caption for Fig. 10.49

Key to wiring diagram for the brake warning indicator and gauges (optional gauge package)

Component	Location
Brake pressure switch	On master cylinder
Coolant temperature transducer	Top front of engine (V6/L4)
Engine oil pressure transducer	Lower rear of engine (V6/L4)
Fuel gage sending unit	Top of gas tank
Fuses	Under right side of instrument panel
Park brake switch	Park brake lever assembly
C100 (12 cavities)	Right cowl, behind shock tower
C101A (16 cavities)	Engine compartment, behind fuse block
C101B (12 cavities)	Engine compartment, behind fuse block
C102A (6 cavities)	Top of fuse block
C103 (6 cavities)	Right rear quarter extension wall
C143 (1 cavity)	In rear next to gas-filled bumper shock
G103	Bottom of instrument panel support
G104	Center rear crossmember above gas tank
G105	Above right headlight

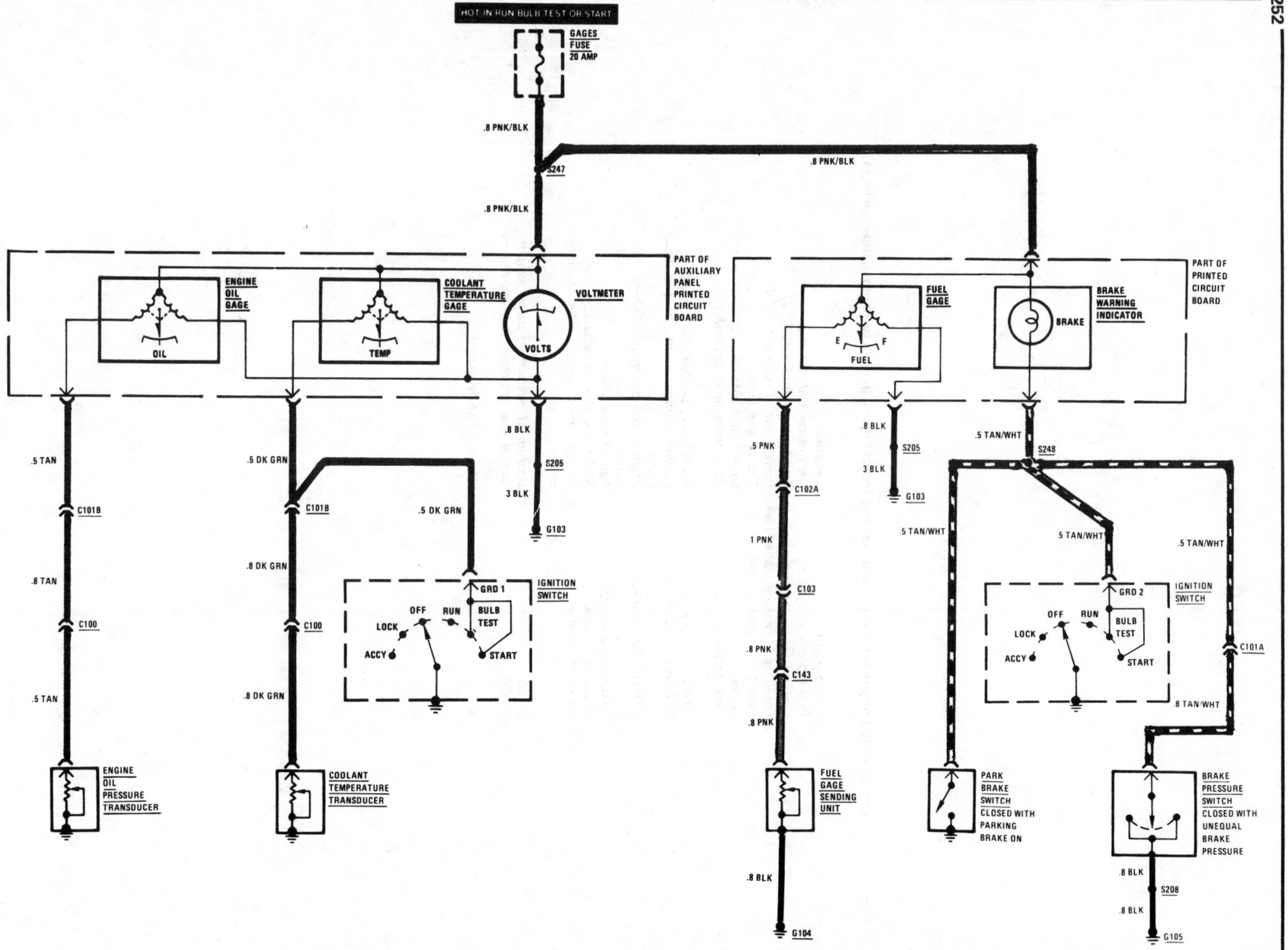

Fig. 10.51 Wiring diagram for the brake warning indicator and gauges (optional gauge package) (Phoenix)

253

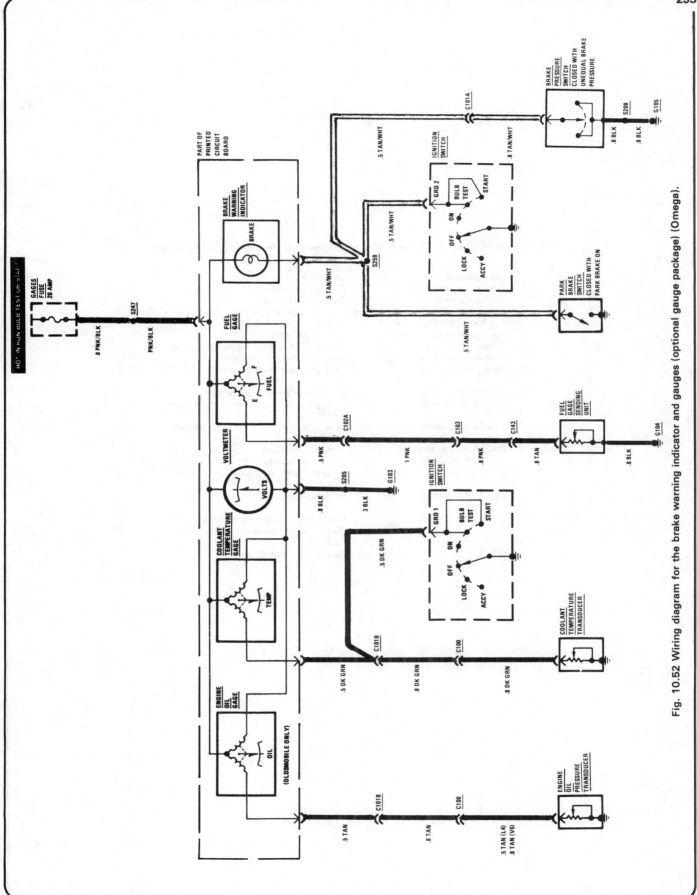

Fig. 10.52 Wiring diagram for the brake warning indicator and gauges (optional gauge package) (Omega).

Key to wiring diagram for the choke heater, warning indicators and fuel gauge

Component	Location
Brake pressure switch	On master cylinder
Choke heater	Side of carburetor
Coolant temperature switch	Top front of engine (V6/L4)
Engine oil pressure switch	Above oil filter (V6/L4)
Fuel gage sending unit	Top of gas tank
Fuses	Under right side of instrument panel
Ignition switch connector	Base of steering column
Park brake switch	Part of brake lever assembly
C100 (12 cavities)	Right cowl behind shock tower
C101A (20 cavities)	In engine compartment, behind fuse block
C101B (20 cavities)	In engine compartment, behind fuse block
C102A (7 cavities)	Top of fuse block
C103 (6 cavities)	Right rear quarter extension wall
C143 (1 cavity)	In rear next to gas-filled bumper shock
C147 (4 cavities)	At fuse block
G103	Bottom of instrument panel support
G104	Center rear crossmember, above tank
G105	Above right headlight

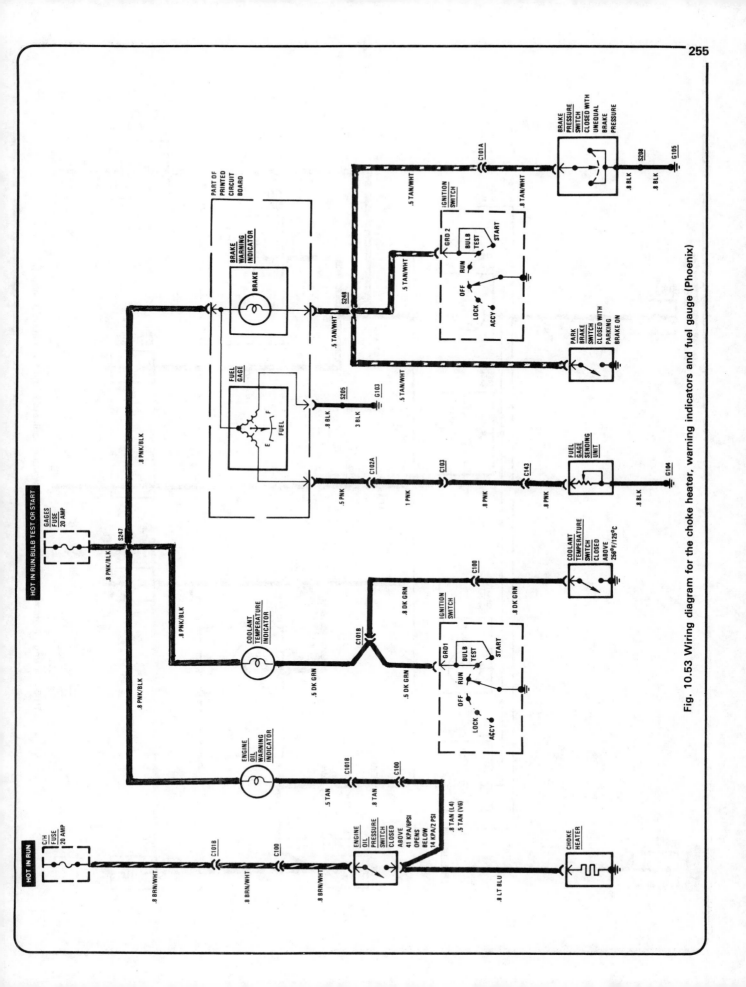

Fig. 10.53 Wiring diagram for the choke heater, warning indicators and fuel gauge (Phoenix)

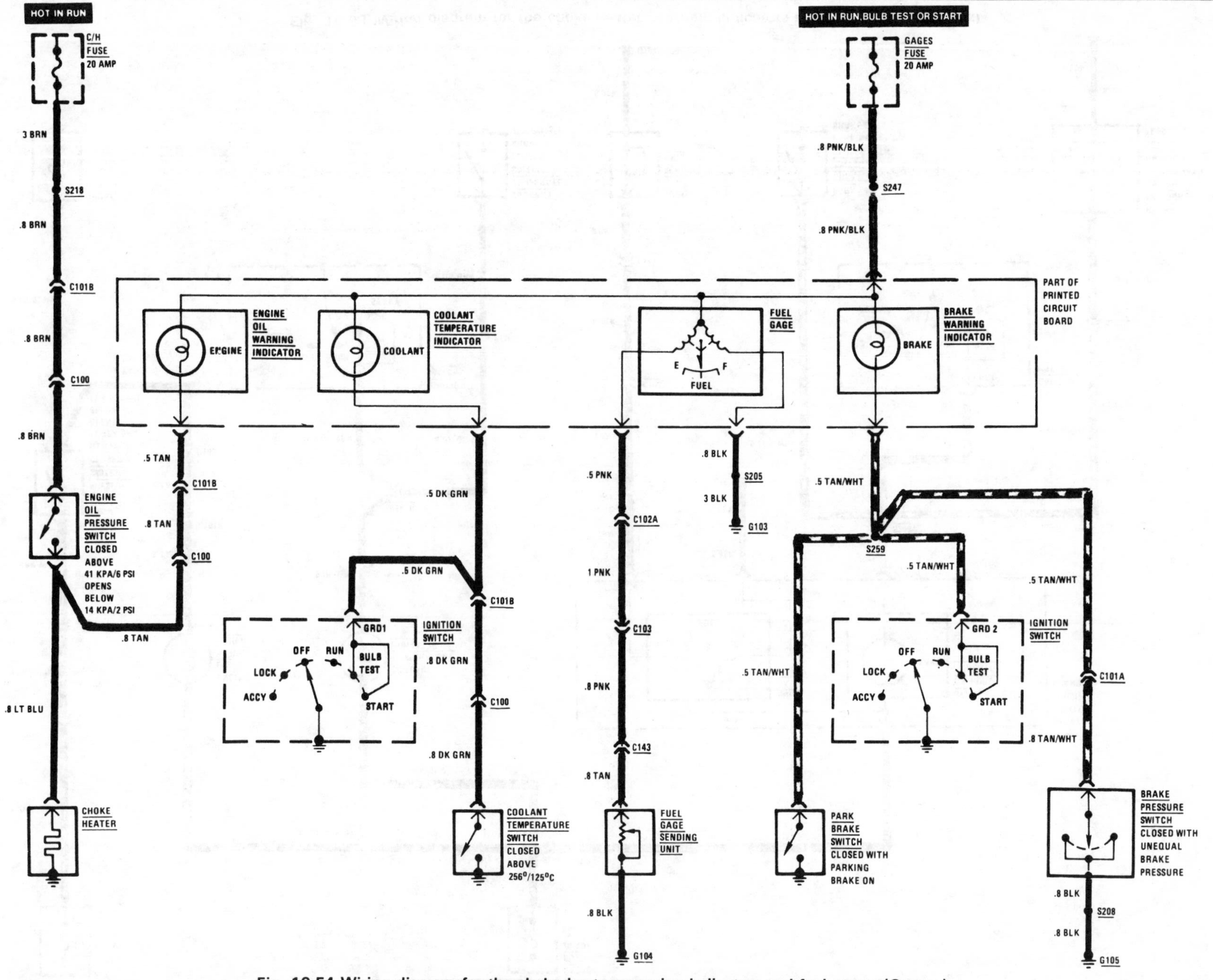

Fig. 10.54 Wiring diagram for the choke heater, warning indicators and fuel gauge (Omega).

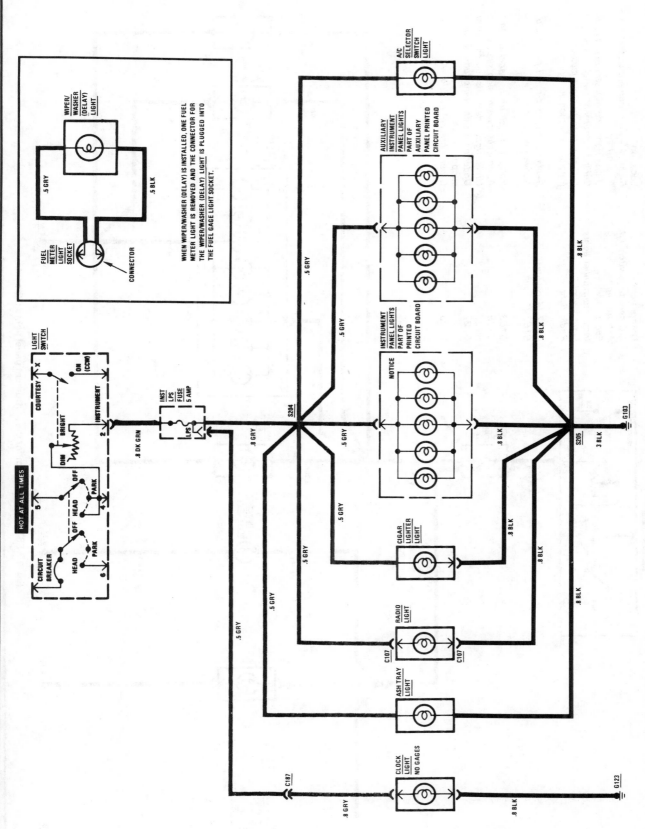

Fig. 10.55 Wiring diagram for the instrument panel lights (Omega). For location of components, refer to the caption for Fig. 10.56

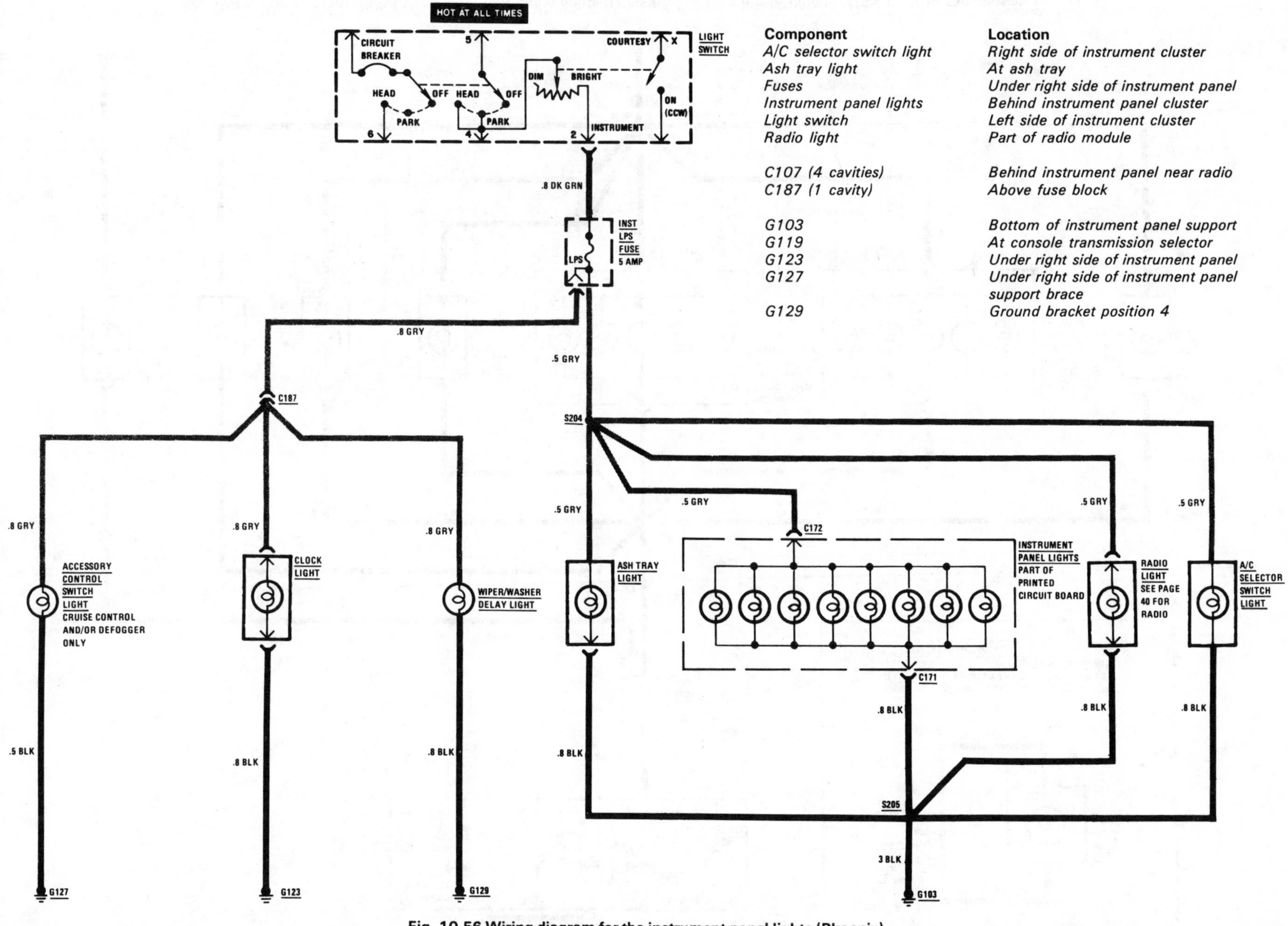

258

Fig. 10.56 Wiring diagram for the instrument panel lights (Phoenix)

Location
Right side of instrument cluster
At ash tray
Under right side of instrument panel
Behind instrument panel cluster
Left side of instrument cluster
Part of radio module

Behind instrument panel near radio
Above fuse block

Bottom of instrument panel support
At console transmission selector
Under right side of instrument panel
Under right side of instrument panel
support brace
Ground bracket position 4

Component
A/C selector switch light
Ash tray light
Fuses
Instrument panel lights
Light switch
Radio light

C107 (4 cavities)
C187 (1 cavity)

G103
G119
G123
G127

G129

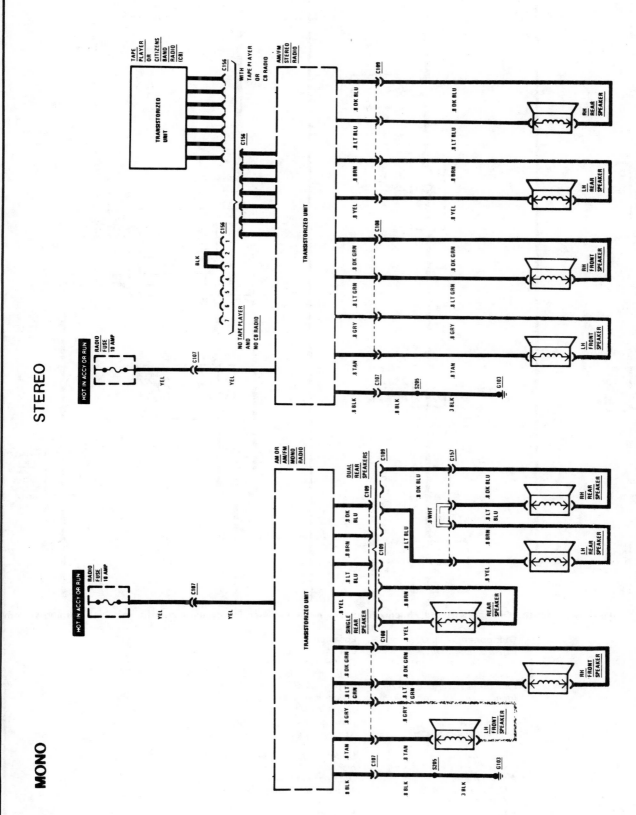

Fig. 10.57 Wiring diagram for the mono and stereo radios. For location of components, refer to the caption for Fig. 10.47

260

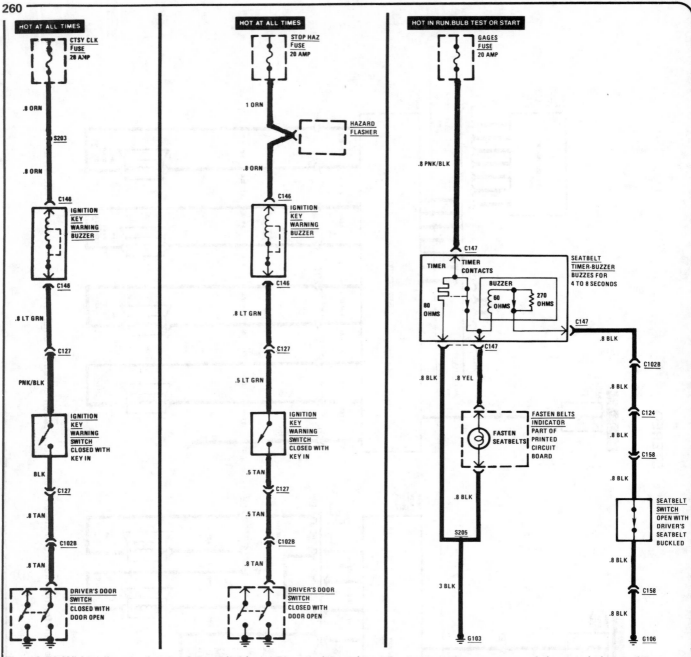

Fig. 10.58 Wiring diagram for the Omega (left) and Phoenix (center) ignition key warning systems and the seat belt warning system (both models)

Component	Location
Driver's door switch	Left door jamb
Fasten belts indicator	Printed circuit board
Fuses	Under right side of instrument panel
Ignition key warning buzzer	At fuse block
Ignition key warning switch	Inside steering column below turn signal switch
Seatbelt switch	Driver's seatbelt retractor
Seatbelt timer-buzzer	At fuse block
C102B (4 cavities)	Under instrument panel, top of fuse block
C124 (1 cavity)	Under driver's seat
C127 (11 cavities)	At base of steering column
C146 (2 cavities)	Fuse block
C147 (4 cavities)	Fuse block
C158 (2 cavities)	At driver's seatbelt retractor
G103	Under driver's seat

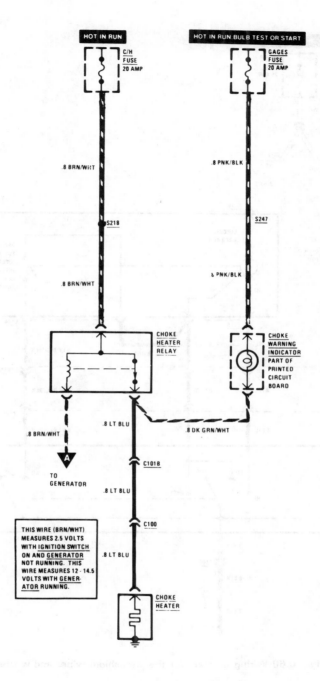

Fig. 10.59 Wiring diagram of the choke heater system (optional gauge package)

Component	Location
Choke heater	On carburetor
Choke heater relay	Behind instrument panel, above ash tray
Choke warning indicator	Part of instrument cluster
Fuses	Under right side of instrument panel at fuse block
C100 (12 cavities)	Right cowl, behind shock tower
C101B (20 cavities)	In engine compartment, behind fuse block
C147 (4 cavities)	Fuse block

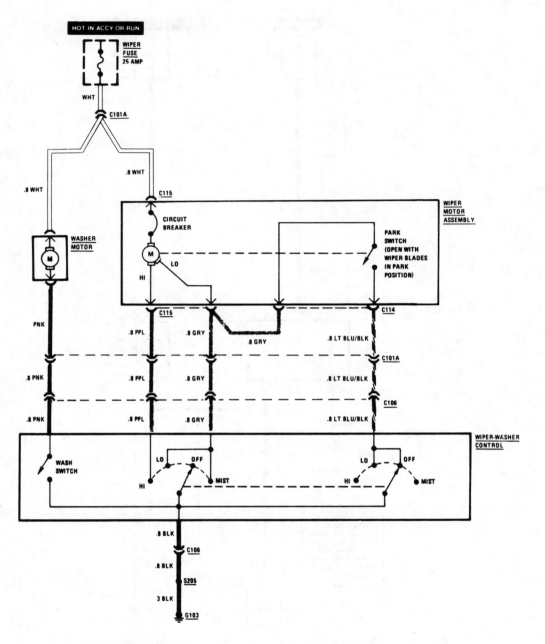

Fig. 10.60 Wiring diagram for the windshield wiper and washer systems

Component	Location
Fuses	Under right side of instrument panel
Washer	Engine compartment, left corner
Wiper motor assembly	Engine compartment, center of cowl
Wiper-washer control	Turn signal lever
C101A (20 cavities)	RH cowl under heater case
C106 (7 cavities)	Base of steering column
C114 (2 cavities)	At wiper motor
C115 (3 cavities)	At wiper motor
G 103	Bottom left instrument panel support

263

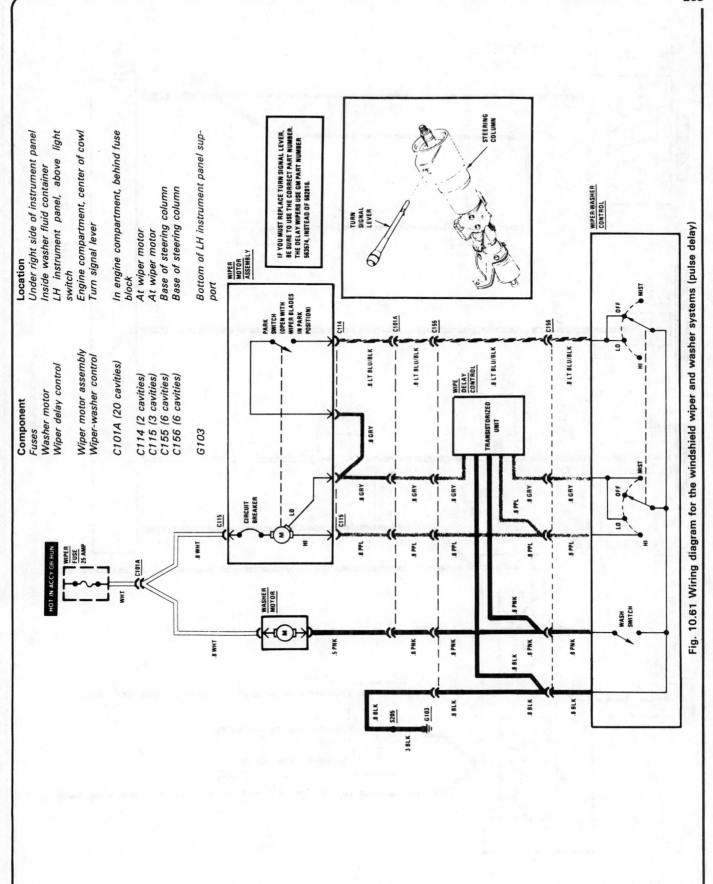

Fig. 10.61 Wiring diagram for the windshield wiper and washer systems (pulse delay)

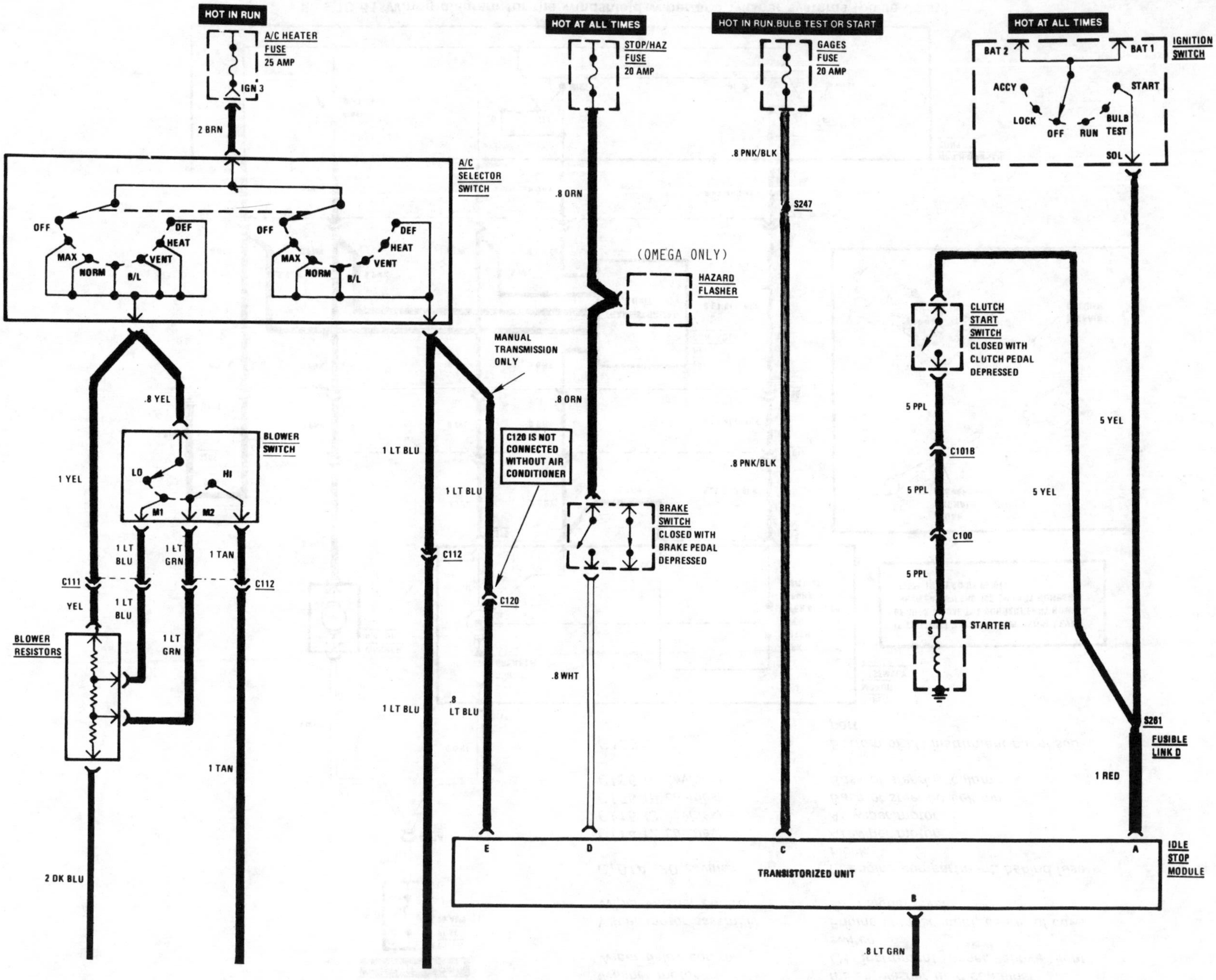

Fig. 10.62 Wiring diagram for the air conditioning system and idle stop solenoid (V6)

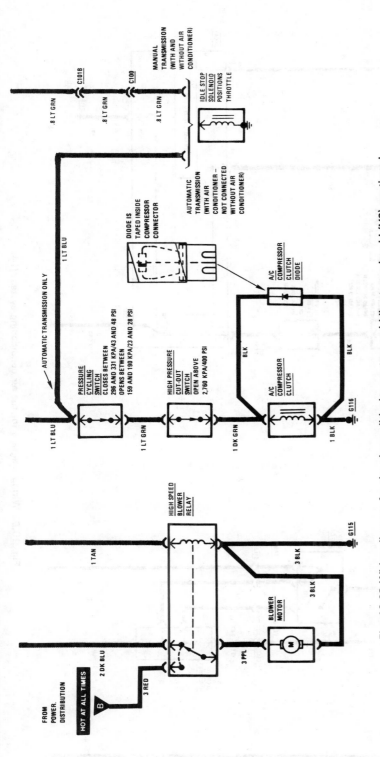

Fig. 10.62 Wiring diagram for the air conditioning system and idle stop solenoid (V6) continued

Component	Location
A/C compressor clutch	On compressor
A/C compressor clutch diode	At compressor
A/C selector switch	Center of instrument panel
Blower motor	Right cowl
Blower resistors	Engine compartment on heater case
Blower switch	Center of instrument panel
Brake switch	Top of brake pedal support
Fuses	Under right side of instrument panel
Fusible link D	AT idle stop module
High pressure cut-out switch	Near compressor
High speed blower relay	Right side of cowl
Idle stop module	Left instrument panel
Idle stop solenoid	Near carburetor
Pressure cylinder switch	On accumulator

Component	Location
C100 (12 cavities)	Right cowl behind shock tower
C101B (20 cavities)	In engine compartment, behind fuse block
C111 (2 cavities)	Behind instrument panel, near fuse block
C112 (3 cavities)	Behind instrument panel, near fuse block
C113 (1 cavity)	Right rear engine
C120 (1 cavity)	Center of instrument panel
G115	Right front cowl, near heater blower case
G116	Right front fender

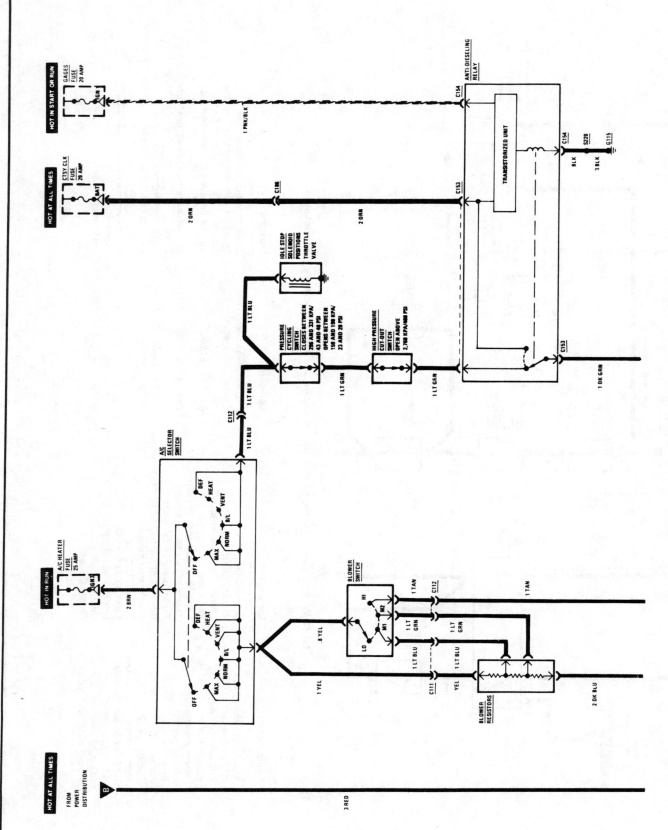

Fig. 10.63 Wiring diagram for the air conditioning system (L4)

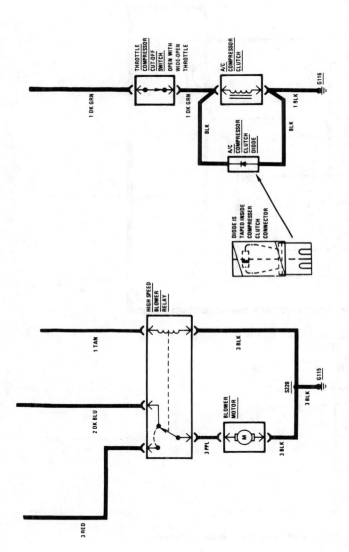

Fig. 10.63 Wiring diagram for the air conditioning system (L4) continued

Component	Location
A/C compressor clutch	On compressor
A/C compressor clutch diode	At compressor
A/C selector switch	On instrument panel, right side of steering column
Anti-dieseling relay	Center instrument panel support brace
Blower motor	Right side of cowl
Blower resistors	Engine compartment, near blower motor
Blower switch	On instrument panel, right side of steering column
Pressure cycling switch	On accumulator
Fuses	Under right side instrument
High pressure cut-out switch	Engine compartment, left side of cowl
High speed blower relay	RH side of cowl
Idle stop solenoid	Near carburetor
Throttle compressor cut-off switch	Top of engine near carburetor

Component	Location
C111 (2 cavities)	Behind instrument panel, near fuse block
C112 (3 cavities)	Behind instrument panel, near fuse block
C113 (1 cavity)	Engine compartment
C153 (3 cavities)	Behind instrument panel at anti-dieseling relay
C154 (2 cavities)	Behind instrument panel at anti-dieseling relay
C186 (1 cavity)	At fuse block
G115	Under instrument panel at support brace
G116	Above right headlight

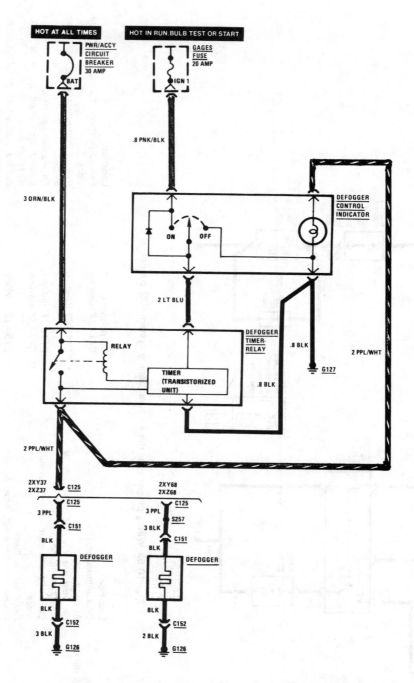

Fig. 10.64 Wiring diagram for the rear window defogger system (Phoenix)

Component	Location
Fuses	Under right side of instrument panel, at fuse block
Defogger	Rear window
Defogger control-indicator	Left side of instrument panel
Defogger timer-relay	Near fuse block
C125 (1 cavity)	Right instrument panel, near fuse block
C151 (1 cavity)	At right rear window counter balance (liftgate)
	At right side of rear window (sedan)
C152 (1 cavity)	At left rear window counter balance (liftgate)
	At left side rear window (sedan)
G126	Near left counter balance (liftgate)
	Left upper corner 'C' pillar (sedan)
G127	Bottom of instrument panel support

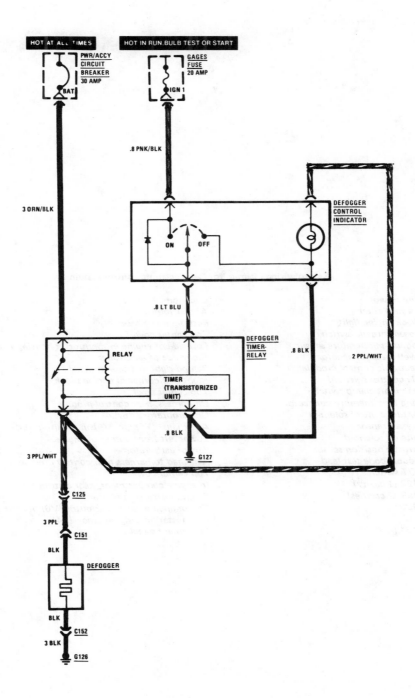

Fig. 10.65 Wiring diagram for the rear window defogger system (Omega). For location of components see the caption for Fig. 10.64

Key to wiring diagram for C-4 electronic control system

Component	Location
C-4 tach filter	At distributor
Check engine light	Part of cluster assembly
Closed throttle switch	Top center cowl
Coolant temperature sensor	Left side of engine in thermostat housing (V6/L4)
Dwell meter connector	Right side of air cleaner
Electronic control module	Behind right instrument panel
Idle control solenoid	Right rear corner of engine block
Lean limit clamp switch	Top center cowl
Long term memory connector	On harness, near control module
Mixture control solenoid	On carburetor (V6/L4)
Oxygen sensor	At exhaust 'Y' pipe (V6)/in manifold (L4)
Pulse air solenoid	Lower left front corner of engine
Throttle position sensor	Part of carburetor
Trouble code test lead	Attached to harness near control module
WOT switch	Top center cowl
C122 (1 cavity)	In engine compartment, near distributor
C198 (2 cavities)	Behind instrument cluster
G130	Top of engine, near distributor (V6) or next to thermostat housing on block (L4)
G131	Instrument panel

271

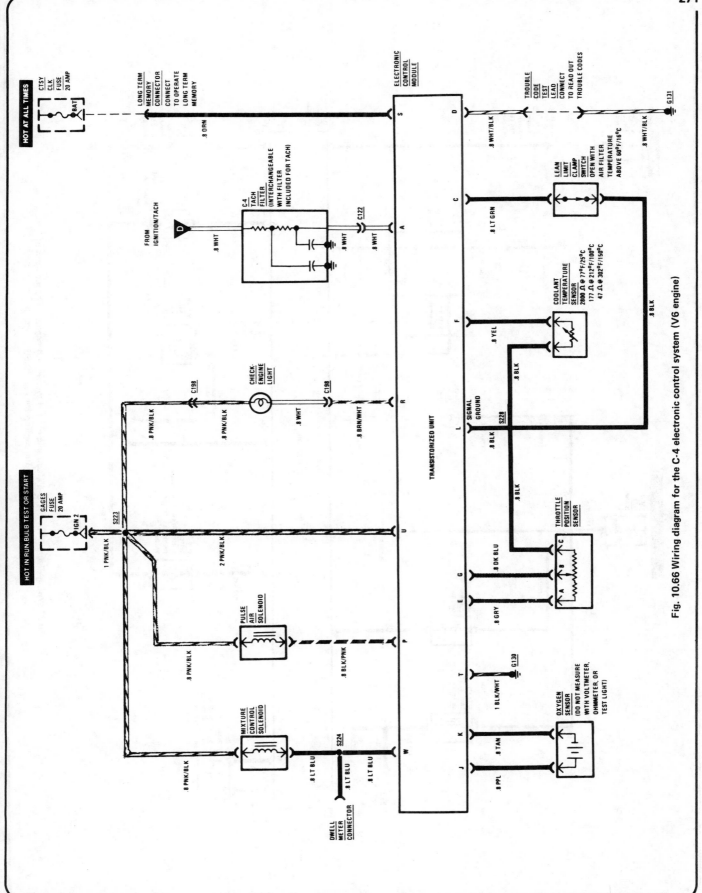

Fig. 10.66 Wiring diagram for the C-4 electronic control system (V6 engine)

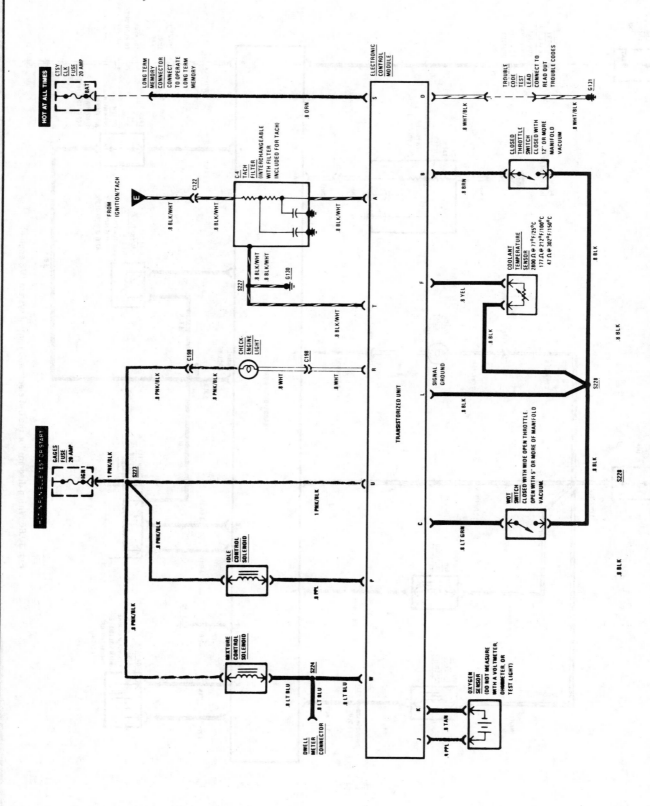

Fig. 10.67 Wiring diagram for the C-4 electronic control system (L4 engine). For location of components, see the caption for Fig. 10.66

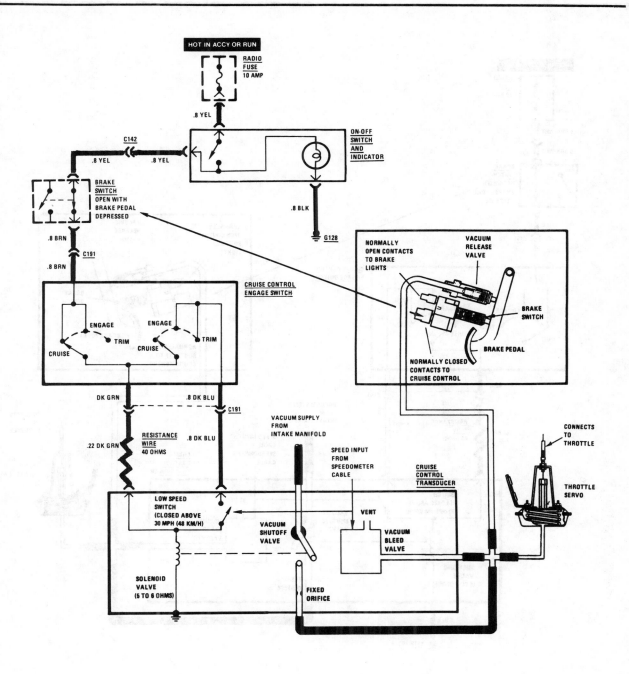

Fig. 10.68 Wiring diagram for the cruise control system (Omega)

Component	Location
Brake switch	Brake pedal lever bracket
Cruise control engage switch	Transmission shift selector lever
Cruise control transducer	Left front shock tower
Fuses	Under right side of instrument panel
Throttle servo	Top left side of engine
C142 (1 cavity)	Right instrument panel near fuse panel
C191 (3 cavities)	Behind left instrument panel
G110	Near cruise control transducer
G128	Bottom of instrument panel support

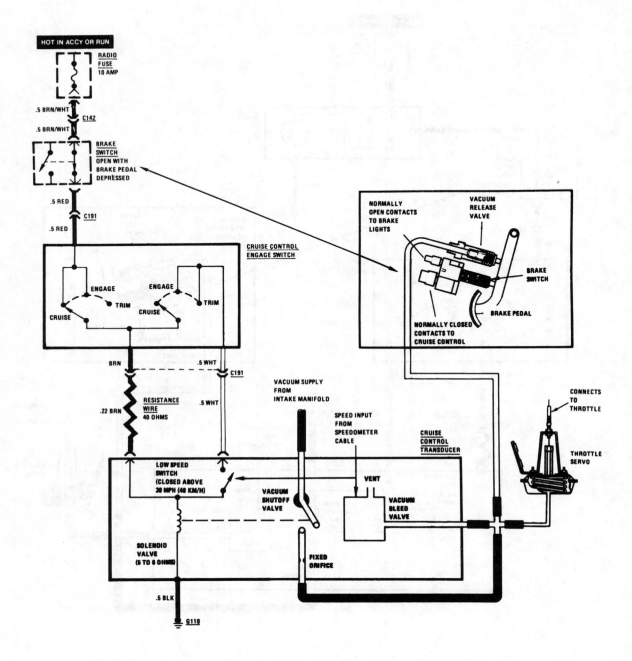

Fig. 10.69 Wiring diagram for the cruise control system (Phoenix)

Component	Location
Brake switch	Brake pedal lever bracket
Cruise control engage switch	Transmission shift selector lever
Cruise control transducer	Left front shock tower
Fuses	Under right side of instrument panel
Throttle servo	Top left side of engine
C142 (1 cavity)	Left side of instrument panel
C191 (3 cavities)	Behind left instrument panel
G110	Near cruise control transducer

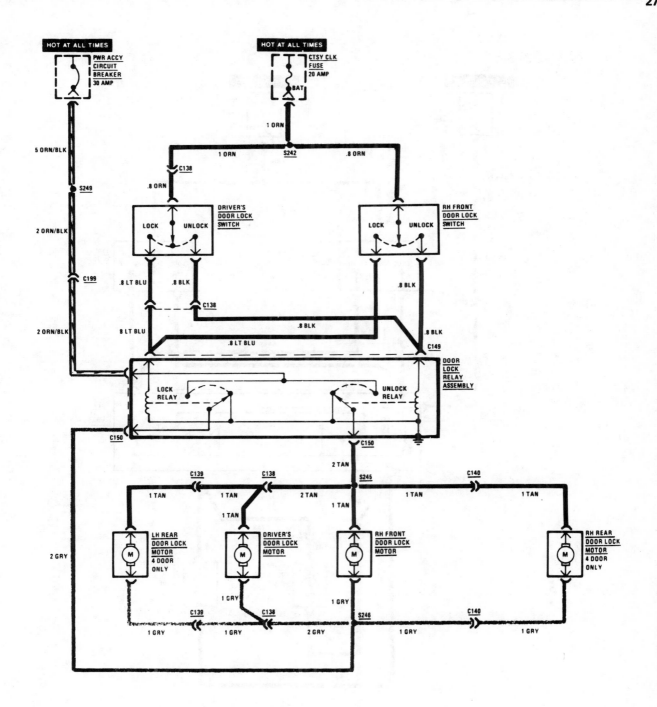

Fig. 10.70 Wiring diagram for the power door lock system (4-door models)

Component	Location
Door lock motors	In doors
Door lock relay assembly	Right shroud
Driver's door lock switch	On driver's door
Fuses	Under right side instrument panel at fuse block
PWR ACCY circuit breaker	Fuse block
Right front door lock switch	On right front door
C138 (5 cavities)	Left shroud at lower access hole
C139 (2 cavities)	Left shroud at lower access hole
C140 (2 cavities)	Right shroud at lower access hole
C149 (2 cavities)	Right shroud top of relay
C150 (3 cavities)	Right shroud top of relay
C199 (1 cavity)	Right instrument panel, near fuse block

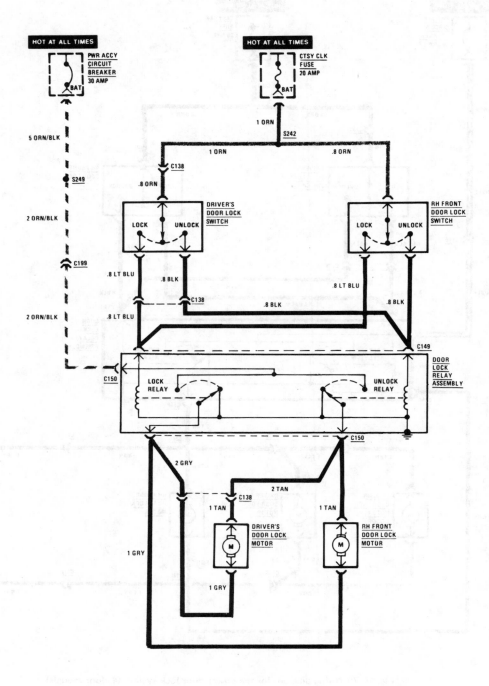

Fig. 10.71 Wiring diagram for the power door lock system (2-door models). For location of components, see the caption for Fig. 10.70

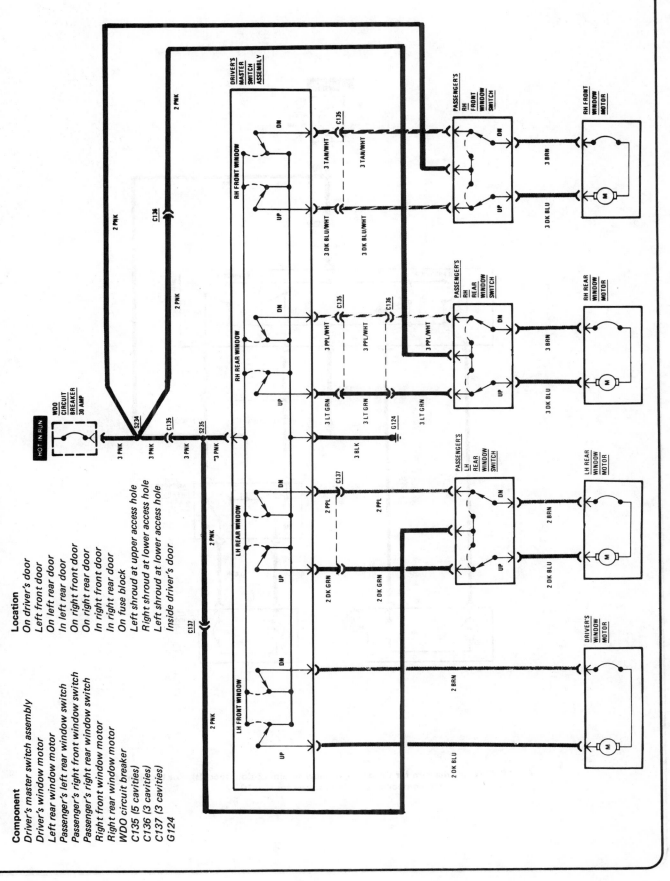

Fig. 10.72 Wiring diagram for the power window system (4-door models)

Component

Driver's master switch assembly
Driver's window motor
Left rear window motor
Passenger's left rear window switch
Passenger's right front window switch
Passenger's right rear window switch
Right front window motor
Right rear window motor
WDO circuit breaker
C135 (5 cavities)
C136 (3 cavities)
C137 (3 cavities)
G124

Location

On driver's door
Left front door
On left rear door
In left rear door
On right front door
On right rear door
In right front door
In right rear door
On fuse block
Left shroud at upper access hole
Right shroud at lower access hole
Left shroud at lower access hole
Inside driver's door

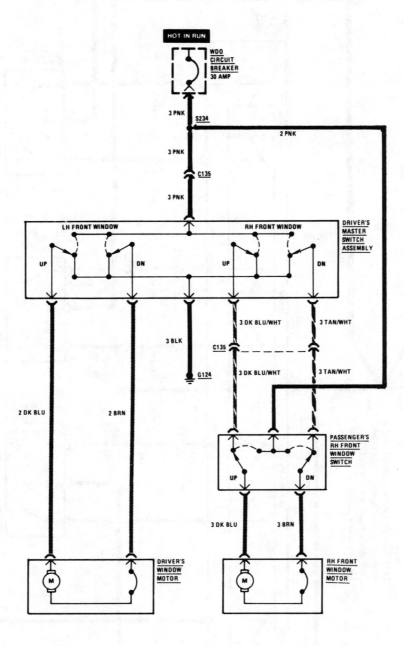

Fig. 10.73 Wiring diagram for the power window system (2-door models). For location of components see the caption for Fig. 10.72

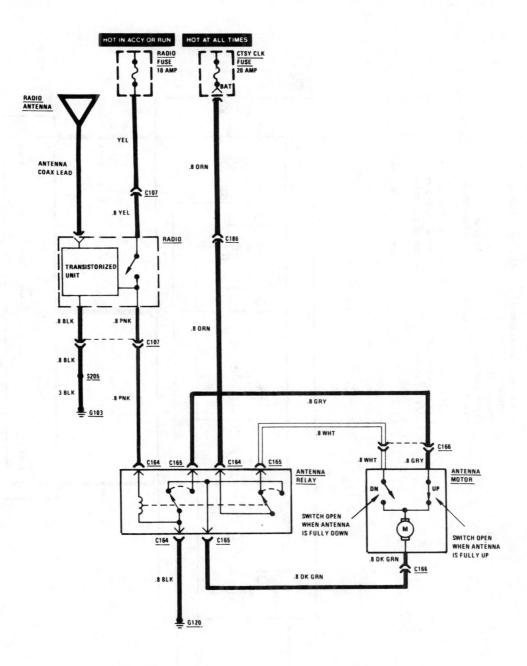

Fig. 10.74 Wiring diagram for the power antenna system

Component	Location
Antenna motor	Bottom right front fender
Antenna relay	Behind right side of instrument panel
C107 (4 cavities)	Behind instrument panel, near radio
C164 (3 cavities)	At antenna relay
C165 (3 cavities)	At antenna relay
C166 (3 cavities)	At antenna motor
C186 (1 cavity)	At fuse panel
G103	Bottom of instrument panel support
G120	Instrument panel center support brace

HOT AT ALL TIMES

Component	Location
Power seat clutch control solenoids	Attached to motor
Power seat motor	Under seat
Power seat relay	Under seat
Power seat switch assembly	Driver's front door
C169 (2 cavities)	Under driver's seat
C181 (3 cavities)	At power seat relay
C182 (2 cavities)	At power seat relay
C122	Under left side of driver's seat

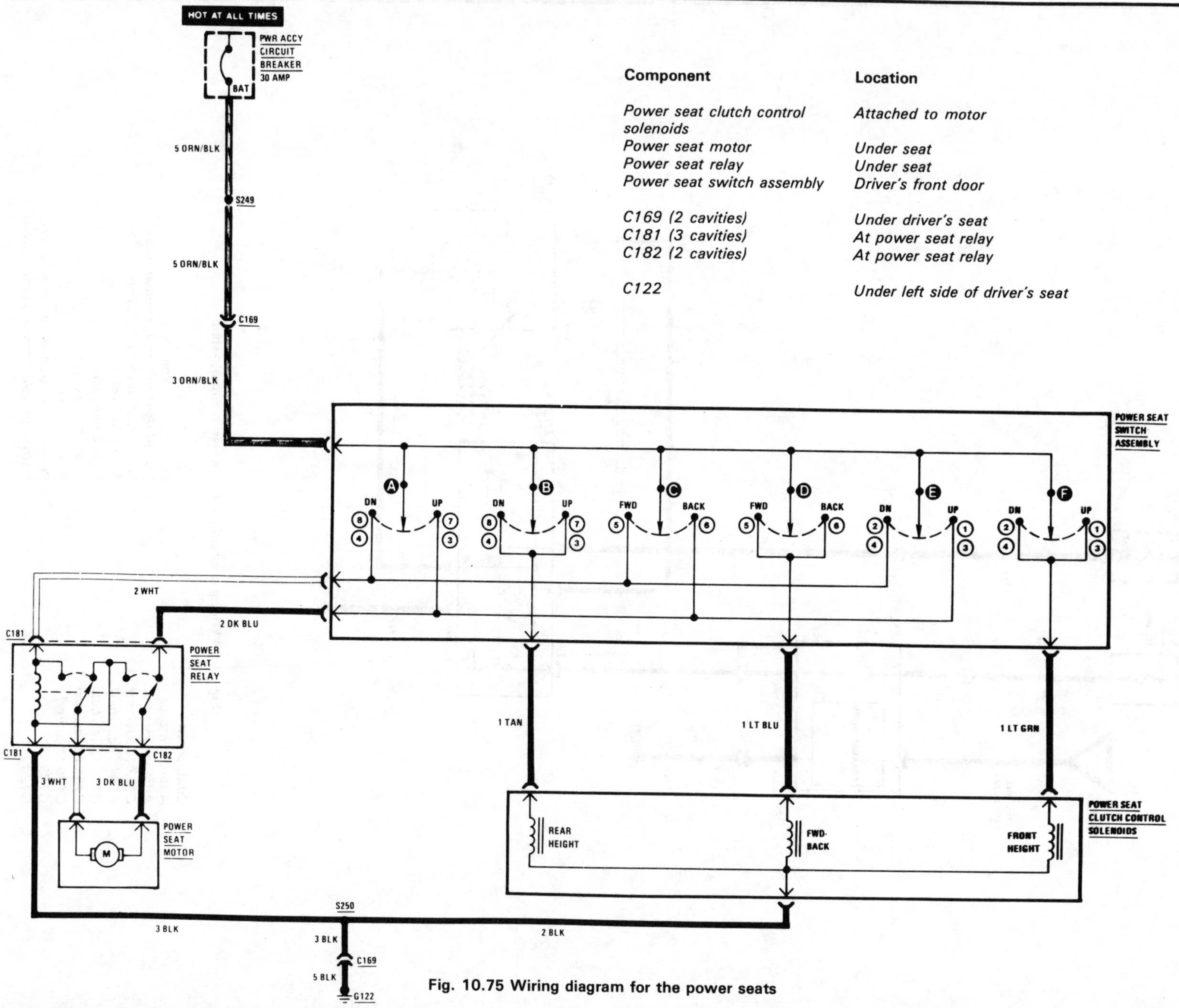

Fig. 10.75 Wiring diagram for the power seats

Chapter 11 Suspension and steering systems

Refer to Chapter 13 for specifications and information related to 1981 through 1984 models

Contents

Specifications

Power steering system capacity .... 3/4 qts (0.7 liters)

Power steering pump capacity .... $\frac{1}{2}$ qts (0.5 liters)

Pinion preload
Power system .... 8 to 16 in-lbs (0.09 to 0.18 m-kg)
Manual system .... 8 to 10 in-lbs (0.09 to 0.11 m-kg)

Front wheel alignment
Camber adjustment .... +.50° ± .50°
Toe-in adjustment (per wheel) .... +2.5 mm ± 2.5 mm (+.10° ± .10°)

Tires
Standard .... P185/80R13 fiberglass belted radial
Optional .... P185/80R13 steel belted radial
Optional .... P207/70R13 steel belted radial
Compact spare .... T125/70D14 fiberglass belted radial

Wheel size .... 13 x 5.5

Compact spare wheel size .... 14 x 4

Superlift shocks
Maximum pressure .... 90 psi (620 kPa)
Minimum pressure .... 10 psi (70 kPa)

Torque specifications	ft-lb	m-kg
Front suspension		
Stabilizer bar retaining plate bolts	40	5.5
Stabilizer bar bracket nuts	35	4.8

	ft-lb	m-kg
Strut damper assembly upper attaching nuts	18	2.5
Strut damper assembly lower attaching nuts	140	19.3
Strut damper assembly upper retaining nut	68	9.4
Balljoint retaining nuts	8	1.1
Balljoint to steering knuckle nut	45	6.2
Lower control arm to engine cradle bolts	48	6.6
Front hub nut	225	31.0
Hub and bearing assembly attaching bolts	63	8.7
Tie rod to steering knuckle nut	40	5.5

Rear suspension

Rear shock absorber upper attaching nut	7	1.0
Rear shock absorber lower attaching nut	34	4.7
Track bar to axle nut	33	4.5
Track bar to underbody nut	34	4.7
Control arm bracket to control arm nut	34	4.7
Control arm bracket to underbody bolt	20	2.7
Brake line bracket to frame screw	8	1.1
Hub and bearing assembly attaching bolts	74	10.2

Steering wheel and column

Steering wheel to shaft nut	30	4.1
Steering column to intermediate shaft	45	6.2
Turn signal switch attaching screws	35 in-lb	0.4
Ignition switch attaching screws	35 in-lb	0.4
Cover to housing screws	100 in-lb	1.15
Column to dash attaching bolts	20	2.7

Rack and pinion assembly

Adjuster plug lock nut	50	6.9
Inner tie rod housing to rack	70	9.6
Outer tie rod jam nut	50	6.9
Cylinder line fittings (power system)	15	2.0
Pinion shaft to intermediate shaft bolt	45	6.2
Rack and pinion assembly attaching bolts	24	3.3
Pinion lock nut (power system)	26	3.6

Power steering pump

Pump attaching bolts and nut (L4 engine)	38	5.2
Pump attaching bolts (V6 engine)	25	3.4
Pump attaching nut (V6 engine)	29	4.0
Pressure hose to pump	20	2.7
Power steering fluid line connections	20	2.7

Wheels

Wheel lug nuts	103	14.2

1 Wheels and tires – general information

1   All X-Body cars are equipped with metric-sized fiberglass or steel belted radial tires. The metric tire size code is shown in Fig. 11.1. Use of other size or type of tires may affect the ride and handling of the car. Do not mix different types of tires such as radials and bias belted on the same car, as handling may be seriously affected.

2   It is recommended that tires be replaced in pairs on the same axle, but if only one tire is being replaced, be sure it is of the same size, structure and tread design as the other.

3   Because tire pressure has a substantial effect on handling and wear, the pressure on all tires should be checked at least once a month or before any extended trips and set to the correct pressure. Tire pressure should be checked and adjusted with the tires cold.

4   To achieve the maximum life of your tires they should be rotated on the car as shown in Fig. 11.2 at 7500 miles and then again at every 15 000-mile interval, as outlined in the car's routine maintenance schedule and detailed in Chapter 1, Section 5.

5   The tires should be replaced when the depth of the tread pattern is worn to a minimum of $\frac{1}{16}$-in (1.5 mm). Correct tire pressures and driving techniques have an important influence on tire life. Heavy cornering, excessively rapid acceleration and sharp braking increase tire wear. Extremely worn tires are not only very susceptible to going flat but are especially dangerous in wet weather conditions.

6   The tire tread pattern can give a good indication of problems in the maintenance or adjustment of tires, suspension and front end compo-

nents. Fig. 11.3 gives some common examples of tire wear patterns and their unusual causes. If a tire exhibits a wear pattern caused by incorrect front end alignment, refer to Section 3.

7   Wheels must be replaced if they are bent, dented, leak air, have elongated bolt holes, are heavily rusted, ovaled, out of vertical symmetry or if the lug nuts won't stay tight. Wheel repairs that use welding or peening are not recommended, as this can weaken the metal.

8   Tire and wheel balance is important in the overall handling, braking and performance of the car. Unbalanced wheels can adversely affect handling and ride characteristics as well as tire life. Whenever a tire is installed on a wheel, the tire and wheel should be balanced by a qualified shop with the proper equipment.

9   All X-Body cars are equipped with a compact spare tire which is designed to save space in the trunk as well as being easier to handle due to its lighter weight. The spare tire pressure should be checked at least once a month, and maintained at 60 psi (412 kPa).

10   The compact spare tire and wheel are designed for use with each other only, and neither the tire nor the wheel should be coupled with other types or sizes of wheels and tires.

11   Because the compact spare is designed as a temporary replacement for an out-of-service standard wheel and tire, the compact spare should be used on the car only until the standard wheel and tire are repaired or replaced. Continuous use of the compact spare at speeds of over 50 mph (80 kph) is not recommended. In addition, the expected tread life of the compact spare is only about 3000 miles (4800 kilometers).

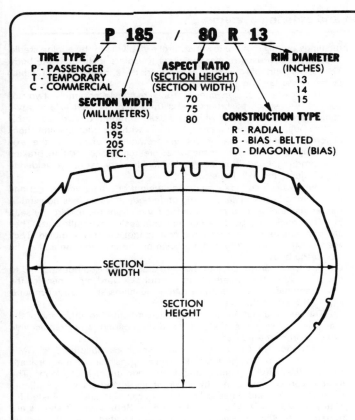

P 185 / 80 R 13

TIRE TYPE
P - PASSENGER
T - TEMPORARY
C - COMMERCIAL

SECTION WIDTH
(MILLIMETERS)
185
195
205
ETC.

ASPECT RATIO
(SECTION HEIGHT)
(SECTION WIDTH)
70
75
80

RIM DIAMETER
(INCHES)
13
14
15

CONSTRUCTION TYPE
R - RADIAL
B - BIAS - BELTED
D - DIAGONAL (BIAS)

SECTION WIDTH

SECTION HEIGHT

Fig. 11.1 Metric tire size code (Sec 1)

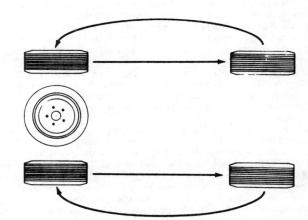

Fig. 11.2 Tires should be rotated as shown at recommended intervals (Sec 1)

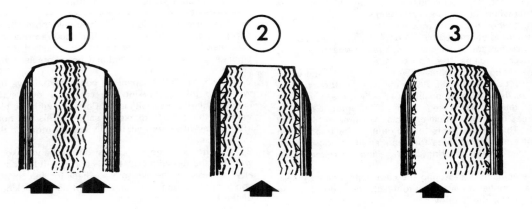

Fig. 11.3 Common tire wear patterns (Sec 1)

1 Wear at outer edges –
   tire underinflated
2 Wear at center – tire
   overinflated

3 Wear at one side –
   incorrect wheel alignment.
   Check camber and toe-in
   adjustments

2 Wheel and tire — removal and installation

1   With the car on a level surface, the parking brake on and the car in gear (manual transaxles should be in 'Reverse'; automatic transaxles should be in 'Park') remove the hub trim ring and loosen, but do not remove, the wheel lug nuts.

2   Using a jack positioned in the proper location on the car, raise the car just enough so that the tire clears the ground surface.

3   Remove the lug nuts.

4   Remove the wheel and tire.

5   If a flat tire is being replaced, ensure that there's adequate ground clearance for the new inflated tire, then mount the wheel and tire on the wheel studs.

6   Apply a light coat of spray lubricant or light oil to the wheel stud threads and install the lug nuts snugly with the cone-shaped end facing the wheel.

7   Lower the car until the tire contacts the ground and the wheel studs are centered in their wheel holes.

8   Tighten the lug nuts evenly and in a cross-pattern, and torque to specs.

9   Lower the car completely and remove the jack.

10 Replace the hub trim ring.

3 Front end alignment

1   A front end alignment refers to the adjustments made to the front wheels so that they are in proper angular relationship to the suspension and the ground. Front wheels that are out of proper alignment not only affect steering control but also increase tire wear. The only front end adjustments required on the X-Body cars are camber and toe-in.

2   Getting the proper front wheel alignment is a very tedious, exacting process and one in which complicated and expensive machines are necessary to perform the job properly. Because of this, it is advisable to have a specialist with the proper equipment perform these tasks.

3   We will, however, use this space to give you a basic idea of what is involved with front end alignment so you can better understand the process and deal intelligently with shops which do this work.

4   Toe in is the turning in of the front wheels. The purpose of a toe specification is to ensure parallel rolling of the front wheels. In a car with zero toe in in the distance between the front edges of the wheels will be the same as the distance between the rear edges of the wheels. The actual amount of toe in is normally only a fraction of an inch. The X-Body cars have a static toe in of approximately 2.5 mm per wheel. Thus the distance between the front edges of the wheels should be about 5 mm less than the distance of the rear edges of the wheels when the car is standing. This is because even when the wheels are set to toe in slightly when the vehicle is standing still, they tend to roll parallel on the road when the car is moving.

5   Toe in adjustment is controlled by the outer tie rod's position on the inner tie rod. Incorrect toe in will cause the tires to wear improperly by making them 'scrub' against the road surface.

6   Camber is the tilting of the front wheels from the vertical when viewed from the front of the vehicle. When the wheels tilt outward at the top, the camber is said to be positive (+). When the wheels tilt inward at the top the camber is negative (−). The amount of tilt is measured in degrees from the vertical and this measurement is called the camber angle. This angle affects the amount of tire tread which contacts the road and compensates for changes in the suspension geometry when the car is cornering or travelling over undulating surfaces.

7   The camber is adjusted by rotating the cam bolts located where the strut damper assemblies are attached to the steering knuckles. The correct camber angle for the X-Body cars is +.50° ± .50°.

4 Suspension system — general information

1   The X-Bodies feature an independent front suspension of the MacPherson Strut design. This design uses a combination strut and shock absorber assembly which is mounted directly to the steering knuckle. A lower control arm which pivots on the engine cradle is also attached to the steering knuckle by way of a balljoint.

2   To minimize the transmission of vibration to the body, rubber bushings are used in the lower control arm pivots in the engine cradle. The cradle also uses rubber bushings to isolate itself from the body. The upper end of the strut is isolated by a rubber mount which contains the bearing for wheel turning.

3   The rear suspension consists of a rear axle assembly, two coil springs, two shock absorbers and a track bar. The rear axle has two control arms welded to it which are used to mount the axle assembly to the body. These control arms, together with the track bar and shock absorbers, maintain the proper geometric relationship of the axle assembly to the body under the forces created by accelerating, braking and cornering. In addition, a non-serviceable stabilizer bar is welded to the inside of the axle housing.

4   The two coil springs support the weight of the car in the rear and are retained between seats in the underbody and rear axle housing. A rubber insulator is used to isolate the spring from the underbody seat.

5   The shock absorbers are conventional sealed hydraulic units. They are non-adjustable, non-refillable and cannot be disassembled. They are mounted at the bottom to a bracket on the axle housing and at the top to the body.

6   The track bar attaches to the right side of the axle housing and to the left side of the underbody to control sideward movement of the axle assembly. Non-replaceable rubber bushings are used for mounting both ends of the bar.

7   The rear hub and bearing assemblies, mounted to either end of the rear axle, are single, sealed units and the bearing is not replaceable separate from the hub assembly.

8   An option to the conventional rear shock absorbers is GM's Superlift system. This is a system which gives the car greater load-carrying flexibility by maintaining a level ride under heavy loads. The system consists of normal hydraulic shock absorbers with a pliable neophrene boot and an air cylinder built around it, and is adjusted for different loads by varying the air pressure. Both Superlift shocks are routed by flexible air lines to one air valve located inside the fuel fill door, so the air pressure is equal in both units at all times. They are mounted in the same location as conventional shocks and are designed so that the shock absorber function is not impaired in the event of accidental air loss.

9   While the air lines used in the Superlift system are flexible, care should be taken not to kink them and to keep them at a safe distance from all exhaust system parts.

10 To maintain the best ride characteristics with an empty car, the air pressure within the Superlift system should be kept at a minimum of 10 psi (70 kPa). To adjust for loads, the air pressure may be increased up to a maximum of 90 psi (620 kPa).

11 Never attempt to heat or straighten any suspension part, as this can weaken the metal or in other ways damage the part.

5 Suspension system — inspection

1   The suspension components should normally last a long time, except in cases where damage has occurred due to an accident. The suspension parts, however, should be checked from time to time for signs of wear which will result in a loss of precision handling and riding comfort.

2   Check that the suspension components have not sagged due to wear. Do this by parking the car on a level surface and visually checking that the car sits level. Compare with the photographs to see whether the car has markedly sagged. This will normally occur only after many miles and will usually appear more on the driver's side of the vehicle.

3   Put the car in gear and take off the handbrake. Grip the steering wheel at the top with both hands and rock it back and forth. Listen for any squeaks or metallic noises. Feel for free play. If any of these conditions is found, have an assistant do the rocking while the source of the trouble is located.

4   Check the shock absorbers, as these are the parts of the suspension system likely to wear out first. If there is any evidence of fluid leakage, they will definitely need replacing. Bounce the car up and down vigorously. It should feel stiff, and well damped by the shock absorbers. As soon as the bouncing is stopped the car should return to its normal position without excessive up and down movement. Do not replace the shock absorbers as single units, but rather in pairs unless a failure has occurred at low mileage.

5   Check all rubber bushings for signs of deterioration and cracking. If necessary, replace the rubber portions of the suspension arm.

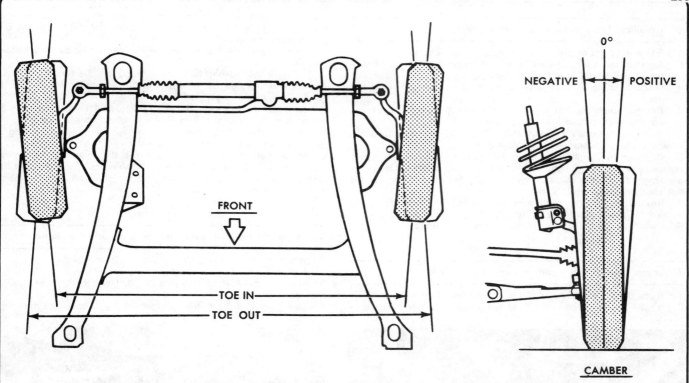

Fig. 11.4 A front end alignment consists of toe-in and camber adjustments as shown (Sec 3)

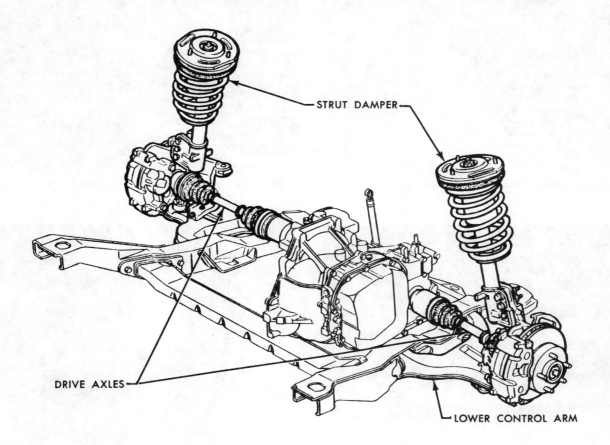

Fig. 11.5 The front suspension and drive axle assemblies (Sec 4)

6 Stabilizer bar – removal and installation

1   Raise the front of the car and support it on jackstands.
2   Remove the spring-loaded bolts that connect the front exhaust crossover pipe to the front intermediate pipe.
3   Disconnect the front crossover pipe from the exhaust manifold and remove.
4   Remove the bolts that secure the stabilizer brackets to the lower control arm and remove the brackets (photo).
5   Remove the bolts that secure the stabilizer mounting plates to the engine cradle and remove both plates (photo).
6   Remove the stabilizer bar from its recesses in the engine cradle, complete with bushings and center brackets. The bushings need not be removed from the stabilizer bar unless either the bushings or the bar are being replaced (photo).
7   Inspect the bearings to be sure they are not hardened, cracked or excessively worn, and replace if necessary.
8   Installation is the reverse of the removal procedure.

7 Lower control arm – removal and installation

1   Raise the front of the car and support it on jackstands.
2   If only one lower control arm is being removed, disconnect only that end of the stabilizer bar. If both lower control arms are being removed, remove the stabilizer bar completely. Refer to Section 6.
3   Remove the wheel.
4   Remove the bolt that retains the balljoint to the steering knuckle (photo).
5   Remove the balljoint from the steering knuckle (photo).
6   Remove the balljoint control arm bushing bolts that secure the control arm to the engine cradle.
7   Remove the control arm. The balljoint does not have to be removed from the control arm unless it needs replacing (photo).
8   Inspect the control arm bushings for hardening, cracking or excessive wear and replace if necessary.
9   Installation of the lower control arm is the reverse of the removal procedure. NOTE: Do not tighten the bushing bolts to their specified torque until the car has been lowered to the ground and its full weight is on the suspension.

8 Lower control arm balljoint – removal and installation

1   Raise the front of the car and support it on jackstands.
2   Remove the wheel.
3   Remove the bolt that retains the balljoint to the brake caliper bracket.
4   Using a $\frac{1}{8}$-in drill bit, drill approximately $\frac{1}{4}$-in deep into the center

6.4 Removing the stabilizer bar bracket from the lower control arm

6.5 Removing the stabilizer bar mounting plate from the engine cradle

6.6 Removing the stabilizer bar, complete with bushings and brackets

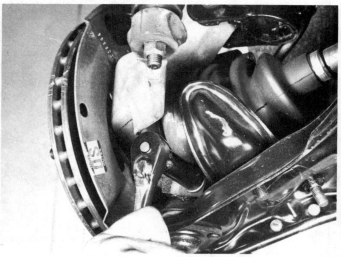
7.4 Removing the pinch bolt that secures the ball joint to the steering knuckle

7.5 Removing the lower control arm's ball joint from the steering knuckle

7.7 Removing the lower control arm from the engine cradle

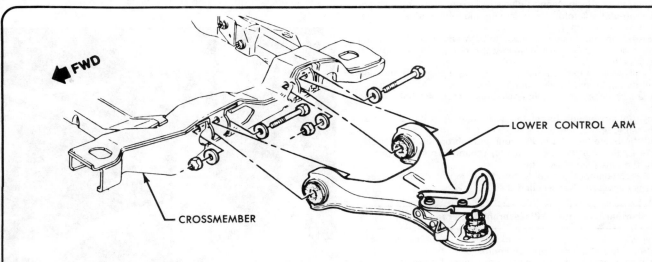

Fig. 11.6 The lower control arm is mounted to the engine cradle by nuts and bolts (Sec 7)

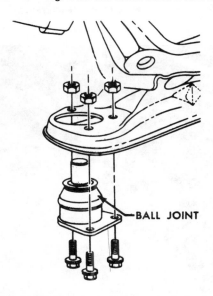

Fig. 11.7 When replacing the balljoint, proper sized nuts and bolts must be used in place of the original mounting rivets (Sec 8)

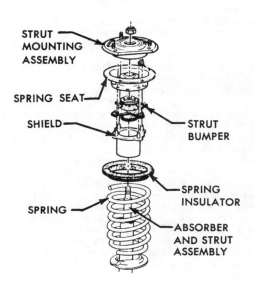

Fig. 11.8 The strut damper assembly (Sec 9)

of the rivets that secure the balljoint to the lower control arm.

5   Using a $\frac{1}{2}$-in drill bit, drill just deep enough to remove the rivet heads.

6   Punch out the remainder of the rivets and remove the ball joint.

7   When reinstalling the balljoint to the lower control arm, use properly sized bolts and nuts to replace the rivets, as shown in Fig. 11.7.

8   Install the balljoint into the steering knuckle, tightening the bolt and nut to their proper torque specs.

9   Mount the wheel and lower the car to the ground.

9 Strut damper assembly – removal and installation

1   Raise the front of the car and support it on jackstands.

2   Remove the wheel.

3   Make a mark on the cam bolt to retain the same camber adjustment upon installation (photo).

4   Loosen, but do not yet remove the strut-to-steering knuckle bolts (photo).

5   Loosen, but do not yet remove the 3 bolts that secure the top of the strut assembly to the shock well, underneath the hood (photo).

6   Disconnect the brake line clip from its mounting tab on the strut.

7   Remove all of the loosened bolts and lift out the strut damper assembly (photo). Be careful not to damage the rubber drive axle boot located below the assembly during removal.

8   If the strut damper assembly needs to be disassembled for spring replacement or any other reason, follow the procedure described in Section 10.

9   To install, position the strut damper assembly in its proper location and install its upper and lower mounting bolts.

10   Place a jack under the hub and disc brake rotor assembly to hold it in position.

11   Lower the car enough to set the cam adjuster in its position as marked in paragraph 3.

12   Install the brake line clip to its mounting tab on the front strut.

13   Torque all the strut damper assembly mounting bolts to specs.

14   Install the wheel and lower the car.

15   If the strut damper assembly has been replaced, a front end alignment is necessary. See Section 3.

10 Strut damper assembly – disassembly and reassembly

1   The spring on the front shock absorber is under considerable pressure, requiring a special spring compressor to be used to safely compress the spring and disengage its components. Do not attempt to disassemble the spring without the proper compressor, as serious injury can occur.

2   A strut spring compressor can either be purchased through GM dealers or though most auto parts stores. Compressors can also be rented on a daily basis from rental agencies and some auto parts stores.

3   Hold the shock in a vise using wood blocks to cushion the jaws to prevent damage to the shock.

4   Following the manufacturer's instructions for the particular spring compressor being used, slightly compress the spring, making sure that the jaws of the compressor are firmly seated around the coils and cannot slip off (photo).

5   Tighten the compressor from side to side, a little at a time, until the spring seat is clear of the uppermost coil.

6   With the spring firmly compressed and clear of its seat, remove the top locknut and washer (photo).

7   Pull the mounting off the top of the shock absorber assembly.

8   Remove the spring seat, bumper, shield and insulator (Fig. 11.8).

9   It is wise at this time to relieve all tension on the spring and remove it from the shock absorber. Loosen the compressor a little at a time until it is free to be lifted off the shock absorber body. Although some compressors would allow you to lift the spring off the shock absorber in its compressed state, this could prove dangerous should the compressor and spring be jostled and accidentally disengaged from each other.

10   The spring should be checked for cracking or deformation of any kind. If the vehicle was sagging in the front, this is an indication that the springs are in need of replacement.

11   Test the front shock absorbers as described in Section 11.

9.3 Mark the position of the camber adjusting bolt cam before removing the strut-to-steering knuckle bolts

9.4 Break loose the strut assembly-to-steering knuckle nuts and bolts

9.5 Removing the strut damper assembly's upper mounting nuts

9.7 Lift out the strut damper assembly

10.4 A suitable spring compressor must be used to disassemble the strut damper assembly

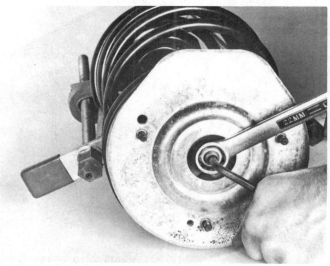

10.6 With the spring compressed, remove the strut assembly upper retaining nut

12.6 Removing the front hub and bearing assembly's mounting bolts

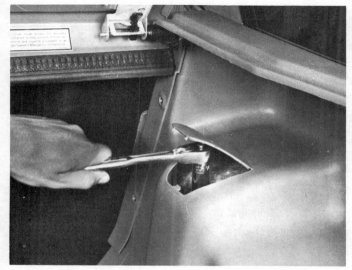

14.1 Open the rear trim cover access panel and remove the rear shock upper mounting nut

14.3 Removing the rear shock lower mounting bolt and nut

12　Using the spring compressor, compress the spring approximately 2 in (50.8 mm). Then with the shock absorber main body mounted in a vise with protective wood blocks, install the spring over the shock absorber body. Make sure the lower coil conforms to the spring seat.

13　Install the insulator, shield and bumper to the shock body.

14　Install the spring seat.

15　Install the mounting assembly.

16　Install the lock washer and locknut to the top of the piston rod. Tighten this nut to a torque of 68 ft-lb (9.3 m-kg).

17　Carefully relieve tension on the \coil spring by loosening the compressor from side to side, a little at a time. Check to be sure the top of the spring is raised properly into its seat.

11　Front shock absorbers – testing

1　To test the shock absorber, hold it in an upright position and work the piston rod up and down its full length of travel, four of five times. If you can feel a strong resistance because of hydraulic pressure, the shock absorber is functioning properly. If you feel no marked resistance or there is a sudden free movement in travel, the shock absorber should be repaired or replaced.

2　If there are excessive amounts of fluid evident on the outside of the shock absorber, the shock absorber should be repaired or replaced.

3　Although it is possible to strip the shock and fit new parts, the work is very intricate and demands extreme cleanliness. Numerous small parts and some special tools will also be necessary. Because of this, it may be wise for the home mechanic to take the shock to a GM dealer or repair shop specializing in MacPherson strut shock absorbers to install a replacement cartridge.

12　Front hub and bearing assembly – removal and installation

1　Break the hub nut loose.

2　Raise the front of the car and support it on jackstands.

3　Remove the front wheel.

4　Remove the disc brake caliper as described in Chapter 9, Section 6. Note: It is not necessary to disconnect the brake line.

5　Remove the hub nut and the brake rotor.

6　Remove the hub and bearing assembly attaching bolts (photo). If the old assembly is to be reinstalled, mark the attaching bolts so they can be installed in the same holes from which they were removed.

7　Using a GM special tool or equivalent puller as shown in Fig. 11.9, remove the hub and bearing assembly from the drive axle.

8　Spin the bearing with your finger and check for any roughness or noise. Also, check the bearing mating surfaces and steering knuckle bore for dirt or nicks. This assembly is a sealed unit and if the bearing needs replacing, the entire hub and bearing assembly must be replaced.

9　If the hub and bearing assembly is being replaced, a new steering knuckle seal must be installed in the steering knuckle prior to installation of the hub and bearing assembly. This is done by applying grease to the seal and its bore in the steering knuckle and then tapping the seal into place using a hammer and the proper sized socket.

10　Install the hub and bearing assembly onto the axleshaft. Then install the hub nut onto the axleshaft and tighten it until the hub and bearing assembly is seated.

11　Install the shield and hub assembly attaching bolts, torquing them to specs.

12　Remove the hub nut, install the rotor on the axleshaft and replace the hub nut on the shaft.

13　Install the brake caliper.

14　Install the wheel and lower the car to the ground.

15　Torque the hub nut to specs.

13　Front wheel stud – removal and installation

1　Raise the front of the car and support it on jackstands.

2　Remove the wheel.

3　Remove the brake caliper as described in Chapter 9, Section 6.

4　Remove the rotor as described in Chapter 9, Section 7.

5　Remove the splash shield.

6　Position the stud to be replaced at either the 5 or 7 o'clock position. Install a lug nut onto the end of the stud and, using a GM

Fig. 11.9 A special puller must be used to remove the front hub and bearing assembly from the drive axle (Sec 12)

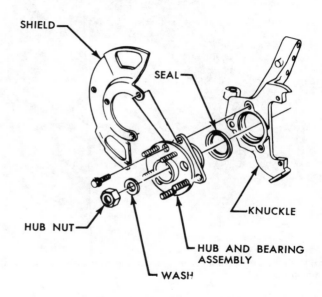

Fig. 11.10 The front hub and bearing assembly and related components (Sec 12)

SHIELD

SEAL

KNUCKLE

HUB NUT

HUB AND BEARING ASSEMBLY

WASH

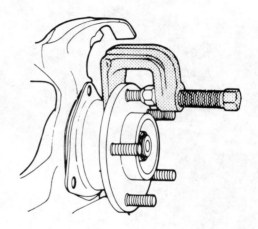

Fig. 11.11 Pressing out a wheel stud from the hub and bearing assembly (Sec 13)

special tool or equivalent as shown in Fig. 11.11, press the stud from its seat.
7   Remove the lug nut, and then the stud.
8   With the stud hole at either the 5 or 7 o'clock position, insert the new stud in the hole, making sure the serrations are aligned with those made by the original bolt.
9   Place four flat washers over the outside end of the stud, and then thread a lug nut onto the stud.
10 Tighten the lug nut until the stud head seats against the rear of the hub. Then remove the lug nut and washer.
11 Reinstall the splash shield, rotor and caliper.
12 Mount the wheel and lower the car to the ground.

14 Rear shock absorber – removal, inspection and installation

1   In the rear compartment of the car, open the upper shock nut access panel in the trim cover (hatchbacks only) and remove the upper shock nut (photo). The upper shock stud must be kept from turning while the nut is loosened.
2   Raise the rear of the car enough to take the weight off of the suspension, but do not lift the tires off the ground. Support the car with jackstands placed at suitable locations under the car's frame. Do not place them under the rear axle. If more clearance is needed under the car, the car can be raised higher, but then the rear axle must also be supported with jackstands.
3   Remove the lower shock attaching bolt and nut and remove the shock (photo). It may be necessary to use a screwdriver to pry the lower end of the shock out of its mounting bracket.
4   The shock should be compressed and then extended its full length a few times to check for any free movement of the shaft, noise, or fluid leakage. If any of these conditions are found the shocks should be replaced with a new set.
5   To install, extend the shock to its full length and place it in its lower mount. Then feed the lower attaching bolt through the mount and shock and install the nut loosely.
6   Lower the car enough to guide the shock's upper stud through the body opening and loosely install the upper attaching nut.
7   Tighten the lower attaching nut, torquing it to specs.

8   Lower the car completely and torque the upper attaching nut to specs. Again the upper shock stud must be kept from turning while tightening the upper nut.
9   On hatchback models, close the access panel in the trim cover.

15 Track bar – removal and installation

1   Raise the rear of the car enough to take the weight off of the suspension, but do not lift the tires off the ground. Support the car with jackstands placed at suitable locations under the frame. Do not place them under the rear axle. If more clearance is needed under the car, the car can be raised higher, but then the rear axle must also be supported with jackstands.
2   Remove the nuts and bolts that secure the track bar at both ends (photo).
3   Remove the track bar.
4   Inspect the bushings for hardening, cracking or excessive wear. If they exhibit any of these conditions, the track bar must be replaced.
5   To install, place the left end of the track bar in its body mount and loosely install the bolt and nut. The open side of the bar must face rearward.
6   Place the other end of the bar in its rear axle mount and loosely install the bolt and nut. Both nuts must face the rear of the car.
7   Lower the car to the ground.
8   Torque both nuts to specs.

16 Rear springs and insulators – removal and installation

1   Raise the rear of the car and support it with jackstands placed at suitable locations under the frame.
2   Support the rear axle with a mobile jack such as a transmission jack or floor jack. Such jacks can be rented on a daily basis from rental agencies and some auto parts stores.
3   Remove the wheels and brake drums.
4   Disconnect the parking brake cable by loosening the adjustment nut and prying forward on the parking brake equalizer lever to disconnect the forward cable from the equalizer lever (photo).

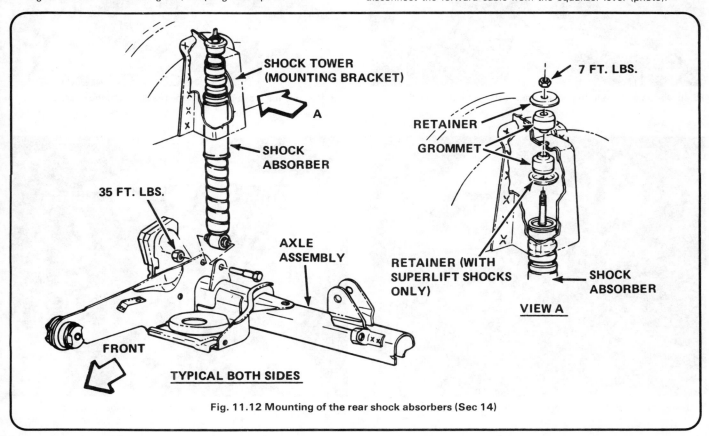

Fig. 11.12 Mounting of the rear shock absorbers (Sec 14)

15.2 Removing the mounting nuts and bolts from both ends of the track bar

16.4a Removing the parking brake adjusting nut

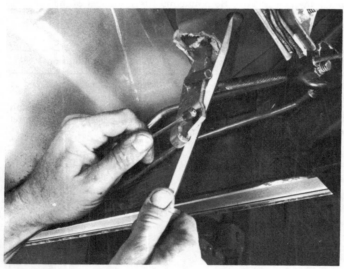

16.4b Disconnect the front parking brake cable from the equalizer lever

16.6 Remove the brake line mounting bracket from the chassis

16.9 After lowering the rear axle, remove the rear springs

17.8 Remove the rear axle control arm bracket mounting bolts

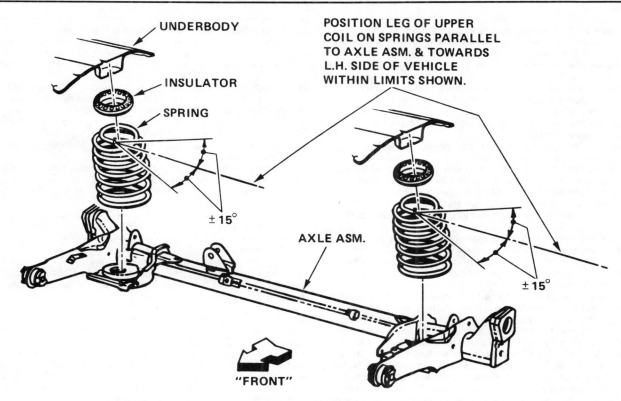

Fig. 11.13 Rear springs and insulators (Sec 16)

5 Twist the equalizer lever and disengage it from the pivot mount on the body.

6 Remove the bolts that attach the brake line brackets to the chassis on both the left and right sides (photo).

7 Remove the track bar as described in Section 15.

8 Remove the lower shock attaching nuts and bolts from both shock absorbers.

9 Lower the rear axle enough to remove the springs and/or insulators (photo). Do not suspend the rear axle by the brake hoses, as this could damage the hoses.

10 If the insulators are worn, cracked or damaged, they should be replaced.

11 Inspect the springs for cracks or other damage. If they exhibit any of these conditions, or if the car has been sagging in the rear, the springs should be replaced. The rear springs should always be replaced as a pair.

12 Installation is the reverse of the removal procedure. NOTE: When installing the springs, be sure they are in the proper position as shown in Fig. 11.13.

13 Adjust the parking brake as described in Chapter 9, Section 15.

17 Control arm bushing – removal and installation

1 Raise the rear of the car and support it with jackstands positioned at suitable locations under the frame.

2 Support the rear axle with a mobile jack such as a transmission jack or floor jack. A jack such as this can be rented on a daily basis from a rental agency or some auto parts stores.

3 Remove the wheels and brake drums.

4 If the right control arm bushing is being replaced, loosen the parking brake adjustment nut and disconnect the forward cable from the parking brake equalizer lever by prying forward on the equalizer lever. Then twist the equalizer lever and disengage it from the pivot mount on the body.

5 Remove the bolts that attach the brake line brackets to the chassis.

6 Remove the lower shock attaching nuts and bolts.

7 Remove the spring(s).

8 Remove the bolts that secure the control arm bracket to the

underbody (photo) and allow the control arm to rotate downward.

9 Remove the control arm bracket from the control arm.

10 Removal of the old bushing and installation of the new one must be done using special GM tools or equivalents, such as the one shown in Fig. 11.14. When installing, the cutouts on the rubber portion of the bushing must face toward the front and rear.

11 Remount the control arm bracket to the control arm and check that it is positioned at a 45° angle to the lower edge of the control arm. See photo 18.12b. When the proper angle is set, tighten the nut and torque it to specs.

12 Install the various components by reversing the removal procedure. Do not torque the lower shock nuts to specifications until the car has been lowered and its full weight is on the suspension.

13 Adjust the parking brake as described in Chapter 9, Section 15.

Fig. 11.14 Removing the control arm bushing (Sec 17)

18 Rear axle assembly – removal and installation

1   Remove the rear springs as described in Section 16.
2   Disconnect the brake lines from the control arm attachment (photo).
3   Disconnect and cap the rigid brake lines from both rear brake cylinders. An effective way of capping the rigid brake lines is shown in Chapter 9, photo 10.8.
4   Disconnect the right rear parking brake cable from the left rear parking brake cable (photo).
5   Disconnect the right rear and left rear parking brake cables from their brackets on the rear axle (photo).
6   Remove the bolts that secure the rear parking brake cable guide to the underbody (photo) and allow the entire parking brake assembly to hang from the right rear backing plate as shown (photo).
7   Remove the bolts that secure the hub and bearing assembly to the rear axle and remove the assemblies along with the brake backing plates.
8   While an assistant steadies the rear axle on the jack, remove the bolts that secure the control arm brackets to the body.
9   Lower the rear axle and remove it from under the car (photo).
10 If the rear axle is being replaced, remove the control arm brackets from the control arms and install on the new axle.
11 Inspect the control arm bushings for cracking, hardening or other damage and replace if necessary as described in Section 17.
12 Prior to installation, lay the axle on a flat surface and, using a suitable angle measuring instrument, make sure the lower edge of the control arms are on a true horizontal plane (photo). Then measure the control arm brackets. These should be at an angle of 45° to the horizontal plane, or the lower edge of the control arm (photo). If they are at a different angle, loosen the bracket nuts and adjust them to a 45° angle. When the proper angle is set torque the nuts to specs.
13 Installation of the rear axle is the reverse of the removal procedure. Do not tighten the lower shock nuts and track arm nuts to specifications until after the car has been lowered and the full weight of the car is on the suspension.
14 Bleed the brake system as described in Chapter 9, Section 3.
15 Adjust the parking brake as described in Chapter 9, Section 15.

19 Rear hub and bearing assembly – removal and installation

1   Raise the rear of the car and support it on jackstands.
2   Remove the wheel and brake drum.
3   Remove the bolts that secure the hub and bearing assembly to the rear axle and remove the assembly.
4   Spin the bearing with your finger and check for any roughness or noise. This assembly is a sealed unit and if the bearing needs replacing the entire hub and bearing assembly must be replaced.
5   Installation is the reverse of the removal procedure.

20 Rear wheel stud – removal and installation

1   Raise the rear of the car and support it on jackstands.
2   Remove the wheel and brake drum as described in Chapter 9, Section 8.
3   Install a lug nut on the end of the stud and, using a GM special tool or equivalent as shown in Fig. 11.11, press the stud from its seat.
4   Remove the lug nut and remove the stud.
5   Insert the new stud in the hole, making sure the serrations are aligned with those made by the original bolt.
6   Place 4 flat washers over the outside end of the stud and thread a lug nut onto the stud.
7   Tighten the lug nut until the stud head seats against the rear of the hub. Then remove the lug nut and washers.
8   Install the brake drum and lower the car to the ground.

21 Steering system – general information

1   All models of the X-Body cars use a rack and pinion steering system. The components that make up the manual system are the steering wheel, steering column, intermediate shaft, rack and pinion assembly, tie rods and steering knuckles. In addition, the power steering system also uses a belt-driven pump to provide hydraulic pressure.
2   In a manual system, the motion of turning the steering wheel is transferred through the column and intermediate shaft to the pinion shaft in the rack and pinion assembly. Teeth on the pinion shaft are meshed with teeth on the rack, so when the shaft is turned, the rack is moved left or right in the rack and pinion housing. Attached to each end of the rack are tie rods which, in turn, are attached to the steering knuckles on the front wheels. This left and right movement of the rack is the direct force which turns the wheels.
3   The power steering system operates in essentially the same way as the manual system, except that the power rack and pinion system uses hydraulic pressure to boost the manual steering force. A rotary control valve in the rack and pinion assembly directs hydraulic fluid from the power steering pump to either side of the integral rack piston, which is attached to the rack. Depending on which side of the piston this hydraulic pressure is applied to, the rack will be forced either left or right, which moves the tie rods, etc.
4   If the power steering system loses its hydraulic pressure it will still function manually, though with increased effort.
5   The steering column is of the collapsible, energy-absorbing type, designed to compress in the event of a front end collision to minimize injury to the driver. The column also houses the ignition switch lock, key warning buzzer, turn signal controls, headlight dimmer control and windshield wiper controls. The ignition and steering wheel can both be locked while the car is parked to inhibit theft.
6   Due to the column's collapsible design, it is important that only

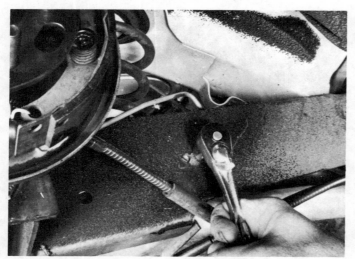

18.2 Disconnect the brake line from the rear axle's control arm

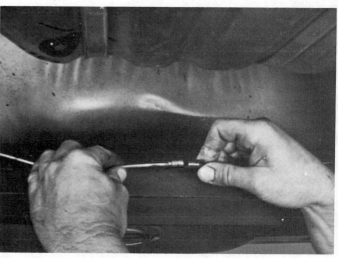

18.4 Disconnect the right rear parking brake cable from the left rear cable

18.5 Disconnect both rear parking brake cables from their rear axle brackets

18.6a Remove the mounting bolts from the rear parking brake cable guide

18.6b Allow the parking brake assembly to hang from the right backing plate

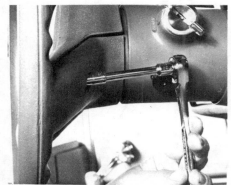
18.9 Remove the rear axle

18.12a Support the rear axle so that the lower edge of the control arm is on a true horizontal line

18.12b The angle of the control arm bracket to the lower edge of the control arm should be 45°

22.2a Removing the horn cover screws from the steering wheel

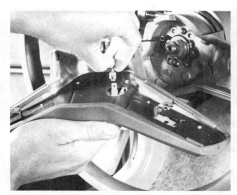
22.2b Removing the horn cover and disconnect the horn wire

22.4 Removing the steering wheel nut retainer

22.6 Mark the relationship of the steering wheel to the steering shaft

22.7 Removing the steering wheel

22.8 Withdraw the horn lead and spring from the column

specified screws, bolts and nuts be used as designated and that they be tightened to the specified torque. Other precautions particular to this design are noted in appropriate Sections.

7   In addition to the standard steering column, optional tilt and key-release versions are also offered. The tilt model can be set in five different positions while with the key release model, the ignition key is locked in the column until a lever is depressed to extract it.

8   Because disassembly of the steering column is more often performed to repair a switch or other electrical part than to correct a problem in the steering functioning, the steering column disassembly and reassembly procedure is included in Chapter 10.

22 Steering wheel – removal and installation

1   Disconnect the negative battery cable.

2   On standard steering wheels remove the 2 screws that secure the horn cover to the steering wheel (photo). Then lift off the horn cover and disconnect the horn wire (photo).

3   On sport steering wheels simply pry off the center cap.

4   Using slip joint pliers, remove the steering wheel nut retainer (photo).

5   Be sure the steering wheel is unlocked, then remove the steering wheel nut.

6   Mark the position of the steering wheel in relation to the steering shaft (photo).

7   Using a GM special tool or equivalent steering wheel puller, remove the steering wheel.

Note: *Under no circumstances should the end of the shaft be hammered on, as impact of this nature could loosen the plastic injections which maintain the column's rigidity (photo).*

8   Remove the horn lead, complete with spring from the steering column (photo).

9   Installation is the reverse of the removal procedure with the following note: when installing the steering wheel on the shaft be sure the alignment marks on the steering wheel and shaft match.

23 Steering column – removal and installation

1   Although it's not mandatory, the steering column removal operation can be made much easier by first removing the front seat as described in Chapter 12.

2   Disconnect the negative battery terminal.

3   If the column is to be disassembled after it is removed from the vehicle, then the steering wheel should be removed, as described in Section 22. If the column is to be kept as one piece, removal of the steering wheel is not necessary.

4   Remove the screws that secure the steering column trim cover to the dash and lift off the cover. On appropriate cars with air-conditioning, disconnect the vent hose when you remove the cover (photo).

5   Disconnect all electrical connections from the steering column including those from the dimmer switch, windshield wiper switch, ignition switch, back-up light switch and turn signal switch as shown in Chapter 10.

6   Disconnect the shift indicator cable by prying the clip from the shaft bowl.

7   Disconnect the shift cable from the column by removing the clip, pin retainer and washer that are used to secure it.

8   Use a screwdriver to pry back the plastic cover over the intermediate shaft so the U-joint is exposed and remove the locking bolt and nut that pinch it to the steering shaft.

9   Remove the 3 bolts and 1 nut that secure the steering column to its support (photo) and remove the column.

10   Because of its collapsible design, the steering column is very susceptible to damage when removed from the car. Be careful not to lean on or drop the column, as this could weaken the column's structure and impair its performance.

11   If the car has been in an accident which resulted in frame damage, major body damage or in which the steering column was impacted, the column could be damaged or misaligned and should be checked by a qualified mechanic.

12   If disassembly of the column is necessary, refer to Chapter 10.

13   The steering column is installed by reversing the sequence of the removal operation, with the following note: when reattaching the shift indicator cable clip to the shift bowl, place the shift lever in the

'Neutral' position, then position the clip on the edge of the bowl so that the shift indicator pointer is pointing to the 'N'. Push the clip onto the bowl to secure it.

24 Steering knuckle – removal and installation

1   Remove the hub and bearing assembly as described in Section 12.

2   Mark the cam bolt so the proper camber alignment can be maintained upon installation.

3   Remove the cam bolt and the upper strut-to-steering knuckle mounting bolt.

4   Remove the nut that secures the tie rod to the steering knuckle.

5   Using a GM special tool or equivalent as shown in Fig. 11.5, disengage the tie rod from the steering knuckle.

6   Remove the bolt that secures the lower balljoint in the lower control arm to the steering knuckle and disengage the balljoint.

7   Remove the steering knuckle from the axleshaft.

8   If the steering knuckle is being replaced, install a new steering knuckle seal into the new knuckle. This is done by greasing both the seal and the knuckle bore and then tapping the seal into place using a hammer and the proper sized socket.

9   Install the steering knuckle onto the axleshaft.

10   Insert the balljoint stud into the steering knuckle, then insert the bolt and nut and tighten the nut to specs.

11   Loosely install the strut to the steering knuckle by installing the cam bolt and upper strut-to-steering knuckle mounting bolt.

12   Install the hub and bearing assembly, shield and rotor.

13   Place a jackstand under the hub and bearing assembly and rotor to support it. Then lower the car enough to align the cam with its mark made during the removal procedure, and tighten the bolts to specs.

14   Engage the tie rod with the steering knuckle using a C-clamp and a $1\frac{1}{8}$-in (27 mm) socket as shown in Fig. 11.15.

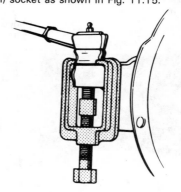

REMOVE TIE ROD END

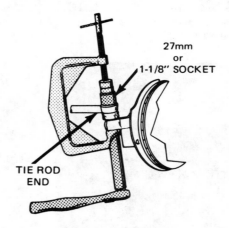

27mm
or
1-1/8" SOCKET

TIE ROD
END

INSTALL TIE ROD END

Fig. 11.15 Engaging and disengaging the outer tie rod and the steering knuckle (Sec 24 and 25)

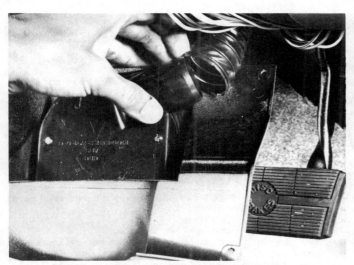

23.4 Removing the steering column trim cover from the dash and disconnect the vent hose if equipped with air conditioner

23.9 Removing the steering column mounting bolts and nut

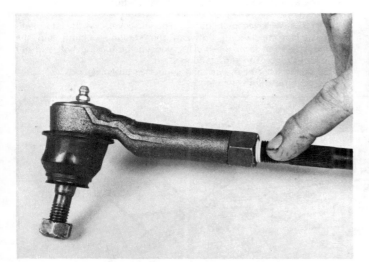

25.6 Mark the position of the jam nut on the inner tie rod

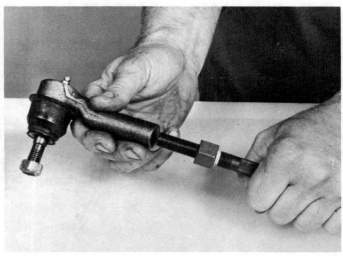

25.8 Unscrew the outer tie rod from the inner tie rod

15 Install the tie rod nut and torque it to specs.
16 Install the brake caliper.
17 Install the wheel and lower the car to the ground.
18 Torque the hub nuts to specs.

25 Outer tie rod – removal and installation

1   In most cases when one or both tie rods must be replaced, the operation can be done with the rack and pinion in the car. For photographic clarity, we performed the operation with the rack and pinion removed.
2   Raise the front of the car and support it with jackstands.
3   Remove the front wheel.
4   Remove the tie rod nut that secures the outer tie rod to the steering knuckle.
5   Using a GM special tool or equivalent as shown in Fig. 11.15, disengage the tie rod from the steering knuckle.
6   Mark the relationship of the jam nut to the inner tie rod threads so similar front end alignment can be maintained upon installation (photo).
7   Back off the jam nut from the outer tie rod.
8   Unscrew the outer tie rod from the inner tie rod (photo).
9   To install, position the jam nut at its mark on the threads. Then

screw the outer tie rod onto the inner tie rod until it's snug against the jam nut.
10 Using a C-clamp and a $1\frac{1}{8}$-in (27 mm) socket as shown in Fig. 11.15, install the tie rod into the steering knuckle.
11 Install the tie rod nut and torque to specs.
12 Torque the jam nut to specs.
13 Mount the front wheel and lower the car to the ground.
14 A front end alignment must now be performed. Refer to Section 3.

26 Rack and pinion boot seals – removal and installation

1   Since the rack and pinion boot seals protect the assembly's internals from dirt and water, they should be checked periodically for holes, cracking and other damage or deterioration. If the boots exhibit such conditions they should be replaced immediately to prevent having to overhaul the entire rack and pinion assembly. The seal boots can be removed and installed with the rack and pinion still in the car, though for photographic clarity we performed the operation with the rack and pinion removed.
2   Remove the outer tie rod as described in Section 25.
3   Remove the jam nut from the inner tie rod.
4   Use pliers to spread the outer boot clamp and remove it from the inner tie rod (photo).

26.4 Removing the outer retaining clamp from the rack and pinion boot seal

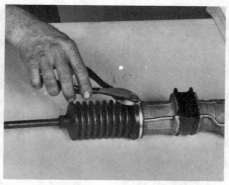

26.5 Removing the inner retaining clamp from the boot seal

26.6 Slide the boot seal off of the inner tie rod

5   Cut off the inner boot clamp and remove (photo).
6   Only if the same boot is to be reinstalled, mark the rack and pinion's breather tube location on the boot and remove the boot (photo).
7   Install a new inner boot clamp or appropriate sized hose clamp over the inner tie rod.
8   Install the seal boot so the large end is over the rack and pinion housing lip and the hole in the boot is aligned with the breather tube. If the old boot is being installed, simply line up the marks made during removal.
9   Install the inner boot clamp over the large end of the boot and tighten.
10 Install the outer boot clamp over the small end of the boot and tighten.

11 Install the jam nut onto the inner tie rod.
12 Install the outer tie rod and engage it in the steering knuckle.
13 Mount the front wheel and lower the car to the ground.
14 Have a front end alignment performed. Refer to Section 3.

27 Rack and pinion – removal and installation

1   Use a screwdriver to pry back the plastic cover over the intermediate shaft so the U-joint between the steering column and the intermediate shaft is exposed. Then loosen the locking bolt and nut that pinch the joint to the steering shaft.
2   Raise the front of the car and support it on jackstands.
3   Remove both front wheels.

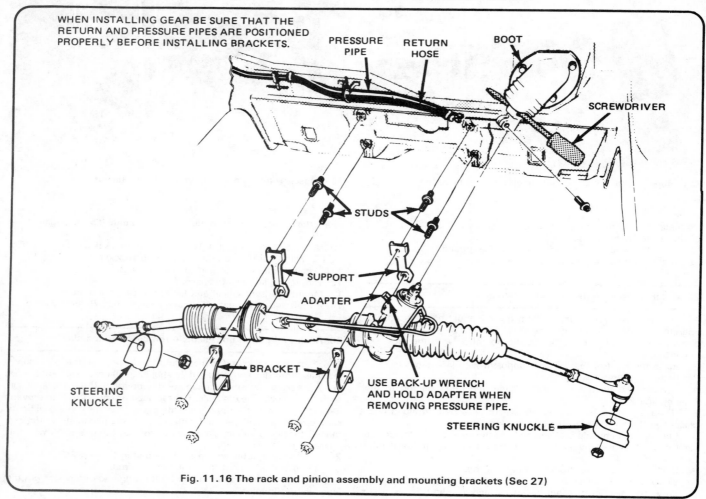

Fig. 11.16 The rack and pinion assembly and mounting brackets (Sec 27)

4   Remove both tie rods from the steering knuckles as described in Section 25.

5   On power steering units, disconnect the pressure pipe from its adapter on the rack and pinion housing. Use a back-up wrench to hold the adapter while removing the pressure pipe.

6   On power steering units, disconnect the return hose from its fitting on the rack and pinion housing.

7   Lift the rubber boot that covers the U-joint between the intermediate shaft and the rack and pinion and insert a screwdriver as shown in Fig. 11.16 to hold the boot out of the way.

8   Remove the bolt that pinches the intermediate shaft to the pinion shaft.

9   Remove the nuts from the 4 rack and pinion mounting studs.

10   Remove the U-brackets and cross-bracket from the mounting studs.

11   Carefully remove the rack and pinion, complete with tie rods, out the left side of the car (photo). Be careful not to damage the emergency brake cable, fuel inlet line or the threads on the mounting studs.

12   Remove the rear support brackets from the mounting studs.

13   If the rack and pinion needs to be repaired, there are several options open to you. A new rack and pinion assembly can be bought as a unit and installed. This, however, is the costliest route. If there is a shop in your area that rebuilds rack and pinion assemblies, taking it to them will be much cheaper than buying a new unit. Rack and pinions in good condition can also be found in junkyards. The final option is to rebuild the assembly yourself, though it is a somewhat difficult operation requiring access to a press for several steps. See Section 28 or 29 for the overhaul procedure for your particular system.

14   Install the right rear support bracket over the mounting studs.

15   Insert the rack and pinion into its cavity, being careful not to damage the emergency brake cable, fuel inlet line or the threads on the mounting studs. See Fig. 11.25. The assembly should be positioned over the top and to the rear of the emergency brake cable.

16   Position the rack and pinion just to the left of its mounting position and install the left rear support bracket on its mounting studs.

17   Set the rack and pinion into its mounting position and match the pinion shaft up with the intermediate shaft U-joint.

18   Insert the pinion into the U-joint and loosely install the bolt.

19   Install the U-brackets onto the mounting studs and loosely install the lower mounting nuts.

20   Install the cross-bracket on the top mounting studs and loosely install the upper mounting nuts. The photo shows the relative position of the brackets.

21   Tighten the mounting nuts evenly and torque to specs.

22   On power steering units, make sure the O-ring is in place on the pressure pipe and install the pressure pipe to its adapter.

23   On power steering units, install the return hose to its fitting.

24   Torque the U-joint bolt to specs.

25   Remove the screwdriver from the intermediate shaft to allow the rubber boot to cover the U-joint.

26   Install the tie rods into the steering knuckles.

27.11 Removing the rack and pinion assembly from the left side of the car

27.20 This is the relative positioning of the rack and pinion assembly mounting brackets

28.4 Slide the shock dampener ring off of the inner tie rod housing

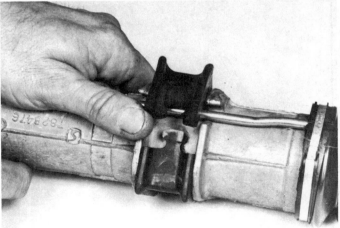

28.15 Removing the rubber grommets from the rack and pinion housing

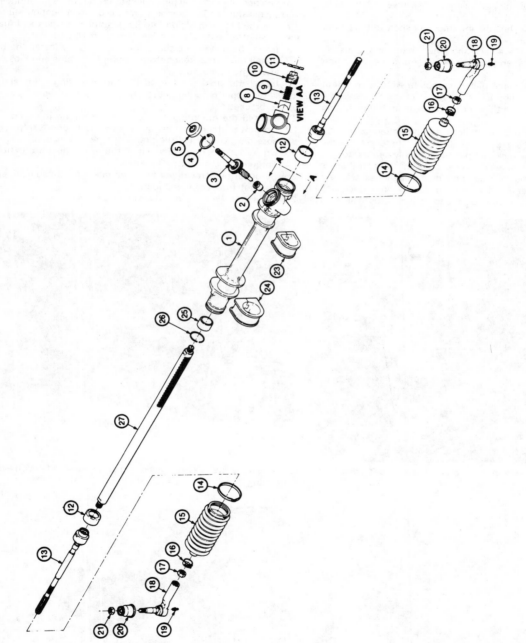

Fig. 11.17 An exploded view of the rack and pinion assembly (manual steering system) (Sec 28)

1 Housing, rack & pinion
2 Bearing assy, roller
3 Pinion assy, bearing &
4 Ring retaining
5 Seal, steering pinion
6 Bolt, pinch

7 Flange assy, coupling & strg.
8 Bearing, rack
9 Spring, adjuster
10 Plug, adjuster
11 Nut, adjuster plug lock
12 Ring, shock dampener

13 Rod assy, inner tie
14 Clamp, boot
15 Boot, rack & pinion
16 Clamp, boot
17 Nut, hex. jam

18 Rod assy, outer tie
19 Fitting, lubrication
20 Seal, tie rod
21 Nut, hex lock
22 Nut

23 Grommet, mounting (LT)
24 Grommet, mounting (RT)
25 Bushing, rack
26 Ring, bushing retaining
27 Rack, steering

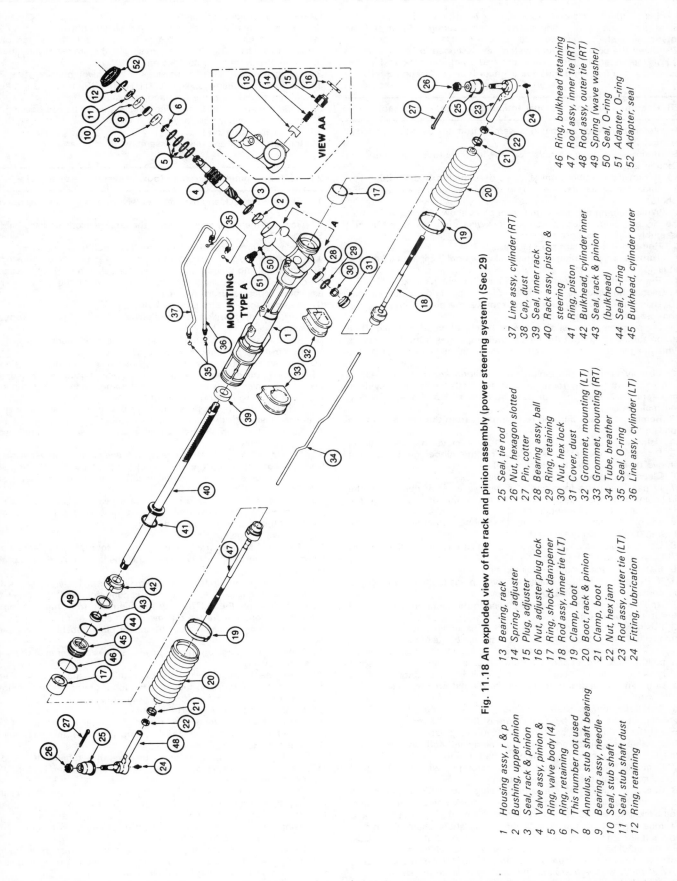

Fig. 11.18 An exploded view of the rack and pinion assembly (power steering system) (Sec 29)

1 Housing assy, r & p
2 Bushing, upper pinion
3 Seal, rack & pinion
4 Valve assy, pinion &
5 Ring, valve body (4)
6 Ring, retaining
7 This number not used
8 Annulus, stub shaft bearing
9 Bearing assy, needle
10 Seal, stub shaft
11 Seal, stub shaft dust
12 Ring, retaining

13 Bearing, rack
14 Spring, adjuster
15 Plug, adjuster
16 Nut, adjuster plug lock
17 Ring, shock dampener
18 Rod assy, inner tie (LT)
19 Clamp, boot
20 Boot, rack & pinion
21 Clamp, boot
22 Nut, hex jam
23 Rod assy, outer tie (LT)
24 Fitting, lubrication

25 Seal, tie rod
26 Nut, hexagon slotted
27 Pin, cotter
28 Bearing assy, ball
29 Ring, retaining
30 Nut, hex lock
31 Cover, dust
32 Grommet, mounting (LT)
33 Grommet, mounting (RT)
34 Tube, breather
35 Seal, O-ring
36 Line assy, cylinder (LT)

37 Line assy, cylinder (RT)
38 Cap, dust
39 Seal, inner rack
40 Rack assy, piston &
   steering
41 Ring, piston
42 Bulkhead, cylinder inner
43 Seal, rack & pinion
   (bulkhead)
44 Seal, O-ring
45 Bulkhead, cylinder outer

46 Ring, bulkhead retaining
47 Rod assy, inner tie (RT)
48 Rod assy, outer tie (RT)
49 Spring (wave washer)
50 Seal, O-ring
51 Adapter, O-ring
52 Adapter, seal

27 Install the wheels and lower the car to the ground.
28 Tighten the U-joint bolt between the steering column and the intermediate shaft, and torque to specs.
29 Bleed the power steering system, as described in Section 34.
30 If the outer tie rods were removed from the rack and pinion assembly, the front end must be aligned. Refer to Section 3.

28 Rack and pinion assembly (manual system) – overhaul

1   Remove the rack and pinion assembly from the car as described in Section 27.
2   Remove the outer tie rods from the inner tie rods as described in Section 25.
3   Remove the rubber boot seals as described in Section 26.
4   Slide the shock dampener ring off of the inner tie rod housing (photo).
5   While holding the rack with a wrench as shown in Fig. 11.20, turn the tie rod pivot housing counterclockwise until the inner tie rod assembly separates from the rack.
6   Remove the adjuster plug locknut.
7   Turn the adjuster plug counterclockwise until it separates from the housing.
8   Remove the rack bearing spring and the rack bearing.
9   Pierce the pinion seal as shown in Fig. 11.21 and pry out the seal.
10 Using internal snap-ring pliers, remove the pinion retaining ring from around the pinion shaft.
11 Support the pinion shaft between blocks of wood in a vise. Then tap on the housing until the pinion shaft separates from the housing. With the pinion shaft removed, the rack will slide right out of the housing.
12 Visually examine the pinion roller bearing and turn the bearing with your finger. If any roughness, noise or other damage is evident, the bearing will have to be pressed from the rack and pinion housing and replaced.
13 Remove the rack bushing retaining ring from the right end of the housing.
14 Using a puller as shown in Fig. 11.22, remove the rack bushing.
15 Disconnect the interlocking tabs on the rubber grommets and remove them from the housing (photo).
16 Clean all of the metal parts in solvent.
17 Inspect the parts for signs of excessive wear or damage. If the pinion seal has been leaking, check for any pitting on the shaft where the seal sits. Replace as necessary.
18 To begin reassembly, install the rubber grommets onto the housing by interlocking their tabs.
19 Using a suitable socket, the same size as the rack bushing, press the bushing into the housing.
20 Install the rack bushing retaining ring.
21 If the roller bearing has been removed, press the new bearing into the housing, again using a suitably sized socket.
22 Apply a coat of lithium-based grease to the teeth on the rack and slide it into the housing.
23 Position the end of the rack so that its edge (not including its threads) is $2\frac{1}{2}$-in (63.5 mm) from the inside lip of the housing. See Fig. 11.23. Apply a coat of grease to the pinion shaft threads, and insert the pinion shaft into its bore with the flat area on the end of the shaft in the 4:30 position. Maintaining the rack in its position with the housing, tap the shaft into its bore until the flat area rotates into the 9:00 position.
24 Install the pinion shaft retaining ring. When installed, the gap between its end should be a minimum of 0.27-in (7 mm).
25 Fill the pinion shaft cavity with anhydrous grease.
26 Install a new pinion seal over the pinion shaft and tap it into place until the top of the seal is flush with the housing.
27 Coat the rack bearing and spring thoroughly with lithium-based grease and install them into the housing.
28 Coat the threads of the adjuster plug with lithium grease and install into the housing. Turn the adjuster clockwise until it bottoms, then back it off 40° to 60°. Using a $\frac{9}{16}$-in (14 mm) 12-point socket and a torque wrench on the end of the pinion shaft, check the pinion torque. It should be 8 to 10 in-lb (.09 to .11 m-kg). If it is more or less, turn the adjuster plug until the proper torque is achieved.
Note: *If the socket is slightly large for the shaft's serrations, wrap a layer of thin cardboard around the shaft to achieve proper fit.*
29 While holding the adjuster plug stationary, install the adjuster plug

locknut and torque it to specs.
30 While holding the rack with a wrench as shown in Fig. 11.20, install the inner tie rod onto the rack and torque the tie rod pivot housing to specs. With the pivot housing at the proper torque, the tie rod should rock freely in its housing.
31 Using a punch, stake both sides of the pivot housing. See Fig. 11.24. When properly staked, a 0.010-in (.25 mm) feeler gauge should not fit between the rack and housing stake.
32 Slide the shock dampener ring over the inner tie rod housing.
33 Install the rubber boot seals.
34 Install the outer tie rods.
35 Install the rack and pinion assembly into the car.

29 Rack and pinion assembly (power system) – overhaul

1   Remove the rack and pinion assembly from the car as described in Section 27.
2   Remove the outer tie rods from the inner tie rods as described in Section 25.
3   Remove the rubber boot seals as described in Section 26.
4   Slide the shock dampener ring off of the inner tie rod housing.
5   While holding the rack with a wrench as shown in Fig. 11.20, turn the tie rod pivot housing counterclockwise until the inner tie rod assembly separates from the rack.
6   Remove the adjuster plug lock nut.
7   Turn the adjuster plug counterclockwise until it separates from the housing.
8   Remove the rack bearing spring and the rack bearing.
9   Remove the retaining ring from the pinion shaft.
10 Remove the dust cover from the bottom of the pinion housing.
11 Place a ratchet wrench with a $\frac{11}{16}$-in 12-point socket over the upper end of the pinion shaft to keep it from turning. Then remove the lock nut from the lower end of the shaft.
12 Using an arbor press, press on the threaded end of the pinion shaft until it is flush with the ball bearing assembly.
13 Remove the stub shaft dust seal, stub shaft seal and the needle bearing assembly.
14 Turn the stub shaft until the ends of the rack are an equal distance from the housing. Mark the position of the pinion to the housing and press the pinion shaft from the housing. Remove the retaining ring and valve body rings from the shaft.
15 Using a brass hammer, drive the rack assembly out of the housing.
16 Remove the bulkhead retaining ring, and remove the outer and inner bulkheads and their related parts.
17 Remove the piston ring from the rack.
18 Using a GM inner rack seal removing tool or equivalent and a piece of rod approximately 12-in long, tap the inner rack seal out of the housing.
19 Turn the pinion shaft ball bearing with your finger to check for roughness or noise. If either of those conditions exist, it must be replaced. Remove the ball bearing retaining ring from the housing.
20 Using a long punch, tap out the pinion shaft ball bearing.
21 Using a long punch, tap out the upper pinion bushing and pinion seal.
22 Loosen the fittings on the fluid cylinder lines and remove the lines from the housing.
23 Mark the location of the breather tube on the housing. Then disconnect the interlocking tabs on the rubber grommets and remove them and the breather tube from the housing.
24 Clean all of the metal parts in solvent.
25 Inspect the parts for signs of excessive wear or damage. If the pinion seal has been leaking, check for any pitting on the shaft where the seal sits. Replace as necessary.
26 To begin reassembly, position the breather tube in its proper location on the housing and install the rubber grommets onto the housing by interlocking their tabs.
27 Place new O-rings on the cylinder lines and install the lines to the housing, tightening them only finger-tight. Once the proper alignment has been obtained, tighten the connectors to specifications.
28 Using a suitable socket, the same size as the upper rack bushing, install a new bushing in the housing.
29 Install the pinion seal into the housing with the seal lip facing up.
30 Using a suitable socket that will press on the outer race of the ball bearing, install the bearing into the pinion housing.
31 Install the ball bearing retaining ring into the housing. Once

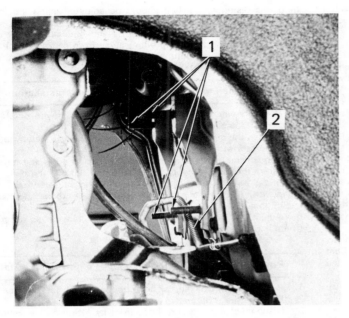

Fig. 11.19 A look at the rack and pinion cavity from the left side of the car (Sec 27)

1   Mounting studs   2   Fuel inlet line

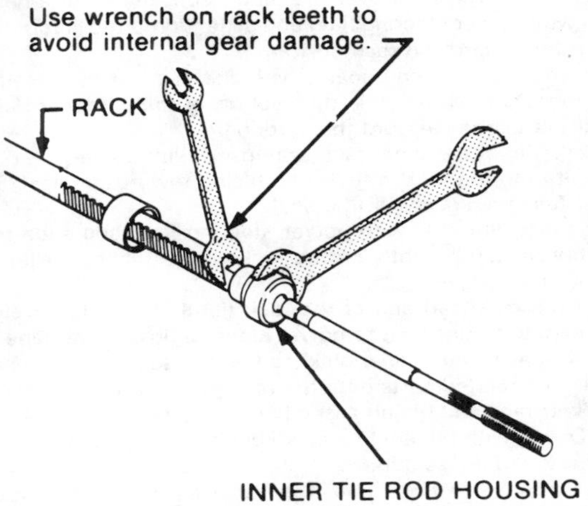

Use wrench on rack teeth to avoid internal gear damage.

─ RACK

INNER TIE ROD HOUSING

Fig. 11.20 Removing the inner tie rod from the rack (Secs 28 and 29)

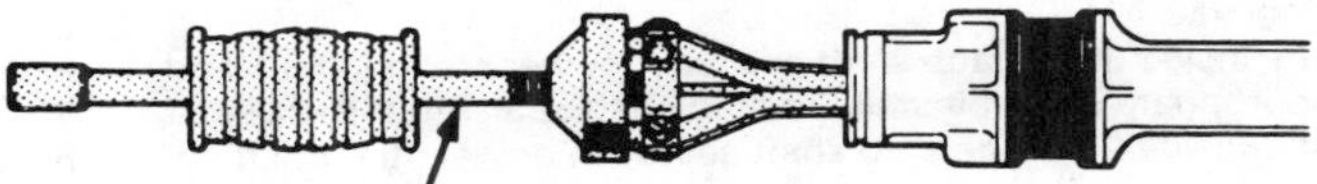

Slip fingers of puller behind bushing.

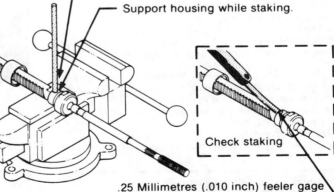

Puller

Fig. 11.22 A puller is needed to remove the rack bushing from the rack and pinion housing (Sec 28)

PINION SEAL

Pierce seal in one of two round spots, pry out seal.

Fig. 11.21 Removing the pinion seal from the pinion shaft (Sec 28)

Stake both sides of housing.

Support housing while staking.

Check staking

.25 Millimetres (.010 inch) feeler gage must not pass between rack and housing stake. (Check both sides.)

Fig. 11.24 The inner tie rod housing must be staked to the rack during installation (Sec 28)

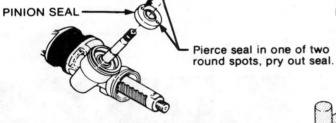

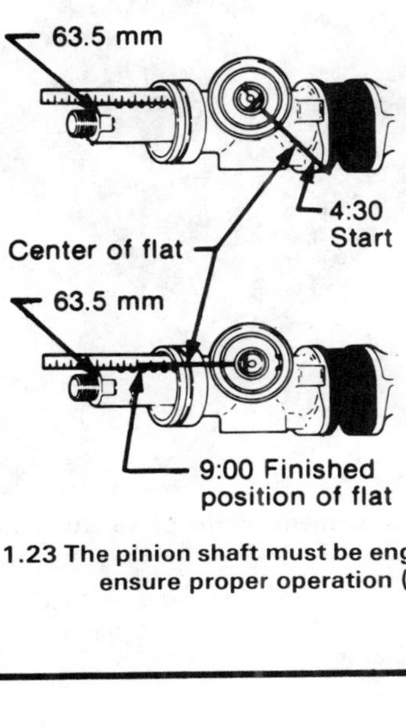

63.5 mm

4:30 Start

Center of flat

63.5 mm

9:00 Finished position of flat

Fig. 11.23 The pinion shaft must be engaged with the rack to ensure proper operation (Sec 28)

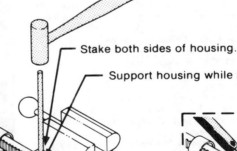

installed, the end of the ring with the large lug should be located counterclockwise from the other end. This ensures that the beveled side of the ring is properly located.

32 Install a new piston ring on the rack.

33 Wrap a thin piece of cardboard tightly around the end of the rack, but make sure it will slide over the teeth. Coat the lip of a new inner rack seal with power steering fluid and slide it onto the cardboard with the lip facing toward the rack position.

34 Slide the piece of cardboard, with the seal on it, over the rack teeth to the piston. Then slide the seal off of the cardboard and seat it against the piston. Discard the cardboard.

35 Coat the lip of the inner rack seal insert with power steering fluid and slide it onto the rack with the lip facing toward the seal. Be sure the insert fully engages with the seal.

36 Coat the entire seal with power steering fluid and slide the rack into the housing. Tap lightly on the rack with a rubber mallet to seat the seal in the housing.

37 Wrap the bulkhead end of the rack tightly with plastic electrical tape, and apply a light coat of power steering fluid to the tape. Install a new rack seal into the inner bulkhead and install the inner and outer bulkheads and related parts onto the rack. Refer to the exploded view of the power rack and pinion assembly for the proper sequence. Coat the new O-ring with fluid before installing it onto the rack. Be sure the retaining ring is fully seated.

38 Install new valve rings onto the valve and pinion assembly. Be careful not to cut them upon installation.

39 Install the retaining ring.

40 Position the rack so its ends are equal distance from the housing. Install the valve and pinion assembly into the housing. When it is fully seated, the alignment marks you made during removal should line up.

41 If the stub shaft needle bearing requires replacement press it from its annulus and press in a new bearing. Then install this assembly onto the pinion shaft.

42 Coat the inside of the stub shaft seal with power steering fluid and using an appropriate socket install the stub shaft seal into the housing.

43 Coat the inside lip of the stub shaft seal with power steering fluid. Then, using an appropriate socket, install the seal into the housing.

44 Install, the stub shaft dust seal and retaining ring onto the shaft.

45 While keeping the shaft from turning with a $\frac{11}{16}$-in 12-point socket, install the lock nut to the bottom of the shaft and torque it to specs.

46 Install the dust cover onto the bottom of the pinion housing.

47 Install the rack bearing and spring into the housing.

48 Install the adjuster plug into the housing. Turn it clockwise until it bottoms, then back it off 40° to 60°. Using a $\frac{11}{16}$-in 12-point socket and a torque wrench on the end of the pinion shaft, check the pinion torque. It should be 8 to 16 in-lb (.1 to .2 m-kg). If it is more or less, turn the adjuster plug until the proper torque is achieved. NOTE: if the socket is slightly large for the shaft's serrations, wrap a layer of thin cardboard around the shaft to achieve proper fit.

49 While holding the adjuster plug stationary, install the adjuster plug locknut and torque it to specs.

50 While holding the rack with a wrench as shown in Fig. 11.20, install the inner tie rod onto the rack and torque the tie rod housing to specs. With the pivot housing at the proper torque the tie rod should rock freely in its housing.

51 Using a punch, stake both sides of the pivot housing. See Fig. 11.24. When properly staked, a 0.010-in (0.25 mm) feeler gauge should not fit between the rack and housing stake.

52 Slide the shock dampener ring over the inner tie rod housing.

53 Install the rubber boot seals.

54 Install the outer tie rods.

55 Install the rack and pinion assembly into the car.

30 Power steering pump belt – adjustment

1 Both the power steering pump and the water pump are driven by a belt which is,. in turn, driven off of the crankshaft. Maintaining the proper tension on this belt is very important because if the belt is either too tight or too loose it can put excessive sidewards strain on the various shafts and bearings.

2 To check the tension of this belt find the upper stretch of belt that goes between the crankshaft and the water pump pulley and, gripping it in the center of the stretch, move the belt up and down to gauge its slack. The distance that the belt can be moved up and down should be about $\frac{1}{2}$-in (13 mm). If the slack allows the belt to move more or less

than this distance, the belt should be adjusted using the following procedure.

3 Loosen the pump attaching bolts and nuts and adjust the belt tension by moving the pump either away from or toward the engine. Tighten the attaching bolts and nuts, and recheck the adjustment.

31 Power steering pump belt – removal and installation

1 If the power steering pump belt becomes frayed or cracked it should be replaced.

2 Loosen the generator/air conditioner compressor belt by loosening the generator attaching bolts.

3 Loosen the power steering pump attaching bolts and nuts.

4 Move the pump toward the engine and remove the belt.

5 Install a new belt over the power steering pump and water pump pulleys and the crankshaft. Adjust to the proper tension as described in Section 30.

6 Adjust the generator belt to the proper tension as described in Chapter 5, Section 14.

32 Power steering pump (L4 engine) – removal and installation

1 Raise the front of the car and support it with jackstands.

2 Remove the radiator hose clamp bolt.

3 Disconnect the pressure hose from its fitting on the rear of the pump.

4 Remove the clamp that secures the flexible return hose to its rigid steel line and disconnect the hose from the line.

5 Loosen the pump's attaching bolts and nuts, move the pump toward the engine and remove the belt from the pulley.

6 Remove the bolt and spacer used in the upper rear mounting location of the pump that holds the pump to the bracket.

7 Remove the 3 bolts that hold the left pump bracket to the engine block.

8 Remove the pump and left pump bracket.

9 Remove the pump from the pump bracket.

10 Remove the 3 bolts that secure the right pump bracket to the pump.

11 If the power steering pump needs replacing, a rebuilt unit can be

Fig. 11.25 Components of the power steering pump (Secs 32 and 33)

1 *Power steering pump*   4 *Return hose*
2 *Pressure hose*   5 *Left pump mounting bracket*
3 *Radiator hose clamp bolt*

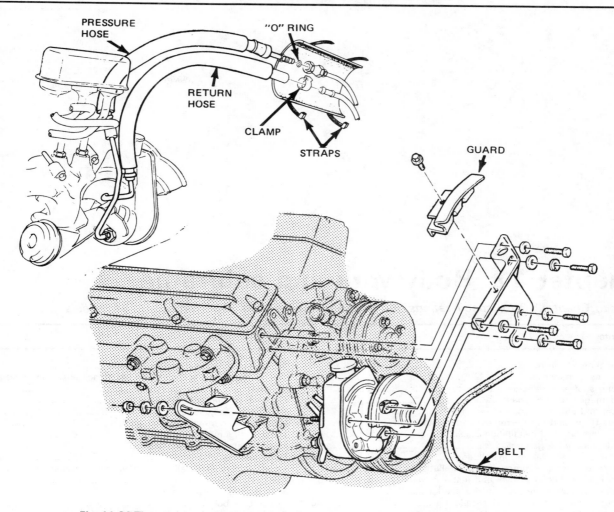

Fig. 11.26 The power steering pump mounting arrangement on the V6 engine (Sec 33)

obtained and is less expensive than a new pump.
12 Install the pump by reversing the removal procedure.
13 Adjust the belt tension as described in Section 30.
14 Bleed the power steering system as described in Section 34.

33 Power steering pump (V6 engine) – removal and installation

1 Disconnect the negative battery terminal.
2 Disconnect the electrical connector from the blower motor.
3 Remove the blower motor.
4 Drain the radiator and disconnect the heater hose at the water pump.
5 Disconnect the pressure and return hoses at the connections shown in Fig. 11.26.
6 Loosen the pump mounting bolts, move the pump toward the engine and remove the belt from the pulley.
7 Remove the 5 bolts that secure the right pump bracket to the pump and rear engine head.
8 Remove the pump from the left pump bracket and remove from the engine compartment.
9 If the power steering pump needs replacing, a rebuilt unit can be obtained and is less expensive than a new pump.
10 Install the pump by reversing the removal procedure.
11 Adjust the belt tension as described in Section 30.

12 Bleed the power steering system as described in Section 34.

34 Bleeding the power steering system

1 Following any operation in which the power steering fluid lines have been disconnected, the power steering system must be bled of air to obtain proper steering performance.
2 With the front wheels turned all the way to the left check the power steering fluid level and, if low, add fluid until it reaches the 'Cold' mark on the dipstick.
3 Start the engine and allow it to run at fast idle. Recheck the fluid level and add more if necessary to reach the 'Cold' mark on the dipstick.
4 Bleed the system by turning the wheels from side to side without hitting the stops. This will work the air out of the system. Be careful that the reservoir does not run empty of fluid.
5 When the air is worked out of the system, return the wheels to the straight-ahead position and leave the car running for several more minutes before shutting it off.
6 Road test the car to be sure the steering system is functioning normally and is free from noise.
7 Recheck the fluid level to be sure it is up to the 'Hot' mark on the dipstick while the engine is at normal operating temperature and add fluid if necessary.

Chapter 12 Bodywork and subframe

Refer to Chapter 13 for specifications and information related to 1981 through 1984 models

Contents

Specifications

Pontiac Phoenix
Overall length
2-door Coupe .... 182.1 in (4626 mm)
5-door Hatchback .... 179.3 in (4555 mm)
Overall width
2-door Coupe .... 69.1 in (1754 mm)
5-door Hatchback .... 69.6 in (1768 mm)
Trackbase .... 104.9 in (2664 mm)
Front .... 58.7 in (1492 mm)
Rear .... 57.0 in (1447 mm)
Curb weight
2-door Coupe .... 2517.9 lb (1143 kg)
5-door Hatchback .... 2563.9 lb (1164 kg)

Oldsmobile Omega
Overall length (all models) .... 181.8 in (4617 mm)
Wheelbase (all models) .... 104.9 in (2664 mm)

Torque specifications

	ft-lb	m-kg
Cradle-to-body bolts	80	11.0
Cradle section attaching bolts	40	5.5
Damper-to-cradle bolt (L4)	18	2.5
Energy absorber-to-bumper bracket nuts	33	4.6
Energy absorber-to-body bolts	25	3.5
Hood hinge screws	20	2.8
Fender attaching screws	7	1.0
Front end panel mounting screws (Omega)	7	1.0
Secondary hood latch bracket screws	5	0.7
Primary hood latch screws	20	2.8
Secondary latch center support screws	7	1.0
Brace mounting screws	40	5.5
Window regulator sash-to-window sash bolts	6	0.8
Door hinge bolts	20	2.8
Door lock attaching screws	7	1.0
Seat belt anchor bolts	30	4.1
Seat belt anchor nuts	45	6.2
Seat adjuster-to-floor pan bolts and nuts	18	2.5
Seat adjuster-to-seat frame bolts	18	2.5

1 Body – general information

1 Both the Omega and the Phoenix are available in two basic body styles. The Omega is available as a four-door sedan or two-door coupe, while the Phoenix is available as a two-door coupe or five-door hatchback. In addition, there are various optional exterior and interior trim packages, such as the Omega Brougham luxury version and the SX sport version for Oldsmobile and the SJ sport version and the LJ luxury version for Pontiac. Differences between the various styles are noted when appropriate in the service procedures within this chapter.
2 All of the X-bodies use a unitized body construction in which the body is designed to provide vehicle rigidity so that a separate frame is not necessary. Mainly for noise and vibration reasons, a subframe is used in the engine compartment and is detailed in Section 40.
3 Certain body panels which are particularly vulnerable to accident damage can be replaced by unbolting them and installing replacement items. These panels include the fenders, inner fender skirts, grille, bumpers and trunk.

2 Body maintenance

1 The condition of your vehicle's bodywork is of considerable importance as it is on this that the resale value will mainly depend. It is much more difficult to repair neglected bodywork than to renew mechanical assemblies. The hidden portions of the body, such as the wheel arches, fender skirts, the underframe and the engine compartment, are equally unimportant, although obviously not requiring such frequent attention as the immediately visible paint.
2 Once a year or every 12 000 miles it is a sound idea to visit your local dealer and have the underside of the body steam cleaned. All traces or dirt and oil will be removed and the underside can then be inspected carefully for rust, damaged hydraulic pipes, frayed electrical wiring and similar trouble areas. The front suspension should be greased on completion of this job.
3 At the same time, clean the engine and the engine compartment either using a steam cleaner or a water-soluble cleaner.
4 The wheel arches and fender shirts should be given particular attention as undercoating can easily come away here and stones and dirt thrown up from the wheels can soon cause the paint to chip and flake and so allow rust to set in. If rust is found, clean down to the bare metal and apply an anti-rust paint.
5 Use a mild detergent and soft sponge to wash the exterior of the car and rinse immediately with clear water. Owners who live in coastal regions and where salt or chemicals are used on the roads should wash the finish religiously to prevent damage to the finish. Do not wash the car in direct sunlight or when the metal is warm. To remove road tar, insects or tree sap use a tar remover rather than a knife or sharp objects which could scratch the surface.
6 A good coat of wax or polish may be your best protection against the elements. Use a good grade of polish or wax suitable for a high-quality synthetic finish. Do not use a wax or polish which contains large amounts of abrasives as these will scratch the finish.

7 Bright metal parts can be protected with wax or a chrome preservative. During winter months or in coastal regions apply a heavier coating or, if necessary, use a non-corrosive compound like petroleum jelly for protection. Do not use abrasive cleaners, strong detergents or materials like steel wool on chrome or anodized aluminium parts as these may damage the protective coating and cause discolouration or deterioration.
8 Interior surfaces can be wiped clean with a damp cloth or with cleaners specifically designed for car interior fabrics. Carefully read the manufacturer's instructions and test any commercial cleaners on an inconspicuous area first. The carpet should be vacuumed regularly and can be covered with mats.
9 Cleaning the mechanical parts of the car serves two useful functions. First, it focuses your attention on parts which may be starting to fail, allowing you to fix or replace them before they cause problems. Second, it is much more pleasant to work on parts which are relatively clean. You will still get dirty on major repair jobs, but it will be less extreme. Large areas like the firewall and inner fender panels should be brushed with detergent, allowed to soak for about 15 minutes, and then carefully rinsed clean. Cover ignition and carburetor points with plastic to prevent moisture from penetrating these critical components.

3 Upholstery and carpets – maintenance

1 Remove the carpets or mats and thoroughly vacuum clean the interior of the vehicle every three months or more frequently if necessary.
2 Beat out the carpets and vacuum clean them if they are very dirty. If the upholstery is soiled apply an upholstery cleaner with a damp sponge and wipe off with a clean dry cloth.
3 Consult your local dealer or auto parts store for cleaners made especially for newer automotive upholstery fabrics. Always test the cleaner in an inconspicuous place

4 Roof covering – maintenance

Under no circumstances try to clean any external vinyl roof covering with detergents, caustic soap or spirit cleaners. Plain soap and water is all that is required, with a soft brush to clean dirt that may be ingrained. Wash the covering as frequently as the rest of the vehicle.

5 Body damage – minor repair

See photo sequences on pages 310 and 311.

Repair of minor scratches in the vehicle's bodywork
If the scratch is very superficial, and does not penetrate to the

metal of the bodywork, repair is very simple. Lightly rub the area of the scratch with a paintwork renovator, or a very fine cutting paste, to remove loose paint from the scratch and to clear the surrounding bodywork of wax polish. Rinse the area with clean water.

Apply touch-up paint to the scratch using a thin paint brush; continue to apply thin layers of paint until the surface of the paint in the scratch is level with the surrounding paintwork. Allow the new paint at least two weeks to harden; then blend it into the surrounding paintwork by rubbing the paintwork, in the scratch area, with a paintwork renovator or a very fine cutting paste. Finally, apply wax polish.

An alternative to painting over the scratch is to use a paint transfer. Use the same preparation for the affected area, then simply pick a patch of a suitable size to cover the scratch completely. Hold the patch against the scratch and burnish its backing paper; the paper will adhere to the paintwork, freeing itself from the backing paper at the same time. Polish the affected area to blend the patch into the surrounding paintwork.

Where the scratch has penetrated right through to the metal of the bodywork, causing the metal to rust, a different repair technique is required. Remove any loose rust from the bottom of the scratch with a penknife, then apply rust inhibiting paint to prevent the formation of rust in the future. Using a rubber or nylon applicator, fill the scratch with bodystopper paste. If required, this paste can be mixed with cellulose thinners to provide a very thin paste which is ideal for filling narrow scratches. Before the stopper-paste in the scratch hardens, wrap a piece of smooth cotton rag around the top of a finger. Dip the finger in cellulose thinners and then quickly sweep it across the surface of the stopper-paste in the scratch; this will ensure that the surface of the stopper-paste is slightly hollowed. The scratch can now be painted over as described earlier in this Section.

Repair of dents in the vehicle's bodywork

When deep denting of the vehicle's bodywork has taken place, the first task is to pull the dent out, until the affected bodywork almost attains its original shape. There is little point in trying to restore the original shape completely, as the metal in the damaged area will have stretched on impact and cannot be reshaped fully to its original contour. It is better to bring the level of the dent up to a point which is about $\frac{1}{8}$-in (3 mm) below the level of the surrounding bodywork. In cases where the dent is very shallow anyway, it is not worth trying to pull it out at all.

If the underside of the dent is accessible, it can be hammered out gently from behind, using a mallet with a wooden or plastic head. Whilst doing this, hold a suitable block of wood firmly against the outside of the panel to absorb the impact from the hammer blows and thus prevent a large area of the bodywork from being 'belled-out'.

Should the dent be in a section of the bodywork which has double skin or some other factor making it inaccessible from behind, a different technique is called for. Drill several small holes through the metal inside the area – particularly in the deeper section. Then screw long self-tapping screws into the holes just sufficiently for them to gain a good purchase in the metal. Now the dent can be pulled out by pulling on the protruding heads of the screws with a pair of pliers.

The next stage of the repair is the removal of the paint from the damaged area, and from an inch or so of the surrounding 'sound' bodywork. This is accomplished most easily by using a wire brush or abrasive pad on a power drill, although it can be done just as effectively by hand using sheets of abrasive paper. To complete the preparation for filling, score the surface of the bare metal with a screwdriver or the tang of a file, or alternatively, drill small holes in the affected area. This will provide a really good 'key' for the filler paste.

To complete the repair see the Section on filling and re-spraying.

Repair of rust holes or gashes in the vehicle's bodywork

Remove all paint from the affected area and from an inch or so of the surrounding 'sound' bodywork, using an abrasive pad or a wire brush on a power drill. If these are not available a few sheets of abrasive paper will do the job just as effectively. With the paint removed you will be able to gauge the severity of the corrosion and therefore decide whether to renew the whole panel (if this is possible) or to repair the affected area. New body panels are not as expensive as most people think and it is often quicker and more satisfactory to fit a new panel than to attempt to repair large areas of corrosion.

Remove all fittings from the affected area except those which will act as a guide to the original shape of the damaged bodywork (eg headlamp shells etc). Then, using tin snips or a hacksaw blade, remove all loose metal and any other metal badly affected by corrosion. Hammer the edges of the hole inward in order to create a slight depression for the filler paste.

Wire brush the affected area to remove the powdery rust from the surface of the remaining metal. Paint the affected area with rust inhibiting paint; if the back of the rusted area is accessible treat this also.

Before filling can take place it will be necessary to block the hole in some way. This can be achieved by the use of Zinc gauze or Aluminum tape.

Zinc gauze is probably the best material to use for a large hole. Cut a piece to the approximate size and shape of the hole to be filled, then position it in the hole so that its edges are below the level of the surrounding bodywork. It can be retained in position by several blobs of filler paste around its periphery.

Aluminum tape should be used for small or very narrow holes. Pull a piece off the roll and trim it to the approximate size and shape required, then pull off the backing paper (if used) and stick the tape over the hole; it can be overlapped if the thickness of one piece is insufficient. Burnish down the edges of the tape with the handle of a screwdriver or similar tool, to ensure that the tape is securely attached to the metal underneath.

Bodywork repairs – filling and re-spraying

Before using this Section, see the Sections on dent, deep scratch, rust holes and gash repairs.

Many types of bodyfiller are available, but generally speaking those proprietary kits which contain a tin of filler paste and a tube of resin hardener are best for this type of repair. A wide, flexible plastic or nylon applicator will be found invaluable for imparting a smooth and well-contoured finish to the surface of the filler.

Mix up a little filler on a clean piece of card or board – measure the hardener carefully (follow the maker's instructions on the pack) otherwise the filler will set too rapidly or too slowly.

Using the applicator apply the filler paste to the prepared area; draw the applicator across the surface of the filler to achieve the correct contour and to level the filler surface. As soon as a contour that approximates the correct one is achieved, stop working the paste – if you carry on too long the paste will become sticky and begin to 'pick up' on the applicator. Continue to add thin layers of filler paste at twenty-minute intervals until the level of the filler is just proud of the surrounding bodywork.

Once the filler has hardened, excess can be removed using a metal plane or file. From then on, progressively finer grades of sandpaper should be used, starting with a 40-grade production paper and finishing with 400-grade wet-and-dry paper. Always wrap the abrasive paper around a flat rubber, cork, or wooden block – otherwise the surface of the filler will not be completely flat. During the smoothing of the filler surface the wet-and-dry paper should be periodically rinsed in water. This will ensure that a very smooth finish is imparted to the filler at the final stage.

At this stage the 'repair area' should be surrounded by a ring of bare metal, which in turn should be encircled by the finely 'feathered' edge of the good paintwork. Rinse the repair area with clean water, until all of the dust produced by the rubbing-down operation has gone.

Spray the whole repair area with a light coat of primer – this will show up any imperfections in the surface of the filler. Repair these imperfections with fresh filler paste or bodystopper, and once more smooth the surface with abrasive paper. If bodystopper is used, it can be mixed with cellulose thinners to form a really thin paste which is ideal for filling small holes. Repeat this spray and repair procedure until you are satisfied that the surface of the filler, and the feathered edge of the paintwork are perfect. Clean the repair area with clean water and allow to dry fully.

The repair area is now ready for final spraying. Paint spraying must be carried out in warm, dry, windless and dust free atmosphere. This condition can be created artificially if you have access to a large indoor working area, but if you are forced to work in the open, you will have to pick your day very carefully. If you are working indoors, dousing the floor in the work area with water will help to settle the dust which would otherwise be in the atmosphere. If the repair area is confined to one body panel, mask off the surrounding panels; this will help to minimize the effects of a slight mis-match in paint colors. Bodywork fittings (eg chrome strips, door handles etc) will also need to be masked off. Use genuine masking tape and several thicknesses of newspaper for the masking operations.

Before commencing to spray, agitate the aerosol can thoroughly, then spray a test area (an old tin, or similar) until the technique is mastered. Cover the repair area with a thick coat of primer; the thickness should be built up using several thin layers of paint rather than one thick one. Using 400-grade wet-and-dry paper, rub down the surface of the primer until it is really smooth. While doing this, the work area should be thoroughly doused with water, and the wet-and-dry paper periodically rinsed in water. Allow to dry before spraying on more paint.

Spray on the top coat, again building up the thickness by using several thin layers of paint. Start spraying in the centre of the repair area and then, using a circular motion, work outward until the whole repair area and about 2 inches of the surrounding original paintwork is covered. Remove all masking material 10 to 15 minutes after spraying on the final coat of paint. Allow the new paint at least two weeks to harden, then, using a paintwork renovator or a very fine cutting paste, blend the edges of the paint into the existing paintwork. Finally, apply wax polish.

6 Body and subframe damage – major repair

1 Major damage must be repaired by competent mechanics with the necessary welding and hydraulic straightening equipment.
2 If the damage has been serious it is vital that the body and subframe be checked for correct alignment as otherwise the handling of the vehicle will suffer and many other faults – such as excessive tire wear, and wear in the transmission and steering – may occur.
3 There is a special body jig which most body repair shops have and to ensure that all is correct it is important that this jig be used for all major repair work.

7 Headlight – adjustment

1 The headlight adjustment screws are located to the side and top of each lamp (photo). The top screw adjusts the lamp's beam vertically and the side screw adjusts the beam horizontally. Although due to legal specifications, proper adjustment of the headlight should be done using appropriate beam setting equipment, the following procedure will get them very close. Final adjustment should be done by a qualified mechanic with the proper equipment.
2 Position the car on level ground, facing and at right angles to a wall, and at a distance of approximately thirty feet.
3 Measure the height of the centers of the headlights from the ground and mark these measurements on the wall.
4 Measure the distance from the center line of the car and the center of each headlight and mark these measurements on the wall, so that you have intersecting lines even with the center of each headlight.
5 Turn on the regular beam of the headlights and turn the horizontal adjusting screws until each beam is centered with their corresponding

marks on the wall. Then, turn the vertical adjusting screw until the top of each beam is level with the horizontal centerline mark on the wall.
6 Bounce the car on its suspension and check that the beams return to their correct positions.

8 Headlight – removal and installation

1 Remove the headlight trim cover (Phoenix) (photo) or grille panel (Omega), as appropriate.
2 Remove the headlight retaining ring (photo).
3 Pull the headlight bulb from its carrier and unplug the bulb from its electrical connector (photo).
4 Installation is the reverse of the removal procedure.

9 Front parking/turn signal lights (Phoenix) – removal, bulb replacement and installation

1 Remove the headlight trim cover.
2 Remove the screws that secure the lamp housing to the body (photo) and lift the lamp off.

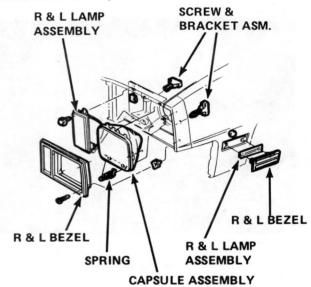

Fig. 12.1 Exploded view of the Phoenix headlight, parking and side marker light components (Section 8)

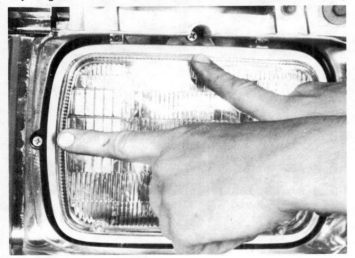

7.1 Headlight adjusting screws

8.1 Removing the Phoenix headlight trim cover

This photo sequence illustrates the repair of a dent and damaged paintwork. The procedure for the repair of a hole is similar. Refer to the text for more complete instructions

After removing any adjacent body trim, hammer the dent out. The damaged area should then be made slightly concave

Use coarse sandpaper or a sanding disc on a drill motor to remove all paint from the damaged area. Feather the sanded area into the edges of the surrounding paint, using progressively finer grades of sandpaper

The damaged area should be treated with rust remover prior to application of the body filler. In the case of a rust hole, all rusted sheet metal should be cut away

Carefully follow manufacturer's instructions when mixing the body filler so as to have the longest possible working time during application. Rust holes should be covered with fiberglass screen held in place with dabs of body filler prior to repair

Apply the filler with a flexible applicator in thin layers at 20 minute intervals. Use an applicator such as a wood spatula for confined areas. The filler should protrude slightly above the surrounding area

Shape the filler with a surform-type plane. Then, use water and progressively finer grades of sandpaper and a sanding block to wet-sand the area until it is smooth. Feather the edges of the repair area into the surrounding paint.

Use spray or brush applied primer to cover the entire repair area so that slight imperfections in the surface will be filled in. Prime at least one inch into the area surrounding the repair. Be careful of over-spray when using spray-type primer

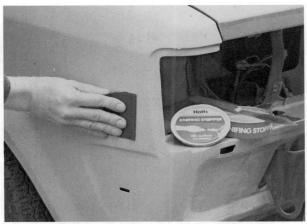

Wet-sand the primer with fine (approximately 400 grade) sandpaper until the area is smooth to the touch and blended into the surrounding paint. Use filler paste on minor imperfections

After the filler paste has dried, use rubbing compound to ensure that the surface of the primer is smooth. Prior to painting, the surface should be wiped down with a tack rag or lint-free cloth soaked in lacquer thinner

Choose a dry, warm, breeze-free area in which to paint and make sure that adjacent areas are protected from over-spray. Shake the spray paint can thoroughly and apply the top coat to the repair area, building it up by applying several coats, working from the center

After allowing at least two weeks for the paint to harden, use fine rubbing compound to blend the area into the original paint. Wax can now be applied

8.2 Removing the headlight retaining ring

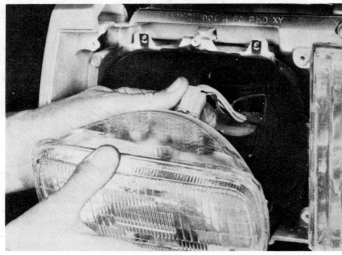

8.3 Unplugging the headlight electrical connector from the headlight

9.2 Removing the Phoenix parking light

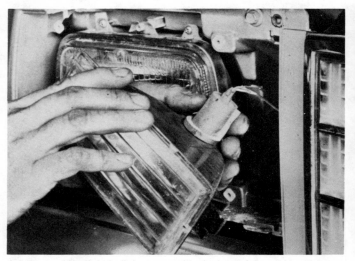

9.3 The parking light bulb is mounted in the rear of the parking light housing

3   Remove the bulb by disconnecting the bulb socket from the rear of the lamp housing (photo).
4   Installation is the reverse of the removal procedure.

10 Front parking/turn signal lights (Omega) – removal, bulb replacement and installation

1   Remove the grille panel.
2   If only the bulb needs to be replaced, simply disconnect the bulb socket from the rear of the lamp housing. Remove the old bulb from the socket, insert the new bulb and reinstall the socket into the lamp housing.
3   If the entire housing needs to be removed, first remove the bulb and socket from the rear of the housing. Then remove the screws that hold the housing to the grille panel.
4   Installation is the reverse of the removal procedure.

11 Grille – removal and installation

1   The grille on the Phoenix is a one-piece unit that is secured to the radiator support by six screws (Fig. 12.3). Removal and installation of the grille simply entails removing and installing the mounting screws.

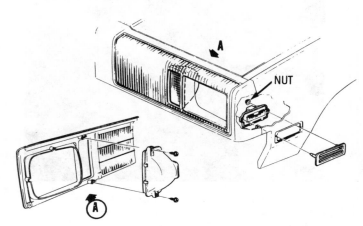

Fig. 12.2 Mounting arrangement of the Omega parking and side marker lights (Section 10)

2   The Omega incorporates two grille panels which are attached to the front end panel by mounting screws (Fig. 12.4).

   a)   *Remove the grille panel mounting screws and lift off the grille panel.*
   b)   *Disconnect the bulb socket from the rear of the parking/turn signal lamp housing.*
   c)   *Remove the screws that attach the lamp housing to the grille panel.*
   d)   *Installation is the reverse of the removal procedure.*

12 Front end panel (Omega) – removal and installation

1   Remove both grille panels as described in Section 11.

2   Remove the screws that attach the front end panel to the body and lift off the panel.
3   Installation is the reverse of the removal procedure.

13 Taillights – bulb replacement

1   Open the rear compartment lid.
2   On Phoenix hatchback models, remove the rear interior trim panel.
3   From inside of the car, remove the plastic wing nuts that secure the taillight assembly to the rear end panel.
4   Pull the taillight assembly forward out of its mounting holes to allow access to the bulb sockets (photo).
5   Replace bulbs as necessary.
6   Installation is the reverse of the removal procedure.

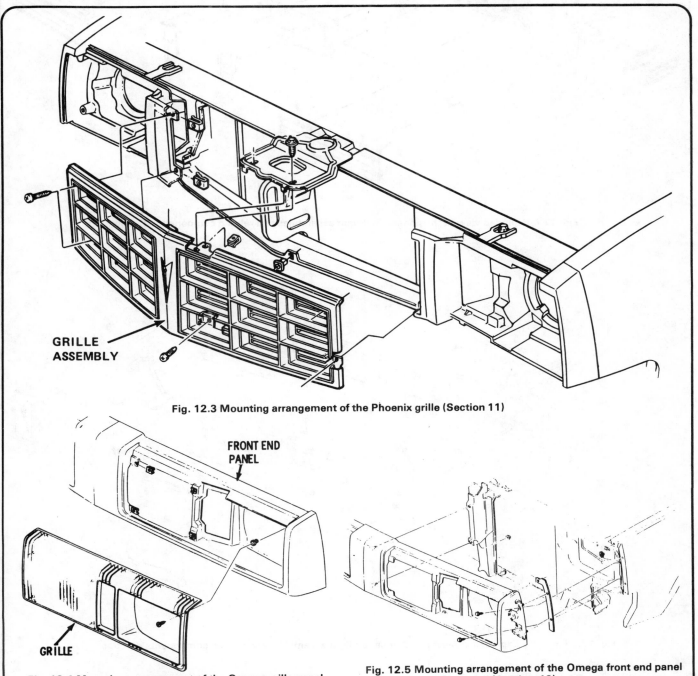

GRILLE
ASSEMBLY

Fig. 12.3 Mounting arrangement of the Phoenix grille (Section 11)

FRONT END
PANEL

GRILLE

Fig. 12.4 Mounting arrangement of the Omega grille panel
(Section 11)

Fig. 12.5 Mounting arrangement of the Omega front end panel
(Section 12)

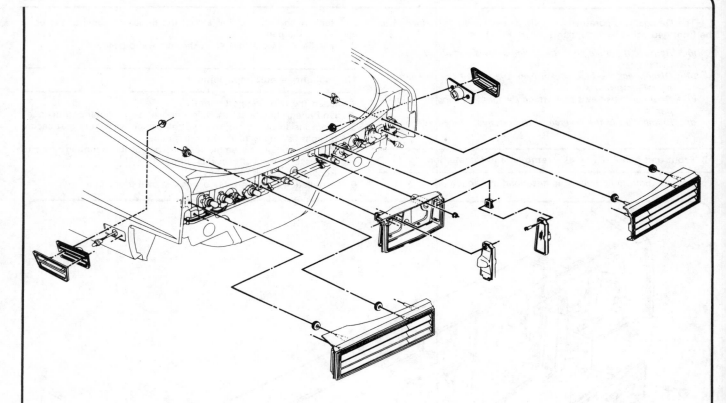

Fig. 12.6 Exploded view of the phoenix tail-light assemblies and related components (Section 13)

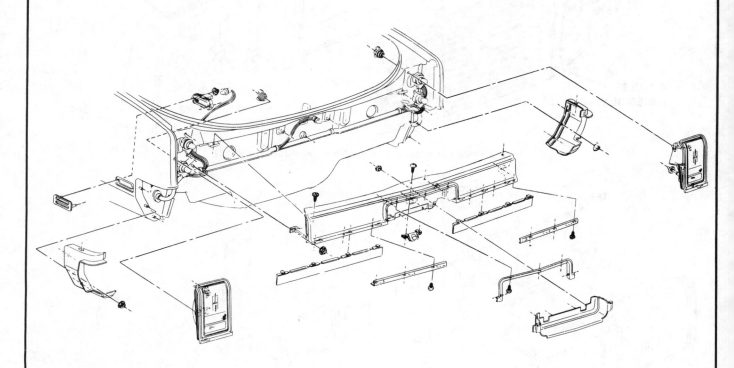

Fig. 12.7 Fig. 12.7 Exploded view of the Omega tail-light assemblies and related components (Section 13)

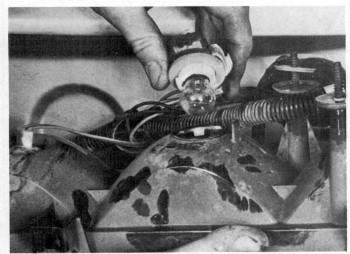

13.4 The tail-light bulbs can be removed from the rear of the tail-light housing after removing it from the car

14 Side-marker lights – general

1 All X-Body models use side marker lights both in the front and rear of the car. Both the front and rear side marker lights work in conjunction with the parking lights circuit.

2 The three basic methods of mounting for the lamp housings are as folows:

   a) *Studs with nuts accessible from the trunk (rear lights) or from inside of the front wheel well (front lights).*
   b) *Studs with nuts accessible after removal of the rear end finishing panel (hatchback rear lights).*
   c) *External screws.*

15 Dome lights – removal and installation

1 The dome lamp works in conjunction with the door jamb switch and/or the headlight switch. The dome lamp wiring harness is routed up the right windshield pillar and across the inner roof panel to the lamp.

2 To remove the dome lamp lens, insert a flat-head screwdriver between the lens and the lamp housing, and press inward and down to disengage the lens retaining tabs from the housing.

3 If bulb replacement is all that is required, simply remove the old bulb from the terminal clips, install a new bulb and snap the lens back in place on the lamp housing.

4 If the lamp housing needs to be removed, remove the two mounting screws.

5 To disengage the wiring harness, use pliers to grasp the terminal clip and push the clips through the back of the housing.

6 To separate the housing assembly, insert a flat-head screwdriver between the reflector and roof bow, and pry upward to disengage the push-on retainers that hold the housing assembly together.

7 To install, reverse the removal procedure.

16 Wiper blade – removal and installation

1 Two methods are used to retain the wiper blades to the wiper arms.

2 One method uses a press-type release tab which, when pressed, allows the wiper blade to be separated from the arm.

3 The other method uses a coil spring retainer. With this design a screwdriver must be inserted on top of the spring and then pressed downward to release the blade.

4 To install, insert the blade over the pin at the tip of the arm and press until the spring retainer or clip engages the groove in the pin.

5 The rubber element is retained in the blade assembly also by two different methods.

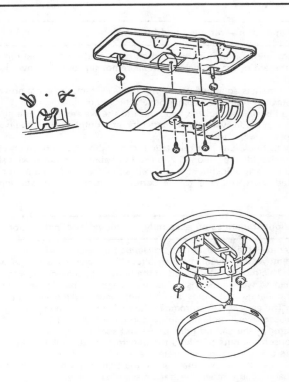

Fig. 12.8 Exploded view of typical dome lights (Section 15)

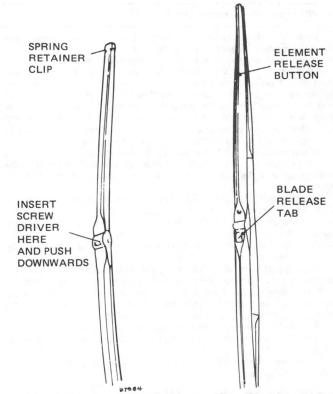

SPRING RETAINER CLIP

ELEMENT RELEASE BUTTON

INSERT SCREW DRIVER HERE AND PUSH DOWNWARDS

BLADE RELEASE TAB

Fig. 12.9 The two types of wiper blades feature different methods of element and blade retention (Section 16)

6 One method uses a press-type button which, when pressed, allows the element to be slid off the blade assembly.

7 The other method uses a spring-type retainer clip in the end of the blade which, when squeezed, allows the element to be slid off the blade assembly.

17 Wiper arm – removal and installation

1   The wiper arm must be pried off of its shaft and is best removed with the aid of the windshield wiper removing tool as shown in Fig. 12.10.
2   On models equipped with a wet blade system, the wiper arm must be detached from the washer hose after removal.
3   To install, connect the wiper arm to the washer hose, if equipped with a wet blade system, and install the arm onto its shaft, again using the special wiper tool.
4   With the wiper arm reinstalled, check the parked position of the arm. It should be positioned 2 in (50 mm) above the lower windshield molding. If any adjustment is required, simply remove the arm from the serrated shaft, rotate it to the correct position and reinstall on the shaft.

18 Wiper transmission assembly – removal and installation

1   Remove the wiper arms as described in Section 17.
2   Remove the reveal molding along the lower edge of the windshield. This molding is secured to the body with slide-on clips that are attached to weld-on studs or screws. A tab on the clip engages the molding flange and holds the molding between the clip and body metal. The easiest way to remove the molding from the retaining clips is to use a reveal molding tool as shown in Fig. 12.12
3   Remove the shroud grille panel and screen (Fig. 12.13).
4   Loosen the nuts that hold the transmission drive link to the wiper motor's crank arm, and separate the two.
5   Remove the screws that secure the transmission assembly to the cowl panel, and remove the transmission assembly.
6   Installation is the reverse of the removal procedure.

19 Wiper motor – removal and installation

1   Proceed with paragraphs 1 through 4 of the wiper transmission assembly removal sequence in Section 18.
2   Disconnect all electrical leads from the wiper motor.
3   On cars equipped with air-conditioning, the A/C evaporator unit and tubing limit removal clearance of the wiper motor, necessitating the removal of the crank arm. To do this, remove the 3 wiper motor mounting bolts. Then while supporting the motor, use locking type pliers to hold the crank arm steady while you remove the crank arm nut. If the nut is removed prior to removing the motor mounting bolts, possible damage to the internal nylon gear could result.
4   If additional clearance is required, the park switch can be removed from the motor by pushing in the retainer tab and pulling out the park switch assembly. The motor can now be removed by rotating it up and outward.
5   On cars not equipped with air-conditioning, simply remove the wiper motor mounting bolts and lift out the motor.
6   The motor can now either be rebuilt or exchanged for a new or rebuilt unit.
7   On cars not equipped with air-conditioning, installation is the reverse of the removal procedure.
8   If equipped with air-conditioning place the motor in its installed position in the engine compartment so that the motor shaft is positioned through the front end panel. Install the crank arm onto the shaft and secure it with its attaching nut. Again a locking type pliers can be used to keep the crank arm from turning.
9   Reinstall the park switch assembly into the motor.
10 Install the wiper motor mounting bolts and reconnect the electrical leads.
11 The remainder of the installation procedure is the reverse of the removal procedure.

20 Windshield and back window – removal and installation

1   These operations are best left to specialists as the glass is retained by quick-setting adhesive/caulk material which leaves no room for error in application or positioning of the windshield.
2   The rear-view mirror support is bonded to the windshield and can only be removed by extremely careful application of heat from an air gun (250° to 350°F) – another job for a specialist.

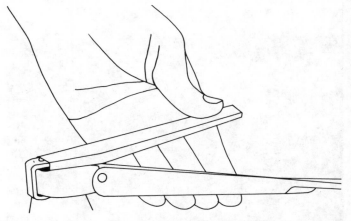

Fig. 12.10 The windshield wiper arm is easily removed by using a wiper arm removing tool (Section 17)

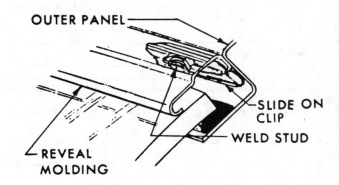

Fig. 12.11 The windshield reveal molding is mounted to the body by slide-on clips secured to welded studs or screws (Sections 18 and 39)

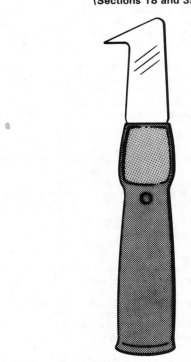

Fig. 12.12 Removing windshield reveal molding is more easily accomplished by using a reveal molding removal tool to separate the molding from the clips (Sections 18 and 39)

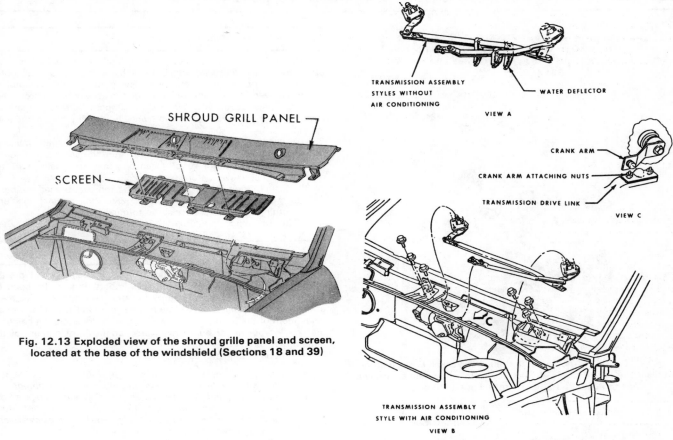

SHROUD GRILL PANEL

SCREEN

TRANSMISSION ASSEMBLY
STYLES WITHOUT
AIR CONDITIONING

WATER DEFLECTOR

VIEW A

CRANK ARM

CRANK ARM ATTACHING NUTS

TRANSMISSION DRIVE LINK

VIEW C

TRANSMISSION ASSEMBLY
STYLE WITH AIR CONDITIONING

VIEW B

Fig. 12.13 Exploded view of the shroud grille panel and screen, located at the base of the windshield (Sections 18 and 39)

Fig. 12.14 Windshield wiper transmission assembly (Section 18)

ON STYLES EQUIPPED WITH AIR CONDITIONING, REMOVE MOTOR ATTACHING BOLTS PRIOR TO REMOVING CRANK ARM ATTACHING NUT. CRANK ARM MUST BE REMOVED BEFORE MOTOR CAN BE LIFTED PAST A/C EVAPORATOR UNIT.

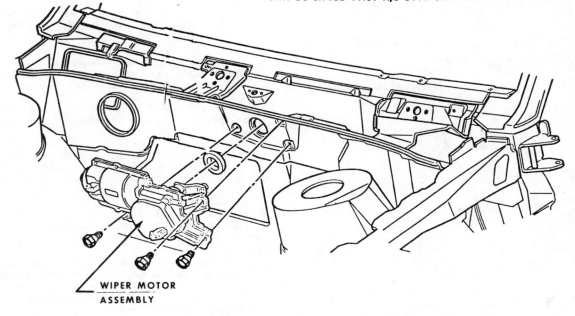

WIPER MOTOR ASSEMBLY

Fig. 12.15 Location of the windshield wiper motor (Section 19)

CRANK ARM MUST BE HELD SECURELY IN PLACE
WHEN REMOVING AND INSTALLING CRANK ARM
RETAINING NUT TO AVOID POSSIBLE DAMAGE
TO INTERNAL GEARS.

NUT

CRANK ARM

SHAFT SEAL
(RUBBER)

SPACER
(PLASTIC)

Fig. 12.16 When removing or installing the crank arm retaining
nut from the wiper motor, the crank arm must be held securely in
place to avoid damage to internal gears (Section 19)

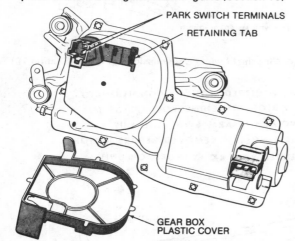

PARK SWITCH TERMINALS

RETAINING TAB

GEAR BOX
PLASTIC COVER

Fig. 12.17 Location of the wiper motor park switch and cover
(Section 19)

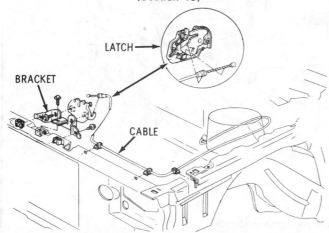

LATCH

BRACKET

CABLE

Fig. 12.18 Hood release cable and latch mechanism (Section 21)

21 Hood latches – general

1   The primary and secondary hood latch assemblies are both
attached to the radiator support. Both latch assemblies have elongated
screw holes for alignment purposes. The primary latch assembly is
easily removed by disconnecting the hood release cable and removing
the screws that secure it to the radiator support. Be sure to mark the
position of the screws before removing, to simplify alignment upon
installation.
2   To remove the secondary latch assembly, the grille must be
removed first, as detailed in Section 11. Then the screws that secure
the latch to the radiator support can be removed. Again, mark the
position of the screws before removing.
3   To install either assembly, reverse the removal procedure, being
sure to match the mounting screws up with their original positions.
The mounting screws should also be torqued to specs.
4   Both assemblies should be lubricated periodically.

22 Hood – alignment

1   To prevent engine compartment fumes from being pulled into the
car interior through the cowl vent it is important that the hood be
properly adjusted and sealed at the cowl area. Fore and aft adjustment
of the hood is made by moving the hinge screws in their slots. Vertical
adjustment of the front of the hood is made by adjusting the height of
the screw-type rubber bumpers located at the front corners of the
radiator support.
2   The hood is adjusted as follows:

   a) *Scribe a line around the entire hinge plate to be repositioned.
       This will enable you to judge the amount of movement.*
   b) *Loosen the appropriate screws on the hood hinge to be
       adjusted and move the hood into the correct alignment. Move
       the hood only a little at a time. Tighten the hinge screws and
       carefully lower the hood to check the position.*
   c) *Adjust the hood bumpers on the radiator support so that the
       hood, when closed, is flush with the fender and grille top
       surfaces.*
   d) *The hood catch and lock assembly is adjustable to provide a
       positive closing of the hood. The hood catch assembly on the
       radiator support section has slotted mounting holes to allow
       the catch to be moved into alignment with the hood lock bolt.
       The lock bolt on the hood can be lengthened or shortened to
       engage with the catch. When closed properly the hood
       bumpers should be slightly compressed.*

3   The catch and lock assembly, as well as the hinges should be
periodically lubricated to prevent sticking or jamming.

23 Hood – removal and installation

1   Raise the hood.
2   Use blankets or cloths to cover the cowl area of the body and the
fenders. This will protect the body and paint as the hood is lifted free
of the car.
3   Disconnect the under-hood lamp wire.
4   Mark the position of the hood on its hinges by outlining the hinge
screws (photo). This will greatly aid alignment when reinstalling.
5   While an assistant supports the hood, remove the hinge-to-hood
screws on both sides.
6   Lift off the hood (photo).
7   Install by reversing the removal procedure.
8   Check the hood alignment and adjust if necessary as described in
Section 22.

24 Hood latch release cable – removal and installation

1   The hood latch cable is a one-piece assembly that includes the pull
handle, control cable and housing.
2   To remove, raise the hood and disengage the cable from the
primary hood latch assembly. Take precautions to keep the hood from
closing and locking while the cable is disconnected.

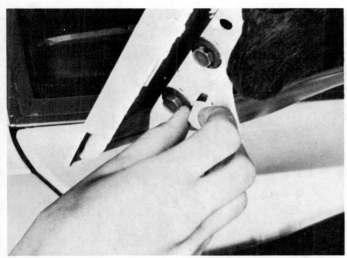

23.4 Prior to removing the hood, the attaching bolts should be marked to maintain proper alignment

23.6 Care should be taken when lifting off the hood so as not to scratch the paint

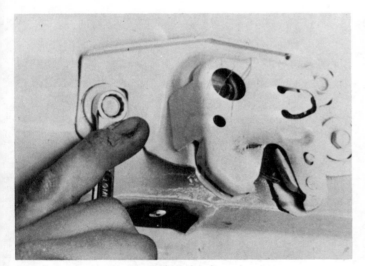

25.2 Removing the hatchback lid lock bolts

26.2 This rivet must be drilled out in order to remove the hatchback lid lock cylinder

3   Unclip the cable from the body.
4   Remove the left shroud side trim panel to the left of the driver's seat.
5   Disengage the control assembly housing from the cable handle cut-out in the trim panel and remove the cable assembly from the panel.
6   Withdraw the cable through the firewall.
7   Installation is the reverse of the removal procedure. When installing, check that the sealing grommet attached to the dash panel is in place.

25 Trunk/hatchback lid lock – removal and installation

1   Open the trunk/hatchback lid. Use a sharp scribe or pencil to mark the outline of the lock on the lid. This will enable you to install the original lock, or its replacement, in the same position.
2   Remove the bolts that secure the lock to the trunk or hatchback lid (photo) and remove the lock.
3   On models with electric lid release units, disconnect the electric connector, remove the solenoid-to-lock bolts and remove the solenoid and lock. See Fig. 12.19.
4   Installation is the reverse of the removal procedure, but use your outline marks for proper positioning.

5   When installation is completed, close the lid and check the engagement of the lock with its striker and adjust if necessary.

26 Trunk/hatchback lid lock cylinder – removal and installation

1   Open the rear compartment lid.
2   Remove the lock cylinder retaining screw, or if a rivet is used (photo), carefully drill out the rivet with a $\frac{5}{32}$-in drill bit.
3   Pull the lock cylinder retainer away from the cylinder and remove it and its gasket.
4   Remove the cylinder from the lid.
5   Installation is the reverse of the removal procedure. Be sure that the lock cylinder shaft engages with the lock, and check its operation with the key before inserting the retaining screw.

27 Gas spring supports (trunk and hatchback lids) – removal and installation

1   Assist in opening trunk and hatchback lids is provided by tubular gas springs which are mounted to the hinge assemblies. These supports are color-coded for each body style and should not be intermixed. When replacing a gas spring, be sure it has the same color

of lettering as the original support.
2   Prop the trunk lid in the full-open position. CAUTION: Do not
attempt to remove or loosen the gas spring supports with the lid in any
other position than fully open.
3   On hatchback models, if equipped with a rear window defogger,
disconnect the wires from both gas springs supports.
4   On hatchback models, if equipped, disconnect the rear compartment cover retainers from the gas springs (Fig. 12.21).
5   Using an awl or similar tool, remove the retaining clips from the
ends of the gas spring supports (photo) and remove the springs.
6   Installation is the reverse of the removal procedure. When
installing the gas springs, the retaining clips will automatically lock
onto the mounting studs.

28 Trunk/hatchback lid – removal and installation

1   Prop the lid fully open.
2   Cover the edges of the rear compartment with cloths or pads to
protect the painted surfaces when the lid is removed.
3   If equipped, disconnect the wiring harness from the lid.
4   On hatchback models, disconnect the gas springs from the
hatchback lid as described in Section 27.
5   Mark the location of the mounting bolts in the hinge.
6   While an assistant supports the lid, remove the mounting bolts
and lift off the lid.
7   Installation is the reverse of the removal procedure.
8   Fore and aft adjustments of the rear trunk lid are controlled by the
position of the hinge bolts in their slots (photo). To adjust, loosen the
hinge bolts, reposition the lid the desired amount and retighten the
bolts.
9   Hatchback lids are also equipped with screw-in rubber bumpers
which control the vertical adjustment of the rear of the lid when closed
(photo).

29 Front seat – removal and installation

1   On a bench-style seat, remove the plastic trim covers over the seat
belt bolts located directly behind the center of the seat.
2   On a bench-style seat, using a serrated-head tool, loosen the seat
belt strap's mounting bolts.
3   Remove the plastic trim covers over the front seat mounts.
4   Remove the mounting nuts or bolts that secure the front seat to
the floor.
5   If equipped, disconnect any electrical wires or connectors to the
front seats.
6   On a bench-style seat, while an assistant lifts the rear of the seat,
pull the seat belts rearward out of their slots in the seat.
7   Remove the seats from the car.
8   Installation is the reverse of the removal procedure.

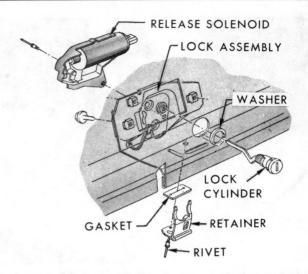

Fig. 12.19 Exploded view of the trunk/hatchback lid lock
mechanism (Section 26)

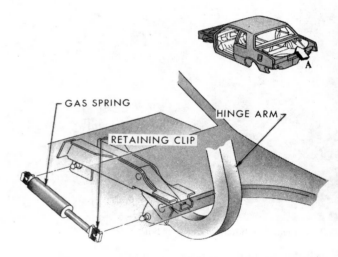

Fig. 12.20 Location of the trunk lid gas springs (Section 27)

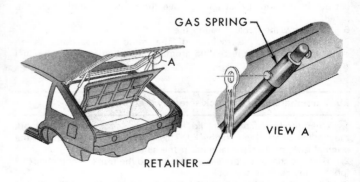

Fig. 12.21 On hatchback models the rear compartment cover
retainers are attached to the gas springs (Section 27)

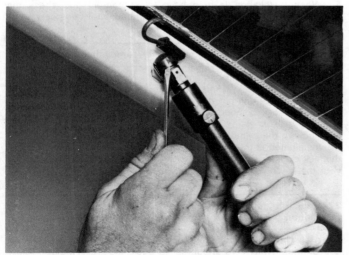

27.5 A small screwdriver or awl can be used to remove the gap spring
attaching clips

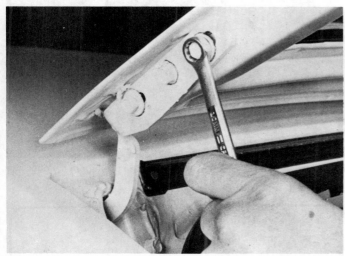

28.8 Loosening the hinge bolts to adjust the hatchback lid

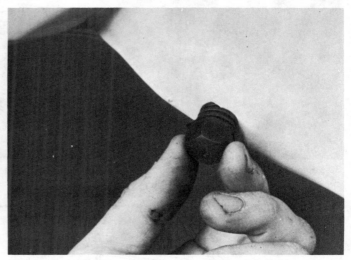

28.9 Vertical adjustment of the hatchback lid is controlled by screw-in rubber bumpers

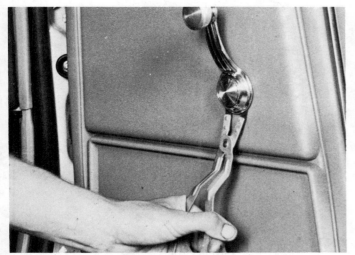

30.1a Removing the spring clip from the window crank handle

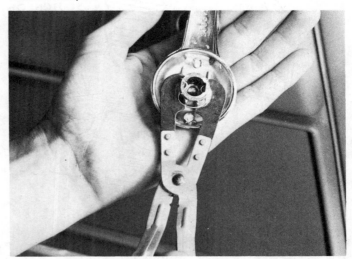

30.1b In order to remove the window crank handle the spring clip removing tool should fit over the clip as shown

30 Door trim panel – removal and installation

1   Remove the window crank handle. This is secured to the regulator shaft with a clip. The trim panel should be pushed away from the handle to expose the shaft and clip. A special spring clip removing tool is available to disengage the clip from its groove (photos). A screwdriver can also be used to remove the clip if care is taken not to tear the panel.
2   Remove the screws that secure the remote control escutcheon to the trim panel.
3   Using a small flat-head screwdriver, insert the blade behind the end of the lock knob and pry it off of its rod (see Fig. 12.22).
4   When the end of the rod is free from the knob, slide the knob rearward and remove it from the escutcheon.
5   Remove the escutcheon from the trim panel (photo).
6   Remove the arm rest mounting screws and remove the arm rest. On models in which the arm rest is molded into the trim panel, remove the screws that secure the pull cup to the arm rest (Fig. 12.23).
7   Remove any exposed screws in the door trim panel.
8   On styles with remote control mirror assemblies, remove the remote mirror escutcheon and disengage the end of the mirror control cable from the escutcheon.
9   On styles with power window controls mounted in the trim panel, remove the switch panel from the trim panel and disconnect the wire harness (Fig. 12.25).

10   The trim panel is attached to the door with plastic retaining clips. To disengage these clips, insert a flat, blunt tool (like a screwdriver blade wrapped with tape) between the metal door skin and the trim panel. Carefully pry the door panel away from the door, keeping the tool close to the clips to prevent damage to the panel. Start at the bottom and work around the door toward the top. The top section is secured at the window channel. Once the retaining clips are pried free, lift the trim panel upward and away from the door (photo).
11   On styles with a courtesy lamp mounted in the lower trim panel, disconnect the wire harness from the lamp.
12   Before installing the trim panel, check that all the trim retaining clips are in good condition and the water shield is correctly applied to the door.
13   If equipped, reconnect the courtesy lamp wire harness.
14   If equipped, reconnect the power window switch wiring harness.
15   Engage the top of the trim panel first and then position the panel correctly on the door. The shaft for the window winder can be used as a rough guide.
16   Press the retaining clips into their respective cups or holes in the door. Pressure can be applied with the palm of your hand or with a clean rubber mallet.
17   Complete the installation procedure by reversing the removal procedure. To install the window crank handle, first install the retaining clip to the handle, align the handle with the one on the opposite door and push the handle onto the shaft. Check that the clip is properly seated in its groove.

30.5 Removing the remote control escutcheon

30.6 Removing the armrest mounting screws

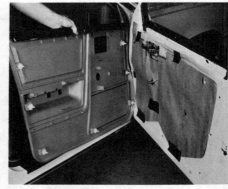

30.10 Lifting the trim panel from the door after disengaging the plastic retaining clips

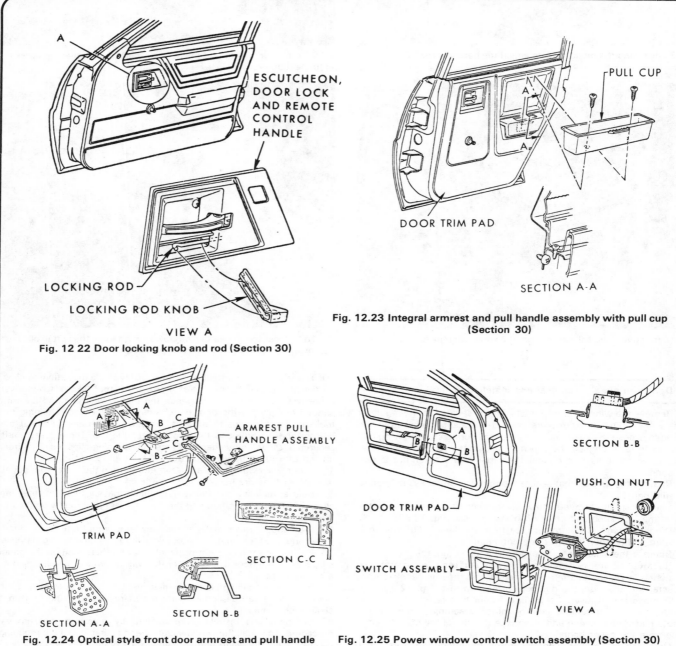

ESCUTCHEON, DOOR LOCK AND REMOTE CONTROL HANDLE

LOCKING ROD

LOCKING ROD KNOB

VIEW A

Fig. 12 22 Door locking knob and rod (Section 30)

PULL CUP

DOOR TRIM PAD

SECTION A-A

Fig. 12.23 Integral armrest and pull handle assembly with pull cup (Section 30)

ARMREST PULL HANDLE ASSEMBLY

TRIM PAD

SECTION C-C

SECTION A-A

SECTION B-B

Fig. 12.24 Optical style front door armrest and pull handle assembly (Section 30)

SECTION B-B

PUSH-ON NUT

DOOR TRIM PAD

SWITCH ASSEMBLY

VIEW A

Fig. 12.25 Power window control switch assembly (Section 30)

31 Door exterior handle – removal and installation

1   Raise the window to the full-up position.
2   Remove the door trim panel as described in Section 30.
3   Pry back the water shield enough to gain access to the exterior handle.
4   Disengage the spring clip from the exterior handle and separate the lock rod from the handle.
5   Remove the two handle mounting nuts.
6   Slide the handle rearward and rotate it up to disengage it from its mounting hole.
7   Installation is the reverse of the removal procedure.

32 Door lock cylinder – removal and installation

1   Raise the window to the full-up position.
2   Remove the trim panel as described in Section 30.
3   Pry back the water shield enough to gain access to the lock cylinder.
4   To help prevent tools or door components from falling down to the bottom of the door cavity, place rags or newspaper inside the cavity.
5   Disenage the lock rod from the lock cylinder.
6   With a screwdriver, slide the lock cylinder retaining clip (on the inboard side of the outer door skin) out of the lock cylinder. Be careful not to damage the outer door skin.
7   With the clip removed, the lock cylinder can be removed from the outside of the door.
8   Installation is a reversal of removal.

33 Door lock assembly – removal and installation

1   Remove the door trim panel as described in Section 30.
2   Pry back the water shield at the rear of the door to gain access to the inside locking assembly.
3   Temporarily install the window crank and roll the window to the full-up position.
4   Disconnect the inside locking rod.
5   Disconnect the lock rod from the interior handle.
6   Disconnect the lock rod from the lock cylinder.
7   If equipped, disconnect the power lock actuator rod.
8   Remove the three lock attaching screws located in the door jamb at the rear of the door. Remove the lock assembly through the access hole.
9   To install, first install the spring clips to the lock assembly, then reverse the removal procedure. Torque the lock assembly mounting screws to specs.

34 Front door window – removal and installation

1   Remove the door trim pad as described in Section 30.
2   Remove the water shield (photo).
3   Raise the window to the full-up position and tape it to the door frame with cloth-backed body tape (photo).
4   Remove the bolts that secure the lower sash channel (attached to the glass), to the regulator sash (photos).
5   If equipped, carefully pull off the rubber down stop at the bottom of the door.
6   Fit the window crank handle over the regulator shaft and run the regulator on the full-down position.
7   Remove the regulator sash by rotating it 90° and pulling it outward.
8   While supporting the glass, remove the tape and carefully lower the glass to the full-down position. Disengage the front edge of the glass from the front run channel retainer. Then slide the glass forward and tilt it slightly to remove the guide clip from the run channel retainer located at the rear leg of the door frame.
9   Carefully raise the glass and while tilting it forward, remove the glass by sliding it out on the inner side of the upper door frame.
10 To remove the guide clip from the glass, wrap tape around a small flat-head screwdriver, then insert the screwdriver between the guide clip and the glass and carefully pry the clip off.
11 The door window sash channel is bonded to the window with a

34.2 Removing the water shield from the door with the aid of a putty knife

34.3 Prior to removing the front door window it should be securely taped to the door frame

34.4a Location of the bolts that secure the lower sash channel to the regulator sash

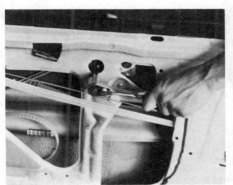

34.1b Removing the lower sash channel bolts with the window up

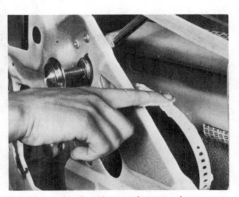

34.14 Lubricating the regulator track

324

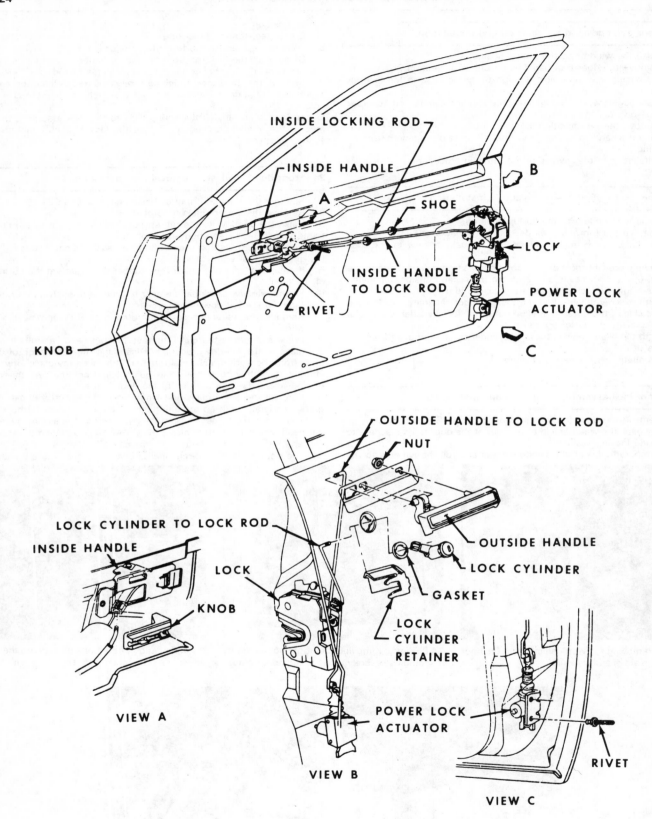

Fig. 12.26 Components of the front door locking system (Sections 32 and 33)

plastisol adhesive. If either the glass or sash channel require replacement, both must be replaced.

12 To install the guide clip onto the glass, first heat the clip with a hot air gun or soak it in hot water for about a minute. Then install the clip by aligning it with the hole in the glass and carefully pressing the clip together at the fastener location.

13 To install the window, lower the glass about halfway into the door and, with one hand on the bottom edge, rotate the glass rearward to snap the guide clip into its retainer.

14 Complete the installation by reversing the removal procedure, with the following notes:

a) *If equipped with a rubber down stop, apply a liquid soap solution to the stop before installing it into the bottom of the door.*

b) *Before installing the trim panel, lubricate the regulator track with a light-duty lithium-based grease, to give it smoother performance (photo).*

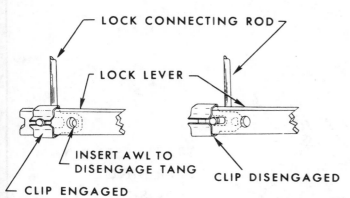

Fig. 12.27 Spring clips are used to secure door control rods and locking rods to their respective levers and handles. Disengagement of the clips is achieved as shown (Sections 33 and 34)

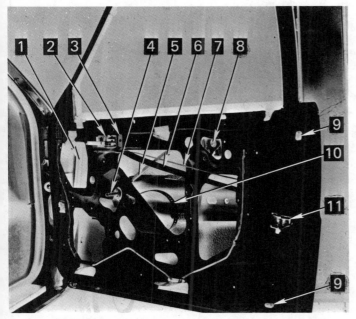

Fig. 12.28 Exposed front door and components (Section 34)

1	Front glass run channel	7	Locking rod
2	Interior door handle	8	Window regulator sash bolts
3	Interior door handle rivet	9	Overslam bumpers
4	Window crank handle shaft	10	Window regulator tape
5	Window regulator track	11	Door lock
6	Door handle to lock rod, in plastic sheath		

35 Front door – removal and installation

1 If equipped with power-operated components:

a) *Disconnect the negative battery cable.*

b) *Remove the trim panel, as described in Section 30.*

c) *Remove the water shield.*

d) *Disconnect the wiring connectors from any power-operated components.*

e) *Remove the rubber conduit from the door and remove the wiring harness from the door through the conduit access hole.*

2 Open the door fully and support it on blocks with cloth pads.

3 Apply cloth-back body tape on the door and body pillars below the upper hinge.

4 Insert a long, flat-head screwdriver underneath the pivot point of the hold-open link and overtop of the spring. Position the screwdriver so it does not apply pressure to the hold-open link.

5 As a safety precaution cover the spring with a shop rag or towel to prevent it from flying off when released. Then lift the screwdriver to disengage the spring.

6 If replacement hinge pin barrel clips are not available, the original clips must be saved. Using two small screwdrivers, spread the clip enough to move it away from its recess toward the pointed end of the pin. The clip will now slide off when the pin is removed.

7 With an assistant supporting the door remove the lower hinge pin by using a rubber or plastic-headed hammer and locking-type pliers.

8 Insert a $\frac{1}{4}$-in x $1\frac{1}{2}$ in bolt into the upper hole of the lower hinge. Then remove the upper pin in the same manner as the lower pin.

9 Remove the bolt from the lower hinge and remove the door from the body.

10 Before installing the door, install the hinge pin clips onto the hinge pins.

11 With the help of an assistant, position the door and insert the small bolt into the $\frac{1}{4}$-in x $1\frac{1}{2}$-in bolt into the upper hole of the lower hinge.

12 With the door in the full-open position, install the upper hinge pin using locking-type pliers and rubber or plastic-headed hammer. A drift punch may also be necessary.

13 Remove the bolt from the lower hinge and install the lower hinge pin.

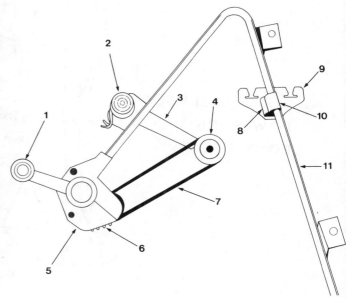

Fig. 12.29 Manual window regulator system (typical) (Section 34)

1	Window crank handle	7	Plastic tape
2	Counter balance spring	8	Block
3	Assist arm	9	Sash
4	Roller	10	Guide
5	Regulator housing	11	Channel
6	Tape attaching tabs		

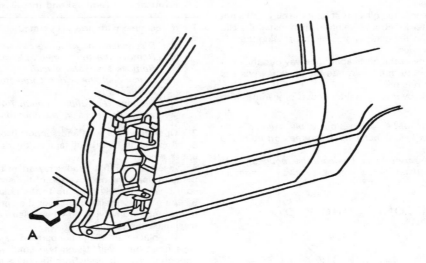

STRAP ASSEMBLY
UPPER HINGE
BODY SIDE

STRAP ASSEMBLY
UPPER HINGE
DOOR SIDE

HINGE SPRING

HOLD-OPEN LINK

HINGE PIN

STRAP ASSEMBLY
LOWER HINGE
BODY SIDE

STRAP ASSEMBLY
LOWER HINGE
DOOR SIDE

VIEW A

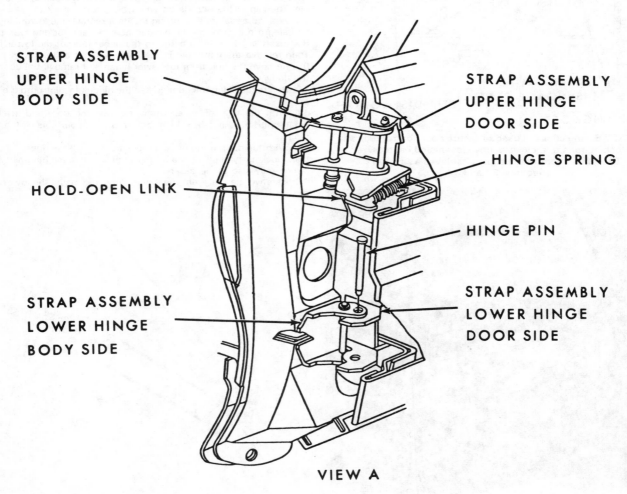

Fig. 12.30 Components of the front door hinge system (Section 35)

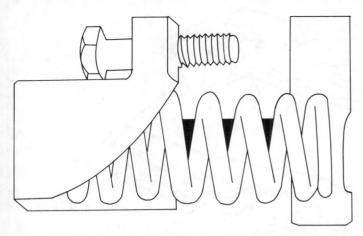

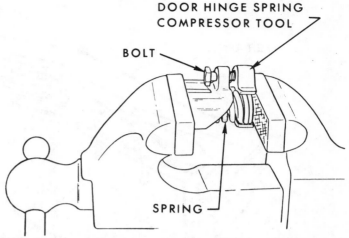

Fig. 12.31 Front door hinge spring compressing tool, with spring (non-compressed) (Section 35)

Fig. 12.32 Using a bench vise to compress the door hinge spring prior to installation (Section 35)

14 The hinge spring must be installed by using a GM hinge-spring installing tool or equivalent. Place the spring in the installing tool and place the tool in a bench vise (Fig. 12.32). Use the vise to compress the tool so the bolt can be threaded into its hole. Tighten the bolt until the spring is fully compressed.

15 Remove the tool, with compressed spring, from the vise and position it in its proper location in the upper hinge. The tool is designed to fit over both the hold-open link and the 'bubble.' Remove the bolt from the tool and allow the spring to extend into its proper position on the hinge. The tool will come out in three pieces.

16 Complete the installation be reversing the removal procedure.

17   The door hinge pins and rollers should be lubricated periodically with 30-weight engine oil. Do not lubricate the contacting surface between the hinge roller and the hold-open link, as this may prevent the roller from rolling properly.

36 Bumpers and energy absorbers – general

1   Both the front and rear bumpers are equipped with gas hydraulic energy absorbers designed to withstand a collision into a fixed barrier at up to 5 mph without damage.

2   The piston tube assembly of these energy absorbers is filled with an inert gas, while the cylinder tube assembly is filled with hydraulic fluid. Upon impact, the energy absorber collapses forcing the hydraulic fluids in the cylinder tube through an orifice and into the piston tube. This provides the energy absorbing action.

3   As the fluid fills the piston tube, the floating piston is forced back in its cylinder, which compresses the gas. After impact, this compressed gas causes the floating piston to force the fluid back into the cylinder tube, which extends the unit to its original position.

4   After any collision, the energy absorbers should be inspected. If obvious physical damage or leaking oil is evident, the unit should be replaced. These absorbers are not designed to be disassembled and, if defective, should be replaced as a unit.

5   Due to the contained gas in the unit, never apply heat to an absorber or weld in its vicinity.

6   A method of testing the condition of the energy absorbers is as follows:

   a)   Position the vehicle in front of a solid, fixed barrier such as a wall, post, etc. The ignition should be off, the shifter should be in 'Park' or 1st gear, depending upon the transaxle, and the parking brake should be on.

   b)   Position a hydraulic or mechanical jack between the barrier and the bumper, so that the jack is in direct line with the absorber being checked. A folded rag between the jack and bumper is recommended to protect the bumper's finish.

   c)   Operate the jack so that it applies pressure and compresses the bumper at least $\frac{3}{8}$-in.

   d)   Release the pressure and the bumper should return to its original position. If it doesn't the absorber needs replacing.

   e)   Repeat the same procedure on all absorbers to be checked.

7   If, following a collision, the absorbers seize in their compressed position and the bumper does not return to its original position, care must be taken in replacing the absorbers. An unexpected spring-back while they're being repaired could cause serious injury. Due to this, it is recommended that a GM dealer or other qualified mechanic perform the repairs.

37 Bumpers (front and rear) – removal and installation

1   Place jack stands under the bumper or have an assistant ready to hold it, so the bumper doesn't drop to the ground when the bolts are removed.

37.4 The Phoenix front bumper is attached to the fender panels as shown

37.5a Removing the nuts that secure the front bumper to the energy absorbers

37.5b Lifting off the front bumper (Phoenix)

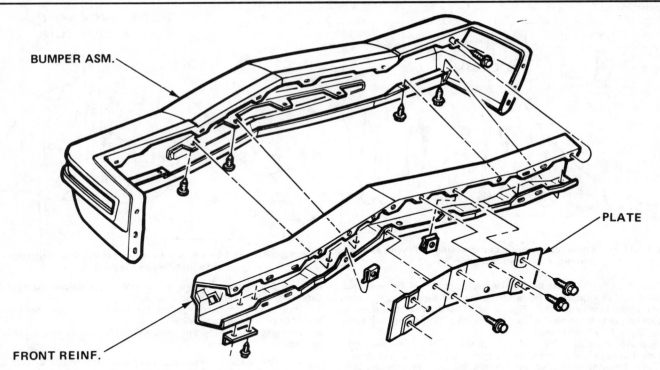

BUMPER ASM.

PLATE

FRONT REINF.

Fig. 12.33 Phoenix front bumper assembly (Section 37)

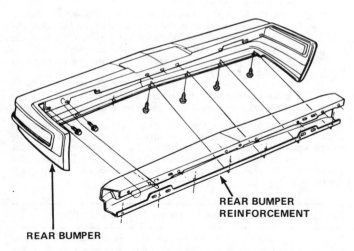

REAR BUMPER

REAR BUMPER
REINFORCEMENT

Fig. 12.34 Phoenix rear bumper assembly (Section 37)

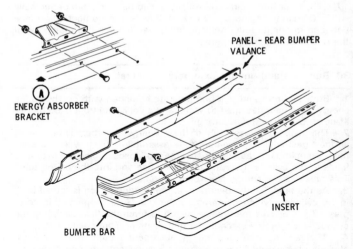

PANEL - REAR BUMPER
VALENCE

(A)
ENERGY ABSORBER
BRACKET

INSERT

BUMPER BAR

Fig. 12.35 Omega rear bumper assembly (Section 37)

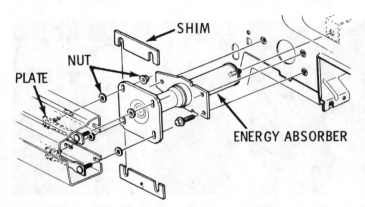

SHIM

NUT

PLATE

ENERGY ABSORBER

Fig. 12.36 Mounting of the energy absorbers to the body and bumpers (Sections 35 and 36)

2   If removing the front bumper, it may be easier to first remove the valence panel, if equipped.
3   If lights are mounted in the bumper, disconnect any wiring connected to the bumper.
4   On the Phoenix, remove the bolts on both sides that attach the bumper to the fender panels (photo).
5   Remove the nuts that secure the bumper to the energy absorbers (4 on each side) (photo) and lift off the bumper (photo).
6   Installation is the reverse of the removal procedure. Be sure to reinstall any shims that were removed from between the energy absorbers and bumper during the removal procedure.
7   After installation, check for proper clearance and alignment between the bumper and the surrounding panels. In-and-out adjustments are made by adding or taking out shims between the bumper and energy absorbers. Up-and-down and side-to-side adjustments can be made by sliding the bumper mounting bolts in their slots, located in the bumper and energy absorber brackets.

38 Energy absorbers (front and rear) – removal and installation

1   Remove the bumper as described in Section 37.
2   Remove the energy absorber mounting bolts (3 on each absorber) and lift out the absorber.
3   Installation is the reverse of the removal procedure.

39 Fender panels (front) – removal and installation

1   Remove the wiper arms as described in Section 17.
2   Remove the reveal molding along the lower edge of the windshield. This molding is secured to the body with slide-on clips that are attached to weld-on studs or screws. A tab on the clip engages the

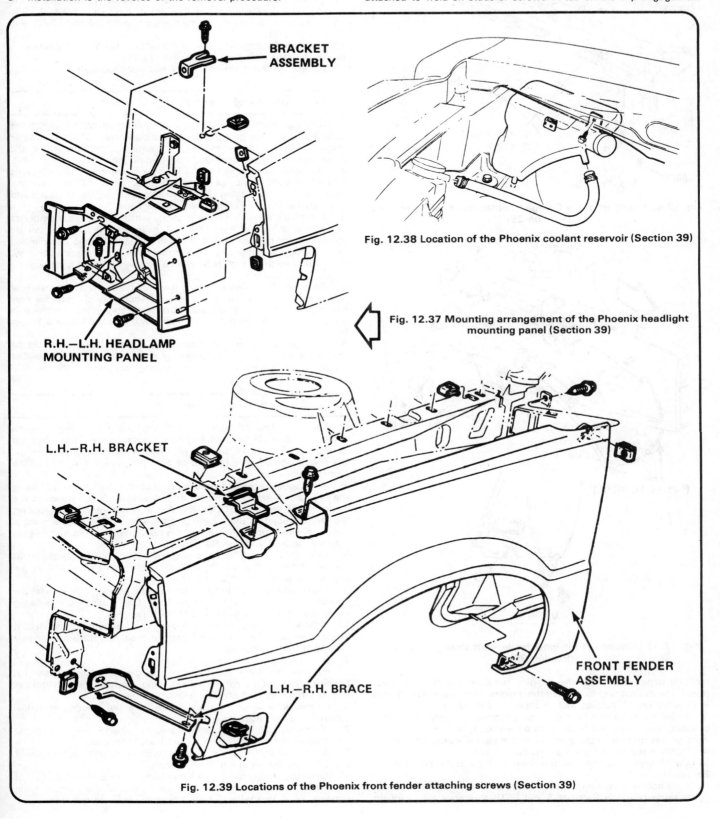

Fig. 12.38 Location of the Phoenix coolant reservoir (Section 39)

Fig. 12.37 Mounting arrangement of the Phoenix headlight mounting panel (Section 39)

BRACKET ASSEMBLY

R.H.–L.H. HEADLAMP MOUNTING PANEL

L.H.–R.H. BRACKET

L.H.–R.H. BRACE

FRONT FENDER ASSEMBLY

Fig. 12.39 Locations of the Phoenix front fender attaching screws (Section 39)

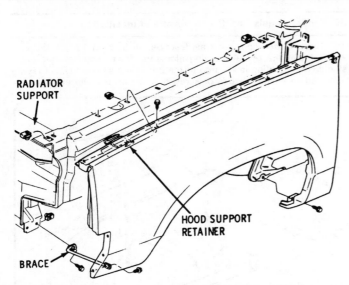

Fig. 12.40 Locations of the Omega front fender attaching screws (Section 39)

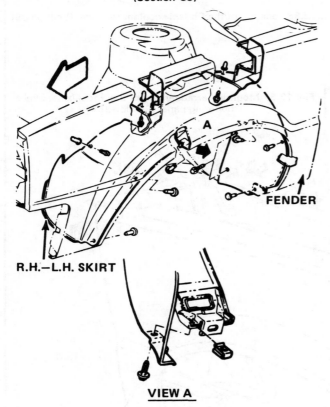

Fig. 12.41 Locations of the inner fender skirt attaching screws (Section 39)

molding flange and holds the molding between the clip and body metal. The easiest way to remove the molding from the retaining clips is to use a reveal molding tool as shown in Fig. 12.12.

3 Raise the hood and be sure it is supported securely in its open position. Note: if the left fender is to be removed, support the hood in another way other than the prop rod, and remove the prop rod bracket.

4 Remove the shroud grille panel (Sec 12.13).

5 On Omega cars, remove the front end panel as described in Section 12.

6 On Phoenix cars, remove the headlights and parking/turn signal lights as described in Sections 8 and 9. Then remove the headlight

mounting panels (Fig. 12.37).

7 If equipped, remove the front valence panel.

8 Remove the front bumper, as described in Section 37.

9 Reach inside the front wheel well and remove the side marker lamp bulb by turning and withdrawing the bulb socket located in the rear of the lamp housing.

10 On Phoenix cars, if removing the right fender panel, remove the radiator coolant reservoir inside the engine compartment (Fig. 12.38).

11 Remove the fender mounting screws (Fig. 12.39 and 12.40) and lift off the fender.

12 The inner fender skirt can be removed from the fender by removing the fender skirt mounting screws (Fig. 12.41).

13 Installation is the reverse of the removal procedure.

40 Cradle (subframe) – general

1 Although the X-Body cars use a unitized construction in which the body is designed to give the car its principal support, a subframe or cradle is used to support the engine, transaxle, front suspension and other mechanical components in the engine area.

2 The cradle is mounted to the body by rubber donut-like cushions located at each corner of the cradle (Fig. 12.42). These cushions minimise the transmission of vibrations from the engine, transaxle and other cradle-mounted components to the body.

3 The cradle consists of two sections which are bolted together at the points shown in Fig. 12.43. If necessary, the cradle can be removed from the car as one piece, or the sections can be unbolted and removed separately, as is the procedure for transaxle removal. With either method, the cradle can be removed without removing the engine or transaxle.

4 Because of the design strength the cradle lends to the car, it is extremely important that the cradle is periodically checked for corrosion or cracking, and be repaired or replaced if either condition is found. Maintaining proper rust-proofing will give the cradle a longer life.

5 Because of the critical dimensions of the cradle, it should be checked and repaired as necessary by a GM dealer or other qualified repair shop following any accident involving the front of the car.

41 Cradle – removal and installation

1 There are two principal ways of supporting the weight of the engine during cradle removal. A special support fixture can be obtained as shown in Fig. 12.44, or an engine hoist can be used. With either, the engine should be supported by the lifting bracket located at the rear of the engine.

2 If the engine support fixture is being used, install it prior to raising the car. On L4 engines, be sure its rear support is positioned in the center of the cowl. CAUTION: This fixture is not intended to support the entire weight of the engine and transaxle. If the engine hoist is being used to support the engine, the hood must be removed to gain sufficient access. Refer to Section 23.

3 Raise the front of the car and support it on jack stands placed at the two forward 4-point lift locations as shown in Fig. 0.4 in the preliminary section of this manual.

4 If an engine support fixture is being used, position a jack under the engine to provide an additional support. If an engine hoist is being used, now is the time to hook it up to the engine.

5 If the entire cradle is being removed, remove both front wheels. If only one section of the cradle is being removed, only the wheel on that side need to be removed.

6 Remove the exhaust crossover pipe.

7 Remove the front stabilizer bar, as described in Chapter 11, Section 6. Note: If the entire cradle is being removed, the stabilizer bar can be left intact until after the cradle is removed.

8 Disconnect one or both ball joints from the steering knuckles, depending upon necessity.

9 Disconnect all engine and transaxle mounts, or only those attached to the cradle section to be removed (photos).

10 If only one cradle section is being removed, unbolt the sections at the locations shown in Fig. 12.43 (photos).

11 While supporting the cradle either with the help of an assistant or with jacks, remove the cradle mounting bolts of the section being removed or all four bolts if the entire cradle is being removed.

41.9a Removing the engine mount retaining nuts

41.9b Removing the front transaxle mount retaining nuts

41.9c Removing the rear transaxle mount retaining nuts

41.10a Removing the rear cradle section attaching bolts

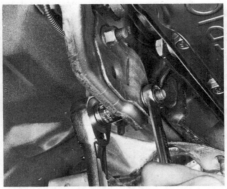

41.10b Removing the right front cradle section attaching bolts

41.12 The left cradle section removed from the car with lower control arm attached

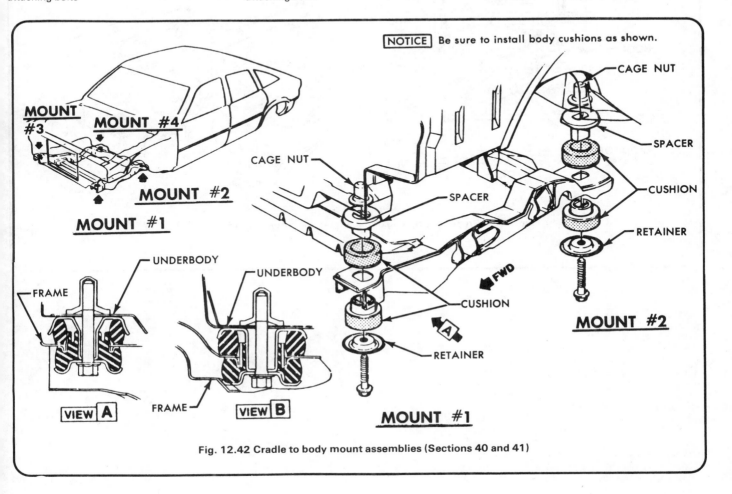

Fig. 12.42 Cradle to body mount assemblies (Sections 40 and 41)

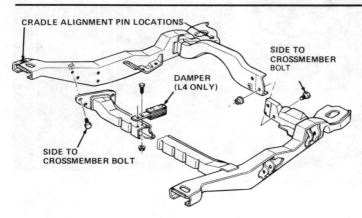

CRADLE ALIGNMENT PIN LOCATIONS

SIDE TO CROSSMEMBER BOLT

DAMPER (L4 ONLY)

SIDE TO CROSSMEMBER BOLT

Fig. 12.43 Cradle assembly (Sections 40 and 41)

mounting cushions for cracking and hardness and replace if necessary.

15 With the aid of an assistant or jacks, raise the cradle to its proper position and insert the mounting bolts, but do not tighten them fully.

16 If only one cradle section has been removed, line it up with the other cradle section and install the attaching bolts.

17 If only the left cradle section is being installed, the body mount bolts can now be tightened and torqued to specs. If the right section or the entire cradle is being installed, then it must be aligned with the body before tightening the mounting bolts. This is done by inserting 2 pins ($\frac{5}{8}$-in (16 mm) diameter and about 8 in long) into the alignment holes shown in Fig. 12.43. With the pins inerted, tighten the body mount bolts to their specified torque. When all the mounting bolts have been properly torqued, the alignment pins can be removed.

18 Connect all engine and transaxle mounts, and tighten to the correct torque. The jack supporting the engine from underneath can now be removed.

19 Install the ball joint(s) into the steering knuckle(s).

20 Install the front stabilizer bar, if not already installed prior to cradle installation.

21 Install the exhaust crossover pipe.

22 Install the front wheel(s).

23 Disconnect the engine hoist (if used).

24 Lower the car to the ground.

25 Remove the engine support fixture, if used.

26 Install the hood, if removed.

27 Have the front end toe-in checked and adjusted if necessary. Refer to Chapter 11, Section 3.

12 Remove the cradle, with control arm(s) attached (photo).

13 If the cradle is being replaced with a new one, transfer the control arms, stabilizer bar (if not previously removed), body mounts and damper (if used) to the new cradle prior to installation.

14 If the old cradle is to be reinstalled, now is a good time to give it a thorough cleaning and inspection, and to repaint with a rust-preventative paint. Be sure to inspect the condition of the rubber

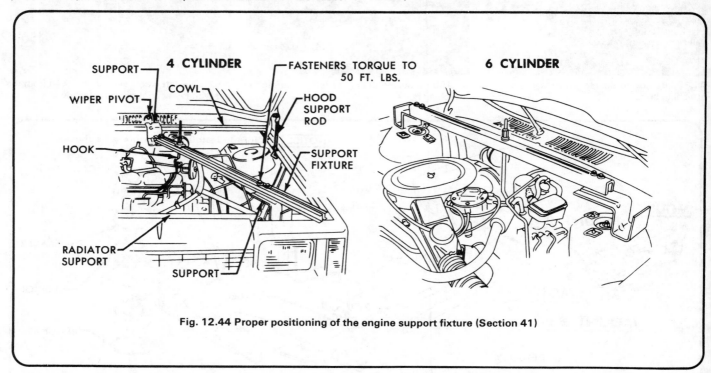

4 CYLINDER

SUPPORT

WIPER PIVOT

COWL

FASTENERS TORQUE TO 50 FT. LBS.

HOOD SUPPORT ROD

HOOK

SUPPORT FIXTURE

RADIATOR SUPPORT

SUPPORT

6 CYLINDER

Fig. 12.44 Proper positioning of the engine support fixture (Section 41)

Chapter 13 Supplement:
Revisions and information on
1981 through 1984 models

Contents

1 Introduction

This supplementary Chapter covers changes made in the Pontiac Phoenix and Oldsmobile Omega during the 1981 through 1984 model years, and the procedures affected by these changes.

Operations that are not included in this Chapter are the same or similar to those described in the first twelve Chapters of this manual.

There have been many small changes made during these years, many the result of more comprehensive emissions systems and the trends toward computerized control of engine operations. This includes the introduction of the Electronic Spark Timing (EST) distributor in 1981.

In 1982 a significant change was made by replacing the carburetor on some models with an Electronic Fuel Injection (EFI) system. Also, the engine cradle (subframe) was redesigned, changing the procedures for some engine and transaxle-related operations.

The recommended way of using this Supplement is, prior to any operation, check here first for any relevant information pertaining to your model. After noting any model differences, particularly in the *Specifications* section, you can then follow the appropriate procedure.

2   Specifications

Note: *The specifications listed here are revised or supplementary to the main specifications given at the beginning of each Chapter. Specifications not listed here are the same as those listed in Chapters 1 through 12.*

Tune-up and routine maintenance

Spark plugs	Type	Gap
1981 to 1983		
L4	R44TSX	0.060 in
V6	R43TS	0.045 in
1984	See emissions decal located under the hood	

Ignition timing

1981
L4
    Manual trans .... 4° BTDC @ 1000 rpm
    Automatic trans (in Drive) .... 4° BTDC @ 675 rpm
V6
    Manual trans .... 6° BTDC @ 850 rpm
    Automatic trans (in Drive) .... 10° BTDC @ 650 rpm
1982 and 1983
L4
    Manual trans .... 8° BTDC @ 1050 rpm
    Automatic trans (in Neutral) .... 8° BTDC @ 1050 rpm
V6 (X code)
    Manual trans .... 10° BTDC @ 800 rpm
    Automatic trans (in Drive) .... 10° BTDC @ 600 rpm
V6 (Z code)
    Manual trans (Federal models) .... 6° BTDC @ 850 rpm
    Manual trans (California models) .... 6° BTDC @ 750 rpm
    Automatic trans (in Drive) .... 10° BTDC @ 750 rpm
1984 .... See emissions decal located under the hood

L4 Engine

Cylinder block
    Out-of-round limit .... 0.0014 in (0.0356 mm)
Pistons
    1981 to 1983
        Comp. ring side clearance .... 0.0015 to 0.0030 in (0.0381 mm to 0.0762 mm)
    1984
        Comp. ring side clearance (top) .... 0.0020 to 0.0030 in (0.050 mm to 0.080 mm)
        Comp. ring side clearance (bottom) .... 0.0010 to 0.0030 in (0.030 mm to 0.080 mm)
        Comp. ring width (top) (1982/83) .... 0.06120 to 0.0625 in (1.575 to 1.583 mm)
        Comp. ring width (top) (1984/85) .... N/A
    1981 to 1983
        Ring gap
            Upper compression .... 0.010 to 0.022 in (0.25 to 0.56 mm)
            Lower compression .... 0.010 to 0.027 in (0.25 to 0.71 mm)
    1984
        Ring gap (both) .... 0.010 to 0.020 in (0.30 to 0.50 mm)
Camshaft
    Lobe lift (intake and exhaust) .... 0.398 in (10.312 mm)

V6 Engine

Pistons
    Clearance (1983/84) .... 0.0007 to 0.0017 in (0.017 to 0.043 mm)
Crankshaft
    Endplay (1982/83) .... 0.002 to 0.007 in (0.05 to 0.17 mm)
    Endplay (1984) .... 0.003 to 0.007 in (0.09 to 0.20 mm)
    Main journal diameter (No. 3) (1983/84) .... 2.493 to 2.494 in (63.327 to 63.351 mm)
    Main bearing clearance (1982/83) .... 0.0017 to 0.0029 in (0.044 to 0.076 mm)
    Main bearing clearance (1984) .... 0.0016 to 0.0032 in (0.041 to 0.081 mm)

Torque specifications (L4)	**Ft-lbs**	**M-kg**
Rocker arm bolt	20	2.8
EFI-to-intake manifold nuts/bolts (1982/83)	15	2.1
Cylinder head bolts (1984)	92	12.6

Cooling system

Capacities (1983)
    L4
        with A/C .... 9.0 qts (8.5 liters)
        without A/C .... 10.5 qts (10.0 liters)

Fuel system

Carburetor identification	with A/C	without A/C
1981		
L4		
Manual trans	17081673	17081670
Automatic trans	17081672	17081670
V6		
Manual trans	17081653	17081651
Automatic trans	17081652	17081650
1982 and 1983		
V6 (X code)		
Manual trans	17082641	17082317
Automatic trans	17082640	17082316
V6 (Z code)		
Manual trans	17082321	17082321
Automatic trans	17082321	17082320
1984	N/A	N/A

Note: *Because certain idle adjustments are controlled by the Electronic Control Module (ECM) and therefore cannot be manually adjusted, if no specification exists for a particular model, no adjustment is required.*

Base idle speed	rpm
1981	
L4 (without A/C)	
Manual trans	800
Automatic trans (in Drive)	550

Curb idle speed	
1981	
L4	
Manual trans	1000
Automatic trans	675
V6	
Manual trans	850
Automatic trans	600
1982 and 1983	
L4	
Manual trans with A/C	900
Without A/C	850
Auto trans (Neutral) A/C	750
Without A/C	680
V6 (X code)	
Manual trans	800
Automatic trans (Drive)	600
V6 (Z code)	
Manual trans (Federal)	850
Manual trans (California)	750
Auto trans (Drive) (Federal)	750
1984	See emissions decal located under the hood

Fast idle speed	
1981	
L4	
Manual trans	2600
Automatic trans (Park)	2600
V6	
Manual trans with A/C	2600
Without A/C	2400
Automatic trans (Park)	2600
1982 and 1983	
V6 (X code)	
Manual trans with A/C	2600
Without A/C	2400
Automatic trans (Neutral)	2600
V6 (Z code)	
Manual trans (Federal)	2600
Manual trans (California)	2800
Automatic trans (Neutral)	2800
1984	See emissions decal located under the hood

Solenoid-activated speed	
1981	
L4	
Manual trans	1000
Automatic trans (Drive)	675
V6	
Manual trans	1100
Auto trans (Drive) with A/C	850

1982 and 1983
  V6 (X code)
    Manual trans   1050
    Auto trans (Drive) with A/C   800
  V6 (Z code)
    Manual trans   1100
    Auto trans (Drive) with A/C   900
  1984   . . . .   See emissions decal located under the hood
Float adjustment
  1981 carburetor number . . . .   Gauge size (in)
    17081650 . . . .   1/4
    17081651 . . . .   1/4
    17081652 . . . .   1/4
    17081653 . . . .   1/4
    17081671 . . . .   5/32
    17081672 . . . .   5/32
    17081673 . . . .   5/32
    17081740 . . . .   1/4
    17081742 . . . .   1/3
  1982 carburetor number . . . .   Gauge size (in)
    17082196 . . . .   5/16
    17082316 . . . .   1/4
    17082317 . . . .   1/4
    17082320 . . . .   1/4
    17082321 . . . .   1/4
    17082640 . . . .   1/4
    17082641 . . . .   1/4
    17082642 . . . .   1/4
  1983 carburetor number . . . .   Gauge size (in)
    17083356 . . . .   13/32
    17083357 . . . .   13/32
    17083358 . . . .   13/32
    17083359 . . . .   13/32
    17083368 . . . .   1/8
    17083370 . . . .   1/8
    17083450 . . . .   1/8
    17083451 . . . .   1/8
    17083452 . . . .   1/8
    17083453 . . . .   1/8
    17083454 . . . .   1/8
    17083455 . . . .   1/8
    17083456 . . . .   1/8
    17083630 . . . .   1/4
    17083631 . . . .   1/4
    17083632 . . . .   1/4
    17083633 . . . .   1/4
    17083634 . . . .   1/4
    17083635 . . . .   1/4
    17083636 . . . .   1/4
    17083650 . . . .   1/8
  1984 carburetor number . . . .   Gauge size (in)
    17084356 . . . .   9/32
    17084357 . . . .   9/32
    17084358 . . . .   9/32
    17084359 . . . .   9/32
    17084368 . . . .   1/8
    17084370 . . . .   1/8
    17084430 . . . .   11/32
    17084431 . . . .   11/32
    17084434 . . . .   11/32
    17084435 . . . .   11/32
    17084452 . . . .   5/32
    17084453 . . . .   5/32
    17084455 . . . .   5/32
    17084456 . . . .   5/32
    17084458 . . . .   5/32
    17084532 . . . .   5/32
    17084632 . . . .   9/32
    17084633 . . . .   9/32
    17084635 . . . .   9/32
    17084636 . . . .   9/32
    17085356 . . . .   9/32
    17085357 . . . .   9/32
    17085358 . . . .   9/32
    17085359 . . . .   9/32

17085369	9/32
17085370	4/32
17085371	9/32
17085452	5/32
17085453	5/32
17085458	5/32

Choke rod adjustment

1981 carburetor number	Degrees
17081650	17
17081651	17
17081652	17
17081653	17
17081670	18
17081671	33.5
17081672	18
17081673	33.5
17081740	17
17081742	17

1982 carburetor number	Degrees
17082196	18
17082316	17
17082317	17
17082320	25
17082321	25
17082640	17
17082641	17
17082642	25

1983 carburetor number	Degrees
17083355	22
17083356	22
17083357	22
17083358	22
17083359	22
17083368	22
17083370	22
17083450	28
17083451	28
17083452	28
17083453	28
17083454	28
17083455	28
17083456	28
17083630	28
17083631	28
17083632	28
17083633	28
17083634	28
17083635	28
17083636	28
17083650	28

1984 carburetor number	Degrees
17084356	22
17084357	22
17084358	22
17084359	22
17084368	22
17084370	22
17084430	15
17084431	15
17084434	15
17084435	15
17084452	28
17084453	28
17084455	28
17084456	28
17084458	28
17084532	28
17084632	28
17084633	28
17084635	28
17084636	28

Primary vacuum break adjustment

1981 L4 carburetor number	Degrees
17081670	19
17081671	21

17081672	19
17081673	21
1981 V6 carburetor number	Degrees
17081650	25
17081651	29
17081652	25
17081653	29
17081740	25
17081742	25
1982 V6 carburetor number	Degrees
17082196	21
17082316	26
17082317	29
17082320	30
17082321	29
17082640	26
17082641	29
17082642	30
1983 V6 carburetor number	Degrees
17083356	25
17083357	25
17083358	25
17083359	25
17083368	25
17083370	25
17083450	27
17083451	27
17083452	27
17083453	27
17083454	27
17083455	27
17083456	27
17083630	27
17083631	27
17083632	27
17083633	27
17083634	27
17083635	27
17083636	27
17083650	27
1984 carburetor number	Degrees
17084356	25
17084357	25
17084358	25
17084359	25
17084368	25
17084370	25
17084430	26
17084431	26
17084434	26
17084435	26
17084452	25
17084453	25
17084455	25
17084456	25
17084458	25
17084532	25
17084632	25
17084633	25
17084635	25
17084636	25
Air valve rod adjustment, all models	1
Secondary vacuum break adjustment	
1981 (V6) carburetor number	Degrees
17081650	34
17081651	34
17081652	34
17081653	34
17081740	34
17081742	34
1982 (V6) carburetor number	Degrees
17082196	19
17082316	34
17082317	35
17082320	35

17082321	35
17082640	34
17082641	35
17082642	35
1983 (V6) carburetor number	**Degrees**
All	35
1984 carburetor number	**Degrees**
17084356	30
17084357	30
17084358	30
17084359	30
17084368	30
17084370	30
17084430	38
17084431	38
17084434	38
17084435	38
17084452	35
17084453	35
17084455	35
17084456	35
17084458	35
17084532	35
17084632	35
17084633	35
17084635	35
17084636	35

Unloader adjustment

1981 carburetor number	**Degrees**
17081650	35
17081651	35
17081652	35
17081653	35
17081670	32
17081671	32
17081672	32
17081673	32
17081740	35
17081742	35
1982 carburetor number	**Degrees**
17082196	27
17082316	35
17032317	35
17032320	33
17032321	35
17032640	35
17032641	35
17032642	33
1983 carburetor number	**Degrees**
17083356	30
17083357	30
17083358	30
17083359	30
17083368	30
17083370	30
17083450	45
17083451	45
17083452	45
17083453	45
17083454	45
17083455	45
17083456	45
17083630	45
17083631	45
17083632	45
17083633	45
17083634	45
17083635	45
17083636	45
17083650	45
1984 carburetor number	**Degrees**
17084356	30
17084357	30
17084358	30
17084359	30

17084368	30
17084370	30
17084430	42
17084431	42
17084434	42
17084435	42
17084452	45
17084453	45
17084455	45
17084456	45
17084458	45
17084532	45
17084632	45
17084633	45
17084635	45
17084636	45

	Gauge size (in)
Secondary lockout adjustment	
1981 (all)	0.012

Air valve spring adjustment	
1982 (all)	One turn
1983 carburetor number	
All except 17083650	One turn
17083650	1/2 turn
1984 carburetor number	
17084356	3/4 turn
17084357	3/4 turn
17084358	3/4 turn
17084359	3/4 turn
17084368	3/4 turn
17084370	3/4 turn
17084430	1 turn
17084431	1 turn
17084434	1 turn
17084435	1 turn
17084452	1/2 turn
17084453	1/2 turn
17084455	1/2 turn
17084456	1/2 turn
17084458	1/2 turn
17084532	1/2 turn
17084632	1/2 turn
17084633	1/2 turn
17084635	1/2 turn
17084636	1/2 turn

Clutch

Torque specifications	Ft-lbs	M-kg
Clutch pedal-to-bracket bolt	35	4.8
Clutch pedal bracket-to-cowl nuts	20	2.8
Clutch pressure plate-to-flywheel bolts	15	2.1

Brake system

Disc diameter	9.72 in (247 mm)
Disc thickness	
Maximum	0.88 in (22.48 mm)
Minimum refinish	0.83 in (21.08 mm)
Wear limit	0.81 in (20.70 mm)
Disc out-of-round limit	0.001 in (0.051 mm)
Brake pedal travel	
Manual systems	4-1/2 in (115 mm)
Power systems	2-1/4 in (57 mm)

Transaxle

Oil capacity (manual)	3 US qts (2.8 liters, 2-1/2 qts Imperial)
Oil capacity (automatic)	Varies (see dipstick markings)

Suspension and steering systems

Front end alignment (1982 to 1984)		
Camber	0° to 0.050° (left and right sides must be within 0.050° of each other)	
Toe-in (per wheel)	0 mm to 0.5 mm or 0° to 0.10°	
Power steering oil capacity	US	Metric
Complete system	1-1/2 pts	0.71 L
Pump only	1-1/16 pts	0.5 L

Torque specifications	Ft-lbs	M-kg
Rear suspension		
Upper shock absorber nut	13	1.8
Lower shock absorber nut	43	5.9
Control arm-to-bracket nut	78	10.8
Hub-to-rear axle bolts	45	6.2

3 Engine

General information

1   Unless included in this Section, all procedures pertaining to the engine remain basically the same as described in Chapter 2. Because of the redesign of some components, minor differences may exist between models. For instance, 1982 through 1984 models with the L4 engine use a fuel injection system in place of the carburetor. Owners servicing these models should ignore references to the carburetor and be aware that some disconnections or removal of fuel injection components may be necessary.

2   Other differences may include emission equipment, such as the AIR pump and bracket, the exhaust crossover pipe on V6 engines and the new design cradle used on 1982 through 1984 models. **Caution:** *Prior to disconnecting any fuel lines in the fuel injection system, the pressure in the system must be relieved. For this procedure refer to Section 5.*

Rocker arm and valve spring (L4 engine) — removal and installation

3   The rocker arm removal and installation procedure is basically the same as described in Chapter 2, except that the rocker arms and balls are now retained by bolts instead of the nut and stud arrangement used previously.

4   If the valve spring is to be removed with the cylinder head attached to the engine, follow the same procedure described in Chapter 2, but once the rocker arm is removed, screw the rocker arm bolt back into place. Then use the bolt with the valve spring compressor tool to depress the spring.

Exhaust manifold (1983 to 1984 V6 models) — removal and installation

Left side removal

5   Disconnect the negative cable from the battery.

6   Remove the air cleaner.

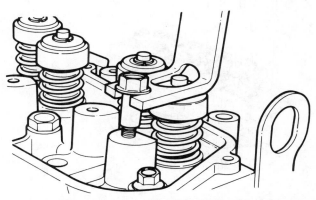

Fig. 13.1 The valve spring can be compressed by using the rocker arm bolt in combination with a valve spring compressor (Sec 3)

7   Disconnect the crossover pipe.

8   Remove the exhaust manifold mounting bolts and lift off the manifold.

Right side removal

9   Disconnect the negative cable from the battery.

10   Remove the air cleaner.

11   Disconnect the Air Injector Reaction (AIR) bracket at the exhaust flange.

12   Raise the front of the car and support it on jackstands.

13   Disconnect the exhaust pipe from the manifold.

14   Lower the car to the ground.

15   Remove the exhaust manifold mounting bolts.

16   Disconnect the oxygen sensor from the manifold.

17   Disconnect the air management hose at the valve.

18   Disconnect the crossover pipe from the manifold.

19   Lift the manifold from the engine compartment.

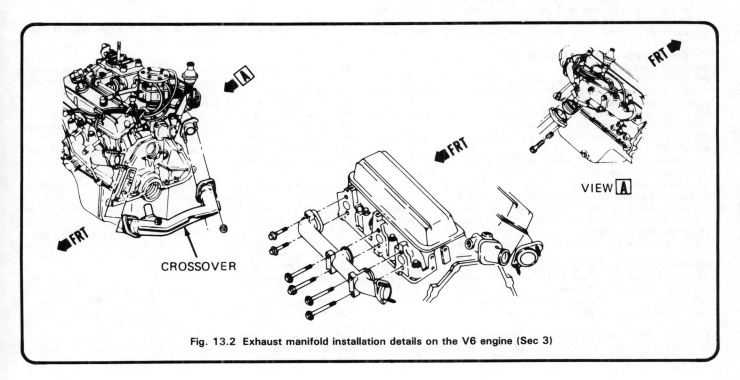

Fig. 13.2 Exhaust manifold installation details on the V6 engine (Sec 3)

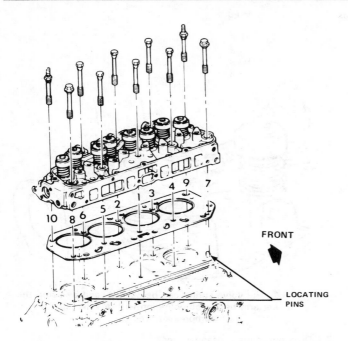

Fig. 13.3 Bolt tightening sequence for the L4 cylinder head
(Sec 3)

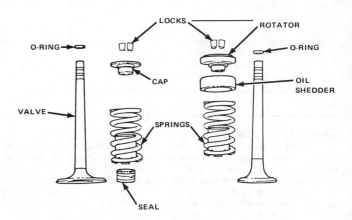

Fig. 13.4 Valve components of the V6 engine (intake on
the left; exhaust on the right) (Sec 3)

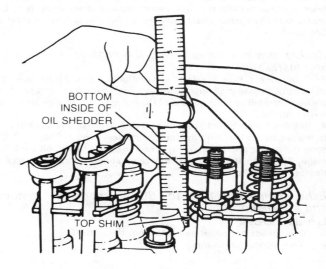

Fig. 13.5 Measuring installed height of exhaust valve spring
(V6 engine) (Sec 3)

Installation (both sides)
20 Prior to installation, be sure that the mating surfaces on both the manifold and cylinder head are clean.
21 Place the manifold in position and install the mounting bolts loosely.
22 Install the crossover pipe.
23 Tighten the manifold mounting bolts to the specified torque.
24 The remainder of the installation is the reverse of the removal procedure.

Intake manifold (V6 engine) — removal and installation
25 The intake manifold removal and installation procedures are the same as described in Chapter 2, except for models equipped with the Air Injection Reaction system. On these models, the air pump and bracket must be removed in order to remove the intake manifold.

Pushrod cover (1982 through 1984 L4 models) —
removal and installation
26 Although the procedure described in Chapter 2 applies to these models, an alternate method is given below which eliminates the need to remove the intake manifold.
27 Raise the front of the vehicle and support it on jackstands placed under the body. Do not place them under the cradle.
28 Place a jack under the cradle rear crossmember to support its weight.
29 Remove the two cradle rear mounting bolts.
30 Remove the two bolts from the exhaust pipe flex joint.
31 Carefully lower the rear of the cradle four to six inches. Check that no engine components are contacting the cowl area as this is done.
32 There should now be sufficient clearance to remove the pushrod cover mounting bolts. Refer to Chapter 2 for the actual cover removal and installation procedure.
33 Installation is the reverse of the removal procedure.

Cylinder head (L4 engine) — installation
34 The installation procedure for the cylinder head remains unchanged from that described in Chapter 2, except that the cylinder head bolt tightening sequence has been changed slightly. Refer to the accompanying illustration for the revised sequence.

Cylinder head (V6 engine) — assembly
35 The cylinder head assembly procedure has been changed from that described in Chapter 2.

36 Make sure all valve mechanism components are perfectly clean and free of abrasive agents which may have been used for valve grinding, reaming, etc.
37 Insert a valve in the proper guide.
38 Install the valve spring and damper.
39 On the intake valves only, install the valve stem seal over the valve stem and valve guide boss.
40 On the exhaust valves, install the oil shedder and valve rotator.
41 On the intake valves, install the valve spring cap over the valve spring.
42 Using a valve spring compressor, compress the spring assembly and hold it in the compressed position.
43 Install the square cut O-ring in the valve stem lower groove. Make sure it is not twisted.
44 Install the valve locks in the upper groove of the valve stem. A dab of grease can be used to hold the locks in place. With the locks properly seated, carefully release the valve spring compressor.
45 Repeat the procedure on all valves.
46 Once installed, check the installed height of the valve springs. Measure from the top of the spring damper to the bottom inside of the oil shedder (exhaust) or from the top of the spring shim to the bottom of the valve cap (intake). Compare this measurement with the specifications. If necessary, shims can be used under the valve spring to bring the unit to the proper specifications. At no time should the spring be shimmed to give an installed height under the minimum specified length.

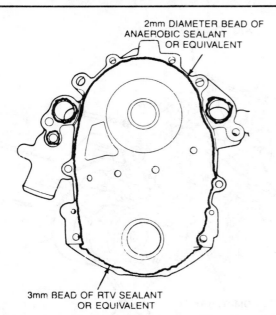

Fig. 13.6 Prior to installing the crankcase front cover, sealant should be applied as shown (Sec 3)

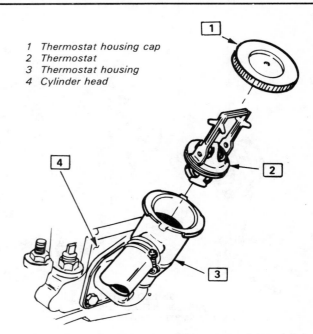

1 Thermostat housing cap
2 Thermostat
3 Thermostat housing
4 Cylinder head

Fig. 3.7 The thermostat on the 1982 and later L4 models is removed by unscrewing the cap and lifting it out (Sec 4)

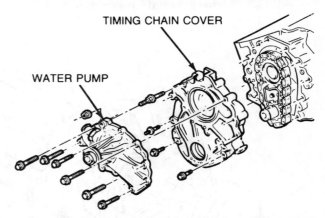

Fig. 13.8 Water pump mounting bolt arrangement (Sec 4)

Crankcase front cover (1983 V6 models) — removal and installation

47 If equipped with air conditioning, remove the Air Injector Reaction (AIR) pump and bracket.
48 Remove the water pump, referring to Chapter 3 if necessary.
49 Raise the front of the vehicle and support it on jackstands.
50 Remove the torsional dampener, referring to Chapter 2.
51 Remove the bolts attaching the oil pan to the front cover.
52 Lower the car to the ground.
53 Remove the remaining front cover bolts and lift off the cover. If it will not easily come off, tap it with a rubber-headed hammer to loosen it. Do not pry on it as this will damage the mating surfaces.
54 Prior to installation make sure that the mating surfaces of the cover, block and oil pan are clean of dirt and old gasket material.
55 Apply a continuous 3/32-inch (2mm) bead of anaerobic sealant to the sealing surface of the front cover. Also apply a continuous 1/8-inch (3mm) bead of RTV or equivalent sealant to the lower sealing surface of the front cover where it contacts the oil pan.
56 Install the front cover.
57 Install the water pump and tighten all of the mounting bolts to the specified torque. This should be done quickly, within five minutes of applying the sealant.
58 Raise the vehicle and support it on jackstands. Install the oil pan-to-cover screws.
59 The remainder of the installation is the reverse of the removal procedure. Be sure to adjust the drivebelts to the proper tension and refill the cooling system.

---

4 Cooling and air conditioning systems

Thermostat (1982 through 1984 L4 models) — removal and installation

1 The thermostat and housing on these models have been redesigned for easier servicing. To remove the thermostat, first remove the thermostat housing cap, then grasp the thermostat handle and pull it out.
2 Installation is accomplished by pushing the thermostat into the housing, making sure it is seated, and installing the cap.

Water pump (V6 engine) — removal and installation

3 The water pump removal and installation procedure remains the same as described in Chapter 3, with the following exception. One of the upper mounting bolts that was used to retain both the water pump and the timing chain cover has been eliminated. A stud is used in this position to retain the timing chain cover. A mounting nut, which screws onto the stud, is used to retain the water pump.

A/C compressor (V6 engine) — removal and installation

4 Prior to disconnecting any A/C lines the vehicle should be taken to a GM dealer or qualified automotive air-conditioning repair shop to have the system pressure discharged.
5 Disconnect the negative cable from the battery.
6 Remove all electrical connections from the A/C compressor and disconnect the high-pressure hoses.
7 Remove the upper through mounting bolt and shim from the rear of the compressor.
8 Remove the upper drivebelt tension adjusting bolt.
9 Remove the bolt attaching the compressor to the lower generator mounting bracket.
10 Push the compressor rearward in the upper bracket.
11 Disengage the drivebelt from the water pump and crankshaft damper and position it to the rear of both pulleys, then slide the belt over the compressor inertia ring.
12 Remove the front radiator support brace bolt and, for clearance, swing the brace toward the right fender.
13 Remove the bolt attaching the compressor manifold to the compressor.
14 Lift the compressor from the car.
15 Installation is the reverse of the removal procedure.
16 Once the compressor and all A/C lines have been securely reconnected, the car must once again be taken to a GM dealer or qualified air conditioning shop to have the system charged.

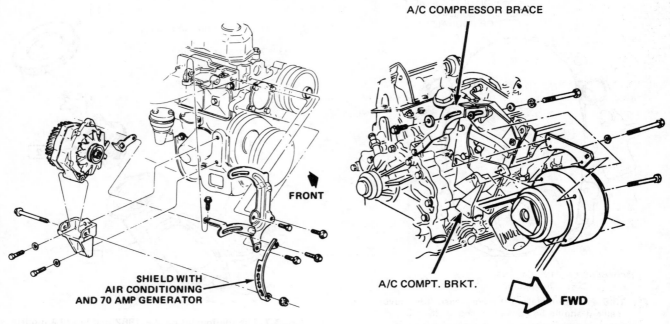

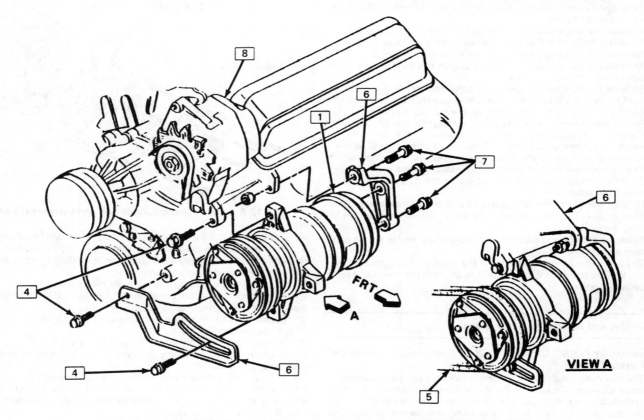

Fig. 13.9 Air conditioning compressor mounting
arrangement (L4 engine) (Sec 4)

Fig. 13.10 Air conditioning compressor mounting
arrangement (1981 through 1983 V6 engine) (Sec 4)

Fig. 13.11 Air conditioning compressor mounting arrangement (1984 V6 engine) (Sec 4)

1 A/C compressor	6 Mounting bracket
4 Bolt	7 Bolt
5 Drive belt	8 Alternator

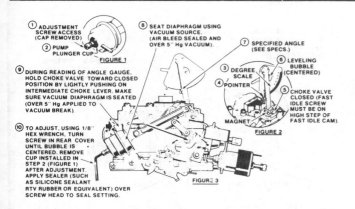

Fig. 13.12 Secondary vacuum break adjustment (1981 and 1982 V6 engine) (Sec 5)

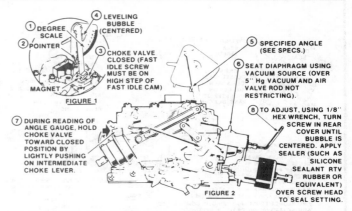

Fig. 13.13 Primary vacuum break adjustment (1981 and 1982 V6 engine) (Sec 5)

5 Fuel system

Carburetor adjustments
Refer to Figs. 13.12 through 13.19

1   Specifications for idle speed adjustments are listed in the *Specifications* at the beginning of this Chapter. Always double-check these specifications with those listed on the emissions control label located on the underside of the hood. If any differences exist, precedence should be given to the emission control label. If no adjustment is listed, none is required.

2   The carburetor pump adjustment is no longer required. In 1981 the pump was changed to a non-adjustable type.

3   The adjustments for the primary and secondary vacuum breaks on 1981 and 1982 model carburetors are the same procedures except for the actual method of adjustment. Instead of bending the vacuum break rod, an adjustment screw is used.
   a) Prior to adjustment, remove the vacuum break from the carburetor. Place the bracket in a vise and carefully grind off the screw cap to gain access to the adjustment screw. Use an accelerator pump plunger cup to plug the end cover of the vacuum break. Reinstall the vacuum break.
   b) Set the choke valve gauge and follow the preliminary steps listed in Chapter 4. Using a 1/8-inch hex wrench, turn the adjustment screw until the bubble in the choke valve gauge is centered. Remove the pump cup from the end cover and apply a silicone sealant over the screw head to seal the setting.

Note: *During the adjustment procedure, be sure the air valve rod is not restricting the vacuum diaphragm from seating. To prevent this, bend the air valve rod just enough so it clears the plunger as necessary. If this procedure is necessary follow the vacuum break adjustment with the air valve rod adjustment.*

Idle mixture needle — removal and installation
Refer to Fig. 13.20

4   In 1981 an alternative method of removing and installing the idle mixture needle was offered by the manufacturer to replace the one given in Chapter 4.

Note: *The idle mixture needle in all models is recessed in the throttle body and sealed with a steel plug. The idle mixture setting is pre-set at the factory and should not be altered. If mixture control adjustments are improperly set, the Computer Command Control system will not maintain precise control of carburetor air/fuel mixture. Proper adjustment must be done while using special emission sensing equipment, making it impractical for the home mechanic. To have the carb mixture settings checked or readjusted, take your car to a GM dealer or other qualified mechanic with the proper equipment. The plug covering the idle mixture needle should not be removed unless the needle needs replacing or normal cleaning procedures fail to clean the idle mixture passages.*

5   Remove the carburetor from the engine and disassemble to separate the throttle body from the rest of the carburetor.

6   Secure the throttle body in a vise with the manifold side up. Use blocks of wood to cushion the throttle body.

7   Locate the idle mixture needle and plug. This will be marked by

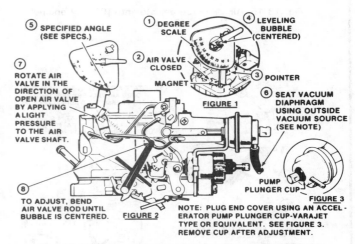

Fig. 13.14 Primary vacuum break adjustment (1981 L4 engine) (Sec 5)

an indented locator point on the underside of the throttle body. Using a hacksaw, make two parallel cuts in the throttle body on either side of this locator mark. The cuts should be deep enough to touch the steel plug, but not extend more than 1/8-inch beyond the locator point.

8   Position a flat punch at a point near the ends of the saw marks. Holding it at a 45° angle, drive the punch into the throttle body until the casting breaks away, exposing the steel plug.

9   Use a center punch to make an indentation in the steel plug. Holding the punch at a 45° angle, drive the plug from the throttle body casting. **Note:** *If the plug breaks apart, be sure to remove all of the pieces.*

10 Use a 3/16-inch deep socket to remove the idle mixture needle and spring from the throttle body.

11 After installation, a bench setting of the idle mixture can be obtained by lightly seating the needle and then backing it off three turns. The final idle mixture adjustment must be made after the carburetor is installed on the engine.

Idle Speed Control (ISC)
General
Refer to Fig. 13.21

12 On carbureted models with an L4 engine and air conditioning, an Idle Speed Control (ISC) motor is attached to the carburetor. Controlled by the car's Electronic Control Module (ECM), the ISC is used to maintain the proper idle speed under certain engine operating conditions. It also acts as a dashpot on acceleration and deceleration.

Note: *The proper curb idle speed is programmed into the ECM, therefore do not use the ISC to alter the curb idle speed.*

13 The ISC motor is removed from the carburetor by disconnecting the wiring connector (the ignition switch must be *Off*) and removing the two screws which attach the ISC bracket to the carburetor.

14 After installing a new ISC motor and connecting it, on-car speed adjustments should be performed as described below.

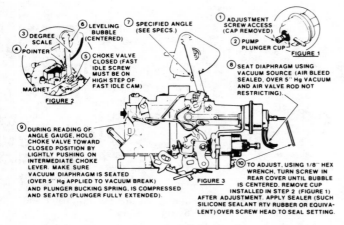

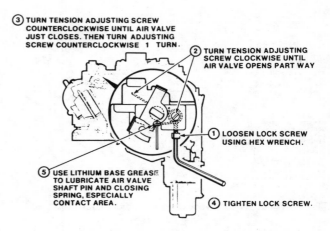

Fig. 13.15 Air valve rod adjustment (1981 L4 engine) (Sec 5)

Fig. 13.16 Air valve spring adjustment (1982 through 1984 V6 engine) (Sec 5)

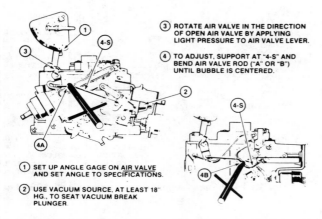

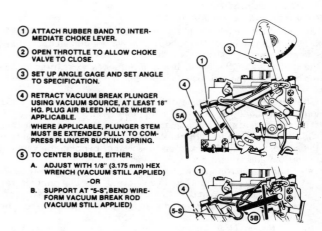

Fig. 13.17 Air valve rod adjustment (1983 to 1984 V6 engine) (Sec 5)

Fig. 13.18 Secondary vacuum break adjustment (1983 to 1984 V6 engine) (Sec 5)

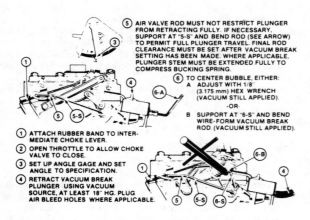

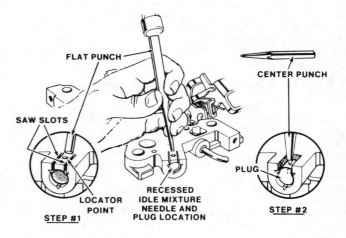

Fig. 13.19 Primary vacuum break adjustment (1983 to 1984 V6 engine) (Sec 5)

Fig. 13.20 After cutting slots with a hacksaw, punches are used to break the casting and remove the idle mixture needle plug (Sec 5)

On-car speed adjustments

15 The transaxle should be in *Neutral* or *Drive* and the parking brake should be set. The air conditioner should be turned off.

16 Connect a tachometer according to the manufacturer's instructions.

17 Connect a dwell meter to the mixture control solenoid dwell lead. The dwell meter should be set on the *Six* cylinder scale.

18 Start the engine and allow it to run until it reaches normal operating temperature and the idle stabilizes. This is indicated by the dwell meter needle starting to vary.

19 Turn the ignition off and disconnect the wiring connector from the ISC motor. **Warning:** *Under no circumstances should the ISC wiring connector be disconnected or connected with the ignition in the* On *position.*

20 The ISC plunger must be retracted. This is done by using jumper wires to ground the D terminal of the ISC motor and connect the C terminal to the positive battery cable. **Note:** *Do not leave the ISC motor connected to the battery any longer than necessary to retract the plunger. Also, do not connect battery voltage to any other terminals as damage to the motor could result.*

21 Start the engine and wait for the dwell meter needle to start to vary.

22 On automatic transaxle models, have an assistant shift the transaxle into *Drive* while holding firm pressure on the brake pedal.

23 Adjust the carburetor idle stop screw so the engine is running at 630 to 650 rpm on automatic transaxle models, or 930 to 950 rpm on manual transaxle models. Be sure the ISC plunger is still fully retracted.

24 Shift the automatic transaxle back to *Park* or *Neutral*.

25 Now the ISC plunger must be extended. Do this by using jumper wires to ground terminal C of the ISC motor and to connect terminal D to the positive battery terminal. Do not connect the battery to any other terminal.

26 With the plunger extended, use an appropriate tool to turn it until the engine speed is 2000 rpm for automatic transaxle models or 2400 rpm for manual transaxle models. Disconnect the jumper wires.

27 Turn off the engine and disconnect the test instruments.

28 Reconnect the wiring connector to the ISC motor.

29 Jumping the terminals will have caused the Check Engine light to come on and an ISC motor trouble code to be stored in the ECM memory. When properly reconnected, the Check Engine light will go out, but to erase the trouble code from the ECM, momentarily remove the ECM fuse at the fuse box.

Electronic Fuel Injection (EFI) system — general

30 Beginning with the 1982 model year, all vehicles with L4 engines come equipped with Electronic Fuel Injection in place of a conventional carburetor.

31 The EFI system is controlled directly by the vehicle's Electronic Control Module (ECM), which automatically adjusts the air/fuel mixture in accordance with engine load and performance requirements. The

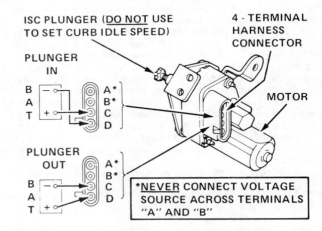

Fig. 13.21 Terminal identification of the Idle Speed Control (ISC) assembly (Sec 5)

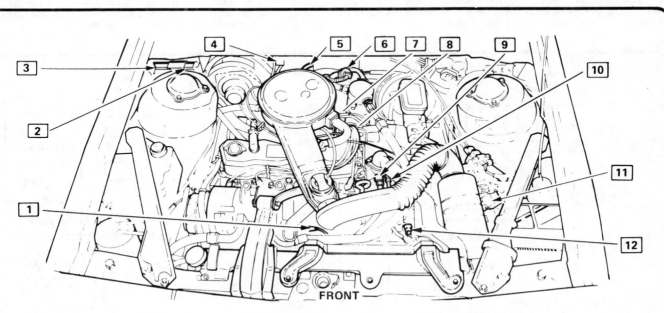

Fig. 13.22 Location of Electronic Fuel Injection (EFI) system components (Sec 5)

1 Oxygen sensor (mounted in exhaust manifold)
2 Fuel pump relay
3 Air conditioner clutch relay
4 MAP sensor

5 Air conditioner compressor control relay (mounted on cowl)
6 Air conditioner cycling switch
7 Oil pressure switch (next to distributor)
8 EST connector (from distributor)

9 Coolant sensor
10 Power steering pressure switch (on pressure line)
11 Coolant fan relay
12 TCC connector

main component of the EFI system is the Throttle Body Injector (TBI), which is mounted on the intake manifold in a similar fashion to a carburetor. The TBI is made up of two major assemblies; the throttle body and the fuel metering assembly.

32 The throttle body contains a single throttle valve, controlled by the accelerator pedal. Attached to the exterior of the body are the Throttle Position Sensor (TPS) which sends throttle position information to the ECM, and the Idle Air Control assembly (IAC), which is used by the ECM to maintain a constant idle speed during normal engine operation.

33 The fuel metering assembly contains the fuel pressure regulator and the single fuel injector. The regulator dampens the pulsations of the fuel pump and maintains a steady pressure to the injector. The fuel injector is controlled by the ECM through an electrically-operated solenoid. The amount of fuel injected into the intake manifold is varied by the length of time the injector plunger is held open.

34 The ECM controlling the EFI system has a learning capability for certain performance conditions. If the battery is disconnected, part of the ECM memory is erased, which makes it necessary to re-teach the computer. This is done by thoroughly warming up the engine and operating the vehicle at part throttle, stop and go and idle conditions.

35 An electric fuel pump, located inside the fuel tank, is used in place of the mechanical pump covered in Chapter 4. When the ignition is turned on, the fuel pump relay immediately supplies current to the fuel pump. If the engine doesn't start after two seconds, the fuel pump will automatically shut off to avoid flooding. If the fuel pump relay fails, the fuel pump will still operate after about four pounds of oil pressure has built up.

36 The fuel filter is an inline type and is located at the rear of the engine on the left side of the car.

37 The throttle stop screw, used to regulate the minimum idle speed, is adjusted at the factory and sealed with a plug to discourage unnecessary readjustment.

38 The complexity of the EFI system prevents many problems from being accurately diagnosed by the home mechanic. Therefore, if a problem should develop in the system, it is best to take the car to a dealer to locate the fault.

39 **Caution:** *Prior to any operation in which a fuel line will be disconnected, the high pressure in the system must first be relieved.* Disconnect the negative cable from the battery to eliminate the possibility of sparks occurring when spilled fuel is present.

Fuel system pressure reduction (fuel injected models)

40 The Electronic Fuel Injection (EFI) system operates under very high pressure. To prevent the spraying of fuel and eliminate the possibility of fire or personal injury, this pressure should be relieved before disconnecting any fuel lines. This is done by using the following procedure.

41 Locate the fuse block and remove the fuel pump fuse.

42 Start the engine and allow it to run until it stops from lack of fuel.

43 Operate the starter for an additional three seconds to eliminate any residual pressure.

44 Turn the ignition to the *Off* position.

45 Do not reinstall the fuel pump fuse until servicing is completed and all fuel lines have been securely connected.

Electric fuel pump (fuel injected models) — removal and installation

46 The electric fuel pump is attached to the fuel level sending unit inside the fuel tank. To remove it, refer to Chapter 4 for removal of the fuel level sender and unbolt the fuel pump from it. **Caution:** *Be sure to relieve the pressure in the fuel system before disconnecting any fuel lines.*

Idle Air Control assembly — removal and installation
Refer to Figs. 13.25 through 13.27

47 Remove the air cleaner.

48 Disconnect the wiring connector from the Idle Air Control assembly.

49 Detach the assembly from the TBI.

50 Prior to reinstalling the IAC assembly, measure the distance between the end of the motor assembly's motor housing and the tip of the conical valve. This valve should be extended from the housing no more than 1.260 in (32 mm) for 1982 models, or 1.125 in (28 mm) for 1983 to 1984 models, or damage may occur to the motor when it is installed. If this distance is greater, first identify the assembly as being either Type 1 (with a collar at the end of the motor) or Type 2 (without a collar). The pintle on a Type 1 assembly can be retracted by pushing on the end of the cone until it's in position. For a Type 2, push the pintle inward and attempt to turn it clockwise. If it turns, continue turning until it is properly set. If it will not turn, exert firm hand pressure to retract it. **Note:** *If the pintle was turned, be sure the spring is in its original position with the straight portion of the spring end aligned with the flat surface under the pintle head.*

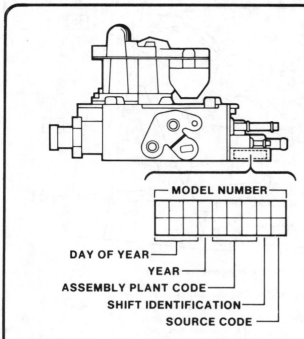

Fig. 13.23 Location of the Throttle Body Injector (TBI) identification number (Sec 5)

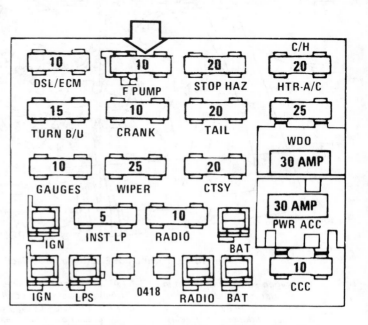

Fig. 13.24 Typical location of the fuel pump fuse (fuel injection models) (Sec 5)

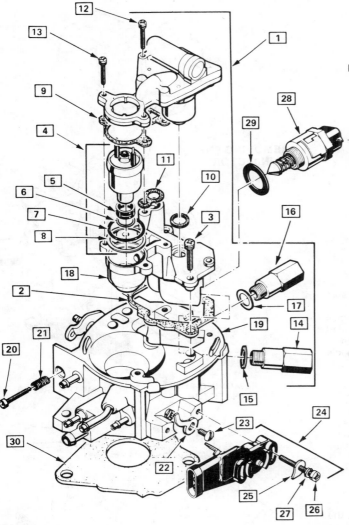

Fig. 13.25 Exploded view of the Throttle Body Injector (TBI) (Sec 5)

1 Fuel meter assembly
2 Fuel meter body gasket
3 Screw and washer assembly
   attachments (3)
4 Fuel injector kit
5 Fuel injector nozzle filter
6 Small O-ring seal
7 Large O-ring seal
8 Fuel injector back-up washer
9 Fuel meter cover gasket
10 Pressure regulator dust seal
11 Fuel meter outlet gasket
12 Screw and washer assembly —
    long (3)
13 Screw and washer assembly —
    short (2)
14 Fuel inlet nut
15 Fuel inlet nut gasket
16 Fuel outlet nut
17 Fuel outlet nut gasket
18 Fuel meter body assembly
19 Throttle body assembly
20 Idle stop screw
21 Idle stop screw spring
22 TPS lever
23 TPS lever attaching screw
24 Throttle position sensor kit
25 TPS retainer (2)
26 TPS attaching screw (2)
27 TPS screw washer (2)
28 Idle air control valve
29 Control valve to TB gasket
30 Flange mounting gasket

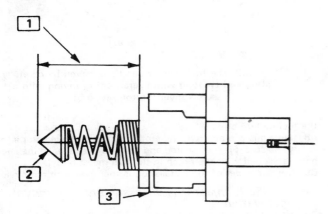

Fig. 13.26 Prior to installing the idle air control valve the distance from the motor (gasket surface) to the tip must be measured (Sec 5)

1 Measured distance
2 Pintle
3 Motor housing

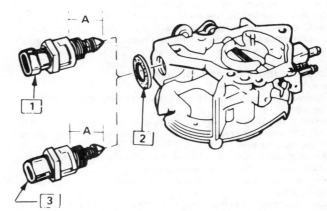

Fig. 13.27 Identification of the idle air control valve types (Sec 5)

1 Type 1 (with collar)
2 Gasket
3 Type 3 (without collar)

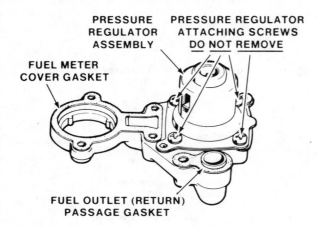

Fig. 13.28 The pressure regulator is attached to the underside of the fuel meter cover (Sec 5)

51 Installation of the IAC assembly is the reverse of removal. Be sure to install the gasket with the assembly.

52 Following installation, start the engine and allow it to reach normal operating temperature. On manual transaxle vehicles, the idle speed will automatically be controlled when operating temperature is reached. On automatic transaxle cars, the assembly will begin controlling idle speed when the engine is at operating temperature and the transaxle is shifted into Drive.

Fuel pressure regulator — removal and installation
Refer to Figs. 13.25 and 13.28

Caution: *The pressure regulator is enclosed in the fuel meter cover. It is under heavy spring tension and should not be removed due to possible personal injury. If the regulator or cover need to be replaced, they must be replaced as a unit.*

53 Relieve the pressure in the fuel system as described elsewhere in this Section.

54 Remove the air cleaner.

55 Disconnect the electrical connector leading to the injector.

56 Remove the five fuel meter cover mounting screws and lift the cover from the body. Note the position of the two shorter screws, as they must be replaced in the same positions.

57 Do not immerse the fuel meter cover in a solvent or cleaner, as this will damage the pressure regulator diaphragm and gaskets.

58 Installation is the reverse of removal procedure. Be sure to use new gaskets and a new regulator dust seal.

Injector — removal and installation
Refer to Fig. 13.29

59 Relieve the pressure in the fuel system as described elsewhere in this Section.

60 Using a pair of small pliers, carefully grasp the center collar of the injector, between the electrical terminals, and use a twisting motion to lift the injector out.

61 An alternative method is to pry it out with a screwdriver, using the accompanying illustration as a guide.

62 Do not push the injector out from underneath as this could damage the injector tip.

63 Do not immerse the injector in a solvent or cleaner. If defective, the injector must be replaced as a unit.

64 Check and clean the fuel filter on the base of the injector. To remove the filter carefully rotate it back and forth to pull it off. The filter is installed by pushing in on the injector until it's seated.

65 Whenever the injector is removed, new O-rings should be installed. Remove the large O-ring and steel back-up washer from the injector cavity. Then remove the small O-ring from the bottom of the cavity.

66 Lubricate a new small O-ring with lithium grease and push it over the nozzle end of the injector so it is seated against the fuel filter.

67 Install the steel back-up washer in the injector cavity. Lubricate the large O-ring with lithium grease and install it in the cavity, directly above the washer. When properly installed, the O-ring is flush with

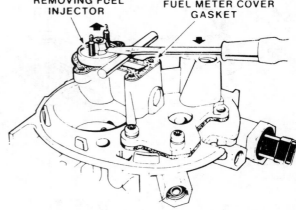

Fig. 13.29 The fuel injector can be removed by carefully pulling and twisting with pliers (top) or prying with a screwdriver (bottom) (Sec 5)

the fuel meter body surface.

68 Use a pushing and twisting motion to install the injector into the cavity. Be sure it is fully seated and that the raised lug in the injector base is aligned with the notch in the fuel meter body.

69 The remainder of the installation is the reverse of removal.

Throttle Body Injector (TBI) assembly — removal and installation

70 Relieve the pressure in the fuel system as described elsewhere in this Section.

71 Remove the air cleaner.

72 Disconnect the electrical connectors leading to the Idle Air Control, Throttle Position Sensor and injector, included in the TBI assembly.

73 Disconnect the throttle linkage and return spring from the TBI.

74 If equipped, disconnect the cruise control linkage from the TBI.

75 Use tape to label the installed locations of all vacuum hoses leading to the TBI, then disconnect them.

76 Disconnect the fuel lines from the TBI.

77 Remove the three TBI mounting bolts and lift it off, along with its gasket.

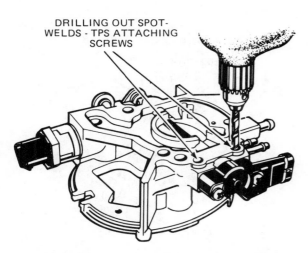

Fig. 13.30 Prior to removing the Throttle Position Sensor (TPS), the spot welds must be drilled out (Sec 5)

DRILLING OUT SPOT-WELDS - TPS ATTACHING SCREWS

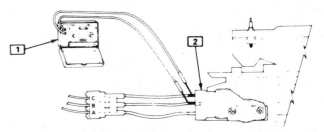

Fig. 13.31 Measuring voltage between Throttle Position Sensor (TPS) terminals (Sec 5)

1 Digital volt/ohmmeter
(10 megaohm input impedance minimum)
2 TPS

78 Prior to installing the TBI, be sure the intake manifold mating surface is clean and that all old gasket material has been scraped off.
79 Using a new gasket, place the TBI in position on the intake manifold. Connect the fuel lines to the assembly. **Note:** *Be sure the fuel line O-rings are not nicked, cut or damaged before connecting the lines.*
80 Install the TBI mounting bolts and tighten them to their proper torque.
81 The remainder of the installation procedure is the reverse of removal.
82 Following installation, start the engine and check for fuel leaks.

Throttle Position Sensor (TPS) — removal and installation
Refer to Figs. 13.30 and 13.31
83 The Throttle Position Sensor is adjusted at the factory and spot welded in place to retain its critical setting. Although the TPS should not be immersed in solvent or cleaner, the throttle body can be disassembled and cleaned with the TPS in place. If replacement is required, use the following procedure.
84 Obtain a TPS service kit from a Buick dealer.
85 Remove the Throttle Body Injector (TBI) from the intake manifold.
86 Remove the fuel meter body as described elsewhere in this Section.
87 Invert the throttle body and place it on a clean, flat surface.
88 Using a 5/16-inch drill bit, drill completely through the two TPS screw access holes in the throttle body base to remove the spot welds holding the screws in place. Refer to the accompanying illustration.
89 Remove the TPS screws, lockwashers and retainers, and lift off the TPS. The screws may be discarded as new ones should be supplied in the service kit.
90 With the throttle valve in the normal closed idle position, install the TPS onto the throttle body with the retainers and two new screws and lockwashers. Be sure the TPS pickup lever is located above the tang on the throttle actuator lever. It is recommended to use a thread-sealing agent on the screws.
91 Following TPS installation, it must be adjusted by using the following procedure:
   a) Install the TBI on the intake manifold.
   b) Remove the EGR valve and heat shield from the engine.
   c) Using three jumper wires connect each of the terminals in the TPS electrical connector to its respective terminal on the TPS. Refer to the accompanying illustration.
   d) Turn the ignition *On* and, using a digital voltmeter, measure the voltage between terminals B and C.
   e) Loosen the TPS mounting screws and slowly rotate the sensor until you obtain a reading of .525 volts ± .075 volts. Tighten the screws securely.
   f) Turn the ignition *Off* and disconnect the jumper wires.
   g) Connect the TPS electrical connector to the TPS.
   h) Reinstall the EGR valve and heat shield. Use a new EGR gasket if necessary.

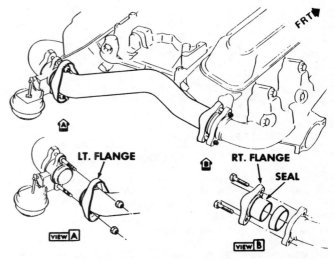

Fig. 13.32 Mounting position of the exhaust crossover pipe (V6 engine) (Sec 6)

FRT
LT. FLANGE
RT. FLANGE
SEAL
VIEW A
VIEW B

Fuel line — repair and replacement
92 The information contained in Chapter 4 remains valid, along with these additional notes.
93 When rubber tubing is used to replace metal pipe, be sure to use only reinforced fuel resistant hose. This should be identified by the word *Fluroelastomer* on the hose. The inside diameter of the hose should match the outside diameter of the metal line.
94 Do not route any hose within four inches of any part of the exhaust system or within ten inches of the catalytic converter.

6 Exhaust system

Exhaust crossover pipe (V6 engine) — installation
Note: *Because the exhaust crossover pipe on the V6 engine has a slip-fit joint on the right side, a special procedure is required for installation. If this sequence is not used, a broken flange ear may result.*
1 Insert the slip-joint (right side) of the crossover pipe into the right manifold and loosely install the nuts.
2 Insert the left side of the crossover pipe into the left manifold.
3 Install the upper nut at this connection and tighten to between one-quarter and one-half of its threaded distance.
4 Install the lower nut and tighten it to the specified torque.
5 Tighten the upper nut to the specified torque.
6 Tighten both right side nuts to the specified torque.

Catalytic converter — general
7 All 1981 X-cars, as well as certain later models, use a special dual bed catalytic converter. This is a monolith-type converter with two different types of catalyst. The front section contains an oxidation catalyst which lowers the levels of hydrocarbons and carbon monoxide.

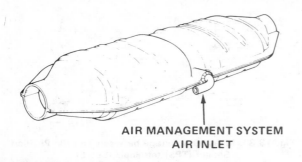

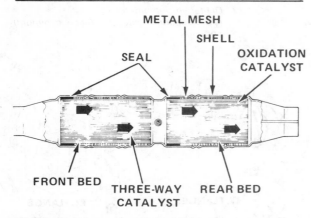

Fig. 13.33 Cross-sectional view of the dual bed catalytic converter and location of the Air Management system fitting (Sec 6)

The rear section contains a three-way catalyst which lowers the levels of oxides of nitrogen (NOX).

8   On vehicles which use an air management valve as part of the Air Injector Reactor system, the fresh air is injected into a fitting located between the two beds of the converter.

9   In 1982 L4 models returned to the use of a single bed converter using the bead-type catalyst. Models with V6 engines continued using a monolith-type converter.

---

7   Engine electrical systems

Distributor — general

1   In 1981, Electronic Spark Timing (EST) was introduced. Used in conjunction with the Computer Command Control System's Electronic Control Module (ECM), the system automatically adjusts the ignition timing to the optimal point depending on engine load and performance.

2   With the incorporation of the EST system, the conventional vacuum and mechanical advance systems were eliminated.

3   The distributor on the L4 engine was redesigned to use an externally-mounted ignition coil.

4   Prior to operations in which the engine must be rotated without the spark plugs firing, such as during compression checks, disconnect the ignition switch feed wire. On V6 engines, this is the pink wire at the distributor. On L4 engines, this is the pink wire at the ignition coil.

5   The location of the tachometer terminal on V6 engines is next to the ignition switch (BAT) connector on the distributor cap, while on the L4 engine it is the brown wire at the ignition coil.

6   Procedures not included in this Chapter are the same as those described in Chapter 5, with the exception of references to vacuum or mechanical advance systems or components. In addition, the distributor also now uses a multi-prong connector which leads to the ECM.

Ignition coil (L4 engine) — removal and installation

7   Remove the bolt that attaches the radio capacitor to the ignition coil.

8   Disconnect the electrical connector from the coil.

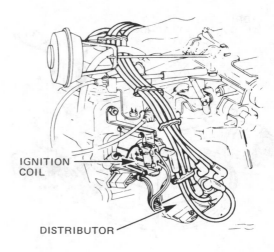

Fig. 13.34 Mounting arrangement of the distributor and ignition coil on L4 engines (Sec 7)

9   Remove the three coil mounting bolts, then disconnect the coil wire. Lift the coil out.

10   Installation is the reverse of the removal procedure.

Distributor (L4 engine) — removal and installation

Removal

11   Remove the ignition coil as described above.

12   Make a mark on the base of the distributor and a matching mark on the block so that the distributor can be replaced in the same position during reinstallation, then loosen the distributor clamp screw and rotate the distributor to gain access to the cap latches.

13   Turn both cap latches counterclockwise and lift the cap off. Do not disconnect the spark plug wires from the cap. Secure the cap out of the way.

14   Disconnect all wiring connectors from the distributor.

15   Remove the distributor clamp screw and holddown clamp.

16   Rotate the distributor until the marks made in Step 12 are in alignment, then mark the position of the rotor on the outside of the distributor body. Slowly lift the distributor from the engine and note the position of the rotor again when it stops turning. Mark this position, also. To ensure correct timing of the distributor upon reinstallation, the rotor should be in this position prior to reinserting the distributor into the engine.

17   Avoid rotating the engine with the distributor removed as the ignition timing will be changed.

Installation (if the engine was not rotated after removal)

18   Position the rotor in the exact location it was in when the distributor was removed from the engine.

19   Lower the distributor down into the engine. To mesh the gears at the bottom of the distributor, it may be necessary to turn the rotor slightly.

20   With the base of the distributor all the way down against the engine block and the marks on the distributor base and the engine block made in Step 12 in alignment, the rotor should be pointed to the first alignment mark made on the distributor housing. If these two marks are not in alignment, repeat the previous steps.

21   Place the clamp into position and install the clamp bolt loosely.

22   Connect the wiring connectors to the distributor.

23   Install the distributor cap. Rotate the distributor to its original position, and tighten the clamp screw securely.

24   Install the ignition coil.

Installation (if the engine was rotated after removal)

25   Turn the crankshaft by applying a wrench to the crankshaft pulley bolt at the front of the engine until the number one piston is at Top Dead Center (TDC). This can be ascertained by removing the number one spark plug and feeling the compression being generated. If you are careful not to scratch the cylinder, you can also use a length of

stiff wire to feel the piston come to the top of the cylinder.

26 With the number one piston at TDC (as indicated by the timing marks on the front cover) the distributor rotor should be pointing to the general area of the number one spark plug wire.

27 Turn the distributor to position the rotor so it is pointing between the number 1 and 3 spark plug towers in the cap.

28 Proceed with installation as detailed in paragraphs 19 through 24. Disregard the rotor mark references in paragraph 23.

Generator — removal and installation

29 Disconnect the negative cable from the battery.

30 Disconnect the two-terminal connector and battery leads from the back of the generator.

31 Remove the upper adjusting bolt.

32 On L4 engines, remove the generator drivebelt. Remove the upper mounting bracket.

33 Remove the right front splash shield.

34 On V6 engines, loosen the lower pivot bolt and remove the drivebelt.

35 Remove the lower pivot bolt and lift the generator from the car.

36 Installation is the reverse of removal procedure. Be sure to adjust the drivebelt tension following installation.

---

8 Emissions control systems

Computer Command Control System — general

1 The Computer Command Control System, described in Chapter 6, has been enlarged to control either completely or in part more of the engine's operating systems, including Electronic Spark Timing, Electronic Fuel Injection (on 1982 and later L4 models) and several of the emissions control systems.

2 A *Check Engine* light, located in the dash, will light if there is a malfunction in the system. If the problem is intermittent, the light will remain lit as long as the problem exists, but will go off 10 seconds after the problem disappears. Despite the light going out, a trouble code will be retained in the Electronic Control Module (ECM) memory for later diagnosis.

Note: *This memory mode is erased whenever battery current is cut off from the ECM. This includes disconnecting the battery terminals, removing the ECM fuse or, on 1982 and later models, by disconnecting the pigtail electrical connector at the positive battery terminal.*

3 Because of the increasing complexity of this system, all diagnosis and servicing of this system and its components should be left to a dealer or other qualified mechanic.

Evaporative Emission Control (EEC) system — general

4 The Evaporative Emission Control (EEC) system described in Chapter 6 remains basically unchanged. An exception is that on the V6 engine, the charcoal canister's purge function is electronically controlled by the vehicle's Electronic Control Module (ECM) through a purge

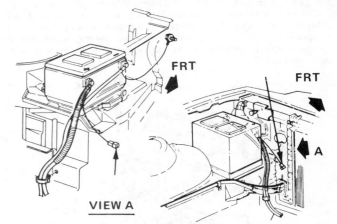

Fig. 13.35 Location of the ECM pigtail connector at the battery (Sec 8)

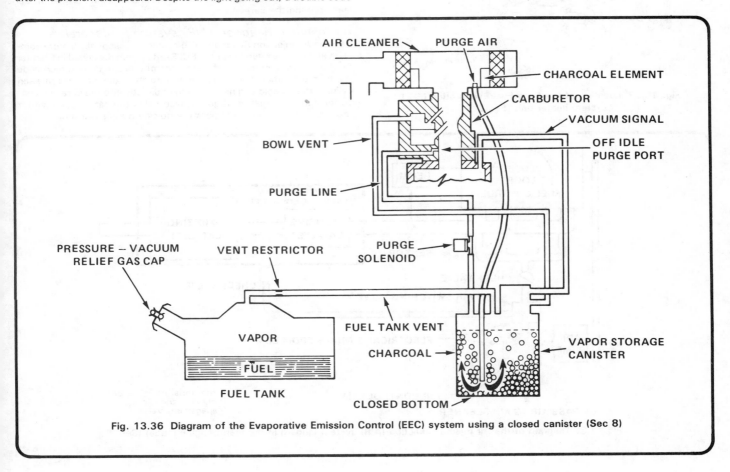

Fig. 13.36 Diagram of the Evaporative Emission Control (EEC) system using a closed canister (Sec 8)

solenoid. During certain periods of engine operation, the ECM cuts off the vacuum signal to the purge valve, preventing canister vapors from being drawn into the intake manifold.

5   If a problem is suspected in the EEC system, an inspection can be performed as described in Chapter 6. However, if no mechanical or vacuum problem can be found, have a dealer or other qualified mechanic check the system out as it relates to the ECM.

6   In addition, some vehicles use canisters that are of the closed design, which draw air from the air cleaner instead of through the bottom of the canister.

Early Fuel Evaporation (EFE) system — general

7   The Early Fuel Evaporation (EFE) system was redesigned for the 1981 model year. It now provides rapid heat to the intake air supply by means of a ceramic heater grid which is integral with the carburetor base gasket and located under the primary bore.

8   The EFE heater unit is controlled by the Electronic Control Module (ECM) through a relay. The ECM senses the coolant temperature level and applies voltage to the heater unit only when the engine temperature is below a predetermined level. At normal operating temperatures the heater unit is off.

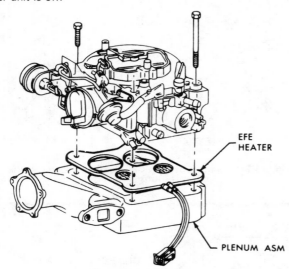

EFE HEATER

PLENUM ASM

Fig. 13.37 Location of the Early Fuel Evaporation (EFE) system heater unit (Sec 8)

9   If the EFE heater is not coming on, poor cold engine performance will be experienced. If the heater is not shutting off when the engine is fully warmed up, the engine will run as if it is out of tune due to the constant flow of hot air through the carburetor.

10 If the EFE system is suspected of malfunctioning while the engine is cold, first visually check all electrical wires and connectors to be sure they are clean, tight and in good condition.

11 With the ignition switch on, use a circuit tester or voltmeter to be sure current is reaching the relay. If not, there is a problem in the wiring leading to the relay, in the ECM thermo switch, or in the ECM itself.

12 With the engine cold and the ignition switch *On*, disconnect the heater unit wiring connector and use a circuit tester or voltmeter to check that current is reaching the heater unit. If so, use a continuity tester to check for continuity in the wiring connector attached to the heater unit. If continuity exists, the system is operating correctly in the cold engine mode.

13 If current was not reaching the heater unit, but was reaching the relay, replace the relay.

14 To check that the system turns off at normal engine operating temperature, first allow the engine to warm up thoroughly. With the engine idling, disconnect the heater unit wiring connector and use a circuit tester or voltmeter to check if current is reaching the heater unit. If not, the system is okay.

15 If current is reaching the heater unit, a faulty ECM is suspect.

16 For confirmation of the ECM's condition, take the car to a dealer or other qualified mechanic.

EFE heater unit — removal and installation

17 Remove the air cleaner.

18 Disconnect all wires, vacuum hoses and fuel lines from the carburetor.

19 Disconnect the wiring connector leading to the EFE unit.

20 Remove the carburetor, referring to Chapter 4 if necessary.

21 Lift off the heater unit.

22 Installation is the reverse of the removal procedure.

23 Following installation start the engine and check for any air or fuel leaks around the carburetor.

Air Injection Reaction (AIR) system — general

24 The Air Injection Reaction (AIR) system is essentially a more complete and complex version of the PULSAIR system described in Chapter 6. The AIR system helps reduce hydrocarbons and carbon monoxide levels in the exhaust by injecting air into the exhaust ports of each cylinder during cold engine operation or directly into the catalytic converter during normal operation. It also helps the catalytic converter reach proper operating temperature quickly during warm-up.

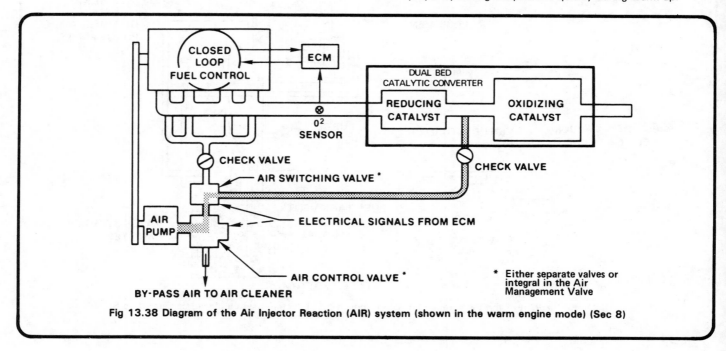

Fig 13.38 Diagram of the Air Injector Reaction (AIR) system (shown in the warm engine mode) (Sec 8)

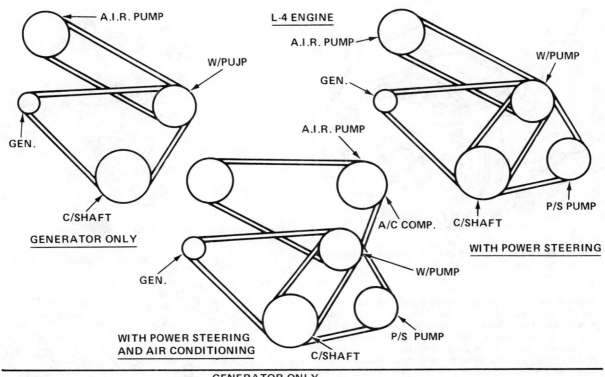

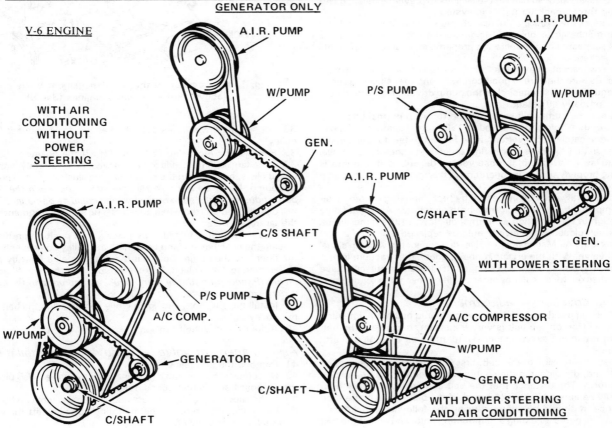

Fig 13.39 Drivebelt arrangement for models equipped with an Air Injector Reaction (AIR) pump (Sec 8)

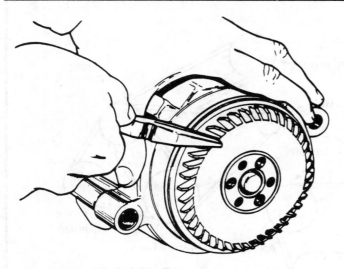

Fig. 13.40 Pliers are used to pull the AIR pump filter from the pump (Sec 8)

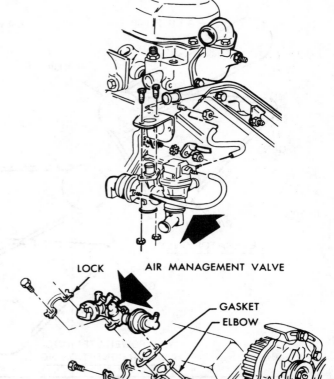

Fig. 13.41 Location of the Air Management Valve on L4 (above) and V6 (below) engines (Sec 8)

25 The AIR system uses an air pump to force the air into the exhaust stream. An Air Management Valve, controlled by the car's Electronic Control Module (ECM), directs the air to the correct location depending on engine temperature and driving conditions. During certain situations, such as during deceleration, the air is diverted to the air cleaner to prevent backfiring from too much oxygen in the exhaust system. One-way check valves are also used in the air lines to prevent exhaust gases from being forced back through the system.

26 Because of the ECM's influence on the system, it is difficult for the home mechanic to properly diagnose the entire system. If the system is suspected of not operating properly, individual components can be checked.

27 Begin any inspection by carefully inspecting all hoses, vacuum lines and wires. Be sure they are in good condition and that all connections are tight and clean. Also check that the pump drivebelt is in good condition and properly adjusted.

28 To check the pump, allow the engine to reach normal operating temperature, then hold engine speed at 1500 rpm. Locate the air hose running to the catalytic converter and squeeze it to feel for pulsations. Have an assistant increase the engine speed and check for a parallel increase in air flow. If this is observed as described, the pump is functioning properly. If it is not operating in this manner, a faulty pump is indicated.

29 The check valve can be inspected by first removing it from its air line. Attempt to blow through it from both directions. Air should only pass through in the direction of normal air flow. If it is either stuck open or stuck closed, the valve should be replaced.

30 To check the Air Management Valve, disconnect the vacuum signal line at the valve. With the engine running, check that vacuum is present in the line. If not, the line is clogged. If vacuum is present, have the valve checked by a dealer or other qualified mechanic for defects.

AIR pump drivebelt — adjustment

31 The AIR pump is driven off of the water pump pulley. Maintaining the proper tension on the belt is very important, because if the belt is too tight it can put excessive sideward strain on the unit's shafts and bearings.

32 To check the tension of this belt, first find the longest free section of the belt and, gripping it in the center of this section, move the belt back and forth. The distance that the belt can be moved back-and-forth should be about 1/2-inch (13 mm). If the belt moves more than this distance, it should be adjusted using the following procedure.

33 Loosen the pump adjusting and mounting bolts and adjust the belt by moving the pump towards or away from the engine. Tighten the adjusting and mounting bolts and recheck the adjustment.

AIR pump pulley and filter — removal and installation

34 Compress the drivebelt to keep the pulley from turning, and loosen the pulley bolts.

35 Loosen the drivebelt as described above and remove it from the pulley.

36 Remove the mounting bolts and lift off the pulley.

37 If the fan-like filter needs to be removed, grasp it firmly with needle-nosed pliers, as shown in the accompanying illustration, and pull it from the pump. **Note:** *Do not insert a screwdriver between the filter and pump housing as the edge of the housing could be damaged.* The filter will usually be distorted when pulled off. Be sure no fragments fall into the air intake hole.

38 The new filter is installed by placing it in position on the pump, placing the pulley over it and tightening the pulley bolts evenly to draw the filter into the pump. Do not attempt to install a filter by pressing or hammering it into place. **Note:** *It is normal for the new filter to have an interference fit with the pump housing, and upon initial operation it may squeal until worn in.*

39 Install the drivebelt, and again while compressing the belt, tighten the pulley bolts.

40 Adjust the drivebelt tension.

Air management valve — removal and installation

41 Remove the air cleaner.

42 Disconnect the vacuum signal line from the valve. Also disconnect the air hoses and wiring connectors.

43 If the mounting bolts are retained by tabbed lockwashers, bend the tabs back, then remove the mounting bolts and lift the valve off of its adapter or bracket.

44 Installation is the reverse of the removal procedure. Be sure to use a new gasket when installing the valve.

Air pump — removal and installation

45 Remove the air management valve and adapter, if equipped.

46 If the pulley needs to be removed from the pump, it should be done

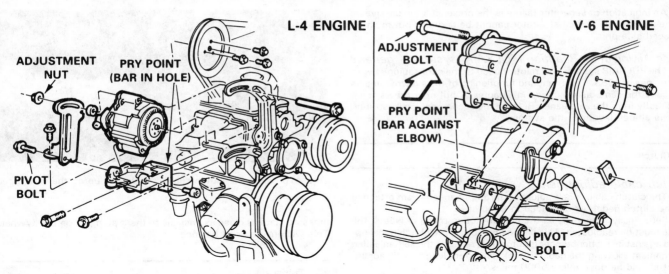

Fig. 13.42 Mounting arrangement of the AIR pump (Sec 8)

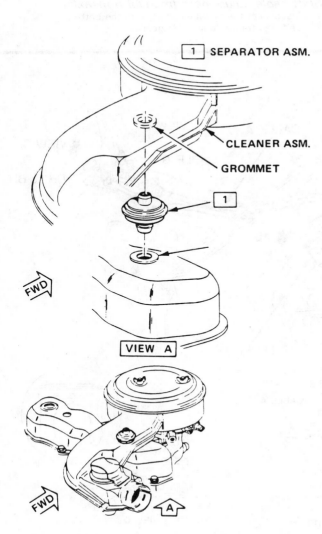

Fig. 13.43 Typical location of the oil separator used in the L4 Positive Crankcase Ventilation (PCV) system (1983 models) (Sec 8)

prior to removing the drivebelt.

47 If the pulley is not being removed, remove the drivebelt.

48 Remove the pump mounting bolts and lift the pump from the engine.

49 Installation is the reverse of the removal procedure. **Note:** *Do not tighten the pump mounting bolts until all components are installed.*

50 Following installation, adjust the drivebelt tension as described elsewhere in this subsection.

Exhaust Gas Recirculation (EGR) system — general

51 In 1983, a new type of EGR valve was introduced; the Pulse Width Modulated type. This valve, used on V6 engines, is controlled entirely by the car's Electronic Control Module (ECM) through a solenoid. This is a complex system and if suspected of not operating properly, is best left to a dealer to diagnose and service.

Positive Crankcase Ventilation (PCV) system — general

52 The PCV system remains basically the same as described in Chapter 7. In 1983, an oil separator was added to the system on models with L4 engines. It is located between the air cleaner snorkel and the rocker cover.

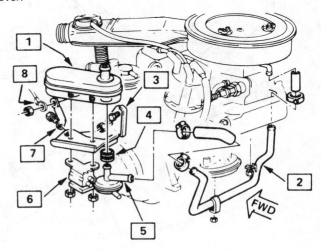

Fig. 13.44 Mounting arrangement of the PULSAIR system (1983 models) (Sec 8)

1	Valve assembly	5	Valve
2	Pipe assembly	6	Actuator
3	Bracket	7	Brace
4	Grommet	8	Ground strap

53 An indication of separator failure is the presence of excessive oil in the air cleaner. The oil separator cannot be serviced but must be replaced as a unit.

Pulse Air Injection Reaction (PULSAIR) system — general
54 The PULSAIR system was reintroduced to the cars equipped with L4 engines in 1983. The intent and functioning of the system remains basically the same as described in Chapter 7, but now draws fresh air directly from the air cleaner. Refer to the accompanying illustration for the altered layout of the system.

9.2 To adjust the clutch cable, simply pull up on the clutch pedal

---

9   Clutch

Clutch cable adjustment
1 The clutch cable is self-adjusting through a mechanism attached to the clutch pedal, as described in Chapter 8.
2 Periodically, however, as the clutch friction material wears, the cable must be readjusted. This is done by pulling the clutch pedal upward against its rubber bumper (photo). This releases the self-adjusting mechanism allowing the cable to seek its correct length. This adjustment should be done every 5000 miles.

Clutch disc and pressure plate — removal and installation
3 The procedure described in Chapter 8 remains the same with the following addition.
4 If installing a new pressure plate, align the paint dab on the new

pressure plate as close as possible to the X stamped on the flywheel. This will ensure good balance.

---

10   Transaxle

Shift cable adjustment (manual transaxle)
1 Disconnect the negative cable from the battery.
2 Shift the transaxle into 1st gear.

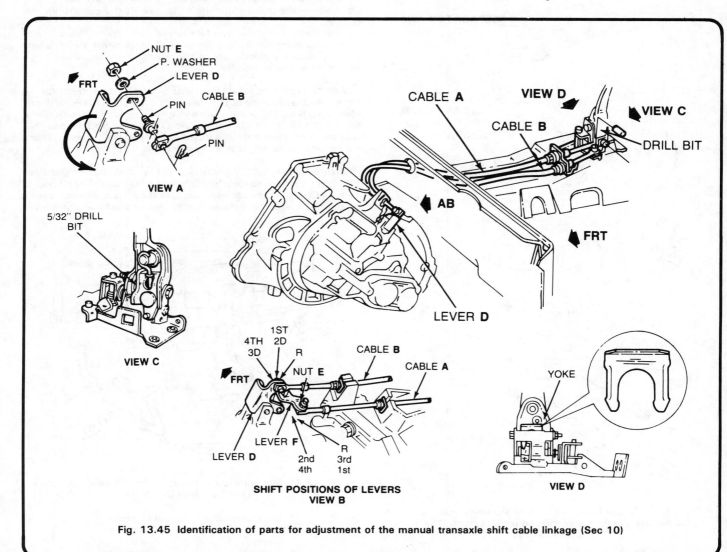

Fig. 13.45 Identification of parts for adjustment of the manual transaxle shift cable linkage (Sec 10)

3   Working under the hood, loosen the shift cable attaching nuts (E) at the transaxle levers (D and F).

4   Move to the interior of the car. Remove the console trim plate and slide the shifter boot up the shifter.

5   Install a yoke clip between the tower and carrier at the base of the shifter, as shown in view D of the accompanying illustration.

6   Install a 5/32 inch (number 22) drill bit into the alignment hole at the side of the shifter assembly. Refer to view C in the accompanying illustration.

7   Refer to view A and rotate the transaxle lever D in the direction of the arrow and tighten the attaching nut E to remove slack from the cable.

8   Tighten the attaching nut E on the transaxle lever F.

9   Remove the drill bit and clip from the shifter assembly.

10   Reinstall the shifter boot and console trim plate.

11   Reconnect the negative battery cable.

12   After adjustment road test the car, checking for a good neutral gate feel during shifting. If necessary, finer adjustments can be made after road testing.

Manual transaxle — removal and installation

13   The removal and installation of the manual transaxle remains basically the same as described in Chapter 7. However some design changes in other components may alter the procedure somewhat, depending on model.

14   If equipped with a V6 engine, you may need to disconnect fuel lines and clamps from the clutch cable bracket and remove the bracket from the transaxle.

15   On V6 engines, the exhaust crossover pipe may need to be removed. Refer to the information in Section 3.

16   For removing the cradle, refer to Section 15 for information on the new design cradle.

Manual transaxle — overhaul

17   The overhaul procedure described in Chapter 7 remains unchanged except for the following.

18   During case reassembly, the following steps should be inserted in place of paragraph 82.

a)   Use a straightedge on both sides of the interlock to see if the de-

tent is out of alignment with the interlock. **Note:** *The straightedge should rest on both sides without interference from the detent paddle.* If any interference is noticed, perform the following step.

b)   With the alignment pin still in position, place the detent and interlock assembly in a vise, with light pressure on the detent paddle to push it into alignment. Loosen the nut securing the detent spring to the interlock. This will allow the spring to achieve proper alignment. Retighten the nut.

c)   Recheck the detent alignment as before.

d)   Once the alignment is correct, place the detent shift lever into the interlock.

Transaxle Converter Clutch (TCC) system — general

19   In 1983 the Transaxle Converter Clutch (TCC) system was introduced to V6 models equipped with automatic transaxles.

20   This system is designed to override the transaxle's hydraulic coupling to the engine by using a mechanical coupling system during high-speed cruising conditions.

21   This mechanical coupling is activated by an electrical solenoid, which is controlled by the car's Electronic Control Module (ECM).

22   A Vehicle Speed Sensor (VSS), located at the speedometer relays information on the speed of the car to the ECM. When the car reaches a predetermined speed, the ECM activates the TCC solenoid, located inside the transaxle, which operates the TCC.

23   During deceleration, passing, or braking the ECM deactivates the solenoid, allowing the transaxle to return to fluid coupling. A special switch, which combines both this TCC function and acts as a brake light switch is mounted at the brake pedal in a similar fashion to the conventional brake light switch.

24   The VSS uses a spinning reflective blade and a Light Emitting Diode (LED) to transmit vehicle speed information to the ECM. As the blades pass through the LED's light beam, light is reflected back to a photo cell, causing a low power signal to be sent to a buffer for amplification and then passed along to the ECM. The VSS can be replaced by first removing the instrument cluster (Chapter 12) to gain access to the rear of the speedometer.

25   Disassembly of the automatic transaxle is required to replace the solenoid or clutch assembly and is therefore best left to a dealer or other qualified mechanic.

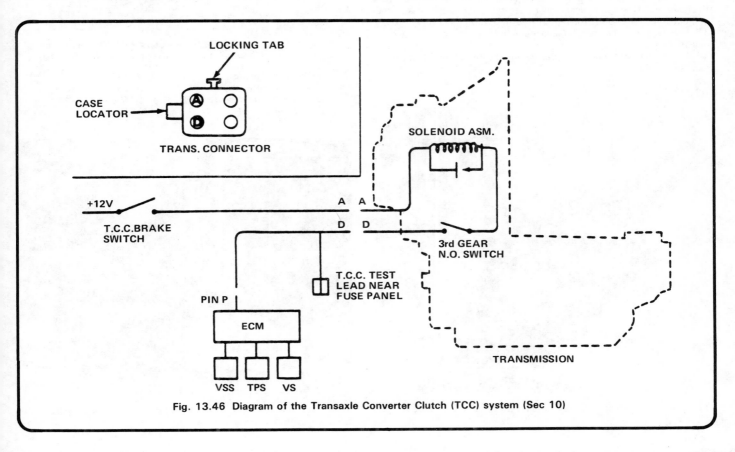

Fig. 13.46 Diagram of the Transaxle Converter Clutch (TCC) system (Sec 10)

26 If the TCC system is suspected of malfunctioning, first be sure that the transaxle fluid level is correct, that the manual linkage and throttle valve cable adjustments are correct and that the trouble is not from the engine or other non-transaxle source. Diagnosis and servicing of the system is best left to a dealer or other qualified mechanic.

11 Driveaxles

Driveaxles — general

Note: *Refer also to Section 14, Front suspension — general*

1   In 1982 a second type of driveaxle was introduced to the X-cars, using a tri-pot type inner joint. The outer joint remains the same as previously used.
2   When removing tri-pot driveaxles, care must be taken to prevent the axle from becoming overextended, which can result in separation of internal components and failure of the joint.
3   To prevent this, when the inner joint is disconnected from the trans-axle, always support the axle with wire in a horizontal position. Likewise, when the entire axle is removed from the car, do not hold it vertically or at an angle. Keep it as horizontal as possible.

Driveaxle (tri-pot type) — disassembly and reassembly

4   The outer joint of this type of driveaxle is removed and disassembled in the same manner as described in Chapter 8.
5   To remove the inner joint, first cut the rubber boot clamps and remove them (photo).
6   Slide the joint housing from the axle.
7   If the spider assembly is not to be disassembled, install a spider bearing retainer tool over the assembly.
8   First remove the inner retaining ring and slide the spider assembly back to expose the end retaining ring, remove the end retaining ring from the axle and slide the spider assembly off (photo).
9   Slide the spacer ring and rubber boot from the axle.
10 If the spider assembly is to be disassembled, refer to the exploded illustration of the driveaxle for the proper order of parts.
11 Use solvent to clean the old grease from the housing.
12 Inspect all parts carefully for excessive wear or damage. Be sure the bearings in the spider assembly rotate without noise or roughness. Inspect the rubber boot for tears or deterioration.
13 It is a good idea to install a new boot whenever the joint is disassembled.
14 Install the boot over the axle, being careful not to cut it on the axle serrations.

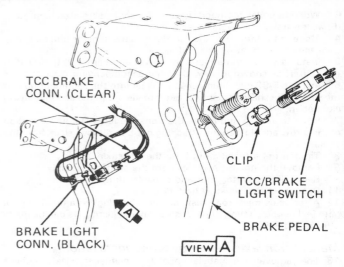

Fig. 13.47 Location of the TCC/brakelight switch (Sec 10)

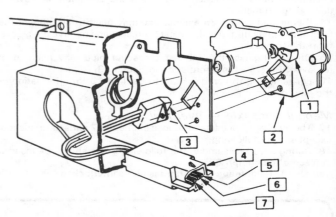

Fig. 13.48 The Vehicle Speed Sensor (VSS) used in the TCC system is located behind the speedometer (Sec 10)

1 Reflector blade
2 Speedometer frame
3 Vehicle speed sensor LED and photocell
4 Buffer circuit
5 Battery voltage
6 Ground
7 VSS output

11.5   A pair of cutters should be used to remove the boot straps

11.8   The rear retaining ring has to be moved back to gain access to the front retaining ring

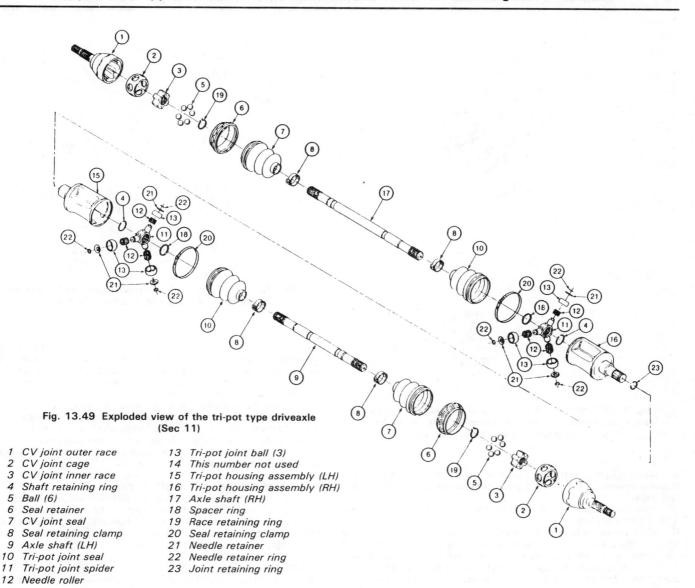

Fig. 13.49 Exploded view of the tri-pot type driveaxle (Sec 11)

1 CV joint outer race
2 CV joint cage
3 CV joint inner race
4 Shaft retaining ring
5 Ball (6)
6 Seal retainer
7 CV joint seal
8 Seal retaining clamp
9 Axle shaft (LH)
10 Tri-pot joint seal
11 Tri-pot joint spider
12 Needle roller

13 Tri-pot joint ball (3)
14 This number not used
15 Tri-pot housing assembly (LH)
16 Tri-pot housing assembly (RH)
17 Axle shaft (RH)
18 Spacer ring
19 Race retaining ring
20 Seal retaining clamp
21 Needle retainer
22 Needle retainer ring
23 Joint retaining ring

11.16 When reinstalling the spider assembly, make sure the recess is facing outward

15 Slide the spacer ring onto the axle and seat it in its groove.
16 Slide the assembled spider bearing assembly onto the axle, so the counterbore in the assembly is facing toward the end of the axle (photo). The assembly should be retained to keep it from coming apart.
17 Install the retaining ring onto the axle.
18 Pack about half the grease supplied with the new boot evenly into the housing and put the remainder in the boot.
19 Insert the housing over the axle and fit the large end of the boot over the housing. Retain it with a new boot clamp.
20 Retain the small boot end with a new clamp, making sure the boot is not twisted, deformed or over-extended.

12 Brakes

Bleeding the brake system
1   If air has entered the system because the master cylinder has been disconnected or the master cylinder reservoir has been low or empty of fluid, or if a complete flushing of the system is needed, the master cylinder must be bled of air prior to bleeding the wheel cylinders or calipers, as described in Chapter 9.
2   Fill the master cylinder reservoirs with fluid.
3   At the master cylinder disconnect the brake line that leads to the left front brake.

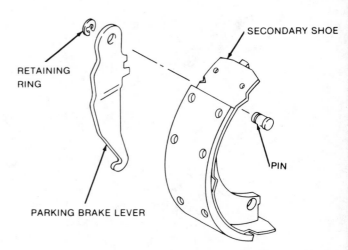

Fig. 13.51 The parking brake lever is attached to the rear brake shoe by a pin and retaining ring (Sec 12)

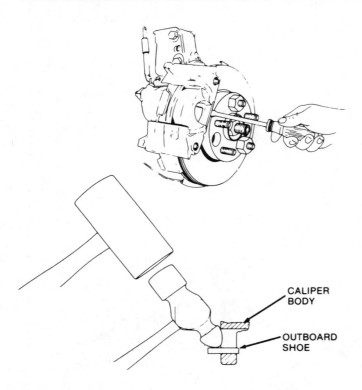

Fig. 13.50 While the outer disc pad is wedged in place with a screwdriver (above), the retaining tabs can be bent over using hammer as shown (Sec 12)

4   When fluid begins to flow from the opening, reconnect the brake line to the master cylinder so it is snug, but can still be loosened quickly and easily.

5   Have an assistant slowly depress the brake pedal one time and hold it firmly depressed.

6   While the pedal is held depressed, loosen the left front brake line again to allow any air to escape from the cylinder, then retighten the connection and have your assistant slowly release the brake pedal.

7   Wait 15 seconds and repeat the operation until all air is bled from the cylinder. This should require only a few repetitions of the procedure. Be sure the master cylinder reservoir is kept at least half full of fluid at all times. Also, be sure to wait 15 seconds between each pedal depression. **Note:** *The pedal must be depressed and released slowly so as not to displace the secondary piston in the master cylinder bore.*

8   When all air is bled from the left front brake line connection, tighten it securely and repeat the entire bleeding procedure at the right front brake line connection.

9   Following the master cylinder bleeding, bleed the wheel cylinders and calipers as described in Chapter 9. **Note:** *As with the master cylinder, when bleeding the remainder of the brake system, depress and release the brake pedal slowly.*

Disc brake pad — removal and installation

10   The procedure for removal and installation of the disc brake pads remains the same as for previous models (described in Chapter 9) with the exception that it is now recommended that the inner pad be installed before the outer pad. Also, there is a new recommended method of locking the outer pads into the caliper.

11   After installation of both pads in the caliper, install the caliper and apply heavy pressure to the brake pedal three times.

12   Seat the outer pad in the caliper by wedging a large flat-blade screwdriver between the pad flange and the hub as shown in the accompanying illustration.

13   With a screwdriver held in this position, have an assistant apply firm, steady pressure to the brake pedal so the outer pad is pressed tightly against the caliper. The screwdriver should be left in place during the following steps.

14   While your assistant maintains pressure on the brake pedal, position an eight-ounce machinist's hammer against the caliper and one of the outer pad retaining tabs as shown in the accompanying figure. Then, strike the machinist's hammer with a heavier hammer to bend the tab and clamp the pad to the caliper.

15   Repeat the procedure with the other retaining tab.

16   Both tabs should be bent to approximately a 45° angle.

17   Release pressure on the brake pedal and check that the outer pad is held tightly to the caliper. If so, remove the screwdriver.

18   These tabs should only be bent once. If they are straightened for any reason, the pad should be replaced.

Rear brake shoes — removal and installation

19   The rear brake shoe removal and installation procedures described in Chapter 9 remain virtually unchanged. The one minor design difference is that the parking brake lever is now attached to the secondary brake shoe by a retaining ring and separate pin. This is in contrast to the integral pin used on 1980 models.

Master cylinder — overhaul

20   In 1981 the master cylinder was redesigned slightly so that the quick take-up valve is now integral with the master cylinder body, and cannot be removed. The remainder of the master cylinder overhaul procedure described in Chapter 9 remains unchanged.

Parking brake adjustment

21   The parking brake does not need maintenance but the cable may stretch over a period of time, necessitating adjustment. Also, the parking brake should be checked for proper adjustment whenever the rear brake cables have been disconnected. If the parking brake pedal travel is less than nine ratchet clicks or more than sixteen ratchet clicks under heavy foot pressure, the parking brake needs adjustment.

22   Depress the parking brake pedal exactly three ratchet clicks.

23   Raise the rear of the car and support it on jackstands.

24   Check that the equalizer nut groove is lubricated with chassis grease. Locate the equalizer at the rear axle, joining the front and rear parking brake cables. See the accompanying parking brake cable illustration.

25   Turn the adjusting nut until the rear wheel can just be turned rearward using two hands but is locked when you attempt to turn it forward.

26   Release the parking brake and check that both rear wheels turn freely and that there is no brake drag in either direction.

27   Lower the car to the ground.

Parking brake cables — removal and installation

28   In 1981, the parking brake cable system was redesigned, necessitating changes in the servicing procedures.

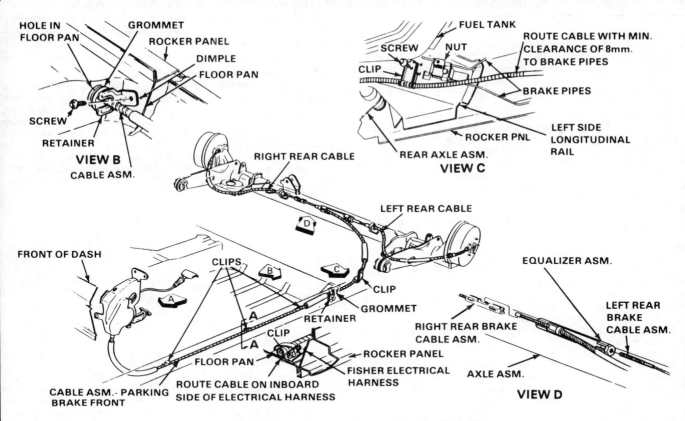

Fig. 13.52 Routing of the parking brake cables (Sec 12)

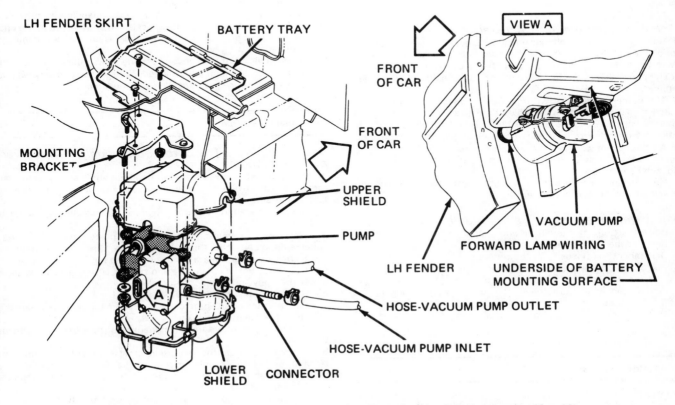

Fig. 13.53 The electric vacuum pump is mounted to the underside of the battery tray (Sec 12)

Front parking brake cable

29 Raise the rear of the car and support it on jackstands.

30 Loosen the equalizer nut, located at the rear axle, until the cable tension is loose enough to allow the front cable to be disengaged from the parking brake lever.

31 Depress the tangs retaining the cable casing to the lever bracket and release the cable.

32 The cable is retained to the floor by clips along its route and by a retainer and screw at its grommet or the point where it is routed through the floor to the rear underside of the vehicle. Lift the carpet (removing the seats, if necessary) to release the cable from the clips and to remove the screw and retainer at the grommet. The grommet can then be unseated by pushing it toward the inside of the vehicle.

33 Disengage the front cable from the equalizer and, returning to the car's interior, pull the cable free.

34 Installation is the reverse of the removal procedure.

35 Following installation, readjust the parking brake as described in this Section.

Rear parking brake cable (right or left)

36 Raise the rear of the car and support it on jackstands.

37 Loosen the equalizer nut to remove any tension from the cable.

38 Remove the wheel and brake drum.

39 With a screwdriver inserted between the brake shoe and the top part of the brake adjuster bracket, push the bracket to the front and release the top adjuster bracket rod.

40 Remove the rear holddown spring and remove the actuator lever and lever return spring.

41 Remove the adjuster screw spring.

42 Remove the top rear brake shoe return spring.

43 Unhook the parking brake cable from the parking brake lever.

44 Compress the locking spring tabs securing the parking brake cable to the backing plate and withdraw the cable.

45 Disconnect the end of the cable from the equalizer.

46 Depress the cable casing retaining tangs and disengage the cable from the axle bracket.

47 Installation is the reverse of the removal procedure.

48 Following installation, readjust the parking brake as described in this Section.

Electric vacuum pump — general

49 Some models use an electric vacuum pump, mounted to the under side of the battery tray, to help maintain a proper vacuum level for the power brake system. The air inlet hose is connected to the brake booster check valve and the air outlet hose is connected to the intake manifold.

50 The pump is equipped with an internal vacuum on-off switch, located in its electrical controller. This automatically activates the pump when the engine vacuum level drops below a predetermined point. The pump only operates when the ignition switch is in the *Run* position.

51 A low vacuum warning light switch, located in the inlet hose, activates a warning light in the instrument panel when the vacuum drops below the set level.

52 Excessive brake pedal effort and lighting of the brake warning light are signs of pump malfunctioning.

Electric vacuum pump — removal and installation

53 Raise the front of the vehicle and support it on jackstands.

54 Remove the splash shield on the left side of the car.

55 Disconnect the hoses from the pump.

56 Disconnect the electrical connector from the pump. This is a locking-type connector and care must be taken when disconnecting it.

57 Remove the three nuts attaching the pump to its mounting bracket and lift the pump out.

58 Installation is the reverse of removal.

13 Electrical system

At the end of this Supplement are wiring diagrams of just those circuits which differ significantly from those included in Chapter 10. If a particular circuit is not shown under the model year of your car, refer to the next most recent diagram covering that circuit, either here or in Chapter 10.

14 Suspension system

Front suspension — general

1 To eliminate the need to readjust the camber settings when servicing the strut mount, jounce bumper, strut shield, spring seat or spring insulator, or when removing the driveaxles, the following marking procedures should be performed prior to such operations. **Note:** *This marking procedure is not necessary when removing the strut damper assembly, front spring or knuckle. The camber setting as well as the toe-in setting will have to be checked and adjusted regardless.*

2 Use a sharp tool to scribe a line on the knuckle marking the position of the lower part of the strut mount. Refer to view A in the accompanying illustration.

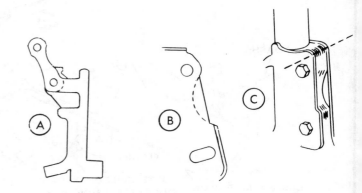

Fig. 13.54 Prior to certain front end operations listed in the text, the positioning of the strut to the knuckle must be carefully marked as shown (Sec 13)

3 Scribe a line on the inner side of the strut flange, along the curve of the knuckle. Refer to view B in the accompanying illustration.

4 Make matching marks on the knuckle and strut mount at the upper corner of the mount as shown in view C of the accompanying illustration.

5 After servicing of the above-mentioned components, be sure that these marks are again properly aligned. **Note:** *After such servicing, the toe-in will still need to be checked and adjusted.*

15 Steering system

Rack and pinion (1982 to 1984 models) — removal and installation

1 Move the steering column intermediate shaft seal upwards and remove the pinch bolt that attaches the intermediate shaft to the rack and pinion stub shaft.

2 On power steering-equipped models, remove the air cleaner for clearance.

3 On power steering-equipped models, place newspapers and a suitable drain pan under the rack and pinion. Disconnect and remove the power steering pipes from the rack and pinion.

4 Raise the front of the vehicle and support it with jackstands placed under the body, not under the cradle.

5 Remove both front wheels.

6 Remove the cotter pins and nuts from both tie-rod ends where they attach to the steering knuckle.

7 If equipped, remove the air management pipe bracket bolt from the crossmember.

8 Place a jack under the rear cradle crossmember to support it and remove the two rear cradle mounting bolts. Carefully lower the rear of the cradle about four to five inches. **Note:** *Lowering more than this may damage engine components near the cowl.*

9 If equipped, remove the rack and pinion heat shield.

10 Remove the two rack and pinion mounting bolts and carefully remove the assembly through the left wheel opening.

11 Installation is the reverse of the removal procedure. **Note:** *Be sure to tighten the rear cradle mounting bolts to their correct torque.*

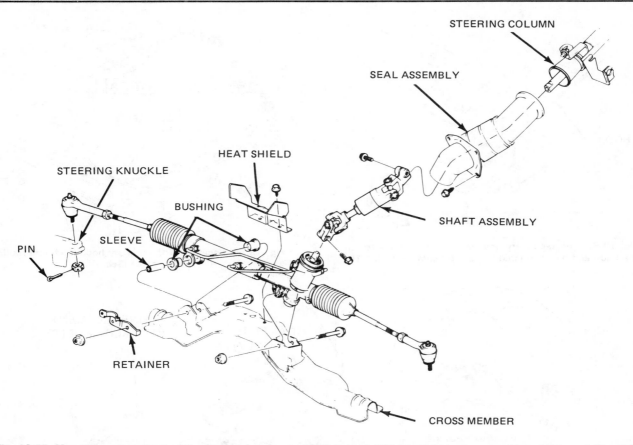

Fig. 13.55 Mounting arrangement of the rack and pinion on 1982 through 1984 models (power steering type shown) (Sec 14)

12 If equipped with power steering, following installation add power steering fluid to the reservoir. Then start the engine, allow it to idle for about ten seconds and stop the engine again. Recheck the power steering fluid level and add more as necessary.

13 On all models, following installation have the toe-in checked, and if necessary, adjusted.

Rack and pinion (power steering system) — overhaul
14 The overhaul procedure for the power steering rack and pinion remains the same as described in Chapter 11, except for the following.

15 In order to prevent damage to the rubber boot when removing it from the inner tie-rod, slide the boot toward the center of the assembly enough to expose the boot groove in the inner tie-rod. Placing a rubber band in this groove will fill it so the boot can be slid over it without damage. Be sure to remove the rubber band again after installing the boot.

16 Prior to installing the valve and pinion assembly, soak the new O-rings in hot water for about ten minutes and install them on the assembly. Be very careful when installing the valve and pinion assembly that the rings are not damaged.

17 Prior to installing the bulkhead, use crocus cloth to remove any burrs or sharp edges from the retaining ring groove in the housing. This will insure the new O-ring is not damaged on reassembly.

16 Body

Plastic wiper blades — general
1   Some vehicles are equipped with plastic wiper blades. To remove this type of blade, insert a screwdriver under the retaining spring and push downward on the screwdriver handle so the spring is raised. The blade assembly can then be separated from the arm.

2   To install the blade assembly to the arm, insert the blade over the pin at the top of the arm and press until the spring retainer engages in the pin groove.

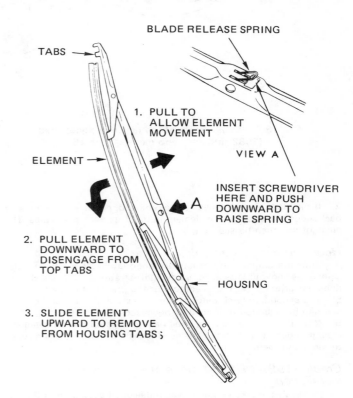

Fig. 13.56 Removal technique for plastic wiper blades (Sec 15)

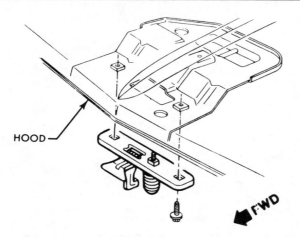

Fig. 13.57 The secondary hood latch catch is mounted to the hood and has elongated holes for adjustment (Sec 15)

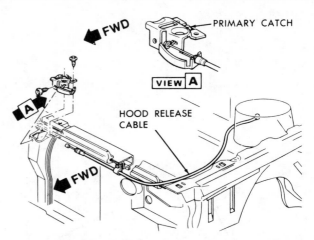

Fig. 13.58 Location of the primary hood latch and routing of the cable (Sec 15)

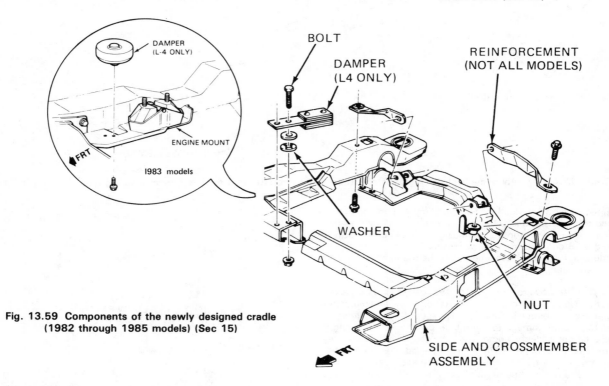

Fig. 13.59 Components of the newly designed cradle (1982 through 1985 models) (Sec 15)

3   If the blade element needs to be removed, pull the blade housing backwards to disengage the element from its upper retaining tabs. The element can then be slid out.

Hood latches — general
4   Both the primary and secondary hood latches have been redesigned, as shown in the accompanying illustrations. The new design does not affect service procedures for the primary hood latch.
5   The secondary latch catch is now mounted directly to the hood and can be unbolted if removal is necessary.
6   Note that both assemblies still have elongated holes for adjustment purposes, necessitating the need to mark the latch positions prior to removing them.

Cradle (1982 to 1984 models) — removal and installation
7   In 1982, the engine cradle was redesigned as shown in the accompanying illustrations, necessitating new procedures for removal and installation. For operations which do not require the removal of the complete cradle, the section forming the front and left side

crossmembers is still detachable from the rest of the cradle. Separate procedures are given for each option.

Partial cradle removal
8   Connect an engine hoist to the engine lifting brackets and raise the hoist just enough to take all slack out of the chain. An alternative method of supporting the engine is with an engine support bracket. Types especially designed for X-cars are available from GM dealers, although more general types can sometimes be rented on a daily basis from an equipment rental agency. If using a support bracket, hook it up according to the instructions accompanying the bracket.
9   With the hood open, have an assistant turn the steering wheel until the bolt attaching the steering column intermediate shaft to the steering gear stub shaft is in the up position. Remove the bolt.
10   Raise the front of the vehicle and support it on jackstands.
11   Place a jack under the engine oil pan to support the engine. Use a block of wood between the pan and the jack.
12   Remove the left front wheel and tire.
13   If equipped, remove the brackets that support the power steering pressure and return lines.

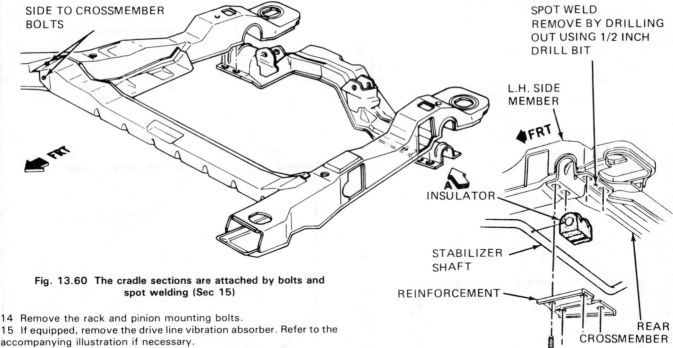

Fig. 13.60 The cradle sections are attached by bolts and spot welding (Sec 15)

14 Remove the rack and pinion mounting bolts.

15 If equipped, remove the drive line vibration absorber. Refer to the accompanying illustration if necessary.

16 Remove the bolts that attach the front stabilizer bar to the left lower control arm.

17 Using an appropriate tool, disconnect the left lower balljoint from the steering knuckle.

18 Remove the front stabilizer bar reinforcements and bushings from the right and left sidemembers.

19 Using a 1/2-inch drill bit, drill through the spot weld located between the left rear mounting holes of the front stabilizer bar.

20 Disconnect the engine and transaxle mounts from the cradle.

21 Remove the bolts that attach the front crossmember to the right sidemember.

22 Remove the bolts that secure the left cradle section to the body.

23 Carefully lower the left cradle section from the car. It may be necessary to pull or carefully pry the section loose.

Partial cradle installation

24 Raise the cradle section into its proper position and loosely install the body mount bolts.

25 Insert the 1/2-inch drill bit through the drilled hole to maintain correct alignment.

26 Install the bolts connecting the front crossmember to the right sidemember and tighten them to their correct torque.

27 Tighten the bolts attaching the left cradle section to the body to their proper torque.

28 Connect the engine and transaxle mounts to the cradle.

29 Install the stabilizer bar bushings and reinforcements, and remove the drill bit.

30 The remainder of the installation procedure is the reverse of the removal procedure.

Complete cradle removal

31 Complete the first four steps listed under partial cradle removal.

32 Remove both front wheels.

33 If equipped, remove the exhaust crossover pipe.

34 If equipped, remove the brackets that support the power steering pressure and return lines.

35 Remove the rack and pinion mounting bolts.

36 If equipped, remove the drive line vibration absorber. Refer to the accompanying illustration if necessary.

37 Remove the front stabilizer bar.

38 Remove the bolts at both lower balljoints and separate them at the steering knuckles.

39 Disconnect all engine and transaxle mounts.

40 With an assistant supporting the cradle, remove the four bolts attaching the cradle to the body.

41 Carefully lower the cradle, complete with both control arms attached.

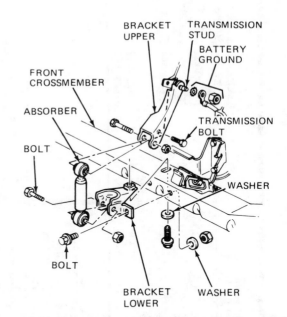

Fig. 13.61 Mounting arrangement of the vibration absorber (Sec 15)

42 Carefully work the cradle toward the rear and lower it from the vehicle with both control arms attached.

43 If a new cradle is being installed, transfer the control arms, frame reinforcements and damper assembly, as equipped, to the new cradle.

Complete cradle installation

44 With the help of an assistant, raise the cradle into its proper position and loosely install the four body mounting bolts.

45 Tighten the cradle-to-body bolts to their proper torque in the following order: 1) right rear, 2) right front, 3) left rear, 4) left front. This sequence is necessary to assure correct body alignment.

46 The remainder of the installation is the reverse of the removal procedure.

47 Following installation have the toe-in checked and adjusted.

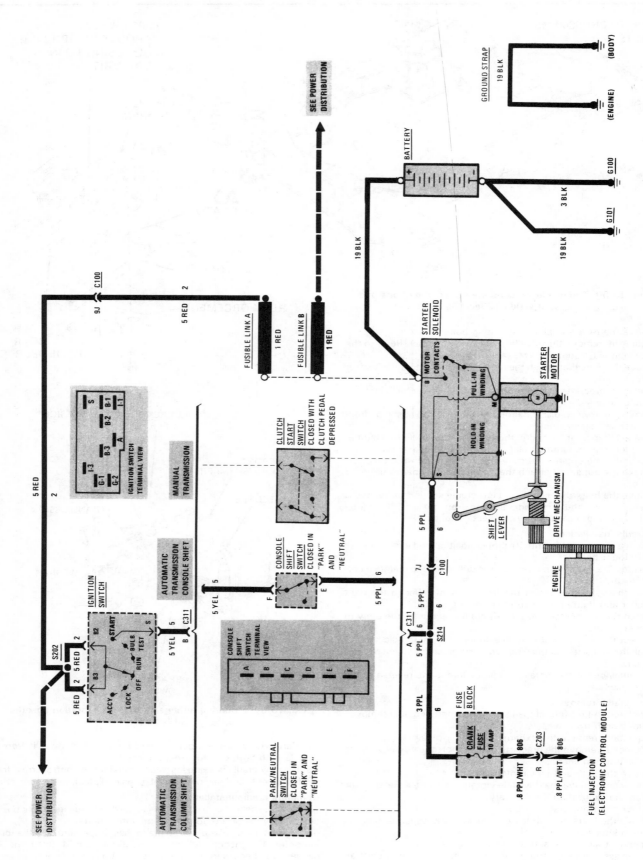

Typical wiring diagram for the starting system (L4)

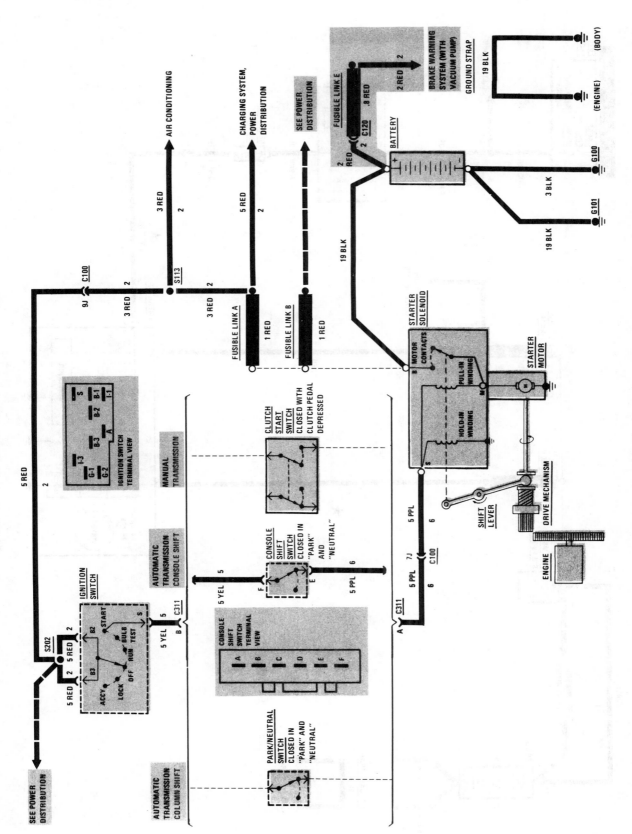

Typical wiring diagram for the starting system (V6)

Typical wiring diagram for the charging system (L4)

370

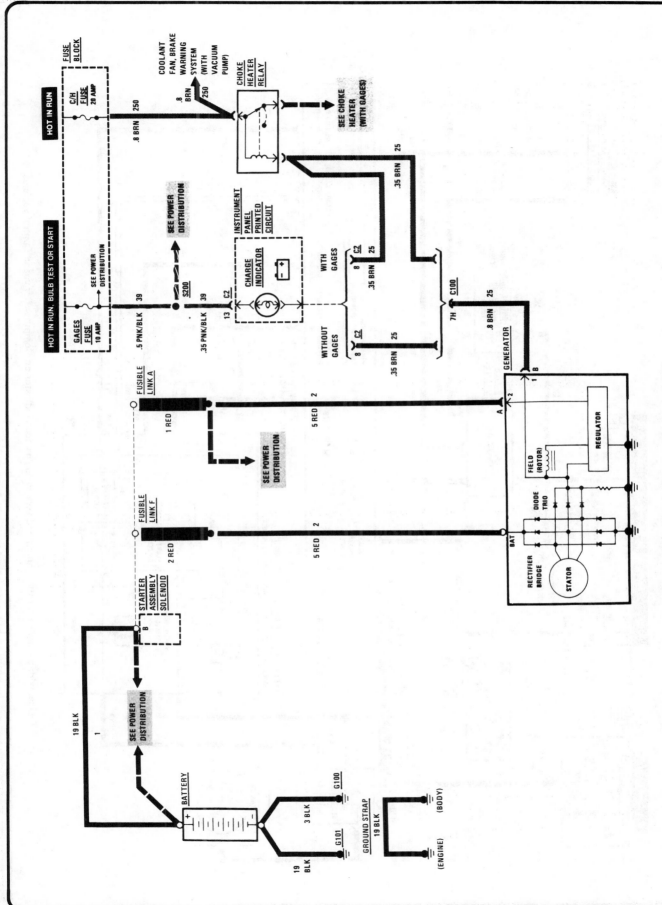

Typical wiring diagram for the charging system (V6)

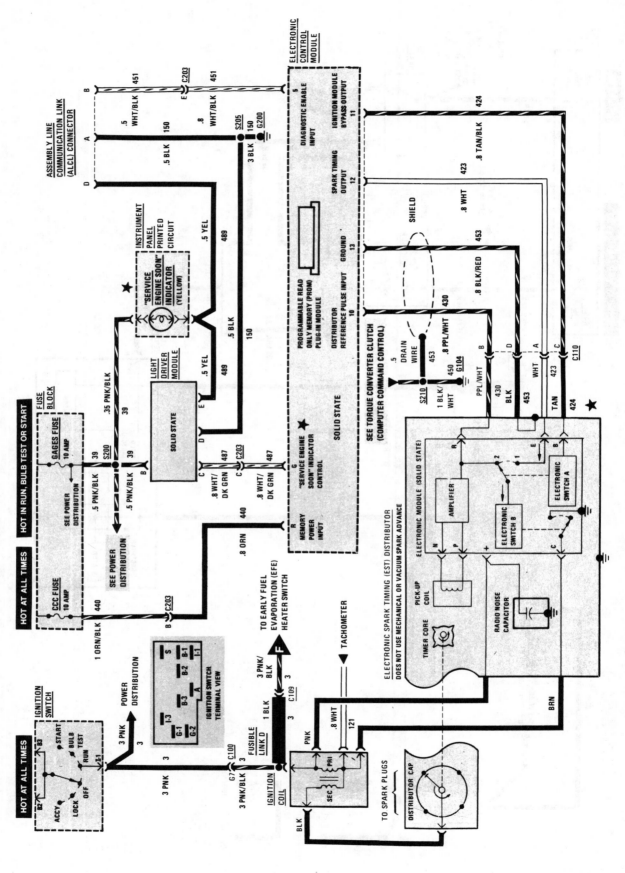

Typical wiring diagram for the ignition and service engine soon indicator on Computer Command Control vehicles

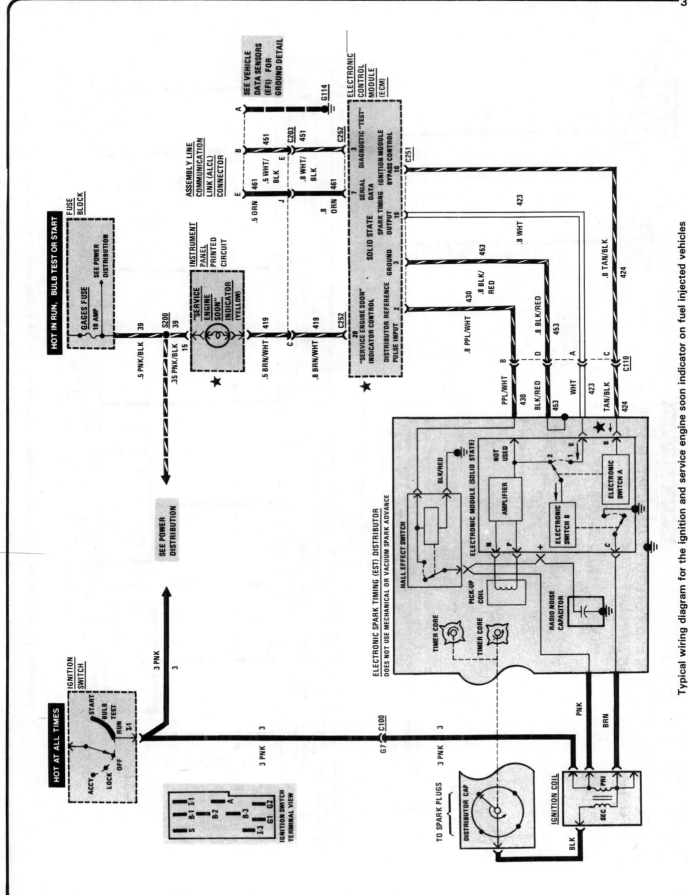

Typical wiring diagram for the ignition and service engine soon indicator on fuel injected vehicles

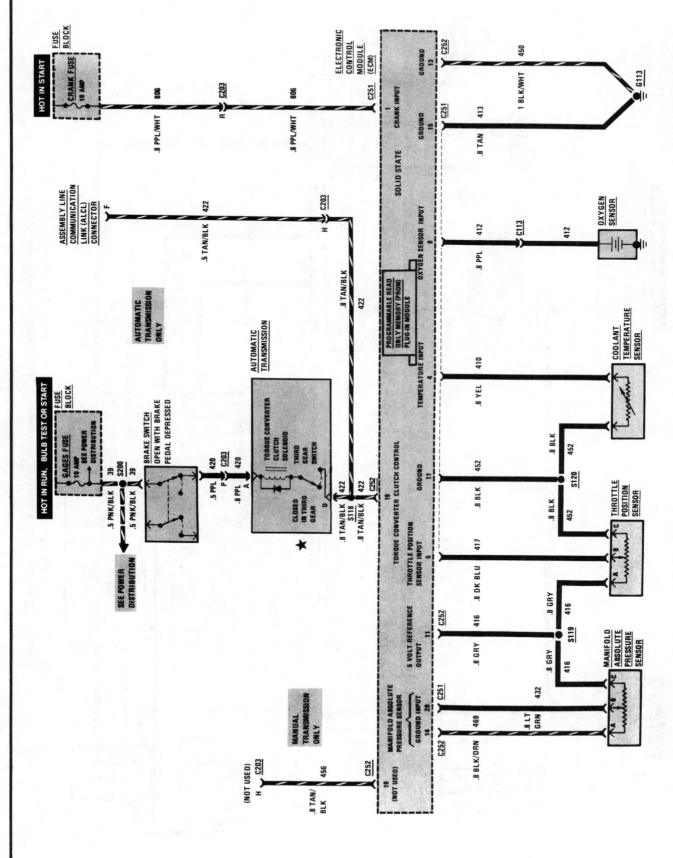

Typical wiring diagram for the engine data sensors and torque converter clutch on fuel injected vehicles

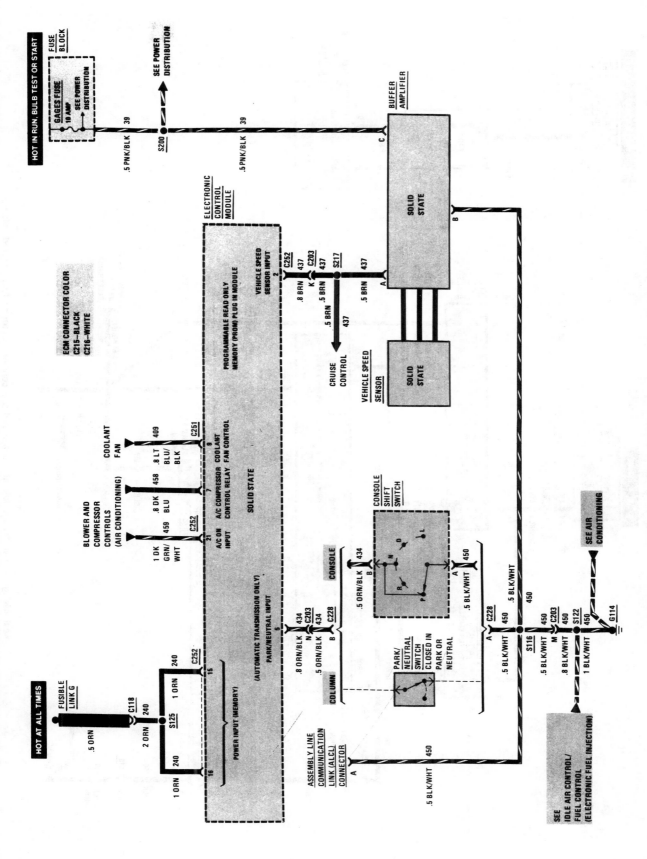

Typical wiring diagram for the vehicle data sensors on fuel injected vehicles

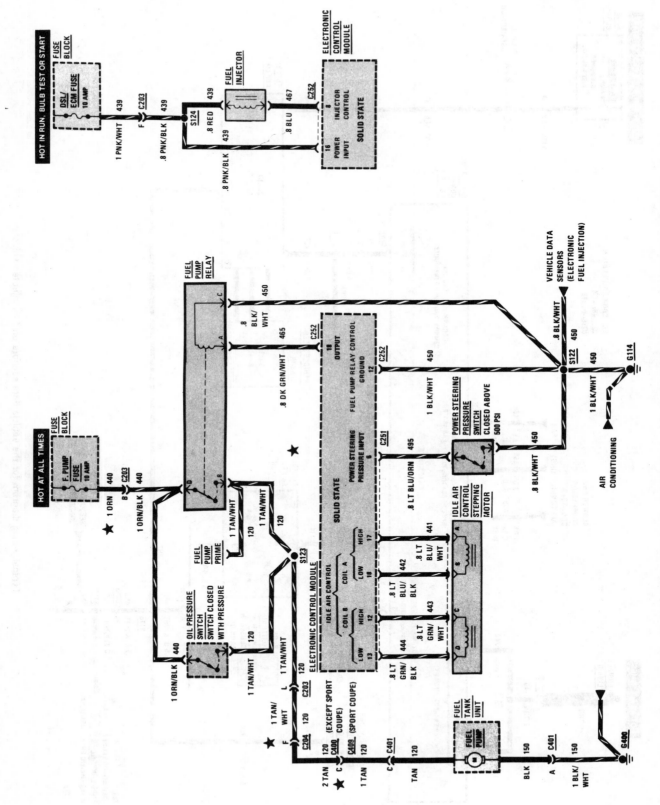

Typical wiring diagram for the idle air control and fuel control system on fuel injected vehicles

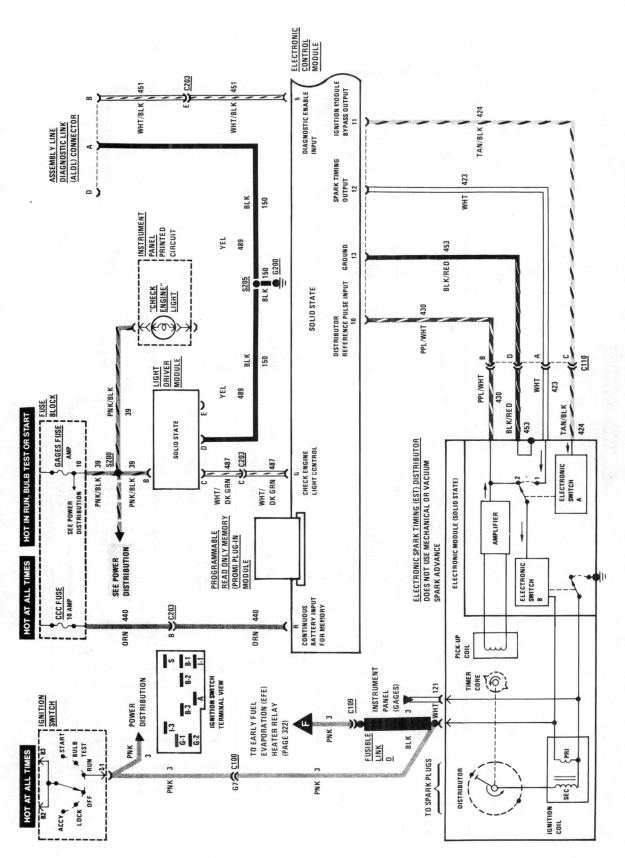

Typical wiring diagram for the ignition and service engine soon indicator on Computer Command Control vehicles (V6) (1980 thru 1984)

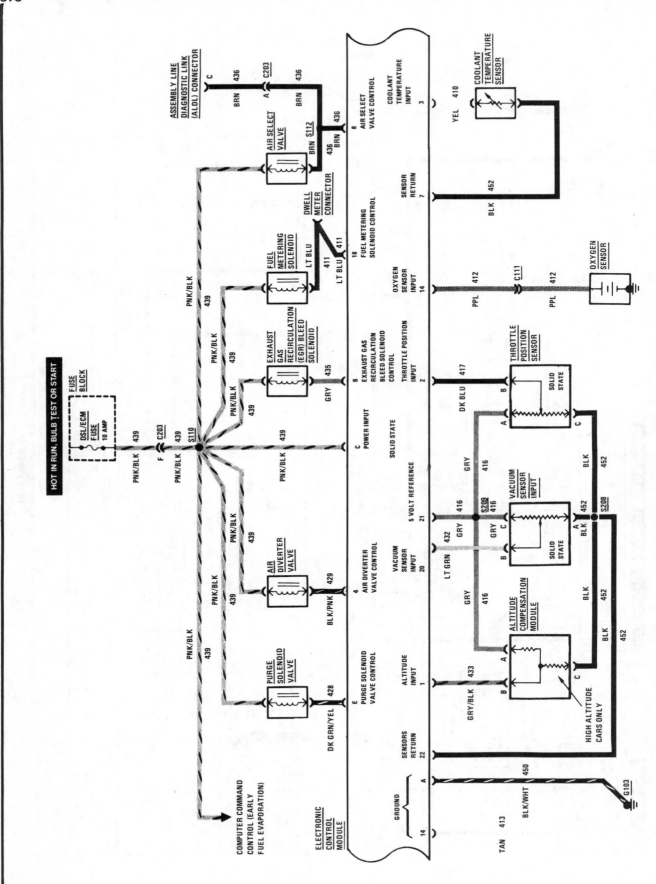

K Typical wiring diagram for the engine data and emission control sensors for Computer Command Control vehicles (V6) (1980 thru 1984)

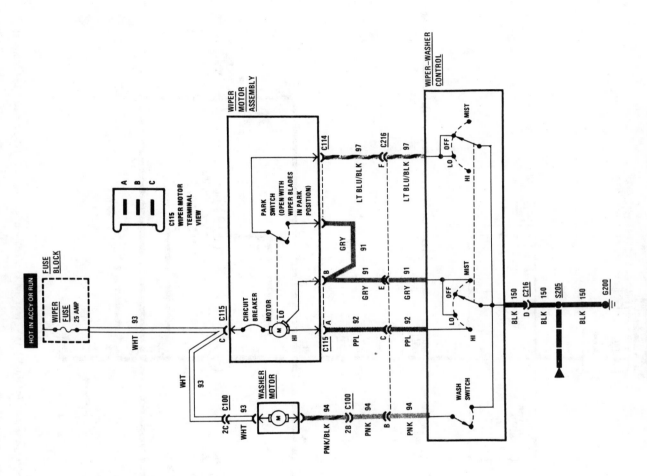

Typical wiring diagram for the windshield wiper and washer circuit

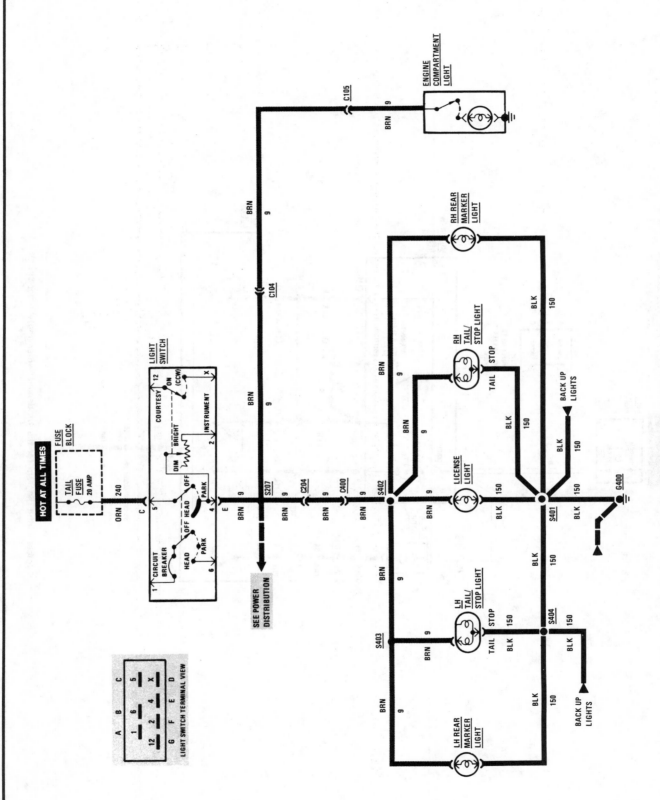

Typical wiring diagram for the lights — rear marker, tail and license plate (1980 thru 1984 Omega)

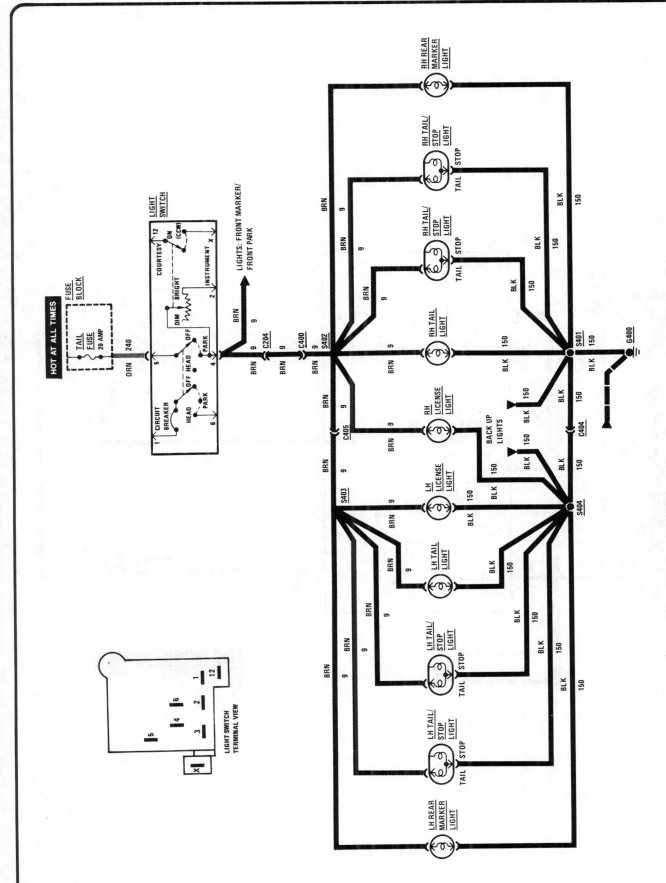

Typical wiring diagram for the lights — rear marker, tail and license plate (1980 thru 1984 Phoenix)

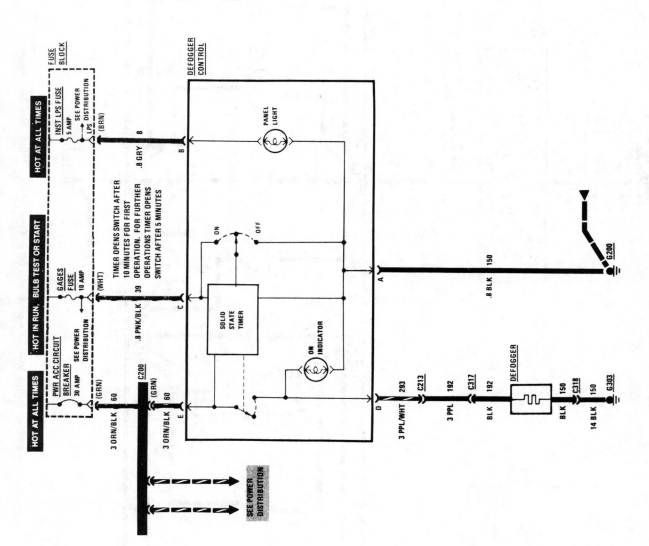

Typical wiring diagram for the defogger circuit (Omega)

383

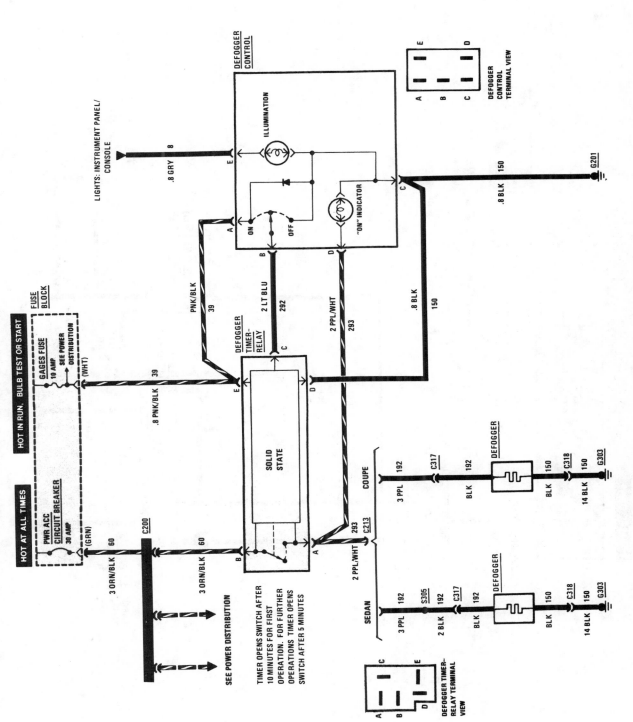

Typical wiring diagram for the defogger circuit (Phoenix)

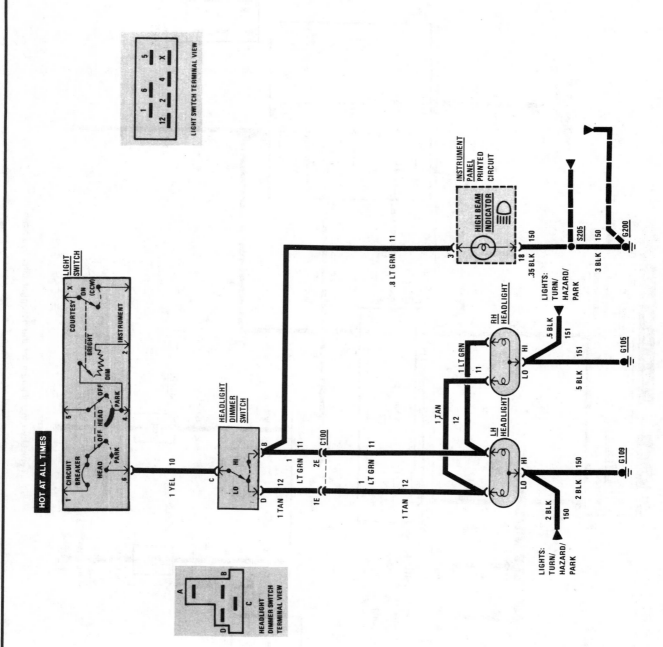

Typical wiring diagram for the headlight circuit

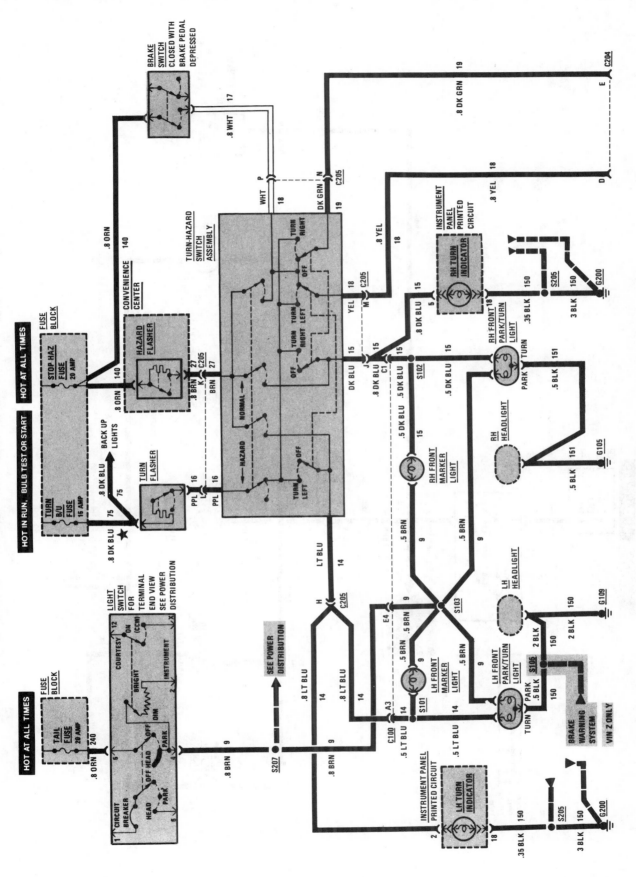

Typical wiring diagram for the lights — turn, hazard and front parking

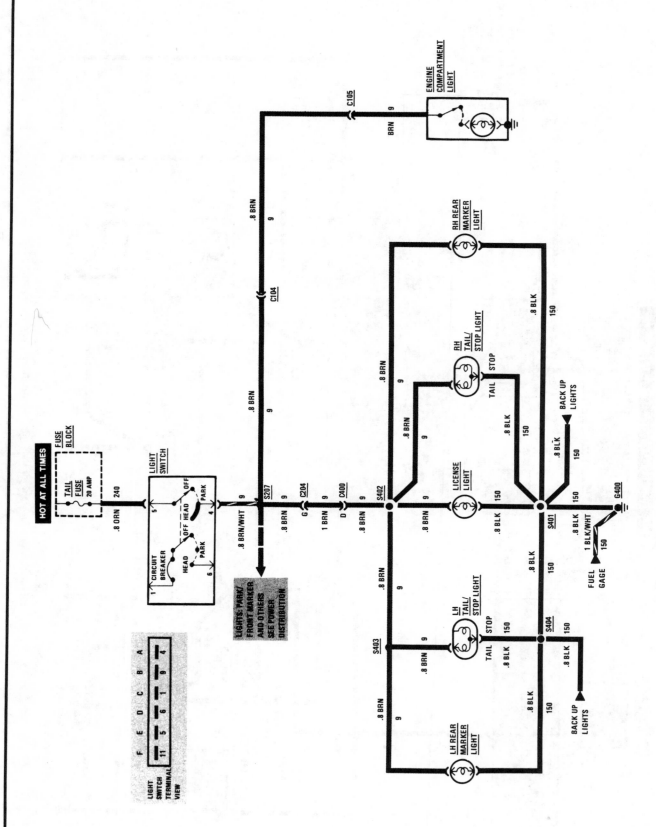

Typical wiring diagram for the lights — rear marker, tail and license plate (1980 thru 1984 Omega)

387

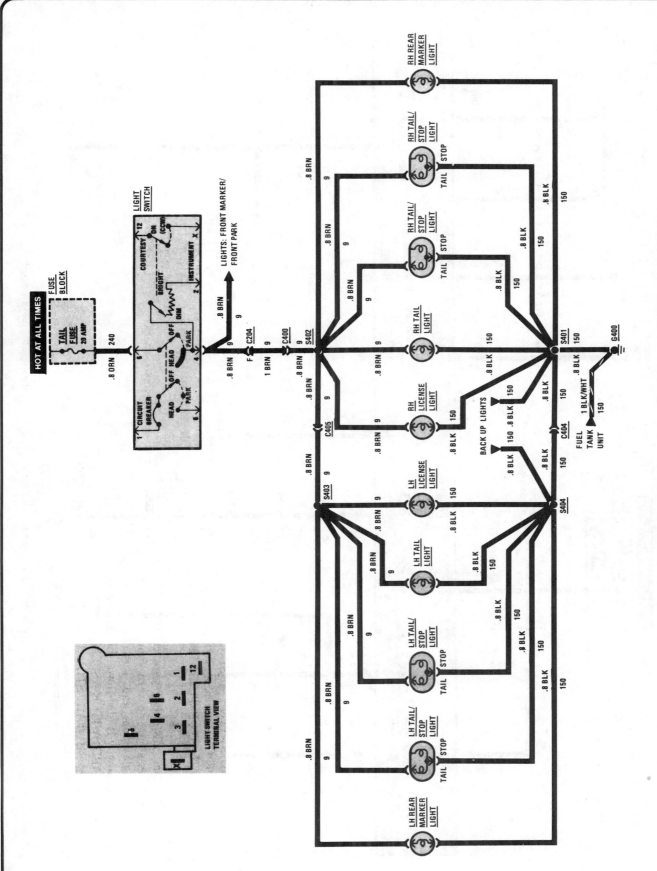

Typical wiring diagram for the lights — rear marker, tail and license plate (1980 thru 1984 Phoenix)

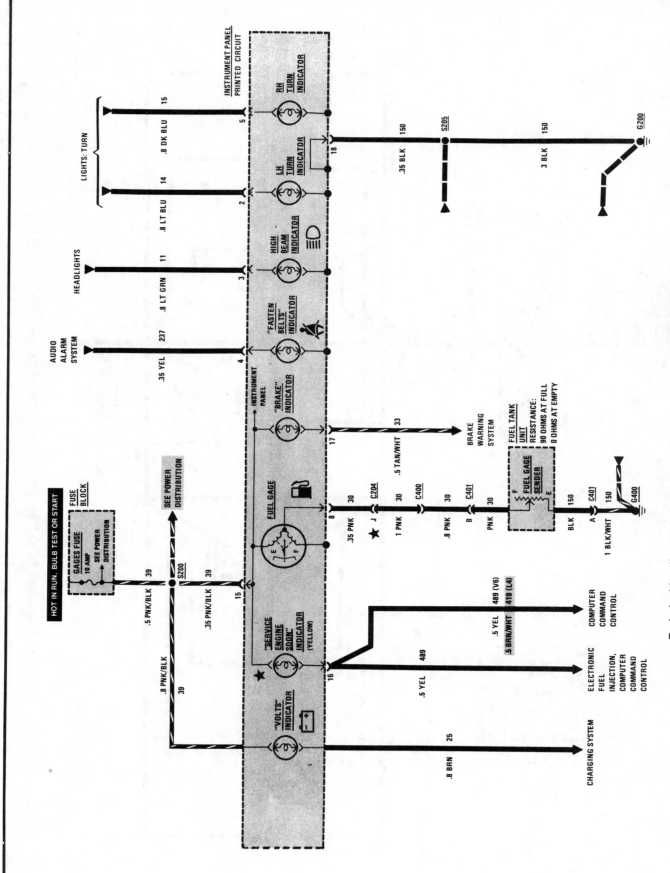

Typical wiring diagram for the indicator circuit — fuel gauge, instrument panel

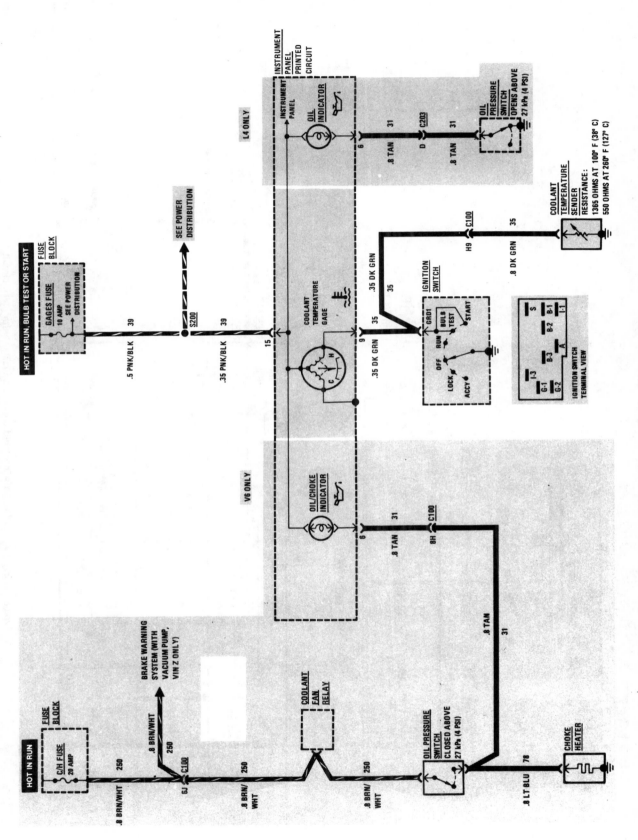

Typical wiring diagram for the indicators circuit — choke heater and instrument panel with gauges

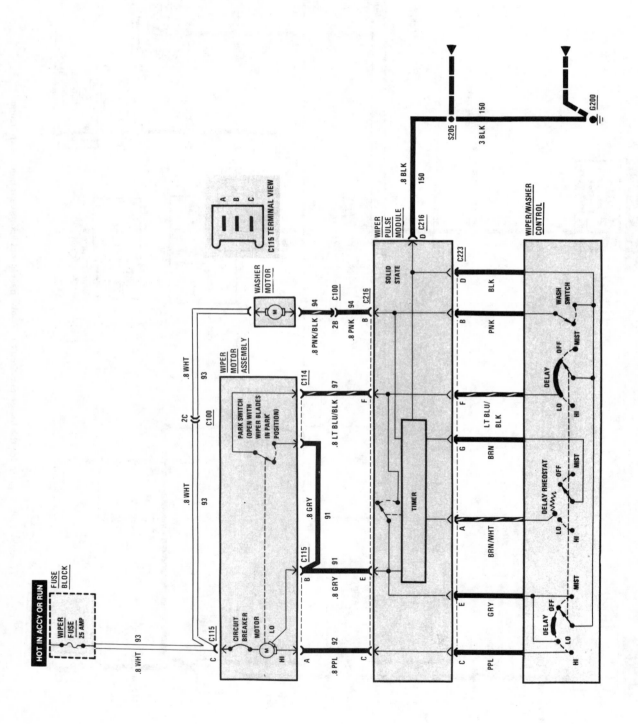

Typical wiring diagram for the windshield wiper and washer with pulse circuit

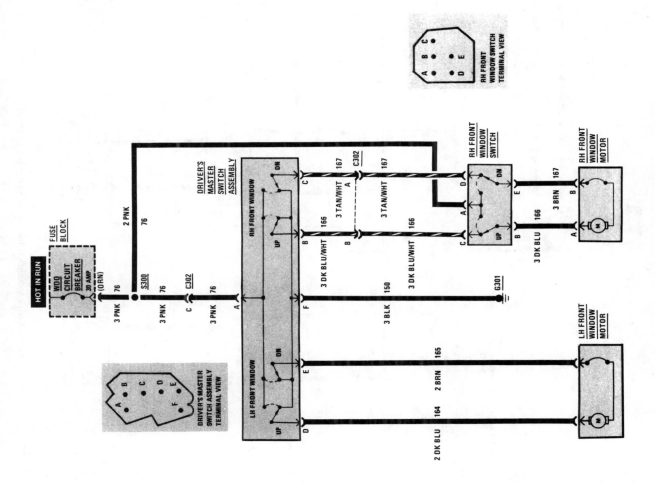

Typical wiring diagram for power windows (2 door)

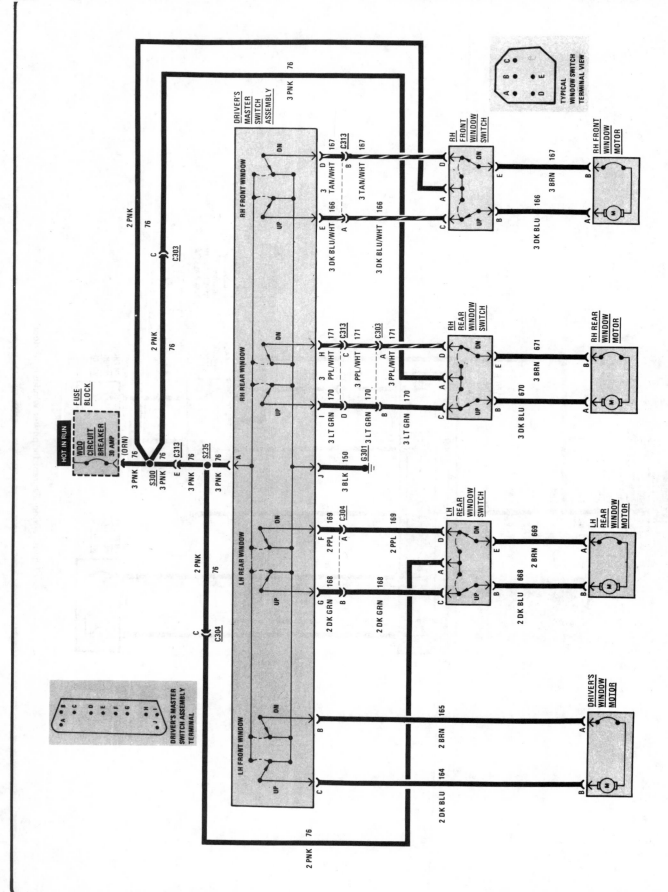

Typical wiring diagram for power windows (4 door)

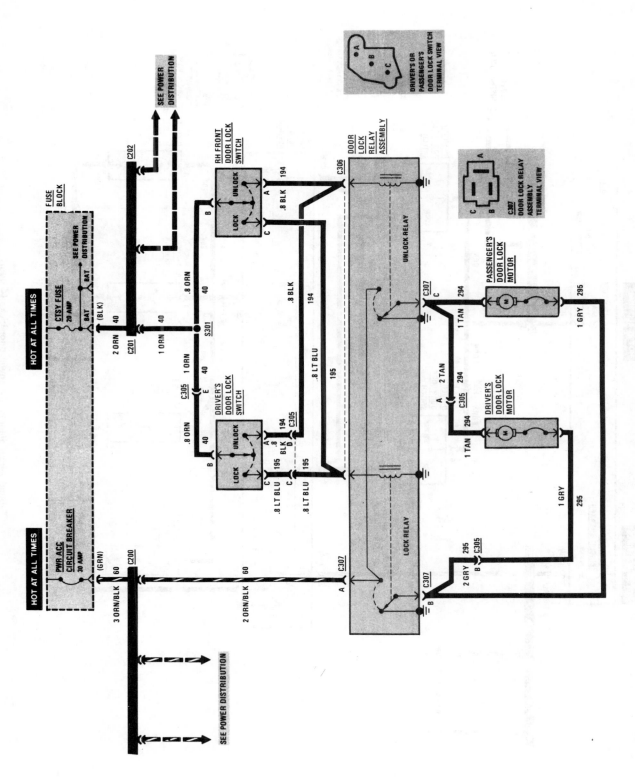

Typical wiring diagram for power door locks (2 door)

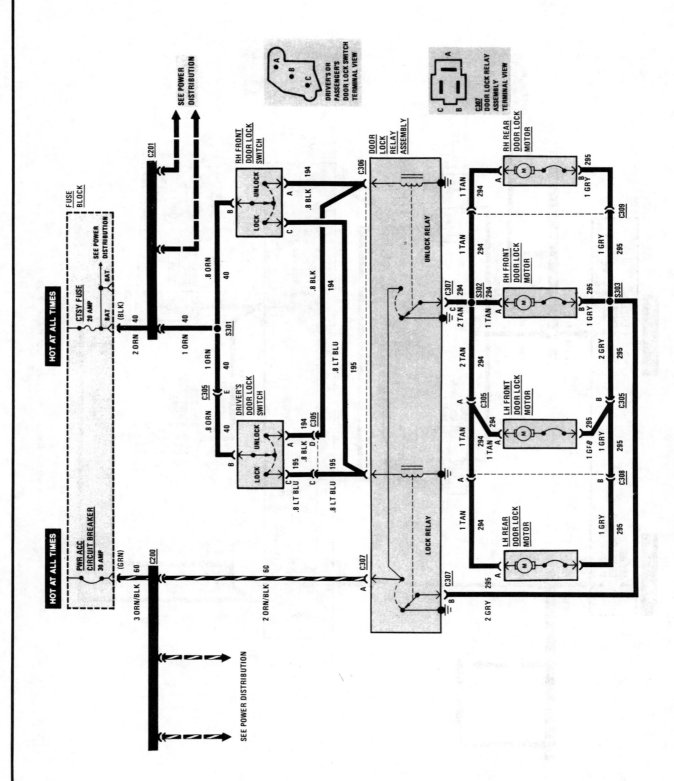

Typical wiring diagram for power door locks (4 door)

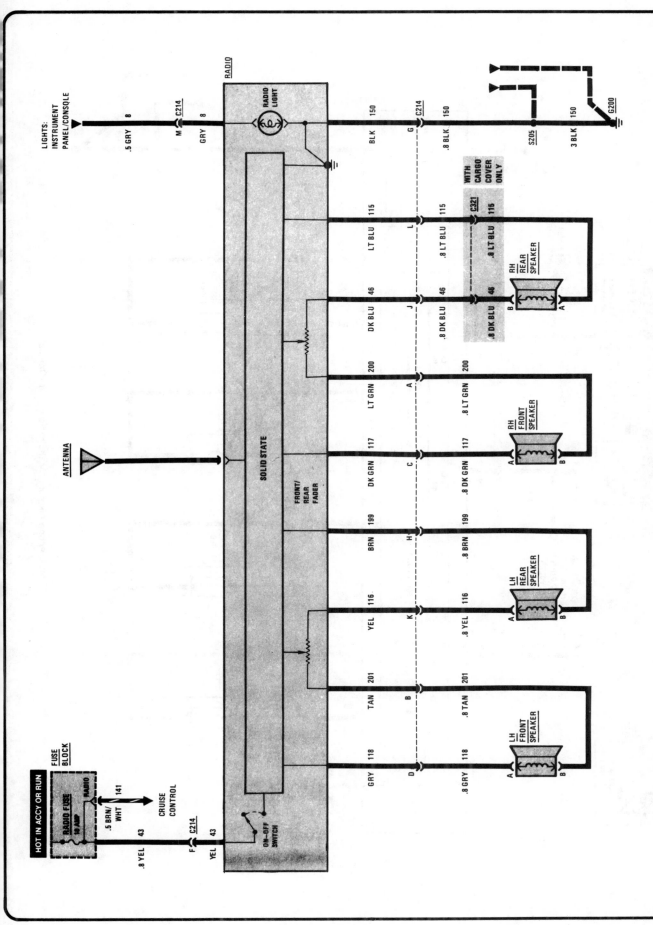

Typical wiring diagram for the radio circuit (Phoenix)

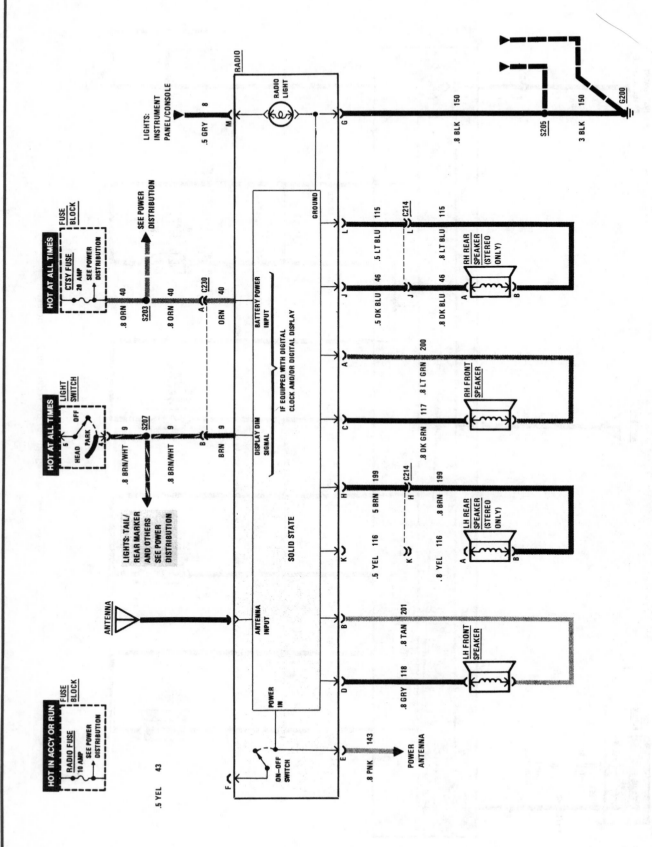

Typical wiring diagram for the radio circuit (Omega)

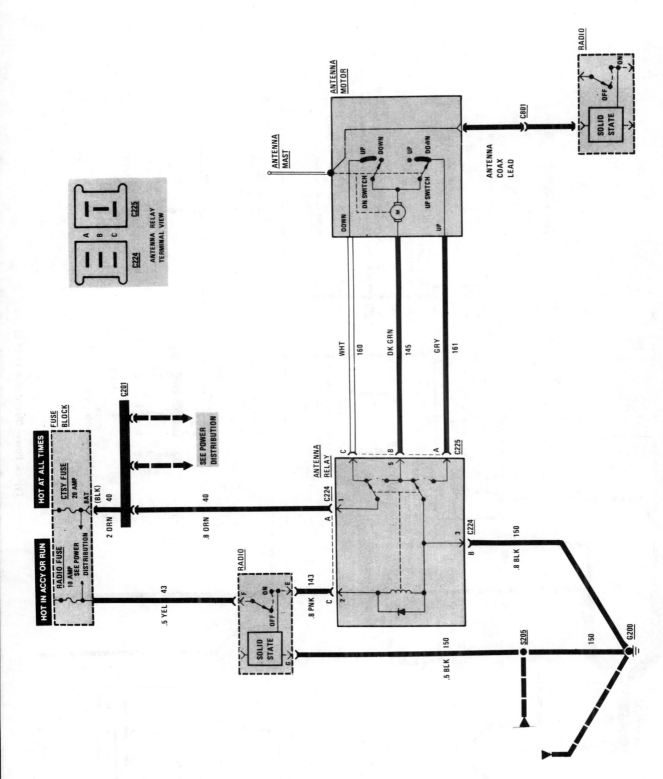

Typical wiring diagram for the power antenna

FUSE BLOCK

40 ORN HORN

40 ORN
40 ORN
40 ORN
40 ORN
40 ORN

INTERIOR LIGHTS/ CLOCK/CIGAR LIGHTER

S203

40 ORN

AUDIO ALARM SYSTEM (CHIME/BUZZER)

C202

40 POWER DOOR LOCKS

40 ORN

CTSY FUSE 20 AMP

BAT

40 (BLK)

40 ORN POWER ANTENNA

40 ORN INTERIOR LIGHTS

BAT

(BLK)

40 ORN TRUNK RELEASE

LIGHT SWITCH

FUSE BLOCK

BRN 8

LPS

INST LPS FUSE 5 AMP

GRY 8

LIGHTS: INSTRUMENT PANEL/CONSOLE, AUDIO ALARM SYSTEM (CHIME/BUZZER)

GRY 8

COURTESY LIGHTS

156 WHT

X

ON (CCW)

COURTESY

INSTRUMENT

SEE GROUND DISTRIBUTION

BLK 150

BLK 150 G200

S205

S/LP FUSE 20 AMP

140 ORN

140

LIGHTS: STOP/ HAZARD

140 ORN

2

BRIGHT

DIM

44 DK GRN

TAIL FUSE 20 AMP

240 ORN

OFF PARK

OFF HEAD

5

PARK

4

9 BRN

9 BRN

LIGHTS: REAR MARKER/ TAIL/LICENSE/ STOP

LIGHTS: TURN/ HAZARD/FRONT PARK/FRONT MARKER/ STOP

C200

60 ORN BLK POWER SEATS

60 ORN BLK POWER DOOR LOCKS

PWR ACC CIRCUIT BREAKER 30 AMP

PWR ACC

(GRN) 60

60 ORN/BLK BLK DEFOGGER

ORN/BLK

CIRCUIT BREAKER

HEAD

OFF HEAD

PARK

6

YEL 10 HEADLIGHTS

1

RED 2

RED 2

CCC FUSE 10 AMP

440 ORN COMPUTER COMMAND CONTROL

RED

2

RED 2

9G

C100

RED 2

CHARGING SYSTEM

RED 2

RED 2

RED 2

S113

RED 2

RED 2

C100

9J

RED 2

S202

RED 2

RED 2

FUSIBLE LINK B

RED

FUSIBLE LINK A

RED

RED 2

RED 2

STARTER ASSEMBLY

BAT

RED 2 AIR CONDITIONING

FUSIBLE LINK C

RED

RED 2 COOLANT FAN

BLK

BATTERY

G101 GROUND STRAP (BODY)

BLK

BLK

G100 (ENGINE)

BLK

+ −

ELECTRONIC FUEL INJECTION (L4 ONLY)

BLK 2

5

4

3

6

2

4

1

12

X

LIGHT SWITCH TERMINAL VIEW

Typical Power Distribution (1 of 2)

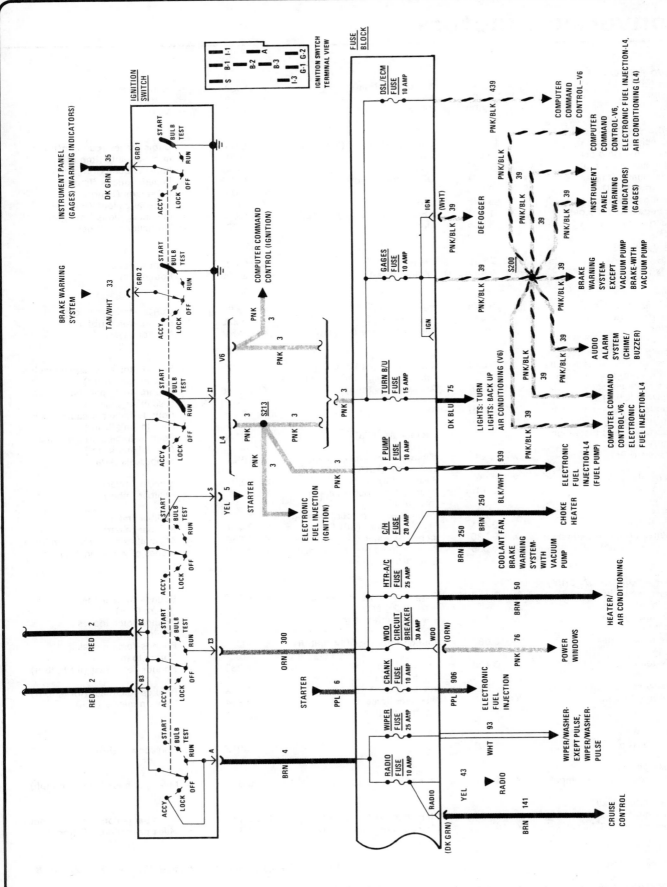

Typical Power Distribution (2 of 2)

Conversion factors

Length (distance)

Inches (in)	X	25.4	= Millimetres (mm)	X	0.0394	=	Inches (in)
Feet (ft)	X	0.305	= Metres (m)	X	3.281	=	Feet (ft)
Miles	X	1.609	= Kilometres (km)	X	0.621	=	Miles

Volume (capacity)

Cubic inches (cu in; in³)	X	16.387	= Cubic centimetres (cc; cm³)	X	0.061	=	Cubic inches (cu in; in³)
Imperial pints (Imp pt)	X	0.568	= Litres (l)	X	1.76	=	Imperial pints (Imp pt)
Imperial quarts (Imp qt)	X	1.137	= Litres (l)	X	0.88	=	Imperial quarts (Imp qt)
Imperial quarts (Imp qt)	X	1.201	= US quarts (US qt)	X	0.833	=	Imperial quarts (Imp qt)
US quarts (US qt)	X	0.946	= Litres (l)	X	1.057	=	US quarts (US qt)
Imperial gallons (Imp gal)	X	4.546	= Litres (l)	X	0.22	=	Imperial gallons (Imp gal)
Imperial gallons (Imp gal)	X	1.201	= US gallons (US gal)	X	0.833	=	Imperial gallons (Imp gal)
US gallons (US gal)	X	3.785	= Litres (l)	X	0.264	=	US gallons (US gal)

Mass (weight)

Ounces (oz)	X	28.35	= Grams (g)	X	0.035	=	Ounces (oz)
Pounds (lb)	X	0.454	= Kilograms (kg)	X	2.205	=	Pounds (lb)

Force

Ounces-force (ozf; oz)	X	0.278	= Newtons (N)	X	3.6	=	Ounces-force (ozf; oz)
Pounds-force (lbf; lb)	X	4.448	= Newtons (N)	X	0.225	=	Pounds-force (lbf; lb)
Newtons (N)	X	0.1	= Kilograms-force (kgf; kg)	X	9.81	=	Newtons (N)

Pressure

Pounds-force per square inch (psi; lbf/in²; lb/in²)	X	0.070	= Kilograms-force per square centimetre (kgf/cm²; kg/cm²)	X	14.223	=	Pounds-force per square inch (psi; lbf/in²; lb/in²)
Pounds-force per square inch (psi; lbf/in²; lb/in²)	X	0.068	= Atmospheres (atm)	X	14.696	=	Pounds-force per square inch (psi; lbf/in²; lb/in²)
Pounds-force per square inch (psi; lbf/in²; lb/in²)	X	0.069	= Bars	X	14.5	=	Pounds-force per square inch (psi; lbf/in²; lb/in²)
Pounds-force per square inch (psi; lbf/in²; lb/in²)	X	6.895	= Kilopascals (kPa)	X	0.145	=	Pounds-force per square inch (psi; lbf/in²; lb/in²)
Kilopascals (kPa)	X	0.01	= Kilograms-force per square centimetre (kgf/cm²; kg/cm²)	X	98.1	=	Kilopascals (kPa)
Millibar (mbar)	X	100	= Pascals (Pa)	X	0.01	=	Millibar (mbar)
Millibar (mbar)	X	0.0145	= Pounds-force per square inch (psi; lbf/in²; lb/in²)	X	68.947	=	Millibar (mbar)
Millibar (mbar)	X	0.75	= Millimetres of mercury (mmHg)	X	1.333	=	Millibar (mbar)
Millibar (mbar)	X	0.401	= Inches of water (inH₂O)	X	2.491	=	Millibar (mbar)
Millimetres of mercury (mmHg)	X	0.535	= Inches of water (inH₂O)	X	1.868	=	Millimetres of mercury (mmHg)
Inches of water (inH₂O)	X	0.036	= Pounds-force per square inch (psi; lbf/in²; lb/in²)	X	27.68	=	Inches of water (inH₂O)

Torque (moment of force)

Pounds-force inches (lbf in; lb in)	X	1.152	= Kilograms-force centimetre (kgf cm; kg cm)	X	0.868	=	Pounds-force inches (lbf in; lb in)
Pounds-force inches (lbf in; lb in)	X	0.113	= Newton metres (Nm)	X	8.85	=	Pounds-force inches (lbf in; lb in)
Pounds-force inches (lbf in; lb in)	X	0.083	= Pounds-force feet (lbf ft; lb ft)	X	12	=	Pounds-force inches (lbf in; lb in)
Pounds-force feet (lbf ft; lb ft)	X	0.138	= Kilograms-force metres (kgf m; kg m)	X	7.233	=	Pounds-force feet (lbf ft; lb ft)
Pounds-force feet (lbf ft; lb ft)	X	1.356	= Newton metres (Nm)	X	0.738	=	Pounds-force feet (lbf ft; lb ft)
Newton metres (Nm)	X	0.102	= Kilograms-force metres (kgf m; kg m)	X	9.804	=	Newton metres (Nm)

Power

Horsepower (hp)	X	745.7	= Watts (W)	X	0.0013	=	Horsepower (hp)

Velocity (speed)

Miles per hour (miles/hr; mph)	X	1.609	= Kilometres per hour (km/hr; kph)	X	0.621	=	Miles per hour (miles/hr; mph)

Fuel consumption*

Miles per gallon, Imperial (mpg)	X	0.354	= Kilometres per litre (km/l)	X	2.825	=	Miles per gallon, Imperial (mpg)
Miles per gallon, US (mpg)	X	0.425	= Kilometres per litre (km/l)	X	2.352	=	Miles per gallon, US (mpg)

Temperature

Degrees Fahrenheit = ($°C \times 1.8$) + 32

Degrees Celsius (Degrees Centigrade; °C) = ($°F - 32$) x 0.56

*It is common practice to convert from miles per gallon (mpg) to litres/100 kilometres (l/100km),
where mpg (Imperial) x l/100 km = 282 and mpg (US) x l/100 km = 235

Index

HAYNES AUTOMOTIVE MANUALS

NOTE: New manuals are added to this list on a periodic basis. If you do not see a listing for your vehicle, consult your local Haynes dealer for the latest product information.

ALFA-ROMEO
531 Alfa Romeo Sedan & Coupe '73 thru '80

AMC
Jeep CJ – *see JEEP (412)*
694 Mid-size models, Concord, Hornet, Gremlin & Spirit '70 thru '83
934 (Renault) Alliance & Encore '83 thru '87

AUDI
162 100 '69 thru '77
615 4000 '80 thru '87
428 5000 '77 thru '83
1117 5000 '84 thru '88
207 Fox '73 thru '79

AUSTIN
049 Healey 100/6 & 3000 Roadster '56 thru '68
Healey Sprite – *see MG Midget Roadster (265)*

BLMC
260 1100, 1300 & Austin America '62 thru '74
527 Mini '59 thru '69
*646 Mini '69 thru '88

BMW
276 320i all 4 cyl models '75 thru '83
632 528i & 530i '75 thru '80
240 1500 thru 2002 exceptTurbo '59 thru '77
348 2500, 2800, 3.0 & Bavaria '69 thru '76

BUICK
Century (front wheel drive) – *see GENERAL MOTORS A-Cars (829)*
*1627 Buick, Oldsmobile & Pontiac Full-size (Front wheel drive) '85 thru '90 Buick Electra, LeSabre and Park Avenue; Oldsmobile Delta 88 Royale, Ninety Eight and Regency; Pontiac Bonneville
*1551 Buick Oldsmobile & Pontiac Full-size (Rear wheel drive) Buick Electra '70 thru '84, Estate '70 thru '90, LeSabre '70 thru '79 Oldsmobile Custom Cruiser '70 thru '90, Delta 88 '70 thru '85, Ninety-eight '70 thru '84 Pontiac Bonneville '70 thru '86, Catalina '70 thru '81, Grandville '70 thru '75, Parisienne '84 thu '86
627 Mid-size all rear-drive Regal & Century models with V6, V8 and Turbo '74 thru '87
Skyhawk – *see GENERAL MOTORS J-Cars (766)*
552 Skylark all X-car models '80 thru '85

CADILLAC
Cimarron – *see GENERAL MOTORS J-Cars (766)*

CAPRI
296 2000 MK I Coupe '71 thru '75
283 2300 MK II Coupe '74 thu '78
205 2600 & 2800 V6 Coupe '71 thru '75
375 2800 Mk II V6 Coupe '75 thru '78
Mercury in-line engines – *see FORD Mustang (654)*
Mercury V6 & V8 engines – *see FORD Mustang (558)*

CHEVROLET
*1477 Astro & GMC Safari Mini-vans '85 thru '90
554 Camaro V8 '70 thru '81
*866 Camaro '82 thru '89
Cavalier – *see GENERAL MOTORS J-Cars (766)*
Celebrity – *see GENERAL MOTORS A-Cars (829)*
625 Chevelle, Malibu & El Camino all V6 & V8 models '69 thru '87
449 Chevette & Pontiac T1000 '76 thru '87
550 Citation '80 thru '85
*1628 Corsica/Beretta '87 thru '90
274 Corvette all V8 models '68 thru '82
*1336 Corvette '84 thru '89
704 Full-size Sedans Caprice, Impala, Biscayne, Bel Air & Wagons, all V6 & V8 models '69 thru '90
319 Luv Pick-up all 2WD & 4WD '72 thru '82
626 Monte Carlo all V6, V8 & Turbo '70 thru '88
241 Nova all V8 models '69 thru '79
*1642 Nova & Geo Prizm front wheel drive '85 thru '90
*420 Pick-ups '67 thru '87 – Chevrolet & GMC, all V8 & in-line 6 cyl 2WD & 4WD '67 thru '87
*1664 Pick-ups '88 thru '90 – Chevlolet & GMC all full-size (C and K) models, '88 thru '90
*831 S-10 & GMC S-15 Pick-ups '82 thru '90
*345 Vans – Chevrolet & GMC, V8 & in-line 6 cyl models '68 thru '89
208 Vega except Cosworth '70 thru '77

CHRYSLER
*1337 Chrysler & Plymouth Mid-size front wheel drive '82 thru '88
K-Cars – *see DODGE Aries (723)*
Laser – *see DODGE Daytona (1140)*

DATSUN
402 200SX '77 thru '79
647 200SX '80 thru '83
228 B-210 '73 thru '78
525 210 '78 thru '82
206 240Z, 260Z & 280Z Coupe & 2+2 '70 thru '78
563 280ZX Coupe & 2+2 '79 thru '83
300ZX – *see NISSAN (1137)*
679 310 '78 thru '82
123 510 & PL521 Pick-up '68 thru '73
430 510 '78 thru '81
372 610 '72 thru '76
277 620 Series Pick-up '73 thru '79
235 710 '73 thru '77
720 Series Pick-up – *see NISSAN Pick-ups (771)*
376 810/Maxima all gasoline models '77 thru '84
124 1200 '70 thru '73
368 F10 '76 thru '79
Pulsar – *see NISSAN (876)*
Sentra – *see NISSAN (982)*
Stanza – *see NISSAN (981)*

DODGE
*723 Aries & Plymouth Reliant '81 thru '88
*1231 Caravan & Plymouth Voyager Mini-Vans '84 thru '89
699 Challenger & Plymouth Saporro '78 thru '83
236 Colt '71 thru '77
419 Colt (rear wheel drive) '77 thru '80
610 Colt & Plymouth Champ (front wheel drive) '78 thru '87
*556 D50 & Plymouth Arrow Pick-ups '79 thru '88
234 Dart & Plymouth Valiant all 6 cyl models '67 thru '76
*1140 Daytona & Chrysler Laser '84 thru '88
*545 Omni & Plymouth Horizon '78 thru '89
*912 Pick-ups all full-size models '74 thru '90
*349 Vans – Dodge & Plymouth V8 & 6 cyl models '71 thru '89

FIAT
080 124 Sedan & Wagon all ohv & dohc models '66 thru '75
094 124 Sport Coupe & Spider '68 thru '78
087 128 '72 thru '79
310 131 & Brava '75 thru '81
038 850 Sedan, Coupe & Spider '64 thru '74
479 Strada '79 thru '82
273 X1/9 '74 thru '80

FORD
*1476 Aerostar Mini-vans '86 thru '88
788 Bronco and Pick-ups '73 thru '79
*880 Bronco and Pick-ups '80 thru '90
014 Cortina MK II except Lotus '66 thru '70
295 Cortina MK III 1600 & 2000 ohc '70 thru '76
268 Courier Pick-up '72 thru '82
789 Escort & Mercury Lynx all models '81 thru '90
560 Fairmont & Mercury Zephyr all in-line & V8 models '78 thru '83
334 Fiesta '77 thru '80
754 Ford & Mercury Full-size, Ford LTD & Mercury Marquis ('75 thru '82); Ford Custom 500, Country Squire, Crown Victoria & Mercury Colony Park ('75 thru '87); Ford LTD Crown Victoria & Mercury Gran Marquis ('83 thru '87)
359 Granada & Mercury Monarch all in-line, 6 cyl & V8 models '75 thru '80
773 Ford & Mercury Mid-size, Ford Thunderbird & Mercury Cougar ('75 thru '82); Ford LTD & Mercury Marquis ('83 thru '86); Ford Torino, Gran Torino, Elite, Ranchero pick-up, LTD II, Mercury Montego, Comet, XR-7 & Lincoln Versailles ('75 thru '86)
*654 Mustang & Mercury Capri all in-line models & Turbo '79 thru '90
*558 Mustang & Mercury Capri all V6 & V8 models '79 thru '89
357 Mustang V8 '64-1/2 thru '73
231 Mustang II all 4 cyl, V6 & V8 models '74 thru '78
204 Pinto '70 thru '74
649 Pinto & Mercury Bobcat '75 thru '80
*1026 Ranger & Bronco II gasoline models '83 thru '89
*1421 Taurus & Mercury Sable '86 thru '90
*1418 Tempo & Mercury Topaz all gasoline models '84 thru '89
1338 Thunderbird & Mercury Cougar/XR7 '83 thru '88
*344 Vans all V8 Econoline models '69 thru '90

GENERAL MOTORS
*829 A-Cars – Chevrolet Celebrity, Buick Century, Pontiac 6000 & Oldsmobile Cutlass Ciera '82 thru '89
*766 J-Cars – Chevrolet Cavalier, Pontiac J-2000, Oldsmobile Firenza, Buick Skyhawk & Cadillac Cimarron '82 thru '89
*1420 N-Cars – Pontiac Grand Am, Buick Somerset and Oldsmobile Calais '85 thru '87; Buick Skylark '86 thru '87

GEO
Tracker – *see SUZUKI Samurai (1626)*
Prizm – *see CHEVROLET Nova (1642)*

GMC
Safari – *see CHEVROLET ASTRO (1477)*
Vans & Pick-ups – *see CHEVROLET (420, 831, 345, 1664)*

HONDA
138 360, 600 & Z Coupe '67 thru '75
351 Accord CVCC '76 thru '83
*1221 Accord '84 thru '89
160 Civic 1200 '73 thru '79
633 Civic 1300 & 1500 CVCC '80 thru '83
297 Civic 1500 CVCC '75 thru '79
*1227 Civic except 16-valve CRX & 4 WD Wagon '84 thru '86
*601 Prelude CVCC '79 thru '89

HYUNDAI
*1552 Excel '86 thru '89

ISUZU
*1641 Trooper & Pick-up all gasolime models '81 thru '89

JAGUAR
098 MK I & II, 240 & 340 Sedans '55 thru '69
*242 XJ6 all 6 cyl models '68 thru '86
*478 XJ12 & XJS all 12 cyl models '72 thru '85
140 XK-E 3.8 & 4.2 all 6 cyl models '61 thru '72

JEEP
*1553 Cherokee, Comanche & Wagoneer Limited '84 thru '89
412 CJ '49 thru '86

LADA
*413 1200, 1300. 1500 & 1600 all models including Riva '74 thru '86

LANCIA
533 Lancia Beta Sedan, Coupe & HPE '76 thru '80

LAND ROVER
314 Series II, IIA, & III all 4 cyl gasoline models '58 thru '86
529 Diesel '58 thru '80

MAZDA
648 626 Sedan & Coupe (rear wheel drive) '79 thru '82
*1082 626 & MX-6 (front wheel drive) '83 thru '90
*267 B1600, B1800 & B2000 Pick-ups '72 thru '90
370 GLC Hatchback (rear wheel drive) '77 thru '83
757 GLC (front wheel drive) '81 thru '86
109 RX2 '71 thru '75
096 RX3 '72 thru '76
460 RX-7 '79 thru '85
*1419 RX-7 '86 thru '89

MERCEDES-BENZ
*1643 190 Series all 4-cyl. gasoline '84 thru '88
346 230, 250 & 280 Sedan, Coupe & Roadster all 6 cyl sohc models '68 thru '72
983 280 123 Series all gasoline models '77 thru '81
698 350 & 450 Sedan, Coupe & Roadster '71 thru '80
697 Diesel 123 Series 200D, 220D, 240D, 240TD, 300D, 300CD, 300TD, 4- & 5-cyl incl. Turbo '76 thru '85

MERCURY
See FORD Listing

MG
475 MGA '56 thru '62
111 MGB Roadster & GT Coupe '62 thru '80
265 MG Midget & Austin Healey Sprite Roadster '58 thru '80

MITSUBISHI
Pick-up – *see Dodge D-50 (556)*

MORRIS
074 (Austin) Marina 1.8 '71 thru '80
024 Minor 1000 sedan & wagon '56 thru '71

NISSAN
*1137 300ZX all Turbo & non-Turbo '84 thru '86
*1341 Maxima '85 thru '89
*771 Pick-ups/Pathfinder gas models '80 thru '88
*876 Pulsar '83 thru '86
*982 Sentra '82 thru '90
*981 Stanza '82 thru '90

OLDSMOBILE
Custom Cruiser – *see BUICK Full-size (1551)*
658 Cutlass all standard gasoline V6 & V8 models '74 thru '88
Cutlass Ciera – *see GENERAL MOTORS A-Cars (829)*
Firenza – *see GENERAL MOTORS J-Cars (766)*
Ninety-eight – *see BUICK Full-size (1551)*
Omega – *see PONTIAC Phoenix & Omega (551)*

OPEL
157 (Buick) Manta Coupe 1900 '70 thru '74

PEUGEOT
161 504 all gasoline models '68 thru '79
663 504 all diesel models '74 thru '83

PLYMOUTH
425 Arrow '76 thru '80
For all other PLYMOUTH titles, see DODGE listing.

PONTIAC
T1000 – *see CHEVROLET Chevette (449)*
J-2000 – *see GENERAL MOTORS J-Cars (766)*
6000 – *see GENERAL MOTORS A-Cars (829)*
1232 Fiero '84 thru '88
555 Firebird all V8 models except Turbo '70 thru '81
*867 Firebird '82 thru '89
Full-size Rear Wheel Drive – *see Buick, Oldsmobile, Pontiac Full-size (1551)*
551 Phoenix & Oldsmobile Omega all X-car models '80 thru '84

PORSCHE
*264 911 all Coupe & Targa models except Turbo '65 thru '87
239 914 all 4 cyl models '69 thru '76
397 924 including Turbo '76 thru '82
*1027 944 including Turbo '83 thru '89

RENAULT
141 5 Le Car '76 thru '83
079 8 & 10 with 58.4 cu in engines '62 thru '72
097 12 Saloon & Estate 1289 cc engines '70 thru '80
768 15 & 17 '73 thru '79
081 16 89.7 cu in & 95.5 cu in engines '65 thru '72
598 18i & Sportwagon '81 thru '86
Alliance & Encore – *see AMC (934)*
984 Fuego '82 thru '85

ROVER
085 3500 & 3500S Sedan 215 cu in engines '68 thru '76
*365 3500 SDI V8 '76 thru '85

SAAB
198 95 & 96 V4 '66 thru '75
247 99 including Turbo '69 thru '80
*980 900 including Turbo '79 thru '88

SUBARU
237 1100, 1300, 1400 & 1600 '71 thru '79
*681 1600 & 1800 2WD & 4Wd '80 thru '88

SUZUKI
1626 Samurai/Sidekick and Geo Tracker '86 thru '89

TOYOTA
*1023 Camry '83 thru '90
150 Carina Sedan '71 thru '74
229 Celica ST, GT & liftback '71 thru '77
437 Celica '78 thru '81
*935 Celica except front-wheel drive and Supra '82 thru '85
680 Celica Supra '79 thru '81
1139 Celica Supra in-line 6-cylinder '82 thru '86
201 Corolla 1100, 1200 & 1600 '67 thru '74
361 Corolla '75 thru '79
961 Corolla (rear wheel drive) '80 thru '87
*1025 Corolla (front wheel drive) '84 thru '88
*636 Corolla Tercel '80 thru '82
230 Corona & MK II all 4 cyl sohc models '69 thru '74
360 Corona '74 thru '82
*532 Cressida '78 thru '82
313 Land Cruiser '68 thru '82
200 MK II all 6 cyl models '72 thru '76
*1339 MR2 '85 thru '87
304 Pick-up '69 thru '78
*656 Pick-up '79 thru '90
787 Starlet '81 thru '84

TRIUMPH
112 GT6 & Vitesse '62 thru '74
113 Spitfire '62 thru '81
028 TR2, 3, 3A, & 4A Roadsters '52 thru '67
031 TR250 & 6 Roadsters '67 thru '76
322 TR7 '75 thru '81

VW
091 411 & 412 all 103 cu in models '68 thru '73
036 Bug 1200 '54 thru '66
039 Bug 1300 & 1500 '65 thru '70
159 Bug 1600 all basic, sport & super (curved windshield) models '70 thru '74
110 Bug 1600 Super (flat windshield) '70 thru '72
238 Dasher all gasoline models '74 thru '81
*884 Rabbit, Jetta, Scirocco, & Pick-up all gasoline models '74 thru '89 & Convertible '80 thru '89
451 Rabbit, Jetta & Pick-up all diesel models '77 thru '84
082 Transporter 1500 '68 thru '79
226 Transporter 1700, 1800 & 2000 all models '72 thru '79
084 Type 3 1500 & 1600 '63 thru '73
1029 Vanagon all air-cooled models '80 thru '83

VOLVO
203 120, 130 Series & 1800 Sports '61 thru '73
129 140 Series '66 thru '74
244 164 '68 thru '75
*270 240 Series '74 thru '90
400 260 Series '75 thru '82
*1550 740 & 760 Series '82 thru '88

SPECIAL MANUALS
1479 Automotive Body Repair & Painting Manual
1654 Automotive Electrical Manual
1480 Automotive Heating & Air Conditioning Manual
482 Fuel Injection Manual
299 SU Carburetors thru '88
393 Weber Carburetors thru '79
300 Zenith/Stromberg CD Carburetors thru '76

See your dealer for other available titles

Over 100 Haynes motorcycle manuals also available

6-1-90

* *Listings shown with an asterisk (*) indicate model coverage as of this printing. These titles will be periodically updated to include later model years — consult your Haynes dealer for more information.*

Haynes Publications Inc., P.O. Box 978, Newbury Park, CA 91320 • (818) 889-5400 • (805) 498-6703

Printed by

J H Haynes & Co Ltd

Sparkford Nr Yeovil

Somerset BA22 7JJ England